An Insider's Guide to the International Criminal Tribunal for the Former Yugoslavia

Volume 2

Map of the Former Yugoslavia

An Insider's Guide to the International Criminal Tribunal for the Former Yugoslavia

A Documentary History and Analysis

Volume 2

By
Virginia Morris
&
Michael P. Scharf

Transnational Publishers, Inc.
Irvington-on-Hudson, New York

Library of Congress Cataloging-in-Publication Data

Morris, Virginia
An insider's guide to the international criminal tribunal for the former Yugoslavia : a documentary history & analysis / Virginia Morris & Michael P. Scharf
p. cm.
Includes bibliographical references (p.) and index.
ISBN 0-941320-92-8
1. International Tribunal for the Prosecution of Persons Responsible for Serious Violations of International Humanitarian Law Committed in the Territory of the Former Yugoslavia since 1991. 2. International criminal courts. 4. Yugoslav War, 1991- —Atrocities. 4. War crimes trials—Yugoslavia. I. Scharf, Michael P. II Title.
JX5430.M67 1994
341.6'9—dc20 94-23553
CIP

Manufactured in the United States of America

Civilization asks whether law is so laggard as to be utterly helpless to deal with crimes of this magnitude by criminals of this order of importance. It does not expect that you can make war impossible. It does expect that your juridical action will put the forces of International Law, its precepts, its prohibitions and, most of all, its sanctions, on the side of peace, so that men and women of good will, in all countries, may have "leave to live by no man's leave, underneath the law."

Robert H. Jackson
Opening speech for the Prosecution
at Nuremberg
21 November 1945.

When we neither punish nor reproach evildoers, we are not simply protecting their trivial old age, we are thereby ripping the foundations of justice from beneath new generations.

A. Solzhenitsyn
The Gulag Archipelago 178
(T. Whitney trans. 1974).

CONTENTS

PART I

REPORT OF THE SECRETARY-GENERAL CONTAINING THE STATUTE OF THE INTERNATIONAL TRIBUNAL, 3 MAY 1993

REPORT OF THE SECRETARY-GENERAL PURSUANT TO PARAGRAPH 2 OF SECURITY COUNCIL RESOLUTION 808 (1993)

S/25704, 3 May 1993

and Corrigendum

S/25704/Corr.1, 30 July 1993.

CONTENTS

CONTENTS (continued)

Introduction

1. By paragraph 1 of resolution 808 (1993) of 22 February 1993, the Security Council decided "that an international tribunal shall be established for the prosecution of persons responsible for serious violations of international humanitarian law committed in the territory of the former Yugoslavia since 1991".

2. By paragraph 2 of the resolution, the Secretary-General was requested "to submit for consideration by the Council at the earliest possible date, and if possible no later than 60 days after the adoption of the present resolution, a report on all aspects of this matter, including specific proposals and where appropriate options for the effective and expeditious implementation of the decision [to establish an international tribunal], taking into account suggestions put forward in this regard by Member States."

3. The present report is presented pursuant to that request. 1/

A

4. Resolution 808 (1993) represents a further step taken by the Security Council in a series of resolutions concerning serious violations of international humanitarian law occurring in the territory of the former Yugoslavia.

5. In resolution 764 (1992) of 13 July 1992, the Security Council reaffirmed that all parties to the conflict are bound to comply with their obligations under international humanitarian law and in particular the Geneva Conventions of 12 August 1949, and that persons who commit or order the commission of grave breaches of the Conventions are individually responsible in respect of such breaches.

6. In resolution 771 (1992) of 13 August 1992, the Security Council expressed grave alarm at continuing reports of widespread violations of international humanitarian law occurring within the territory of the former Yugoslavia and especially in Bosnia and Herzegovina, including reports of mass forcible expulsion and deportation of civilians, imprisonment and abuse of civilians in detention centres, deliberate attacks on non-combatants, hospitals and ambulances, impeding the delivery of food and medical supplies to the civilian population, and wanton devastation and destruction of property. The Council

1/ On 19 April 1993, the Secretary-General addressed a letter to the President of the Security Council informing him that the report would be made available to the Security Council no later than 6 May 1993.

strongly condemned any violations of international humanitarian law, including those involved in the practice of "ethnic cleansing", and demanded that all parties to the conflict in the former Yugoslavia cease and desist from all breaches of international humanitarian law. It called upon States and international humanitarian organizations to collate substantiated information relating to the violations of humanitarian law, including grave breaches of the Geneva Conventions, being committed in the territory of the former Yugoslavia and to make this information available to the Council. Furthermore, the Council decided, acting under Chapter VII of the Charter of the United Nations, that all parties and others concerned in the former Yugoslavia, and all military forces in Bosnia and Herzegovina, should comply with the provisions of that resolution, failing which the Council would need to take further measures under the Charter.

7. In resolution 780 (1992) of 6 October 1992, the Security Council requested the Secretary-General to establish an impartial Commission of Experts to examine and analyse the information as requested by resolution 771 (1992), together with such further information as the Commission may obtain through its own investigations or efforts, of other persons or bodies pursuant to resolution 771 (1992), with a view to providing the Secretary-General with its conclusions on the evidence of grave breaches of the Geneva Conventions and other violations of international humanitarian law committed in the territory of the former Yugoslavia.

8. On 14 October 1992 the Secretary-General submitted a report to the Security Council pursuant to paragraph 3 of resolution 780 (1992) in which he outlined his decision to establish a five-member Commission of Experts (S/24657). On 26 October 1992, the Secretary-General announced the appointment of the Chairman and members of the Commission of Experts.

9. By a letter dated 9 February 1993, the Secretary-General submitted to the President of the Security Council an interim report of the Commission of Experts (S/25274), which concluded that grave breaches and other violations of international humanitarian law had been committed in the territory of the former Yugoslavia, including wilful killing, "ethnic cleansing", mass killings, torture, rape, pillage and destruction of civilian property, destruction of cultural and religious property and arbitrary arrests. In its report, the Commission noted that should the Security Council or another competent organ of the United Nations decide to establish an ad hoc international tribunal, such a decision would be consistent with the direction of its work.

10. It was against this background that the Security Council considered and adopted resolution 808 (1993). After recalling the provisions of resolutions 764 (1992), 771 (1992) and 780 (1992) and, taking into consideration the interim report of the Commission of Experts, the Security Council expressed once again its grave alarm at continuing reports of widespread violations of international humanitarian law occurring within the territory of the former Yugoslavia, including reports of mass killings and the continuation of the practice of "ethnic cleansing". The Council determined that this situation constituted a threat to international peace and security, and stated that it was determined to put an end to such crimes and to take effective measures to bring to justice the persons who are responsible for them. The Security Council stated its conviction that in the particular circumstances of the former Yugoslavia the establishment of an international tribunal would enable this aim to be achieved and would contribute to the restoration and maintenance of peace.

11. The Secretary-General wishes to recall that in resolution 820 (1993) of 17 April 1993, the Security Council condemned once again all violations of international humanitarian law, including in particular, the practice of "ethnic cleansing" and the massive, organized and systematic detention and rape of women, and reaffirmed that those who commit or have committed or order or have ordered the commission of such acts will be held individually responsible in respect of such acts.

B

12. The Security Council's decision in resolution 808 (1993) to establish an international tribunal is circumscribed in scope and purpose: the prosecution of persons responsible for serious violations of international humanitarian law

committed in the territory of the former Yugoslavia since 1991. The decision does not relate to the establishment of an international criminal jurisdiction in general nor to the creation of an international criminal court of a permanent nature, issues which are and remain under active consideration by the International Law Commission and the General Assembly.

C

13. In accordance with the request of the Security Council, the Secretary-General has taken into account in the preparation of the present report the suggestions put forward by Member States, in particular those reflected in the following Security Council documents submitted by Member States and noted by the Council in its resolution 808 (1993): the report of the committee of jurists submitted by France (S/25266), the report of the commission of jurists submitted by Italy (S/25300), and the report submitted by the Permanent Representative of Sweden on behalf of the Chairman-in-Office of the Conference on Security and Cooperation in Europe (CSCE) (S/25307). The Secretary-General has also sought the views of the Commission of Experts established pursuant to Security Council resolution 780 (1992) and has made use of the information gathered by that Commission. In addition, the Secretary-General has taken into account suggestions or comments put forward formally or informally by the following Member States since the adoption of resolution 808 (1993): Australia, Austria, Belgium, Brazil, Canada, Chile, China, Denmark, Egypt,* Germany, Iran (Islamic Republic of),* Ireland, Italy, Malaysia,* Mexico, Netherlands, New Zealand, Pakistan,* Portugal, Russian Federation, Saudi Arabia,* Senegal,* Slovenia, Spain, Sweden, Turkey,* United Kingdom of Great Britain and Northern Ireland, United States of America and Yugoslavia. He has also received suggestions or comments from a non-member State (Switzerland).

14. The Secretary-General has also received comments from the International Committee of the Red Cross (ICRC), "the International Criminal Police Organization" and from the following non-governmental organizations: Amnesty International, Association Internationale des Jeunes Avocats, Ethnic Minorities Barristers' Association, Fédération internationale des femmes des carrières juridiques, Jacob Blaustein Institution for the Advancement of Human Rights, Lawyers Committee for Human Rights, National Alliance of Women's Organizations (NAWO), and Parliamentarians for Global Action. Observations have also been received from international meetings and individual experts in relevant fields.

15. The Secretary-General wishes to place on record his appreciation for the interest shown by all the Governments, organizations and individuals who have offered valuable suggestions and comments.

D

16. In the main body of the report which follows, the Secretary-General first examines the legal basis for the establishment of the International Tribunal foreseen in resolution 808 (1993). The Secretary-General then sets out in detail the competence of the International Tribunal as regards the law it will apply, the persons to whom the law will be applied, including considerations as to the principle of individual criminal responsibility, its territorial and temporal reach and the relation of its work to that of national courts. In succeeding chapters, the Secretary-General sets out detailed views on the organization of the international tribunal, the investigation and pre-trial proceedings, trial and post-trial proceedings, and cooperation and judicial assistance. A concluding chapter deals with a number of general and organizational issues such as privileges and immunities, the seat of the international tribunal, working languages and financial arrangements.

* On behalf of the members of the Organization of the Islamic Conference (OIC) and as members of the Contact Group of OIC on Bosnia and Herzegovina.

17. In response to the Security Council's request to include in the report specific proposals, the Secretary-General has decided to incorporate into the report specific language for inclusion in a statute of the International Tribunal. The formulations are based upon provisions found in existing international instruments, particularly with regard to competence ratione materiae of the International Tribunal. Suggestions and comments, including suggested draft articles, received from States, organizations and individuals as noted in paragraphs 13 and 14 above, also formed the basis upon which the Secretary-General prepared the statute. Texts prepared in the past by United Nations or other bodies for the establishment of international criminal courts were consulted by the Secretary-General, including texts prepared by the United Nations Committee on International Criminal Jurisdiction, 2/ the International Law Commission, and the International Law Association. Proposals regarding individual articles are, therefore, made throughout the body of the report; the full text of the statute of the International Tribunal is contained in the annex to the present report.

I. THE LEGAL BASIS FOR THE ESTABLISHMENT OF THE INTERNATIONAL TRIBUNAL

18. Security Council resolution 808 (1993) states that an international tribunal shall be established for the prosecution of persons responsible for serious violations of international humanitarian law committed in the territory of the former Yugoslavia since 1991. It does not, however, indicate how such an international tribunal is to be established or on what legal basis.

19. The approach which, in the normal course of events, would be followed in establishing an international tribunal would be the conclusion of a treaty by which the States parties would establish a tribunal and approve its statute. This treaty would be drawn up and adopted by an appropriate international body (e.g., the General Assembly or a specially convened conference), following which it would be opened for signature and ratification. Such an approach would have the advantage of allowing for a detailed examination and elaboration of all the issues pertaining to the establishment of the international tribunal. It also would allow the States participating in the negotiation and conclusion of the treaty fully to exercise their sovereign will, in particular whether they wish to become parties to the treaty or not.

20. As has been pointed out in many of the comments received, the treaty approach incurs the disadvantage of requiring considerable time to establish an instrument and then to achieve the required number of ratifications for entry into force. Even then, there could be no guarantee that ratifications will be received from those States which should be parties to the treaty if it is to be truly effective.

21. A number of suggestions have been put forward to the effect that the General Assembly, as the most representative organ of the United Nations, should have a role in the establishment of the international tribunal in addition to its role in the administrative and budgetary aspects of the question. The involvement of the General Assembly in the drafting or the review of the statute of the International Tribunal would not be reconcilable with the urgency expressed by the Security Council in resolution 808 (1993). The Secretary-General believes that there are other ways of involving the authority and prestige of the General Assembly in the establishment of the International Tribunal.

22. In the light of the disadvantages of the treaty approach in this particular case and of the need indicated in resolution 808 (1993) for an effective and expeditious implementation of the decision to establish an international tribunal, the Secretary-General believes that the International Tribunal should be established by a decision of the Security Council on the basis of Chapter VII of the Charter of the United Nations. Such a decision would constitute a measure to maintain or restore international peace and security, following the requisite determination of the existence of a threat to the peace, breach of the peace or act of aggression.

2/ The 1953 Committee on International Criminal Jurisdiction was established by General Assembly resolution 687 (VII) of 5 December 1952.

23. This approach would have the advantage of being expeditious and of being immediately effective as all States would be under a binding obligation to take whatever action is required to carry out a decision taken as an enforcement measure under Chapter VII.

24. In the particular case of the former Yugoslavia, the Secretary-General believes that the establishment of the International Tribunal by means of a Chapter VII decision would be legally justified, both in terms of the object and purpose of the decision, as indicated in the preceding paragraphs, and of past Security Council practice.

25. As indicated in paragraph 10 above, the Security Council has already determined that the situation posed by continuing reports of widespread violations of international humanitarian law occurring in the former Yugoslavia constitutes a threat to international peace and security. The Council has also decided under Chapter VII of the Charter that all parties and others concerned in the former Yugoslavia, and all military forces in Bosnia and Herzegovina, shall comply with the provisions of resolution 771 (1992), failing which it would need to take further measures under the Charter. Furthermore, the Council has repeatedly reaffirmed that all parties in the former Yugoslavia are bound to comply with the obligations under international humanitarian law and in particular the Geneva Conventions of 12 August 1949, and that persons who commit or order the commission of grave breaches of the Conventions are individually responsible in respect of such breaches.

26. Finally, the Security Council stated in resolution 808 (1993) that it was convinced that in the particular circumstances of the former Yugoslavia, the establishment of an international tribunal would bring about the achievement of the aim of putting an end to such crimes and of taking effective measures to bring to justice the persons responsible for them, and would contribute to the restoration and maintenance of peace.

27. The Security Council has on various occasions adopted decisions under Chapter VII aimed at restoring and maintaining international peace and security, which have involved the establishment of subsidiary organs for a variety of purposes. Reference may be made in this regard to Security Council resolution 687 (1991) and subsequent resolutions relating to the situation between Iraq and Kuwait.

28. In this particular case, the Security Council would be establishing, as an enforcement measure under Chapter VII, a subsidiary organ within the terms of Article 29 of the Charter, but one of a judicial nature. This organ would, of course, have to perform its functions independently of political considerations; it would not be subject to the authority or control of the Security Council with regard to the performance of its judicial functions. As an enforcement measure under Chapter VII, however, the life span of the international tribunal would be linked to the restoration and maintenance of international peace and security in the territory of the former Yugoslavia, and Security Council decisions related thereto.

29. It should be pointed out that, in assigning to the International Tribunal the task of prosecuting persons responsible for serious violations of international humanitarian law, the Security Council would not be creating or purporting to "legislate" that law. Rather, the International Tribunal would have the task of applying existing international humanitarian law.

30. On the basis of the foregoing considerations, the Secretary-General proposes that the Security Council, acting under Chapter VII of the Charter, establish the International Tribunal. The resolution so adopted would have annexed to it a statute the opening passage of which would read as follows:

> Having been established by the Security Council acting under Chapter VII of the Charter of the United Nations, the International Tribunal for the Prosecution of Persons Responsible for Serious Violations of International Humanitarian Law Committed in the Territory of the Former Yugoslavia since 1991 (hereinafter referred to as "the International Tribunal") shall function in accordance with the provisions of the present Statute.

II. COMPETENCE OF THE INTERNATIONAL TRIBUNAL

31. The competence of the International Tribunal derives from the mandate set out in paragraph 1 of resolution 808 (1993). This part of the report will examine and make proposals regarding these fundamental elements of its competence: ratione materiae (subject-matter jurisdiction), ratione personae (personal jurisdiction), ratione loci (territorial jurisdiction) and ratione temporis (temporal jurisdiction), as well as the question of the concurrent jurisdiction of the International Tribunal and national courts.

32. The statute should begin with a general article on the competence of the International Tribunal which would read as follows:

Article 1

Competence of the International Tribunal

The International Tribunal shall have the power to prosecute persons responsible for serious violations of international humanitarian law committed in the territory of the former Yugoslavia since 1991 in accordance with the provisions of the present Statute.

A. Competence ratione materiae (subject-matter jurisdiction)

33. According to paragraph 1 of resolution 808 (1993), the international tribunal shall prosecute persons responsible for serious violations of international humanitarian law committed in the territory of the former Yugoslavia since 1991. This body of law exists in the form of both conventional law and customary law. While there is international customary law which is not laid down in conventions, some of the major conventional humanitarian law has become part of customary international law.

34. In the view of the Secretary-General, the application of the principle nullum crimen sine lege requires that the international tribunal should apply rules of international humanitarian law which are beyond any doubt part of customary law so that the problem of adherence of some but not all States to specific conventions does not arise. This would appear to be particularly important in the context of an international tribunal prosecuting persons responsible for serious violations of international humanitarian law.

35. The part of conventional international humanitarian law which has beyond doubt become part of international customary law is the law applicable in armed conflict as embodied in: the Geneva Conventions of 12 August 1949 for the Protection of War Victims; 3/ the Hague Convention (IV) Respecting the Laws and Customs of War on Land and the Regulations annexed thereto of 18 October 1907; 4/ the Convention on the Prevention and Punishment of the Crime of Genocide of 9 December 1948; 5/ and the Charter of the International Military Tribunal of 8 August 1945. 6/

3/ Convention for the Amelioration of the Condition of the Wounded and Sick in Armed Forces in the Field of 12 August 1949, Convention for the Amelioration of the Condition of the Wounded, Sick and Shipwrecked Members of Armed Forces at Sea of 12 August 1949, Convention relative to the Treatment of Prisoners of War of 12 August 1949, Convention relative to the Protection of Civilian Persons in Time of War of 12 August 1949 (United Nations, Treaty Series, vol. 75, No. 970-973).

4/ Carnegie Endowment for International Peace, The Hague Conventions and Declarations of 1899 and 1907 (New York, Oxford University Press, 1915), p. 100.

5/ United Nations, Treaty Series, vol. 78, No. 1021.

6/ The Agreement for the Prosecution and Punishment of the Major War Criminals of the European Axis, signed at London on 8 August 1945 (United Nations, Treaty Series, vol. 82, No. 251); see also Judgement of the International Military Tribunal for the Prosecution and Punishment of the Major War Criminals of the European Axis (United States Government Printing Office, Nazi Conspiracy and Aggression, Opinion and Judgement) and General Assembly resolution 95 (I) of 11 December 1946 on the Affirmation of the Principles of International Law Recognized by the Charter of the Nürnberg Tribunal.

36. Suggestions have been made that the international tribunal should apply domestic law in so far as it incorporates customary international humanitarian law. While international humanitarian law as outlined above provides a sufficient basis for subject-matter jurisdiction, there is one related issue which would require reference to domestic practice, namely, penalties (see para. 111 below).

Grave breaches of the 1949 Geneva Conventions

37. The Geneva Conventions constitute rules of international humanitarian law and provide the core of the customary law applicable in international armed conflicts. These Conventions regulate the conduct of war from the humanitarian perspective by protecting certain categories of persons: namely, wounded and sick members of armed forces in the field; wounded, sick and shipwrecked members of armed forces at sea; prisoners of war, and civilians in time of war.

38. Each Convention contains a provision listing the particularly serious violations that qualify as "grave breaches" or war crimes. Persons committing or ordering grave breaches are subject to trial and punishment. The lists of grave breaches contained in the Geneva Conventions are reproduced in the article which follows.

39. The Security Council has reaffirmed on several occasions that persons who commit or order the commission of grave breaches of the 1949 Geneva Conventions in the territory of the former Yugoslavia are individually responsible for such breaches as serious violations of international humanitarian law.

40. The corresponding article of the statute would read:

Article 2

Grave breaches of the Geneva Conventions of 1949

The International Tribunal shall have the power to prosecute persons committing or ordering to be committed grave breaches of the Geneva Conventions of 12 August 1949, namely the following acts against persons or property protected under the provisions of the relevant Geneva Convention:

(a) wilful killing;

(b) torture or inhuman treatment, including biological experiments;

(c) wilfully causing great suffering or serious injury to body or health;

(d) extensive destruction and appropriation of property, not justified by military necessity and carried out unlawfully and wantonly;

(e) compelling a prisoner of war or a civilian to serve in the forces of a hostile power;

(f) wilfully depriving a prisoner of war or a civilian of the rights of fair and regular trial;

(g) unlawful deportation or transfer or unlawful confinement of a civilian;

(h) taking civilians as hostages.

Violations of the laws or customs of war

41. The 1907 Hague Convention (IV) Respecting the Laws and Customs of War on Land and the Regulations annexed thereto comprise a second important area of conventional humanitarian international law which has become part of the body of international customary law.

42. The Nürnberg Tribunal recognized that many of the provisions contained in the Hague Regulations, although innovative at the time of their adoption were, by 1939, recognized by all civilized nations and were regarded as being declaratory of the laws and customs of war. The Nürnberg Tribunal also recognized that war crimes defined in article 6(b) of the Nürnberg Charter were already recognized as war crimes under international law, and covered in the Hague Regulations, for which guilty individuals were punishable.

43. The Hague Regulations cover aspects of international humanitarian law which are also covered by the 1949 Geneva Conventions. However, the Hague Regulations also recognize that the right of belligerents to conduct warfare is not unlimited and that resort to certain methods of waging war is prohibited under the rules of land warfare.

44. These rules of customary law, as interpreted and applied by the Nürnberg Tribunal, provide the basis for the corresponding article of the statute which would read as follows:

Article 3

Violations of the laws or customs of war

The International Tribunal shall have the power to prosecute persons violating the laws or customs of war. Such violations shall include, but not be limited to:

(a) employment of poisonous weapons or other weapons calculated to cause unnecessary suffering;

(b) wanton destruction of cities, towns or villages, or devastation not justified by military necessity;

(c) attack, or bombardment, by whatever means, of undefended towns, villages, dwellings, or buildings;

(d) seizure of, destruction or wilful damage done to institutions dedicated to religion, charity and education, the arts and sciences, historic monuments and works of art and science;

(e) plunder of public or private property.

Genocide

45. The 1948 Convention on the Prevention and Punishment of the Crime of Genocide confirms that genocide, whether committed in time of peace or in time of war, is a crime under international law for which individuals shall be tried and punished. The Convention is today considered part of international customary law as evidenced by the International Court of Justice in its Advisory Opinion on Reservations to the Convention on the Prevention and Punishment of the Crime of Genocide, 1951. 7/

46. The relevant provisions of the Genocide Convention are reproduced in the corresponding article of the statute, which would read as follows:

7/ Reservations to the Convention on the Prevention and Punishment of the Crime of Genocide: Advisory Opinion of 28 May 1951, International Court of Justice Reports, 1951, p. 23.

Article 4

Genocide

1. The International Tribunal shall have the power to prosecute persons committing genocide as defined in paragraph 2 of this article or of committing any of the other acts enumerated in paragraph 3 of this article.

2. Genocide means any of the following acts committed with intent to destroy, in whole or in part, a national, ethnical, racial or religious group, as such:

(a) killing members of the group;

(b) causing serious bodily or mental harm to members of the group;

(c) deliberately inflicting on the group conditions of life calculated to bring about its physical destruction in whole or in part;

(d) imposing measures intended to prevent births within the group;

(e) forcibly transferring children of the group to another group.

3. The following acts shall be punishable:

(a) genocide;

(b) conspiracy to commit genocide;

(c) direct and public incitement to commit genocide;

(d) attempt to commit genocide;

(e) complicity in genocide.

Crimes against humanity

47. Crimes against humanity were first recognized in the Charter and Judgement of the Nürnberg Tribunal, as well as in Law No. 10 of the Control Council for Germany. 8/ Crimes against humanity are aimed at any civilian population and are prohibited regardless of whether they are committed in an armed conflict, international or internal in character. 9/

48. Crimes against humanity refer to inhumane acts of a very serious nature, such as wilful killing, torture or rape, committed as part of a widespread or systematic attack against any civilian population on national, political, ethnic, racial or religious grounds. In the conflict in the territory of the former Yugoslavia, such inhumane acts have taken the form of so-called "ethnic cleansing" and widespread and systematic rape and other forms of sexual assault, including enforced prostitution.

49. The corresponding article of the statute would read as follows:

8/ Official Gazette of the Control Council for Germany, No. 3, p. 22, Military Government Gazette, Germany, British Zone of Control, No. 5, p. 46, Journal Officiel du Commandement en Chef Français en Allemagne, No. 12 of 11 January 1946.

9/ In this context, it is to be noted that the International Court of Justice has recognized that the prohibitions contained in common article 3 of the 1949 Geneva Conventions are based on "elementary considerations of humanity" and cannot be breached in an armed conflict, regardless of whether it is international or internal in character. Case concerning Military and Paramilitary Activities in and against Nicaragua (Nicaragua v. United States of America), Judgement of 27 June 1986: I.C.J. Reports 1986, p. 114.

Article 5

Crimes against humanity

The International Tribunal shall have the power to prosecute persons responsible for the following crimes when committed in armed conflict, whether international or internal in character, and directed against any civilian population:

(a) murder;

(b) extermination;

(c) enslavement;

(d) deportation;

(e) imprisonment;

(f) torture;

(g) rape;

(h) persecutions on political, racial and religious grounds;

(i) other inhumane acts.

B. Competence ratione personae (personal jurisdiction) and individual criminal responsibility

50. By paragraph 1 of resolution 808 (1993), the Security Council decided that the International Tribunal shall be established for the prosecution of persons responsible for serious violations of international humanitarian law committed in the territory of the former Yugoslavia since 1991. In the light of the complex of resolutions leading up to resolution 808 (1993) (see paras. 5-7 above), the ordinary meaning of the term "persons responsible for serious violations of international humanitarian law" would be natural persons to the exclusion of juridical persons.

51. The question arises, however, whether a juridical person, such as an association or organization, may be considered criminal as such and thus its members, for that reason alone, be made subject to the jurisdiction of the International Tribunal. The Secretary-General believes that this concept should not be retained in regard to the International Tribunal. The criminal acts set out in this statute are carried out by natural persons; such persons would be subject to the jurisdiction of the International Tribunal irrespective of membership in groups.

52. The corresponding article of the statute would read:

Article 6

Personal jurisdiction

The International Tribunal shall have jurisdiction over natural persons pursuant to the provisions of the present Statute.

Individual criminal responsibility

53. An important element in relation to the competence *ratione personae* (personal jurisdiction) of the International Tribunal is the principle of individual criminal responsibility. As noted above, the Security Council has reaffirmed in a number of resolutions that persons committing serious violations of international humanitarian law in the former Yugoslavia are individually responsible for such violations.

54. The Secretary-General believes that all persons who participate in the planning, preparation or execution of serious violations of international humanitarian law in the former Yugoslavia contribute to the commission of the violation and are, therefore, individually responsible.

55. Virtually all of the written comments received by the Secretary-General have suggested that the statute of the International Tribunal should contain provisions with regard to the individual criminal responsibility of heads of State, government officials and persons acting in an official capacity. These suggestions draw upon the precedents following the Second World War. The Statute should, therefore, contain provisions which specify that a plea of head of State immunity or that an act was committed in the official capacity of the accused will not constitute a defence, nor will it mitigate punishment.

56. A person in a position of superior authority should, therefore, be held individually responsible for giving the unlawful order to commit a crime under the present statute. But he should also be held responsible for failure to prevent a crime or to deter the unlawful behaviour of his subordinates. This imputed responsibility or criminal negligence is engaged if the person in superior authority knew or had reason to know that his subordinates were about to commit or had committed crimes and yet failed to take the necessary and reasonable steps to prevent or repress the commission of such crimes or to punish those who had committed them.

57. Acting upon an order of a Government or a superior cannot relieve the perpetrator of the crime of his criminal responsibility and should not be a defence. Obedience to superior orders may, however, be considered a mitigating factor, should the International Tribunal determine that justice so requires. For example, the International Tribunal may consider the factor of superior orders in connection with other defences such as coercion or lack of moral choice.

58. The International Tribunal itself will have to decide on various personal defences which may relieve a person of individual criminal responsibility, such as minimum age or mental incapacity, drawing upon general principles of law recognized by all nations.

59. The corresponding article of the statute would read:

Article 7

Individual criminal responsibility

1. A person who planned, instigated, ordered, committed or otherwise aided and abetted in the planning, preparation or execution of a crime referred to in articles 2 to 5 of the present Statute, shall be individually responsible for the crime.

2. The official position of any accused person, whether as Head of State or Government or as a responsible Government official, shall not relieve such person of criminal responsibility nor mitigate punishment.

3. The fact that any of the acts referred to in articles 2 to 5 of the present Statute was committed by a subordinate does not relieve his superior of criminal responsibility if he knew or had reason to know that the subordinate was about to commit such acts or had done so and the superior failed to take the necessary and reasonable measures to prevent such acts or to punish the perpetrators thereof.

4. The fact that an accused person acted pursuant to an order of a Government or of a superior shall not relieve him of criminal responsibility, but may be considered in mitigation of punishment if the International Tribunal determines that justice so requires.

C. Competence ratione loci (territorial jurisdiction) and ratione temporis (temporal jurisdiction)

60. Pursuant to paragraph 1 of resolution 808 (1993), the territorial and temporal jurisdiction of the International Tribunal extends to serious violations of international humanitarian law to the extent that they have been "committed in the territory of the former Yugoslavia since 1991".

61. As far as the territorial jurisdiction of the International Tribunal is concerned, the territory of the former Yugoslavia means the territory of the former Socialist Federal Republic of Yugoslavia, including its land surface, airspace and territorial waters.

62. With regard to temporal jurisdiction, Security Council resolution 808 (1993) extends the jurisdiction of the International Tribunal to violations committed "since 1991". The Secretary-General understands this to mean anytime on or after 1 January 1991. This is a neutral date which is not tied to any specific event and is clearly intended to convey the notion that no judgement as to the international or internal character of the conflict is being exercised.

63. The corresponding article of the statute would read:

Article 8

Territorial and temporal jurisdiction

> The territorial jurisdiction of the International Tribunal shall extend to the territory of the former Socialist Federal Republic of Yugoslavia, including its land surface, airspace and territorial waters. The temporal jurisdiction of the International Tribunal shall extend to a period beginning on 1 January 1991.

D. Concurrent jurisdiction and the principle of non-bis-in-idem

64. In establishing an international tribunal for the prosecution of persons responsible for serious violations committed in the territory of the former Yugoslavia since 1991, it was not the intention of the Security Council to preclude or prevent the exercise of jurisdiction by national courts with respect to such acts. Indeed national courts should be encouraged to exercise their jurisdiction in accordance with their relevant national laws and procedures.

65. It follows therefore that there is concurrent jurisdiction of the International Tribunal and national courts. This concurrent jurisdiction, however, should be subject to the primacy of the International Tribunal. At any stage of the procedure, the International Tribunal may formally request the national courts to defer to the competence of the International Tribunal. The details of how the primacy will be asserted shall be set out in the rules of procedure and evidence of the International Tribunal.

66. According to the principle of *non-bis-in-idem*, a person shall not be tried twice for the same crime. In the present context, given the primacy of the International Tribunal, the principle of *non-bis-in-idem* would preclude subsequent trial before a national court. However, the principle of *non-bis-in idem* should not preclude a subsequent trial before the International Tribunal in the following two circumstances:

(a) The characterization of the act by the national court did not correspond to its characterization under the statute; or

(b) Conditions of impartiality, independence or effective means of adjudication were not guaranteed in the proceedings before the national courts.

67. Should the International Tribunal decide to assume jurisdiction over a person who has already been convicted by a national court, it should take into consideration the extent to which any penalty imposed by the national court has already been served.

68. The corresponding articles of the statute would read:

Article 9

Concurrent jurisdiction

1. The International Tribunal and national courts shall have concurrent jurisdiction to prosecute persons for serious violations of international humanitarian law committed in the territory of the former Yugoslavia since 1 January 1991.

2. The International Tribunal shall have primacy over national courts. At any stage of the procedure, the International Tribunal may formally request national courts to defer to the competence of the International Tribunal in accordance with the present Statute and the Rules of Procedure and Evidence of the International Tribunal.

Article 10

Non-bis-in-idem

1. No person shall be tried before a national court for acts constituting serious violations of international humanitarian law under the present Statute, for which he or she has already been tried by the International Tribunal.

2. A person who has been tried by a national court for acts constituting serious violations of international humanitarian law may be subsequently tried by the International Tribunal only if:

(a) the act for which he or she was tried was characterized as an ordinary crime; or

(b) the national court proceedings were not impartial or independent, were designed to shield the accused from international criminal responsibility, or the case was not diligently prosecuted.

3. In considering the penalty to be imposed on a person convicted of a crime under the present Statute, the International Tribunal shall take into account the extent to which any penalty imposed by a national court on the same person for the same act has already been served.

III. THE ORGANIZATION OF THE INTERNATIONAL TRIBUNAL

69. The organization of the International Tribunal should reflect the functions to be performed by it. Since the International Tribunal is established for the prosecution of persons responsible for serious violations of international humanitarian law committed in the territory of the former Yugoslavia, this presupposes an international tribunal composed of a judicial organ, a prosecutorial organ and a secretariat. It would be the function of the prosecutorial organ to investigate cases, prepare indictments and prosecute persons responsible for committing the violations referred to above. The judicial organ would hear the cases presented to its Trial Chambers, and consider appeals from the Trial Chambers in its Appeals Chamber. A secretariat or Registry would be required to service both the prosecutorial and judicial organs.

70. The International Tribunal should therefore consist of the following organs: the Chambers, comprising two Trial Chambers and one Appeals Chamber; a Prosecutor; and a Registry.

71. The corresponding article of the statute would read as follows:

Article 11

Organization of the International Tribunal

The International Tribunal shall consist of the following organs:

(a) The Chambers, comprising two Trial Chambers and an Appeals Chamber;

(b) The Prosecutor; and

(c) A Registry, servicing both the Chambers and the Prosecutor.

A. The Chambers

1. Composition of the Chambers

72. The Chambers should be composed of 11 independent judges, no 2 of whom may be nationals of the same State. Three judges would serve in each of the two Trial Chambers and five judges would serve in the Appeals Chamber.

73. The corresponding article of the statute would read as follows:

Article 12

Composition of the Chambers

The Chambers shall be composed of eleven independent judges, no two of whom may be nationals of the same State, who shall serve as follows:

(a) Three judges shall serve in each of the Trial Chambers;

(b) Five judges shall serve in the Appeals Chamber.

2. Qualifications and election of judges

74. The judges of the International Tribunal should be persons of high moral character, impartiality and integrity who possess the qualifications required in their respective countries for appointment to the highest judicial offices. Impartiality in this context includes impartiality with respect to the acts falling within the competence of the International Tribunal. In the overall composition of the Chambers, due account should be taken of the experience of the judges in criminal law, international law, including international humanitarian law and human rights law.

75. The judges should be elected by the General Assembly from a list submitted by the Security Council. The Secretary-General would invite nominations for judges from States Members of the United Nations as well as non-member States maintaining permanent observer missions at United Nations Headquarters. Within 60 days of the date of the invitation of the Secretary-General, each State would nominate up to two candidates meeting the qualifications mentioned in paragraph 74 above, who must not be of the same nationality. The Secretary-General would forward the nominations received to the Security Council. The Security Council would, as speedily as possible, establish from the nominations transmitted by the Secretary-General, a list of not less than 22 and not more than 33 candidates, taking due account of the adequate representation of the principal legal systems of the world. The President of the Security Council would then transmit the list to the General Assembly. From that list, the General Assembly would proceed as speedily as possible to elect the 11 judges of the International Tribunal. The candidates declared elected shall be those who have received an absolute majority of the votes of the States Members of the United Nations and of the States maintaining permanent observer missions at United Nations Headquarters. Should two candidates of the same nationality obtain the required majority vote, the one who received the higher number of votes shall be considered elected.

76. The judges shall be elected for a term of four years. The terms and conditions of service shall be those of the Judges of the International Court of Justice. They shall be eligible for re-election.

77. In the event of a vacancy occurring in the Chambers, the Secretary-General, after consultation with the Presidents of the Security Council and the General Assembly, would appoint a person meeting the qualifications of paragraph 74 above, for the remainder of the term of office concerned.

78. The corresponding article of the statute would read as follows:

Article 13

Qualifications and election of judges

1. The judges shall be persons of high moral character, impartiality and integrity who possess the qualifications required in their respective countries for appointment to the highest judicial offices. In the overall composition of the Chambers due account shall be taken of the experience of the judges in criminal law, international law, including international humanitarian law and human rights law.

2. The judges of the International Tribunal shall be elected by the General Assembly from a list submitted by the Security Council, in the following manner:

(a) The Secretary-General shall invite nominations for judges of the International Tribunal from States Members of the United Nations and non-member States maintaining permanent observer missions at United Nations Headquarters;

(b) Within sixty days of the date of the invitation of the Secretary-General, each State may nominate up to two candidates meeting the qualifications set out in paragraph 1 above, no two of whom shall be of the same nationality;

(c) The Secretary-General shall forward the nominations received to the Security Council. From the nominations received the Security Council shall establish a list of not less than twenty-two and not more than thirty-three candidates, taking due account of the adequate representation of the principal legal systems of the world;

(d) The President of the Security Council shall transmit the list of candidates to the President of the General Assembly. From that list the General Assembly shall elect the eleven judges of the International Tribunal. The candidates who receive an absolute majority of the votes of States Members of the United Nations and of the non-member States maintaining permanent observer missions at United Nations Headquarters, shall be declared elected. Should two candidates of the same nationality obtain the required majority vote, the one who received the higher number of votes shall be considered elected.

3. In the event of a vacancy in the Chambers, after consultation with the Presidents of the Security Council and of the General Assembly, the Secretary-General shall appoint a person meeting the qualifications of paragraph 1 above, for the remainder of the term of office concerned.

4. The judges shall be elected for a term of four years. The terms and conditions of service shall be those of the Judges of the International Court of justice. They shall be eligible for re-election.

3. Officers and members of the Chambers

79. The judges would elect a President of the International Tribunal from among their members who would be a member of the Appeals Chamber and would preside over the appellate proceedings.

80. Following consultation with the members of the Chambers, the President would assign the judges to the Appeals Chamber and to the Trial Chambers. Each judge would serve only in the chamber to which he or she was assigned.

81. The members of each Trial Chamber should elect a presiding judge who would conduct all of the proceedings before the Trial Chamber as a whole.

82. The corresponding article of the statute would read as follows:

Article 14

Officers and members of the Chambers

1. The judges of the International Tribunal shall elect a President.

2. The President of the International Tribunal shall be a member of the Appeals Chamber and shall preside over its proceedings.

3. After consultation with the judges of the International Tribunal, the President shall assign the judges to the Appeals Chamber and to the Trial Chambers. A judge shall serve only in the Chamber to which he or she was assigned.

4. The judges of each Trial Chamber shall elect a Presiding Judge, who shall conduct all of the proceedings of the Trial Chamber as a whole.

4. Rules of procedure and evidence

83. The judges of the International Tribunal as a whole should draft and adopt the rules of procedure and evidence of the International Tribunal governing the pre-trial phase of the proceedings, the conduct of trials and appeals, the admission of evidence, the protection of victims and witnesses and other appropriate matters.

84. The corresponding article of the statute would read as follows:

Article 15

Rules of procedure and evidence

The judges of the International Tribunal shall adopt rules of procedure and evidence for the conduct of the pre-trial phase of the proceedings, trials and appeals, the admission of evidence, the protection of victims and witnesses and other appropriate matters.

B. The Prosecutor

85. Responsibility for the conduct of all investigations and prosecutions of persons responsible for serious violations of international humanitarian law committed in the territory of the former Yugoslavia since 1 January 1991 should be entrusted to an independent Prosecutor. The Prosecutor should act independently as a separate organ of the International Tribunal. He or she shall not seek or receive instructions from any Government or from any other source.

86. The Prosecutor should be appointed by the Security Council, upon nomination by the Secretary-General. He or she should possess the highest level of professional competence and have extensive experience in the conduct of investigations and prosecutions of criminal cases. The Prosecutor should be appointed for a four-year term of office and be eligible for reappointment. The terms and conditions of service of the Prosecutor shall be those of an Under-Secretary-General of the United Nations.

87. The Prosecutor would be assisted by such other staff as may be required to perform effectively and efficiently the functions entrusted to him or her. Such staff would be appointed by the Secretary-General on the recommendation of the Prosecutor. The Office of the Prosecutor should be composed of an investigation unit and a prosecution unit.

88. Staff appointed to the Office of the Prosecutor should meet rigorous criteria of professional experience and competence in their field. Persons should be sought who have had relevant experience in their own countries as investigators, prosecutors, criminal lawyers, law enforcement personnel or medical experts. Given the nature of the crimes committed and the sensitivities of victims of rape and sexual assault, due consideration should be given in the appointment of staff to the employment of qualified women.

89. The corresponding article of the statute would read as follows:

Article 16

The Prosecutor

1. The Prosecutor shall be responsible for the investigation and prosecution of persons responsible for serious violations of international humanitarian law committed in the territory of the former Yugoslavia since 1 January 1991.

2. The Prosecutor shall act independently as a separate organ of the International Tribunal. He or she shall not seek or receive instructions from any Government or from any other source.

3. The Office of the Prosecutor shall be composed of a Prosecutor and such other qualified staff as may be required.

4. The Prosecutor shall be appointed by the Security Council on nomination by the Secretary-General. He or she shall be of high moral character and possess the highest level of competence and experience in the conduct of investigations and prosecutions of criminal cases. The Prosecutor shall serve for a four-year term and be eligible for reappointment. The terms and conditions of service of the Prosecutor shall be those of an Under-Secretary-General of the United Nations.

5. The staff of the Office of the Prosecutor shall be appointed by the Secretary-General on the recommendation of the Prosecutor.

C. The Registry

90. As indicated in paragraph 69 above, a Registry would be responsible for the servicing of the International Tribunal. The Registry would be headed by a Registrar, whose responsibilities shall include but should not be limited to the following:

(a) Public information and external relations;

(b) Preparation of minutes of meetings;

(c) Conference-service facilities;

(d) Printing and publication of all documents;

(e) All administrative work, budgetary and personnel matters; and

(f) Serving as the channel of communications to and from the International Tribunal.

91. The Registrar should be appointed by the Secretary-General after consultation with the President of the International Tribunal. He or she would be appointed to serve for a four-year term and be eligible for reappointment. The terms and conditions of service of the Registrar shall be those of an Assistant Secretary-General of the United Nations.

92. The corresponding article of the statute would read as follows:

Article 17

The Registry

1. The Registry shall be responsible for the administration and servicing of the International Tribunal.

2. The Registry shall consist of a Registrar and such other staff as may be required.

3. The Registrar shall be appointed by the Secretary-General after consultation with the President of the International Tribunal. He or she shall serve for a four-year term and be eligible for reappointment. The terms and conditions of service of the Registrar shall be those of an Assistant Secretary-General of the United Nations.

4. The staff of the Registry shall be appointed by the Secretary-General on the recommendation of the Registrar.

IV. INVESTIGATION AND PRE-TRIAL PROCEEDINGS

93. The Prosecutor would initiate investigations ex officio, or on the basis of information obtained from any source, particularly from Governments or United Nations organs, intergovernmental and non-governmental organizations. The Prosecutor would assess the information received or obtained and decide whether there is a sufficient basis to proceed.

94. In conducting his investigations, the Prosecutor should have the power to question suspects, victims and witnesses, to collect evidence and to conduct on-site investigations. In carrying out these tasks, the Prosecutor may, as appropriate, seek the assistance of the State authorities concerned.

95. Upon the completion of the investigation, if the Prosecutor has determined that a prima facie case exists for prosecution, he would prepare an indictment containing a concise statement of the facts and the crimes with which the accused is charged under the statute. The indictment would be transmitted to a judge of a Trial Chamber, who would review it and decide whether to confirm or to dismiss the indictment.

96. If the investigation includes questioning of the suspect, then he should have the right to be assisted by counsel of his own choice, including the right to have legal assistance assigned to him without payment by him in any such case if he does not have sufficient means to pay for it. He shall also be entitled to the necessary translation into and from a language he speaks and understands.

97. Upon confirmation of the indictment, the judge would, at the request of the Prosecutor, issue such orders and warrants for the arrest, detention, surrender and transfer of persons, or any other orders as may be necessary for the conduct of the trial.

98. The corresponding articles of the statute would read as follows:

Article 18

Investigation and preparation of indictment

1. The Prosecutor shall initiate investigations ex officio or on the basis of information obtained from any source, particularly from Governments, United Nations organs, intergovernmental and non-governmental organizations. The Prosecutor shall assess the information received or obtained and decide whether there is sufficient basis to proceed.

2. The Prosecutor shall have the power to question suspects, victims and witnesses, to collect evidence and to conduct on-site investigations. In carrying out these tasks the Prosecutor may, as appropriate, seek the assistance of the State authorities concerned.

3. If questioned, the suspect shall be entitled to be assisted by counsel of his own choice, including the right to have legal assistance assigned to him without payment by him in any such case if he does not have sufficient means to pay for it, as well as to necessary translation into and from a language he speaks and understands.

4. Upon a determination that a prima facie case exists, the Prosecutor shall prepare an indictment containing a concise statement of the facts and the crime or crimes with which the accused is charged under the Statute. The indictment shall be transmitted to a judge of the Trial Chamber.

Article 19

Review of the indictment

1. The judge of the Trial Chamber to whom the indictment has been transmitted shall review it. If satisfied that a prima facie case has been established by the Prosecutor, he shall confirm the indictment. If not so satisfied, the indictment shall be dismissed.

2. Upon confirmation of an indictment, the judge may, at the request of the Prosecutor, issue such orders and warrants for the arrest, detention, surrender or transfer of persons, and any other orders as may be required for the conduct of the trial.

V. TRIAL AND POST-TRIAL PROCEEDINGS

A. Commencement and conduct of trial proceedings

99. The Trial Chambers should ensure that a trial is fair and expeditious and that proceedings are conducted in accordance with the rules of procedure and evidence and with full respect for the rights of the accused. The Trial Chamber should also provide appropriate protection for victims and witnesses during the proceedings.

100. A person against whom an indictment has been confirmed would, pursuant to an order or a warrant of the International Tribunal, be informed of the contents of the indictment and taken into custody.

101. A trial should not commence until the accused is physically present before the International Tribunal. There is a widespread perception that trials in absentia should not be provided for in the statute as this would not be consistent with article 14 of the International Covenant on Civil and Political Rights, 10/ which provides that the accused shall be entitled to be tried in his presence.

102. The person against whom an indictment has been confirmed would be transferred to the seat of the International Tribunal and brought before a Trial Chamber without undue delay and formally charged. The Trial Chamber would read the indictment, satisfy itself that the rights of the accused are respected, confirm that the accused understands the indictment, and instruct the accused to enter a plea. After the plea has been entered, the Trial Chamber would set the date for trial.

103. The hearings should be held in public unless the Trial Chamber decides otherwise in accordance with its rules of procedure and evidence.

104. After hearing the submissions of the parties and examining the witnesses and evidence presented to it, the Trial Chamber would close the hearing and retire for private deliberations.

105. The corresponding article of the statute would read:

10/ United Nations, Treaty Series, vol. 999, No. 14668, p. 171 and vol. 1057, p. 407 (proces-verbal of rectification of authentic Spanish text).

Article 20

Commencement and conduct of trial proceedings

1. The Trial Chambers shall ensure that a trial is fair and expeditious and that proceedings are conducted in accordance with the rules of procedure and evidence, with full respect for the rights of the accused and due regard for the protection of victims and witnesses.

2. A person against whom an indictment has been confirmed shall, pursuant to an order or an arrest warrant of the International Tribunal, be taken into custody, immediately informed of the charges against him and transferred to the International Tribunal.

3. The Trial Chamber shall read the indictment, satisfy itself that the rights of the accused are respected, confirm that the accused understands the indictment, and instruct the accused to enter a plea. The Trial Chamber shall then set the date for trial.

4. The hearings shall be public unless the Trial Chamber decides to close the proceedings in accordance with its rules of procedure and evidence.

B. Rights of the accused

106. It is axiomatic that the International Tribunal must fully respect internationally recognized standards regarding the rights of the accused at all stages of its proceedings. In the view of the Secretary-General, such internationally recognized standards are, in particular, contained in article 14 of the International Covenant on Civil and Political Rights. 10/

107. The corresponding article of the statute would read as follows:

Article 21

Rights of the accused

1. All persons shall be equal before the International Tribunal.

2. In the determination of charges against him, the accused shall be entitled to a fair and public hearing, subject to article 22 of the Statute.

3. The accused shall be presumed innocent until proved guilty according to the provisions of the present Statute.

4. In the determination of any charge against the accused pursuant to the present Statute, the accused shall be entitled to the following minimum guarantees, in full equality:

(a) to be informed promptly and in detail in a language which he understands of the nature and cause of the charge against him;

(b) to have adequate time and facilities for the preparation of his defence and to communicate with counsel of his own choosing;

(c) to be tried without undue delay;

(d) to be tried in his presence, and to defend himself in person or through legal assistance of his own choosing; to be informed, if he does not have legal assistance, of this right; and to have legal assistance assigned to him, in any case where the interests of justice so require, and without payment by him in any such case if he does not have sufficient means to pay for it;

(e) to examine, or have examined, the witnesses against him and to obtain the attendance and examination of witnesses on his behalf under the same conditions as witnesses against him;

(f) to have the free assistance of an interpreter if he cannot understand or speak the language used in the International Tribunal;

(g) not to be compelled to testify against himself or to confess guilt.

C. Protection of victims and witnesses

108. In the light of the particular nature of the crimes committed in the former Yugoslavia, it will be necessary for the International Tribunal to ensure the protection of victims and witnesses. Necessary protection measures should therefore be provided in the rules of procedure and evidence for victims and witnesses, especially in cases of rape or sexual assault. Such measures should include, but should not be limited to the conduct of in camera proceedings, and the protection of the victim's identity.

109. The corresponding article of the statute would read as follows:

Article 22

Protection of victims and witnesses

The International Tribunal shall provide in its rules of procedure and evidence for the protection of victims and witnesses. Such protection measures shall include, but shall not be limited to, the conduct of in camera proceedings and the protection of the victim's identity.

D. Judgement and penalties

110. The Trial Chambers would have the power to pronounce judgements and impose sentences and penalties on persons convicted of serious violations of international humanitarian law. A judgement would be rendered by a majority of the judges of the Chamber and delivered in public. It should be written and accompanied by a reasoned opinion. Separate or dissenting opinions should be permitted.

111. The penalty to be imposed on a convicted person would be limited to imprisonment. In determining the term of imprisonment, the Trial Chambers should have recourse to the general practice of prison sentences applicable in the courts of the former Yugoslavia.

112. The International Tribunal should not be empowered to impose the death penalty.

113. In imposing sentences, the Trial Chambers should take into account such factors as the gravity of the offence and the individual circumstances of the convicted person.

114. In addition to imprisonment, property and proceeds acquired by criminal conduct should be confiscated and returned to their rightful owners. This would include the return of property wrongfully acquired by means of duress. In this connection the Secretary-General recalls that in resolution 779 (1992) of 6 October 1992, the Security Council endorsed the principle that all statements or commitments made under duress, particularly those relating to land and property, are wholly null and void.

115. The corresponding articles of the statute would read as follows:

Article 23

Judgement

1. The Trial Chambers shall pronounce judgements and impose sentences and penalties on persons convicted of serious violations of international humanitarian law.

2. The judgement shall be rendered by a majority of the judges of the Trial Chamber, and shall be delivered by the Trial Chamber in public. It shall be accompanied by a reasoned opinion in writing, to which separate or dissenting opinions may be appended.

Article 24

Penalties

1. The penalty imposed by the Trial Chamber shall be limited to imprisonment. In determining the terms of imprisonment, the Trial Chambers shall have recourse to the general practice regarding prison sentences in the courts of the former Yugoslavia.

2. In imposing the sentences, the Trial Chambers should take into account such factors as the gravity of the offence and the individual circumstances of the convicted person.

3. In addition to imprisonment, the Trial Chambers may order the return of any property and proceeds acquired by criminal conduct, including by means of duress, to their rightful owners.

E. Appellate and review proceedings

116. The Secretary-General is of the view that the right of appeal should be provided for under the Statute. Such a right is a fundamental element of individual civil and political rights and has, *inter alia*, been incorporated in the International Covenant on Civil and Political Rights. For this reason, the Secretary-General has proposed that there should be an Appeals Chamber.

117. The right of appeal should be exercisable on two grounds: an error on a question of law invalidating the decision or, an error of fact which has occasioned a miscarriage of justice. The Prosecutor should also be entitled to initiate appeal proceedings on the same grounds.

118. The judgement of the Appeals Chamber affirming, reversing or revising the judgement of the Trial Chamber would be final. It would be delivered by the Appeals Chamber in public and be accompanied by a reasoned opinion to which separate or dissenting opinions may be appended.

119. Where a new fact has come to light which was not known at the time of the proceedings before the Trial Chambers or the Appeals Chamber, and which could have been a decisive factor in reaching the decision, the convicted person or the Prosecutor should be authorized to submit to the International Tribunal an application for review of the judgement.

120. The corresponding articles of the statute would read as follows:

Article 25

Appellate proceedings

1. The Appeals Chamber shall hear appeals from persons convicted by the Trial Chambers or from the Prosecutor on the following grounds:

(a) an error on a question of law invalidating the decision; or

(b) an error of fact which has occasioned a miscarriage of justice.

2. The Appeals Chamber may affirm, reverse or revise the decisions taken by the Trial Chambers.

Article 26

Review proceedings

Where a new fact has been discovered which was not known at the time of the proceedings before the Trial Chambers or the Appeals Chamber and which could have been a decisive factor in reaching the decision, the convicted person or the Prosecutor may submit to the International Tribunal an application for review of the judgement.

F. Enforcement of sentences

121. The Secretary-General is of the view that, given the nature of the crimes in question and the international character of the tribunal, the enforcement of sentences should take place outside the territory of the former Yugoslavia. States should be encouraged to declare their readiness to carry out the enforcement of prison sentences in accordance with their domestic laws and procedures, under the supervision of the International Tribunal.

122. The Security Council would make appropriate arrangements to obtain from States an indication of their willingness to accept convicted persons. This information would be communicated to the Registrar, who would prepare a list of States in which the enforcement of sentences would be carried out.

123. The accused would be eligible for pardon or commutation of sentence in accordance with the laws of the State in which sentence is served. In such an event, the State concerned would notify the International Tribunal, which would decide the matter in accordance with the interests of justice and the general principles of law.

124. The corresponding article of the statute would read as follows:

Article 27

Enforcement of sentences

Imprisonment shall be served in a State designated by the International Tribunal from a list of States which have indicated to the Security Council their willingness to accept convicted persons. Such imprisonment shall be in accordance with the applicable law of the State concerned, subject to the supervision of the International Tribunal.

Article 28

Pardon or commutation of sentences

If, pursuant to the applicable law of the State in which the convicted person is imprisoned, he or she is eligible for pardon or commutation of sentence, the State concerned shall notify the International Tribunal accordingly. The President of the International Tribunal, in consultation with the judges, shall decide the matter on the basis of the interests of justice and the general principles of law.

VI. COOPERATION AND JUDICIAL ASSISTANCE

125. As pointed out in paragraph 23 above, the establishment of the International Tribunal on the basis of a Chapter VII decision creates a binding obligation on all States to take whatever steps are required to implement the decision. In practical terms, this means that all States would be under an obligation to cooperate with the International Tribunal and to assist it in all stages of the proceedings to ensure compliance with requests for assistance in the gathering of evidence, hearing of witnesses, suspects and experts, identification and location of persons and the service of documents. Effect shall also be given to orders issued by the Trial Chambers, such as warrants of arrest, search warrants, warrants for surrender or transfer of persons, and any other orders necessary for the conduct of the trial.

126. In this connection, an order by a Trial Chamber for the surrender or transfer of persons to the custody of the International Tribunal shall be considered to be the application of an enforcement measure under Chapter VII of the Charter of the United Nations.

127. The corresponding article of the statute would read as follows:

Article 29

Cooperation and judicial assistance

1. States shall cooperate with the International Tribunal in the investigation and prosecution of persons accused of committing serious violations of international humanitarian law.

2. States shall comply without undue delay with any request for assistance or an order issued by a Trial Chamber, including, but not limited to:

(a) the identification and location of persons;

(b) the taking of testimony and the production of evidence;

(c) the service of documents;

(d) the arrest or detention of persons;

(e) the surrender or the transfer of the accused to the International Tribunal.

VII. GENERAL PROVISIONS

A. The status, privileges and immunities of the International Tribunal

128. The Convention on the Privileges and Immunities of the United Nations of 13 February 1946 would apply to the International Tribunal, the judges, the Prosecutor and his staff, and the Registrar and his staff. The judges, the Prosecutor, and the Registrar would be granted the privileges and immunities, exemptions and facilities accorded to diplomatic envoys in accordance with international law. The staff of the Prosecutor and the Registrar would enjoy the privileges and immunities of officials of the United Nations within the meaning of articles V and VII of the Convention.

129. Other persons, including the accused, required at the seat of the International Tribunal would be accorded such treatment as is necessary for the proper functioning of the International Tribunal.

130. The corresponding article of the statute would read:

Article 30

The status, privileges and immunities of the International Tribunal

1. The Convention on the Privileges and Immunities of the United Nations of 13 February 1946 shall apply to the International Tribunal, the judges, the Prosecutor and his staff, and the Registrar and his staff.

2. The judges, the Prosecutor and the Registrar shall enjoy the privileges and immunities, exemptions and facilities accorded to diplomatic envoys, in accordance with international law.

3. The staff of the Prosecutor and of the Registrar shall enjoy the privileges and immunities accorded to officials of the United Nations under articles V and VII of the Convention referred to in paragraph 1 of this article.

4. Other persons, including the accused, required at the seat of the International Tribunal shall be accorded such treatment as is necessary for the proper functioning of the International Tribunal.

B. Seat of the International Tribunal

131. While it will be for the Security Council to determine the location of the seat of the International Tribunal, in the view of the Secretary-General, there are a number of elementary considerations of justice and fairness, as well as administrative efficiency and economy which should be taken into account. As a matter of justice and fairness, it would not be appropriate for the International Tribunal to have its seat in the territory of the former Yugoslavia or in any State neighbouring upon the former Yugoslavia. For reasons of administrative efficiency and economy, it would be desirable to establish the seat of the International Tribunal at a European location in which the United Nations already has an important presence. The two locations which fulfil these requirements are Geneva and The Hague. Provided that the necessary arrangements can be made with the host country, the Secretary-General believes that the seat of the International Tribunal should be at The Hague.

132. The corresponding article of the statute would read:

Article 31

Seat of the International Tribunal

The International Tribunal shall have its seat at The Hague.

C. Financial arrangements

133. The expenses of the International Tribunal should be borne by the regular budget of the United Nations in accordance with Article 17 of the Charter of the United Nations.

134. The corresponding article of the statute would read:

Article 32

Expenses of the International Tribunal

The expenses of the International Tribunal shall be borne by the regular budget of the United Nations in accordance with Article 17 of the Charter of the United Nations.

D. Working languages

135. The working languages of the Tribunal should be English and French.

136. The corresponding article of the statute would read as follows:

Article 33

Working languages

The working languages of the International Tribunal shall be English and French.

E. Annual report

137. The International Tribunal should submit an annual report on its activities to the Security Council and the General Assembly.

138. The corresponding article of the statute would read:

Article 34

Annual report

The President of the International Tribunal shall submit an annual report of the International Tribunal to the Security Council and to the General Assembly.

Annex

Statute of the International Tribunal

Having been established by the Security Council acting under Chapter VII of the Charter of the United Nations, the International Tribunal for the Prosecution of Persons Responsible for Serious Violations of International Humanitarian Law Committed in the Territory of the Former Yugoslavia since 1991 (hereinafter referred to as "the International Tribunal") shall function in accordance with the provisions of the present Statute.

Article 1

Competence of the International Tribunal

The International Tribunal shall have the power to prosecute persons responsible for serious violations of international humanitarian law committed in the territory of the former Yugoslavia since 1991 in accordance with the provisions of the present Statute.

Article 2

Grave breaches of the Geneva Conventions of 1949

The International Tribunal shall have the power to prosecute persons committing or ordering to be committed grave breaches of the Geneva Conventions of 12 August 1949, namely the following acts against persons or property protected under the provisions of the relevant Geneva Convention:

(a) wilful killing;

(b) torture or inhuman treatment, including biological experiments;

(c) wilfully causing great suffering or serious injury to body or health;

(d) extensive destruction and appropriation of property, not justified by military necessity and carried out unlawfully and wantonly;

(e) compelling a prisoner of war or a civilian to serve in the forces of a hostile power;

(f) wilfully depriving a prisoner of war or a civilian of the rights of fair and regular trial;

(g) unlawful deportation or transfer or unlawful confinement of a civilian;

(h) taking civilians as hostages.

Article 3

Violations of the laws or customs of war

The International Tribunal shall have the power to prosecute persons violating the laws or customs of war. Such violations shall include, but not be limited to:

(a) employment of poisonous weapons or other weapons calculated to cause unnecessary suffering;

(b) wanton destruction of cities, towns or villages, or devastation not justified by military necessity;

(c) attack, or bombardment, by whatever means, of undefended towns, villages, dwellings, or buildings;

(d) seizure of, destruction or wilful damage done to institutions dedicated to religion, charity and education, the arts and sciences, historic monuments and works of art and science;

(e) plunder of public or private property.

Article 4

Genocide

1. The International Tribunal shall have the power to prosecute persons committing genocide as defined in paragraph 2 of this article or of committing any of the other acts enumerated in paragraph 3 of this article.

2. Genocide means any of the following acts committed with intent to destroy, in whole or in part, a national, ethnical, racial or religious group, as such:

(a) killing members of the group;

(b) causing serious bodily or mental harm to members of the group;

(c) deliberately inflicting on the group conditions of life calculated to bring about its physical destruction in whole or in part;

(d) imposing measures intended to prevent births within the group;

(e) forcibly transferring children of the group to another group.

3. The following acts shall be punishable:

(a) genocide;

(b) conspiracy to commit genocide;

(c) direct and public incitement to commit genocide;

(d) attempt to commit genocide;

(e) complicity in genocide.

Article 5

Crimes against humanity

The International Tribunal shall have the power to prosecute persons responsible for the following crimes when committed in armed conflict, whether international or internal in character, and directed against any civilian population:

(a) murder;

(b) extermination;

(c) enslavement;

(d) deportation;

(e) imprisonment;

(f) torture;

(g) rape;

(h) persecutions on political, racial and religious grounds;

(i) other inhumane acts.

Article 6

Personal jurisdiction

The International Tribunal shall have jurisdiction over natural persons pursuant to the provisions of the present Statute.

Article 7

Individual criminal responsibility

1. A person who planned, instigated, ordered, committed or otherwise aided and abetted in the planning, preparation or execution of a crime referred to in articles 2 to 5 of the present Statute, shall be individually responsible for the crime.

2. The official position of any accused person, whether as Head of State or Government or as a responsible Government official, shall not relieve such person of criminal responsibility nor mitigate punishment.

3. The fact that any of the acts referred to in articles 2 to 5 of the present Statute was committed by a subordinate does not relieve his superior of criminal responsibility if he knew or had reason to know that the subordinate was about to commit such acts or had done so and the superior failed to take the necessary and reasonable measures to prevent such acts or to punish the perpetrators thereof.

4. The fact that an accused person acted pursuant to an order of a Government or of a superior shall not relieve him of criminal responsibility, but may be considered in mitigation of punishment if the International Tribunal determines that justice so requires.

Article 8

Territorial and temporal jurisdiction

The territorial jurisdiction of the International Tribunal shall extend to the territory of the former Socialist Federal Republic of Yugoslavia, including its land surface, airspace and territorial waters. The temporal jurisdiction of the International Tribunal shall extend to a period beginning on 1 January 1991.

Article 9

Concurrent jurisdiction

1. The International Tribunal and national courts shall have concurrent jurisdiction to prosecute persons for serious violations of international humanitarian law committed in the territory of the former Yugoslavia since 1 January 1991.

2. The International Tribunal shall have primacy over national courts. At any stage of the procedure, the International Tribunal may formally request national courts to defer to the competence of the International Tribunal in accordance with the present Statute and the Rules of Procedure and Evidence of the International Tribunal.

Article 10

Non-bis-in-idem

1. No person shall be tried before a national court for acts constituting serious violations of international humanitarian law under the present Statute, for which he or she has already been tried by the International Tribunal.

2. A person who has been tried by a national court for acts constituting serious violations of international humanitarian law may be subsequently tried by the International Tribunal only if:

(a) the act for which he or she was tried was characterized as an ordinary crime; or

(b) the national court proceedings were not impartial or independent, were designed to shield the accused from international criminal responsibility, or the case was not diligently prosecuted.

3. In considering the penalty to be imposed on a person convicted of a crime under the present Statute, the International Tribunal shall take into account the extent to which any penalty imposed by a national court on the same person for the same act has already been served.

Article 11

Organization of the International Tribunal

The International Tribunal shall consist of the following organs:

(a) The Chambers, comprising two Trial Chambers and an Appeals Chamber;

(b) The Prosecutor, and

(c) A Registry, servicing both the Chambers and the Prosecutor.

Article 12

Composition of the Chambers

The Chambers shall be composed of eleven independent judges, no two of whom may be nationals of the same State, who shall serve as follows:

(a) Three judges shall serve in each of the Trial Chambers;

(b) Five judges shall serve in the Appeals Chamber.

Article 13

Qualifications and election of judges

1. The judges shall be persons of high moral character, impartiality and integrity who possess the qualifications required in their respective countries for appointment to the highest judicial offices. In the overall composition of the Chambers due account shall be taken of the experience of the judges in criminal law, international law, including international humanitarian law and human rights law.

2. The judges of the International Tribunal shall be elected by the General Assembly from a list submitted by the Security Council, in the following manner:

(a) The Secretary-General shall invite nominations for judges of the International Tribunal from States Members of the United Nations and non-member States maintaining permanent observer missions at United Nations Headquarters;

(b) Within sixty days of the date of the invitation of the Secretary-General, each State may nominate up to two candidates meeting the qualifications set out in paragraph 1 above, no two of whom shall be of the same nationality;

(c) The Secretary-General shall forward the nominations received to the Security Council. From the nominations received the Security Council shall establish a list of not less than twenty-two and not more than thirty-three candidates, taking due account of the adequate representation of the principal legal systems of the world;

(d) The President of the Security Council shall transmit the list of candidates to the President of the General Assembly. From that list the General Assembly shall elect the eleven judges of the International Tribunal. The candidates who receive an absolute majority of the votes of the States Members of the United Nations and of the non-Member States maintaining permanent observer missions at United Nations Headquarters, shall be declared elected. Should two candidates of the same nationality obtain the required majority vote, the one who received the higher number of votes shall be considered elected.

3. In the event of a vacancy in the Chambers, after consultation with the Presidents of the Security Council and of the General Assembly, the Secretary-General shall appoint a person meeting the qualifications of paragraph 1 above, for the remainder of the term of office concerned.

4. The judges shall be elected for a term of four years. The terms and conditions of service shall be those of the judges of the International Court of Justice. They shall be eligible for re-election.

Article 14

Officers and members of the Chambers

1. The judges of the International Tribunal shall elect a President.

2. The President of the International Tribunal shall be a member of the Appeals Chamber and shall preside over its proceedings.

3. After consultation with the judges of the International Tribunal, the President shall assign the judges to the Appeals Chamber and to the Trial Chambers. A judge shall serve only in the Chamber to which he or she was assigned.

4. The judges of each Trial Chamber shall elect a Presiding Judge, who shall conduct all of the proceedings of the Trial Chamber as a whole.

Article 15

Rules of procedure and evidence

The judges of the International Tribunal shall adopt rules of procedure and evidence for the conduct of the pre-trial phase of the proceedings, trials and appeals, the admission of evidence, the protection of victims and witnesses and other appropriate matters.

Article 16

The Prosecutor

1. The Prosecutor shall be responsible for the investigation and prosecution of persons responsible for serious violations of international humanitarian law committed in the territory of the former Yugoslavia since 1 January 1991.

2. The Prosecutor shall act independently as a separate organ of the International Tribunal. He or she shall not seek or receive instructions from any Government or from any other source.

3. The Office of the Prosecutor shall be composed of a Prosecutor and such other qualified staff as may be required.

4. The Prosecutor shall be appointed by the Security Council on nomination by the Secretary-General. He or she shall be of high moral character and possess the highest level of competence and experience in the conduct of investigations and prosecutions of criminal cases. The Prosecutor shall serve for a four-year term and be eligible for reappointment. The terms and conditions of service of the Prosecutor shall be those of an Under-Secretary-General of the United Nations.

5. The staff of the Office of the Prosecutor shall be appointed by the Secretary-General on the recommendation of the Prosecutor.

Article 17

The Registry

1. The Registry shall be responsible for the administration and servicing of the International Tribunal.

2. The Registry shall consist of a Registrar and such other staff as may be required.

3. The Registrar shall be appointed by the Secretary-General after consultation with the President of the International Tribunal. He or she shall serve for a four-year term and be eligible for reappointment. The terms and conditions of service of the Registrar shall be those of an Assistant Secretary-General of the United Nations.

4. The staff of the Registry shall be appointed by the Secretary-General on the recommendation of the Registrar.

Article 18

Investigation and preparation of indictment

1. The Prosecutor shall initiate investigations ex-officio or on the basis of information obtained from any source, particularly from Governments, United Nations organs, intergovernmental and non-governmental organizations. The Prosecutor shall assess the information received or obtained and decide whether there is sufficient basis to proceed.

2. The Prosecutor shall have the power to question suspects, victims and witnesses, to collect evidence and to conduct on-site investigations. In carrying out these tasks, the Prosecutor may, as appropriate, seek the assistance of the State authorities concerned.

3. If questioned, the suspect shall be entitled to be assisted by counsel of his own choice, including the right to have legal assistance assigned to him without payment by him in any such case if he does not have sufficient means to pay for it, as well as to necessary translation into and from a language he speaks and understands.

4. Upon a determination that a prima facie case exists, the Prosecutor shall prepare an indictment containing a concise statement of the facts and the crime or crimes with which the accused is charged under the Statute. The indictment shall be transmitted to a judge of the Trial Chamber.

Article 19

Review of the indictment

1. The judge of the Trial Chamber to whom the indictment has been transmitted shall review it. If satisfied that a prima facie case has been established by the Prosecutor, he shall confirm the indictment. If not so satisfied, the indictment shall be dismissed.

2. Upon confirmation of an indictment, the judge may, at the request of the Prosecutor, issue such orders and warrants for the arrest, detention, surrender or transfer of persons, and any other orders as may be required for the conduct of the trial.

Article 20

Commencement and conduct of trial proceedings

1. The Trial Chambers shall ensure that a trial is fair and expeditious and that proceedings are conducted in accordance with the rules of procedure and evidence, with full respect for the rights of the accused and due regard for the protection of victims and witnesses.

2. A person against whom an indictment has been confirmed shall, pursuant to an order or an arrest warrant of the International Tribunal, be taken into custody, immediately informed of the charges against him and transferred to the International Tribunal.

3. The Trial Chamber shall read the indictment, satisfy itself that the rights of the accused are respected, confirm that the accused understands the indictment, and instruct the accused to enter a plea. The Trial Chamber shall then set the date for trial.

4. The hearings shall be public unless the Trial Chamber decides to close the proceedings in accordance with its rules of procedure and evidence.

Article 21

Rights of the accused

1. All persons shall be equal before the International Tribunal.

2. In the determination of charges against him, the accused shall be entitled to a fair and public hearing, subject to article 22 of the Statute.

3. The accused shall be presumed innocent until proved guilty according to the provisions of the present Statute.

4. In the determination of any charge against the accused pursuant to the present Statute, the accused shall be entitled to the following minimum guarantees, in full equality:

(a) to be informed promptly and in detail in a language which he understands of the nature and cause of the charge against him;

(b) to have adequate time and facilities for the preparation of his defence and to communicate with counsel of his own choosing;

(c) to be tried without undue delay;

(d) to be tried in his presence, and to defend himself in person or through legal assistance of his own choosing; to be informed, if he does not have legal assistance, of this right; and to have legal assistance assigned to him, in any case where the interests of justice so require, and without payment by him in any such case if he does not have sufficient means to pay for it;

(e) to examine, or have examined, the witnesses against him and to obtain the attendance and examination of witnesses on his behalf under the same conditions as witnesses against him;

(f) to have the free assistance of an interpreter if he cannot understand or speak the language used in the International Tribunal;

(g) not to be compelled to testify against himself or to confess guilt.

Article 22

Protection of victims and witnesses

The International Tribunal shall provide in its rules of procedure and evidence for the protection of victims and witnesses. Such protection measures shall include, but shall not be limited to, the conduct of *in camera* proceedings and the protection of the victim's identity.

Article 23

Judgement

1. The Trial Chambers shall pronounce judgements and impose sentences and penalties on persons convicted of serious violations of international humanitarian law.

2. The judgement shall be rendered by a majority of the judges of the Trial Chamber, and shall be delivered by the Trial Chamber in public. It shall be accompanied by a reasoned opinion in writing, to which separate or dissenting opinions may be appended.

Article 24

Penalties

1. The penalty imposed by the Trial Chamber shall be limited to imprisonment. In determining the terms of imprisonment, the Trial Chambers shall have recourse to the general practice regarding prison sentences in the courts of the former Yugoslavia.

2. In imposing the sentences, the Trial Chambers should take into account such factors as the gravity of the offence and the individual circumstances of the convicted person.

3. In addition to imprisonment, the Trial Chambers may order the return of any property and proceeds acquired by criminal conduct, including by means of duress, to their rightful owners.

Article 25

Appellate proceedings

1. The Appeals Chamber shall hear appeals from persons convicted by the Trial Chambers or from the Prosecutor on the following grounds:

(a) an error on a question of law invalidating the decision; or

(b) an error of fact which has occasioned a miscarriage of justice.

2. The Appeals Chamber may affirm, reverse or revise the decisions taken by the Trial Chambers.

Article 26

Review proceedings

Where a new fact has been discovered which was not known at the time of the proceedings before the Trial Chambers or the Appeals Chamber and which could have been a decisive factor in reaching the decision, the convicted person or the Prosecutor may submit to the International Tribunal an application for review of the judgement.

Article 27

Enforcement of sentences

Imprisonment shall be served in a State designated by the International Tribunal from a list of States which have indicated to the Security Council their willingness to accept convicted persons. Such imprisonment shall be in accordance with the applicable law of the State concerned, subject to the supervision of the International Tribunal.

Article 28

Pardon or commutation of sentences

If, pursuant to the applicable law of the State in which the convicted person is imprisoned, he or she is eligible for pardon or commutation of sentence, the State concerned shall notify the International Tribunal accordingly. The President of the International Tribunal, in consultation with the judges, shall decide the matter on the basis of the interests of justice and the general principles of law.

Article 29

Cooperation and judicial assistance

1. States shall cooperate with the International Tribunal in the investigation and prosecution of persons accused of committing serious violations of international humanitarian law.

2. States shall comply without undue delay with any request for assistance or an order issued by a Trial Chamber, including, but not limited to:

(a) the identification and location of persons;

(b) the taking of testimony and the production of evidence;

(c) the service of documents;

(d) the arrest or detention of persons;

(e) the surrender or the transfer of the accused to the International Tribunal.

Article 30

The status, privileges and immunities of the International Tribunal

1. The Convention on the Privileges and Immunities of the United Nations of 13 February 1946 shall apply to the International Tribunal, the judges, the Prosecutor and his staff, and the Registrar and his staff.

2. The judges, the Prosecutor and the Registrar shall enjoy the privileges and immunities, exemptions and facilities accorded to diplomatic envoys, in accordance with international law.

3. The staff of the Prosecutor and of the Registrar shall enjoy the privileges and immunities accorded to officials of the United Nations under articles V and VII of the Convention referred to in paragraph 1 of this article.

4. Other persons, including the accused, required at the seat of the International Tribunal shall be accorded such treatment as is necessary for the proper functioning of the International Tribunal.

Article 31

Seat of the International Tribunal

The International Tribunal shall have its seat at The Hague.

Article 32

Expenses of the International Tribunal

The expenses of the International Tribunal shall be borne by the regular budget of the United Nations in accordance with Article 17 of the Charter of the United Nations.

Article 33

Working languages

The working languages of the International Tribunal shall be English and French.

Article 34

Annual report

The President of the International Tribunal shall submit an annual report of the International Tribunal to the Security Council and to the General Assembly.

PART II

THE RULES OF PROCEDURE AND EVIDENCE OF THE INTERNATIONAL TRIBUNAL, 5 MAY 1994

RULES OF PROCEDURE AND EVIDENCE
(Adopted on 11 February 1994)
(As Amended 5 May 1994)
(As Further Amended 4 October 1994)
(As Revised 30 January 1995)*

IT/32/Rev. 3, 30 January 1995.

CONTENTS

*The text of Rule 96, as initially amended on 5 May 1994, is reproduced in Document IX.C.2 below. The text of Rule 70(B), as initially amended on 4 October 1994, is reproduced at 356n. 945. The following provisions were affected by the revisions adopted on 30 January 1995: Rule 2 Definitions; Rule 3 Languages; Rule 5 Non-compliance with Rules; Rule 8 Request for Information; Rule 9 Prosecutor's Request for Deferral; Rule 10 Formal Request for Deferral; Rule 12 Determinations of Courts of any State; Rule 13 *Non Bis in Idem*; Rule 15 Disqualification of Judges; Rule 28 Assignment to Review Indictments; Rule 36 Record Book; Rule 37 Functions of the Prosecutor; Rule 39 Conduct of Investigations; Rule 40 Provisional Measures; Rule 42 Rights of Suspects during Investigation; Rule 43 Recording Questioning of Suspects; Rule 45 Assignment of Counsel; Rule 47 Submission of Indictment by the Prosecutor; Rule 53 Non-disclosure; Rule 54 General Rule [orders and warrants]; Rule 55 Execution of Arrest Warrants; Rule 57 Procedure after Arrest; Rule 61 Procedure in Case of Failure to Execute a Warrant; Rule 62 Initial Appearance of Accused; Rule 65 Provisional Release; Rule 66 Disclosure by the Prosecutor; Rule 68 Disclosure of Exculpatory Evidence; Rule 70 Matters not Subject to Disclosure; Rule 72 General Provisions [preliminary motions]; Rule 75 Measures for the Protection of Victims and Witnesses; Rule 77 Contempt of the Tribunal; Rule 88 Judgement; Rule 90 Testimony of Witnesses; Rule 91 False Testimony under Solemn Declaration; Rule 93 Evidence of Consistent Pattern of Conduct; Rule 95 Evidence Obtained by Means Contrary to Internationally Protected Human Rights; Rule 96 Evidence in Cases of Sexual Assault; Rule 101 Penalties; Rule 105 Restitution of Property; Rule 108 Notice of Appeal; Rule 116*bis* Expedited Appeals Procedure; Rule 117 Judgement on Appeal.

Part One

GENERAL PROVISIONS

Rule 1
Entry into Force

These Rules of Procedure and Evidence, adopted pursuant to Article 15 of the Statute of the Tribunal, shall come into force on 14 March 1994.

Rule 2
Definitions

(A) In the Rules, unless the context otherwise requires, the following terms shall mean:

Rules: The Rules referred to in Rule 1;

Statute: The Statute of the Tribunal adopted by Security Council resolution 827 of 25 May 1993;

Tribunal: The International Tribunal for the Prosecution of Persons Responsible for Serious Violations of International Humanitarian Law Committed in the Territory of the Former Yugoslavia since 1991, established by Security Council resolution 827 of 25 May 1993.

* * *

Accused: A person against whom an indictment has been submitted in accordance with Rule 47;

Arrest: The act of taking a suspect or an accused into custody by a national authority;

Bureau: A body composed of the President, the Vice-President and the Presiding Judges of the Trial Chambers;

Investigation: All activities undertaken by the Prosecutor under the Statute and the Rules for the collection of information and evidence;

Party: The Prosecutor or the accused;

President: The President of the Tribunal;

Prosecutor: The Prosecutor appointed pursuant to Article 16 of the Statute;

Regulations: The provisions framed by the Prosecutor pursuant to Sub-rule 37 (A) for the purpose of directing the functions of his Office;

State: A State Member or non-Member of the United Nations or a self-proclaimed entity de facto exercising governmental functions, whether recognised as a State or not;

Suspect: A person concerning whom the Prosecutor possesses reliable information which tends to show that he may have committed a crime over which the Tribunal has jurisdiction;

Transaction: A number of acts or omissions whether occurring as one event or a number of events, at the same or different locations and being part of a common scheme, strategy or plan;

Victim: A person against whom a crime over which the Tribunal has jurisdiction has allegedly been committed.

(B) In the Rules, the masculine shall include the feminine and the singular the plural, and vice-versa.

Rule 3
Languages

(A) The working languages of the Tribunal shall be English and French.

(B) An accused shall have the right to use his own language.

(C) Any other person appearing before the Tribunal, other than as counsel, who does not have sufficient knowledge of either of the two working languages, may use his own language.

(D) Counsel for an accused may apply to the Presiding Judge of a Chamber for leave to use a language other than the two working ones or the language of the accused. If such leave is granted, the expenses of interpretation and translation shall be borne by the Tribunal to the extent, if any, determined by the President, taking into account the rights of the defence and the interests of justice.

(E) The Registrar shall make any necessary arrangements for interpretation and translation into and from the working languages.

Rule 4
Meetings away from the Seat of the Tribunal

A Chamber may exercise its functions at a place other than the seat of the Tribunal, if so authorised by the President in the interests of justice.

Rule 5
Non-compliance with Rules

Any objection by a party to an act of another party on the ground of non-compliance with the Rules or Regulations shall be raised at the earliest opportunity; it shall be upheld, and the act declared null, only if the act was inconsistent with the fundamental principles of fairness and has occasioned a miscarriage of justice.

Rule 6
Amendment of the Rules

(A) Proposals for amendment of the Rules may be made by a Judge, the Prosecutor or the Registrar and shall be adopted if agreed to by not less than seven Judges at a plenary meeting of the Tribunal convened with notice of the proposal addressed to all Judges.

(B) An amendment to the Rules may be otherwise adopted, provided it is unanimously approved by the Judges.

(C) An amendment shall enter into force immediately, but shall not operate to prejudice the rights of the accused in any pending case.

Rule 7
Authentic Texts

The English and French texts of the Rules shall be equally authentic. In case of discrepancy, the version which is more consonant with the spirit of the Statute and the Rules shall prevail.

Part Two

PRIMACY OF THE TRIBUNAL

Rule 8
Request for Information

Where it appears to the Prosecutor that a crime within the jurisdiction of the Tribunal is or has been the subject of investigations or criminal proceedings instituted in the courts of any State, he may request the State to forward to him all relevant information in that respect, and the State shall transmit to him such information forthwith in accordance with Article 29 of the Statute.

Rule 9
Prosecutor's Request for Deferral

Where it appears to the Prosecutor that in any such investigations or criminal proceedings instituted in the courts of any State:

(i) the act being investigated or which is the subject of those proceedings is characterized as an ordinary crime;

(ii) there is a lack of impartiality or independence, or the investigations or proceedings are designed to shield the accused from international criminal responsibility, or the case is not diligently prosecuted; or

(iii) what is in issue is closely related to, or otherwise involves, significant factual or legal questions which may have implications for investigations or prosecutions before the Tribunal, the Prosecutor may propose to the Trial Chamber designated by the President that a formal request be made that such court defer to the competence of the Tribunal.

Rule 10

Formal Request for Deferral

(A) If it appears to the Trial Chamber seised of a proposal for deferral that, on any of the grounds specified in Rule 9, deferral is appropriate, the Trial Chamber may issue a formal request to the State concerned that its court defer to the competence of the Tribunal.

(B) A request for deferral shall include a request that the results of the investigation and a copy of the court's records and the judgement, if already delivered, be forwarded to the Tribunal.

(C) Where deferral to the Tribunal has been requested by a Trial Chamber, any subsequent proceedings shall be held before the other Trial Chamber.

Rule 11

Non-compliance with a Request for Deferral

If, within sixty days after a request for deferral has been notified by the Registrar to the State under whose jurisdiction the investigations or criminal proceedings have been instituted, the State fails to file a response which satisfies the Trial Chamber that the State has taken or is taking adequate steps to comply with the order, the Trial Chamber may request the President to report the matter to the Security Council.

Rule 12

Determinations of Courts of any State

Subject to Article 10(2) of the Statute, determinations of courts of any State are not binding on the Tribunal.

Rule 13

Non Bis in Idem

When the President receives reliable information to show that criminal proceedings have been instituted against a person before a court of any State for a crime for which that person has already been tried by the Tribunal, a Trial Chamber shall, following *mutatis mutandis* the procedure provided in Rule 10, issue a reasoned order requesting that court permanently to discontinue its proceedings. If that court fails to do so, the President may report the matter to the Security Council.

Part Three

ORGANIZATION OF THE TRIBUNAL

Section 1 The Judges

Rule 14
Solemn Declaration

(A) Before taking up his duties each Judge shall make the following solemn declaration:

"I solemnly declare that I will perform my duties and exercise my powers as a Judge of the International Tribunal for the Prosecution of Persons Responsible for Serious Violations of International Humanitarian Law Committed in the Territory of the Former Yugoslavia since 1991 honourably, faithfully, impartially and conscientiously".

(B) The declaration, signed by the Judge and witnessed by the Secretary-General of the United Nations or his representative, shall be kept in the records of the Tribunal.

Rule 15
Disqualification of Judges

(A) A Judge may not sit on a trial or appeal in any case in which he has a personal interest or concerning which he has or has had any association which might affect his impartiality. He shall in any such circumstance withdraw, and the President shall assign another Judge to sit in his place.

(B) Any party may apply to the Presiding Judge of a Chamber for the disqualification and withdrawal of a Judge of that Chamber from a trial or appeal upon the above grounds. The Presiding Judge shall confer with the Judge in question, and if necessary the Bureau shall determine the matter. If the Bureau upholds the application, the President shall assign another Judge to sit in place of the disqualified Judge.

(C) The Judge of the Trial Chamber who reviews an indictment against an accused, pursuant to Article 19 of the Statute and Rule 47, shall not sit as a member of the Trial Chamber for the trial of that accused.

(D) No member of the Appeals Chamber shall sit on any appeal in a case in which he sat as a member of the Trial Chamber.

(E) If a Judge is, for any reason, unable to continue sitting in a part-heard case, the Presiding Judge may, if that inability seems likely to be of short duration, adjourn the proceedings; otherwise he shall report to the President who may assign another Judge to the case and order either a rehearing or, with the consent of the accused, continuation of the proceedings from that point.

Rule 16
Resignation

A Judge who decides to resign shall communicate his resignation in writing to the President who shall transmit it to the Secretary-General of the United Nations.

Rule 17
Precedence

(A) All Judges are equal in the exercise of their judicial functions, regardless of dates of election, appointment, age or period of service.

(B) The Presiding Judges of the Trial Chambers shall take precedence according to age after the President and the Vice-President.

(C) Judges elected or appointed on different dates shall take precedence according to the dates of their election or appointment; Judges elected or appointed on the same date shall take precedence according to age.

(D) In case of re-election, the total period of service as a Judge of the Tribunal shall be taken into account.

Section 2 The Presidency

Rule 18
Election of the President

(A) The President shall be elected for a term of two years, or such shorter term as shall coincide with the duration of his term of office as a Judge. He may be re-elected once.

(B) If the President ceases to be a member of the Tribunal or resigns his office before the expiration of his term, the Judges shall elect from among their number a successor for the remainder of the term.

(C) The President shall be elected by a majority of the votes of the Judges composing the Tribunal. If no Judge obtains such a majority, the second ballot shall be limited to the two Judges who obtained the greatest number of votes on the first ballot. In the case of equality of votes on the second ballot, the Judge who takes precedence in accordance with Rule 17 shall be declared elected.

Rule 19
Functions of the President

The President shall preside at all plenary meetings of the Tribunal; he shall coordinate the work of the Chambers and supervise the activities of the Registry as well as exercise all the other functions conferred on him by the Statute and the Rules.

Rule 20
The Vice-President

(A) The Vice-President shall be elected for a term of two years, or such shorter term as shall coincide with the duration of his term of office as a Judge. He may be re-elected once.

(B) The Vice-President may sit as a member of a Trial Chamber or of the Appeals Chamber.

(C) Sub-rules 18(B) and (C) shall apply *mutatis mutandis* to the Vice-President.

Rule 21
Functions of the Vice-President

Subject to Sub-rule 22(B), the Vice-President shall exercise the functions of the President in case of his absence or inability to act.

Rule 22
Replacements

(A) If neither the President nor the Vice-President can carry out the functions of the President, these shall be assumed by the senior Judge, determined in accordance with Rule 17.

(B) If the President is unable to exercise his functions as Presiding Judge of the Appeals Chamber, that Chamber shall elect a Presiding Judge from among its number.

Section 3 Internal Functioning of the Tribunal

Rule 23
The Bureau

(A) The Bureau shall be composed of the President, the Vice-President and the Presiding Judges of the Trial Chambers.

(B) The President shall consult the other members of the Bureau on all major questions relating to the functioning of the Tribunal.

(C) A Judge may draw the attention of any member of the Bureau to issues that in his opinion ought to be discussed by the Bureau or submitted to a plenary meeting of the Tribunal.

Rule 24
Plenary Meetings of the Tribunal

The Judges shall meet in plenary to:

(i) elect the President and Vice-President;

(ii) adopt and amend the Rules;

(iii) adopt the Annual Report provided for in Article 34 of the Statute;

(iv) decide upon matters relating to the internal functioning of the Chambers and the Tribunal;

(v) determine or supervise the conditions of detention;

(vi) exercise any other functions provided for in the Statute or in the Rules.

Rule 25
Dates of Plenary Sessions

(A) The dates of the plenary sessions of the Tribunal shall normally be agreed upon in July of each year for the following calendar year.

(B) Other plenary meetings shall be convened by the President if so requested by at least six Judges, and may be convened whenever the exercise of his functions under the Statute or the Rules so requires.

Rule 26
Quorum and Vote

(A) The quorum for each plenary meeting of the Tribunal shall be seven Judges.

(B) Subject to Sub-rules 6(A) and (B) and Sub-rule 18(C), the decisions of the plenary meetings of the Tribunal shall be taken by the majority of the Judges present. In the event of an equality of votes, the President or the Judge who acts in his place shall have a casting vote.

Section 4 The Chambers

Rule 27
Rotation

(A) Judges shall rotate on a regular basis between the Trial Chambers and the Appeals Chamber. Rotation shall take into account the efficient disposal of cases.

(B) The Judges shall take their places in their new Chamber as soon as the President thinks it convenient, having regard to the disposal of part-heard cases.

(C) The President may at any time temporarily assign a member of a Trial Chamber or of the Appeals Chamber to another Chamber.

Rule 28
Assignment to Review Indictments

The President shall, in July of each year and after consultation with the Judges, assign for each month of the next calendar year one Judge from each Trial Chamber as the Judges to whom indictments shall be transmitted for review under Rule 47, and shall publish the list of assignments.

Rule 29
Deliberations

The deliberations of the Chambers shall take place in private and remain secret.

Section 5 The Registry

Rule 30
Appointment of the Registrar

The President shall seek the opinion of the Judges on the candidates for the post of Registrar, before consulting with the Secretary-General of the United Nations pursuant to Article 17(3) of the Statute.

Rule 31
Appointment of the Deputy Registrar and Registry Staff

The Registrar, after consultation with the Bureau, shall make his recommendations to the Secretary-General of the United Nations for the appointment of the Deputy Registrar and other Registry staff.

Rule 32
Solemn Declaration

(A) Before taking up his duties, the Registrar shall make the following declaration before the President:

"I solemnly declare that I will perform the duties incumbent upon me as Registrar of the International Tribunal for the Prosecution of Persons Responsible for

Serious Violations of International Humanitarian Law Committed in the Territory of the Former Yugoslavia since 1991 in all loyalty, discretion and good conscience and that I will faithfully observe all the provisions of the Statute and the Rules of Procedure and Evidence of the Tribunal".

(B) Before taking up his duties, the Deputy Registrar shall make a similar declaration before the President.

(C) Every staff member of the Registry shall make a similar declaration before the Registrar.

Rule 33
Functions of the Registrar

The Registrar shall assist the Chambers, the plenary meetings of the Tribunal, the Judges and the Prosecutor in the performance of their functions. Under the authority of the President, he shall be responsible for the administration and servicing of the Tribunal and shall serve as its channel of communication.

Rule 34
Victims and Witnesses Unit

(A) There shall be set up under the authority of the Registrar a Victims and Witnesses Unit consisting of qualified staff to:

(i) recommend protective measures for victims and witnesses in accordance with Article 22 of the Statute; and

(ii) provide counselling and support for them, in particular in cases of rape and sexual assault.

(B) Due consideration shall be given, in the appointment of staff, to the employment of qualified women.

Rule 35
Minutes

Except where a full record is made under Rule 81, the Registrar, or Registry staff designated by him, shall take minutes of the plenary meetings of the Tribunal and of the sittings of the Chambers, other than private deliberations.

Rule 36
Record Book

The Registrar shall keep a Record Book which shall list, subject to Rule 53, all the particulars of each case brought before the Tribunal. The Record Book shall be open to the public.

Section 6 The Prosecutor

Rule 37
Functions of the Prosecutor

(A) The Prosecutor shall perform all the functions provided by the Statute in accordance with the Rules and such Regulations, consistent with the Statute and the Rules, as may be framed by him. Any alleged inconsistency in the Regulations shall be brought to the attention of the Bureau to whose opinion the Prosecutor shall defer.

(B) His powers under Parts Four to Eight of the Rules may be exercised by staff members of the Office of the Prosecutor authorised by him, or by any person acting under his direction.

Rule 38
Deputy Prosecutor

(A) The Prosecutor shall make his recommendations to the Secretary-General of the United Nations for the appointment of a Deputy Prosecutor.

(B) The Deputy Prosecutor shall exercise the functions of the Prosecutor in the event of his absence or inability to act or upon the Prosecutor's express instructions.

Part Four

INVESTIGATIONS AND RIGHTS OF SUSPECTS

Section 1 Investigations

Rule 39
Conduct of Investigations

In the conduct of an investigation, the Prosecutor may:

(i) summon and question suspects, victims and witnesses and record their statements, collect evidence and conduct on-site investigations;

(ii) undertake such other matters as may appear necessary for completing the investigation and the preparation and conduct of the prosecution at the trial, including the taking of special measures to provide for the safety of potential witnesses and informants;

(iii) seek, to that end, the assistance of any State authority concerned, as well as of any relevant international body including the International Criminal Police Organization (INTERPOL); and

(iv) request such orders as may be necessary from a Trial Chamber or a Judge.

Rule 40
Provisional Measures

In case of urgency, the Prosecutor may request any State:

(i) to arrest a suspect provisionally;

(ii) to seize physical evidence;

(iii) to take all necessary measures to prevent the escape of a suspect or an accused, injury to or intimidation of a victim or witness, or the destruction of evidence.

The State concerned shall comply forthwith, in accordance with Article 29 of the Statute.

Rule 41
Retention of Information

The Prosecutor shall be responsible for the retention, storage and security of information and physical evidence obtained in the course of his investigations.

Rule 42
Rights of Suspects during Investigation

(A) A suspect who is to be questioned by the Prosecutor shall have the following rights, of which he shall be informed by the Prosecutor prior to questioning, in a language he speaks and understands:

(i) the right to be assisted by counsel of his choice or to have legal assistance assigned to him without payment if he does not have sufficient means to pay for it;

(ii) the right to have the free assistance of an interpreter if he cannot understand or speak the language to be used for questioning; and

(iii) the right to remain silent, and to be cautioned that any statement he makes shall be recorded and may be used in evidence.

(B) Questioning of a suspect shall not proceed without the presence of counsel unless the suspect has voluntarily waived his right to counsel. In case of waiver, if the suspect subsequently expresses a desire to have counsel, questioning shall thereupon cease, and shall only resume when the suspect has obtained or has been assigned counsel.

Rule 43
Recording Questioning of Suspects

Whenever the Prosecutor questions a suspect, the questioning shall be tape-recorded or video-recorded, in accordance with the following procedure:

(i) the suspect shall be informed in a language he speaks and understands that the questioning is being tape-recorded or video-recorded;

(ii) in the event of a break in the course of the questioning, the fact and the time of the break shall be recorded before tape-recording or video-recording ends and the time of resumption of the questioning shall also be recorded;

(iii) at the conclusion of the questioning the suspect shall be offered the opportunity to clarify anything he has said, and to add anything he may wish, and the time of conclusion shall be recorded;

(iv) the tape shall then be transcribed as soon as practicable after the conclusion of questioning and a copy of the transcript supplied to the suspect, together with a copy of the recorded tape or, if multiple recording apparatus was used, one of the original recorded tapes; and

(v) after a copy has been made, if necessary, of the recorded tape for purposes of transcription, the original recorded tape or one of the original tapes shall be sealed in the presence of the suspect under the signature of the Prosecutor and the suspect.

Section 2 Of Counsel

Rule 44
Appointment and Qualifications of Counsel

Counsel engaged by a suspect or an accused shall file his power of attorney with the Registrar at the earliest opportunity. A counsel shall be considered qualified to represent a suspect or accused if he satisfies the Registrar that he is admitted to the practice of law in a State, or is a University professor of law.

Rule 45
Assignment of Counsel

(A) A list of counsel who speak one or both of the working languages of the Tribunal, meet the requirements of Rule 44 and have indicated their willingness to be assigned by the Tribunal to indigent suspects or accused, shall be kept by the Registrar.

(B) The criteria for determination of indigency shall be established by the Registrar and approved by the Judges.

(C) In assigning counsel to an indigent suspect or accused, the following procedure shall be observed:

(i) a request for assignment of counsel shall be made to the Registrar;

(ii) the Registrar shall enquire into the means of the suspect or accused and determine whether the criteria of indigency are met;

(iii) if he decides that the criteria are met, he shall assign counsel from the list; if he decides to the contrary, he shall inform the suspect or accused that the request is refused.

(D) If a request is refused, a further request may be made by a suspect or an accused to the Registrar upon showing a change in circumstances.

(E) The Registrar shall, in consultation with the Judges, establish the criteria for the payment of fees to assigned counsel.

(F) If a suspect or an accused elects to conduct his own defence, he shall so notify the Registrar in writing at the first opportunity.

(G) Where an alleged indigent person is subsequently found not to be indigent, the Chamber may make an order of contribution to recover the cost of providing counsel.

Rule 46
Misconduct of Counsel

(A) A Chamber may, after a warning, refuse audience to counsel if, in its opinion, his conduct is offensive, abusive or otherwise obstructs the proper conduct of the proceedings.

(B) A Judge or a Chamber may also, with the approval of the President, communicate any misconduct of counsel to the professional body regulating the conduct of counsel in his State of admission or, if a professor and not otherwise admitted to the profession, to the governing body of his University.

Part Five

PRE-TRIAL PROCEEDINGS

Section 1 Indictments

Rule 47
Submission of Indictment by the Prosecutor

(A) If in the course of an investigation the Prosecutor is satisfied that there is sufficient evidence to provide reasonable grounds for believing that a suspect has committed a crime within the jurisdiction of the Tribunal, he shall prepare and forward to the Registrar an indictment for confirmation by a Judge, together with supporting material.

(B) The indictment shall set forth the name and particulars of the suspect, and a concise statement of the facts of the case and of the crime with which the suspect is charged.

(C) The Registrar shall forward the indictment and accompanying material to one of the Judges currently assigned under Rule 28, who will inform the Prosecutor of the date fixed for review of the indictment.

(D) On reviewing the indictment, the Judge shall hear the Prosecutor, who may present additional material in support of any count. The Judge may confirm or dismiss each count or may adjourn the review.

(E) The dismissal of a count in an indictment shall not preclude the Prosecutor from subsequently bringing a new indictment based on the acts underlying that count if supported by additional evidence.

Rule 48
Joinder of Accused

Persons accused of the same or different crimes committed in the course of the same transaction may be jointly charged and tried.

Rule 49
Joinder of Crimes

Two or more crimes may be joined in one indictment if the series of acts committed together form the same transaction, and the said crimes were committed by the same accused.

Rule 50
Amendment of Indictment

The Prosecutor may amend an indictment, without leave, at any time before its confirmation, but thereafter only with leave of the Judge who confirmed it or, if at trial, with leave of the Trial Chamber. If leave to amend is granted, the amended indictment shall be transmitted to the accused and to his counsel and where necessary the date for trial shall be postponed to ensure adequate time for the preparation of the defence.

Rule 51
Withdrawal of Indictment

(A) The Prosecutor may withdraw an indictment, without leave, at any time before its confirmation, but thereafter only with leave of the Judge who confirmed it or, if at trial, only with leave of the Trial Chamber.

(B) The withdrawal of the indictment shall be promptly notified to the suspect or the accused and to his counsel.

Rule 52
Public Character of Indictment

Subject to Rule 53, upon confirmation by a Judge of a Trial Chamber, the indictment shall be made public.

Rule 53
Non-disclosure of Indictment

(A) When confirming an indictment the Judge may, in consultation with the Prosecutor, order that there be no public disclosure of the indictment until it is served on the accused, or, in the case of joint accused, on all the accused.

(B) A Judge or Trial Chamber may, in consultation with the Prosecutor, also order that there be no disclosure of an indictment, or part thereof, or of all or any part of any particular document or information, if satisfied that the making of such an order is required to give effect to a provision of the Rules, to protect confidential information obtained by the Prosecutor, or is otherwise in the interests of justice.

Section 2 Orders and Warrants

Rule 54
General Rule

At the request of either party or *proprio motu*, a Judge or a Trial Chamber may issue such orders, summonses, subpoenas and warrants as may be necessary for the purposes of an investigation or for the preparation or conduct of the trial.

Rule 55
Execution of Arrest Warrants

(A) A warrant of arrest shall be signed by a Judge and shall bear the seal of the Tribunal. It shall be accompanied by a copy of the indictment, and a statement of the rights of the accused. These rights include those set forth in Article 21 of the Statute, and in Rules 42 and 43 *mutatis mutandis*, together with the right of the accused to remain silent, and to be cautioned that any statement he makes shall be recorded and may be used in evidence.

(B) A warrant for the arrest of the accused and an order for his surrender to the Tribunal shall be transmitted by the Registrar to the national authorities of the State in whose territory or under whose jurisdiction or control the accused resides, or was last known to be, together with instructions that at the time of arrest the indictment and the statement of the rights of the accused be read to him in a language he understands and that he be cautioned in that language.

(C) When an arrest warrant issued by the Tribunal is executed, a member of the Prosecutor's Office may be present as from the time of arrest.

Rule 56
Cooperation of States

The State to which a warrant of arrest is transmitted shall act promptly and with all due diligence to ensure proper and effective execution thereof, in accordance with Article 29 of the Statute.

Rule 57
Procedure after Arrest

Upon the arrest of the accused, the State concerned shall detain him, and shall promptly notify the Registrar. The transfer of the accused to the seat of the Tribunal shall be arranged between the State authorities concerned, the authorities of the host country and the Registrar.

Rule 58
National Extradition Provisions

The obligations laid down in Article 29 of the Statute shall prevail over any legal impediment to the surrender or transfer of the accused to the Tribunal which may exist under the national law or extradition treaties of the State concerned.

Rule 59
Failure to Execute a Warrant

(A) Where the State to which a warrant of arrest has been transmitted has been unable to execute the warrant, it shall report forthwith its inability to the Registrar, and the reasons therefore.

(B) If, within a reasonable time after the warrant of arrest has been transmitted to the State, no report is made on action taken, this shall be deemed a failure to execute the warrant of arrest and the Tribunal, through the President, may notify the Security Council accordingly.

Rule 60
Advertisement of Indictment

At the request of the Prosecutor, a form of advertisement shall be transmitted by the Registrar to the national authorities of any State or States in whose territory the Prosecutor has reason to believe that the accused may be found, for publication in newspapers having wide circulation in that territory, intimating to the accused that service of an indictment against him is sought.

Rule 61

Procedure in Case of Failure to Execute a Warrant

(A) If a warrant of arrest has not been executed, and personal service of the indictment has consequently not been effected, and the Prosecutor satisfies a Judge of a Trial Chamber that:

(i) he has taken all reasonable steps to effect personal service, including recourse to the appropriate authorities of the State in whose territory or under whose jurisdiction and control the person to be served resides or was last known to him to be; and

(ii) he has otherwise tried to inform the accused of the existence of the indictment by seeking publication of newspaper advertisements pursuant to Rule 60,

the Judge shall order that the indictment be submitted by the Prosecutor to the Trial Chamber.

(B) Upon obtaining such an order the Prosecutor shall submit the indictment to the Trial Chamber in open court, together with all the evidence that was before the Judge who initially confirmed the indictment. The Prosecutor may also call before the Trial Chamber and examine any witness whose statement has been submitted to the confirming Judge.

(C) If the Trial Chamber is satisfied on that evidence, together with such additional evidence as the Prosecutor may tender, that there are reasonable grounds for believing that the accused has committed all or any of the crimes charged in the indictment, it shall so determine. The Trial Chamber shall have the relevant parts of the indictment read out by the Prosecutor together with an account of the efforts to effect service referred to in Sub-rule (A) above.

(D) The Trial Chamber shall also issue an international arrest warrant in respect of the accused which shall be transmitted to all States.

(E) If the Prosecutor satisfies the Trial Chamber that the failure to effect personal service was due in whole or in part to a failure or refusal of a State to cooperate with the Tribunal in accordance with Article 29 of the Statute, the Trial Chamber shall so certify, in which event the President shall notify the Security Council.

Rule 62
Initial Appearance of Accused

Upon his transfer to the seat of the Tribunal, the accused shall be brought before a Trial Chamber without delay, and shall be formally charged. The Trial Chamber shall:

(i) satisfy itself that the right of the accused to counsel is respected;

(ii) read or have the indictment read to the accused in a language he speaks and understands, and satisfy itself that the accused understands the indictment;

(iii) call upon the accused to enter a plea of guilty or not guilty; should the accused fail to do so, enter a plea of not guilty on his behalf;

(iv) in case of a plea of not guilty, instruct the Registrar to set a date for trial;

(v) in case of a plea of guilty, instruct the Registrar to set a date for the pre-sentencing hearing;

(vi) instruct the Registrar to set such other dates as appropriate.

Rule 63
Questioning of Accused

After the initial appearance of the accused the Prosecutor shall not question him unless his counsel is present and the questioning is tape-recorded or video-recorded in accordance with the procedure provided for in Rule 43. The Prosecutor shall at the beginning of the questioning caution the accused that he is not obliged to say anything unless he wishes to do so but that whatever he says may be given in evidence.

Rule 64
Detention on Remand

Upon his transfer to the seat of the Tribunal, the accused shall be detained in facilities provided by the host country, or by another country. The President may, on the application of a party, request modification of the conditions of detention of an accused.

Rule 65
Provisional Release

(A) Once detained, an accused may not be released except upon an order of a Trial Chamber.

(B) Release may be ordered by a Trial Chamber only in exceptional circumstances, after hearing the host country and only if it is satisfied that the accused will appear for trial and, if released, will not pose a danger to any victim, witness or other person.

(C) The Trial Chamber may impose such conditions upon the release of the accused as it may determine appropriate, including the execution of a bail bond and the observance of such conditions as are necessary to ensure his presence for trial and the protection of others.

(D) If necessary, the Trial Chamber may issue a warrant of arrest to secure the presence of an accused who has been released or is for any other reason at liberty.

Section 3 Production of Evidence

Rule 66
Disclosure by the Prosecutor

(A) The Prosecutor shall make available to the defence, as soon as practicable after the initial appearance of the accused, copies of the supporting material which accompanied the indictment when confirmation was sought as well as all prior statements obtained by the Prosecutor from the accused or from prosecution witnesses.

(B) The Prosecutor shall on request, subject to Sub-rule (C), permit the defence to inspect any books, documents, photographs and tangible objects in his custody or control, which are material to the preparation of the defence, or are intended for use by the Prosecutor as evidence at trial or were obtained from or belonged to the accused.

(C) Where information is in the possession of the Prosecutor, the disclosure of which may prejudice further or ongoing investigations, or for any other reasons may be contrary to the public interest or affect the security interests of any State, the Prosecutor may apply to the Trial Chamber sitting *in camera* to be relieved from the obligation to disclose pursuant to Sub-rule (B). When making such application the Prosecutor shall provide the Trial Chamber (but only the Trial Chamber) with the information that is sought to be kept confidential.

Rule 67
Reciprocal Disclosure

(A) As early as reasonably practicable and in any event prior to the commencement of the trial:

(i) the Prosecutor shall notify the defence of the names of the witnesses that he intends to call in proof of the guilt of the accused and in rebuttal of any defence plea of which the Prosecutor has received notice in accordance with Sub-rule (ii) below;

(ii) the defence shall notify the Prosecutor of its intent to offer:

(a) the defence of alibi; in which case the notification shall specify the place or places at which the accused claims to have been present at the time of the alleged crime and the names and addresses of witnesses and any other evidence upon which the accused intends to rely to establish the alibi;

(b) any special defence, including that of diminished or lack of mental responsibility; in which case the notification shall specify the names and addresses of witnesses and any other evidence upon which the accused intends to rely to establish the special defence.

(B) Failure of the defence to provide notice under this Rule shall not limit the right of the accused to testify on the above defences.

(C) If the defence makes a request pursuant to Sub-rule 66(B), the Prosecutor shall be entitled to inspect any books, documents, photographs and tangible objects, which are within the custody or control of the defence and which it intends to use as evidence at the trial.

(D) If either party discovers additional evidence or material which should have been produced earlier pursuant to the Rules, that party shall promptly notify the other party and the Trial Chamber of the existence of the additional evidence or material.

Rule 68
Disclosure of Exculpatory Evidence

The Prosecutor shall, as soon as practicable, disclose to the defence the existence of evidence known to the Prosecutor which in any way tends to suggest the innocence or mitigate the guilt of the accused or may affect the credibility of prosecution evidence.

Rule 69
Protection of Victims and Witnesses

(A) In exceptional circumstances, the Prosecutor may apply to a Trial Chamber to order the non-disclosure of the identity of a victim or witness who may be in danger or at risk until such person is brought under the protection of the Tribunal.

(B) Subject to Rule 75, the identity of the victim or witness shall be disclosed in sufficient time prior to the trial to allow adequate time for preparation of the defence.

Rule 70
Matters not Subject to Disclosure

(A) Notwithstanding the provisions of Rules 66 and 67, reports, memoranda, or other internal documents prepared by a party, its assistants or representatives in connection with the investigation or preparation of the case, are not subject to disclosure or notification under those Rules.

(B) If the Prosecutor is in possession of information which has been provided to him on a confidential basis and which has been used solely for the purpose of generating new evidence, that initial information and its origin shall not be disclosed by the Prosecutor without the consent of the person or entity providing the initial information and shall in any event not be given in evidence without prior disclosure to the accused.

Section 4 Depositions

Rule 71
Depositions

(A) At the request of either party, a Trial Chamber may, in exceptional circumstances and in the interests of justice, order that a deposition be taken for use at trial, and appoint, for that purpose, a Presiding Officer.

(B) The motion for the taking of a deposition shall be in writing and shall indicate the name and whereabouts of the person whose deposition is sought, the date and place at which the deposition is to be taken, a statement of the matters on which the person is to be examined, and of the exceptional circumstances justifying the taking of the deposition.

(C) If the motion is granted, the party at whose request the deposition is to be taken shall give reasonable notice to the other party, who shall have the right to attend the taking of the deposition and cross-examine the person whose deposition is being taken.

(D) Deposition evidence may also be given by means of a video-conference.

(E) The Presiding Officer shall ensure that the deposition is taken in accordance with the Rules and that a record is made of the deposition, including cross-examination and objections raised by either party for decision by the Trial Chamber. He shall transmit the record to the Trial Chamber.

Section 5 Preliminary Motions

Rule 72
General Provisions

(A) After the initial appearance of the accused, either party may move before a Trial Chamber for appropriate relief or ruling. Such motions may be written or oral, at the discretion of the Trial Chamber.

(B) The Trial Chamber shall dispose of preliminary motions *in limine litis* and without interlocutory appeal, save in the case of dismissal of an objection based on lack of jurisdiction.

Rule 73
Preliminary Motions by Accused

(A) Preliminary motions by the accused shall include:

(i) objections based on lack of jurisdiction;

(ii) objections based on defects in the form of the indictment;

(iii) applications for the exclusion of evidence obtained from the accused or having belonged to him;

(iv) applications for severance of crimes joined in one indictment under Rule 49, or for separate trials under Sub-rule 82(B);

(v) objections based on the denial of request for assignment of counsel.

(B) Any of the motions by the accused referred to in Sub-rule (A) shall be brought within sixty days after his initial appearance, and in any case before the hearing on the merits.

(C) Failure to apply within the time-limit prescribed shall constitute a waiver of the right. Upon a showing of good cause, the Trial Chamber may grant relief from the waiver.

Part Six

PROCEEDINGS BEFORE TRIAL CHAMBERS

Section 1 General Provisions

Rule 74
Amicus Curiae

A Chamber may, if it considers it desirable for the proper determination of the case, invite or grant leave to a State, organization or person to appear before it and make submissions on any issue specified by the Chamber.

Rule 75
Measures for the Protection of Victims and Witnesses

(A) A Judge or a Chamber may, *proprio motu* or at the request of either party, or of the victim or witness concerned, order appropriate measures for the privacy and protection of victims and witnesses, provided that the measures are consistent with the rights of the accused.

(B) A Chamber may hold an *in camera* proceeding to determine whether to order:

(i) measures to prevent disclosure to the public or the media of the identity or whereabouts of a victim or a witness, or of persons related to or associated with him by such means as:

(a) expunging names and identifying information from the Chamber's public records;
(b) non-disclosure to the public of any records identifying the victim;
(c) giving of testimony through image- or voice-altering devices or closed circuit television; and
(d) assignment of a pseudonym;

(ii) closed sessions, in accordance with Rule 79;

(iii) appropriate measures to facilitate the testimony of vulnerable victims and witnesses, such as one-way closed circuit television.

(C) A Chamber shall, whenever necessary, control the manner of questioning to avoid any harassment or intimidation.

Rule 76

Solemn Declaration by Interpreters and Translators

Before performing any duties, an interpreter or a translator shall solemnly declare to do so faithfully, independently, impartially and with full respect for the duty of confidentiality.

Rule 77

Contempt of the Tribunal

(A) Subject to the provisions of Sub-rule 90(E), a witness who refuses or fails contumaciously to answer a question relevant to the issue before a Chamber may be found in contempt of the Tribunal. The Chamber may impose a fine not exceeding US$10,000 or a term of imprisonment not exceeding six months.

(B) The Chamber may, however, relieve the witness of the duty to answer, for reasons which it deems appropriate.

(C) Any person who attempts to interfere with or intimidate a witness may be found guilty of contempt and sentenced in accordance with Sub-rule (A).

(D) Any judgement rendered under this Rule shall be subject to appeal.

(E) Payment of a fine shall be made to the Registrar to be held in a separate account.

Rule 78

Open Sessions

All proceedings before a Trial Chamber, other than deliberations of the Chamber, shall be held in public, unless otherwise provided.

Rule 79

Closed Sessions

(A) The Trial Chamber may order that the press and the public be excluded from all or part of the proceedings for reasons of:

(i) public order or morality;

(ii) safety, security or non-disclosure of the identity of a victim or witness as provided in Rule 75; or

(iii) the protection of the interests of justice.

(B) The Trial Chamber shall make public the reasons for its order.

Rule 80
Control of Proceedings

(A) The Trial Chamber may exclude a person from the courtroom in order to protect the right of the accused to a fair and public trial, or to maintain the dignity and decorum of the proceedings.

(B) The Trial Chamber may order the removal of an accused from the courtroom and continue the proceedings in his absence if he has persisted in disruptive conduct following a warning that he may be removed.

Rule 81
Records of Proceedings and Evidence

(A) The Registrar shall cause to be made and preserve a full and accurate record of all proceedings, including audio recordings, transcripts and, when deemed necessary by the Trial Chamber, video recordings.

(B) The Trial Chamber may order the disclosure of all or part of the record of closed proceedings when the reasons for ordering its non-disclosure no longer exist.

(C) The Registrar shall retain and preserve all physical evidence offered during the proceedings.

(D) Photography, video-recording or audio-recording of the trial, otherwise than by the Registry, may be authorised at the discretion of the Trial Chamber.

Section 2 Case Presentation

Rule 82
Joint and Separate Trials

(A) In joint trials, each accused shall be accorded the same rights as if he were being tried separately.

(B) The Trial Chamber may order that persons accused jointly under Rule 48 be tried separately if it considers it necessary in order to avoid a conflict of interests that might cause serious prejudice to an accused, or to protect the interests of justice.

Rule 83

Instruments of Restraint

Instruments of restraint, such as handcuffs, shall not be used except as a precaution against escape during transfer or for security reasons, and shall be removed when the accused appears before a Chamber.

Rule 84

Opening Statements

Before presentation of evidence by the Prosecutor, each party may make an opening statement. The defence may however elect to make its statement after the Prosecutor has concluded his presentation of evidence and before the presentation of evidence for the defence.

Rule 85

Presentation of Evidence

(A) Each party is entitled to call witnesses and present evidence. Unless otherwise directed by the Trial Chamber in the interests of justice, evidence at the trial shall be presented in the following sequence:

(i) evidence for the prosecution;

(ii) evidence for the defence;

(iii) prosecution evidence in rebuttal;

(iv) defence evidence in rejoinder;

(v) evidence ordered by the Trial Chamber pursuant to Rule 98.

(B) Examination-in-chief, cross-examination and re-examination shall be allowed in each case. It shall be for the party calling a witness to examine him in chief, but a Judge may at any stage put any question to the witness.

(C) The accused may, if he so desires, appear as a witness in his own defence.

Rule 86

Closing Arguments

After the presentation of all the evidence, the Prosecutor may present an initial argument, to which the defence may reply. The Prosecutor may, if he wishes, present a rebuttal argument, to which the defence may present a rejoinder.

Rule 87

Deliberations

(A) When both parties have completed their presentation of the case, the Presiding Judge shall declare the hearing closed, and the Trial Chamber shall deliberate in private. A finding of guilt may be reached only when a majority of the Trial Chamber is satisfied that guilt has been proved beyond reasonable doubt.

(B) The Trial Chamber shall vote separately on each charge contained in the indictment. If two or more accused are tried together under Rule 48, separate findings shall be made as to each accused.

Rule 88

Judgement

(A) The judgement shall be pronounced in public, on a date of which notice shall have been given to the parties and counsel and at which they shall be entitled to be present.

(B) If the Trial Chamber finds the accused guilty of a crime and concludes from the evidence that unlawful taking of property by the accused was associated with it, it shall make a specific finding to that effect in its judgement. The Trial Chamber may order restitution as provided in Rule 105.

(C) The judgement shall be rendered by a majority of the Judges. It shall be accompanied or followed as soon as possible by a reasoned opinion in writing, to which separate or dissenting opinions may be appended.

Section 3 Rules of Evidence

Rule 89

General Provisions

(A) The rules of evidence set forth in this Section shall govern the proceedings before the Chambers. The Chambers shall not be bound by national rules of evidence.

(B) In cases not otherwise provided for in this Section, a Chamber shall apply rules of evidence which will best favour a fair determination of the matter before it and are consonant with the spirit of the Statute and the general principles of law.

(C) A Chamber may admit any relevant evidence which it deems to have probative value.

(D) A Chamber may exclude evidence if its probative value is substantially outweighed by the need to ensure a fair trial.

(E) A Chamber may request verification of the authenticity of evidence obtained out of court.

Rule 90

Testimony of Witnesses

(A) Witnesses shall, in principle, be heard directly by the Chambers unless a Chamber has ordered that the witness be heard by means of a deposition as provided for in Rule 71.

(B) Every witness shall, before giving evidence, make the following solemn declaration: "I solemnly declare that I will speak the truth, the whole truth and nothing but the truth".

(C) A child who, in the opinion of the Chamber, does not understand the nature of a solemn declaration, may be permitted to testify without that formality, if the Chamber is of the opinion that he is sufficiently mature to be able to report the facts of which he had knowledge and that he understands the duty to tell the truth. A judgement, however, cannot be based on such testimony alone.

(D) A witness, other than an expert, who has not yet testified shall not be present when the testimony of another witness is given. However, a witness who has heard the testimony of another witness shall not for that reason alone be disqualified from testifying.

(E) A witness may object to making any statement which might tend to incriminate him. The Chamber may, however, compel the witness to answer the question. Testimony compelled in this way shall not be used as evidence in a subsequent prosecution against the witness for any offence other than perjury.

Rule 91

False Testimony under Solemn Declaration

(A) A Chamber, on its own initiative or at the request of a party, may warn a witness of the duty to tell the truth and the consequences that may result from a failure to do so.

(B) If a Chamber has strong grounds for believing that a witness has knowingly and wilfully given false testimony, it may direct the Prosecutor to investigate the matter with a view to the preparation and submission of an indictment for false testimony.

(C) The rules of procedure and evidence in Parts Four to Eight shall apply *mutatis mutandis* to proceedings under this Rule.

(D) No Judge who sat as a member of the Trial Chamber before which the witness appeared shall sit for the trial of the witness for false testimony.

(E) The maximum penalty for false testimony under solemn declaration shall be a fine of US$10,000 or a term of imprisonment of twelve months, or both. The payment of any fine imposed shall be made to the Registrar to be held in the account referred to in Sub-rule 77(E).

Rule 92

Confessions

A confession by the accused given during questioning by the Prosecutor shall, provided the requirements of Rule 63 were strictly complied with, be presumed to have been free and voluntary unless the contrary is proved.

Rule 93

Evidence of Consistent Pattern of Conduct

(A) Evidence of a consistent pattern of conduct may be admissible in the interests of justice.

(B) Acts tending to show such a pattern of conduct shall be disclosed by the Prosecutor to the defence pursuant to Rule 66.

Rule 94

Judicial Notice

A Trial Chamber shall not require proof of facts of common knowledge but shall take judicial notice thereof.

Rule 95

Evidence Obtained by Means Contrary to Internationally Protected Human Rights

No evidence shall be admissible if obtained by methods which cast substantial doubt on its reliability or if its admission is antithetical to, and would seriously damage, the integrity of the proceedings.

Rule 96 *

Evidence in Cases of Sexual Assault

In cases of sexual assault:

(i) no corroboration of the victim's testimony shall be required;

(ii) consent shall not be allowed as a defence if the victim

(a) has been subjected to or threatened with or has had reason to fear violence, duress, detention or psychological oppression, or

(b) reasonably believed that if she did not submit, another might be so subjected, threatened or put in fear;

*In Rule 96, subparagraph (ii)(b), line one, the word "she" should be replaced by the words "the victim." U.N. Doc. IT/32/Rev.3/ Corr.1 (1995).

(iii) before evidence of the victim's consent is admitted, the accused shall satisfy the Trial Chamber *in camera* that the evidence is relevant and credible;

(iv) prior sexual conduct of the victim shall not be admitted in evidence.

Rule 97

Lawyer-Client Privilege

All communications between lawyer and client shall be regarded as privileged, and consequently not subject to disclosure at trial, unless:

(i) the client consents to such disclosure; or

(ii) the client has voluntarily disclosed the content of the communication to a third party, and that third party then gives evidence of that disclosure.

Rule 98

Power of Chambers to Order Production of Additional Evidence

A Trial Chamber may order either party to produce additional evidence. It may itself summon witnesses and order their attendance.

Section 4 Sentencing Procedure

Rule 99

Status of the Acquitted Person

(A) In case of acquittal, the accused shall be released immediately.

(B) If, at the time the judgement is pronounced, the Prosecutor advises the Trial Chamber in open court of his intention to file notice of appeal pursuant to Rule 108, the Trial Chamber may, at the request of the Prosecutor, issue a warrant for the arrest of the accused to take effect immediately.

Rule 100

Pre-sentencing Procedure

If a Trial Chamber finds the accused guilty of a crime, the Prosecutor and the defence may submit any relevant information that may assist the Trial Chamber in determining an appropriate sentence.

Rule 101

Penalties

(A) A convicted person may be sentenced to imprisonment for a term up to and including the remainder of his life.

(B) In determining the sentence, the Trial Chamber shall take into account the factors mentioned in Article 24(2) of the Statute, as well as such factors as:

(i) any aggravating circumstances;

(ii) any mitigating circumstances including the substantial cooperation with the Prosecutor by the convicted person before or after conviction;

(iii) the general practice regarding prison sentences in the courts of the former Yugoslavia;

(iv) the extent to which any penalty imposed by a court of any State on the convicted person for the same act has already been served, as referred to in Article 10(3) of the Statute.

(C) The Trial Chamber shall indicate whether multiple sentences shall be served consecutively or concurrently.

(D) The sentence shall be pronounced in public and in the presence of the convicted person, subject to Sub-rule 102(B).

(E) Credit shall be given to the convicted person for the period, if any, during which the convicted person was detained in custody pending his surrender to the Tribunal or pending trial or appeal.

Rule 102

Status of the Convicted Person

(A) The sentence shall begin to run from the day it is pronounced under Sub-rule 101(D). However, as soon as notice of appeal is given, the enforcement of the judgement shall thereupon be stayed until the decision on the appeal has been delivered, the convicted person meanwhile remaining in detention, as provided in Rule 64.

(B) If, by a previous decision of the Trial Chamber, the convicted person has been released, or is for any other reason at liberty, and he is not present when the judgement is pronounced, the Trial Chamber shall issue a warrant for his arrest. On arrest, he shall be notified of the conviction and sentence, and the procedure provided in Rule 103 shall be followed.

Rule 103

Place of Imprisonment

(A) Imprisonment shall be served in a State designated by the Tribunal from a list of States which have indicated their willingness to accept convicted persons.

(B) Transfer of the convicted person to that State shall be effected as soon as possible after the time-limit for appeal has elapsed.

Rule 104

Supervision of Imprisonment

All sentences of imprisonment shall be supervised by the Tribunal or a body designated by it.

Rule 105

Restitution of Property

(A) After a judgement of conviction containing a specific finding as provided in Sub-rule 88(B), the Trial Chamber shall, at the request of the Prosecutor, or may, at its own initiative, hold a special hearing to determine the matter of the restitution of the property or the proceeds thereof, and may in the meantime order such provisional measures for the preservation and protection of the property or proceeds as it considers appropriate.

(B) The determination may extend to such property or its proceeds, even in the hands of third parties not otherwise connected with the crime of which the convicted person has been found guilty.

(C) Such third parties shall be summoned before the Trial Chamber and be given an opportunity to justify their claim to the property or its proceeds.

(D) Should the Trial Chamber be able to determine the rightful owner on the balance of probabilities, it shall order the restitution either of the property or the proceeds or make such other order as it may deem appropriate.

(E) Should the Trial Chamber not be able to determine ownership, it shall notify the competent national authorities and request them so to determine.

(F) Upon notice from the national authorities that an affirmative determination has been made, the Trial Chamber shall order the restitution either of the property or the proceeds or make such other order as it may deem appropriate.

(G) The Registrar shall transmit to the competent national authorities any summonses, orders and requests issued by a Trial Chamber pursuant to Sub-rules (C),(D),(E) and (F).

Rule 106

Compensation to Victims

(A) The Registrar shall transmit to the competent authorities of the States concerned the judgement finding the accused guilty of a crime which has caused injury to a victim.

(B) Pursuant to the relevant national legislation, a victim or persons claiming through him may bring an action in a national court or other competent body to obtain compensation.

(C) For the purposes of a claim made under Sub-rule (B) the judgement of the Tribunal shall be final and binding as to the criminal responsibility of the convicted person for such injury.

Part Seven

APPELLATE PROCEEDINGS

Rule 107

General Provision

The rules of procedure and evidence that govern proceedings in the Trial Chambers shall apply *mutatis mutandis* to proceedings in the Appeals Chamber.

Rule 108

Notice of Appeal

(A) Subject to Sub-rule (B), a party seeking to appeal a judgement or sentence shall, not more than thirty days from the date on which the judgement or sentence was pronounced, file with the Registrar and serve upon the other parties a written notice of appeal, setting forth the grounds.

(B) Such delay shall be fixed at fifteen days in case of an appeal from a judgement dismissing an objection based on lack of jurisdiction or a decision rendered under Rule 77 or Rule 91.

Rule 109

Record on Appeal

(A) The record on appeal shall consist of the parts of the trial record, as certified by the Registrar, designated by the parties.

(B) The parties, within thirty days of the certification of the trial record by the Registrar, may by agreement designate the parts of that record which, in their opinion, are necessary for the decision on the appeal.

(C) Should the parties fail so to agree within that time, the Appellant and the Respondent shall each designate to the Registrar, within sixty days of the certification, the parts of the trial record which he considers necessary for the decision on the appeal.

(D) The Appeals Chamber shall remain free to call for the whole of the trial record.

Rule 110

Copies of Record

The Registrar shall make a sufficient number of copies of the record on appeal for the use of the Judges of the Appeals Chamber and of the parties.

Rule 111

Appellant's Brief

An Appellant's brief of argument and authorities shall be served on the other party and filed with the Registrar within ninety days of the certification of the record.

Rule 112

Respondent's Brief

A Respondent's brief of argument and authorities shall be served on the other party and filed with the Registrar within thirty days of the filing of the Appellant's brief.

Rule 113

Brief in Reply

An Appellant may file a brief in reply within fifteen days after the filing of the Respondent's brief.

Rule 114

Date of Hearing

After the expiry of the time-limits for filing the briefs provided for in Rules 111, 112 and 113, the Appeals Chamber shall set the date for the hearing and the Registrar shall notify the parties.

Rule 115

Additional Evidence

(A) A party may apply by motion to present before the Appeals Chamber additional evidence which was not available to it at the trial. Such motion must be served on the other party and filed with the Registrar not less than fifteen days before the date of the hearing.

(B) The Appeals Chamber shall authorise the presentation of such evidence if it considers that the interests of justice so require.

Rule 116

Extension of Time-Limits

The Appeals Chamber may grant a motion to extend a time-limit upon a showing of good cause.

Rule 116 *bis*

Expedited Appeals Procedure

(A) An appeal under Sub-rule 108(B) shall be heard expeditiously on the basis of the original record of the Trial Chamber and without the necessity of any written brief.

(B) All delays and other procedural requirements shall be fixed by an order of the President issued on an application by one of the parties, or *proprio moto* should no such application have been made within fifteen days after the filing of the notice of appeal.

(C) Rules 109 to 114 shall not apply to such appeals.

Rule 117

Judgement on Appeal

(A) The Appeals Chamber shall pronounce judgement on the basis of the record on appeal together with such additional evidence as has been presented to it.

(B) The judgement shall be rendered by a majority of the Judges. It shall be accompanied or followed as soon as possible by a reasoned opinion in writing, to which separate or dissenting opinions may be appended.

(C) In appropriate circumstances the Appeals Chamber may order that the accused be re-tried according to law.

(D) The judgement shall be pronounced in public, on a date of which notice shall have been given to the parties and counsel and at which they shall be entitled to be present.

Rule 118

Status of the Accused Following Appeal

(A) A sentence pronounced by the Appeals Chamber shall be enforced immediately.

(B) Where the accused is not present when the judgement is due to be delivered, either as having been acquitted on all charges or as a result of an order issued pursuant to Rule 65, or for any other reason, the Appeals Chamber may deliver its judgement in the absence of the accused and shall, unless it pronounces his acquittal, order his arrest or surrender to the Tribunal.

Part Eight

REVIEW PROCEEDINGS

Rule 119

Request for Review

Where a new fact has been discovered which was not known to the moving party at the time of the proceedings before a Trial Chamber or the Appeals Chamber, and could not have been discovered through the exercise of due diligence, the defence or, within one year after the final judgement has been pronounced, the Prosecutor, may make a motion to that Chamber for review of the judgement.

Rule 120

Preliminary Examination

If a majority of Judges of the Chamber that pronounced the judgement agree that the new fact, if proved, could have been a decisive factor in reaching a decision, the Chamber shall review the judgement, and pronounce a further judgement after hearing the parties.

Rule 121

Appeals

The judgement of a Trial Chamber on review may be appealed in accordance with the provisions of Part Seven.

Rule 122

Return of Case to Trial Chamber

If the judgement to be reviewed is under appeal at the time the motion for review is filed, the Appeals Chamber may return the case to the Trial Chamber for disposition of the motion.

Part Nine

PARDON AND COMMUTATION OF SENTENCE

Rule 123

Notification by States

If, according to the law of the State in which a convicted person is imprisoned, he is eligible for pardon or commutation of sentence, the State shall, in accordance with Article 28 of the Statute, notify the Tribunal of such eligibility.

Rule 124

Determination by the President

The President shall, upon such notice, determine, in consultation with the Judges, whether pardon or commutation is appropriate.

Rule 125

General Standards for Granting Pardon or Commutation

In determining whether pardon or commutation is appropriate, the President shall take into account, *inter alia*, the gravity of the crime or crimes for which the prisoner was convicted, the treatment of similarly-situated prisoners, the prisoner's demonstration of rehabilitation, as well as any substantial cooperation of the prisoner with the Prosecutor.

PART III

DIRECTIVE ON ASSIGNMENT OF DEFENCE COUNSEL, 1 AUGUST 1994

DIRECTIVE ON ASSIGNMENT OF DEFENCE COUNSEL
(Directive No. 1/94)
IT/73/Rev 1, 1 August 1994.

TABLE OF CONTENTS

SUMMARY OF CONTENT

INTRODUCTION

(PREAMBLE)

This directive has been drawn up in accordance with the provisions set out in the preamble and which govern the International Tribunal for Crimes in the former Yugoslavia.

The text also has its origins in reference documents relating to legal assistance and, among them, the Rules of the European Commission and European Court of Human Rights and their addenda, and French and Dutch law relating to legal aid and their implementing texts.

(ARTICLE 1) ENTRY INTO FORCE

This directive is intended to enter into force as early as possible, and in any event as soon as the Office of the Prosecutor commences his investigative inquiries.

(ARTICLE 2) DEFINITIONS

The directive is an implementing text of the Statute and of the various rules adopted by the Tribunal in plenary session, which the Registrar must adopt in order to ensure implementation of the provisions concerning the right to counsel and the principle of assignment of counsel. It is therefore unnecessary to define in this directive, terms which are already defined in the basic texts.

GENERAL PRINCIPLES

(ARTICLES 3 to 5)

These principles reiterate respectively the general right to a defence, the right to assignment of counsel and the principle of indigency as laid down in the instruments establishing the Tribunal and developed during the proceedings of the Tribunal's third plenary session relating to assignment of counsel.

ASSIGNMENT PROCEDURE

(ARTICLES 6 to 13)

These provisions set out the detailed procedures for the assignment of counsel, including the application made by the suspect or the accused, the applicant's declaration of means and its certification, the particulars and analysis of his financial situation, the decision by the Registrar, the intimation of this decision and the avenues of appeal available against a decision to reject a request.

STATUS OF ASSIGNED COUNSEL

(ARTICLES 14 to 22)

After noting the qualifying requirements for assigned counsel, the text defines the scope of their assignment, the legal implications of the assignment of counsel, and the bearing of costs and expenses and their recovery.

Three further situations have been envisaged, namely the assignment of counsel away from the seat of the Tribunal, the withdrawal of assignment of counsel and the discontinuance of the services of counsel.

REMUNERATION AND TRAVEL EXPENSES

(ARTICLES 23 to 31)

The remuneration paid to assigned counsel on completion of his engagement will comprise three categories, namely, a retainer, fees, and a daily allowance whose rates and method of calculation are set out.

The payment of such remuneration, and of all the other costs which fall to be paid rests upon the presentation of a detailed statement on a standard form provided by the Registry and submitted for payment on completion of the engagement of assigned counsel to the Financial Officer of the Registry.

All payments in respect of the assignment of counsel must receive the prior approval of the Registrar, who will countersign any statement presented to the financial department for this purpose.

THE ADVISORY PANEL

(ARTICLES 32 AND 33)
A consultative body is established, consisting of seven members to be appointed on the recommendation of representatives of the legal profession. The Advisory Panel will be consulted as and when appropriate by the Registrar or the President on questions relating to the assignment of counsel or on any other questions relating to the assignment of counsel of which the Tribunal is seized. The Advisory Panel may of its own initiative consult the Registrar on any matter relating to the assignment of counsel. The members of the Advisory Panel will be appointed every two years on the anniversary date of the entry into force of the Directive.

FACILITIES

(ARTICLE 34)
Subject to the availability of space and resources, some basic facilities would be provided for assigned counsel.

DIRECTIVE ON THE ASSIGNMENT OF DEFENCE COUNSEL

(Directive No. 1/94)

PREAMBLE

The Registrar of the Tribunal,

Considering the Statute of the Tribunal as adopted by the Security Council under Resolution 827 (1993) of 25 May 1993, and in particular Articles 18 and 21 thereof;

Considering the Rules of Procedure and Evidence as adopted by the Tribunal on 11 February 1994 and amended on 5 May 1994, and in particular Rules 42, 45 and 55 thereof;

Considering	the Rules for the Detention of persons pending trial or appeal before the Tribunal or detained on the orders of the Tribunal as adopted by the Tribunal on 5 May 1994, and in particular Rule 67 thereof;
Considering	the host country agreement between the United Nations and the Kingdom of the Netherlands concerning the seat of the Tribunal signed at New York on 29 July 1994, and in particular Article XX thereof;
Considering	the approval of this Directive no. 1/94 by the Tribunal on 28 July 1994;

ISSUES THE DIRECTIVE ON THE ASSIGNMENT
OF DEFENCE COUNSEL AS FOLLOWS:

ARTICLE 1. ENTRY INTO FORCE

This directive lays down the conditions and arrangements for assignment of counsel and shall enter into force on the first day of August nineteen hundred and ninety four (1 August 1994).

ARTICLE 2. DEFINITIONS

Under this directive, the following terms shall mean:

Directive:	directive No. 1/94 on the assignment of defence counsel as approved by the Tribunal on 28 July 1994;
President:	the President of the Tribunal;
Registrar:	the Registrar of the Tribunal;
Rules:	the Rules of Procedure and Evidence adopted by the Tribunal 11 February 1994;
Rules of detention:	the Rules for the detention of persons pending trial or appeal before the Tribunal or detained on the orders of the Tribunal;
Statute:	the Statute of the Tribunal adopted by the Security Council under Resolution 827 (1993) of 25 May 1993;
Tribunal:	the International Tribunal for the Prosecution of Persons Responsible for Serious Violations of International Humanitarian Law Committed in the Territory of the Former Yugoslavia since 1991;

Stage of procedure: each of the stages of procedure laid down by the Rules in which the suspect or the accused may be involved (investigation, indictment, proceedings in the trial chamber, appeal, review).

ARTICLE 3. RIGHT TO COUNSEL

Without prejudice to the right of an accused to conduct his own defence, a suspect during an investigation and an accused upon whom personal service of the indictment has been effected, shall have the right to be assisted by counsel provided that he has not waived his right to counsel.

ARTICLE 4. PERSON TO WHOM COUNSEL IS ASSIGNED

(A) If he has insufficient means, the suspect during an investigation or the accused prosecuted before the Tribunal may be assigned counsel free of charge on the following terms and conditions:

(B) If the suspect or accused,

(i) either requests assignment of counsel but does not comply with the requirements set out below within a reasonable time,

(ii) or fails to obtain counsel or to request assignment of counsel, or to elect in writing that he intends to conduct his own defence,

the Registrar shall nevertheless assign him counsel in the interests of justice in accordance with Rule 45 (E) of the Rules and without prejudice to Article 19.

ARTICLE 5. INDIGENCY

A person shall be considered to be indigent if he does not have sufficient means to engage counsel of his choice and to have himself legally represented or assisted by counsel of his choice.

ARTICLE 6. REQUEST FOR ASSIGNMENT OF COUNSEL

Subject to the provisions of Article 22, a suspect or accused who wishes to be assigned counsel shall make a request to the Registrar of the Tribunal by means of the form included in Annex I. A request shall be lodged with the Registry, or transmitted to it, by the suspect or accused himself or by a person authorized by him to do so on his behalf.

ARTICLE 7. APPLICANT'S FINANCIAL SITUATION

(A) A suspect or accused who requests the assignment of counsel, must fulfil the requirement of indigency as defined in Article 5.

(B) In order to determine whether the suspect or accused is indigent, there shall be taken into account means of all kinds of which he has direct or indirect enjoyment or freely disposes, excluding any family or social benefits to which he may be entitled. In assessing such means, account shall also be taken of the means of the spouse of a suspect or accused, as well as those of persons with whom he habitually resides.

(C) Account shall also be taken of the apparent lifestyle of a suspect or accused, and of his enjoyment of any property, movable or immovable, and whether or not he derives income from it.

ARTICLE 8. DECLARATION OF MEANS

For the purposes of Article 7, the Registrar shall invite a suspect or accused requesting the assignment of counsel to make a declaration of his means on the form included in Annex II.

ARTICLE 9. CERTIFICATION OF THE DECLARATION OF MEANS

A declaration must, so far as possible, be certified by an appropriate authority, either that of the place where the suspect or accused resides or is found or that of any other place considered appropriate in the circumstances which it shall be for the Registrar to assess. If the declaration is not certified within a reasonable period of time, the Registrar may assign counsel and without prejudice to Articles 10 and 19.

ARTICLE 10. INFORMATION

For the purpose of establishing whether the suspect or accused satisfies the requisite conditions for assignment of counsel, the Registrar may request the gathering of any information, hear the suspect or accused, consider any representation, or request the production of any documents likely to support the request.

ARTICLE 11. DECISION BY THE REGISTRAR

After examining the declaration of means laid down in Article 8 and relevant information obtained pursuant to Article 10, the Registrar shall determine if the suspect or accused is indigent or not, and he shall decide:

(i) without prejudice to Article 19, either to assign counsel and choose for this purpose a name from the list drawn up in accordance with Article 14; or,

(ii) not to grant the request for assignment of counsel, in which case his decision shall be reasoned.

ARTICLE 12. NOTIFICATION OF THE DECISION

(A) The Registrar shall notify the suspect or accused his decision.

(B) He shall also notify his decision to the counsel so assigned and to his professional or governing body.

ARTICLE 13. REMEDY AGAINST A DECISION NOT TO ASSIGN COUNSEL

(A) The suspect whose request for assignment of counsel has been denied may seek the President's review of the decision of the Registrar. The President may either confirm the Registrar's decision or decide that a counsel should be assigned.

(B) The accused whose request for assignment of counsel for his initial appearance has been denied, may make a motion to the Trial Chamber before which he is due to appear for immediate review of the Registrar's decision. The Trial Chamber may either confirm the Registrar's decision or decide that a counsel should be assigned.

(C) After the initial appearance of the accused, an objection against the denial of his request for the assignment of counsel shall take the form of a preliminary motion by him before the Trial Chamber not later than 60 days after his first appearance and, in any event, before the hearing on the merits.

ARTICLE 14. PRE-REQUISITES FOR THE ASSIGNMENT OF COUNSEL

Any person may be assigned as counsel if the Registrar is satisfied that he fulfils the following pre-requisites:

(i) he is admitted to practice law in a State or is a professor of law at a university or similar academic institution,

(ii) he speaks one of the working languages of the Tribunal, namely, French and English,

(iii) he agrees to be assigned as counsel by the Tribunal to represent a suspect or accused, and

(iv) his name has been included in the list envisaged in Article 45 (A) of the Rules.

ARTICLE 15. PROFESSIONAL CERTIFICATION

In support of the pre-requisite provided for in Article 14 (i), the Registrar shall be supplied with certification of professional qualification issued by the competent professional or governing body.

ARTICLE 16. SCOPE OF THE ASSIGNMENT

(A) A suspect or accused shall only be entitled to have one counsel assigned to him and that counsel shall deal with all stages of procedure and all matters arising out of the representation of the suspect or accused or of the conduct of his defence.

(B) Where persons accused of the same or different crimes are jointly charged or tried, each accused shall separately be entitled to request assignment of counsel.

ARTICLE 17. APPLICABLE LAW

In the performance of their duties, counsel assigned shall be subject to the relevant provisions of the Statute, of the Rules, of the Rules of Detention, of any other rules or regulations adopted by the Tribunal, of the Host Country Agreement and of this Directive, and of the codes of practice and ethics governing their profession.

ARTICLE 18. RESPONSIBILITY FOR COSTS AND EXPENSES

(A) Where counsel has been assigned, the costs and expenses of legal representation of the suspect or accused necessarily or reasonibly incurred shall be met by the Tribunal subject to any budgetary constraints.

(B) Such costs and expenses to be met by the Tribunal shall include costs relating to investigative and procedural steps, measures taken for the production of evidence to assist or support the defence, as well as expenses for ascertainment of the facts, consultancy and expert opinion, transportation and accommodation of witnesses, postal charges, registration fees, taxes or similar duties, and all remuneration due to counsel in accordance with Articles 23 and 30.

(C) The Financial Officer of the Registry shall reimburse the sums claimed by assigned counsel for the expenses as provided in paragraph (A) and (B) above on receipt of a statement of expenses made out using the form included in Annex III which must be approved by the Registrar.

ARTICLE 19. WITHDRAWAL OF ASSIGNMENT

(A) Assignment of counsel may be withdrawn by the Registrar if, after his decision, the suspect or accused comes into means which, had they been available at the time the request in Article 6 was made, would have caused the Registrar not to grant the request.

(B) Assignment of counsel may be withdrawn if information obtained according to Article 10 establishes that the suspect or accused has sufficient means to allow him to pay for the cost of his defence.

(C) The decision to withdraw the assignment shall be reasoned and notified to the suspect or accused and to the counsel assigned. Such withdrawal shall take effect from the date of receipt of the notification.

(D) After the notification of the withdrawal of the assignment of counsel, all the costs and expenses incurred by the representation of the suspect or accused shall cease to be met by the Tribunal upon replacement.

(E) The provisions of Article 13 shall apply *mutatis mutandis* where there is dissatisfaction against the decision withdrawing the assignment of counsel.

ARTICLE 20. WITHDRAWAL UPON DECISION BY A CHAMBER

(A) Upon decision by a Chamber either to refuse audience to assigned counsel for misconduct under Rule 46 (A), or to grant the request of an accused to be assigned another counsel, the Registrar shall then withdraw the assignment.

(B) The withdrawal shall be notified to the accused, to the counsel concerned and to his professional or governing body.

(C) The Registrar shall immediately assign a new counsel to the suspect or accused.

ARTICLE 21. REPLACEMENT

Where the assignment of counsel is withdrawn by the Registrar or where the services of assigned counsel are discontinued, the counsel assigned may not withdraw from acting until either a replacement counsel has been provided by the Tribunal or by the suspect or accused, or the suspect or accused has declared his intention in writing to conduct his own defence.

ARTICLE 22. ASSIGNMENT OF COUNSEL AWAY FROM THE SEAT OF THE TRIBUNAL

(A) Away from the seat of the Tribunal, and in a case of urgency, a suspect who, during the investigation, requests assignment of counsel, may indicate the name of counsel if he knows one who may be assigned in accordance with the provisions of this Directive.

(B) Where the suspect fails to indicate a name, the Prosecutor, or a person authorized by him or acting under his direction, may contact the local Bar

Association and obtain the name of counsel who may be assigned in accordance with the provisions of this Directive.

(C) In the situations envisaged in paragraphs (A) and (B), the procedure for assignment of counsel as set out in this Directive shall apply *mutatis mutandis* but shall be accelerated where necessary.

ARTICLE 23. REMUNERATION PAID TO ASSIGNED COUNSEL

(A) The remuneration paid to assigned counsel for any one case and at any one stage of the procedure shall include:

(i) a fixed rate,

(ii) fees calculated on the basis of a fixed daily rate applied at any stage of the procedure to the number of days of work, and

(iii) a daily allowance calculated on the basis of fixed rates as established by the United Nations Schedule of Daily Subsistence Allowance Rates applied to the number of days of work;

(B) Assigned counsel who receives remuneration from the Tribunal, shall not be entitled to receive remuneration from any other source.

ARTICLE 24. FIXED RATE

The fixed rate envisaged in Article 23 (A) (i) shall be equivalent to four hundred US Dollars (US$ 400.00).

ARTICLE 25. FEES

The fixed daily rate for fees envisaged in Article 23 (A) (ii) shall be equivalent to two hundred US Dollars(US$ 200.00).

ARTICLE 26. DAILY ALLOWANCE

(A) The fixed rate for the daily allowance envisaged in Article 23 (A) (iii) shall apply to the first period of two weeks.

(B) For successive periods of two weeks, a progressive reduction of the rates set out in paragraph (A) above shall be applied as follows:

- 20% for the second period of two weeks,
- 40% for the third period of two weeks,
- 60% for additional weeks.

ARTICLE 27. STATEMENT OF REMUNERATION

(A) Subject to the provisions of Article 28, payment of the fees envisaged in Article 23 (A) shall be made at the conclusion of the relevant stage of procedure, on presentation by counsel of a detailed statement using the form included in Annex IV.

(B) The statement shall indicate, inter alia, the name of the suspect or the accused, the registration number in the Record Book, the stage of the procedure at which assigned counsel was involved and the number of days of work.

ARTICLE 28. PROVISIONAL PAYMENT

(A) When the engagement of assigned counsel has lasted more than two weeks, a provisional payment of the fees and daily allowance set out in Article 23 (A) (ii) and (iii) above may be made for each period of two weeks served, on presentation by counsel of a provisional statement covering the corresponding period.

(B) Subject to the provisions of Article 29 the fixed rate shall be paid in accordance with Article 27 on presentation of the final statement by assigned counsel.

ARTICLE 29. PAYMENT *PRO RATA TEMPORIS*

When, during engagement, an assigned counsel is replaced in the same capacity by another assigned counsel for whatever reason, the remuneration shall be paid to each of them *pro rata temporis*.

ARTICLE 30. TRAVEL EXPENSES

(A) Travel expenses shall be reimbursed for an assigned counsel who does not usually reside in the territory of the host country or in the country where the particular stage of the procedure is being conducted, on the basis of one economy class round trip air ticket by the shortest route or within limits laid down by the Registrar, on presentation of a statement of travel expenses using the form included in Annex V, accompanied by the original counterfoil of the ticket.

(B) Travel expenses shall be reimbursed to assigned counsel residing in the territory of the country but not in the town where he is serving, on the basis of fixed rates as established by the United Nations Schedule of Rates of Reimbursement for Travel by Private Motor Vehicle applicable to differents groups of Countries and Territories, per kilometre travelled on the outward and return journeys by the shortest route, on presentation of a statement of travel expenses using the form included in Annex V.

(C) Notwithstanding paragraphs (A) and (B), the Registrar shall assess, after consulting the President and depending on the circumstances of the case, whether the Tribunal, in the interests of justice and in order to ensure the full exercise of defence rights, is required to meet other travel expenses of assigned counsel.

ARTICLE 31. FINANCIAL OFFICER OF THE REGISTRY

(A) All sums payable to assigned counsel under the provisions of this Directive shall be paid by the Financial Officer of the Registry.

(B) The statement of expenses, the statement of remuneration (be it provisional or final) and the statement of travel expenses envisaged under Articles 18, 27, 28 and 30, must receive the prior approval of the Registrar.

ARTICLE 32. ADVISORY PANEL

(A) An Advisory Panel shall be set up consisting of two members chosen by the President by ballot from the list referred to in Article 14, two members proposed by the International Bar Association, two members proposed by the Union International des Avocats, and the President of the Nederlandse Orde van Advokaten or his representative.

(B) The President of the Advisory Panel will be the President of the Nederlandse Orde van Advokaten or his representative. The membership of the Advisory Panel shall come up for appointment every two years on the anniversary date of the entry into force of this Directive.

(C) The Advisory Panel may be consulted as and when necessary by the Registrar or the President on matters relating to assignment of counsel .

(D) The Advisory Panel may also of its own initiative refer to the Registrar any matter relating to the assignment of counsel.

ARTICLE 33. SETTLEMENT OF DISPUTES

In the event of disagreement on questions relating to calculation and payment of remuneration or to reimbursement of expenses, the Registrar shall make a decision, after consulting the President and, if necessary, the Advisory Panel, on an equitable basis.

ARTICLE 34. PROVISION OF FACILITIES

(A) Assigned counsel who do not have professional facilities close to the seat of the Tribunal shall, subject to availability of space and resources, be provided with reasonable facilities and equipment such as photocopiers, computer equipment, various types of office equipment, and telephone lines.

(B) At the seat of the Tribunal, assigned counsel may use the libraries and the documentation centre used by the Judges of the Tribunal.

LIST OF ANNEXES TO DIRECTIVE NO.1/94

Annex I: Request for assignment of counsel (form D1/1)

Annex II: Declaration of means (form D1/2)

Annex III: Statement for reimbursement of expenses (form D1/3)

Annex IV: Statement of fees (form D1/4)

Annex V: Statement of travel expenses (form D1/5)

PART IV

RULES GOVERNING THE DETENTION OF PERSONS AWAITING TRIAL OR APPEAL BEFORE THE INTERNATIONAL TRIBUNAL, 5 MAY 1994

RULES GOVERNING THE DETENTION OF PERSONS AWAITING TRIAL OR APPEAL BEFORE THE TRIBUNAL OR OTHERWISE DETAINED ON THE AUTHORITY OF THE TRIBUNAL (Adopted on 5 May 1994)

IT/38/Rev. 3, 10 May 1994.

TABLE OF CONTENTS

RULES GOVERNING THE DETENTION OF PERSONS AWAITING TRIAL OR APPEAL BEFORE THE TRIBUNAL OR OTHERWISE DETAINED ON THE AUTHORITY OF THE TRIBUNAL

("RULES OF DETENTION")

PREAMBLE

The purpose of these Rules of Detention is to govern the administration of the detention unit for detainees awaiting trial or appeal at the Tribunal or any other person detained on the authority of the Tribunal and to ensure the continued application and protection of their individual rights while in detention. The primary principles on which these Rules of Detention rest reflect the overriding requirements of humanity, respect for human dignity and the presumption of innocence.

In particular, these Rules of Detention are intended to regulate, in general terms, the rights and obligations of detainees at all stages from reception to release, and to provide the basic criteria for management of the detention unit.

DEFINITIONS

(i) In these Rules of Detention the following terms shall mean:

Bureau: the body comprised of the President, the Vice-President and the Presiding Judges of the Trial Chambers established pursuant to Rule 23 of the Rules of Procedure and Evidence;

Commanding Officer: the official of the United Nations appointed as the head of the staff responsible for the administration of the detention unit;

Detainee: any person detained awaiting trial or appeal before the Tribunal, or being held pending transfer to another institution, and any other person detained on the authority of the Tribunal;

Detention unit: the unit for detainees erected within the grounds of the host prison;

General Director: the head of the host prison appointed by the authorities of the Host State;

Host prison: the penitentiary complex maintained by the authorities of the Host State and located at The Hague;

Host State: the Kingdom of the Netherlands;

Medical officer: the medical officer for the time being appointed by agreement between the Registrar and the General Director of the host prison;

Prosecutor: the Prosecutor appointed pursuant to Article 18 of the Statute of the Tribunal adopted by Security Council resolution 827 of 25 May 1993, or any person authorized by him or acting under his direction;

Registrar:	the Registrar of the Tribunal appointed pursuant to Article 17(3) of the Statute of the Tribunal, or any person authorized by him or acting under his direction;
Rules of Procedure and Evidence:	the Rules of Procedure and Evidence of the Tribunal as adopted on 11 February 1994 or as subsequently amended;
Staff of the detention unit:	the staff employed by the United Nations to run the detention unit;
Tribunal:	the International Tribunal for the Prosecution of Persons Responsible for Serious Violations of International Humanitarian Law Committed in the Territory of the Former Yugoslavia since 1991, established by Security Council resolution 827 of 25 May 1993.

(ii) In these Rules of Detention, the masculine shall include the feminine and the singular the plural and vice-versa.

(iii) These Rules of Detention shall enter into force as of 1 August 1994.

BASIC PRINCIPLES

1. These Rules of Detention are to be applied in conjunction with the relevant provisions of the Headquarters Agreement entered into between the Host State and the United Nations and, in particular, the Annex on matters relating to security and order.

2. The United Nations shall retain the ultimate responsibility and liability for all aspects of detention pursuant to these Rules of Detention. All detainees shall be subject to the sole jurisdiction of the Tribunal at all times that they are so detained, even though physically absent from the detention unit, until final release or transfer to another institution. Subject to the overriding jurisdiction of the Tribunal, the Commanding Officer shall have sole responsibility for all aspects of the day-to-day management of the detention unit, including security and order, and may make all decisions relating thereto, except where otherwise provided in these Rules of Detention.

3. These Rules of Detention shall be applied impartially. There shall be no discrimination on grounds of race, colour, sex, language, religion, political or other opinion, national, ethnic or social origin, property, birth, economic or other status.

4. A detainee is entitled to observe the religious beliefs and moral precepts of the group to which he belongs and that right shall be respected at all times.

5. All detainees, other than those who have been convicted by the Tribunal, are presumed to be innocent until found guilty and are to be treated as such at all times.

6. The Bureau may, at any time, appoint a judge of the Tribunal to inspect the detention unit and to report to the Tribunal on the general conditions of implementation of these Rules of Detention or of any particular aspect thereof. In addition, there shall be regular and unannounced inspections of the detention unit and its services by qualified and experienced inspectors appointed by the Tribunal. Their task shall be to ensure that the detention unit is administered in accordance with the requirements of these Rules of Detention and to protect the individual rights of detainees with special regard to the legality of the detention measures adopted in the detention unit and to report to the Tribunal thereon. The Bureau shall act upon all such reports as it sees fit, in consultation with the relevant authorities of the Host State where necessary.

7. These Rules of Detention and any regulations made hereunder shall be made readily available to the staff of the detention unit in the working languages of the Tribunal and that of the host State.

8. These Rules of Detention and any regulations made hereunder shall be made readily available to each detainee in those languages and in the language of the detainee.

MANAGEMENT OF THE DETENTION UNIT

Reception

9. No person shall be received in the detention unit without a warrant of arrest duly issued by a judge or a Chamber of the Tribunal.

10. A complete, secure and current record shall be kept concerning each detainee received. It shall include:

a. information concerning the identity of the detainee and his next of kin;
b. the date of issue of the indictment against the detainee and of the warrant of arrest;
c. the date and time of admission;
d. the name of counsel, if known;
e. the date, time and reason for all absences from the detention unit, whether to attend at the Tribunal, for medical or other approved reasons, or on final release or transfer to another institution.

11. All information concerning detainees shall be treated as confidential and made accessible only to the detainee, his counsel and persons authorized by the Registrar. The detainee shall be informed of this fact upon his arrival at the detention unit.

12. As soon as practicable after admission, each detainee shall be provided with information concerning legal, diplomatic and consular representation available to him. The detainee shall be given the opportunity at this time to notify, within reason, his family, his counsel, the appropriate diplomatic or consular representative and, at the discretion of the Commanding Officer, any other person, of his whereabouts, at the expense of the Tribunal. The detainee shall be asked at this time to name a person or authority to be notified of special events affecting him.

13. On arrival at the detention unit, the Commanding Officer shall order that a detainee's body and clothes may be searched for articles that may constitute a danger to the security and proper running of the detention unit, or which may constitute a danger to the detainee, any other detainee or any member of the staff of the detention unit and shall remove any such items.

14. An inventory shall be made of all money, valuables, clothing and other effects belonging to a detainee which, under these Rules of Detention or the rules of the host prison, he is not permitted to retain. The inventory shall be signed by the detainee. All such items shall be placed in safe custody or, at the request and expense of the detainee, sent to an address provided by him. If the items are retained within the detention unit, all reasonable steps shall be taken by the staff of the detention unit to keep them in good condition. If it is found necessary to destroy an item, this shall be recorded and the detainee informed.

15. Each detainee shall be examined by the medical officer or his deputy on the day of admission and thereafter as necessary, with a view particularly to the discovery of physical or mental illness and the taking of all necessary measures for medical treatment and the segregation of detainees suspected of infectious or contagious conditions.

Accommodation

16. Each detainee shall occupy a cell unit by himself except in exceptional circumstances or in cases where the Commanding Officer, with the approval of the Registrar, considers that there are advantages in sharing accommodation.

17. Each detainee shall be provided with a separate bed and with appropriate bedding which shall be kept in good order and changed on a regular basis so as to ensure its cleanliness.

18. The detention unit shall, at all times, meet all requirements of health and hygiene, due regard being paid to climatic conditions, lighting, heating and ventilation.

19. Each detainee shall be permitted unrestricted access to the sanitary, hygiene and drinking water arrangements in his cell unit.

20. All parts of the detention unit shall be properly maintained and kept clean at all times. In particular, each detainee shall be expected to keep his cell unit clean and tidy at all times.

Personal hygiene

21. Detainees shall be required to keep themselves clean, and shall be provided with such toilet articles as are necessary for health and cleanliness.

22. Facilities shall be provided by the host prison for the proper care of the hair and beard, and male detainees shall be enabled to shave regularly.

Clothing

23. Detainees may wear their own civilian clothing if, in the opinion of the Commanding Officer, it is clean and suitable. An indigent detainee shall be provided with suitable and sufficient civilian clothing at the cost of the Tribunal.

24. All clothing shall be clean and kept in proper condition. Underclothing shall be changed and washed as often as necessary for the maintenance of hygiene, in accordance with the regime of the host prison.

Food

25. The host prison shall provide each detainee at the normal hours with food which is suitably prepared and presented, and which satisfies in quality and quantity the standards of dietetics and modern hygiene and takes into account the age, health, religious and, as far as possible, cultural requirements of the detainee.

Physical exercise and sport

26. Each detainee shall be allowed at least one hour of walking or other suitable exercise in the open air daily, if the weather permits. Where possible, arrangements may be made with the General Director for use by detainees of indoor and outdoor sporting facilities outside the detention unit but within the host prison.

27. A properly organized programme of physical education, sport and other recreational activities shall be arranged by the Commanding Officer to ensure physical fitness, adequate exercise and recreational opportunities.

28. The Commanding Officer, acting on the advice of the medical officer, shall ensure that any detainee who participates in such a programme is physically fit to do so. Special arrangements shall be made, under medical direction, for remedial or therapeutic treatment for any detainee who is unable to participate in the regular programme.

Medical services

29. The medical services of the host prison, including psychiatric and dental care, shall be fully available to detainees, subject to any practical arrangements made with the General Director. A person capable of providing first-aid shall be present at the detention unit at all times.

30. Detainees may be visited by, and consult with, a doctor or dentist of their choice at their own expense. All such visits shall be made by prior arrangement with the Commanding Officer as to the time and duration of the visit and shall be subject to the same security controls as are imposed under Rule 63. The Commanding Officer shall not refuse a request for such a visit without reasonable grounds. Any treatment or medication recommended by such a doctor or dentist shall be administered solely by the medical officer or his deputy. The medical officer may, in his sole discretion, refuse to administer any such treatment or medication.

31. Detainees who require specialist or in-patient treatment shall be treated within the host prison to the fullest extent possible or transferred to a civil hospital.

32. The Registrar shall be informed immediately upon the death or serious illness or injury of a detainee. The Registrar shall immediately inform the spouse or nearest relative of the detainee and shall, in any event, inform any other person previously designated by the detainee. In the event of the death of a detainee, an inquest will be conducted in accordance with the legal requirements of the Host State. The President may also order an inquiry into the circumstances surrounding the death or serious injury of any detainee.

33. The medical officer shall have the care of the physical and mental health of the detainees and shall see, on a daily basis or more often if necessary, all sick detainees, all who complain of illness and any detainee to whom his attention is specially directed.

34. The medical officer shall report to the Commanding Officer whenever he considers that the physical or mental health of a detainee has been or will be adversely affected by any condition of his detention. The Commanding Officer shall immediately submit the report to the Registrar who, after consultation with the President, shall take all necessary action.

35. A competent authority appointed by the Tribunal pursuant to Rule 6 shall regularly inspect the detention unit and advise the Commanding Officer and the Registrar upon:

a. the quantity, quality, preparation and serving of food;
b. the hygiene and cleanliness of the detention unit and of the detainees;
c. the sanitation, heating, lighting and ventilation of the detention unit;
d. the suitability and cleanliness of the detainees' clothing and bedding.

36. The Registrar shall, if he concurs with the recommendations made, take immediate steps to give effect to those recommendations; if he does not concur with them, he shall immediately submit both a personal report and a copy of the recommendations to the Tribunal.

Discipline

37. Discipline and order shall be maintained by the staff of the detention unit in the interests of safe custody and the well-ordered running of the detention unit.

38. The Commanding Officer, in consultation with the Registrar, shall issue regulations:
   a. defining conduct constituting a disciplinary offence;
   b. regulating the type of punishment that can be imposed;
   c. specifying the authority that can impose such punishment;
   d. providing for a right of appeal to the President.

39. The disciplinary regulations shall provide a detainee with the right to be heard on the subject of any offence which he is alleged to have committed.

Segregation

40. The Registrar, acting on the request of the Prosecutor, or on his own initiative, and after seeking medical advice, may order that a detainee be segregated from all or some of the other detainees so as to avoid any potential conflict within the detention unit, or danger to the detainee in question.

41. At any time, the Commanding Officer may also order that a detainee be segregated from some or all of the other detainees for the preservation of security and good order in the detention unit or for the protection of the detainee in question. The Commanding Officer shall report all incidents of segregation to the medical officer who shall confirm the physical and mental fitness of the detainee for such segregation. Segregation is not to be used as a disciplinary measure.

42. A detainee may ask to be segregated from all or some of the other detainees. Upon receipt of such a request, the Commanding Officer shall consult the medical officer to determine whether such segregation is medically acceptable. A request for segregation will be granted unless, in the opinion of the medical officer, such segregation would be injurious to the mental or physical health of the detainee.

43. The Commanding Officer shall review all cases of individual segregation of detainees at least once a week and report to the Registrar thereon.

44. The Commanding Officer may organize the use of communal areas of the detention unit so as to segregate certain groups of detainees from others in the interests of the safety of the detainees and the proper conduct and operation of the detention unit. If such segregation is put into practice, care shall be taken to ensure that all such groupings are treated on an equal basis, having regard to the number of detainees falling within each group. All such segregations must be reported to the Tribunal, which may vary the nature, basis or conditions of such segregation.

Isolation unit

45. A detainee may be confined to the isolation unit only in the following circumstances:
   a. by order of the Registrar, acting in consultation with the President; such an order may be based upon a request from any interested person, including the Prosecutor;
   b. by order of the Commanding Officer in order to prevent the detainee from inflicting injury on other detainees or to preserve the security and good order of the detention unit;
   c. as a punishment pursuant to Rule 38.

A record shall be kept of all events concerning a detainee confined to the isolation unit.

46. All cases of use of the isolation unit shall be reported to the medical officer who shall confirm the physical and mental fitness of the detainee for such isolation. A detainee who has been confined to the isolation unit shall be visited by the medical officer or his deputy as often as the medical officer deems necessary.

47. A detainee who has been confined to the isolation unit may at any time request a visit from the medical officer, such visit to be made as soon as possible and, in any event, within twenty-four hours of the request.

48. All cases of use of the isolation unit shall be reported to the Registrar immediately, who shall report the matter to the President. The President may order the release of a detainee from the isolation unit at any time.

49. In principle, no detainee may be kept in the isolation unit for more than seven consecutive days. If further isolation is necessary, the Commanding Officer shall report the matter to the Registrar before the end of the seven-day period and the medical officer shall confirm the physical and mental fitness of the detainee to continue such isolation for a further period not to exceed seven days. Each and every extension of use of the isolation unit shall be subject to the same procedure.

Instruments of restraint and the use of force

50. Instruments of restraint, such as handcuffs, shall only be used in the following exceptional circumstances:

a. as a precaution against escape during transfer from the detention unit to any other place, including access to the premises of the host prison for any reason;
b. on medical grounds by direction and under the supervision of the medical officer;
c. to prevent a detainee from self-injury, injury to others or to prevent serious damage to property.

In all incidents involving the use of instruments of restraint, the Commanding Officer shall consult the medical officer and report to the Registrar, who may report the matter to the President.

51. Instruments of restraint shall be removed at the earliest possible opportunity.

52. If the use of any instrument of restraint is required under Rule 50, the restrained detainee shall be kept under constant and adequate supervision.

53. The staff of the detention unit shall not use force against a detainee except in self-defence or in cases of attempted escape or active or passive resistance to an order based upon these Rules of Detention or any regulations issued hereunder. Staff who have recourse to force must use no more than is strictly necessary and must report the incident immediately to the Commanding Officer, who shall provide a report on the matter to the Registrar.

54. A detainee against whom force has been used shall have the right to be examined immediately and treated, if necessary, by the medical officer. The medical examination shall be conducted in private and in the absence of any non-medical staff. The results of the examination, including any relevant statement by the detainee and the medical officer's opinion, shall be formally recorded and made available to the detainee, in a language accessible to him, to the Commanding Officer, to the President and to the Prosecutor.

55. A record shall be kept of every instance of the use of force against a detainee.

Disturbances

56. If, in the opinion of the Commanding Officer, a situation exists or is developing which threatens the security and good order of the detention unit, the Commanding Officer shall contact the General Director who will request the immediate assistance of the authorities of the Host State to maintain control within the detention unit. All such requests must be reported to the Registrar and the President immediately.

Suspension of the Rules of Detention

57. If there is serious danger of disturbances occurring within the detention unit or the host prison, the Commanding Officer or the General Director, as appropriate, may temporarily suspend the operation of all or part of these Rules of Detention for a maximum of two days. Any such suspension must be reported to the Registrar immediately. Thereupon, the President, acting in consultation with the Bureau, shall consult with the relevant authorities of the Host State and take such action in connection therewith as may be seen fit at the time.

Information to detainees

58. In addition to the copies of these Rules of Detention and any regulations to be provided to each detainee pursuant to Rule 8, each detainee shall on admission be provided with written information in the working languages of the Tribunal or in his own language concerning the rights and treatment of detainees, the disciplinary requirements of the detention unit, the authorized methods of seeking information and making complaints, and all other matters necessary to enable him to understand both his rights and obligations and to adapt himself to the routine of the detention unit.

59. At any time at which there is a detainee in the detention unit who speaks and understands neither of the working languages of the Tribunal nor that spoken by any of the staff of the detention unit, arrangements shall be made for an interpreter to be available on reasonable notice and, in any event, in cases of emergency, to permit the detainee to communicate freely with the staff and administration of the detention unit.

RIGHTS OF DETAINEES

Communications and visits

60. Subject to the provisions of Rule 66, detainees shall be entitled, under such conditions of supervision and time-restraints as the Commanding Officer deems necessary, to communicate with their families and other persons with whom it is in their legitimate interest to correspond by letter and by telephone at their own expense. In the case of an indigent detainee, the Registrar may agree that the Tribunal will bear such expenses within reason.

61. All correspondence and mail, including packages, shall be inspected for explosives or other irregular material. The Commanding Officer, in consultation with the Registrar, shall lay down conditions as to the inspection of correspondence, mail and packages in the interests of maintaining order in the detention unit and to obviate the danger of escape.

62. A detainee shall be informed at once of the death or serious illness of any near relative.

63. Detainees shall be entitled to receive visits from family, friends and others, subject only to the provisions of Rule 66 and to such restrictions and supervision as the Commanding Officer, in consultation with the Registrar, may impose. Such restrictions and supervision must be necessary in the interests of the administration of justice or the security and good order of the host prison and the detention unit. All visitors must also comply with the separate requirements of the visiting regime of the host prison. These restrictions may include personal searches of clothing and X-ray examination of possessions on entry to either or both of the detention unit and the host prison. Any person, including defence counsel for a detainee or a diplomatic or consular representative accredited to the Host State, who refuses to comply with such requirements, whether of the detention unit or of the host prison, may be refused access.

64. A detainee must be informed of the identity of each visitor and may refuse to see any visitor other than a representative of the Prosecutor.

65. Detainees shall be allowed to communicate with and receive visits from the diplomatic and consular representative accredited to the Host State of the State to which they belong or, in the case of detainees who are without diplomatic or consular representation in the Host State and refugees or stateless persons, with the diplomatic representative accredited to the Host State of the State which takes charge of their interests or of a national or international authority whose task it is to serve the interests of such persons.

66. The Prosecutor may request the Registrar or, in cases of emergency, the Commanding Officer, to prohibit contact between a detainee and any other person if he has reasonable grounds for believing that such contact is for the purposes of attempting to arrange the escape of the detainee from the detention unit, or could prejudice or otherwise affect the outcome of the proceedings against the detainee, or of any other investigation, or that such contact could be harmful to the detainee or any other person. If the request is made to the Commanding Officer on grounds of urgency, the Prosecutor shall immediately inform the Registrar of the request, together with the reasons therefor. The detainee shall immediately be informed of the fact of any such request. A detainee may at any time request the President to deny or reverse such a request for prohibition of contact.

Legal assistance

67. Each detainee shall be entitled to communicate fully and without restraint with his defence counsel, with the assistance of an interpreter where necessary. Unless such counsel and interpreter have been provided by the Tribunal on the basis of the indigency of the detainee, all such communications shall be at the expense of the detainee. All such correspondence and communications shall be privileged. All visits shall be made by prior arrangement with the Commanding Officer as to the time and duration of the visit and shall be subject to the same security controls as are imposed under Rule 63. The Commanding Officer shall not refuse a request for such a visit without reasonable grounds. Interviews with legal counsel and interpreters shall be conducted in the sight but not within the hearing, either direct or indirect, of the staff of the detention unit.

Spiritual welfare

68. Every detainee shall be entitled to indicate, on arrival at the detention unit or thereafter, whether he wishes to establish contact with any of the ministers or spiritual advisers of the host prison.

69. A qualified representative of each religion or system of beliefs held by any detainee shall be appointed and approved by the Bureau. Such representative shall be permitted to hold regular services and activities within the detention unit and to pay pastoral visits to any detainee of his religion, subject to the same considerations of the security and good order of the detention unit and of the host prison as apply to other visits.

70. Access to a representative of any religion shall not be refused to any detainee, subject only to the same restrictions and conditions provided for in Rule 63. A detainee may refuse to see any such religious representative.

71. So far as is practicable, every detainee shall be allowed to satisfy the needs of his religious, spiritual and moral life by attending services or meetings held in the detention unit and having in his possession any necessary books or literature. By arrangement with the General Director, a detainee may, on request, be permitted to visit any religious facility within the grounds of the host prison.

Work programme

72. The Commanding Officer, after consultation with the General Director, and as far as is practicable, shall institute a work programme to be performed by detainees either in the individual cell units or in the communal areas of the detention unit.

73. Detainees shall be offered the opportunity to enrol in such work programme but shall not be required to work. A detainee who chooses to work shall be paid for his work at rates to be established by the Commanding Officer in consultation with the Registrar and may use part of his earnings to purchase articles for his own use pursuant to Rule 82. The balance of any monies earned shall be held to his account in accordance with Rule 14.

Recreational activities

74. Detainees shall be allowed to procure at their own expense books, newspapers, reading and writing materials and other means of occupation as are compatible with the interests of the administration of justice and the security and good order of the detention unit and of the host prison.

75. In particular, detainees shall be entitled to keep themselves regularly informed of the news by reading newspapers, periodicals and other publications and by radio and television broadcasts, all necessary equipment to be provided at their own expense. The Commanding Officer may refuse the installation of any such equipment which he considers to be a potential risk to the safety and good order of the detention unit or to any of the detainees.

76. If, in the opinion of the Prosecutor, the interests of justice would not be served by allowing a particular detainee unrestricted access to the news, or that such unrestricted access could prejudice the outcome of the proceedings against the detainee or of any other investigation, the Prosecutor may request the Registrar, or in cases of urgency, the Commanding Officer to restrict such access. If the request is made to the Commanding Officer on grounds of urgency, the Prosecutor shall immediately inform the Registrar of the request, together with the reasons therefor. The detainee shall immediately be informed of the fact of any such request. A detainee may at any time request the President to deny or reverse such a request for restriction of access.

77. By arrangement with the General Director, detainees may use the library and such vocational or other facilities of the host prison as may be made available.

Personal possessions of detainees

78. A detainee may keep in his possession all clothing and personal items for his own use or consumption unless, in the opinion of the Commanding Officer or the General Director, such items constitute a threat to the security or good order of the detention unit or the host prison, or to the health or safety of any person therein. All items so removed shall be retained by the staff of the detention unit as provided for in Rule 14.

79. Any item received from outside, including any item introduced by any visitor to a detainee, shall be subject to separate security controls by both the detention unit and the host prison and may be transported through the host prison to the detention unit by staff of either the detention unit or of the host prison. The General Director may refuse access to the host prison of any item intended for consumption by detainees.

80. As far as practicable, any item received for a detainee from outside shall be treated as provided for in Rule 14 unless intended and permitted under these Rules of Detention and the rules of the host prison for use during imprisonment.

81. The possession and use of any medication shall be subject to the control and supervision of the medical officer. Detainees may possess cigarettes and smoke them at such times and places as the Commanding Officer permits. The possession or consumption of alcohol is not permitted.

82. Each detainee shall be authorized to spend his own money to purchase items of a personal nature from the store operated by the host prison. In the case of an indigent detainee, the Registrar may authorize the purchase of such items, within reason, for the account of the Tribunal. Detainees shall have the right to purchase such items within seven days of arrival and at least once a week thereafter.

83. On release of the detainee from the detention unit, or transfer to another institution, all articles and money retained within the detention unit shall be returned to the detainee except in so far as he has been authorized to spend money or send such property out of the detention unit, or it has been found necessary on hygienic grounds to destroy any article of clothing. The detainee shall sign a receipt for the articles and money returned to him.

Complaints

84. Each detainee may make a complaint to the Commanding Officer or his representative at any time.

85. A detainee, if not satisfied with the response from the Commanding Officer, has the right to make a written complaint, without censorship, to the Registrar, who shall forward it to the President or to the authority competent to carry out inspections pursuant to Rule 6.

86. Each detainee may make a complaint to the competent inspecting authority during an inspection of the detention unit. The detainee shall have the opportunity to talk to the inspector in the sight but not within sound of the staff of the detention unit.

87. The right of complaint shall include confidential access to the relevant authority pursuant to Rules 85 and 86.

88. Every complaint made to the Registrar shall be acknowledged within twenty-four hours. Each complaint shall be dealt with promptly and replied to without delay and, in any event, no later than two weeks of receipt.

REMOVAL AND TRANSPORT OF DETAINEES

89. When detainees are being removed to or from the detention unit, they shall be exposed to public view as little as possible and all proper safeguards shall be adopted to protect them from insult, injury, curiosity and publicity in any form.

90. Detainees shall at all times be transported in vehicles with adequate ventilation and light and in such a way as will not subject them to unnecessary physical hardship or indignity.

91. The transport of detainees through the host prison shall be conducted jointly by personnel of the detention unit and of the host prison.

AMENDMENT OF THE RULES OF DETENTION

92. Proposals for amendment of the Rules of Detention may be made by a judge, the Prosecutor or the Registrar and shall be adopted if agreed to by not less than seven judges at a plenary meeting of the Tribunal convened with notice of the proposal addressed to all judges. An amendment to the Rules of Detention may be otherwise adopted, provided it is unanimously approved by the judges. Any such amendment shall enter into force immediately unless the Tribunal decides otherwise.

PART V

HEADQUARTERS AGREEMENT FOR THE INTERNATIONAL TRIBUNAL, 27 MAY 1994

LETTER DATED 14 JULY 1994 FROM THE SECRETARY-GENERAL ADDRESED TO THE PRESIDENT OF THE SECURITY COUNCIL

Agreement Between the United Nations and the Kingdom of the Netherlands Concerning the Headquarters of the International Tribunal for the Prosecution of Persons Responsible for Serious Violations of International Humanitarian Law Committed in the Territory of the Former Yugoslavia Since 1991

S/1994/848, 19 July 1994

and Corrigendum

S/1994/848/Corr. 1, 25 August 1994.

I have the honour to refer to paragraph 6 of Security Council resolution 827 (1993) of 25 May 1993, whereby the Council decided that the determination of the seat of the International Tribunal would be subject to the conclusion of appropriate arrangements between the United Nations and the Netherlands acceptable to the Council.

Following extensive negotiations between representatives of the United Nations and the Government of the Kingdom of the Netherlands and representatives of Aegon Nederland nv., instruments concerning the headquarters of the Tribunal and the lease of its premises have been initialled. I am satisfied that in their present form these instruments constitute acceptable arrangements within the meaning of paragraph 6 of Security Council resolution 827 (1993).

Copies of the Agreement between the United Nations and the Kingdom of the Netherlands Concerning the Headquarters of the International Tribunal for the Prosecution of Persons Responsible for Serious Violations of International Humanitarian Law Committed in the Territory of the Former Yugoslavia since 1991 (see annex) and the Agreement for Tenancy of Churchillplein 1, the Hague,* are attached for the information of the Council.

I would be grateful if you could confirm to me that the Security Council has found these arrangements acceptable and that the seat of the Tribunal has been determined to be at The Hague.

(<u>Signed</u>) Boutros BOUTROS-GHALI

---

* The text of the Agreement for Tenancy, may be consulted in room S-3520.

Annex

PROTOCOL OF DISCUSSIONS

Delegations representing the Government of the Kingdom of the Netherlands and the United Nations met in New York on 26 and 27 May 1994 in order to discuss the conclusion of an Agreement Concerning the Headquarters of the International Tribunal for the Prosecution of Persons Responsible for Serious Violations of International Humanitarian Law.

Agreement was reached on the text for such an Agreement. This text, as initialed by the Chairmen of both delegations, is attached to this Protocol.

For the Government of the Kingdom of the Netherlands

For the United Nations

New York, 27 May 1994

AGREEMENT
BETWEEN
THE UNITED NATIONS
AND
THE KINGDOM OF THE NETHERLANDS
CONCERNING THE HEADQUARTERS OF THE INTERNATIONAL TRIBUNAL
FOR THE PROSECUTION OF PERSONS RESPONSIBLE FOR
SERIOUS VIOLATIONS OF INTERNATIONAL HUMANITARIAN LAW
COMMITTED IN THE TERRITORY OF THE FORMER YUGOSLAVIA SINCE 1991

The United Nations and the Kingdom of the Netherlands,

Whereas the Security Council acting under Chapter VII of the Charter of the United Nations decided, by paragraph 1 of its resolution 808 (1993) of 22 February 1993, inter alia "that an international tribunal shall be established for the prosecution of persons responsible for serious violations of international humanitarian law committed in the territory of the former Yugoslavia since 1991";

Whereas the International Tribunal is established as a subsidiary organ within the terms of Article 29 of the Charter of the United Nations;

Whereas the Security Council, in paragraph 6 of its resolution 827(1993) of 25 May 1993 further inter alia decided that "the determination of the seat of the International Tribunal is subject to the conclusion of appropriate arrangements between the United Nations and the Netherlands acceptable to the Council";

Whereas the Statute of the International Tribunal, in its Article 31, provides that "the International Tribunal shall have its seat at The Hague";

Whereas the United Nations and the Kingdom of the Netherlands wish to conclude an Agreement regulating matters arising from the establishment and necessary for the proper functioning of the International Tribunal in the Kingdom of the Netherlands;

Have agreed as follows.

ARTICLE I

DEFINITIONS

For the purpose of the present Agreement, the following definitions shall apply:

(a) "the Tribunal" means the International Tribunal for the Prosecution of Persons Responsible for Serious Violations of International Humanitarian Law Committed in the Territory of the Former Yugoslavia since 1991, established by the Security Council pursuant to its resolutions 808(1993) and 827(1993);

(b) "the premises of the Tribunal" means buildings, parts of buildings and areas, including installations and facilities made available to, maintained, occupied or used by the Tribunal in the host country in connection with its functions and purposes;

(c) "the host country" means the Kingdom of the Netherlands;

(d) "the Government" means the Government of the Kingdom of the Netherlands;

(e) "the United Nations" means the United Nations, an international governmental organization established under the Charter of the United Nations;

(f) "the Security Council" means the Security Council of the United Nations;

(g) "the Secretary-General" means the Secretary-General of the United Nations;

(h) "the competent authorities" means national, provincial, municipal and other competent authorities under the law of the host country;

(i) "the Statute" means the Statute of the Tribunal adopted by the Security Council by its resolution 827(1993);

(j) "the Judges" means the Judges of the Tribunal as elected by the General Assembly of the United Nations pursuant to Article 13 of the Statute;

(k) "the President" means the President of the Tribunal as referred to in Article 14 of the Statute;

(l) "the Prosecutor" means the Prosecutor of the Tribunal as appointed by the Security Council pursuant to Article 16 of the Statute;

(m) "the Registrar" means the Registrar of the Tribunal as appointed by the Secretary-General pursuant to Article 17 of the Statute;

(n) "the officials of the Tribunal" means the staff of the Office of the Prosecutor as referred to in paragraph 5 of Article 16 of the Statute and the staff of the Registry as referred to in paragraph 4 of Article 17 of the the Statute;

(o) "persons performing missions for the Tribunal" means persons performing certain missions for the Tribunal in the investigation or prosecution or in the judicial or appellate proceedings;

(p) "the witnesses" means persons referred to as such in the Statute;

(q) "experts" means persons called at the instance of the Tribunal, the Prosecutor, the suspect or the accused to present testimony based on special knowledge, skills, experience or training;

(r) "counsel" means a person referred to as such in the Statute;

(s) "the suspect" means a person referred to as such in the Statute;

(t) "the accused" means a person referred to as such in the Statute;

(u) "the General Convention" means the Convention on the Privileges and Immunities of the United Nations adopted by the General Assembly of the United Nations on 13 February 1946, to which the Kingdom of the Netherlands acceded on 19 April 1948;

(v) "the Vienna Convention" means the Vienna Convention on Diplomatic Relations done at Vienna on 18 April 1961, to which the Kingdom of the Netherlands acceded on 7 September 1984;

(w) "the regulations" means the regulations adopted by the Tribunal pursuant to Article VI, paragraph 3 of this Agreement.

ARTICLE II
PURPOSE AND SCOPE OF THE AGREEMENT

This Agreement shall regulate matters relating to or arising out of the establishment and the proper functioning of the Tribunal in the Kingdom of the Netherlands.

ARTICLE III
JURIDICAL PERSONALITY OF THE TRIBUNAL

1. The Tribunal shall possess in the host country full juridical personality. This shall, in particular, include the capacity:

a) to contract;

b) to acquire and dispose of movable and immovable property;

c) to institute legal proceedings.

2. For the purpose of this Article the Tribunal shall be represented by the Registrar.

ARTICLE IV
APPLICATION OF THE GENERAL AND VIENNA CONVENTIONS

The General Convention and the Vienna Convention shall be applicable mutatis mutandis to the Tribunal, its property, funds and assets, to the premises of the Tribunal, to the Judges, the Prosecutor and the Registrar, the officials of the Tribunal and persons performing missions for the Tribunal.

ARTICLE V
INVIOLABILITY OF THE PREMISES OF THE TRIBUNAL

1. The premises of the Tribunal shall be inviolable. The competent authorities shall take whatever action may be necessary to ensure that the Tribunal shall not be dispossessed of all or any part of the premises of the Tribunal without the express consent of the Tribunal. The property, funds and assets of the Tribunal, wherever located and by whomsoever held, shall be immune from search, seizure, requisition, confiscation, expropriation and any other form of interference, whether by executive, administrative, judicial or legislative action.

2. The competent authorities shall not enter the premises of the Tribunal to perform any official duty, except with the express consent, or at the request of, the Registrar or an official designated by him. Judicial actions and the service or execution of legal process, including the seizure of private property, cannot be enforced on the premises of the Tribunal except with the consent of and in accordance with conditions approved by the Registrar.

3. In case of fire or other emergency requiring prompt protective action, or in the event that the competent authorities have reasonable cause to believe that such an emergency has occured or is about to occur on the premises of the Tribunal, the consent of the Registrar, or an official designated by him, to any necessary entry into the premises of the Tribunal shall be presumed if neither of them can be reached in time.

4. Subject to paragraphs 1, 2 and 3 above, the competent authorities shall take the necessary action to protect the premises of the Tribunal against fire or other emergency.

5. The Tribunal may expel or exclude persons from the premises of the Tribunal for violation of its regulations.

ARTICLE VI
LAW AND AUTHORITY ON THE PREMISES OF THE TRIBUNAL

1. The premises of the Tribunal shall be under the control and authority of the Tribunal, as provided in this Agreement.

2. Except as otherwise provided in this Agreement or in the General Convention, the laws and regulations of the host country shall apply on the premises of the Tribunal.

3. The Tribunal shall have the power to make regulations operative on the premises of the Tribunal for the purpose of establishing therein the conditions in all respects necessary for the full execution of its functions. The Tribunal shall promptly inform the competent authorities of regulations thus enacted in accordance with this paragraph. No law or regulation of the host country which is inconsistent with a regulation of the Tribunal shall, to the extent of such inconsistency, be applicable within the premises of the Tribunal.

4. Any dispute between the Tribunal and the host country, as to whether a regulation of the Tribunal is authorised by this Article, or as to whether a law or regulation of the host country is inconsistent with any regulation of the Tribunal authorised by this Article, shall be promptly settled by the procedure set out in Article XXVIII, paragraph 2 of this Agreement. Pending such settlement, the regulation of the Tribunal shall apply and the law or regulation of the host country shall be inapplicable on the premises of the Tribunal to the extent that the Tribunal claims it to be inconsistent with its regulation.

ARTICLE VII
PROTECTION OF THE PREMISES OF THE TRIBUNAL AND THEIR VICINITY

1. The competent authorities shall exercise due diligence to ensure the security and protection of the Tribunal and to ensure that the tranquility of the Tribunal is not disturbed by the intrusion of persons or groups of persons from outside the premises of the Tribunal or by disturbances in their immediate vicinity and shall provide to the premises of the Tribunal the appropriate protection as may be required.

2. If so requested by the President or the Registrar of the Tribunal, the competent authorities shall provide adequate police force necessary for the preservation of law and order

on the premises of the Tribunal or in the immediate vicinity thereof, and for the removal of persons therefrom.

ARTICLE VIII

FUNDS, ASSETS AND OTHER PROPERTY

1. The Tribunal, its funds, assets and other property, wherever located and by whomsoever held, shall enjoy immunity from every form of legal process, except insofar as in any particular case the Tribunal has expressly waived its immunity. It is understood, however, that no waiver of immunity shall extend to any measure of execution.

2. Without being restricted by financial controls, regulations or moratoria of any kind, the Tribunal:

a) may hold and use funds, gold or negotiable instruments of any kind and maintain and operate accounts in any currency and convert any currency held by it into any other currency;

b) shall be free to transfer its funds, gold or currency from one country to another, or within the host country, to the United Nations or any other agency.

ARTICLE IX

INVIOLABILITY OF ARCHIVES AND ALL DOCUMENTS OF THE TRIBUNAL

The archives of the Tribunal, and in general all documents and materials made available, belonging to or used by it, wherever located in the host country and by whomsoever held, shall be inviolable.

ARTICLE X

EXEMPTION FROM TAXES AND DUTIES

1. Within the scope of its official functions, the Tribunal, its assets, income and other property shall be exempt from all direct taxes, which include inter alia, income tax, capital tax, corporation tax as well as direct taxes levied by local and provincial authorities.

2. The Tribunal shall:

(a) on application be granted exemption from motor-vehicle tax in respect of motor vehicles used for its official activities;

(b) be exempt from stock exchange tax, insurance tax, tax on capital duty and real property transfer tax;

(c) be exempt from all import duties and taxes in respect of goods, including publications and motor vehicles, whose import or export by the Tribunal is necessary for the exercise of its official activities;

(d) be exempt from value-added tax paid on any goods, including motor vehicles, or services of substantial value, which are necessary for its official activities. Such claims for exemption will be made only in respect of goods or services supplied on a recurring basis or involving considerable expenditure;

(e) be exempt from excise duty included in the price of alcoholic beverages, tobacco products and hydrocarbons such as fuel oils and motor fuels purchased by the Tribunal and necssary for its official activities;

(f) be exempt from the Tax on Private Passenger Vehicles and Motorcycles (Belasting van personenauto's en motorrijwielen, BPM) with respect to motor vehicles for its official activities.

3. The exemptions provided for in paragraph 2(d) and (e) above may be granted by way of a refund. The exemptions referred to in paragraph 2 above shall be applied in accordance with the formal requirements of the host country. These requirements, however, shall not affect the general principles laid down in this Article.

4. The provisions of this Article shall not apply to taxes and duties which are considered to be charges for public utility services, provided at a fixed rate according to the amount of services rendered and which can be specifically identified, described and itemized.

5. Goods acquired or imported under paragraph 2 above shall not be sold, given away, or otherwise disposed of, except in accordance with conditions agreed upon with the Government.

ARTICLE XI
COMMUNICATIONS FACILITIES

1. The Tribunal shall enjoy, in respect of its official communications, treatment not less favourable than that accorded by the Government to any diplomatic mission in matters of establishment and operation, priorities, tariffs, charges on mail and cablegrams and on

teleprinter, facsimile, telephone and other communications, as well as rates for information to the press and radio.

2. No official correspondence or other communication of the Tribunal shall be subject to censorship by the Government. Such immunity from censorship shall extend to printed matter, photographic and electronic data communications, and other forms of communications as may be used by the Tribunal. The Tribunal shall be entitled to use codes and to dispatch and receive correspondence and other material or communications either by courier or in sealed bags, all of which shall be inviolable and shall have the same privileges and immunities as diplomatic couriers and bags.

3. The Tribunal shall have the right to operate radio and other telecommunications equipment on United Nations registered frequencies and those allocated to it by the Government, between the Tribunal offices, installations, facilities and means of transport, within and outside the host country, and in particular with the International Court of Justice in The Hague, United Nations Headquarters in New York, United Nations Offices in Vienna and Geneva and the territory of the former Yugoslavia.

4. For the fulfilment of its purposes, the Tribunal shall have the right to publish freely and without restrictions within the host country in conformity with this Agreement.

ARTICLE XII
PUBLIC SERVICES FOR THE PREMISES OF THE TRIBUNAL

1. The competent authorities shall secure, on fair conditions and upon the request of the Registrar or on his behalf, the public services needed by the Tribunal such as, but not limited to, postal, telephone and telegraphic services, electricity, water, gas, sewage, collection of waste, fire protection, local transportation and cleaning of public streets.

2. In cases where electricity, water, gas or other services referred to in paragraph 1 above are made available to the Tribunal by the competent authorities, or where the prices thereof are under their control, the rates for such services shall not exceed the lowest comparable rates accorded to essential agencies and organs of the Government.

3. In case of force majeure resulting in a complete or partial disruption of the aforementioned services, the Tribunal shall for the performance of its functions be accorded the priority given to essential agencies and organs of the Government.

4. Upon request of the competent authorities, the Registrar, or an official designated by him, shall make suitable arrangements to enable duly authorized representatives of the appropriate public services to inspect, repair, maintain, reconstruct and relocate utilities, conduits, mains and sewers on the premises of Tribunal under conditions which shall not unreasonably disturb the carrying out of the functions of the Tribunal. Underground constructions may be undertaken by the competent authorities on the premises of the Tribunal only after consultation with the Registrar, or an official designated by him, and under conditions which shall not disturb the carrying out of the functions of the Tribunal.

ARTICLE XIII
FLAG, EMBLEM AND MARKINGS

The Tribunal shall be entitled to display its flag, emblem and markings on the premises of the Tribunal, and to display its flag on vehicles used for official purposes.

ARTICLE XIV
PRIVILEGES AND IMMUNITIES OF THE JUDGES, THE PROSECUTOR AND THE REGISTRAR

1. The Judges, the Prosecutor and the Registrar shall, together with members of their families forming part of their household and who do not have Netherlands nationality or permanent residence status in the host country, enjoy the privileges and immunities, exemptions and facilities accorded to diplomatic agents, in accordance with international law and in particular under the General Convention and the Vienna Convention. They shall inter alia enjoy:

a) personal inviolability, including immunity from arrest or detention;

b) immunity from criminal, civil and administrative jurisdiction in conformity with the Vienna Convention;

c) inviolability for all papers and documents;

d) exemption from immigration restrictions, alien registration or national service obligations;

e) the same facilities in respect of currency or exchange restrictions as are accorded to representatives of foreign governments on temporary official missions;

f) the same immunities and facilities in respect of their personal baggage as are accorded to diplomatic agents.

2. In the event the Tribunal operates a system for the payments of pensions and annuities to former Judges, Prosecutors and Registrars and their dependants, exemption from income tax in the host country shall not apply to such pensions and annuities.

3. Privileges and immunities are accorded to the Judges, the Prosecutor and the Registrar in the interest of the Tribunal and not for the personal benefit of individuals themselves. The right and the duty to waive the immunity in any case where it can be waived without prejudice to the purpose for which it is accorded shall lie, as concerns the Judges, with the Tribunal in accordance with its rules; as concerns the Prosecutor and the Registrar, with the Secretary-General in consultation with the President.

ARTICLE XV
PRIVILEGES AND IMMUNITIES OF OFFICIALS OF THE TRIBUNAL

1. The officials of the Tribunal shall, regardless of their nationality, be accorded the privileges and immunities as provided for in Articles V and VII of the General Convention. They shall inter alia:

a) enjoy immunity from legal process in respect of words spoken or written and all acts performed by them in their official capacity. Such immunity shall continue to be accorded after termination of employment with the Tribunal;

b) enjoy exemption from taxation on the salaries and emoluments paid to them by the Tribunal;

c) enjoy immunity from national service obligations;

d) enjoy immunity, together with members of their families forming part of their household, from immigration restrictions and alien registration;

e) be accorded the same privileges in respect of exchange facilities as are accorded to the members of comparable rank of the diplomatic missions established in the host country;

f) be given, together with members of their families forming part of their household, the same repatriation facilities in time of international crisis as diplomatic agents;

g) have the right to import free of duties and taxes, except payments for services, their furniture and effects at the time of first taking up their post in the host country.

2. Internationally-recruited staff of P-5 level and above who do not have Netherlands nationality or permanent residence status in the host country shall, together with members of their families forming part of their household who do not have Netherlands nationality or permanent residence status in the host country, be accorded the privileges, immunities and facilities as are accorded to members of comparable rank of the diplomatic staff of missions accredited to the Government.

3. Internationally-recruited staff shall also be entitled to export with relief from duties and taxes, on the termination of their function in the host country, their furniture and personal effects, including motor vehicles.

4. In the event that the Tribunal operates a system for the payments of pensions and annuities to former officials of the Tribunal and their dependants, exemption from income tax in the host country shall not apply to such pensions and annuities.

5. The privileges and immunities are granted to the officials of the Tribunal in the interest of the Tribunal and not for their personal benefit. The right and the duty to waive the immunity in any particular case, where it can be waived without prejudice to the purpose for which it is accorded shall lie with the Secretary-General.

6. The rights and entitlements referred to in paragraphs 1(g) and 3 above shall be exercised in accordance with the formal requirements of the host country. These requirements, however, shall not affect the general principles laid down in this Article.

ARTICLE XVI
PERSONNEL RECRUITED LOCALLY AND ASSIGNED TO HOURLY RATES

Personnel recruited by the Tribunal locally and assigned to hourly rates shall be accorded immunity from legal process in respect of words spoken or written and acts performed by them in their official capacity for the Tribunal. Such immunity shall continued to be accorded after termination of employment with the Tribunal. They shall also be accorded such other facilities as may be necessary for the independent exercise of their functions for the Tribunal. The terms and conditions of their employment shall be in accordance with the relevant United Nations resolutions, decisions, regulations, rules and policies.

ARTICLE XVII
PERSONS PERFORMING MISSIONS FOR THE TRIBUNAL

1. Persons performing missions for the Tribunal shall enjoy the privileges, immunities and facilities under Articles VI and VII of the General Convention, which are necessary for the independent exercise of their duties for the Tribunal.

2. The right and the duty to waive the immunity referred to in paragraph 1 above in any particular case where it can be waived without prejudice to the administration of justice by the Tribunal and the purpose for which it is granted, shall lie with the President of the Tribunal.

ARTICLE XVIII
WITNESSES AND EXPERTS APPEARING BEFORE THE TRIBUNAL

1. Without prejudice to the obligation of the host country to comply with requests for assistance made, or orders issued by, the Tribunal pursuant to Article 29 of its Statute, witnesses and experts appearing from outside the host country on a summons or a request of the Tribunal or the Prosecutor shall not be prosecuted or detained or subjected to any other restriction of their liberty by the authorities of the host country in respect of acts or convictions prior to their entry into the territory of the host country.

2. The immunity provided for in paragraph 1 above shall cease when the witness or expert having had, for a period of fifteen consecutive days from the date when his or her presence is no longer required by the Tribunal or the Prosecutor, an opportunity of leaving, has nevertheless remained in the territory of the host country, or having left it, has returned, unless such return is on another summons or request of the Tribunal or the Prosecutor.

3. Witnesses and experts referred to in paragraph 1 above shall not be subjected by the host country to any measure which may affect the free and independent exercise of their functions for the Tribunal.

ARTICLE XIX
COUNSEL

1. The counsel of a suspect or an accused who has been admitted as such by the Tribunal shall not be subjected by the host country to any measure which may affect the free and independent exercise of his or her functions under the Statute.

2. In particular, the counsel shall, when holding a certificate that he or she has been admitted as a counsel by the Tribunal, be accorded:

(a) exemption from immigration restrictions;

(b) inviolability of all documents relating to the exercise of his or her functions as a counsel of a suspect or accused;

(c) immunity from criminal and civil jurisdiction in respect of words spoken or written and acts performed by them in their official capacity as counsel. Such immunity shall continue to be accorded to them after termination of their functions as a counsel of a suspect or accused.

3. This Article shall be without prejudice to such disciplinary rules as may be applicable to the counsel.

4. The right and the duty to waive the immunity referred to in paragraph 2 above in any particular case where it can be waived without prejudice to the administration of justice by the Tribunal and the purpose for which it is granted, shall lie with the Secretary-General.

ARTICLE XX
THE SUSPECT OR ACCUSED

1. The host country shall not exercise its criminal jurisdiction over persons present in its territory, who are to be or have been transferred as a suspect or an accused to the premises of the Tribunal pursuant to a request or an order of the Tribunal, in respect of acts, omissions or convictions prior to their entry into the territory of the host country.

2. The immunity provided for in this Article shall cease when the person, having been acquitted or otherwise released by the Tribunal and having had for a period of fifteen consecutive days from the date of his or her release an opportunity of leaving, has nevertheless remained in the territory of the host country, or having left it, has returned.

ARTICLE XXI
CO-OPERATION WITH THE COMPETENT AUTHORITIES

1. Without prejudice to their privileges and immunities, it is the duty of all persons enjoying such privileges and immunities to respect the laws and regulations of the host country. They also have a duty not to interfere in the internal affairs of the host country.

2. The Tribunal shall cooperate at all times with the competent authorities to facilitate the proper administration of justice, secure the observance of police regulations and prevent the occurrence of any abuse in connection with the privileges, immunities and facilities accorded under this Agreement.

3. The Tribunal shall observe all security directives as agreed with the host country or as issued, in coordination with the United Nations Security Service, by the competent authorities responsible for security conditions within the penitentiary institution of the host country where the Tribunal area for detention is located, as well as all directives of the competent authorities responsible for fire prevention regulations.

ARTICLE XXII
NOTIFICATION

1. The Registrar shall notify the Government of the names and categories of persons referred to in this Agreement, in particular the Judges, the Prosecutors, the officials of the Tribunal, persons performing missions for the Tribunal, counsel admitted by the Tribunal, witnesses and experts called to appear before the Tribunal or the Prosecutor, and of any change in their status.

2. The Registrar shall also notify the Government of the name and identity of each official of the Tribunal who is entitled to carry fire arms on the premises of the Tribunal, as well as the name, type, caliber and serial number of the arm or arms at his or her disposition.

ARTICLE XXIII
ENTRY INTO, EXIT FROM AND MOVEMENT WITHIN THE HOST COUNTRY

All persons referred to in Article XIV, XV, XVII, XVIII and XIX of this Agreement as notified as such by the Registrar to the Government shall have the right of unimpeded entry into, exit from, and movement within, the host country, as appropriate and for the purposes of the Tribunal. They shall be granted facilities for speedy travel. Visas, entry permits or licenses, where required, shall be granted free of charge and as promptly as possible. The same facilities shall be accorded to persons accompanying witnesses who have been notified as such by the Registrar to the Government.

ARTICLE XXIV
UNITED NATIONS LAISSEZ-PASSER AND CERTIFICATE

1. The Government shall recognise and accept United Nations Laissez-passer as a valid travel document.

2. In accordance with the provisions of Section 26 of the General Convention, the Government shall recognise and accept the United Nations certificate issued to persons travelling on the business of the Tribunal. The Government agrees to issue any required visas on such certificates.

ARTICLE XXV
IDENTIFICATION CARDS

1. At the request of the Tribunal, the Government shall issue identification cards to persons referred to in Articles XIV, XV, XVIII, XIX and XX of this Agreement certifying their status under this Agreement.

2. The Security Service of the Tribunal shall maintain photographic and other appropriate records of the suspect and accused persons referred to in Article XXI.

ARTICLE XXVI
SECURITY, SAFETY AND PROTECTION OF PERSONS REFERRED TO IN THIS AGREEMENT

The competent authorities shall take effective and adequate action which may be required to ensure the appropriate security, safety and protection of persons referred to in this Agreement, indispensable for the proper functioning of the Tribunal, free from interference of any kind.

ARTICLE XXVII
SOCIAL SECURITY AND PENSION FUND

1. Officials of the Tribunal are subject to the United Nations Staff Regulations and Rules and, if they have an appointment of six months' duration or more, become participants in the United Nations Pension Fund. Accordingly, such officials shall be exempt from all compulsory contributions to the Netherlands social security organizations. Consequently, they shall not be covered against the risks described in the Netherlands social security regulations.

2. The provisions of paragraph 1 above shall apply mutatis mutandis to the members of the family forming part of the hosehold of the persons referred to in paragraph 1 above, unless they are employed or self-employed in the host country or receive Netherlands social security benefits.

ARTICLE XXVIII

SETTLEMENT OF DISPUTES

1. The Tribunal shall make provisions for appropriate modes of settlement of:

a) disputes arising out of contracts and other disputes of a private law character to which the Tribunal is a party;

b) disputes involving an official of the Tribunal who, by reason of his or her official position, enjoys immunity, if such immunity has not been waived.

2. Any dispute between the Parties concerning the interpretation or application of this Agreement or the regulations of the Tribunal, which cannot be settled amicably, shall be submitted, at the request of either Party to the dispute, to an arbitral tribunal, composed of three members. Each Party shall appoint one arbitrator and the two arbitrators thus appointed shall together appoint a third arbitrator as their chairman. If one of the Parties fails to appoint its arbitrator and has not proceeded to do so within two months after an invitation from the other Party to make such an appointment, the other Party may request the President of the International Court of Justice to make the necessary appointment. If the two arbitrators are unable to reach agreement, in the two months following their appointment, on the choice of the third arbitrator, either Party may invite the President of the International Court of Justice to make the necessary appointment. The Parties shall draw up a special agreement determining the subject of the dispute. Failing the conclusion of such an agreement within a period of two months from the date on which arbitration was requested, the dispute may be brought before the arbitral tribunal upon application of either Party. Unless the Parties decide otherwise, the arbitral tribunal shall determine its own procedure. The arbitral tribunal shall reach its decision by a majority of votes on the basis of the applicable rules of international law. In the absence of such rules, it shall decide ex aequo et bono. The decision shall be final and binding on the Parties to the dispute, even if rendered in default of one of the Parties to the dispute

ARTICLE XXIX
FINAL PROVISIONS

1. The provisions of this Agreement shall be complementary to the provisions of the General Convention and the Vienna Convention, the latter Convention only insofar as it is relevant for the diplomatic privileges, immunities and facilities accorded to the appropriate categories of persons referred to in this Agreement. Insofar as any provision of this Agreement and any provisions of the General Convention and the Vienna Convention relate to the same subject matter, each of these provisions shall be applicable and neither shall narrow the effect of the other.

2. This Agreement may be amended by mutual consent at any time at the request of either Party.

3. This Agreement shall cease to be in force if the seat of the Tribunal is removed from the territory of the host country or if the Tribunal is dissolved, except for such provisions as may be applicable in connection with the orderly termination of the operations of the Tribunal at its seat in the host country and the disposition of its property therein, as well as provisions granting immunity from legal process of every kind in respect of words spoken or written or acts done in an official capacity, even after termination of employment with the Tribunal.

4. The provisions of this Agreement will be applied provisionally as from the date of signature.

5. This Agreement shall enter into force on the day after both Parties have notified each other in writing that the legal requirements for entry into force have been complied with.

6. With respect to the Kingdom of the Netherlands, this Agreement shall apply to the part of the Kingdom in Europe only.

IN WITNESS WHEREOF, the undersigned, duly authorized thereto, have signed this Agreement.

DONE at............on ....1994 in duplicate, in the English language.

For the Government of the Kingdom of the Netherlands	For the United Nations

DRAFT LETTER OF EXCHANGE BY THE GOVERNMENT OF THE NETHERLANDS

ADDRESSED TO THE UNITED NATIONS

Dear Sir,

On the occasion of the signing of the Agreement between the Kingdom of the Netherlands and the United Nations Concerning the Headquarters of the International Tribunal for the Prosecution of Persons Responsible for Serious Violations of International Humanitarian Law Committed in the Territory of the Former Yugoslavia Since 1991, I would like to refer to discussions held between the representatives of the Government of the Kingdom of the Netherlands and the representatives of the United Nations concerning the interpretation and implementation of certain provisions of the Agreement.

I have the honour to confirm on behalf of the Government of the Netherlands the following understanding.

It is the understanding of the Parties that none of the regulations made operative by the Tribunal based on the power given to it under Article VI, paragraph 3, of the Agreement, shall relate to any question of the treatment of the suspect, accused or other persons detained on the premises of the Tribunal; these matters shall be dealt with by the Tribunal in accordance with its competence under Article 15 of the Statute of the Tribunal adopted by the Security Council by its resolution 827 (1993) of 25 May 1993.

It is the understanding of the Parties that the exemptions, rights and entitlements referred to in Article X, paragraph 2, and Article XV, paragraphs 1(g) and 3, shall be granted in accordance with the formal requirements of the host country which, however, shall not have the effect of depriving the Tribunal or its officials of these exemptions, rights or entitlements or in any way diminishing the extent thereof.

With respect to the provisions of paragraph 1(g), it is understood that the expression "furniture and effects" includes motor vehicles.

It is further the understanding of the Parties that all official motor vehicles of the Tribunal will be covered by the appropriate liability insurance, and that all officials of the Tribunal and persons performing missions, who will own or operate motor vehicles, will be directed to acquire an appropriate insurance against third party risks in the Netherlands.

It is the understanding of the Parties that, if so requested by the Tribunal, the competent authorities of the host country shall not create impediments to either entry into and exit from the Netherlands or the transport between the detention facility and the Tribunal of persons detained on the authority of the Tribunal.

I should be grateful if you could confirm that the above is also the understanding of the United Nations.

DRAFT LETTER OF EXCHANGE BY THE UNITED NATIONS
ADDRESSED TO THE GOVERNMENT OF THE NETHERLANDS

Dear Sir,

I have the honour to acknowledge receipt of Your Excellency's letter of .... 1994, in which you confirm your Government's understanding regarding the interpretation and implementation of certain provisions of the Agreement between the United Nations and the Kingdom of the Netherlands concerning the Headquarters of the International Tribunal for the Prosecution of Persons Responsible for Serious Violations of International Humanitarian Law Committed in the Territory of the Former Yugoslavia since 1991.

In accordance with your Your Excellency's request, I wish to confirm, on behalf of the United Nations that the understandings reflected in your above-mentioned letter fully correspond to the views of the United Nations on the subject.

LETTER DATED 25 JULY 1994 FROM THE PRESIDENT OF THE SECURITY COUNCIL ADDRESSED TO THE SECRETARY-GENERAL

S/1994/849, 25 July 1994.

I have the honour to refer to your letter of 14 July 1994 (S/1994/848) enclosing copies of the Agreement between the United Nations and the Kingdom of the Netherlands concerning the Headquarters of the International Tribunal for the Prosecution of Persons Responsible for Serious Violations of International Humanitarian Law Committed in the Territory of the Former Yugoslavia since 1991 and the Agreement for Tenancy of Churchillplein 1, The Hague.

I have the honour to inform you that, in accordance with paragraph 6 of its resolution 827 (1993) and without prejudice to consideration of the arrangements by the General Assembly, the Security Council finds the arrangements between the United Nations and the Netherlands acceptable. The Council confirms that the seat of the Tribunal has been determined to be in The Hague.

(*Signed*) Jamsheed K. A. MARKER
President of the
Security Council

PART VI

SECURITY COUNCIL RESOLUTIONS AND RECORD OF DEBATES

A. RESOLUTION 780 (1992)
Adopted by the Security Council at its 3119th Meeting, on 6 October 1992

S/RES/780 (1992), 6 October 1992.

The Security Council,

Reaffirming its resolution 713 (1991) of 25 September 1991 and all subsequent relevant resolutions,

Recalling paragraph 10 of its resolution 764 (1992) of 13 July 1992, in which it reaffirmed that all parties are bound to comply with the obligations under international humanitarian law and in particular the Geneva Conventions of 12 August 1949, 1/ and that persons who commit or order the commission of grave breaches of the Conventions are individually responsible in respect of such breaches,

Recalling also its resolution 771 (1992) of 13 August 1992, in which, inter alia, it demanded that all parties and others concerned in the former Yugoslavia, and all military forces in Bosnia and Herzegovina, immediately cease and desist from all breaches of international humanitarian law,

Expressing once again its grave alarm at continuing reports of widespread violations of international humanitarian law occurring within the territory of the former Yugoslavia and especially in Bosnia and Herzegovina, including reports of mass killings and the continuance of the practice of "ethnic cleansing",

1. Reaffirms its call, in paragraph 5 of resolution 771 (1992), upon States and, as appropriate, international humanitarian organizations to collate substantiated information in their possession or submitted to them relating to the violations of humanitarian law, including grave breaches of the Geneva Conventions being committed in the territory of the former Yugoslavia, and requests States, relevant United Nations bodies, and relevant organizations to make this information available within thirty days of the adoption of the present resolution and as appropriate thereafter, and to provide other appropriate assistance to the Commission of Experts referred to in paragraph 2 below;

2. Requests the Secretary-General to establish, as a matter of urgency, an impartial Commission of Experts to examine and analyse the information submitted pursuant to resolution 771 (1992) and the present resolution, together with such further information as the Commission of Experts may obtain through its own investigations or efforts, of other persons or bodies pursuant to resolution 771 (1992), with a view to providing the Secretary-General with its conclusions on the evidence of grave breaches of the Geneva Conventions and other violations of international humanitarian law committed in the territory of the former Yugoslavia;

3. Also requests the Secretary-General to report to the Council on the establishment of the Commission of Experts;

4. Further requests the Secretary-General to report to the Council on the conclusions of the Commission of Experts and to take account of these conclusions in any recommendations for further appropriate steps called for by resolution 771 (1992);

5. Decides to remain actively seized of the matter.

1/ United Nations Treaty Series, vol. 75, Nos. 970-973.

PROVISIONAL VERBATIM RECORD OF THE THREE THOUSAND ONE HUNDRED AND NINETEENTH MEETING Held at Headquarters, New York, on Tuesday, 6 October 1992, at 6:20 p.m.

S/PV. 3119, 6 October 1992.

President:	Mr. MERIMEE	(France)
Members:	Austria	Mr. HOHENFELLNER
	Belgium	Mr. NOTERDAEME
	Cape Verde	Mr. JESUS
	China	Mr. JIN Yongjian
	Ecuador	Mr. POSSO SERRANO
	Hungary	Mr. ERDOS
	India	Mr. SREENIVASAN
	Japan	Mr. HATANO
	Morocco	Mr. SNOUSSI
	Russian Federation	Mr. VORONTSOV
	United Kingdom of Great Britain and Northern Ireland	Sir David HANNAY
	United States of America	Mr. PERKINS
	Venezuela	Mr. ARRIA
	Zimbabwe	Mr. MUMBENGEGWI

The PRESIDENT (interpretation from French): I should like to inform the Council that I have received letters from the representatives of Bosnia and Herzegovina and Croatia in which they request to be invited to participate in the discussion of the item on the Council's agenda. In accordance with the usual practice, I propose, with the consent of the Council, to invite those representatives to participate in the discussion without the right to vote, in accordance with the relevant provisions of the Charter and rule 37 of the Council's provisional rules of procedure.

There being no objection, it is so decided.

At the invitation of the President, Mr. Sacirbey (Bosnia and Herzegovina) and Mr. Nobilo (Croatia) took places at the Council table.

The PRESIDENT (interpretation from French): The Security Council will now begin its consideration of the item on its agenda. The Security Council is meeting in accordance with the understanding reached in its prior consultations.

Members of the Council have before them document S/24618, which contains the text of a draft resolution submitted by Belgium, France, Morocco, the

United Kingdom of Great Britain and Northern Ireland, the United States of America, and Venezuela.

I should like to inform the Council that Hungary has joined as a sponsor of the draft resolution.

I should like to draw the attention of the Council to the following documents: S/24473, letter dated 17 August 1992 from the Permanent Representative of Bolivia to the United Nations addressed to the President of the Security Council; S/24478, S/24525 and S/24537, letters dated 24 August, 4 September and 5 September 1992, respectively, from the Permanent Representative of Bosnia and Herzegovina to the United Nations addressed to the President of the Security Council; S/24489, letter dated 24 August 1992 from the Chargé d'Affaires ad interim of the Permanent Mission of Singapore to the United Nations addressed to the Secretary-General; S/24494, letter dated 26 August 1992 from the Chargé d'Affaires ad interim of the Permanent Mission of Malaysia to the United Nations addressed to the Secretary-General; S/24508, letter dated 31 August 1992 from the Permanent Representative of Cyprus to the United Nations addressed to the Secretary-General; S/24516, note by the Secretary-General transmitting the report on the situation of human rights in the territory of the former Yugoslavia submitted by Mr. Tadeusz Mazowiecki, Special Rapporteur of the Commission on Human Rights; and S/24583, letter dated 22 September 1992 from the Deputy Permanent Representative of the United States of America to the United Nations addressed to the Secretary-General.

Members of the Council also have before them photocopies of a letter dated 5 October 1992 from the representatives of Egypt, the Islamic Republic of Iran, Pakistan, Saudi Arabia, Senegal and Turkey addressed to the President of the Security Council. This letter will be published as a Security Council document under the symbol S/24620.

It is my understanding that the Security Council is ready to proceed to the vote on the draft resolution before it. If I hear no objection, I shall take it that that is the case.

There being no objection, it is so decided.

Before putting the draft resolution to the vote, I shall call on those members of the Council who wish to make statements before the voting.

Mr. ARRIA (Venezuela) (interpretation from Spanish): I wish first to convey to you, Mr. President, my delegation's congratulations as you guide the work of the Council; we are sure you will do so with your known qualities and talents.

(spoke in English)

"The powerful do what they will, and the poor suffer what they must".

(spoke in Spanish)

That was the barbarous philsophy that, according to Thucydides, obtained during the Peloponnesian Wars and cost the lives of thousands of children, women and old people and the massacre of defenceless civilian populations.

History is being repeated today against the equally defenceless civilian population of the Republic of Bosnia and Herzegovina. Without question, the implementation of this criminal, uncivilized philosophy, which has been under way for nearly a year, constitutes genuine trampling underfoot of all the values that guide and inspire the United Nations. The Security Council is duty-bound to address this situation firmly and swiftly.

The decision to establish a commission of experts to investigate all such violations of international humanitarian law would be inspired by the commission that was set up in 1943 for similar purposes and later served as the basis for the proceedings of the Nuremberg tribunal. In our view, this would not only serve to establish responsibility and punish the guilty, but would also, we believe - and most particularly - constitute an important deterrent in the context of the process the United Nations has undertaken to bring peace to the population of the former Yugoslavia, and especially to the suffering Republic of Bosnia and Herzegovina.

The Special Rapporteur of the Commission on Human Rights, Mr. Tadeusz Mazowiecki, former Prime Minister of Poland, in his eloquent and valuable report of 3 September 1992, noted the need to prosecute all those responsible for human rights violations. Not only should his recommendations be taken into account by this commission of experts, but Mr. Mazowiecki should be invited to be a member of that commission.

It is our understanding that the commission established by the draft resolution before us would collect the information that will make it possible to prosecute those who may be found to be responsible for the criminal or vandalistic acts that have been perpetrated against thousands upon thousands of citizens of the Republic of Bosnia and Herzegovina, and of crimes defined as war crimes by the 1907 Hague Convention respecting the Laws and Customs of War, the Geneva Conventions of 1949, the Nuremburg Charter of 1945, the Nuremburg Principles of 1950, the 1977 Additional Protocol I to the Geneva Conventions of 1949 and the United Nations Convention on the Prevention and Punishment of the Crime of Genocide.

All those instruments classify as war crimes those crimes committed against peace, including the initiation of acts of war, aggression and all other crimes against humanity, including those committed against civilian populations such as indiscriminate bombing, mistreatment of prisoners, mass deportations, "ethnic cleansing" and so forth. It is precisely such crimes that justified the sentences of execution or long prison terms meted out to the criminals of the Second World War.

Nor must we forget that the United Nations Convention on the Prevention and Punishment of the Crime of Genocide clearly states that genocide means inflicting on a group of human beings conditions of life calculated to bring about its physical destruction in whole or in part. Article 54 of the 1977 Additional Protocol I to the Geneva Conventions also prohibits the destruction of infrastructures basic to life, such as electricity, drinking water, sewage and other basic public services. Such are the acts today being perpetrated in the Republic of Bosnia and Herzegovina.

History abounds in enemies of mankind - what the ancients called hostis humanis generis - ranging from slave traders to the criminals responsible for the Holocaust. The only crime that has not been committed in the case of Bosnia and Herzegovina is that which in another place and another time Bertrand Russell called the crime of silence. Here we find the opposite: through the mass media, the world has been witnessing the greatest and most terrible devastation - the systematic attempt to destroy the city of Sarajevo, the capital of the Republic of Bosnia and Herzegovina.

The draft resolution before us today is a specific reflection of the will and determination of the Security Council, as expressed in the preamble to the Charter of the United Nations, which begins,

> "We, the peoples of the [world], determined to save succeeding generations from the scourge of war ... and to reaffirm faith in fundamental human rights, in the dignity and worth of the human person, in the equal rights of men and women and of nations large and small".

As a State party to the Fourth Geneva Convention of 1949, and as a contracting party to the 1948 United Nations Convention on the Prevention and Punishment of the Crime of Genocide, Venezuela supports all efforts contributing to stopping and punishing all those who commit crimes against human dignity, wherever they may occur. The lack of an international penal jurisdiction should not exempt these criminals from trial and punishment. We trust that the commission of experts that would be established under the draft resolution will begin its work urgently and will frame its mandate in an objective and impartial manner. That would be the first step in a process responding to the mass murders and to the practice of "ethnic cleansing" - a process that will assign personal responsibility to those found guilty of grave violations of international humanitarian law.

We know that war constitutes the greatest tragedy. That is why it becomes imperative to make all those who initiate or promote acts of war or conquest understand clearly that they shall be held accountable to the international community for their responsibility in crimes against humanity. This is how the delegation of Venezuela understands its obligation to the international community, which we in the Security Council represent.

The PRESIDENT (interpretation from French): I thank the representative of Venezuela for his kind words addressed to me.

I now put the draft resolution (S/24618) to the vote.

A vote was taken by show of hands.

In favour: Austria, Belgium, Cape Verde, China, Ecuador, France, Hungary, India, Japan, Morocco, Russian Federation, United Kingdom of Great Britain and Northern Ireland, United States of America, Venezuela, Zimbabwe

The PRESIDENT: There were 15 votes in favour. The draft resolution has therefore been adopted unanimously as resolution 780 (1992).

I shall now call on those members of the Council who wish to make statements following the vote.

Mr. PERKINS (United States of America): My delegation is pleased to have joined the other Council members in adopting this resolution. The resolution, first, sends a clear message that those responsible for the atrocities and gross violations of international humanitarian law, including violations involved in the process of "ethnic cleansing" and other war crimes in the former Yugoslavia, must be brought to justice. Second, the resolution will hopefully act as a deterrent to those in other parts of the world who may be contemplating similar violations and crimes.

If I may, I would like to amplify on our interpretation of operative paragraph 1 of the resolution. First, my delegation believes that the term "relevant United Nations bodies" includes the Special Rapporteur. Furthermore, we believe that the phrase "to provide other appropriate assistance to the Commission of Experts" in this paragraph allows the Commission to request follow-up by these other bodies, including the Special Rapporteur.

Mr. NOTERDAEME (Belgium) (interpretation from French): First of all, I should like to congratulate you very sincerely, Sir, on your election to the presidency of the Security Council, and to thank sincerely your predecessor for his good work during the month of September.

My delegation participated in the drafting of, and co-sponsored, the draft resolution our Council has just adopted. The position of Belgium was based on the intolerable nature of the grave, systematic breaches of the Geneva Conventions on the territory of the former Yugoslavia.

As if further proof were needed, let me refer to the recent statement by the President of the International Committee of the Red Cross, Mr. Sommaruga, who said that the most elementary principles of international humanitarian law continue to be disregarded on the territory of the former Yugoslavia, and that the consequences of this are incalculable.

In the wake of resolution 771 (1992), our Council has thus sent an even clearer signal to the perpetrators of these violations of humanitarian law. The establishment of a Commission makes this signal more credible by making more operational the principle contained in the Geneva Conventions regarding the personal responsibility of war criminals.

It is the desire of the Belgian authorities that our Organization, upon receipt of the conclusions of this Commission and of the recommendations of the Secretary-General, should be able to provide itself with the means to punish the perpetrators who will have been so identified.

The PRESIDENT (interpretation from French): I thank the representative of Belgium for his kind words addressed to me.

Mr. ERDOS (Hungary) (interpretation from French): Hungary sincerely welcomes the unanimous adoption of resolution 780 (1992). In that respect, I should like to make three points.

Firstly, Hungary interprets the resolution we have just adopted as the beginning of a process which should lead us, within a reasonable period of time, to the logical conclusion of the enterprise represented by resolution 780 (1992), namely, the establisment of the appropriate means and the compilation of the necessary information to bring to justice those responsible for the crimes that continue to be committed systematically and on a daily basis in the former Yugoslavia. This genocide and blind barbarity cannot be left without suitable punishment by the international community.

Secondly, it is our understanding that the request addressed to States, relevant United Nations bodies, and relevant organizations to collate information represents an appeal to all bodies, organs and individuals concerned with the cause of human rights, with no exceptions, and of course including the Commission on Human Rights, to do so; the information should, most particularly, include the detailed and substantive report on the human rights situation in the territory of the former Yugoslavia submitted by Mr. Tadeusz Mazowiecki, Special Rapporteur of the Commission on Human Rights.

Thirdly, we expect the Commission of Experts provided for under the resolution to be set up as soon as possible.

Mr. SNOUSSI (Morocco) (interpretation from French): First of all, I should like to welcome the adoption of this resolution, to which we gave our total support. This action, in the view of all the members of the Organization of the Islamic Conference, should be considered as no more than one stage in a whole range of measures which the Council, unfortunately, will have to take in order to put an end to the terrible acts which are continuing to be perpetrated with impunity in Bosnia and Herzegovina.

Tomorrow, alas, we will have to think about other steps and other provisions if we want to arrest this frenzy that has been unleashed against a peaceful people which wanted only to live in freedom, a people that 200 years ago was free, sovereign and respected; at that time, it had diplomatic relations with my country.

It is now going through a veritable nightmare. The crimes being committed there are unpardonable; these are crimes against people and property, and against a culture and a civilization. Today, we have forged a vital link; but tomorrow, alas, we shall be forced to think about courts and so on if we continue to enounter the same blindness and obstinacy.

Mr. VORONTSOV (Russian Federation): The Russian delegation voted for resolution 780 (1992) that we have just adopted, viewing it as an additional means to influence the opposing parties with a view to alleviating the sufferings of the peaceful population on the territory of the former Yugoslavia, and in particular in Bosnia and Herzegovina, and by so doing to bring about the quickest possible solution of the Yugoslav conflict.

We hope that the impartial Commission of Experts provided for in the resolution will, on the basis of carefully substantiated information, give us the true picture of the violations of the Geneva Conventions and other violations of international humanitarian law taking place on the territory of the former Yugoslavia.

The resolution, which we have unanimously adopted as a follow-up to Security Council resolution 771 (1992), should, in our view, be a serious warning to any political and military leaders who allow mass breaches of the norms of international humanitarian law on the territory of the former Yugoslavia and warn them of their personal responsibility for such act.

The Russian delegation would particularly like to emphasize that the significance of the resolution goes beyond the framework of a settlement of the Yugoslav question and that it is also a warning to all who violate the norms of international humanitarian law in other spheres of conflict.

The PRESIDENT (interpretation from French): I shall now make a statement in my capacity as the representative of France.

Confronted with the horror that the crimes daily being reported inspire in us, crimes of impermissible violations of international humanitarian law being committed in the territory of the former Yugoslavia, and in Bosnia and Herzegovina in particular, I should like to emphasize how vital, in my view, this resolution is.

For indeed it is very important that the Security Council send a clear warning to the perpetrators of those violations, who must understand that their personal responsibility is involved. I would add that the resolution we have just adopted is a part of the prospective creation by the appropriate bodies of an international penal jurisdiction to rule on such acts.

My Government considers that it goes without saying that the Council's request in paragraph 1 of the resolution to "relevant United Nations bodies" includes the Special Rapporteur of the Commission on Human Rights on the former Yugoslavia. The contributions that the Special Rapporteur can make to the impartial Commission of Experts will be one of the essential elements in drawing up that Commission's conclusions.

I now resume my functions as President of the Council.

There are no further speakers inscribed on my list. The Security Council has thus concluded the present stage of its consideration of the item on its agenda. The Security Council will remain seized of the matter.

B. RESOLUTION 808 (1993)

Adopted by the Security Council at its 3175th Meeting, on 22 February 1993

S/RES/808 (1993), 22 February 1993.

The Security Council,

Reaffirming its resolution 713 (1991) of 25 September 1991 and all subsequent relevant resolutions,

Recalling paragraph 10 of its resolution 764 (1992) of 13 July 1992, in which it reaffirmed that all parties are bound to comply with the obligations under international humanitarian law and in particular the Geneva Conventions of 12 August 1949, and that persons who commit or order the commission of grave breaches of the Conventions are individually responsible in respect of such breaches,

Recalling also its resolution 771 (1992) of 13 August 1992, in which, inter alia, it demanded that all parties and others concerned in the former Yugoslavia, and all military forces in Bosnia and Herzegovina, immediately cease and desist from all breaches of international humanitarian law,

Recalling further its resolution 780 (1992) of 6 October 1992, in which it requested the Secretary-General to establish, as a matter of urgency, an impartial Commission of Experts to examine and analyse the information submitted pursuant to resolutions 771 (1992) and 780 (1992), together with such further information as the Commission of Experts may obtain, with a view to providing the Secretary-General with its conclusions on the evidence of grave breaches of the Geneva Conventions and other violations of international humanitarian law committed in the territory of the former Yugoslavia,

Having considered the interim report of the Commission of Experts established by resolution 780 (1992) (S/25274), in which the Commission observed that a decision to establish an ad hoc international tribunal in relation to events in the territory of the former Yugoslavia would be consistent with the direction of its work,

Expressing once again its grave alarm at continuing reports of widespread violations of international humanitarian law occurring within the territory of the former Yugoslavia, including reports of mass killings and the continuance of the practice of "ethnic cleansing",

Determining that this situation constitutes a threat to international peace and security,

Determined to put an end to such crimes and to take effective measures to bring to justice the persons who are responsible for them,

Convinced that in the particular circumstances of the former Yugoslavia the establishment of an international tribunal would enable this aim to be achieved and would contribute to the restoration and maintenance of peace,

Noting in this regard the recommendation by the Co-Chairmen of the Steering Committee of the International Conference on the Former Yugoslavia for the establishment of such a tribunal (S/25221),

Noting also with grave concern the "report of the European Community investigative mission into the treatment of Muslim women in the former Yugoslavia" (S/25240, annex I),

Noting further the report of the committee of jurists submitted by France (S/25266), the report of the commission of jurists submitted by Italy (S/25300), and the report transmitted by the Permanent Representative of Sweden on behalf of the Chairman-in-Office of the Conference on Security and Cooperation in Europe (CSCE) (S/25307),

1. Decides that an international tribunal shall be established for the prosecution of persons responsible for serious violations of international humanitarian law committed in the territory of the former Yugoslavia since 1991;

2. Requests the Secretary-General to submit for consideration by the Council at the earliest possible date, and if possible no later than 60 days after the adoption of the present resolution, a report on all aspects of this matter, including specific proposals and where appropriate options for the effective and expeditious implementation of the decision contained in paragraph 1 above, taking into account suggestions put forward in this regard by Member States;

3. Decides to remain actively seized of the matter.

PROVISIONAL VERBATIM RECORD OF THE THREE THOUSAND ONE HUNDRED AND SEVENTY-FIFTH MEETING

Held at Headquarters, New York, on Monday, 22 February 1993, at 11 a.m.

S/PV. 3175, 22 February 1993.

President:	Mr. SNOUSSI	(Morocco)
Members:	Brazil	Mr. DE ARAUJO CASTRO
	Cape Verde	Mr. BARBOSA
	China	Mr. CHEN Jian
	Djibouti	Mr. DORANI
	France	Mr. MERIMEE
	Hungary	Mr. ERDOS
	Japan	Mr. MARUYAMA
	New Zealand	Mr. O'BRIEN
	Pakistan	Mr. MARKER
	Russian Federation	Mr. VORONTSOV
	Spain	Mr. YAÑEZ BARNUEVO
	United Kingdom of Great Britain and Northern Ireland	Sir David HANNAY
	United States of America	Ms. ALBRIGHT
	Venezuela	Mr. ARRIA

The PRESIDENT (interpretation from French): I should like to inform the Council that I have received letters from the representatives of Bosnia and Herzegovina and Croatia in which they request to be invited to participate in the discussion of the item on the Council's agenda. In conformity with the usual practice, I propose, with the consent of the Council, to invite those representatives to participate in the discussion, without the right to vote, in accordance with the relevant provisions of the Charter and rule 37 of the Council's provisional rules of procedure.

There being no objection, it is so decided.

At the invitation of the President, Mr. Sacirbey (Bosnia and Herzegovina) and Mr. Nobilo (Croatia) took places at the Council table.

The PRESIDENT (interpretation from French): The Council will now begin its consideration of the item on the agenda.

The Security Council is meeting in accordance with the understanding reached in its prior consultations.

Members of the Council have before them the following documents: S/25266, letter dated 10 February 1993 from the Permanent Representative of France to the United Nations addressed to the Secretary-General; S/25300, letter dated 16 February 1993 from the Permanent Representative of Italy to the United Nations addressed to the Secretary-General; and S/25307, letter dated 18 February 1993 from the Permanent Representative of Sweden to the United Nations addressed to the Secretary-General.

Members of the Council also have before them document S/25221, report of the Secretary-General on the activities of the International Conference on the Former Yugoslavia; document S/25274, letter dated 9 February 1993 from the Secretary-General addressed to the President of the Security Council; and document S/25240, letter dated 2 February 1993 from the Permanent Representative of Denmark to the United Nations addressed to the Secretary-General.

Lastly, members of the Council have before them document S/25314, which contains the text of a draft resolution prepared in the course of the Council's prior consultations.

It is my understanding that the Council is ready to proceed to the vote on the draft resolution before it. If I hear no objection, I shall take it that that is the case.

There being no objection, it is so decided.

Before putting the draft resolution to the vote, I shall call on those members of the Council who wish to make statements before the voting.

Mr. de ARAUJO CASTRO (Brazil): Mr. President, allow me to begin by congratulating you on the able and effective manner in which you have been conducting the work of the Security Council. Allow me, also, to express our recognition to Ambassador Yoshio Hatano of Japan for his accomplishments as President of the Council for the month of January.

I have been instructed to make the following statement in connection with the draft resolution we are about to adopt.

The serious violations of international humanitarian law which have been taking place in the territory of the former Yugoslavia have outraged the conscience of humanity. It is with deep sorrow and concern that the Brazilian Government, and Brazilian society at large, have received the repeated news of unspeakable atrocities committed within the context of this senseless conflict on European soil, which must be brought to an end.

The information gathered by the Commission of Experts established pursuant to Security Council resolution 780 (1992) and by the Special Rapporteur of the Commission on Human Rights have provided substantial evidence of grave breaches of humanitarian law being committed on a massive scale and in a systematic fashion. These include reports of mass killings, torture, rape and the unacceptable practices that are referred to by the equally unacceptable expression "ethnic cleansing".

The international community cannot allow this to continue or to go unpunished. These grave breaches of the most elementary norms of humanity must be treated as what in fact they are: criminal acts, crimes against women and children and other defenceless victims, but also, in the most proper sense of the expression, crimes against humanity. A cry for justice breaks from every heart, and that cry cannot go unheeded.

Brazil favours strong action to ensure the full ascertainment of the truth about each of the cases of war crimes and crimes against humanity committed in the territory of the former Yugoslavia. Convinced that effective prosecution and punishment of the perpetrators of these crimes is a matter of high moral duty, Brazil supports the establishment of an international criminal tribunal to bring to justice the individuals found to be responsible for such abominable acts. It is in that spirit that we will vote in favour of the draft resolution before the Security Council.

We will support, and we stand ready to contribute to, the work to be carried out by the Secretary-General in elaborating specific proposals and options for the implementation of the decision to be taken today.

It is of particular importance that the international tribunal to be established rest on a solid legal foundation, which will ensure the effectiveness of its actions. To that end, we believe that in dealing with many of the issues at hand, it should prove useful to draw on the studies and discussions that over the years have been undertaken within the United Nations on the exceedingly complex legal question of an international criminal jurisdiction.

As regards the definition of the best method for the establishment of an ad hoc international criminal tribunal, it should be borne in mind that the authority of the Security Council is not self-constituted but originates from a delegation of powers by the whole membership of the Organization. It is never too much to recall that the Security Council, in the exercise of its responsibilities, acts on behalf of the States Members of the United Nations, in accordance with Article 24, paragraph 1, of the Charter.

Just as the authority of the Council does not spring from the Council itself but derives from the fact that certain responsibilities have been conferred upon it by all the Members of the United Nations, the powers of the Council cannot be created, recreated or reinterpreted creatively by decisions of the Council itself, but must be based invariably on specific Charter provisions.

It is precisely because the Council exercises a delegated responsibility in a field as politically sensitive as the maintenance of international peace and security that the task of interpreting its competences calls for extreme caution, in particular when invoking language of Chapter VII of the Charter. Especially when the Council is being increasingly called upon to fully exercise the considerable powers entrusted to it, the definition of such powers must be construed strictly on the basis of the text of the relevant Charter provisions. To go beyond that would be legally inconsistent and politically unwise.

The Security Council can and should play a strong and positive role in promoting the implementation of the various elements that would contribute to the peace efforts developed by the Conference on the Former Yugoslavia. That role, however, can and should remain within the scope of the powers expressly granted to the Security Council in accordance with the United Nations Charter.

In this rapidly changing world, we consider it increasingly important to promote the rule of law in international relations by acting to ensure strict respect for the provisions of our Charter and other norms of international law.

The PRESIDENT (interpretation from French): I thank the representative of Brazil for the kind words he addressed to me.

Mr. CHEN Jian (China) (interpretation from Chinese): The Chinese delegation supports the thrust of the draft resolution before us and will therefore vote in favour.

Based on our understanding of the nature of the draft resolution before us, I should like to reiterate for the record that its expected adoption and my delegation's participation in it do not prejudge China's position on future Security Council actions on the subject.

The PRESIDENT (interpretation from French): I shall now put to the vote the draft resolution contained in document S/25314.

A vote was taken by show of hands.

In favour: Brazil, Cape Verde, China, Djibouti, France, Hungary, Japan, Morocco, New Zealand, Pakistan, Russian Federation, Spain, United Kingdom of Great Britain and Northern Ireland, United States of America, Venezuela

The PRESIDENT (interpretation from French): There were 15 votes in favour. The draft resolution has therefore been adopted unanimously as resolution 808 (1993).

I shall now call on those members who wish to make statements following the voting.

Mr. MERIMEE (France) (interpretation from French): When the first news and accounts of the atrocities committed on the territory of the former Yugoslavia began to come in, the collective memory of our peoples had to relive the horror of times we had thought long past.

But there are lessons to be learned from history. Conditions have changed since the Second World War. The United Nations now has the responsibility of maintaining and restoring international peace and security. Indeed, through the Security Council, the United Nations has firmly committed itself to this cause in the former Yugoslavia since the adoption on 25 September 1991 of resolution 713 (1991).

The atrocities committed by all sides in the Yugoslav crisis have given rise to an intolerable situation which is fanning the flames of conflict and therefore constitutes a threat to international peace and security.

Prosecuting the guilty is necessary if we are to do justice to the victims and to the international community. Prosecuting the guilty will also send a clear message to those who continue to commit these crimes that they will be held responsible for their acts. And finally, prosecuting the guilty is, for the United Nations and particularly for the Security Council, a matter of doing their duty to maintain and restore peace.

It is with these considerations in mind that the French Minister for Foreign Affairs asked a group of jurists to draw up a report on setting up an international criminal tribunal that could prosecute persons responsible for the serious violations of international humanitarian law that have been committed in the territory of the former Yugoslavia since the beginning of that State's process of dissolution. The report, which contains specific proposals for the establishment of such a tribunal, was concluded in record time - three weeks. It was made public by the French authorities and published as a Security Council document. The report concludes in particular that the creation of an international tribunal for the former Yugoslavia could be decided on by the Security Council within the framework of its powers under Chapter VII of the Charter to maintain or restore international peace and security.

France has endorsed this conclusion and has taken the initiative of proposing to the Security Council a draft resolution for its implementation.

By adopting unanimously resolution 808 (1993) in pursuance of this initiative, the Security Council has just taken a decision of major significance. For the first time in history, the United Nations will be setting up an international criminal jurisdiction - one that will be competent to try those who have committed serious violations of international humanitarian law in the territory of the former Yugoslavia. We already know from the interim report of the Commission of Experts established pursuant to Security Council resolution 780 (1992) and through the considerable evidence that has come in that these atrocities take many forms, from the systematic rape of women to the sinister practice of "ethnic cleansing" and wholesale massacres, and that they are committed in many parts of the territory of the former Yugoslavia. The Security Council has today taken the solemn decision that it will not allow these crimes to go unpunished and will not countenance their continuation.

The tribunal that we have just decided to create should be established as soon as possible. It should be set up through a further decision of the Security Council under the provisions of Chapter VII, which establishes its competence in the maintenance and restoration of international peace and security.

In that respect, we expect from the Secretary-General some concrete proposals of a practical nature that will allow our Council to respond to the urgency of the situation facing us. The results of all the efforts and contributions made by France and other countries and in other forums will be available to him. We have every confidence that Mr. Boutros-Ghali and his colleagues will succeed in this task, which is of such far-reaching significance.

We trust that the Security Council will then act with the authority and unanimity that it has just strikingly displayed in adopting resolution 808 (1993) in order to impose respect for the law.

Ms. ALBRIGHT (United States of America): There is an echo in this Chamber today. The Nuremberg Principles have been reaffirmed. We have preserved the long-neglected compact made by the community of civilized nations 48 years ago in San Francisco to create the United Nations and enforce the Nuremberg Principles.

The lesson that we are all accountable to international law may have finally taken hold in our collective memory. This will be no victor's tribunal. The only victor that will prevail in this endeavour is the truth. Unlike the world of the 1940s, international humanitarian law today is impressively codified, well understood, agreed upon and enforceable. The debates over the state of international law that so encumbered the Nuremberg Trials will not burden this tribunal.

The United States strongly supports the Council's adoption of today's historic resolution, which takes the first step in establishing an ad hoc tribunal to prosecute persons accused of war crimes and other serious violations of international humanitarian law in the territory of the former Yugoslavia. Virtually all of the parties that have examined this issue, including the General Assembly, the Co-Chairmen of the International Conference on the Former Yugoslavia and the Commission of Experts established by Security Council resolution 780 (1992) have urged the creation of such a tribunal.

President Bill Clinton has long supported the establishment of a war-crimes tribunal at the United Nations to bring justice and deter further atrocities in the former Yugoslavia. Just 12 days ago, Secretary of State

Warren Christopher, speaking on the President's behalf, explained why the United States believes that this and other actions are urgently required. As the Secretary said:

"We cannot ignore the human toll. Serbian ethnic cleansing has been pursued through mass murders; systematic beatings and the rapes of Muslims and others; prolonged shellings of innocents in Sarajevo and elsewhere; forced displacement of entire villages; inhumane treatment of prisoners in the detention camps; and the blockading of relief to the sick and starving civilians. Atrocities have been committed by other parties as well. Our conscience revolts at the idea of passively accepting such brutality".

The Secretary also explained that there is another reason for urgent action now:

"There is a broader imperative here. The world's response to the violence in the former Yugoslavia is an early and concrete test of how we will address the concerns of the ethnic and religious minorities in the post-cold-war period".

I quote from the Secretary again:

"The events in the former Yugoslavia raise the questions of whether a State may address the rights of its minorities by eradicating those minorities to achieve ethnic purity. Bold tyrants and fearful minorities are watching to see whether ethnic cleansing is a policy the world will tolerate. If we hope to promote the spread of freedom, or if we hope to encourage the emergence of peaceful, multi-ethnic democracies, our answers must be a resounding 'no'".

The United States has so far submitted five reports to the Council pursuant to Security Council resolution 771 (1992), which contains substantiated information about the atrocities that have taken place in the former Yugoslavia. The Council's action today begins the process of establishing a war-crimes tribunal. We look forward to working with the Secretary-General to accomplish expeditiously his task of providing the Council with options for the statute and rules of procedure of such a tribunal.

Once the Secretary-General's report is received, we, along with the other members, will act quickly within the Council to establish a tribunal under

Chapter VII. We will also, in cooperation with the United Nations, exert every effort to ensure that those individuals involved in these outrageous, heinous crimes are identified and held accountable for their actions, which so affront the world's collective conscience.

It is worthwhile recalling that the Nuremberg Principles on war crimes, crimes against the peace, and crimes against humanity were adopted by the General Assembly in 1948. By its action today, with resolution 808 (1993) the Security Council has shown that the will of this Organization can be exercised, even if it has taken nearly half a century for the wisdom of our earliest principles to take hold. I hope that it will not take another half century to achieve the peace and security that will render the hideous crimes we suspect have been committed strictly historical phenomena.

Mr. RICHARDSON (United Kingdom of Great Britain and Northern Ireland): We have been receiving for many months now continued reports of massive breaches of international humanitarian law and human rights in Bosnia. I want to mention in particular the abuse of women, the deliberate obstruction of humanitarian relief convoys, the forcible movements of population, the forcible surrender of property and the deliberate targeting of civilian populations.

There has been an outburst of anger at these shocking developments. All parties share responsibility for these breaches. We believe that the Serbs have been most culpable in these hideous practices, but we also believe that all such actions must be condemned; they must be investigated; and the perpetrators must be called to account, whoever is responsible, throughout the territory of the former Yugoslavia. Those who have perpetrated these shocking breaches of international humanitarian law should be left in no doubt that they will be held individually responsible for their actions.

We think it is vital that an international legal mechanism be established to bring those accused of war crimes, from whatever party to the conflict, to justice. Whatever mechanism is proposed to give effect to this resolution should reflect this and should have jurisdiction over all of the parties. We welcome the valuable work on possible mechanisms by the French and Italian legal experts and by Ambassador Corell and his colleagues of the Conference on Security and Co-operation in Europe. This work is a valuable contribution to the study by the Secretary-General, which we have requested in the resolution we have just adopted, of the most effective and feasible way of establishing a tribunal or a court.

The Secretary-General's task will not be easy. The Commission of Experts' interim report notes the difficulties of identifying the perpetrators of these crimes. It is vital that whatever court or tribunal is established be provided with the necessary evidence. The Commission must therefore be given adequate resources to continue its work, and the Secretary-General will need to take account of legal difficulties such as those I have mentioned in examining the options to put to this Council.

The court is, of course, an ad hoc legal framework to deal with war crimes committed only in the territory of the former Yugoslavia. In the longer term, we shall continue to support the study by the International Law Commission towards an international criminal court with general jurisdiction. We hope that the Secretary-General will be able to carry out his examination of the options for establishing a court as quickly as possible, consistent of course with a thorough examination of the many problems that the reports so far submitted have already identified. We look forward to his report to the Council in the near future and we recognize, of course, that a further resolution by this Council will be necessary once we have received the Secretary-General's report.

Mr. VORONTSOV (Russian Federation) (interpretation from Russian): Russia has pursued an unwavering course of putting an end to war crimes and cannot remain indifferent to the flagrant mass violations of international humanitarian law in the territory of the former Yugoslavia. Murder, rape and "ethnic cleansing" must cease immediately, and the guilty - whatever their affiliation - must be duly punished.

We believe that the Security Council's adoption of a resolution deciding that an international tribunal shall be established for the prosecution of persons responsible for serious violations of international humanitarian law committed in the territory of the former Yugoslavia reflects the international community's will to exert its influence on all parties to the conflict in order to accelerate the peace process. The legal basis, status, composition and powers of the international tribunal and the modalities for its establishment and functioning will, as provided by the resolution, be decided by the Council subsequently, on the basis of a report on the subject by the Secretary-General. But even today the resolution should serve the purpose of bringing to their senses those who are ready to sacrifice for the sake of their political ambitions the lives and dignity of hundreds and thousands of totally innocent people.

Nor should we forget that violations of international humanitarian law are also taking place in the course of other armed conflicts. We believe that the Council's adoption of today's resolution will also serve as a serious warning to those guilty of mass crimes and flagrant violations of human rights in other parts of the world.

Mr. ARRIA (Venezuela) (interpretation from Spanish): When the Nuremberg war-crimes tribunal began its work on 18 October 1945, Judge Robert H. Jackson said that

> "This first trial of crimes against world peace places a very heavy responsibility upon us. The crimes we intend to condemn and punish were so deliberate and so devastating that our civilization cannot allow them to be ignored, for mankind could not survive a repetition of such crimes."

Not quite 48 years after the beginning of the Nuremberg trial, the world is horrified to see that organized barbarism - which, it was thought, was possible only in that age and could never be repeated - has come again, this time before the eyes of all mankind. And unlike the experience of the past, no one can escape his responsibility by claiming ignorance of the atrocities.

The policies of scorched earth, of what was initially called "ethnic cleansing" and today can more accurately be called "ethnic extermination", of concentration camps and of torture carried out by the Serb militias, who resort even to the savage policy of raping women as a technique of war, have attained sinister levels previously unthinkable to mankind. The authoritative testimony given by Mr. Cornelio Sommaruga, President of the International Committee of the Red Cross (ICRC), and by Mr. David Andrews, former Foreign Minister of Ireland, on behalf of the European Community, among other equally qualified persons, leads to the clear conclusion that the rapes and other crimes have become an instrument of war, not a consequence of war.

Many organizations such as ICRC and the European Community have issued unequivocal statements on all the atrocities that have been and continue to be committed. Sarajevo remains a city under siege; the siege has lasted 10 terrible months; the cemetery cannot hold all the dead, and it is now necessary to bury them in the sports stadium. The survivors bury their dead without ceremony.

Medical centres are the scene of daily horrors: the horror of individual tragedies and the horror of the collective tragedy of having no way and no materials to help the victims of these systematic killings.

In that connection, former United States Secretary of State Lawrence Eagleburger himself has suggested to world public opinion the names of the most prominent candidates for trial by the future war-crimes tribunal.

Venezuela believes that the resolution we have just adopted is consistent with the principles and the plan of action agreed to by all parties concerned in the context of the International Conference on the Former Yugoslavia and that it is also consistent with the provisions of Article 41 of the Charter. My delegation congratulates the Government of France on its initiative in submitting to the Council the draft resolution adopted today.

We eagerly await the specific recommendations the Secretary-General will present to the Council, with a view to activating the machinery. If the purpose of that machinery is to be fully achieved, there must also be very substantial support for the Commission of Experts established by the Council, so that the Commission may complete its work of laying the foundations for the process to be advanced by the war-crimes tribunal.

Mr. ERDOS (Hungary) (interpretation from French): One of the most tragic, grim and alarming aspects of the bloody conflict in the former Yugoslavia is the planned and systematic mass violation of the most elementary norms of international humanitarian law. Since the end of the Second World War, Europe has not known such terrible upheavals or human-rights violations of such magnitude and such cruelty.

It is the view of world public opinion that efforts to bring to justice those responsible for these crimes must be an integral part of a broad endeavour to achieve a just and lasting settlement of the entire conflict that is now savaging the former Yugoslavia.

As in 1945, the conscience of Europe and the world cannot allow those who have ordered and committed violations of international humanitarian law - and who cynically and blindly continue to do so - to escape justice.

The way the international community deals with questions relating to the events in the former Yugoslavia will leave a profound mark on the future of that part of Europe, and beyond. It will make either easier or more painful, or even impossible, the healing of the psychological wounds the conflict has inflicted upon peoples who for centuries have lived together in harmony and good-neighbourliness, regardless of what we may hear today from certain parties to the conflict. We cannot forget that the peoples, the ethnic communities and the national minorities of Central and Eastern Europe are watching us and following our work with close attention.

The results of our activities, whether positive or negative, our successes or our failures within the United Nations and the Security Council, will inevitably have repercussions and direct effects upon that entire part of the world and, I am convinced, elsewhere too.

We consider that the Security Council's decision of last October to set up a Commission of Experts charged with studying and analysing information on the grave violations of international humanitarian law in the former Yugoslavia is of great importance. Information and reports from various sources confirm and strengthen our conviction that the gravity and massive nature of these violations constitute a threat to international peace and security. Consequently, there should be no doubt about the competence of the Security Council to deal with this matter. Resolution 808 (1993) contains a clear and unequivocal political message for those who are responsible and who are committing almost-unimaginable crimes.

Hungary is ready, when the time comes, to embark on the second stage of our work, which will be the report of the Secretary-General containing concrete proposals and options for the implementation of the resolution that the Council has solemnly adopted today.

Mr. YAÑEZ-BARNUEVO (Spain) (interpretation from Spanish): The Council has recently taken decisions of great import, but few deserve to be called "historic" as much as the resolution we have just adopted. Indeed, as the provisional report of the Commission of Experts established by Security Council resolution 780 (1992) clearly states, this is the first time the

Security Council has decided to establish a tribunal to try those deemed responsible for grave violations of international humanitarian law perpetrated in an armed conflict - in this instance, the grave acts committed in the territory of the former Yugoslavia. In that provisional report, the Commission concludes that grave offences and other violations of international humanitarian law have been committed, including murder, "ethnic cleansing", mass killings, torture, rape, looting and destruction of civilian property, destruction of cultural and religious property and arbitrary detention.

We understand that some may harbour certain doubts about the competence of the Council to take this step, for it is a novel one. However, we do not share those doubts. We understand that this is a limited and precise action with the clear objective of restoring peace, which is perfectly in keeping with the competence of the Council. In fact, the Council is not attempting to establish any new jurisdictional or legislative framework of a permanent nature. It is not setting itself up as a permanent judge or legislator. It is only attempting to create an ad hoc mechanism that, by applying existing laws, will assign responsibility for acts committed in an ongoing conflict that has already been seen to threaten and undermine peace; a mechanism that contributes, by means of recourse to justice and punishment of the guilty, to restoring the peace and ensuring its maintenance, so as to deter the repetition of similar acts in the future.

For these reasons, the States members of the European Community have on various occasions declared themselves to be in favour of the establishment of an international criminal tribunal for the prosecution of those engaged in such grave misconduct.

Spain would have preferred the establishment of a criminal tribunal with universal jurisdiction, but it recognizes that to create one would have required more time than is now at our disposal if we wish to contribute to the early restoration of peace in the former Yugoslavia. Nevertheless, we are confident that this is the first step towards the future creation of an international, universal, permanent criminal jurisdiction, and we shall continue to support and promote the efforts towards this end now being made in other forums within this Organization.

While we are aware of the need to act swiftly in order that the establishment of an international criminal tribunal on the former Yugoslavia fulfils its dual objective of meting out justice and discouraging such grave violations in the future, we believe that this undertaking is so important and so sensitive that it is necessary to ensure the maximum respect for legal rigour in its functioning. We therefore fully support a two-stage process, such as the one we are initiating today, in which, following the adoption of a decision in principle, a thorough, detailed study is conducted so that the institution established will live up to the expectations of the international community and will meet all the requirements of full respect for international law. It is imperative that norms relating to human rights be respected, in particular the rights of defence. It is also essential to resolve difficult questions such as the nature of the sentences to be imposed, the places they are to be served, the statutes of the organs entrusted with the investigation and the indictment, the possibility of appealing the decisions of the tribunal and other questions of no less importance.

From the foregoing, it is clear that there is a tremendous amount of work to be done. We have no doubt that the Secretary-General, to whom we entrust this enormous task, will carry it out with his characteristic speed and effectiveness. In so doing he will have at his disposal some excellent studies that have already been done - and here I wish to mention those prepared by expert jurists from France and Italy and by an ad hoc Committee of the Conference on Security and Cooperation in Europe, which have already been distributed as Security Council documents - and the full cooperation, I have no doubt, of all the States Members of the United Nations and those bodies competent in the field of international law that the Secretary-General deems it appropriate to consult. From this moment we shall await with great interest the result of his labours, with its concrete proposals for the Council regarding the organization, operation and other points pertaining to the smooth functioning of the tribunal.

We have stated that the establishment of the tribunal will contribute, in our view, to the restoration and maintenance of peace in accordance with the principles of justice and international law. At the same time, we wish to recall that it is not an attempt to supplant the bold efforts currently under way for the achievement of a just and lasting political agreement. Genuine peace must be founded on justice and, at the same time, a dialogue that ensures that the parties involved agree to the terms of any solution to the underlying problems of the former Yugoslavia.

For all those reasons we encourage the two Co-Chairmen of the Steering Committee of the International Conference to continue their efforts to bring about agreement between all the parties to the conflict. We pledge our full cooperation to that end. Crimes such as those committed in the territory of the former Yugoslavia should never remain unpunished. By its decision today, the Security Council has made that crystal clear. All those responsible for such acts are therefore warned of the international community's resolve.

Mr. O'BRIEN (New Zealand): It is indeed a momentous decision that the Council has taken this morning. We owe a great deal, Mr. President, to your skill and purpose in getting the resolution adopted. Our decision has not been taken lightly. No one can deny the enormity of the crimes, of which previous speakers have spoken very eloquently. No one can deny the deep significance of the issues that must guide the Council in its follow-up to its decision today.

New Zealand has long supported the principle of international criminal jurisdiction. Therefore, we stand ready with others to offer a contribution to the Secretary-General's upcoming important work on the basis of which the Council will take a decision about the further vital matter of the actual tribunal machinery for the territory of the former Republic of Yugoslavia. We believe that it is absolutely essential that the Council, having taken this significant decision today, proceed with purpose and resolve to translate the decision into practical and effective results on the basis of the Secretary-General's proposal; in our opinion, the momentum must not be allowed to diminish.

The PRESIDENT (interpretation from French): I shall now make a statement in my capacity as representative of my country.

My country has just participated responsibly and following its conscience in the adoption of the resolution, which confirms the will of the Security Council not to allow to go unpunished all the horrible crimes in Bosnia and Herzegovina that we have been hearing about for several months. Not content with carrying out a disgraceful genocide, the Serbs have systematically perpetrated a whole range of atrocities, torture and violence, all of them totally inadmissible, acts and practices that we had thought belonged to a bygone age.

In establishing the principle of a war crimes tribunal, the Council is responding to the unanimous wish of the international community, which for almost two years has been deploring and condemning the acts in question and strongly calling for punishment and action.

The step we have taken is serious. Until yesterday the crimes continued unabated. Today the criminals know they will be pursued and punished. This warning is important with regard to those who have respected no moral values; it will surely deter those who are afraid only of force. Let us hope that our action will be followed by deterrent steps. Perhaps it will then finally be understood in the former Yugoslavia that resolutions are passed to be respected and that human life is to be safeguarded and protected.

I hardly need repeat our congratulations to the French delegation on its valuable contribution to the establishment of peace and harmony. I hope that the historic action we have just taken will mark the beginning of a return to wisdom in a region that has suffered too much death and upheaval.

I now resume my functions as President.

There are no further speakers on my list. The Security Council has thus concluded the present stage of its consideration of the item on the agenda. The Security Council will remain seized of the matter.

C. RESOLUTION 827 (1993)
Adopted by the Security Council at its 3217th Meeting, on 25 May 1993

S/RES/827 (1993), 25 May 1993.

The Security Council,

Reaffirming its resolution 713 (1991) of 25 September 1991 and all subsequent relevant resolutions,

Having considered the report of the Secretary-General (S/25704 and Add.1) pursuant to paragraph 2 of resolution 808 (1993),

Expressing once again its grave alarm at continuing reports of widespread and flagrant violations of international humanitarian law occurring within the territory of the former Yugoslavia, and especially in the Republic of Bosnia and Herzegovina, including reports of mass killings, massive, organized and systematic detention and rape of women, and the continuance of the practice of "ethnic cleansing", including for the acquisition and the holding of territory,

Determining that this situation continues to constitute a threat to international peace and security,

Determined to put an end to such crimes and to take effective measures to bring to justice the persons who are responsible for them,

Convinced that in the particular circumstances of the former Yugoslavia the establishment as an ad hoc measure by the Council of an international tribunal and the prosecution of persons responsible for serious violations of international humanitarian law would enable this aim to be achieved and would contribute to the restoration and maintenance of peace,

Believing that the establishment of an international tribunal and the prosecution of persons responsible for the above-mentioned violations of international humanitarian law will contribute to ensuring that such violations are halted and effectively redressed,

Noting in this regard the recommendation by the Co-Chairmen of the Steering Committee of the International Conference on the Former Yugoslavia for the establishment of such a tribunal (S/25221),

Reaffirming in this regard its decision in resolution 808 (1993) that an international tribunal shall be established for the prosecution of persons responsible for serious violations of international humanitarian law committed in the territory of the former Yugoslavia since 1991,

Considering that, pending the appointment of the Prosecutor of the International Tribunal, the Commission of Experts established pursuant to resolution 780 (1992) should continue on an urgent basis the collection of information relating to evidence of grave breaches of the Geneva Conventions and other violations of international humanitarian law as proposed in its interim report (S/25274),

Acting under Chapter VII of the Charter of the United Nations,

1. Approves the report of the Secretary-General;

2. Decides hereby to establish an international tribunal for the sole purpose of prosecuting persons responsible for serious violations of international humanitarian law committed in the territory of the former Yugoslavia between 1 January 1991 and a date to be determined by the Security Council upon the restoration of peace and to this end to adopt the Statute of the International Tribunal annexed to the above-mentioned report;

3. Requests the Secretary-General to submit to the judges of the International Tribunal, upon their election, any suggestions received from States for the rules of procedure and evidence called for in Article 15 of the Statute of the International Tribunal;

4. Decides that all States shall cooperate fully with the International Tribunal and its organs in accordance with the present resolution and the Statute of the International Tribunal and that consequently all States shall take any measures necessary under their domestic law to implement the provisions of the present resolution and the Statute, including the obligation of States to comply with requests for assistance or orders issued by a Trial Chamber under Article 29 of the Statute;

5. Urges States and intergovernmental and non-governmental organizations to contribute funds, equipment and services to the International Tribunal, including the offer of expert personnel;

6. Decides that the determination of the seat of the International Tribunal is subject to the conclusion of appropriate arrangements between the United Nations and the Netherlands acceptable to the Council, and that the International Tribunal may sit elsewhere when it considers it necessary for the efficient exercise of its functions;

7. Decides also that the work of the International Tribunal shall be carried out without prejudice to the right of the victims to seek, through appropriate means, compensation for damages incurred as a result of violations of international humanitarian law;

8. Requests the Secretary-General to implement urgently the present resolution and in particular to make practical arrangements for the effective functioning of the International Tribunal at the earliest time and to report periodically to the Council;

9. Decides to remain actively seized of the matter.

PROVISIONAL VERBATIM RECORD OF THE THREE THOUSAND TWO HUNDRED AND SEVENTEENTH MEETING

Held at Headquarters, New York, on Tuesday, 25 May 1993, at 9 p.m.

S/PV. 3217, 25 May 1993.

President:	Mr. VORONTSOV	(Russian Federation)
Members:	Brazil	Mr. SARDENBERG
	Cape Verde	Mr. BARBOSA
	China	Mr. LI Zhaoxing
	Djibouti	Mr. OLHAYE
	France	Mr. MERIMEE
	Hungary	Mr. ERDOS
	Japan	Mr. MARUYAMA
	Morocco	Mr. SNOUSSI
	New Zealand	Mr. O'BRIEN
	Pakistan	Mr. MARKER
	Spain	Mr. YAÑEZ BARNUEVO
	United Kingdom of Great Britain and Northern Ireland	Sir David HANNAY
	United States of America	Mrs. ALBRIGHT
	Venezuela	Mr. ARRIA

The PRESIDENT: I should like to inform the Council that I have received letters from the representatives of Bosnia and Herzegovina and Croatia, in which they request to be invited to participate in the discussion of the item on the Council's agenda. In accordance with the usual practice, I propose, with the consent of the Council, to invite those representatives to participate in the discussion without the right to vote, in conformity with the relevant provisions of the Charter and rule 37 of the Council's provisional rules of procedure.

There being no objection, it is so decided.

At the invitation of the President, Mr.Sacirbey (Bosnia and Herzegovina) and Mr. Drobnjak (Croatia) took places at the Council table.

The PRESIDENT: The Security Council will now begin its consideration of the item on its agenda.

The Security Council is meeting in accordance with the understanding reached in its prior consultations.

Members of the Council have before them the report of the

Secretary-General pursuant to paragraph 2 of Security Council resolution 808 (1993), documents S/25704 and Addendum 1. Members of the Council also have before them document S/25826, which contains the text of a draft resolution submitted by France, New Zealand, the Russian Federation, Spain, the United Kingdom of Great Britain and Northern Ireland and the United States of America.

I should like to draw the attention of the members of the Council to the following other documents: S/25417, note verbale dated 12 March 1993 from the Permanent Mission of Mexico to the United Nations addressed to the Secretary-General; S/25504, letter dated 31 March from the Chargé d'affaires a.i. of the Permanent Mission of Canada to the United Nations addressed to the Secretary-General; S/25594, letter dated 13 April 1993 from the Permanent Representative of Canada to the United Nations addressed to the Secretary-General; S/25537, letter dated 5 April 1993 from the Permanent Representative of the Russian Federation to the United Nations addressed to the Secretary-General; S/25540, letter dated 6 April 1993 from the Permanent Representative of Brazil to the United Nations addressed to the Secretary-General; S/25575, letter dated 5 April 1993 from the Permanent Representative of the United States of America to the United Nations addressed to the Secretary-General; S/25652, letter dated 20 April 1993 from the Permanent Representative of Slovenia to the United Nations addressed to the Secretary-General; S/25716, note verbale dated 30 April 1993 from the Permanent Representative of the Netherlands to the United Nations addressed to the Secretary-General; S/25765, letter dated 11 May 1993 from the Chargé d'affaires a.i.of the Permanent Mission of Canada to the United Nations addressed to the Secretary-General; S/25801, letter dated 19 May 1993 from the Chargé d'affaires a.i. of the Permanent Mission of Yugoslavia to the United Nations addressed to the Secretary-General; and S/25829, letter dated 24 May 1993 from the Permanent Representatives of France, the Russian Federation, Spain, the United Kingdom of Great Britain and Northern Ireland and the United States of America to the United Nations addressed to the President of the Security Council.

It is my understanding that the Council is ready to proceed to the vote on the draft resolution before it. Unless I hear any objection, I shall now put the draft resolution to the vote.

There being no objection, it is so decided.

A vote was taken by show of hands.

In favour: Brazil, Cape Verde, China, Djibouti, France, Hungary, Japan, Morocco, New Zealand, Pakistan, Russian Federation, Spain, United Kingdom of Great Britain and Northern Ireland, United States of America, Venezuela

The PRESIDENT (interpretation from Russian): There were 15 votes in favour. The draft resolution has therefore been adopted unanimously as resolution 827 (1993).

I shall now call on those members of the Council who wish to make statements following the voting.

Mr. ARRIA (Venezuela) (interpretation from Spanish): The evolution of international society reveals the need to create a corrective and punitive forum, particularly in the case of crimes affecting the very essence of the civilized conscience, as in the case of crimes against humanity.

In Nüremberg and Tokyo we saw the emergence of international courts to try those guilty of the crimes committed during the course of the Second World War. Now the Security Council has decided to act on behalf of the global community of States by establishing an International Tribunal which, as a forum representing all humanity, will bring to trial and punish those guilty of abominable crimes. This is the vital significance of the step the Council has taken today as a substantive part of the Vance-Owen peace process.

The search for justice cannot be tainted by diplomatic or political considerations. Too many grave violations of human rights have taken place in many parts of the world while those responsible for them have escaped the hand of justice, such as the Khmer Rouge in Cambodia and the warlords in Somalia; Sudan, Iraq and Haiti are other instances.

But there comes a time when one must ask oneself: "If we do not act now, when will we? If we do not act in a case such as this, when will we act?" The Security Council has asked itself that question. It has reflected upon it and agreed unanimously to take immediate action in the case of the former

Yugoslavia, while at the same time issuing a warning to others elsewhere that they cannot continue violating international humanitarian law with impunity. The Council goes even further by encouraging the establishment of a permanent International Tribunal, as my country among many others has been advocating.

The delegation of Venezuela voted in favour of resolution 808 (1993), which decided to establish the Tribunal, because it is convinced of the duty incumbent upon the international community to reaffirm that the commission of such crimes as those that have clearly been committed in this case cannot pass without political condemnation and penal sanctions. Such a situation would be intolerable in modern society.

My delegation recognizes that the Tribunal is intended to deal with a specific and limited crisis that the Council has been addressing under Chapter VII of the Charter. It also recognizes that the Tribunal, as a subsidiary organ of the Council, would not be empowered with - nor would the Council be assuming - the ability to set down norms of international law or to legislate with respect to those rights. It simply applies existing international humanitarian law.

Venezuela recognizes that in adopting the draft Statute of the Tribunal the Council is also taking exceptional action. It is on the basis of this exceptional nature of the action that we can accept aspects of the Statute with respect to which suggestions for its refinement or improvement and adaptation might have been made with a view to addressing the specific features of the legal régimes of various Member States. Venezuela believes that this ad hoc Tribunal has thus been established to act in support of the purposes and principles of the Charter.

My delegation trusts that the ad hoc Tribunal will indeed be impartial, because it is conceived as the expression of a commitment to an indispensable system of international justice and in no way as an act of retaliation against the Serbs or any other specific group. It is being established in an attempt to bring to trial and punish anyone who proves to be guilty of the horrible crimes that have been committed in the former Yugoslavia, as well as to reverse the consequences of the crime of genocide committed for territorial gain and to provide financial compensation to the victims, as the resolution we have adopted this evening provides.

My delegation stresses that the central function of the Tribunal will be exercised by the chief prosecutor who, as of now, should be provided with all the necessary financial and administrative support. Otherwise, the Tribunal will not be able to fulfil its mandate. In this respect, we suggest that the Prosecutor should not confine himself to bringing cases before the Tribunal, but should also present an overall report on all of the violations of international humanitarian law that come to his knowledge, which will provide him with an historical record of great importance.

Finally, I would call attention to that unfinished part of our Organization's agenda, which refers to the creation of a permanent international penal jurisdication. The creation of such a jurisdiction has been debated for many years. Today, the global scope of organized criminal activity requires a concomitant global political will to prosecute and punish it. Accountability for criminal conduct affecting and offending humanity should also entail global accountability. We need appropriate machinery to address that situation, before events overwhelm us.

Pain and indignation at certain types of crimes and an outcry for justice have become global. No one can deny that organized crime today is transnational, defying national laws and extending beyond all national jurisdictions. Such crimes as terrorism, money laundering, drug trafficking, the illicit traffic in conventional and non-conventional weapons, financial speculation and other offences committed by cartels, mafias and gangs have grown so widespread that they are not only increasingly serious but also increasingly sophisticated, easily able to flout national jurisdictions. Just as there is "ethnic cleansing", there is also a "cleansing" of judges, journalists, police officers and political leaders who dare to oppose organized crime. Undoubtedly, the rights of these persons are just as fundamental as those to be dealt with by the ad hoc Tribunal for the former Yugoslavia.

Nothing encourages crime more than impunity, and thus the international community cannot continue to put off a global response such as a permanent tribunal. Humanity is suffering in too many corners of the world, not only in the former Yugoslavia.

This horrible dimension and reality of global crime and offenses against international humanitarian law must come to an end. We must put an end to the interminable legal discussions that, in delaying the establishment of international jurisdiction, are merely encouraging impunity. That is the reality.

Mr. MERIMEE (France) (interpretation from French): In adopting resolution 827 (1993), the Security Council has just established an International Tribunal that will prosecute, judge and punish people from any community who have committed or continue to commit crimes in the territory of the former Yugoslavia.

The Nuremberg Tribunal and the Tokyo Tribunal judged, on behalf of humanity in its entirety, those who had breached the most elementary rules. Those Tribunals were established by the victors at the end of a war. Today, through the Security Council, it is the international community that is establishing the International Tribunal for Yugoslavia.

The Statute of the Tribunal that we have adopted under resolution 827 (1993) defines its competence and mandate. The Statute was worked out at the request of the Security Council, pursuant to resolution 808 (1993), by the Secretary-General and his colleagues, in particular Mr. Carl-August Fleischhauer, in a very short period of time, and my delegation wishes to pay a tribute to the outstanding quality of their work. That work has made it possible for us to adopt the draft Statute very quickly and without amendment.

I should like to make a few brief comments on this subject: firstly, the expression "laws or customs of war" used in Article 3 of the Statute covers specifically, in the opinion of France, all the obligations that flow from the humanitarian law agreements in force on the territory of the former Yugoslavia at the time when the offences were committed.

Secondly, with regard to Article 5, that Article applies to all the acts set out therein when committed in violation of the law during a period of armed conflict on the territory of the former Yugoslavia, within the context of a widespread or systematic attack against a civilian population for national, political, ethnic, racial or religious reasons.

Thirdly, we believe that, pursuant to Article 9, paragraph 2, the

Tribunal may intervene at any stage of the procedure and assert its primacy, including from the stage of investigation where appropriate, in the situations covered under Article 10, paragraph 2.

Resolution 827 (1993) was adopted under Chapter VII of the Charter. The threat to international peace and security created by the serious situation in the former Yugoslavia justifies recourse to those provisions. This resolution, which is a decision within the meaning of Article 25 of the Charter, thus now applies to all States. This means, specifically, that all States are required to cooperate fully with the Tribunal, even if this obliges them to amend certain provisions of their domestic law.

France is pleased, therefore, that the initiative that it took this past February has led to such a resounding expression by the United Nations of our common resolve not to tolerate infamy and to assert the rule of law. My country hopes that this message will be understood by all and that it will help silence the guns on the territory of the former Yugoslavia.

Mrs. ALBRIGHT (United States of America): Today we begin to cleanse the hatred that has torn apart the former Yugoslavia. A few months ago, I said:

> "This will be no victors' tribunal. The only victor that will prevail in this endeavour is the truth." (S/PV.3175, p. 11)

Truth is the cornerstone of the rule of law, and it will point towards individuals, not peoples, as perpetrators of war crimes. And it is only the truth that can cleanse the ethnic and religious hatreds and begin the healing process.

Included among the millions who will learn of this resolution are the hundreds of thousands of civilians who are the victims of horrific war crimes and crimes against humanity in the former Yugoslavia. To these victims we declare by this action that your agony, your sacrifice, and your hope for justice have not been forgotten. And to those who committed these heinous crimes, we have a very clear message: war criminals will be prosecuted and justice will be rendered.

The crimes being committed, even as we meet today, are not just isolated acts of drunken militiamen, but often are the systematic and orchestrated crimes of Government officials, military commanders, and disciplined artillerymen and foot soldiers. The men and women behind these crimes are individually responsible for the crimes of those they purport to control; the fact that their power is often self-proclaimed does not lessen their culpability.

Those sceptics - including the war criminals - who deride this Tribunal as being powerless because the suspects may avoid arrest should not be so confident. The Tribunal will issue indictments whether or not suspects can be taken into custody. They will become international pariahs. While these individuals may be able to hide within the borders of Serbia or in parts of Bosnia or Croatia, they will be imprisoned for the rest of their lives within their own land. Under today's resolution, every Government, including each one in the former Yugoslavia, will be obligated to hand over those indicted by the Tribunal.

We must ensure that the voices of the groups most victimized are heard by the Tribunal. I refer particularly to the detention and systematic rape of women and girls, often followed by cold-blooded murder. Let the tens of thousands of women and girls who courageously survived the brutal assault of cowards who call themselves soldiers know this: your dignity survives, as does that of those who died.

The Honourable Geraldine Ferraro, who recently represented the United States on the Human Rights Commission, said of this crime:

> "Rape should not be used as a weapon of war. It should also not be used as a tool for revenge... Women's rights are human rights, and must be respected as such."

The International Tribunal will prosecute the rapists and murderers and their superiors.

My Government is also determined to see that women jurists sit on the Tribunal and that women prosecutors bring war criminals to justice. Our view is shared by all of the women Permanent Representatives of this Organization. We also take note of the recommendation of the Organization of the Islamic Conference that gender be duly represented on the Tribunal.

Today's resolution contains important provisions designed to ensure the expeditious establishment of the Tribunal. It is imperative that I take some time to state clearly and completely the understandings which underpin my Government's support for this resolution and for the Statute of the Tribunal. To begin, we want to stress the importance of three provisions in particular.

Today's resolution ensures that the United Nations Commission of Experts will continue to pursue its work of establishing a database and preparing evidence during the interim period before the appointment of the Tribunal's Prosecutor and hiring of staff to begin authoritative investigations and preparations for trials. We expect that the Secretary-General will provide the Commission with the space, resources and personnel necessary to continue its mandate, and we urge other countries to follow our lead in pledging financial contributions to the Commission. At the appropriate time, we expect the Commission would cease to exist and that its work would be folded into the Prosecutor's office.

The resolution also encourages States to submit proposals for the rules of evidence and procedure for consideration by the judges of the Tribunal. We hope to contribute to this critical process of developing the rules that the Tribunal can expeditiously adopt so that the Prosecutor will then be in a position to begin prosecuting cases without further delay.

In addition, the resolution recognizes that States may find it necessary to take measures under their domestic law to enable them to implement the provisions of the Statute, and pledges them to endeavour to take any such measures as soon as possible. That is certainly the intention of the United States.

We commend the Secretariat for its outstanding report, which has laid the foundation for today's action by the Council. While the Council has adopted the Statute for the Tribunal as proposed in that report, the members of the Council have recognized that the Statute raises several technical issues that can be addressed through interpretive statements.

In particular, we understand that other members of the Council share our view regarding the following clarifications related to the Statute:

Firstly, it is understood that the "laws or customs of war" referred to in Article 3 include all obligations under humanitarian law agreements in force in the territory of the former Yugoslavia at the time the acts were committed, including common article 3 of the 1949 Geneva Conventions, and the 1977 Additional Protocols to these Conventions.

Secondly, it is understood that Article 5 applies to all acts listed in that article, when committed contrary to law during a period of armed conflict in the territory of the former Yugoslavia, as part of a widespread or systematic attack against any civilian population on national, political, ethnic, racial, gender, or religious grounds.

Thirdly, it is understood that the primacy of the International Tribunal referred to in paragraph 2 of Article 9 only refers to the situations described in Article 10.

The United States wishes also to offer several other clarifications related to the provisions of the Statute:

With respect to paragraph 1 of Article 7, it is our understanding that individual liability arises in the case of a conspiracy to commit a crime referred to in Articles 2 through 5, or the failure of a superior - whether political or military - to take reasonable steps to prevent or punish such crimes by persons under his or her authority. It is, of course, a defence that the accused was acting pursuant to orders where he or she did not know the orders were unlawful and a person of ordinary sense and understanding would not have known the orders to be unlawful.

With respect to Article 10, it is our understanding that the Tribunal is authorized to conduct proceedings against persons previously tried by a national court for the same crime when national proceedings - including clemency, parole, and other similar relief - were not impartial or independent, were designed to shield the accused from international criminal responsibility, or were not diligently prosecuted.

With respect to Article 19, we understand that the reference to "prima facie" case in paragraph 1 means a reasonable basis to believe that a crime as defined in Articles 2 through 5, has been committed by the person named in the indictment.

Finally, with respect to Article 24, it is our understanding that compensation to victims by a convicted person may be an appropriate part of decisions on sentencing, reduction of sentences, parole or commutation. We also understand that the Tribunal may impose a sentence of life imprisonment, or consecutive sentences for multiple offences, in any appropriate case.

With the adoption of the Statute for the Tribunal, we have completed the most difficult part of the task we began in February with resolution 808 (1993) when that was approved by the Council. We must now move without delay to the next steps, particularly the appointment of the prosecutor and the selection of judges.

Finally, of this we are certain: the Tribunal must succeed, for the sake of the victims and for the credibility of international law in this new era.

Sir David HANNAY (United Kingdom): The United Kingdom Government has been horrified at the continued evidence of massive breaches of international humanitarian law and human rights in the former Yugoslavia, the abuse of women, the deliberate obstruction of humanitarian relief convoys, forced population movements, forcible surrender of property and the deliberate military targeting of civilian populations. Above all, the practice of "ethnic cleansing" has managed to combine the commitment of the most odious of crimes for the most base purposes. All parties in the former Yugoslavia share some responsibility for these crimes, and it is important to emphasize that the action the Council is taking today is not aimed at one party alone. The Security Council has repeatedly demanded the immediate cessation of such atrocities, but these demands have not been heeded. It is essential that those who commit such acts be in no doubt that they will be held individually responsible. It is essential that these atrocities be investigated and the perpetrators called to account, whoever and wherever they may be.

It is against this background, and in the very special circumstances pertaining in the former Yugoslavia, that the Council has decided to establish, as an ad hoc measure, a Tribunal for the prosecution of those responsible for serious violations of international humanitarian law in the former Yugoslavia. This is an exceptional step needed to deal with exceptional circumstances. At the same time, my Government continues to support the work of the International Law Commission, which will result, we hope, in the establishment of an international criminal court with general jurisdiction.

We therefore fully supported resolution 808 (1993), in which the Council decided in principle on the establishment of an ad hoc Tribunal to deal with the serious violations of international humanitarian law committed in the former Yugoslavia since 1991. We welcome and endorse the Secretary-General's excellent report on the most effective and expeditious means of establishing the Tribunal.

It is of the greatest importance for the effective functioning of the Tribunal that the judges, prosecutor and staff are persons with considerable practical experience in the field of criminal prosecution. The Tribunal has very specific purposes, to try persons for serious criminal offences, and it is essential that all involved are experts in the field.

Articles 9 and 10 of the Statute deal with the relationship between the International Tribunal and national courts. In our view, the primacy of the Tribunal, referred to in Article 9, paragraph 2, relates primarily to the courts in the territory of former Yugoslavia: elsewhere it will only be in the kinds of exceptional circumstances outlined in Article 10, paragraph 2, that primacy should be applicable.

Articles 2 to 5 of the draft Statute describe the crimes within the jurisdiction of the Tribunal. The Statute does not, of course, create new law, but reflects existing international law in this field. In this connection, it would be our view that the reference to the laws or customs of war in Article 3 is broad enough to include applicable international conventions and that Article 5 covers acts committed in time of armed conflict.

As the resolution makes clear, it will be necessary for States to establish their own procedures for implementing their obligations under the Statute. Thus, for example, domestic procedures will be needed to give effect to the obligation under Article 29 to comply with a request or order concerning the surrender or transfer of an accused to the International Tribunal.

It will be for the General Assembly to make the necessary budgetary allocations for the effective functioning of the Tribunal, and in due course its appropriate subordinate bodies will need to scrutinize very carefully the financial arrangements and provisions for the Tribunal.

We strongly support the resolution that has just been adopted. The establishment of the Tribunal sends a clear message to all in the former Yugoslavia that they must stop immediately violations of international humanitarian law or face the consequences. We hope that message will be heeded.

Mr. ERDOS (Hungary) (interpretation from French): Hungary attaches the greatest importance to the unanimous adoption of resolution 827 (1993) of the Security Council. This is the first time that the United Nations establishes an international criminal jurisdiction to prosecute persons who commit grave violations of international humanitarian law.

This initiative is a logical follow-up of the process begun by Security Council resolution 764 (1992) which emphasized the individual responsibilities for grave violations of the 1949 Geneva Conventions in former Yugoslavia, violations which constitute horrific crimes without precedent in Europe since the end of the Second World War.

On the basis of the information that has reached us from several sources, as well as from the Commission of Experts established by the Security Council, the Council, in resolution 808 (1993), noted that the violations of international humanitarian law, because of their gravity and their generalized character, constituted a threat to international peace and security, which, in our view, fully justifies the competence of the Security Council in this sphere.

We believe that resolution 827 (1993) represents a balance between the complex political and legal requirements and, above all, creates the specific conditions necessary for the Tribunal to be set up and to begin its activity promptly.

We note also the importance of the fact that the jurisdiction of the Tribunal covers the whole range of international humanitarian law and the entire duration of the conflict throughout the territory of former Yugoslavia. The Statute of the Tribunal allows the prosecution of all persons - not communities - charged with crimes where the crime was committed in the territory of former Yugoslavia and without regard to their ethnic affiliation. We note also that the official status of the individual brought to court, whatever it might be, does not immunize him from his criminal liability. In the light of the significance of implementing the goals set for the Tribunal and in the light of their complexity, it is important that the Tribunal be made up of highly qualified persons, both in theory and in practice, in order properly to carry out under optimal conditions the tasks that are conferred on them.

Hungary has firmly supported all resolutions of the Security Council concerning grave violations of international humanitarian law. Hungary is convinced that persons who commit or order the commission of grave and systematic violations of that law should not escape the hand of justice, and their acts cannot enjoy impunity. We are deeply convinced that it is impossible to envisage a lasting settlement of the conflict in the former Yugoslavia, including in the Republic of Bosnia and Herzegovina, without the prosecution of those who massacre and burn children, women and elderly people; who, with diabolical regularity, shell innocent civilian populations; who practice "ethnic cleansing", the true tragic implications of which have not yet been fully appreciated; who cut off the water supplies of besieged communities; who deliberately destroy cultural or religious property, and so on.

On the basis of these considerations, Hungary voted in favour of the draft resolution in the hope that its adoption and the expeditious establishment of the Tribunal will contribute effectively to bringing an end to violations of international humanitarian law and will send the right message to those at whom this resolution is aimed.

Mr. O'BRIEN (New Zealand): New Zealand welcomes the adoption of this resolution, which it co-sponsored. We particularly commend the report of the Secretary-General, including the Statute for the Tribunal to try persons responsible for violations of international humanitarian law in the territory of the former Yugoslavia. Like others here tonight, we congratulate the Secretary-General for the lucidity of his report and for the comprehensiveness of the Statute, which in large measure accords with New Zealand's own perceptions of what the Tribunal should do. We consider that it is appropriate that the Council has approved the Statute in toto here tonight.

The atrocities reportedly committed in the territory of the former Yugoslavia, notably in Bosnia and Herzegovina, have horrified and continue to horrify all of us. New Zealand considers that it is imperative that persons responsible for acts of "ethnic cleansing", the forced expulsion of people, systematic rape, torture and murder are brought to trial and are punished. The establishment of the Tribunal by this resolution ensures that we have in place an effective mechanism to achieve these ends.

As is noted in the resolution and in the Secretary-General's report, the establishment of the Tribunal and the prosecution of persons suspected of crimes against international humanitarian law is closely related to the wider efforts to restore peace and security to the former Yugoslavia. This is an important point. We recall that in the Secretary-General's report of 2 February, the Co-Chairmen of the International Conference specifically state that human rights and humanitarian issues are the core elements of the peacemaking process in the former Yugoslavia. In restating then their advocacy of the creation of the Tribunal, Messrs. Vance and Owen stated that the situation on the ground was not acceptable. Since February, of course, that situation has not improved; quite the contrary. It is important here to underline this, because our decision tonight, and indeed the tribunal itself, does have a context. The Co-Chairmen set it explicitly within the peacemaking process. Implementation of that process and the work of the Tribunal must mutually reinforce one another.

We must remember, however, that the Tribunal is a court. Its task is to apply independently and impartially the rules of customary international law and, we believe, conventional law applicable in the territory of the former Yugoslavia. The Tribunal must be left to carry out its work until it has discharged its mandate under its Statute or until the Council decides that its work shall be brought to an end.

Mr. MARUYAMA (Japan): I do not believe it is necessary to elaborate on the appalling situation in the former Yugoslavia. The violations of international humanitarian law in the region are extraordinary in their scope, gravity and persistence. The humanitarian implications are enormous, not only for the present generation but also for generations to come.

The magnitude of the crisis is clearly demonstrated in unanimously adopted resolution 808 (1993), which declared the situation to be a threat to international peace and security. Its particular circumstances indeed demand exceptional measures and have motivated the Security Council to take action under Chapter VII of the United Nations Charter.

Japan is fully aware of the extraordinary and complex nature of the effort to establish an ad hoc Tribunal. It is incumbent upon us to ensure that the Tribunal is independent and neutral and that it reflects the universal authority of the United Nations. We are also required to work out a sound legal basis for the establishment and functioning of the Tribunal, and to seek adequate resources. This should be accomplished without delay, with a view to enabling the international community to respond to the tragic humanitarian situation very quickly and in the cause of justice.

Prompted by the imminent danger and accommodating a number of difficult issues, the Secretary-General has provided us with an excellent report which strikes a proper balance among a variety of factors, particularly between political and legal demands. Japan believes that his report has enabled us to take an immediate decision and deserves our sincere appreciation.

Perhaps more extensive legal studies could have been undertaken on various aspects of the Statute, such as the question of the principle of _nullum crimen sine lege_ and on measures to establish a bridge with domestic legal systems. In this connection, Japan has kept in close consultation with the President as well as with the Secretariat. At the same time, Japan fully shares the determination of the international community, which calls for the exhaustion of all possible measures, including the expeditious establishment of the Tribunal, to put an end to the ongoing atrocities in the former Yugoslavia and restore justice. This is the reason why Japan supported the adoption of the resolution and why it intends to cooperate in its implementation to the best of its ability, in accordance with the spirit of internationally established principles on criminal matters and within our Constitution.

The Statute of the International Tribunal itself reflects the way of thinking of the Security Council. First, it is obvious that the commencement of activities by the Tribunal in no way relieves the parties concerned of their obligation to enforce international humanitarian law.

Secondly, it is equally obvious that such legal remedies in no way relieve the Security Council of its enormous responsibility to address the Yugoslav crisis in its entirety.

Thirdly, cooperation and assistance on the part of the States concerned is essential to guarantee the smooth functioning of the Tribunal. If there is any politically misguided effort to block such cooperation, our exercise could be seriously hampered. All States must exhaust all means to cooperate in good faith. Japan stands ready to implement the common spirit of the international community and make the best use of the relevant laws and regulations in extending its maximum possible cooperation.

The Security Council is obliged to take the exceptional measures it is taking today. Yet it cannot be argued that these measures lie outside the Council's jurisdiction, for the very complexity of the threat and the gravity of the crisis have made the Council's action inevitable. On the contrary, it may be argued that, without a comprehensive strategy on the part of the international community, the complex situation in the former Yugoslavia cannot be properly addressed. We must respond to this formidable problem immediately.

Mr. SNOUSSI (Morocco) (interpretation from French): I wish at the outset to congratulate you, Sir, on the very effective way in which you have performed the duties of President this month.

Nor can I fail to say how much we appreciated the presidency of Ambassador Marker of Pakistan, which was marked by great skill and wisdom.

It gives me pleasure also to pay a well-deserved tribute to the Secretary-General for his remarkable report, which enabled us to prepare the resolution adopted this evening.

The resolution we have just adopted will certainly breathe new life into the Council's daily efforts in a tragic situation where the prospects for a just and final solution are, unfortunately, not encouraging. Despite all our resolutions, despite the positions we have taken on these grave violations, the Bosnian Serbs have not responded to the urgent appeals of the Security Council. On the contrary, they have persisted in their defiance of the international community.

Thus, no one can doubt that the urgent establishment of this International Tribunal marks a turning-point in this tragedy. Yet, however important it may be, this special measure can be fully effective only within the context of overall action by the Council to settle this terrible conflict and restore international peace and security in the region. That is why it has always been our view that an international tribunal must be but one element of a plan, based on the principles of the United Nations Charter, to put an end to Serb aggression, to demand the return of territory acquired by force and "ethnic cleansing" and fully to restore the territorial integrity, unity and sovereignty of Bosnia and Herzegovina.

We are convinced that the International Tribunal will promote the justice to which we all aspire and will strengthen the rule of law in international relations. The tribunal must seek to punish serious violations of humanitarian law in the broadest sense as crimes against international peace and security. No guilty party will be spared the punishment commensurate with the seriousness of the crime. By virtue of the rule of universal jurisdiction, national courts will also have a role to play with respect to crimes beyond the purview of the International Tribunal. The legitimacy and legality of the Tribunal should not be questioned; the Tribunal should hand down deterrent sentences both for those who commit crimes and for their accomplices, and should not ignore appropriate compensation for victims and their families. Nor should the International Tribunal's sentences ignore the responsibility of States for breaches of international law attributable to them.

Yet we must recall that the effectiveness and credibility of the Tribunal, which must be independent and neutral, will depend on the political, legal, financial and technical support of the international community. All States have the obligation to cooperate with and support the Tribunal so it can carry out its mandate to the satisfaction of the victims and their families.

In conclusion, my delegation hopes sincerely that the establishment of this International Tribunal will restore hope to the civilian populations and, especially, restore its trust in the international community, whose moral norms and laws have been flouted for too long.

The PRESIDENT (interpretation from Russian): I thank the representative of Morocco for the kind words he addressed to me and to my predecessor.

Mr. BARBOSA (Cape Verde) (interpretation from French): The grave violations of international humanitarian law committed every day in the territory of the former Yugoslavia, in particular in Bosnia and Herzegovina, shock the conscience of mankind. In this Council, my country has repeatedly expressed its profound indignation and its condemnation of these acts of massive torture, murder and rape, and of the abominable practice of "ethnic cleansing", all of which have been confirmed by the Commission of Experts established pursuant to the relevant provisions of resolution 780 (1992) and by the Special Rapporteur of the Commission on Human Rights.

Thus, we strongly favoured the Council's adoption of its resolution 808 (1993), since which the situation in Bosnia and Herzegovina has dangerously deteriorated, jeopardizing efforts to implement a peace plan for that country. This situation is no longer tolerable, and it justifies the adoption of this evening's resolution. My delegation was an active participant in the process leading to its adoption, and hence voted in favour of it.

The sense that its adoption was important and urgent must not make us lose our orientation and forget the Council's weighty responsibilities under the Charter of the United Nations. We believe that the establishment of the International Tribunal, which begins today, however important it may be, must be but the first step in a long and complex process. First of all, we must overcome all the difficulties and obstacles that will certainly appear as we seek to establish the Tribunal, starting with financial problems that do not appear easily resolved.

Moreover, my delegation considers that the establishment of the Tribunal will be a positive step only if it is viewed as closely connected to a suitably comprehensive peace plan capable of preserving international peace and security throughout the territory of the Socialist Federal Republic of Yugoslavia. Needless to say, this will be impossible unless an end is put to the aggression against the Republic of Bosnia and Herzegovina, unless the freedom of its people is fully achieved, and unless its sovereignty and territorial integrity are respected.

As we see it, the establishment of this Tribunal to judge and punish war crimes is an instrument for the promotion of international peace and security. That was the basis of the Council's recourse to this procedure to establish it. We therefore hope that approval of this step will encourage us to act in our search for effective solutions to the problems that we confront in that part of Europe, in keeping with the peace plan regarded by all members of the Council as the only realistic framework for providing a solution giving lasting peace for the territory of the former Yugoslavia.

Before I conclude, I am happy to convey to the Secretary-General, Mr. Boutros Boutros-Ghali, and to the Secretariat team headed by Mr. Fleischhauer, the high commendation of the Government of Cape Verde for the outstanding work they have done in such a short time. We also salute all the countries that have made important contributions to the concept of the Tribunal, beginning with France, as well as international and intergovernmental bodies.

Mr. MARKER: (Pakistan) Together with the other members of the Organization of the Islamic Conference, Pakistan has consistently and strongly advocated the early establishment of a special tribunal for the prosecution of persons responsible for serious violations of international humanitarian law committed in the territory of the former Yugoslavia since 1991. My delegation is therefore pleased with the adoption of resolution 827 (1993) by the Council.

In this connection, my delegation wishes to express its sincere appreciation and thanks for the excellent report of the Secretary-General, together with the Statute of the International Tribunal, contained in document S/25704, which we regard as a document of historic proportions and a landmark in the process of the implementation of human rights and humanitarian law.

We believe that "ethnic cleansing", genocide and other heinous crimes have been committed in the Republic of Bosnia and Herzegovina, in flagrant violation of international humanitarian law, with the specific objective of acquiring territory and as a deliberate campaign to exterminate the Republic of Bosnia and Herzegovina, a sovereign State Member of the United Nations. We trust that the establishment of an international tribunal and the prosecution of persons responsible for crimes against humanity and international humanitarian law will contribute to ensuring that such crimes are halted and that territories forcefully occupied as a result of such crimes are vacated by the aggressors. This will also contribute towards the full restoration of the unity, territorial integrity and sovereignty of the Republic of Bosnia and Herzegovina.

My delegation is committed to the comprehensive implementation of the peace plan in the Republic of Bosnia and Herzegovina, based on the principles of the United Nations Charter. We believe that the resolution we have just adopted is an important element of the Vance-Owen peace process and falls squarely within its ambit.

The international community must halt the aggression, reverse it through withdrawals from all territories occupied by the use of force and "ethnic cleansing" and restore international legality. The Security Council must move swiftly to take further appropriate and effective enforcement actions in this direction. We cannot accept, even by implication, the status quo imposed by aggression, the use of force and "ethnic cleansing". This would set a most dangerous precedent for the civilized world.

Mr. LI Zhaoxing (China) (interpretation from Chinese): China has consistently opposed crimes that violate international humanitarian law and advocated that criminals in this category should be brought to justice. Bearing in mind the particular circumstances in the former Yugoslavia and the urgency of restoring and maintaining world peace, the Chinese delegation voted in favour of the resolution we have just adopted.

This political position of ours, however, should not be construed as our endorsement of the legal approach involved. We have always held that, to avoid setting any precedent for abusing Chapter VII of the Charter, a prudent attitude should be adopted with regard to the establishment of an international tribunal by means of Security Council resolutions under Chapter VII. It is the consistent position of the Chinese delegation that an international tribunal should be established by concluding a treaty so as to provide a solid legal foundation for it and ensure its effective functioning.

Furthermore, the Statute of the International Tribunal just adopted is a legal instrument with the attributes of an international treaty involving complicated legal and financial questions. It ought to become effective only after having been negotiated and concluded by sovereign States and ratified by their national legislative organs in accordance with domestic laws. Therefore, to adopt by a Security Council resolution the Statute of the International Tribunal which gives the Tribunal both preferential and exclusive jurisdiction is not in compliance with the principle of State judicial sovereignty. The adoption of the Statute of the International Tribunal by the Security Council through a resolution by invoking Chapter VII means that United Nations Member States must implement it to fulfil their obligations provided for in the Charter. This will bring many problems and difficulties both in theory and in practice. For this reason, China has consistently maintained its reservations.

In short, the Chinese delegation emphasizes that the International Tribunal established in the current manner can only be an ad hoc arrangement suited only to the special circumstances of the former Yugoslavia and shall not constitute any precedent.

Mr. SARDENBERG (Brazil): Sometimes exceptionally grave circumstances may demand exceptional action on the part of the United Nations and of Member States. The action taken today by the Security Council on the establishment of an ad hoc international tribunal on war crimes in the former Yugoslavia falls clearly into that category.

The reports of widespread violations of international humanitarian law in the territory of the former Yugoslavia have caused deep shock and outrage in Brazil, as in other countries. The strongest words would not be strong enough to express the depth of our condemnation of the atrocities committed in the context of the armed conflict in that subregion of the European continent.

In the conflict in the former Yugoslavia, the most basic norms of humanity have been systematically trodden underfoot. Innocent civilians, including children, have been the victims of acts of unspeakable brutality, in utter disregard of the protection which, under international law, they are entitled to enjoy in a situation of armed conflict. That has included widespread violence against women of all ages, including a horrifying pattern of sexual assault against Muslim women. Religious persecution and racially motivated crimes have been brought to a new abhorrent level, expressed by the unacceptable phrase "ethnic cleansing".

Such criminal events could not in any way be tolerated by the international community. A cry for justice was voiced by each of the victims of the crimes committed in the conflict in the former Yugoslavia, and that cry has echoed in this Chamber. In resolution 808 (1993), the Security Council had already decided that an international tribunal should be established for the prosecution of persons responsible for serious violations of international humanitarian law.

Brazil examined with great care the proposals for the establishment, by the Security Council itself, of such an international tribunal. In that consideration, we found that such proposals posed intricate and not unimportant legal difficulties, many of which were not resolved to our satisfaction.

Given the legal difficulties involved, which in the normal course of events would have required much more extensive study and deliberation and could have prevented us from supporting the initiative, it was only the consideration of the unique and exceptionally serious circumstances in the former Yugoslavia that determined the vote we cast on the resolution we have just adopted. Our positive vote is to be understood as a political expression of our condemnation of the crimes committed in the former Yugoslavia and of our heartfelt wish to contribute to bringing to justice, with the urgency that is imposed on us by the facts, all persons responsible for such acts. It should not be construed as an overall endorsement of legal formulas involved in the foundation or in the Statute of the International Tribunal.

We would certainly have preferred that an initiative bearing such far-reaching political and legal implications had received a much deeper examination in a context that allowed a broader participation by all States Members of the United Nations. To that end, we believe it would have been appropriate for this matter also to be brought to the attention of the General Assembly.

The views of the Brazilian Government on the main legal issues involved in the establishment and functioning of the Tribunal were expressed in the statement made on the occasion of the adoption of resolution 808 (1993) and in the memorandum submitted by Brazil and circulated in connection with that resolution in document S/25540. In particular, Brazil expressed the view that the most appropriate and effective method for establishing the International Tribunal would be the conclusion of a convention setting up an ad hoc international criminal jurisdiction and containing the terms of reference for its exercise.

The option of establishing the Tribunal exclusively through a resolution of the Security Council, which we did not favour, leaves unresolved a number of serious legal issues relating to the powers and competences attributed to the Council by the United Nations Charter. That fact will not and should not limit the effectiveness of the work of the International Tribunal. It does limit, however, in our understanding, the conclusions that could be drawn from the adoption of this resolution as regards the legal and political framework for the work of the Security Council.

It is our view that the resolution is aimed at addressing a specific and unique situation with a view to producing one specific result: bringing to justice the persons responsible for serious violations of international humanitarian law in the former Yugoslavia. Both the resolution and the Statute it adopts are thus not meant to establish new norms or precedents of international law. At any rate, it would not be for the Security Council to do that. The report of the Secretary-General, which is approved by the resolution, makes it clear that by adopting this resolution the Security Council is not creating or purporting to legislate international humanitarian law and that the International Tribunal will have the task of applying existing norms of international humanitarian law.

For the work of the International Tribunal to be effective, it will be essential that it receive the fullest cooperation of all States. That is a clear obligation resulting from the resolution adopted today. For its part, the Brazilian Government is determined, should the need arise, to cooperate fully with the International Tribunal in strict accordance with the relevant Brazilian legislation, which includes the observance of the constitutional competence of the Brazilian Supreme Court to process and judge requests for extradition.

Mr. YAÑEZ BARNUEVO (Spain) (interpretation from Spanish): Resolution 827 (1993), which the Council has just adopted, is the logical consequence of resolution 808 (1993), adopted last February. On that occasion, the Council decided to establish an international tribunal to bring to trial those charged with serious violations of international humanitarian law perpetrated since 1991 in the territory of the former Yugoslavia. It also urged the Secretary-General to submit a report containing specific proposals for the implementation of that decision. The Secretary-General, with the efficient assistance of the Legal Counsel, has completed that task and submitted an excellent report. On that basis, the Council is now proceeding to establish the Tribunal. Spain has already expressed its support in principle for the establishment of the International Tribunal and has now confirmed its support for that establishment in co-sponsoring and voting in favour of resolution 827 (1993).

The Secretary-General's report and the Statute of the Tribunal that it contains in its annex respond to a great extent to the concerns of the Spanish Government in this area as expressed in the comments and suggestions which it transmitted to the Secretary-General pursuant to the provisions of resolution 808 (1993). Naturally, the Statute can be improved upon and we might have benefited from certain particular improvements, especially in determining the substantive subject matter and temporal jurisdiction of the Tribunal and the characterization of crimes and penalties. Nevertheless, we have preferred to retain the form proposed by the Secretary-General in its entirety for several reasons.

First, certain clarifications can be found by reading the Statute in the light of the explanations provided in the Secretary-General's report with respect to each Article. Other clarifications can be contributed by the Tribunal itself when it drafts its rules of procedure and begins carrying out its judicial activities, which will consist in applying abstract rules to concrete cases, thus spelling out their content. Finally, and most importantly, the goal of restoring peace in the territory of the former Yugoslavia requires prompt action, which might have been compromised through a prolonged and detailed discussion of a Statute which satisfies the fundamental prerequisites for ensuring the achievement of that goal.

Indeed, although the Statute lacks express provisions in this respect, the Tribunal does appear as a clearly independent organ. This derives both from the qualifications required of its members and from the procedure for their selection, which includes the participation of the Security Council and the General Assembly. It derives above all from the autonomy of its machinery, which is not subject to any external review. In this connection, we should recall that this independence is not at all incompatible with its formal character as a subsidiary organ of the Council, as is borne out by the jurisprudence of the International Court of Justice with respect to the United Nations Administrative Tribunal and its relations with the General Assembly.

Secondly, we have here an impartial body governed by the law itself in fulfilling its duties. Its jurisdiction encompasses all of the territory of the former Yugoslavia and actions by all parties involved in the conflict or conflicts in that area. Moreover, its activity is governed by the general principles of law, in particular respect for the guarantees of due process and the rights of the accused. We should especially emphasize that the Statute rules out any trial of the accused in absentia or the imposition of the death penalty.

Thirdly, we are creating a body that we wish to be effective. To that end, it is indispensable to impose upon States an obligation to cooperate with the Tribunal that is based upon Chapter VII of the Charter. That obligation implies the duty to promulgate any domestic legal measures that may be necessary. A particularly important feature of this obligation is the primacy accorded the International Tribunal over national courts.

Lastly, the resolution creates an ad hoc body with a jurisdiction limited not only geographically and temporally but also materially, in that it will be circumscribed to applying the international law in force. In fact, with the establishment of the Tribunal, we are not seeking not to create new international law or to change existing law but to guarantee effectively respect for that law.

In the final analysis, the Council, by adopting resolution 827 (1993) is seeking to make a reality of the determination contained in the preamble of the Charter to reaffirm faith in fundamental human rights, in the dignity and worth of the human person, and indeed to establish conditions for the maintenance of justice and respect for international law in so tragic a situation as that unfortunately still being experienced by the peoples of the former Yugoslavia.

It is our hope that this crucial step that was taken today by the Council will also serve to encourage the speedy completion in the General Assembly of the work leading to the establishment of an international criminal tribunal of a permanent kind and with universal jurisdiction, the need for which is becoming increasingly imperative, as demonstrated by the conflicts not only in the former Yugoslavia but also in similar situations elsewhere that also call for justice to be done by the international community.

Mr. OLHAYE (Djibouti) (interpretation from French): Resolution 827 (1993), which we have just adopted following the report of the Secretary-General, to whom we pay a tribute, is a new measure taken by the Council to judge those charged with serious violations of international humanitarian law committed on the territory of the former Yugoslavia since 1991, in particular in the Republic of Bosnia and Herzegovina.

Since the Serbian forces in Bosnia, supported by the Belgrade Government, started the war in the Republic of Bosnia and Herzegovina, they have, faithful to animal instincts, never stopped carrying out their insane policy of dismantling a sovereign, independent State and of wiping from the face of the Earth all that was Bosnia.

Those forces, which have death squad commandos operating in their midst who are quite rightly being called war criminals, have been hired and paid by former Bosnian Serb political chiefs such as Karadzic and his ilk, who are thirsty for blood and for absolute power. This is why it is not appropriate to lump the whole thing together and call it a civil war in Bosnia and Herzegovina.

The concentration camps, the mass expulsion and deportation of civilians, the raping of women - in short, the "ethnic cleansing" practiced by the Serbs in Bosnia most particularly - are not only an insult to humanity but, unfortunately, a yet unanswered challenge to the international community.

The resolution just adopted by the Council is just one measure among so many others that we hope will be taken in the days to come. Let us, I beg, not lose sight of the fact that bringing the guilty to justice, whatever their ethnic origin, and compensating the victims must be considered as two factors that are indissolubly linked and are the ultimate goal of the resolution.

The right of a people to territorial integrity is sacred, the more so because the Bosnian pluralism is deeply rooted in Bosnian soil: it cannot be shifted and cannot, either in the south or in the north, in the east or in the west, suffer any amputation.

That country will have its peace and its unity restored once the guns have been silenced, the militias have been dissolved, the causes of the conflict have been rooted out, the barriers between the regions have fallen, when all the refugees have gone back to their homes and, lastly, when all citizens have rallied round their State, the Republic of Bosnia and Herzegovina.

The PRESIDENT (interpretation from Russian): I shall now make a statement in my capacity as representative of the Russian Federation.

First of all, I should like to express my gratitude to the Secretary-General and to his colleagues in the Secretariat, in particular Mr. Fleischhauer, for his well-prepared report that includes the Statute of the International Tribunal.

The Russian Federation not only supported but in fact co-sponsored the draft resolution that establishes the International Tribunal to prosecute those responsible for serious violations of international humanitarian law committed on the territory of the former Yugoslavia since the beginning of 1991.

Today the need for this decision has become quite self-evident to us all. This has also been shown by the fact that the need for the Tribunal to be set up quickly was noted in the joint action programme adopted on 22 May by the Ministers for Foreign Affairs of the United States, Britain, France, Spain and Russia. Those guilty of mass crimes covered by the 1949 Geneva Protocols, violations of the laws and customs of war, crimes of genocide and crimes against humanity must be duly punished.

It is of particular importance that for the first time in history, it is not the victors who are judging the vanquished, but the entire international community that, through the Tribunal, will be passing sentence on those who are grossly violating not only the norms of international law but even quite simply our human concepts of morality and humanity.

We favour the establishment of the International Tribunal because we see in it not a place for summary justice, nor a place for settling scores or for seeking vengeance, but an instrument of justice which is called upon to restore international legality and the faith of the world community in the triumph of justice and reason. That is why, today, while the flames of war continue to rage in the territory of the former Yugoslavia, where already tens of thousands of lives have been taken, the Security Council, as the principal organ of the United Nations responsible for the maintenance of international peace and security, assumed, in accordance with the Charter of the United Nations, the responsibility for implementing the appropriate specific measures, which include the establishment of the International Tribunal.

In taking this decision to establish the International Tribunal, we are simultaneously approving its Statute, which determines the sphere of competence of that body, the form it work will take and the methods it will use, the rules governing its composition and so on. In this connection, my delegation is authorized to state the following.

While believing that the text of the Statute addresses the tasks that face the Tribunal, and for that reason supporting it, we deem it appropriate to note that, according to our understanding, Article 5 of the Statute encompasses criminal acts committed on the territory of the former Yugoslavia during an armed conflict - acts which were widespread or systematic, were aimed against the civilian population and were motivated by that population's national, political, ethnic, religious or other affiliation.

While supporting the establishment of this organ of international criminal justice for the punishment of persons guilty of having committed serious violations of international humanitarian law on the territory of the former Yugoslavia, we also believe that this body will not abolish nor replace national justice organs.

As we understand it, the provisions of Article 9, paragraph 2, denote the duty of a State to give very serious consideration to a request by the Tribunal to refer to it a case that is being considered in a national court. But this is not a duty automatically to refer the proceedings to the Tribunal on such a matter. A refusal to refer the case naturally has to be justified. We take it that this provision will be reflected in the rules of procedure and the rules of evidence of the Tribunal.

The establishment of the International Tribunal, apart from the great juridical meaning of this step, is also an extremely important political act taken by the international community which at the same time fulfils a preventive function and also promotes the restoration of peace in the region.

I now resume my functions as President of the Security Council.

There are no further speakers inscribed on my list. The Security Council has thus concluded the present stage of its consideration of the item on its agenda.

The Security Council will remain seized of the matter.

PART VII*

PROPOSALS OF STATES AND ORGANIZATIONS FOR THE STATUTE OF THE INTERNATIONAL TRIBUNAL

*(Some States submitted informal proposals which were not issued as public documents and are not, therefore, reproduced in this volume. This also applies to the proposals submitted by States concerning the Rules.)

A. PROPOSAL FOR AN INTERNATIONAL WAR CRIMES TRIBUNAL FOR THE FORMER YUGOSLAVIA

By Rapporteurs (Corell–Türk–Thune) under the CSCE Moscow Human Dimension Mechanism to Bosnia-Herzegovina and Croatia

9 February 1993.*

Table of Contents

* Some portions of this Document have been omitted. The table of contents and a summary of this proposal were circulated as U.N. Doc. S/25307 dated 18 February 1993.

SUMMARY

On 28 September 1992 the Rapporteurs (Corell-Türk-Thune) under the CSCE Moscow Human Dimension Mechanism to Bosnia-Herzegovina and Croatia were given the mandate i.a. "to investigate reports of atrocities against unarmed civilians in Croatia and Bosnia, and to make recommendations as to the feasibility of attributing responsibility for such acts".

The Rapporteurs visited Croatia during the period of 30 September - 5 October 1992. On 7 October 1992 they issued a report on this visit. One of the proposals contained in this report was that a Committee of Experts from interested States should be convened as soon as possible in order to prepare a draft treaty establishing an international _ad hoc_ tribunal for certain crimes committed in the former Yugoslavia.

In view of the fact that the Rapporteurs had been unable to visit Bosnia-Herzegovina, on 24 November 1992 they offered to make an interim report on that State, analyzing the relevant penal law, and to draft a convention establishing an international _ad hoc_ tribunal to deal with war crimes and crimes against humanity committed in the former Yugoslavia. In a decision on 15 December 1992, the CSCE Council welcomed the offer of the Rapporteurs to refine their proposals on making the principle of personal accountability effective, including the possibility of the establishment of an _ad hoc_ tribunal. The CSCE Council foresaw continuing consultations in the matter with the Commission of Experts established pursuant to Security Council Resolution 780 (1992).

Having studied the question further and after consultations with the UN Expert Commission and contacts with i.a. representatives for the Rapporteur on the former Yugoslavia under the United Nations Commission on Human Rights, the International Conference on the former Yugoslavia and the Minister for Foreign Affairs of Bosnia-Herzegovina, the Rapporteurs decided to draw up the present report in spite of the fact that they were not able to visit Bosnia-Herzegovina.

* N.B. to the draft Convention.

The main part of the report consists of a proposal for an International War Crimes Tribunal for the former Yugoslavia. The purpose of this Tribunal is to try individuals accused of war crimes and crimes against humanity as defined in international law and the domestic criminal law provisions of the former Yugoslavia and determined in scope by the proposed Convention.

The law to be applied by the Tribunal consists of a number of provisions from the Penal Code of the Former Socialist Federative Republic of Yugoslavia. This law is still in force in the territory of the former Yugoslavia, either directly, or, as in the case of Bosnia-Herzegovina and Croatia, through reference with or without modifications. In accordance with the proposal, the Tribunal will have jurisdiction over war crimes and crimes against humanity, as specified in the Convention, committed in the territory of the former Yugoslavia as from 1 January 1991.

The main features of the Tribunal are as follows.

The Tribunal consists of five bodies: the Court, the Procuracy, the Secretariat, the Board on Clemency and the Standing Committee.

The responsibility for the administration of the Tribunal rests with the Standing Committee which consists of representatives of States parties to the Convention. The Court has two instances to meet current obligations under international law concerning the right of appeal. The task of the first instance is to adjudicate cases in Chambers composed of three judges. The Court of Appeal shall adjudicate cases appealed from the first instance and shall sit in Chambers composed of five judges. The task of the Plenary Court is to decide mainly on administrative matters. The Procuracy is independent in relation to the Court. It is obliged to indict the accused, if the findings in the criminal inquiry indicate that the case is reasonably founded in fact and law. The task of the Secretariat is to serve the Tribunal with a particular responsibility for the Court.

The jurisdiction of the Tribunal is exclusive and compulsory in relation to States parties to the Convention in the territory of the former Yugoslavia. However, the draft Convention provides for the transfer of jurisdiction back to those States when they have the appropriate means to adjudicate effectively and fairly cases falling under the jurisdiction of the Tribunal.

The Court is competent to impose deprivation of liberty and fines. It may not pass sentence of capital punishment. Sentences are to be served in the territory of the former Yugoslavia under international supervision.

The draft Convention provides that victims can participate in the criminal proceedings. There is also a limited possibility for victims to claim restitution of property and compensation.

The text of the draft Convention should be supplemented by Rules of the Tribunal, to be drawn up by the Plenary Court. These rules will i.a. provide for legal aid and defence counsel.

The costs of the Tribunal are to be distributed among the States parties to the Convention. However, the costs for the enforcement of judgments will rest with the State responsible for execution.

The report does not take a stand on the question in which forum the Convention should be negotiated. However, the draft is designed in order to facilitate action by the CSCE participating States or some of these States within the framework of the CSCE or any other appropriate framework.

The main conclusions of the Rapporteurs are:

* In view of the urgency of the situation in certain areas of the territory of the former Yugoslavia the adjudication of cases concerning war crimes and crimes agains humanity should dealt with by an ad hoc Tribunal (Section 8.1).

* The Rapporteurs advise strongly against waiting for the work done on the project for the elaboration of a draft statute for an international criminal court entrusted to the International Law Commission (Section 8.1).

* National law, interpreted in the light of the international commitments which underlie this legislation, forms a sufficient basis for adjudication (Section 8.2).

* A general and well-structured method of information collection with a view to assisting prosecutors must be implemented <u>as soon as possible</u> (Section 8.3).

* The costs for a Tribunal of the kind foreseen by the Rapporteurs will be marginal in comparison to the amounts spent on various other efforts necessary for the restauration of peace in the area (Section 8.10).

* It is not only desirable but also feasible from a legal point of view to establish an international war crimes Tribunal for the former Yugoslavia. In view of this conclusion, the establishment of such a Tribunal is primarily a question of political will (Section 10).

1 INTRODUCTION

The following is a report of the Rapporteurs (Corell-Türk-Thune) under the CSCE Moscow Human Dimension Mechanism mission to Bosnia-Herzegovina and Croatia, drawn up in response to their mandate and to a decision by the CSCE Council on 15 December 1992.

The report contains a description of the background to the Rapporteur mission (Section 2) and some general reflections on the mandate of the mission and the publication of the present report (Section 3). Subsequently, the Rapporteurs make some observations on the situation in Bosnia-Herzegovina (Section 4). They then go on to describe relevant legislation in Bosnia-Herzegovina, the corresponding information on Croatia appearing in their report on this country, issued on 7 October 1992 (Section 5). They then proceed to discuss questions of principle in relation to the prospect of attributing responsibility (Section 6) and to deliberate on a competent jurisdiction (Section 7).

The main part of the report contains a proposal for an International War Crimes Tribunal for the Former Yugoslavia. The proposal consists of a general part, a draft Convention and a Commentary on the proposed articles (Section 8 and Annexes 6 - 8).

Acknowledgements and a few concluding remarks appear at the end of the report (Sections 9 and 10). There are eight annexes to the report.

The Rapporteurs wish to emphasize that the subject matter is of a complex nature and that they have had limited time at their disposal. They also wish to draw the attention to the fact that according to the rules a rapporteur mission is a mission of short duration; its report should be produced three weeks after the last rapporteur has been appointed, or, they presume, after their mandate has been finalized if this occurs at a later date. In the present case, conditions have been somewhat different, particularly after the decision by the CSCE Council on 15 December 1992 (cf. Section 2.4).

Nonetheless, the Rapporteurs consider it necessary to strike a balance between their ambitions and the urgency of the question; no matter how much time they spent on drafting a proposal, this proposal would still have to be subjected to a very close scrutiny and, finally, if the suggested course of action was to be followed, to deliberations at a diplomatic conference.

The Rapporteurs have attempted to deal with the complex materia in as limited space as possible. On the other hand, they have also tried to elaborate a fairly complete proposal. To increase legibility they have avoided using too many legal concepts and have tried to explain the meaning of those which have been used. Furthermore, they have not included references and the multitude of foot-notes that usually accompany a document of the present nature. They hope that their proposal will be of service for future decisions taken by the CSCE participating States.

This report represents the unanimous opinion of the Rapporteurs. The Commentary on the draft Convention was exclusively elaborated by Ambassador Corell, who had also prepared the basic draft for the statute of the Tribunal.

2 BACKGROUND

2.1 Formation of the Rapporteur Mission

On 5 August 1992 the United Kingdom informed the Office for Democratic Institutions and Human Rights (ODIHR) in Warsaw that the United Kingdom, with the support of Italy, Portugal, Denmark, the United States, Greece, Spain, the Netherlands, Ireland and Germany, had decided to invoke the Moscow Human Dimension Mechanism with respect to Bosnia-Herzegovina and Croatia. Subsequently, ODIHR was informed that France and Belgium had also joined the supporting States.

The rules of the Moscow Human Dimension Mechanism are laid down in the Document of the Moscow Meeting of the Conference on the Human Dimension of the CSCE. The relevant provisions appear as Annex 1 to this report. The United Kingdom had invoked Paragraph 12 of the Document which allows for engaging this mechanism in case a participating State considers that a particularly serious threat to the fulfilment of the provisions of the CSCE human dimension has arisen in another participating State.

On 19 August 1992 the ODIHR was informed that the United Kingdom had appointed Ambassador Hans Corell, Under-Secretary for Legal and Consular Affairs, Ministry for Foreign Affairs of Sweden, as Rapporteur.

On 29 August 1992 the ODIHR informed the United Kingdom that the Republic of Bosnia-Herzegovina and the Republic of Croatia had appointed as Rapporteur for the mission to their respective countries Ambassador Helmut Türk, Deputy Secretary-General and Legal Advisor of the Federal Ministry for Foreign Affairs of Austria.

On 4 September 1992 Ambassador Corell and Ambassador Türk informed the ODIHR that they had on that day appointed Mrs. Gro Hillestad Thune, member of the European Commission of Human Rights, from Norway, as the third Rapporteur for the mission to Bosnia-Herzegovina and to Croatia.

Consequently, the Moscow Human Dimension Mechanism in the present case was established and ready to enter into function on 4 September 1992. The participants in the Rapporteur Mission for the preparation of this report appear in Annex 2.

2.2 The mandate

Originally, the mandate for this Rapporteur Mission was to enable investigation of reports of attacks on unarmed civilians in Bosnia-Herzegovina, especially in Sarajevo and Gorazde, and in Croatia.

Due to circumstances which prevailed after the initiation of the Mission, the mandate was further discussed among the initiators. On 28 September 1992 the mandate of the Mission was finalized. The Rapporteurs were informed through the Foreign and Commonwealth Office of the following mandate:

> "To investigate reports of atrocities against unarmed civilians in Croatia and Bosnia, and to make recommendations as to the feasibility of attributing responsibility for such acts.
>
> The additional mandate, depending on how much can be accomplished in the time available and in the light of any organisational difficulties which may arrive, is to visit areas which may be under threat of ethnic cleansing, and to investigate allegations of the arbitrary arrests of Serbs in Croatia."

Due to the time which had lapsed since the original contact with the Rapporteurs, in particular since Ambassador Corell was first approached, they had difficulties in performing their task as a whole immediately. Furthermore, the United Kingdom informed the Rapporteurs that the Foreign and Commonwealth Office would need some time to prepare a visit to Bosnia-Herzegovina in view of the security situation. In consultation between the United Kingdom, the ODIHR, and the Rapporteurs it was decided that the Rapporteur Mission should perform its task in two steps. It was thus decided that they should first visit Croatia, commencing on 30 September 1992, i.e. two days after the mandate was finalized. The visit to Bosnia-Herzegovina was contemplated for mid-November 1992.

2.3 The report on Croatia

The Rapporteurs visited Croatia on 30 September - 5 October 1992. On 7 October 1992 they issued their report. For the purpose of the present report it may suffice to quote the following from the summary:

> "There are numerous reports regarding atrocities perpetrated against unarmed civilians as well as the practice of "ethnic cleansing" in territory of the Republic of Croatia. Although

> responsibility for these grave violations of human rights and the norms of international humanitarian law is to be attributed to both parties to the conflict, it appears that the scale and gravity of the crimes committed by the Yugoslav National Army, Serbian paramilitary groups and the police forces of the Knin authorities are by far the most serious. On the Serbian side, such violations of generally accepted international norms seem to form part of an officially tolerated or even supported systematic policy.
>
> Besides the fact-finding elements of their mission the Rapporteurs saw their main task to be investigation of the possibilities of attributing responsibility for acts of atrocities against unarmed civilians. In this connection, they examined the relevant national legislation and the administration of justice in Croatia as well as pertinent international legal instruments. On the basis of this examination, the Rapporteurs conclude that there is a sufficient legal basis for international prosecution."

In connection with this part of their mandate the Rapporteurs made the following two proposals.

First: A committee of experts should be convened immediately to examine the possibility of establishing a system for the administration of collected information. The mandate of the committee should be to propose within a very short time the necessary rules as well as the administrative and technical solutions for the collection of information, and to make an estimate of costs.

Second: Since there is a viable possibility for establishing an international jurisdiction to deal with the alleged war crimes and crimes against humanity committed in the former Yugoslavia, a committee of experts from interested States should be convened as soon as possible in order to prepare a draft treaty establishing an international ad hoc tribunal for certain crimes committed in the former Yugoslavia. The committee should also make an estimate of costs for such a jurisdiction.

The Rapporteurs note that no genuine action was taken regarding their recommendations.

2.4 Relevant decisions by the CSCE Council and the CSO

The report on Croatia was examined by the Committee of Senior Officials (CSO) at their meeting in Prague on 5 and 6 November 1992. On 6 November the CSO took a decision on the report. The decision contains i.a. the following:

> "Decides that the mission of the Rapporteurs Ambassador Corell, Ambassador Türk and Mrs. Thune, should be completed as soon as it is possible, bearing in mind the need to assure the safety of the Rapporteurs;
>
> Asks the Chairman-in-Office to release the report to the public and to transmit it to the Committee of Experts drawn up by UNSCR 780;
>
> Welcomed the report's recommendations and invited the Rapporteurs to report on their findings to the appropriate UN bodies.
>
> The CSO asks the Chairman-in-Office to draw the attention of the UN Secretary-General to the report's recommendation and particularly to the urgency of its implementation within the appropriate international framework. The UN Commission of Experts should give particular attention to the principle of personal responsibility for war crimes and examine how this principle could be put into practice by an ad hoc tribunal.
>
> Endorses the urgency of the exhumation of mass graves in UNPA Sector East and strongly calls on the Belgrade authorities to fully co-operate in providing conditions for the safe exhumation of the mass graves in the UNPA Sector East of Croatia. Having noted also the activities and resources of UN Special Rapporteur Mazowiecki in this respect, the CSO considered that the recommendation should be referred to the Special Rapporteur and the SCR 780 Commission of Experts, via the UN Secretary General, for follow-up action."

In view of the fact that it was difficult to organize a visit to Bosnia-Herzegovina and the increasing demand that suspected war criminals should be brought to justice, the Rapporteurs communicated on 24 November 1992 the following message to the Government of the United Kingdom with reference to the decision by the CSO:

> "The Rapporteurs would in this context like to mention that Ambassador Corell was asked to attend a meeting of the UN Commission of Experts on 5 November. At this meeting the chairman of the Commission expressed the opinion that it was not for the Commission to study the question of an ad hoc tribunal. Neither was it their task to set up a more structured system for collection of information in line with the proposal made by the Rapporteurs.
>
> In the meantime the Rapporteurs were informed that it could take some time before they could go to Bosnia-Herzegovina, since UNPROFOR was not in a position to guarantee their safety. The request yesterday about our preparedness to visit Bosnia-Herzegovina in the near future therefore came

somewhat unexpected. Naturally, we are prepared to visit Bosnia-Herzegovina if reasonable guarantees for our safety could be given. But we must also agree on the mandate. This is not clear to us, although we assume that it would be the same as for Croatia mutatis mutandis.

As the matter now stands we would like to make the following proposal.

The fact that war crimes and crimes against humanity are committed in Bosnia-Herzegovina is obvious. This appears from various sources of information, i.a. the reports of the mission of Sir John Thomson and the special rapporteur of the United Nations Commission on Human Rights, Mr Tadeusz Mazowiecki.

As can be seen from the Report on their visit to Croatia the Rapporteurs paid special attention to the part of their mandate which concerned the attribution of personal responsibility.

It seems quite clear that the UN Commission of Experts has no mandate to make proposals for an ad hoc tribunal. Since a number of declarations to the effect that those who have committed war crimes should be brought to justice (i.a. by the EC Ministers of Foreign Affairs on 5 October and by the CSO on 7 November) the Rapporteurs think that, for the moment, the best manner to carry on their mandate would be:

1) to make an interim report on Bosnia-Herzegovina, analyzing the relevant penal law, and

2) to draft a convention establishing an international ad hoc tribunal to deal with war crimes and crimes against against humanity committed in the former Yugoslavia.

This work could be carried out promptly and would not presuppose a visit to Bosnia-Herzegovina. It would, however, presuppose a mandate given by the States concerned. The Rapporteurs would appreciate a reaction to their proposal as soon as possible, not least due to the fact that Ambassador Türk is taking up his post as Austria's Ambassador to the United States on 28 January 1993."

The matter was subsequently discussed among the States which had invoked the Moscow Mechanism and within the CSO. It was further deliberated at the meeting of the CSCE Council in Stockholm on 14 and 15 December 1992. In its decision on the former Yugoslavia on 15 December the CSCE Council included the following language (paragraph 14):

"The Ministers welcomed the offer of the rapporteurs on Croatia and Bosnia-Herzegovina under the Moscow Human Dimension Mechanism to refine their proposals on making the principle of personal accountability effective including the possibility of the establishment of an ad hoc tribunal, and to do so through continuing

> consultations with the Commission of Experts established pursuant to Security Council resolution 780 (1992)."

2.5 Co-ordination with other missions and other contacts

Before their visit to Croatia the Rapporteurs had contacts with the office of the Special Rapporteur appointed by the United Nations Commission on Human Rights, former Prime Minister Tadeusz Mazowiecki of Poland, and Sir John Thomson, appointed by the CSO to head a Mission to the former Yugoslavia.

On 5 November 1992, Ambassador Corell presented the report on Croatia to the Commission of Experts established pursuant to Security Council Resolution 780 (1992). Following the decision by the CSO on 6 November, and in view of the fact that the UN Commission had scheduled its second meeting for 14 December, Ambassador Corell contacted the Chairman of the Commission, Professor Frits Kalshoven. In a letter to Professor Kalshoven on 10 December Ambassador Corell said on behalf of the Rapporteurs that it would be very helpful if they could receive a message as soon as possible about the outcome of the deliberations of the Commission. In this way the Rapporteurs could inform - in accordance with the CSO-decision - the competent bodies within the CSCE about their contacts with the UN Commission. The Commission was also informed about the CSCE Council meeting on 14 och 15 December 1992.

On 16 December 1992 Ambassador Corell informed Professor Kalshoven about the decision of the CSCE Council of the day before.

In a letter of 18 December 1992, Professor Kalshoven informed the Rapporteurs i.a. as follows:

> "As regards the idea of consultations between your mission and the Commission of Experts on matters relating to the principle of personal accountability for violations of international humanitarian law, including the possibility of the establishment of an _ad hoc_ tribunal, the Commission in its recent session decided that there would be no objections to such consultations, it being understood that as far as the Commission is concerned, this cooperation will have an entirely informal character and will have to remain within the confines of its terms of reference as set out in SC Resolution 780 (1992).

> The Commission decided further to mandate Professor M. Cherif Bassiouni as its representative in these informal consultations."

On 24 January 1993 the Rapporteurs met with three of the members of the UN Commission, namely the Chairman Professor Frits Kalshoven, Professor Cherif Bassiouni and Mr William Fenrick. They further had consultations with Professor Bassiouni on legal and technical issues on 25 January. During their talks the members of the Commission expressed the view that the Commission was not mandated to occupy itself with the question of the establishment of an international criminal court. However, they demonstrated a profound interest in the establishment of such a court, and the Rapporteurs were able to draw on their thinking in this field.

On 25 January 1993 the Rapporteurs met with Dr. Georg Mautner-Markhof and Professor Roman Wieruszewski, advisers to Mr. Tadeusz Mazowiecki, Special Rapporteur of the UN Commission on Human Rights on former Yugoslavia.

During the meeting it was underlined that there is at present an urgent need to co-ordinate the flow of information concerning atrocities committed in the former Yugoslavia. The view was also expressed that an international tribunal which can convict those reasonsible for such acts is highly needed. The Rapporteurs were in this context asked to transmit a copy of the present report to the Special Rapporteur as soon as possible, notably before he is presenting his next report to the Human Right Commission in February. The Rapporteurs said that it was not within their competence to disseminate the report but that they would bring this request to the attention of the appropriate bodies of the CSCE.

With respect to the International Conference on the former Yugoslavia, the Rapporteurs had noted the following part of the opening statement of Mr. Cyrus Vance to the Ministerial Meeting of the Steering Committee of the Conference on 16 December 1992:

> "We have also taken action on allegations of war crimes and other breaches of international humanitarian law. We have sought to help the Commission of Experts bring about a forensic examination of the mass grave site at Ovcara near Vukovar and this is in train this week. Lord Owen and I believe that atrocities committed in

> the former Yugoslavia are unacceptable, and persons guilty of war crimes should be brought to justice. We, therefore, recommend the establishment of an international criminal court."

On 26 January 1993 the Rapporteurs had a meeting with Ambassador Peter Hall, Deputy to Lord Owen, in order to inform the Co-chairmen of the International Conference on the former Yugoslavia about their proposals regarding the establishment of an international tribunal. Ambassador Hall reacted favourably to the idea of establishing such a tribunal and said that the idea undoubtedly had the support of both Co-chairmen. At the same time he stressed that it was important that such an international instance function even-handed without discriminating against any particular group of the population in the former Yugoslavia. Furthermore, he pointed to the importance of precisely targetting the persons who are alleged to have committed war crimes and crimes against humanity.

On 25 January 1993 the Rapporteurs had a meeting with H.E. Haris Silajdzic, Minister for Foreign Affairs of the Republic of Bosnia-Herzegovina, Professor Dr. Muhamed Filipovic, Vice-President of the Academy of Science and Art of the Republic of Bosnia-Herzegovina and Member of the Assembly of the Republic of Bosnia-Herzegovina and Dr. Kasim Trnka, Member of the Constitutional Court of the Republic of Bosnia-Herzegovina.

The Rapporteurs outlined the main elements of their proposal regarding the establishment of an international criminal tribunal to deal with war crimes and crimes against humanity committed in the territory of the former Yugoslavia. Minister Silajdzic stated in this connection that the Government of the Republic of Bosnia-Herzegovina insisted on the establishment, as soon as possible, of such an international tribunal. He shared the view of the Rapporteurs that such an instance should be designed to permit the punishment of any person having committed such crimes, irrespective of that person's nationality or religion.

The Rapporteurs also held an exchange of views with Minister Silajdzic and his colleagues on the actual human rights situation in Bosnia-Herzegovina which was documented by a great number of reports drawn up by various institutions, presenting a vivid picture of the appalling violations of human rights and norms of international humanitarian law. The Bosnian side shared the view of the Rapporteurs that therefore it did not seem necessary to draw up a further report on the human rights situation, i.e. by the Rapporteurs, but rather to take speedy action on the already existing reports.

On 26 January 1993 the Rapporteurs met with the President of the parliament of Bosnia-Herzegovina, Mr. Miro Lazovic.

Mr. Lazovic confirmed that the parliament has not been able to meet since 14 April 1992 when its functions were transferred to the Presidency. Efforts are being made to reassemble its members outside Sarajevo.

Mr. Lazovic expressed his strong conviction that there is an urgent need for an international tribunal in order to prosecute perpetrators of war crimes - regardless of ethnic origin. He saw no legal or formal obstacles to this and told the Rapporteurs that he expected that parliament without any difficulties would ratify a treaty establishing such a tribunal.

Mr. Lazovic, who presented himself as a Serb, stressed the urgency of the matter and held the view that the Government of Bosnia-Herzegovina should insist on the publication of the present report immediately after having been transmitted to the initiating States within the CSCE.

On 29 January 1993 Ambassador Corell met with Dr. Ove Bring of Sir John Thomson's mission. Dr. Bring had returned from a visit to Serbia and was finalizing a report on that visit to be presented to the CSO at their meeting on 2 - 4 February 1993. The report was communicated to the Rapporteurs on 4 February 1993.

The Rapporteurs finally note in this context that the Standing Committee of the CSCE Parliamentary Assembly (comprising the Heads of the national delegations) met in Copenhagen on 13 - 14 January 1993. The resolution adopted by the Committee includes the following language (paragraph 8):

"s t r e s s e s the need to establish international forums, including an international court, under which those responsible for mass rape, torture, murder, imprisonment, and other criminal acts can be held fully accountable for their crimes."

2.6 Relevant documents

There are a great number of reports and documents concerning the situation in the former Yugoslavia. The Rapporteurs have tried to study as many of them as possible. In their report on Croatia they mentioned in particular the following:

- Report of the CSCE Mission to Bosnia-Herzegovina 29 August to 4 September, headed by Sir John Thomson

- Report on the situation of human rights in the territory of the former Yugoslavia submitted by Mr. Tadeusz Mazowiecki, Special Rapporteur of the Commission on Human Rights pursuant to paragraph 14 of Commission resolution 1992/S-1/1 of 14 August 1992 (E/CN. 4/1997/S-1/ 9:28/8-1992)

- Further report of the Secretary-General pursuant to Security Council Resolution 743 (1992) and 762 (1992) of 28 September 1992 (S/24600)

- War Crimes in Bosnia-Herzegovina: A Helsinki Watch Report - August 1992

- Submissions of Information to the United Nations Security Council by the US-Government in accordance with paragraph 5 of Resolution 771 (1992) of 22 September 1992.

At the present juncture the Rapporteurs should like to refer in particular to the following documents:

- The documents enumerated in <u>Annex 3</u>.

- Report of the Secretary-General on the Financing of the United Nations Protection Force of 2 December 1992 (Doc. A/47/741)

- Report of the Secretary-General on the International Conference on the Former Yugoslavia of 24 December 1992 (S/25015)

- Report of the Secretary-General on the Activities of the International Conference on the Former Yugoslavia of 6 January 1993 (S/25050)

- Further report of the Secretary-General pursuant to Security Council Resolution 787 (1992) of 8 January 1993 (S/25000/Add. 1)

3 REFLECTIONS ON THE MANDATE AND THE PUBLICATION OF THE REPORT

As appears from Paragraph 11 of the Document of the Moscow Meeting of the Conference on Human Dimension of the CSCE (cf. Annex 1), CSCE Rapporteurs "will establish the facts, report on them and may give advice on possible solutions to the question raised". The Rapporteurs of the present Mission assume that the idea of the rules was basically to make proposals to the receiving States. The rules also mirror tasks of a quite different nature from the one which has been entrusted to the present Mission.

There are two significant features, which the Rapporteurs would like to highlight, namely the fact that both of the requested States actually turn to the international community and ask for help in establishing an international criminal jurisdiction, and the fact that the CSCE Council has taken a step which endorses the proposal by the Rapporteurs made in the report on Croatia and specified in a message to the initiating States on 24 November 1992; the Rapporteurs are asked to refine their proposal on making the principle of personal accountability effective including the possibility of the establishment of an ad hoc tribunal (emphasis added here) (cf. Section 2.4).

The Rapporteurs assume, however, that the Mission is still governed by the rules on the Moscow Human Dimension Mechanism. They therefore intend to apply those rules and to report according to the same. They note in this context that the United Kingdom, which according to the Moscow Rules is the initiating State, has handed over this responsibility to Denmark, which holds the Presidency of the European Community as from 1 January 1993.

As will be seen, a significant feature of the proposal in

this report is that the "advice on possible solutions" is directed to the CSCE participating States in general.

They note in this context that the Rapporteurs according to the rules shall submit their report to the participating State or States concerned and, unless all the States concerned agree otherwise, to the CSCE Institution, i.e. the Office for Democratic Institutions and Human Rights (ODIHR), no later than three weeks after the last Rapporteur has been appointed. The requested State will submit any observations on the report to the CSCE Institution, unless all the States concerned agree otherwise, no later than three weeks after the submission of the report. The CSCE Institution will then transmit the report, as well as any observations by the requested State or any other participating State, to all participating States without delay. The report may then be placed on the agenda of the next regular meeting of the CSO, which may decide on any possible follow-up action. The report will remain confidential until after that meeting of the Committee.

In the view of the Rapporteurs this is a most unfortunate situation. They have all the time been concerned that a mission of the present kind does not fit very well under the Rules of the Moscow Mechanism. If these rules were to be followed in this case, the report cannot be made public until the end of March at the earliest. At the same time the United Nations Commission of Human Rights is debating the question of the former Yugoslavia during its meeting at Geneva from 1 February to 12 March 1993. National groups are also being set up in different States to study the question of a possible war crimes tribunal. The Rapporteurs know of such initiatives in Canada, France, Italy and Switzerland. They have been approached by participants in such national groups asking for information and preferably drafts prepared by the Rapporteurs. The Rapporteurs are naturally not in a position to hand out any documentation, but have to follow the Moscow Rules scrupulously.

However, they are very concerned if the report cannot be made public immediately upon delivery. They note in particular the plea by the Minister for Foreign Affairs of Bosnia-Herzegovina and the urgent request by representatives of the United Nations to have access to the report as soon as possible (cf. Section 2.5). They therefore request that the report be published immediately upon delivery.

4 REPORTS ON THE HUMAN RIGHTS SITUATION IN BOSNIA-HERZEGOVINA

General observations

Numerous reports about the human rights situation in Bosnia-Herzegovina have been submitted by governmental and non-governmental institutions. A list of these reports is contained in Annex 3. These reports bear witness to gross violations of human rights and norms of international humanitarian law, including war crimes and crimes against humanity, in Bosnia-Herzegovina. The reports reveal a recognizable pattern of appalling human rights violations in that country.

The reports ascribe responsibility for the human rights violations to all ethnic groups involved in the armed conflict: the Croats, the Bosnian Muslims and the (Bosnian) Serbian forces. The reports, however, emphasize that human rights violations by Croats and Bosnian Muslims are not comparable to those committed by Serbian and Bosnian Serbian forces.

Abuses of individuals, mostly unarmed civilians, take every conceivable form: torture, killing, rape and other humiliations. Reports attribute the most serious human rights violations by Serbian and Bosnian Serbian forces to the policy of "ethnic cleansing".

By the end of 1992 between 25 000 (UN figure) and 130 000 (figures of the Bosnian government) people had died as a result of the war; more than 1,5 million people (i.e. one-third of the total population and one-half of the Muslim population) are reported to be displaced. Approximately 70 per cent of Bosnian territory (mostly northern and western) is presently under Serbian control.

Human Rights violations, including "ethnic cleansing" and rape

The Serbian policy of "involuntary transfers of the Muslim population from Serbian controlled territory" is generally seen as the basis of all human rights violations by the (Bosnian) Serbian forces. The victims are mainly Muslim civilians. So far, hundreds of thousands of Muslims have been affected by the policy of "ethnic cleansing". "Ethnic cleansing" is carried out either by direct means (random executions, maltreatments, rapes, destruction of homes, threats) or indirectly (confiscation or compulsion to sign away property).

According to some reports Croat forces also destroyed Muslim villages. The policy of "ethnic cleansing" is, however, in general considered being part of the Serbian strategy to expel Muslims from Serbian controlled areas.

Situations of armed conflict tend to contribute to a high incidence or rape; rape is therefore often referred to - tragically enough - as being a by-product, a "casuality" of war. The various reports on rape in Bosnia-Herzegovina provide disturbing information on rapes of Croatian and Serbian women as well as sexual abuse of men in detention camps. However, the great majority of rapes is said to be committed by (Bosnian) Serbian forces on Muslim women. These rapes are viewed to be too systematic to be mere by-products of the conflict, but rather considered to form part of the Serbian policy in Bosnia and to serve as a strategic purpose in itself. It is beyond doubt that the number of rapes is substantial and that they often have been committed in extremely humiliating and violent circumstances.

The reports on human rights violations in Bosnia-Herzegovina also provide information on executions of civilians by military and paramilitary forces; arbitrary arrests, torture, disappearances and destruction of property.

The reports, in general, blame the (Bosnian) Serbian forces for more serious human rights violations and more cruel abuses of the civilian population than the other parties to the conflict.

Human rights violations in detention camps

The various reports blame all parties to the conflict for arbitrary arrests of civilians, for torture and inhuman treatment of prisoners. The sanitary and medical situation in the camps are considered most worrysome, humanitarian aid is desperately needed. According to the reports, however, human rights violations in Serbian camps, by far, exceed those in other camps. The reports also give examples of rape and sexual abuse of women and of men in detention camps. Cases are known where women are explicitely detained in order to be sexually abused in detention.

Violations of International Humanitarian Law

International humanitarian law and international conventions on the treatment of civilians are found to be heavily and systematically violated in Bosnia-Herzegovina. Reports by non-governmental organizations on investigations of alleged war crimes in Bosnia-Herzegovina describe numerous cases of executions and disappearances of civilians, "ethnic cleansing", aggression against medical assistants and journalists and widespread destruction of property.

Further sources point to indiscriminate attacks against civilians, including massacres; detention of civilians and the worst kinds of torture and killings of prisoners; forced movement of populations; use of paramilitary groups, including criminals.

While in the reports all sides are considered guilty of violence against civilians, attacks on population centers and prevention of delivery of humanitarian aid are reported as features of the behaviour of the Serbian forces and their paramilitary allies.

5 RELEVANT LEGISLATION AND ADMINISTRATION OF JUSTICE IN BOSNIA-HERZEGOVINA

5.1 Relevant legislation

Constitutional law

It is to be recalled that the negotiations within the framework of the International Conference on the former Yugoslavia are aiming at the adoption of a new constitution for Bosnia-Herzegovina. The present situation is therefore somewhat unclear. The only constitution formally in force seems to be the Constitution of the Socialist Republic of Bosnia-Herzegovina. Before the elections in November 1990, this Constitution had been supplemented by the Federal Yugoslav Constitution, which contains a number of provisions applicable to all six Republics in the former Yugoslavia. These provisions were not repeated in the constitutions of these Republics.

The coalition consisting of the three parties which won the elections in Bosnia-Herzegovina (Croatian Democratic Community, Serbian Democratic Party and the Party of Democratic Action) intended to elaborate a new constitution for this State. They were, however, not successful in their efforts to find a common ground for this endeavour. These efforts have later been continued through international assistance from EC States and within the framework of the Conference just mentioned. At present there is no agreement as to the contents of a new constitution for Bosnia-Herzegovina.

As far as the Rapporteurs have been able to establish, the legal constitutional situation is characterized by certain lacunae; parts of the old Constitution of Bosnia-Herzegovina, as well as the Constitution of the former Yugoslavia, are not considered relevant to the new situation.

Two constitutional aspects come to the forefront. First, whether under domestic law in Bosnia-Herzegovina there are any constitutional obstacles against transferring jurisdiction to an international judicial body. Secondly, the question what legal status international treaties carry in the internal legal order in Bosnia-Herzegovina.

As regards the first question, the Rapporteurs have found no such legal obstacle. This conclusion is based on written material and oral submissions, in particular information given at the meetings at Geneva between the Rapporteurs and representatives of the Government and Parliament of Bosnia-Herzegovina and their legal advisers on 25 and 26 January 1993.

As regards the second question, the Rapporteurs note Article 210.2 of the Yugoslav Constitution of 1974. According to this provision international treaties and conventions are directly applicable in domestic law. The Rapporteurs have, however, not been able to establish the exact status of this provision in Bosnia-Herzegovina at present.

Criminal law

No new Criminal Code has yet been adopted in Bosnia-Herzegovina following the elections in November 1990.

During consultations with representatives of the Government of Bosnia-Herzegovina as well as with legal experts, the Rapporteurs have been informed that the applicable criminal law is almost identical to the Criminal Code of the former Yugoslavia. The exceptions concern an increase in the possible length of sentences for certain serious crimes. It follows that serious crimes such as war crimes and crimes against humanity are punishable according to the provisions of Chapter 16 of the Criminal Code of the former Yugoslavia (attached to Annex 6) regardless of whether such acts have been committed before or after the change of the

constitutional situation in Bosnia-Herzegovina.

5.2 Administration of justice

Criminal procedure was uniform throughout the former Yugoslavia, including Bosnia-Herzegovina, and was governed by the Code of Criminal Procedure and the Criminal Code. In Bosnia-Herzegovina the adaptation to the new State Constitution is still going on, but the two Codes mentioned are still in force.

There are three court instances. The first instance is the Municipal Court. These courts handle all cases except the more serious ones. The second instance is the District Court. These courts have jurisdiction over serious crimes and also act as Courts of Appeal with respect to judgments by the Municipal Courts. The Supreme Court is the Court of Appeal in matters where the District Court is the court of first resort.

The court sits in panels of three judges (one professional judge and two lay judges). In cases of serious crimes, the panel consists of five judges (three professional judges and two lay judges). Simple cases are adjudicated by one professional judge. The lay judges are appointed by the court from among the members of the Municipal counsels. The former Yugoslavia court system does not include jury trials.

The judges are appointed by representative bodies at the different territorial levels. Their term of office is six years, and they can be re-appointed.

The prosecutor generally does not have the freedom to decide not to prosecute. He may decline to prosecute only those acts which are "almost not dangerous for the society". Only conduct that is "dangerous to society" can be characterized as a criminal offence under the criminal law of the former Yugoslavia.

The criminal procedure consists of four stages: the pre-trial phase, the preliminary judicial inquiry, the trial process (which includes the main hearing) and appealate review. In the first phase the prosecutor may request a preliminary judicial inquiry. If he has already sufficient evidence, he may bring out a formal accusation immediately.

A preliminary judicial inquiry is initiated by the Examining Magistrate when he considers that there is sufficient ground to believe that an offence has been committed. The Prosecutor can decide to forego further prosecution and dismiss the case at any time during the preliminary judicial inquiry.

In the trial process the prosecutor must bring out the formal accusation within fifteen days after the preliminary judicial inquiry is closed. After the formal accusation, the court examines whether all the formal requirements are fulfilled and starts a main hearing. A written judgment should be filed within eight days, or, in complicated cases, within fifteen days after the pronouncement.

As regards the appeal procedures, both the defendant and the prosecutor have the right to appeal within fifteen days of the written judgment. The Court of Appeal appoints a panel which makes a decision on the basis of a meeting to which all the parties are invited. The panel may order a new hearing if there is new evidence. The Court of Appeal may:

(i) leave the judgment unchanged;
(ii) vacate the judgment and refer the case back to the court of first resort for a new panel of judges;
(iii) change the judgment; however, if only the defendant has appealed, the Court of Appeal can neither increase the punishment nor issue a sanction for a more serious crime.

It is obvious to the Rapporteurs that the legal system in Bosnia-Herzegovina will have little possibilities to deal within a foreseeable future with all war crimes and crimes against humanity which have been committed and continue to be committed in that country (cf. Section 7).

6 ATTRIBUTING RESPONSIBILITY

The question of attributing responsibility was examined by the Rapporteurs already in their report on Croatia (see Section 7 of that report). The examination was made with respect to principles, collection of information and administration of justice.

In the opinion of the Rapporteurs, this examination applies equally to Bosnia-Herzegovina. As they indicated already in the report on Croatia a possible proposal on their part would also inevitably have an impact on other parts of the former Yugoslavia.

The Rapporteurs identified and defined the following requirements which should be met by a criminal justice system in the present case:

- Suspects should be brought to justice as soon as possible
- The justice system must comply with international norms
- The system must be as cost-effective and accessible as possible
- The persons sentenced must be treated according to the applicable standards for the treatment of prisoners and this should be done under international supervision.

The Rapporteurs found that it was necessary to investigate several options before a definite decision could be taken. They also contemplated the possibility of combining different solutions.

The contents of the present report reflects the further thinking of the Rapporteurs on this matter.

7 DELIBERATIONS ON A COMPETENT JURISDICTION

The question of a competent jurisdiction was also examined by the Rapporteurs in their report on Croatia (see Section 9 of that report).

They deliberated on three options: national courts, the establishment of an international criminal court and the establishment of an international ad hoc tribunal for certain crimes committed in the former Yugoslavia.

As far as national courts are concerned the Rapporteurs saw no real possibility of an effective prosecution of war crimes and crimes against humanity at the national level. The following part of Section 9.1 of their report on Croatia, reflecting the reasons for this conclusion, could be quoted:

> "First, the Croatian courts are still in a transformation process from the court system under communist rule into a judiciary which would meet the prerequisites for courts in States operating under the rule of law.
>
> Second, the antagonism which the Rapporteurs have experienced between Croats and Serbs as a result of the armed conflict is so intense at the moment, that it is unlikely that the courts in Croatia would be considered as impartial and independent by many of the persons concerned.
>
> Third, the trials will inevitably mean that witnesses and other persons concerned will have to appear before the courts. In such cases, it can be assumed that persons from e.g. Serbia would hesitate to go to Croatia to appear as witnesses against suspected Croatian war criminals. The same would apply vice versa.
>
> Fourth, the bringing to justice of suspected war criminals presumably encompasses persons of high level in the respective countries. In such cases, it could be argued that it is less appropriate that the administration of justice be entrusted to any of the parties to the conflict.
>
> Fifth, a reassuring impression from the visit of the Rapporteurs to Croatia is that the Government of Croatia is, in principle, in favour of an international tribunal and would seem to be ready to cooperate with other States in order to establish such a jurisdiction. - - - "

These reasons would in the opinion of the Rapporteurs apply a fortiori to Bosnia-Herzegovina.

As far as the establishment of an international criminal court is concerned, the Rapporteurs in their report on Croatia made reference to the on-going work within the United Nations. They stated that, although they were very much in favour of the establishment of such a court, they would strongly advise against waiting for such a court to be established before action was taken against serious criminal acts committed in connection with the armed conflict in the territory of the former Yugoslavia.

They then went on to deliberate the third option and discussed questions on applicable law, procedural law, establishment of a jurisdiction, prosecution, implementation of sentences, and languages. They then made the following summary:

> "The foregoing discussion demonstrates that there is a viable possibility of establishing an international jurisdiction to deal with alleged war crimes and crimes against humanity committed in the former Yugoslavia. The review which the Rapporteurs have made is certainly not exhaustive. They are anxious to stress that the review is made only for the purpose of making an illustration of the problems which would have to be solved if an international jurisdiction were contemplated. There are no shortcuts, and an international jurisdiction must be set up to meet the highest standards of legal protection as well as efficiency. This examination would have to be made by experts in the field."

The Rapporteurs then proposed that a committee of experts from interested States be convened as soon as possible to prepare a draft treaty establishing an international _ad hoc_ tribunal for certain crimes committed in the former Yugoslavia. The committee should be instructed to elaborate such a draft and to make an estimation of costs.

It seems that the Rapporteurs are now themselves faced with this very task. The present report contains their proposals in the matter.

8 PROPOSAL FOR AN INTERNATIONAL WAR CRIMES TRIBUNAL FOR THE FORMER YUGOSLAVIA

8.1 General considerations

In its report on Croatia on 7 October 1992 the Rapporteurs proposed that an international _ad hoc_ tribunal for certain crimes committed in the former Yugoslavia be established. The Rapporteurs subsequently offered to prepare a draft treaty on such a tribunal (cf. Section 2.4). This offer was welcomed by the CSCE Council on 15 December 1992 (ibdm). After consultations with the Commission of Experts established pursuant to Security Council Resolution 780 (1992) and after talks with representatives of other organisations involved in the situation in the former Yugoslavia as well as with representatives of Bosnia-Herzegovina, the Rapporteurs have decided to make a proposal for an _ad hoc_ tribunal. The proposal consists of a general part, a draft Convention and a Commentary to the provisions of the draft.

The Rapporteurs are anxious to emphasize that the setting up of an _ad hoc_ tribunal is a major undertaking. First of all the establishment of the tribunal is a complex issue _per se_. Secondly, such a tribunal may have implications for the efforts to stop the armed conflicts and bring peace to the area. Furthermore, the tribunal also entails costs and has to be maintained for a number of years. In principle, the establishment of an international tribunal requires the same rules as the establishment of courts at the national level, which rules govern every stage of the process, from the inquiry and apprehension of suspects to the implementation of sentences.

Efforts to establish an international criminal jurisdiction have been going on for quite some time. The latest development is reflected in the report of the International Law Commission on the work of its forty-fourth session (4 May - 24 July 1992; General Assembly, Official records, 47th session, Supplement no. 10; A/47/10). Based on this report and the debate in the Sixth Committee of the United Nations General Assembly, the Assembly decided to request the Commission to continue its work on this question by undertaking the project for the elaboration of a draft statute for an international criminal court as a matter of priority as from its next session (G.A. Res. 47/33, 25 November 1992).

The Rapporteurs, however, advised already in their report on Croatia (Section 9.2 of that report) strongly against waiting for the work of the United Nations in this field to be completed. Instead they encouraged the establishment of an _ad hoc_ tribunal.

Having given this idea further thought, the Rapporteurs feel even more convinced today of this course of action. The situation in the former Yugoslavia lends itself to a sui generis solution, which should be chosen in particular in view of the urgency of the matter. The Rapporteurs have decided not to engage in any extensive deliberations in this report on arguments for or against an international court. Judging from the many statements made by representatives of States, in particular CSCE participating States, the Rapporteurs assume that there is a determination common to a number of concerned States to take action with a view to attributing personal accountability for war crimes and crimes against humanity committed in the former Yugoslavia. The Rapporteurs also note that two of the States in the territory of the former Yugoslavia have advocated the establishment of an international jurisdiction: Bosnia-Herzegovina in a letter to the Secretary-General of the United Nations on 10 August 1992 (Annex 4) and in contacts with the Rapporteurs (See Section 2.5), and Croatia in contacts with the Rapporteurs (See Section 13 of the report on Croatia) and in a statement in the Sixth Committee of the United Nations General Assembly on 6 November 1992 (Annex 5).

As will be explained in the following (Section 8.2) the Rapporteurs are of the opinion that the jurisdiction of an ad hoc tribunal should not be limited to the territory of those two States. In view of the fact that the acts in question are criminal in accordance with applicable national law in the entire territory of the former Yugoslavia, the Rapporteurs are of the opinion that a tribunal should be established to administer justice with respect to acts committed in that territory.

With respect to the creation of a tribunal and its administration, the Rapporteurs think that it should be governed by its own statute, in the form of a convention. This is particular so in view of the sui generis solution which the Rapporteurs propose and the fact that the proposal can be described as a system of "ceded jurisdiction" (cf. Section 8.2). One feasible option is that the convention should be open to the CSCE participating States.

There are three arguments voiced against the creation of an international jurisdiction for the former Yugoslavia which the Rapporteurs should like to address.

One argument which the Rapporteurs have heard since their report on Croatia was established is that there are so many technical and legal difficulties involved that States would be reluctant to engage in the establishment of such a jurisdiction. The Rapporteurs do not believe that the problems are insurmountable. They note in particular that the Working Group of the ILC in its excellent report has come to the conclusion that the technical problems connected with the establishment of an international criminal court can be resolved (cf. para. 432 of the ILC report). This conclusion would apply _a fortiori_ to the establishment of an _ad hoc_ tribunal for a specific territory and in a context where it is not necessary to solve the problem of the relation between the tribunal and an international code of crimes.

A second argument is that an _ad hoc_ tribunal would hamper the efforts to establish peace in the area. The Rapporteurs think that this is a dangerous argument. In every armed conflict there would be efforts to end the fighting and to establish peace. This means that the argument could be advanced in connection with any conflict. To avoid the question of criminal responsibility or to yield to demands for abolition would in the view of the Rapporteurs be contrary to the idea of rule of law. Furthermore, the establishment of an international tribunal would be a demonstration of international co-operation which would have immediate preventive effects.

A third argument is that an _ad hoc_ tribunal for the former Yugoslavia would be detrimental to the work towards the establishment of an international criminal jurisdiction presently being done within the United Nations, and in particular by the International Law Commission. The Rapporteurs are not at all convinced by that argument. Two of the Rapporteurs have been involved in this work in the UN General Assembly for a number of years, and they fail to see that an _ad hoc_ tribunal in the present case, based on the national law in the area, can in any way be contrary to what is being done within the United Nations. The obvious question to put as a counter-argument is: Should war criminals go unpunished just because we are expecting in some future the results of a work which has been going on within the United Nations for over forty years?

Even if the problems connected with an international tribunal can be overcome, it is - as already said - a major undertaking to create such an organ. The crucial question is naturally the level of ambition. The proposals for an international criminal court which have been presented so far reflect a relatively limited organ. In the present situation and judging from the reports emanating from the former Yugoslavia, it can be assumed that there are hundreds, not to say thousands of suspected war criminals and persons having committed crimes against humanity in the area. The need for an international jurisdiction apply equally to almost all of these suspects. The Rapporteurs have therefore chosen to model their proposal in such a way that the tribunal can deal with all crimes which fall under the provisions in question. The system of "ceded jurisdiction" foreseen by the Rapporteurs is furthermore a system which contracting States can implement to live up to their obligation to try suspected war criminals at the national level which follows i.a. from the 1949 Geneva Convention Relative to the Protection of Civilian Persons in Time of War.

Based on these considerations the Rapporteurs propose that an International ad hoc tribunal for war crimes and crimes against humanity committed in the former Yugoslavia be established. In the following sections they address some of the questions of principle connected with such establishment. The tribunal is referred to as the International War Crimes Tribunal for the Former Yugoslavia, or in short the Tribunal.

A draft Convention, establishing the Tribunal, appears as Annex 6 to this report.

8.2 Jurisdiction and applicable law

Jurisdiction - General remarks

A basic feature in criminal law is that States have jurisdiction over individuals within their territory. But national jurisdiction is wider than that, and comprises individuals of the nationality of the States in question also outside the territory, e.g. on board vessels flying the national flag of the State, or aircraft registered in the same State. They would also have jurisdiction over crimes committed against their own citizens irrespective of where the crime is committed. A comparative study would, however, show that rules on jurisdiction differ widely from State to State; in some cases jurisdiction is rather limited, in other cases a State would assume jurisdiction over crimes committed also outside the territory of the same State and committed by persons with little or no connection with the State in question.

A common feature of many conventions, in which States agree to criminalize acts as international crimes, is the principle of aut dedere, aut judicare. The principle means that a State is under the obligation either to prosecute an accused individual or to deliver him for trial in another contracting State. The ways in which States observe these rules under their national law differ. In case the State has a wide jurisdiction, these rules could correspond to rather restrictive rules on extradition and vice versa. Depending therefore on the scope of national jurisdiction and the possibilities to extradite, States would make their choice. In many cases, States would not be in a position to extradite their own citizens. If that is the case, they would have to establish jurisdiction over crimes committed by these citizens abroad in order to comply with international commitments under the clause just referred to.

Irrespective of which system applies in a particular case, the common denominator is that the jurisdiction is national. Subject to the rules of national constitutions, States would however have the possibility of conferring jurisdiction upon an international judicial body. This is one of the key questions which has been discussed in connection with the various efforts made in the past to establish an international criminal jurisdiction. The question is closely related to the matter of applicable law.

In this context it may suffice to note one important reason for this link between jurisdiction and applicable law; it must be ascertained that an international jurisdiction is wholly in conformity with general principles of criminal law, in particular the principle of legality, expressed in the Latin sentence: nullum crimen sine lege, nulla poena sine lege (no act is criminal unless this is laid down in law; no act can be punished unless punishment is prescribed by law). However, provided that this principle is respected and the applicable law is clear enough, there is no legal restraint on the possibility for States to confer their jurisdiction to an international body which fulfils international legal requirements for a court. Among the most prominent features of such a court is that it should be independent, impartial and established by law (or treaty at the international level). Reference is made i.a. to Articles 14 and 15 of the International Covenant on Civil and Political Rights and Articles 5 and 6 of the European Convention on Human Rights.

Another question is whether the international jurisdiction contemplated should be exclusive or concurrent with national jurisdiction. Yet another question is whether jurisdiction should be general or dependent on the decision in the particular case by national organs to hand over the jurisdiction to the international entity. In case an international criminal court would be established, it is necessary to investigate the various options.

In the present case the Rapporteurs are convinced that the method to be used is in principle the one of compulsory exclusive jurisdiction conveyed to the Tribunal. The reasons for this are those that appear in Section 7 and the fact that two of the States in the territory of the former Yugoslavia have asked for international co-operation. To confer exclusive jurisdiction on the Tribunal would mean that all suspected war criminals from the area would be treated on an equal basis, and that there would be no reason for allegations of bias on the part of the judicial organs.

Since the proposal foresees that a number of States outside the area of the former Yugoslavia will become parties to the treaty it is also necessary to examine the question whether they too should confer jurisdiction to the Tribunal. In this context it is important to note that all States concerned can be assumed to be parties to the 1949 Geneva Convention III relative to the Treatment of Prisoners of War and the 1949 Geneva Convention IV relative to the Protection of Civilian Persons in Time of War. As such they are under the obligation to establish jurisdiction over persons alleged to have committed grave breaches as defined in the Conventions (Articles 130 and 147, respectively).

In the view of the Rapporteurs it could be a considerable merit in designing the Convention in such a way that also States outside the former Yugoslavia confer, or "cede", jurisdiction to the Tribunal. The greatest merit with such a solution would be that it would not be possible for suspects to take refuge in contracting States who might be inclined to deal more leniently with those persons than would the Tribunal. However, the Rapporteurs recognize that this is a matter which may influence the preparedness of States to become parties to the Convention. It might therefore prove feasible to design the Convention in such a way that States in the territory of the former Yugoslavia are always obliged to deliver suspects to the Tribunal, whereas other States parties to the Convention can apply the principle of *aut dedere, aut judicare*. This solution is reflected in the draft Convention (Article 59).

In this context it should be noted that the expression "ceded jurisdiction" is used by the Working Group of the ILC to describe the situation where a State has jurisdiction to try an offender under a relevant treaty or under general international law, and it consents to an international court exercising jurisdiction instead (cf. para. 456 of the ILC report). The Working Group, however, is not certain that the "ceded jurisdiction" argument would work. The reason is that other States - presumably not parties to the treaty establishing the international criminal court - could have jurisdiction based on the international rules on universal jurisdiction. This third State could be said to be "concerned" and have rights, or potential rights, of jurisdiction which cannot be affected without their consent.

Since this situation may occur in the present case, the Rapporteurs should like to forward the argument that they think that "ceded jurisdiction" would work. There can already today be a competition, where several States ask for extradition and where the requested State has to decide which application should be granted. In case there is a dispute between the States concerned, this matter can ultimately be brought before the International Court of Justice. In the present situation the Tribunal established under the draft Convention would be in a similar position to a "State". In case a third State argues that an individual should be extradited to it rather than delivered to the Tribunal, the matter would, if pursued, ultimately have to be settled in the same way. The Rapporteurs assume, however, that a request from the Tribunal to have a person delivered would carry particular weight, since the Tribunal is a joint effort by a number of States concerned having conferred their jurisdiction to this international body.

Another important question is which persons should be subject to the jurisdiction of the Tribunal. This matter is dealt with below.

Yet another matter is the fact that jurisdiction would have to be limited to crimes committed in the territory of the former Yugoslavia (Article 3). This definition is certainly not as clear as the Rapporteurs would have wanted. In particular problems might arise in connection with preparation, conspiracy and complicity. In the view of the Rapporteurs it is, however, not necessary to solve in detail these questions in the Convention. Irrespective of efforts in this direction there would still be an area where the treaty-maker has no other choice but to leave the matter to be decided upon within the framework of the jurisdiction of the competent organs of the Convention, n.b. the Court.

Applicable law

The question which law to apply is one of the central issues in connection with the establishment of an international criminal jurisdiction. In this context reference is often made to Article 38 of the Statute of the International Court of Justice. This Article reads as follows:

> "1. The Court, whose function is to decide in accordance with international law such disputes as are submitted to it, shall apply:
>
> a. international conventions, whether general or particular, establishing rules expressly recognized by the contesting states;
>
> b. international custom as evidence of a general practice accepted as law;

c. the general principles of law recognized by civilized nations;

d. subject to the provisions of Article 59, judicial decisions and the teachings of the most highly qualified publicists of the various nations, as subsidiary means for the determination of rules of law.

2. This provision shall not prejudice the power of the Court to decide a case ex aequo et bono, if the parties agree thereto."

Note: Article 59 lays down that the decision of the Court has no binding force except between the parties and in respect of that particular case.

In writings on international criminal jurisdiction it is often mentioned that this provision, although included in the statute of a court which has no criminal jurisdiction, is indispensable also in such jurisdiction. The Rapporteurs are not convinced. And even if the provision would be referred to, it is certainly not sufficient. As already stated, the principle of legality (nullum crimen sine lege, nulla poena sine lege) must be observed.

A significant feature of the conventions in which contracting States undertake to criminalize acts as international crimes is that the international instrument does not contain a complete provision which would fulfil the requirements of the principle of legality. The question of punishment is left to the contracting States to regulate in the national law. This means that, even if a State ratifies a convention containing a provision which makes a certain act criminal, this provision is not sufficient for courts to apply, if they are seized with a concrete case. They need in addition a penal provision which lays down the punishment which the court should mete out, in case the accused is found guilty.
This system is aptly demonstrated by the 1949 Geneva Convention IV. To illustrate, Articles 146 and 147 of this Convention could be quoted:

"Article 146

The High Contracting Parties undertake to enact any legislation necessary to provide effective penal sanctions for persons committing, or ordering to be committed, any of the grave breaches of the present Convention defined in the following Article.

Each High Contracting Party shall be under the obligation to search for persons alleged to have committed, or to have ordered to be committed, such

> grave breaches, and shall bring such persons, regardless of their nationality, before its own courts. It may also, if it prefers, and in accordance with the provisions of its own legislation, hand such persons over for trial to another High Contracting Party concerned, provided such High Contracting Party has made out a prima facie case.
>
> Each High Contracting Party shall take measures necessary for the suppression of all acts contrary to the provisions of the present Convention other than the grave breaches defined in the following Article.
>
> In all circumstances, the accused persons shall benefit by safeguards of proper trial and defence, which shall not be less favourable than those provided by Article 105 and those following of the Geneva Convention relative to the Treatment of Prisoners of War of August 12, 1949.
>
> Article 147
>
> Grave breaches to which the preceding Article relates shall be those involving any of the following acts, if committed against persons or property protected by the present Convention: wilful killing, torture or inhuman treatment, including biological experiments, wilfully causing great suffering or serious injury to body or health, unlawful deportation or transfer or unlawful confinement of a protected person, compelling a protected person to serve in the forces of a hostile Power, or wilfully depriving a protected person of the rights of fair and regular trial prescribed in the present Convention, taking of hostages and extensive destruction and appropriation of property, not justified by military necessity and carried out unlawully and wantonly."

The situation in which the treaty-maker finds himself in the setting up of an international criminal tribunal is therefore to identify the applicable substantive law. (A distinction should be made between the substantial law and the procedural law, see below.) The options are here either to draft an international criminal code or at least include complete penal provisions in the treaties in question, or to rely on national provisions fulfilling the requirements of the principle of legality.

It is at this juncture which the United Nations finds itself. The ILC has been entrusted with the task of drafting a statute for an international criminal tribunal. The question which law this tribunal should apply is not yet resolved. An international code of crimes has reached the stage of first reading in the ILC, and Member States were asked to submit their views on this draft to the Secretary-General before 1 January 1993. It is obvious that the question of an international criminal code is a very difficult issue, and that there is still a long way to go before such a code can see the light of the day.

An international court can however be set up independently of an international code. But the question would still be which law this court should apply. The choice would again be the same: to identify acts which are considered criminal under international law and to add to them international penal provisions, or, as appears from the above, to rely on national legislation.

It is against this background which the conclusions by the Rapporteurs in their report on Croatia should be seen. The Rapporteurs recall the statement on this matter in the said report:

> "A special feature in this connection is the principle *nullum crimen sine lege*. The meaning of this principle is that the alleged crime must have been punishable at the time it was committed. In other words, the suspect should have been under the obligation to observe the rule in question when he committed the act. Whether he in fact did know about the rule is of no relevance.
>
> The question in this connection is whether international instruments such as the 1948 United Nations Convention on the Prevention and Punishment of the Crime of Genocide would be a sufficient basis for action by an international jurisdiction. The same holds true of the 1949 Geneva Conventions and the additional Protocols of 1977. The characteristic of these instruments is that they require contracting States to provide penal sanctions for violations of certain provisions in the instruments in question. The instruments themselves, however, do not contain any provisions as to the punishments which should follow upon conviction. Such provisions ought, therefore, to be found in national laws.
>
> If an international jurisdiction is set up, one option would be to formulate international provisions laying down the punishment which should follow upon the finding that a person is guilty of a crime against any of the provisions in question, e.g. the Geneva Conventions. Another solution is to examine whether the national legislation in force is a sufficient basis for legal action."

The Rapporteurs then went on to examine Articles 141 through 155c of the Penal Code of the Socialist Federal Republic of Yugoslavia (Annex 6 to the report on Croatia) as well as the corresponding provisions in the Penal Code presently in force in Croatia. The Rapporteurs found that those provisions provided a sufficient legal basis for the administration of justice with respect to suspected war criminals in the former Yugoslavia.

The Rapporteurs have now deliberated further on this matter and have come to the conclusion that the Tribunal should apply national law, nota bene the Penal Code of the Socialist Federal Republic of Yugoslavia. However, it is not sufficient to rely only on the provisions just mentioned (they are annexed to the draft Convention appearing as Annex 6 to the present report). It is also necessary to look into a number of provisions, which are normally drafted in a general way so as to be applicable to all penal provisions. As examples of such provisions could be mentioned provisions on attempt, preparation, conspiracy, complicity, and extenuating circumstances. Other important provisions are the general provisions on penalties (maximum and minimum periods of imprisonment, time to serve, parole, etc.) and also provisions on damages and restitution of property. These questions are further dealt with in the Commentary to Articles 28-30, 46 and 47.

If this method is chosen there would be no problem with respect to the principle of legality. The acts in question were criminal and punishable at the time they were committed. This means that the suspect or accused was under the obligation to observe the pertinent rule when the act was committed. It is irrelevant whether the person in question in fact did know about the relevant rule or not (ignorantia juris nocet).

It must, however, be stressed that the Penal Code of the former Yugoslavia may not be in force today in all States in the territory of the former Yugoslavia. As in Croatia there might be a new Penal Code. Whether this is a problem or - like in Croatia - will not hamper the possibilities of bringing the accused to justice, is a matter to be investigated in a future drafting exercise.

A related matter is the question of double criminality, which is dealt with in the Commentary to Article 59.

Turning now to the substantive law to be applied by the Tribunal, this matter has to be examined in relation to the following three factors: jurisdiction in relation to the time factor (ratione temporis), subject-matter jurisdiction (ratione materiae), and personal jurisdiction (ratione personae).

Jurisdiction ratione temporis

It is evident that the convention establishing the Tribunal must lay down a point in time from which acts committed should fall under the competence of the Tribunal. It is important to underline that here, at least as the Rapporteurs see it, there is no problem with respect to the principle of legality. This principle does not really limit enactment of new procedural rules, e.g. which court should be competent to try acts which are criminal. Normally rules on procedure take immediate effect and can be applied to cases which are pending or cases which are initiated later but concern crimes which were committed before the change in the procedural rules was made.

Against this background the Rapporteurs propose that a date is set which determines the competence of the Tribunal. This means that, if a case pertaining to a point in time before the date set would be brought to the attention of the Tribunal, the organ of the Tribunal seized with the matter would have to declare the case inadmissible. The Rapporteurs suggest that this date should be 1 January 1991.

As will appear, the Rapporteurs do not propose any provision laying down the point in time when the jurisdiction of the Tribunal should cease. The reason for this is that it would in their view be unfortunate if such a date was set. It would merely lead to speculations and calculated actions on the part of various actors under the system with a view to eventually avoiding the jurisdiction of the Tribunal. Instead the Rapporteurs have designed their proposal in such a way that the activities of the Tribunal could be phased out in the light of development, in particular the ability of national courts to take over jurisdiction. This means that the functions of the Tribunal after some time could be reduced to a supervisory function and the decision-making concentrated to a quick review of cases before a decision is taken to transfer the proceedings from the Tribunal back to States in the territory of the former Yugoslavia (See Section 8.9).

Jurisdiction ratione materiae

The Rapporteurs are of the opinion that one should be careful not to make the jurisdiction of the Tribunal too wide. It should rather be limited to the most serious crimes, in particular in view of the fact that international proceedings are always more complex, costly and time-consuming than proceedings at the national level. Also the interest of prosecuting serious crimes is greater than in other cases. As a starting point the Rapporteurs have taken international law and the most important conventions in this context, namely the 1948 United Nations Convention on the Prevention and Punishment of the Crime of Genocide, the 1949 Geneva Conventions III and IV, the Additional Protocols of 1977, and the 1954 Hague Convention (cf. Commentary to Preamble).

The following provisions of the Convention against Genocide should be quoted in order to facilitate the understanding of the reasoning of the Rapporteurs:

> "Article II
>
> In the present Convention, genocide means any of the following acts committed with intent to destroy, in whole or in part, a national, ethnical, racial or religious group, as such:
> (a) Killing members of the group;
> (b) Causing serious bodily or mental harm to members of the group;
> (c) Deliberately inflicting on the group conditions of life calculated to bring about its physical destruction in whole or in part;
> (d) Imposing measures intended to prevent births within the group;
> (e) Forcibly transferring children of the group to another group.
>
> Article III
>
> The following acts shall be punishable:
> (a) Genocide;
> (b) Conspiracy to commit genocide;
> (c) Direct and public incitement to commit genocide;
> (d) Attempt to commit genocide;
> (e) Complicity in genocide."

Having studied these provisions and having studied further the above mentioned Penal Code of the former Yugoslavia, as well as available reports on the situation in the former Yugoslavia and against the background of their own observations, the Rapporteurs have come to the conclusion that the substantial provisions to be applied by the Tribunal should be Articles 141 (Genocide), 142 (War crimes against the civilian population), 144 (War crimes against prisoners of war), 150 (Rude treatment of the wounded, sick or prisoners of war), and 151 (Destruction of cultural and historical monuments) of the Penal Code of the former Yugoslavia.

Among the considerations which the Rapporteurs have made in arriving at this conclusion they would like to mention the following:

- The law is known in the whole territory of the former Yugoslavia, and would create no problems with respect to the principle of legality;

- The law is based on international commitments laid down in the Conventions just mentioned, which would mean that corresponding provisions would appear also in the Penal Codes of other contracting States, which, in fact, are under the obligation to try or extradite persons accused of crimes against those provisions, should the suspects appear on their territories or otherwise come under their jurisdiction;

- The law would cause no problem in a system which is designed to phase out the activities of the Tribunal and transfer jurisdiction back to the States in the territory of the former Yugoslavia;

- The law would limit the jurisdiction of the Tribunal so as to deal with cases where an international support in the bringing of those responsible to justice is mostly needed.

Another question is how to categorize the crimes falling under the jurisdiction of the Tribunal as suggested by the Rapporteurs.

In the discussion over the years the following concepts have been employed: crimes against peace, war crimes, and crimes against humanity. The rapporteurs certainly do not intend to enter into a discussion on whether these categories are appropriate or whether other ways of structuring should be employed. They simply note that these concepts are well-known, and that they have been used in the past.

If this categorization is employed, it is apparent that the crimes which the Rapporteurs suggest should fall under the jurisdiction of the Tribunal belong to the categories of war crimes and crimes against humanity. The Rapporteurs have therefore chosen to describe the crimes in those categories, and this method is employed throughout the report. However, in proposing the title of the draft Convention the Rapporteurs deemed it more appropriate only to refer to war crimes (cf. the Commentary to Title and Preamble).

The reasoning in regard to the present topic is further developed in the Commentary to Article 28.

Jurisdiction ratione personae

The third criterion to be examined is which persons should fall under the jurisdiction of the Tribunal. This question is naturally of utmost importance. The Rapporteurs assume that all those who should be regarded as responsible under international law should fall under the jurisdiction of the Tribunal. Article 2 of the draft Convention is therefore formulated accordingly.

The Rapporteurs are aware of the fact that jurisdiction over both individuals and legal persons have been contemplated in previous efforts of establishing international criminal jurisdiction. They think, however, that the jurisdiction now contemplated should be confined to individuals. There are many reasons for this. One of the most obvious is that a wider jurisdiction might bar possible contracting States from joining in the international effort.

The Rapporteurs are finally of the opinion that the Tribunal should not have jurisdiction over disputes between States parties to the Convention relating to the application of the Convention.

8.3 Collection of information

As already mentioned (Section 2.3) the Rapporteurs proposed in their Report on Croatia that a committee of experts should be convened immediately to propose the necessary rules and the administrative and technical solutions for collection of information on suspected war criminals, and to make an estimation of costs.

The Rapporteurs recall that they stated in their report on Croatia that there is an urgent need to co-ordinate the efforts in the present collection of information. They had observed frustration among persons serving in the various organizatons engaged in the collection of such information because of the fact that there was no central and competent authority to whom they could forward the information. The Rapporteurs, therefore, saw a need to institutionalize the collection of information and to entrust the responsibility for this collection to a particular organ on a more permanent basis. They expressed the view that a system for such collection should:

- make it possible to establish personal responsibility,

- make it possible for victims or their relatives to participate and at the same time to ease their grief,

- give the possibility for witnesses and organizations to deposit their statements or contributions in order to assist in the establishment of personal responsibility,

- give a clear signal to the world that the international community is prepared to take action and to pursue such efforts,

- save the possibilities for different options with respect to actions needed, in particular the bringing of suspects to justice.

Since that proposal was made, the Security Council of the United Nations has appointed the Commission of Experts under Resolution 780 (1992). The mandate of this Commission is as follows:

> "to examine and analyse the information submitted pursuant to resolution 771 (1992) and the present resolution, together with such further information as the Commission of Experts may obtain through its own investigations or efforts, of other persons or bodies pursuant to resolution 771 (1992), with a view to providing the Secretary-General with its conclusions on the evidence of grave breaches of the Geneva Conventions and other violations of international humanitarian law committed in the territory of the former Yugoslavia;"

During the first contacts between the Rapporteur mission and the UN Commission, the latter made clear that it was not in their mandate to elaborate a system of administration of information of the kind foreseen in the Report on Croatia.

In order to find out whether the preoccupations of the Rapporteurs with respect to data collection were correct, Ambassador Corell had a short interview with two experienced criminal investigators in Stockholm. From this interview appears the following.

There are various methods to be used in connection with the investigation of crimes of the character which would have to be investigated in the former Yugoslavia. An important factor in this context is also the extent to which investigators can rely upon existent systems in the States in question.

There is a clear distinction between investigation of cases where there is a suspect, on the one hand, and investigations where there is no suspect or where there is a considerable number of persons among whom the perpetrator is to be sought, on the other hand. In particular in the latter category of cases it is imperative that a rational system to retrieve information is developed. In this context computers are often used. There are different systems with a different degree of elaboration. Irrespective of which system one would chose, there would still be need for analysis and assessment of different options, to be followed by purchase and education of the personnel to be entrusted with the operation of the system. It is also important that there is a registrator to supervise the persons who operate the computers.

In the actual registration it is necessary to use criteria of the kind already mentioned by the Rapporteurs: name of depositor; plaintiff/witness/other; suspects, if any; the alleged violation; time; place, etc. But important factors are also the ability of the persons involved and their professional capacity in organizing the police work, since cases differ widely in character.

It is important that registration is started at an early stage, since collected information which is not registered and organized tends to be very difficult to deal with the longer the time elapses. It is equally important to start investigations and to allow people to give information to the investigators at an early stage.

Once a person emerges as clear suspect the situation changes. In that situation the computers are not used in the same way, although all new information must be registered. But when a suspect is there, the investigation is concentrated on this person and in gathering evidence with respect to that case. Here the investigators are in a better position to collect information and to make the proper documentation to be presented to the prosecutor and also to the defence counsel, when time comes.

The conclusion which the Rapporteurs draw from this information is that their preoccupations in the report on Croatia on 7 October 1992 were justified. It is imperative that this first step in a process towards bringing war criminals to justice is examined thoroughly by experts in the way the Rapporteurs suggested. It would seem that in cases where there are already suspects, and where witnesses have given statements (the Rapporteurs have been informed that there are a considerable number of such cases), one could relatively quickly arrive at a stage where the prosecutor can take a decision on indictment. The Rapporteurs note, however, the caution by the investigators interviewed that information not registered properly as soon as it has been delivered will become very difficult to administer at a later stage. Therefore, even if there are already now cases which could be presented to a court in a relatively short time, it is necessary to decide at the outset on a more general framework of the registration of information. This decision must also contain rules on secrecy etc.

The Rapporteurs are aware that the UN Commission under Security Council Resolution 780 (1992) are at present collecting information. It must be observed, however, that it is a different matter to collect information in a more general way and to collect information within the framework of a criminal investigation with the intention to bring suspects to justice. The Rapporteurs see a risk for duplication of work if collection of information is to be made for different purposes. No doubt, the information collected by the UN Commission will be of help to investigators acting within the framework of an international tribunal. But the sooner a decision is taken on a general and well structured method of information collection with a view to assist prosecutors, the better.

From the contacts which the Rapporteurs have had with professor Cherif Bassiouni (cf. Section 2.5) it appears that he has on his own initiative paid attention to these questions and that he has, within the framework of the UN Expert Commission, organized a separate system for collection and storage of data related to war crimes and crimes against humanity. This system might serve as the starting-point for a system of the kind which the Rapporteurs foresee.

8.4 Organization of the Tribunal

The Rapporteurs would first like to refer to the prerequisites to be met by an international jurisdiction which they have identified. They appear in Section 7.

If a Tribunal is set up, it would need at least four organs: a court, a prosecutorial function, a secretariat and a standing committee of contracting States. The Rapporteurs also foresee an organ to deal with matters of clemency.

As far as the court is concerned, it is obvious that this instance would perform exactly the same functions as national courts. As the Rapporteurs have stated in their report on Croatia (Section 7.1) the administration of justice by an international jurisdiction must fulfil the international standards for criminal proceedings. Among those are the right to appeal. The Rapporteurs cannot foresee that a tribunal containing only one instance to deliver judgments without appeal could be contemplated in this case. Therefore, it is necessary to create within the Tribunal an instance of appeal.

The question arises whether judges could alternate from adjudicating cases in the first instance and in the instance of appeal. The Rapporteurs strongly advise against mixing these functions. There are many draw-backs with such a system, the most significant being the risk for disqualification, the impropriateness of judges alternating as the examiner and the examined, and the risk for general confusion in the administration of the court. They therefore propose that the judges of appeal be a category separate from the other judges.

A significant feature of existing international courts is that they are entitled to draw up their own rules of procedure. The Rapporteurs think that such competence is necessary also in the present case. This task and other tasks of an administrative matter mean that the court must be able to meet and make decisions also in an administrative capacity. Since all the judges should be entitled to participate in such decisions, it is necessary to create a forum where they can participate irrespective of whether they belong to the first instance or the instance of appeal.

Based on these considerations, the Rapporteurs propose that the Court shall consist of a Court of First Instance, which shall perform its judicial functions in Chambers of three judges, a Court of Appeal, which shall perform its judicial functions in Chambers of five judges, and the Plenary Court, which shall perform its functions with the participation of all the judges of the Court.

It is imperative that the system is flexible and that the number of judges could be increased or decreased in relation to work-load and possible back-log. The Rapporteurs therefore propose that the judges be appointed directly by the States parties to the Convention. Each State should appoint two judges for the Court of First Instance and one judge of appeal. However, no judge should serve on the Court until called by the Standing Committee (see below).

If twelve ratifications are required for the entry into force of the proposed Convention the number of appointed judges would be 24 + 12 at the outset. From these a sufficient number would be called to serve.

As far as the system of prosecution is concerned, the Rapporteurs recommend that an independent prosecutorial system be implemented. With such a system there would be no need for a formal preliminary hearing by a small chamber of the court, as foreseen in earlier draft treaties for an international criminal court. The Rapporteurs note that their view coincides with the view taken by the Working group of the International Law Commission (cf. paras. 509 and 512 of the ILC report).

A Procurator-General should be appointed to act as chief officer of the prosecutorial authority. This authority should have an independent power - and duty - to prosecute all the cases where substantiated charges can be made. The Rapporteurs also foresee a possibility to appeal against decisions by prosecutors.

The initiation of cases should not be limited to complaints, but the prosecutor should examine all prospective cases independent of their origin. Since the Rapporteurs foresee that the proposed Court should in principle assume exclusive jurisdiction over the crimes in question, there can be no limitation as to who should be able to communicate with the prosecutorial authority.

The need for a Secretariat is obvious. Reference is made to the draft Convention and the Commentary.

There is also an obvious need for a Standing Committee of the States parties to the Convention. The task of this Committee should be to administer the Convention, and in particular to decide on questions of budget. In view of the method suggested for the appointment of judges, the Standing Committee should also have the important duty of calling appointed judges to serve on the Court. The Committee would be in the same position as Governments and Parliaments at the national level; it would be responsible for the allocation of sufficient resources for the proper administration of justice. This argument applies not only to the resources of the Court but to the Tribunal as a whole.

Finally, the question of clemency cannot be overlooked. There must in the view of the Rapporteurs also be a body established by the Convention to exercise with respect to persons sentenced by the Court this function in lieu of competent national organs of the States parties to the Convention (cf. Article 48 of the draft Convention). Hence the Rapporteurs foresee a Board of Clemency.

A graphic presentation of the organization of the Tribunal appears in Annex 7.

8.5 Seat of the Tribunal

The question of the seat of the Tribunal needs careful consideration. The Rapporteurs are aware that this question also has important political connotations. They therefore abstain from making any concrete proposal, but would nevertheless like to point out the following in this connection.

The Rapporteurs foresee a great number of cases to be heard by the Court, and it is obvious that these hearings will involve not only the presence of the accused, but also of victims and witnesses from the area. This means that the Court must be very close to those who shall appear before it. On the other hand, it could be considered as a bias, if the formal seat of the Tribunal would be located in any one of the States in the territory of the former Yugoslavia.

The most appropriate solution might therefore be that the formal seat of the Tribunal is established in a place outside the territory of the former Yugoslavia with a possibility for the Court (i.e. the Chambers) to meet at locations in the territory of the former Yugoslavia. This would on the other hand mean a drawback to the co-operation between the different organs of the Tribunal, in particular the co-operation between the Chambers of the Court and the Secretariat; the prosecutors would obviously have to "follow" the Court. The need for the Plenary Court to meet must also be observed.

Other important aspects to be looked into are the premises as such, in particular the Court rooms, archives, as well as the security for those connected with the Tribunal and persons appearing before its organs. The question of arranging for the detention of persons accused while their cases are being dealt with must also be resolved.

An important aspect is also that it would be necessary to conclude a headquarters agreement between the Tribunal and the State where the seat of the Tribunal is located. It should be observed in this context that special arrangement might be needed, if hearings are contemplated at the seat, in particular concerning the premises necessary for keeping detained persons under appropriate custody. The relation between the Tribunal and States where Chambers may meet should preferably be covered by the general provisions on co-operation in the Convention itself. All these formalities must perhaps not necessarily be regulated under public law; to some extent contract might be feasible.

8.6 International judicial assistance to the Tribunal

It is obvious that the establishment of an international *ad hoc* tribunal of the kind which the Rapporteurs foresee presupposes a close co-operation between the Tribunal and the contracting States.

The Rapporteurs take it for granted that accused persons will not be tried *in absentia* (cf. Report on Croatia, Section 9.3). It will therefore be necessary to bring accused persons before the Court. Here the Rapporteurs think that it is necessary to distinguish between cases where the accused is present in a State party to the Convention within the territory of the former Yugoslavia, and present in another State party to the Convention. Yet another case is where the accused is present in a third State. In the discussion on an international criminal court the argument has been advanced that the statute of the court should provide that transfer to the court was not to be regarded as extradition (cf. paras. 519-527 of the ILC report). The Rapporteurs do not think that it is necessary to resolve the question whether a transfer should be regarded as extradition or not. This matter could be left to the requested State, which has to ascertain that obligations towards the Tribunal can be respected under national law.

The draft treaty also provides for the application of the principle *aut dedere, aut judicare* (cf. Article 59). According to the draft this option is, however, not open to States parties to the Convention within the territory of the former Yugoslavia. The way in which the draft is designed, such States undertake to respect compulsory jurisdiction of the Tribunal, which means that they must always be prepared to transfer the accused to the Court.

As already stated with respect to the seat of the Tribunal assistance and co-operation must also cover the situation when Chambers of the Court must arrange hearings in other States than the State where the seat of the Tribunal is (cf. Section 8.5).

In addition to this there are a number of means of legal assistance and co-operation. In general it should suffice to apply the system of legal assistance and co-operation which is applied between States today. The Rapporteurs refer to Articles 53 - 58 of the draft Convention, which contain general rules and rules on communications and requests, provisional measures, delivery of persons, the so called speciality rule, and rules on costs.

8.7 Legal aid and defence counsel

As the Rapporteurs have already stated (cf. Section 6) the justice system to be set up must comply with international norms. This means that a number of judicial guarantees must be ascertained for the accused persons. Among these guarantees are the right for the accused to have adequate time and facilities for the preparation of his defence and to communicate with counsel of his own choosing, and to have legal assistance assigned to him and without payment by him in any such case if he does not have sufficient means to pay for it.

The Rapporteurs have contemplated whether to include in the draft Convention provisions to this effect. Except for a general provision on judicial guarantees (Article 31) the draft Convention does not contain any provisions on this subject; this matter could be left to the Rules of the Tribunal. It should be observed, however, that adequate funds have to be allocated by the Standing Committee in order to pay for legal assistance, since it can be assumed that very few of the defendants will be anywhere near the possibility of paying the costs for this assistance. This related in particular to the fees which will be granted by the Court to defence counsel.

8.8 Sanctions, enforcement of judgments and supervision thereof

The sentence nullum crimen sine lege requires that punishments for criminal acts must be laid down in law when the crime was committed in order that the Court may mete out this punishment. As already explained (Section 8.2) it will be necessary for the Tribunal to rely on the pertinent national legislation in this respect.

According to the criminal law of the former Socialist Federal Republic of Yugoslavia the following punishments may be imposed: capital punishment, imprisonment and fines.

Already in their report on Croatia the Rapporteurs concluded that it was in their opinion inconceivable that the CSCE should endorse the death penalty (cf. Section 7.1 of that report). The draft Convention therefore includes a provision to the effect that the Court shall not pass a sentence of capital punishment, although this punishment appears in the provisions of the national law (Article 29, paragraph 2).

Since capital punishment will be excluded, it is necessary to examine more in detail how imprisonment is imposed according to the pertinent national law. It appears that the general rule on imprisonment (Article 38 of the Penal Code) lays down that imprisonment may not be shorter than fifteen days, nor exceed fifteen years. However, for crimes for which capital punishment is prescribed, the Court may also impose the punishment of imprisonment for twenty years. The question is, therefore, if it is possible to lay down in the Convention the possibility of imposing imprisonment for life. A first look at the national law may indicate that this is not possible. On the other hand, it could be argued that, if capital punishment cannot be imposed, there would be a possibility of imposing imprisonment for more than twenty years, n.b. lifetime, according to the principle majus includit minus. The Rapporteurs are, however, not prepared to make any proposal in this respect since the question undoubtedly needs further study.

Otherwise, the Rapporteurs foresee, that imprisonment in accordance with the national legislation will be a normal sanction imposed by the Court. Fines should, however, not be excluded. Fines could be imposed as a principal and as an accessory punishment. One must also bear in mind that the Court may not find that the act for which the accused is indicted is of such a grave nature that imprisonment must follow; the prosecutor must of course accept that the Court can make another assessment in this respect than the one made in the indictment.

A major issue is to decide where imprisonment is to be served. The Rapporteurs hold the view that the rule should be - subject to a narrow field of exception - that the sentences shall be served in the territory of the former Yugoslavia (cf. Article 46). This undoubtedly puts a heavy burden on the States in that territory. But unless they are prepared to take upon themselves to accept enforcement, the Rapporteurs foresee little possibility that justice can be done in the present case; the number of prisoners will probably be considerable.

The proposed solution also raises other important questions. The arguments putting the possibilities for national jurisdiction in the present case in question (cf. Section 7) could partly be invoked also against the idea of prisoners serving sentences in the territory of the former Yugoslavia. There is a risk that prisoners, with whom the population in the province where the sentence is served might sympathize, would be treated in an unduly favourable way, while prisoners belonging to the "opposite side" might even risk maltreatment. It is therefore necessary to have a rigorous international supervision of the enforcement. The Rapporteurs trust, however, that it would be in the interest of the States in the territory of the former Yugoslavia to build up societies under the rule of law. One of the hallmarks of such a society is that it should respect also the personal dignity of those who have violated the laws of that very society.

In sum, the Rapporteurs foresee that the question of sanctions, enforcement of judgments and supervision thereof needs careful consideration in the future deliberations. Further reflections on these questions appear in the Commentary to Articles 29, 46 and 47.

8.9 Transfer of proceedings from the Tribunal to States in the territory of the former Yugoslavia

As appears from Section 8.2, the Rapporteurs propose that the jurisdiction of the Tribunal should be exclusive with respect to States in the territory of the former Yugoslavia. This means that the States in which the crimes have been committed do not any more have jurisdiction over these crimes, if they become parties to the Convention.

As appears, the draft Convention, which limits jurisdiction to crimes committed after a ceratin date, does not contain any provision on the time when jurisdiction of the Tribunal should cease. The reasons for this have already been explained (Section 8.2).

In the view of the Rapporteurs it is necessary to create a flexible system. The greatest flexibility can be achieved if the Court would be given the right to transfer proceedings back to States in the territory of the former Yugoslavia. This would make it possible for the Court to assess the situation and gradually phase out the activities of the Tribunal.

The Rapporteurs foresee that a provision to this effect could be applied gradually and with respect to certain parts of the territory, while other parts would have to wait.

The Rapporteurs are anxious to emphasize that the formulation of the provision (Article 60) must in no way be construed as showing disrespect to the States in question. On the contrary, the Rapporteurs fully understand the difficulties which these States are facing. Their conclusions concerning jurisdiction by national courts reflected in Section 7 should also be borne in mind. The way in which the draft Convention is formulated, a transfer back to national jurisdiction means that the Court no longer has jurisdiction in the case. A decision on transfer should in their view be final. On the other hand it should not be made without the consent of the State to which the transfer is intended.

8.10 Financing

One of the most important issues to be regulated in the Convention is the financing. Matters pertaining to financing should be dealt with in the same way as is normal at the national level. This means that the organs of the Tribunal will have to provide the Standing Committee with sufficient basis in order for the Committee to be able to take a decision on the establishment of the annual budget.

The Convention and in particular its Annex 2 is drafted so as to provide the maximum of flexibility. This means that the budget may have to provide for certain resources which can be used, if necessary.

The items of the budget, as the Rapporteurs can foresee them at present, could be:

- Cost for the office

- Salaries for the judges

- Salaries for the Procurator-General and the members of the staff of the Procuracy

- Salaries for the Secretary and the members of the staff of the Secretariat

- Costs for legal aid

- Costs for witnesses and other evidence

- Travelling expenses and per diems

- Costs for interpretation and translation

- Unforeseen.

The main rule of the costs of the Tribunal appears in Article 52 of the draft Convention. The substantive provisions are, however, laid down in a Financial Protocol in order not to burden the Convention itself with too much detail. The protocol is partly modelled after the draft Financial Protocol to the Stockholm Convention on Conciliation and Arbitration within the CSCE.

The Rapporteurs suggested in their report on Croatia that experts looking into the matter of drafting a treaty on an <u>ad hoc</u> tribunal should also make an estimation of costs. This is a question which requires thorough knowledge of many aspects of the establishment of international organizations, a field in which the Rapporteurs unfortunately lack much experience. They have, however, collected some information from the organs operating in the Hague. Some experience has also been drawn from the present work on the drafting of the Financial Protocol just mentioned. Based on this knowledge the following very - the Rapporteurs underline very - general calculations could be made.

In order not to create expectations the Rapporteurs prefer not to itemize the posts, but their assumptions are that the Court of First Instance would at the outset consist of 15 judges and the Court of Appeal of 7 judges. There would be 15 prosecutors, and the staff - including investigators - would consist of approximately 50 persons.

The annual cost for salaries to such a personnel would be approximately USD 8 - 10,000,000.

To this would come rental and maintenance of premises, miscellaneous equipment, audit services, transport of detained persons etc., counsel's fees and travel expenses etc. as well as costs for witnesses and other persons called before the court.

A very rough calculation would indicate a total cost of USD 16,000,000 per year, or USD 0.044 million per day.

In this context it is interesting to make a comparison with the costs for the United Nations Protection Force (UNPROFOR). From the Secretary General's report of 2 December 1992 (Doc. A/47/741) appears i.a. the following (cf. Annex IV to the report). The net total for UNPROFOR for the period 12 January - 14 October 1992 (revised aportionment) was USD 260,000,000. The cost estimate for the period 15 October 1992 - 20 February 1993 is USD 290,924,000, and the cost estimate for the period 21 February 1993 - 20 February 1994 is USD 569,548,200. The latter figure corresponds to USD 1.56 million per day.

In the Secretary-General's report of 8 January 1993 (Doc. S/25000/Add. 1) there are estimates of the additional costs to the United Nations arising from the proposal to enlarge the mandate and strength of UNPROFOR. It is estimated that the costs associated with the additional responsibilities of monitoring crossing-points on the borders of Bosnia and Herzegovina with the Federal Republic of Yugoslavia would amount to some USD 694,125,000 for an initial six-month period. It is further estimated that the monthly cost thereafter will be approximately USD 69,155,000.

The Rapporteurs certainly do not intend to make any comparison whatsoever between UNPROFOR and a Tribunal; they have themselves observed the indispensable efforts in which this force is engaged, and they were very kindly assisted by UNPROFOR during their visit to Croatia. But it is nevertheless interesting to note that a forceful international jurisdiction could be set up at a cost which is only marginal - perhaps one or two per cent - in comparison to the costs for UNPROFOR.

The Rapporteurs would, however, not look only at the figures in relation to the Tribunal as such. One of the basic ideas of the international co-operation today is the rule of law. At the national level considerable funds are allocated to various institutions set up in defence of this idea. An important factor in the assessment of funds to be allocated to this end is the benefit which the judicial system brings to the society as a whole: the benefit of prevention.

In the view of the Rapporteurs the same reasoning should be applied also at the international level. The preventive effect of establishing the rule of law at the international level must also be recognized. Experiences from financing international operations for peace-keeping and for the monitoring of different international crises demonstrate that the costs for such undertakings tend to be soaring. A clear demonstration of determination and international co-operation in the matter with which this report is concerned would in the view of the Rapporteurs have a preventive effect, which in the long run would balance the costs foreseen at the present juncture.

8.11 Proceedings before the Tribunal

The preceding sections deal with some important questions of principle. The Rapporteurs are aware that it may be difficult to get a clear picture of the entire proceedings before the Tribunal. They therefore decided to present in this section a brief outline of the proceedings. They have chosen to do so by making reference to a case proceeded before the different organs of the Tribunal.

The first stage would be the investigation. A prosecutor would probably indicate what cases the investigators should concentrate on. But there would also be a general work concentrated on retrieving information which can indicate starting points.

There would be several sources of information (cf. Section 8.3). The investigators would have to rely on contacts and assistance at the national level. Victims and witnesses would have to be interviewed.

When the investigation has reached a stage where it is

possible to start preparing an indictment, the prosecutor will get more directly involved. If the suspect is under arrest at the national level (the Convention should not prevent such actions at the national level) the prosecutor might request the Court to issue a warrant of arrest, whereby the Court would take over responsibility for the person detained. If the suspect is not to be found, a warrant of arrest could nevertheless be granted, and States parties to the Convention as well as Interpol might be engaged. This would mean that the suspect would be apprehended if found, e.g. at a border-crossing or an airport.

When there is enough material gathered, the prosecutor has to take a stand whether to terminate the inquiry or to indict the suspect.

The indictment is then filed with the Secretary of the Tribunal, who allocates the case to one of the Chambers of the Court of First Instance. The Court makes an overview of the case and decides to serve the indictment on the accused. The accused would then be summoned (or brought) to a main hearing before the Court. He will have access to counsel, and the principle of "equality of arms" requires that he should be able to call witnesses and present evidence in the same manner as the prosecutor.

The main hearing will in principle be in public. When the proceedings are closed, the Court will withdraw and eventually pronounce its judgment. If the accused is acquitted, the case is closed unless the judgment is appealed. If the accused is found guilty, the judgment will be enforced. If the judgment is appealed, enforcement will depend on the outcome of the proceedings before the Court of Appeal.

If the case is appealed, the proceedings before the Court of Appeal will be very similar to the proceedings before the Court of First Instance. It should be noted, though, that the case before the Court of Appeal could be limited to certain questions or certain parts of the judgment. A common feature in appeal proceedings in criminal cases is that the accused may accept the fact that he is found guilty of a certain crime, but he wants the Court of Appeal to impose a more lenient sanction.

The judgment of the Court of Appeal will be final. If the accused is sentenced to imprisonment, the care for the convict will be transferred from the Tribunal to the national prison authorities in a State in the territory of the former Yugoslavia. The convict will be placed in an appropriate prison. General rules in this field may require that he should serve the sentence in such a way that his possibilities of receiving visits from members of his family are not impeded.

The case will now also be registered with the Supervising Judge, who must always be kept informed about the whereabouts of the prisoner. The prisoner will be informed about his right to communicate with the Supervising Judge, who may also visit prisons in the former Yugoslavia.

Eventually, the prisoner might ask for a modification of the sentence or for conditional release. This matter would have to be dealt with by the ordinary competent national organs. Their decision is, however, dependent on the approval by the Supervising Judge.

If the prisoner applies for clemency, this will not be a matter for national authorities but for the Board of Clemency.

Eventually, the prisoner will have served his term, and the matter will be closed also with the Supervising Judge.

9 ACKNOWLEDGEMENTS

The Rapporteurs wish to express their gratitude to the Government of the Republic of Bosnia-Herzegovina for the co-operation extended to them despite the fact that the Rapporteurs were not able to visit that country. In particular they are grateful for the material provided which has made it possible for the Rapporteurs to examine the most important legal aspects of the subject matter entrusted to them. The Rapporteurs furthermore wish to express their gratitude to the Minister of Foreign Affairs of Bosnia-Herzegovina, Mr. Haris Silajdzic, the President of the Parliament of Bosnia-Herzegovina, Mr. Miro Lazovic, and to the other members of the Bosnian delegation for answering to their call for a meeting at Geneva at a time when they were otherwise engaged in the negotiations within the International Conference on the former Yugoslavia.

They would also like to thank Professor Frits Kalshoven and the other members of the Expert Commission established under United Nations Security Council Resolution No. 780 (1992), and in particular Professor M. Cherif Bassiouni, for a valuable exchange of views and information about the work of the Commission.

They furthermore thank Dr. Georg Mautner-Markhof and Professor Roman Wieruszewski, advisers to Mr. Janusz Mazowiecki, Special Rapporteur of the United Nations Commission on Human Rights on the former Yugoslavia, for informing them about the Rapporteur mission and for their kind advice. They are also grateful to Ambassador Peter Hall, Deputy to Lord Owen, and Mr. David Ludlow, Private Secretary to Lord Owen, for informing them about the present situation in the International Conference on the Former Yugoslavia and for offering helpful comments in relation to their mandate.

The Rapporteurs also extend their gratitude to Ms. Birgit Kofler and Ms. Karin Proidl, Legal Officers of the Federal Ministry for Foreign Affairs of Austria, for preparing Annex 3, and to Ms. Ann Marie Pennegård, Counsellor, Permanent Delegation of Sweden to the United Nations at Geneva, who assisted them during their visit to Geneva on 24-26 January 1993.

They also express their gratitude to the Government of Norway for financial support of the translation of legal texts into English.

Finally, the Rapporteurs wish to thank the Ministry for Foreign Affairs of Sweden and the staff of the Legal Office of the Ministry, in particular Ms. Ulla-Britt Lagell and Ms. Anna Nilsson, for making possible the prompt completion of this report, and Ms. Ritva Manoli, for the graphic design of the cover and Annex 7.

10 CONCLUDING REMARKS

The Rapporteurs would like to reiterate their statement in the concluding remarks in their report on Croatia:

> "It is beyond any doubt that gross violations of human rights and norms of international humanitarian law,

> including war crimes and crimes against humanity, have been committed in connection with the armed conflict in the former Yugoslavia. It is also common knowledge that every day atrocities continue to be committed. The evidence is overwhelming and undeniable. The international community cannot allow this horrifying situation to persist. In various fields, decisive measures should be taken to put an end to this tragic situation. One such field is the legal field."

The Rapporteurs can only note that the atrocities in the former Yugoslavia have continued since their report was issued on 7 October 1992. Many examples could be mentioned. The Rapporteurs are, however, especially concerned about numerous reports on extensive abuse of women in Bosnia-Herzegovina.

The Rapporteurs have noted the increased concern by the international community regarding this appalling situation; a concern demonstrated by a number of activities in different fields, i.e. by the United Nations, the CSCE, the EC, and the International Conference on the former Yugoslavia. They have noted in particular the resolutions adopted by the United Nations Security Council and the work performed by the Commission established under Security Council Resolution No. 780 (1992), and they are aware of all the efforts undertaken in various fields in order to protect the civilian population in the area. However, the time has come to act with increased determination in the legal field. As the Rapporteurs stated in their report on Croatia, the international community shares a common responsibility to bring to justice those who have committed crimes in connection with the armed conflict in the former Yugoslavia.

The Rapporteurs wish to point out that a wealth of information has already been gathered by various governmental and non-governmental organizations and institutions. Much of this information in their view would be sufficient to serve as a legal basis for criminal proceedings against suspected perpetrators. If no action is taken in the near future, it will become increasingly difficult to prosecute.

The Rapporteurs are convinced that the States on the territory of the former Yugoslavia which have declared their willingness to co-operate will do so. Persons under the jurisdiction of those States and suspected of having committed war crimes and crimes against humanity would therefore be delivered for trial by the Tribunal.

The Rapporteurs trust that in due course all the States on the territory of the former Yugoslavia will bow to the dictates of public conscience and accept the prosecution of suspected war criminals by the proposed Tribunal.

The message should be clear: Nobody committing war crimes and crimes against humanity will escape justice!

The Rapporteurs reiterate their conviction that the establishment of an International War Crimes Tribunal for the former Yugoslavia is not only desirable but also feasable from a legal point of view. The establishment of such a Tribunal is therefore primarily a question of political will.

Stockholm, Washington and Oslo, 9 February 1993

Hans Corell Helmut Türk Gro Hillestad Thune

* * *

Annex 6

DRAFT CONVENTION ON AN INTERNATIONAL WAR CRIMES TRIBUNAL FOR THE FORMER YUGOSLAVIA

The States parties to this Convention, being States participating in the Conference on Security and Co-operation in Europe,

Gravely alarmed by the numerous reports on war crimes and crimes against humanity, committed in the former Yugoslavia, and by the fact that such crimes continue to be committed in certain areas thereof;

Mindful of their obligations under the 1949 Geneva Convention III relative to the Treatment of Prisoners of War and the 1949 Geneva Convention IV relative to the Protection of Civilian Persons in Time of War to establish jurisdiction over persons alleged to have committed grave breaches as defined in Article 130 and Article 147, respectively, of those Conventions, and aware of the 1977 Protocols I and II to these Conventions;

Mindful also of their obligation under Article 28 of the 1954 Hague Convention for the Protection of Cultural Property in the Event of an Armed Conflict to take, within the framework of their ordinary criminal jurisdiction, all necessary steps to prosecute and impose penal or disciplinary sanctions upon those persons, of whatever nationality, who commit or order to be committed a breach of that Convention;

Reaffirming their determination, as expressed in their previous statements, that suspected war criminals in the former Yugoslavia should be held personally accountable for their acts;

Responding to the appeals from States in the territory of the former Yugoslavia to establish an international jurisdiction to try individuals accused of war crimes and crimes against humanity committed in that territory,

Have agreed as follows:

CHAPTER I - GENERAL PROVISIONS

Article 1
Establishment of the Tribunal

There is hereby established an International War Crimes Tribunal for the former Socialist Federative Republic of Yugoslavia ("the former Yugoslavia").

Article 2
Purpose of the Tribunal

The purpose of the Tribunal is to try individuals accused of war crimes and crimes against humanity as defined in international law and the domestic criminal law provisions of the former Yugoslavia and determined in scope by this Convention.

Article 3
Crimes Punishable under this Convention

Crimes punishable under this Convention are the crimes referred to in this Convention and committed in the territory of the former Yugoslavia as from 1 January 1991.

Article 4
Organs of the Tribunal

The Tribunal shall consist of the following organs:

(a) the Court, comprising the Court of First Instance, the Court of Appeal, and the Plenary Court;

(b) the Procuracy;

(c) the Secretariat;

(d) the Board on Clemency; and

(e) the Standing Committee of States parties to this Convention, hereinafter referred to as the Standing Committee.

Article 5

Legal Capacity

The Tribunal shall enjoy in the territory of each of the States parties to this Convention such legal capacity as may be necessary for the exercise of its functions and the fulfilment of its purposes.

Article 6

Seat

1. The seat of the Tribunal shall be established at ...

2. The Court may upon approval of the Standing Committee meet in the territory of any State party to this Convention.

CHAPTER II - THE COURT

A. THE COURT OF FIRST INSTANCE

Article 7

Appointment of Judges

1. Each State party to this Convention shall appoint, within two months following its entry into force, two judges, both of whom shall be nationals of that State. A State which becomes party to this Convention after its entry into force shall appoint its judges within thirty days following the entry into force of this Convention for the State concerned.

2. The judges shall have no official function on the Tribunal until they are called to serve on the Court of First Instance by the Standing Committee.

3. Judges shall be persons of high moral character and have the legal competence and qualifications required for appointment to a criminal court of their States.

4. In the event of death or resignation or if there is a vacancy for any other reason, the State concerned shall appoint a new judge. The term of office of the new judge shall be the remainder of the term of office of the predecessor.

5. The names of the judges shall be notified to the Secretary of the Tribunal, who shall enter them into a list, which shall be communicated to each State party to this Convention.

Article 8
Terms of Office

1. Judges shall be appointed for a term of five years. They may be re-appointed once.

2. A judge shall continue in office beyond his term in order to complete work on any pending matter in which he was involved until final disposition of that matter.

3. In the case of the resignation of a judge, the resignation shall be addressed to the President of the Tribunal, who shall transmit it to the Standing Committee. This transmission shall make the place vacant.

Article 9
Solemn Declaration

Each judge shall, before taking up his duties, make a solemn declaration in open court that he will perform his functions impartially and conscientiously.

Article 10
Privileges and Immunities

The judges shall enjoy, while performing their functions in the territory of the States parties to this Convention, the privileges and immunities accorded to members of the International Court of Justice.

Article 11
Occupation of Judges

1. Once appointed judges may not have any occupation or business other than that of a judge in the State from which they have been appointed, or a member of the faculty of a university. Judges shall not engage in any activity which interferes with their judicial functions at the Tribunal and avoid any appearance of lack of impartiality.

2. Any doubt on this point shall be settled by the decision of the Plenary Court.

Article 12
Disability of Judges

A judge shall perform no function on the Tribunal with respect to any matter in which he may have had any involvement prior to his appointment to the Tribunal, nor with respect to any matter involving actual, apparent or potential conflict of interest.

Article 13
Disqualification of Judges

1. A judge who considers that he should not participate in a particular proceeding shall so inform the President of the Plenary Court, who may excuse the judge.

2. A party to a proceeding may submit that a judge should not participate in a particular proceeding. Such submission shall be addressed to the President of the Plenary Court.

3. If the President of the Plenary Court upon receipt of a submission under paragraph 2 or of his own motion considers that a judge should not participate in a particular proceeding, the President shall so advise the judge.

4. If the President of the Plenary Court and the judge disagree on issues referred to in this Article, the Plenary Court shall decide.

Article 14
Dismissal of Judges

1. A judge may be removed by a unanimous vote of the Plenary Court for incapacity to fulfil his functions.

2. The President of the Court shall transmit such decision to the Standing Committee. This transmission shall make the place vacant.

Article 15
Emoluments

The Standing Committee shall determine the salary of judges.

Article 16
Chambers

1. For the consideration of each case brought before it the Court of First Instance shall consist of a Chamber composed of three judges.

2. Election of the judges to the Chambers shall be by the Plenary Court by lot.

3. The President of the Court shall request the Standing Committee to call judges to serve on the Court of First Instance when the need arises. The answer to this request by the Standing Committee shall be within thirty days of the request.

Article 17
Decision-making

1. The decisions of the Chambers shall be taken by a majority of their members, who may not abstain from voting.

2. In the event that there is no majority, the judges shall make a renewed effort in order to arrive at a decision. If this is not possible, the vote of the presiding judge shall prevail.

B. THE COURT OF APPEAL

Article 18
Appointment of Judges

1. Each State party to this Convention shall appoint, within two months following its entry into force, one judge of appeal who shall be a national of that State. A State which becomes party to this Convention after its entry into force shall appoint its judge of appeal within thirty days following the entry into force of this Convention for the State concerned.

2. The judges of appeal shall have no official function on the

Tribunal until they are called to serve on the Court of Appeal by the Standing Committee.

3. Judges of appeal shall fulfil the requirements laid down in Article 7, paragraph 3. In addition, they shall fulfil the requirements for appointment to a criminal court of appeal of their States.

4. In the event of death or resignation or if there is a vacancy for any other reason, the State concerned shall appoint a new judge of appeal. The term of office of the new judge of appeal shall be the remainder of the term of office of the predecessor.

5. The names of the judges of appeal shall be notified to the Secretary of the Tribunal, who shall enter them into a list, which shall be communicated to each State party to this Convention.

Article 19
Chambers

1. For the consideration of each case brought before it the Court of Appeal shall consist of a Chamber composed of five judges of appeal.

2. The Standing Committee shall elect one Chamber and two alternate judges of appeal by lot. Should the need arise, the Standing Committee shall elect two Chambers and two alternate judges of appeal by lot.

3. If there is a need for more than two Chambers, the provisions of Article 16, paragraphs 2 and 3 shall apply *mutatis mutandis*.

Article 20
Other Provisions

The provisions of Articles 8-15 and 17 shall apply to the Court of Appeal *mutatis mutandis*.

C. THE PLENARY COURT

Article 21
Constitution and Functions

1. All the judges called to serve on the Court of First Instance and the Court of Appeal constitute the Plenary Court.

2. The Plenary Court shall elect from among the judges of appeal a President and a vice-President. The President shall serve for a term of two years, and may be re-elected, although not for more than two consecutive terms.

3. The Plenary Court shall decide on matters entrusted to it by this Convention.

4. A quorum of twelve judges shall suffice to constitute the Plenary Court. The Rules of the Tribunal may lay down a higher number.

5. The decisions of the Plenary Court shall be taken by a majority of the judges participating in the vote. Those abstaining shall not be considered participating in the vote. In the event of a tied vote, the vote of the President shall prevail.

6. In case this Convention lays down special rules on the decision-making procedure of the Plenary Court, such rules shall apply instead of paragraph 5.

CHAPTER III - THE PROCURACY

Article 22
Functions

The Procuracy shall investigate and prosecute the crimes as determined in scope by this Convention.

Article 23
The Procurator-General and Members of the Staff of the Procuracy

1. The Procurator-General is the chief officer of the Procuracy and the Chief Public Prosecutor. He shall be elected by the Standing Committee from a list of at least three nominees

submitted by the States parties to the Convention. He shall serve for a renewable term of five years, barring resignation or removal by a two-third's vote of the Plenary Court for incompetence, conflict of interest, or manifest disregard of the provisions of this Convention or the Rules of the Tribunal.

2. The salary of the Procurator-General shall be the same as that of the judges of appeal.

3. The Procuracy shall employ other prosecutors, investigators and clerical staff as necessary to carry out its responsibilities and consistent with the budget established by the Standing Committee. The members of the staff of the Procuracy shall be appointed and removed by the Procurator-General. Their salaries shall be determined by the Procurator-General subject to the budget established by the Standing Committee.

CHAPTER IV - THE SECRETARIAT

Article 24
Functions

1. The Secretariat is the administrative, financial, and clerical organ of the Tribunal.

2. The Secretariat shall:

(a) prepare a budget proposal for the ensuing financial year for each of the organs of the Tribunal on the basis of the information provided thereto by the other organs;

(b) publish an annual financial report and a report on the activities of the Tribunal on the basis of information provided by the President of the Court and the Procurator-General; and

(c) perform any other function provided in this Convention.

Article 25
The Secretary and Members of the Staff of the Secretariat

1. The Secretary of the Tribunal is the chief officer of the Secretariat. He is the clerk of the Tribunal as a whole but has

a particular responsibility with respect to the Court. He shall be elected by the Plenary Court and serve for a renewable term of five years, barring resignation or removal by the Plenary Court for incompetence, conflict of interests or manifest disregard of the provisions of this Convention or the Rules of the Tribunal.

2. The salary of the Secretary shall be the same as that of the judges of appeal.

3. The Secretariat shall employ such staff as appropriate to perform its functions consistent with the budget established by the Standing Committee. The members of the staff of the Secretariat shall be appointed and removed by the Secretary. Their salaries shall be determined by the Secretary subject to the budget established by the Standing Committee.

CHAPTER V - THE STANDING COMMITTEE

Article 26
Functions

1. The Standing Committee shall represent the States parties to this Convention. It shall perform the functions expressly assigned to it under the Convention, and any other functions that it determines appropriate in furtherance of the purposes of the Tribunal and are not inconsistent with the Convention. These functions may in no way impair the independence and integrity of the Court as a judicial body.

2. The Standing Committee shall:

(a) call judges to serve on the Court;

(b) elect the Procurator-General;

(c) establish the annual budget of the Tribunal;

(d) assist the Tribunal in carrying out its functions;

(e) monitor compliance by the States parties with the provisions of this Convention;

(f) ensure compliance with judgments and other decisions of the Court; and

(g) perform any other function provided in this Convention.

Article 27
Composition and Procedure

1. The Standing Committee shall consist of one representative and one alternate representative appointed by each State party to this Convention. If no appointment is made, the permanent representative to the State where the seat of the Tribunal is located shall be regarded as representative.

2. The Standing Committee shall elect from among the representatives a presiding officer and an alternate presiding officer. The presiding officer shall have the right to have one or more assistants who are not members of the staff of the Secretariat.

3. The presiding officer shall convene regular meetings at least twice a year at the seat of the Tribunal. At the request of one third of the representatives he shall call extraordinary meetings. The Standing Committee can also decide to meet in a location other than the seat of the Tribunal.

4. The Standing Committee may exclude from participation at a given session the representative of a State party that:

(a) has failed to provide financial support for the Tribunal in accordance with the established budget; or

(b) has failed to carry out any other obligation under this Convention.

5. The Standing Committee may form an executive board or any other sub-committee as it may deem appropriate.

6. The Standing Committee may adopt rules of procedure as necessary.

7. The decisions of the Standing Committee shall be taken by a majority of the members participating in the vote. Those abstaining shall not be considered participating in the vote. In the event of a tied vote, the vote of the presiding officer shall prevail.

8. In case this Convention lays down special rules on the decision-making procedure of the Standing Committee, such rules shall apply instead of paragraph 7.

CHAPTER VI - JURISDICTION AND APPLICABLE LAW

Article 28
Jurisdiction and Applicable Law

1. The Tribunal shall, subject to the provisions of this Convention, apply the substantive law set forth in Annex 1, to be construed in the light of the pertinent international instruments. Annex 1 constitutes an integral part of this Convention.

2. With respect to general substantive law, such as rules on attempt, preparation, conspiracy and complicity, the provisions of the Penal Code of the former Yugoslavia shall apply. In passing sentence the Court shall observe the provisions on aggravating or extenuating circumstances of the same Code.

3. In all cases before the Tribunal, the procedures, rules, and standards of the Tribunal shall apply.

4. If the jurisdiction of the Tribunal is challenged by a party to the trial, the matter shall be decided by the pertinent Chamber of the Court of First Instance at once. If it is made later, the matter shall be decided by the Court at such time as the Court thinks fit.

CHAPTER VII - PENALTIES AND REMEDIES

Article 29
Penalties

1. The Court shall have the power to impose the penalties provided for in the Penal Code of the former Yugoslavia. Such penalties include:

(a) deprivation of liberty;

(b) fines; and

(c) confiscation of the proceeds of criminal conduct.

2. The Court shall not pass sentence of capital punishment.

Article 30
Remedies

1. The Court shall have the power to order in conformity with the legislation of the former Yugoslavia:

(a) restitution of property; and
(b) provision for damages.

2. The Court may decide not to hear matters referred to in paragraph 1, if this would impede or delay the criminal case with which the Court is seized.

CHAPTER VIII - GENERAL PROVISIONS ON PROCEDURE

Article 31
Judicial Guarantees

An individual charged with a crime under the provisions of this Convention shall be entitled without discrimination to the guarantees provided for in the International Covenant on Civil and Political Rights and the European Convention on Human Rights.

Article 32
Double Jeopardy

1. No person who has been tried, acquitted, or convicted by the Court shall be subsequently tried for the same crime in any court within the jurisdiction of any State party to this Convention.

2. A person who has been tried in any national court shall not be tried again for the same crime before the Tribunal.

Article 33
Rights and Interests of the Victim

The rights and interests of the victim of a crime shall be protected. In particular, a victim shall have:

(a) the opportunity to participate in the criminal proceedings in accordance with the provisions of this Convention and the Rules of the Tribunal; and

(b) the right to claim restitution of property and appropriate compensation.

CHAPTER IX - CRIMINAL INQUIRY AND INITIATION OF THE PROCESS

Article 34
Criminal Inquiry

1. A criminal inquiry shall be conducted as soon as there is reason to believe that a crime falling within the jurisdiction of the Tribunal has been committed.

2. The Procurator-General shall appoint one of the prosecutors of the Procuracy to conduct the inquiry in the capacity of Public Prosecutor.

3. The Public Prosecutor shall have the right to call witnesses for examination, to request evidence and to call experts.

4. The person subject to inquiry shall have the right to be heard in respect of the complaint. He shall also have the right to be assisted at the inquiry by a counsel of his own choice, to submit information, and to inspect any document introduced during the inquiry.

5. The Public Prosecutor may request national authorities of States parties to this Convention to assist in the performance of his function and to supply relevant information.

6. A State party to this Convention shall render such assistance in conformity with the Convention and with national law.

Article 35
Initiation of the Process

1. Having regard to the facts established at the criminal inquiry, the Public Prosecutor shall either:

(a) terminate the inquiry against the alleged offender, should the complaint or suspicion appear to be unfounded in law or in fact, or

(b) decide to indict the accused based on the findings in the inquiry, if the case is reasonably founded in fact and law.

2. In the case referred to in paragraph 1 (a), a State party to this Convention or an alleged victim may appeal the determination to the Procurator-General.

3. In the case referred to in paragraph 1 (b), the Public Prosecutor shall prepare an indictment of the accused based on the findings of the inquiry and shall file it with the Secretary of the Tribunal. He shall also be responsible for conducting the prosecution before the Court.

CHAPTER X - PROCEDURES BEFORE THE COURT OF FIRST INSTANCE

Article 36
Pre-trial Processes

1. The Public Prosecutor may request the Court of First Instance to issue orders in aid or development of a case, in particular:

(a) warrants of arrests;

(b) subpoenas;

(c) injunctions;

(d) search warrants; and

(e) warrants for surrender of an accused so as to enable the bringing of the accused before the Court.

2. Requests for such orders may be granted without prior notice to the accused, if such notice would jeopardize the pursuit of justice.

3. All such orders shall be executed pursuant to the relevant laws of the State in which they are supposed to be executed.

4. A warrant of arrest may be issued when there exists a strong suspicion on reasonable and probable grounds that the accused person has committed the alleged offence and that the Tribunal has jurisdiction in the case. Subsequent to the arrest of the accused, the Court may request the concerned State to detain the accused or to release him provisionally. The Court may impose conditions of provisional release.

Article 37
Indictment

1. The indictment shall contain a concise statement of the facts which constitute each alleged offence and a specific reference to the legal provisions under which the accused is charged. The Court may authorize amendments to this indictment as regards the extent of crimes included.

2. The Court is not bound to apply the legal provisions which are referred to by the Public Prosecutor in the indictment but it may apply other legal provisions which appear in Annex 1 or in this Convention as it may find appropriate to the case after having given reasonable notice to the parties.

Article 38
Notice of Indictment

1. The Court shall bring the indictment to the notice of the accused.

2. The Court shall not proceed with the trial unless satisfied that the accused has had the indictment and any amendment thereof served upon him and has had sufficient time and facilities to prepare his defense.

Article 39
Withdrawal of Prosecution, Dismissal or Acquittal

1. If the Public Prosecutor withdraws the indictment, the Court shall dismiss the case. However, if the accused so requests, the Court shall discharge him.

2. If, after hearing the case, the Court does not find sufficient evidence of guilt, it shall acquit the accused.

Article 40

Main Hearing

1. The Court shall hear the case in public, unless it decides for reasons of public order or the protection of the private life of victims or to the extent strictly necessary in special circumstances where publicity would prejudice the interests of justice that the hearing shall be held in camera.

2. The Court shall have the right to call witnesses for examination and to request evidence from witnesses and other appropriate evidential material, and to call experts. The Court may call upon any State to supply information which may appear to be relevant to the case.

3. When all evidence respecting guilt and innocence has been presented and argued by the parties, the Court shall close the hearing and retire for deliberations. These shall take place in private and shall not be disclosed.

Article 41

Judgments

1. The Court shall announce its judgments orally, in full or in summary, in open court. A judgment shall state, in relation to each accused, the reasons upon which it is based.

2. The judgment shall contain the names of the judges who have taken part in the decision. It shall be signed by the presiding judge and the Secretary.

3. A judge may issue a concurring or dissenting opinion. If such opinion is issued, the judgment shall contain the same.

4. The judgment shall contain information on how to appeal.

5. Unless appealed the judgment shall be final.

CHAPTER XI - PROCEDURES BEFORE THE COURT OF APPEAL

Article 42

Initiation of the Process

1. Judgments of the Court of First Instance may be appealed by

the accused upon written notice filed with the Secretariat within thirty days of the date on which the judgment was rendered in writing.

2. The Procuracy may appeal questions of law in the same manner as an accused under paragraph 1.

3. Other appeals against actions of the Court of First Instance may be examined before a final judgment is handed down only if such actions relate to procedural matters.

Article 43
The Trial

The provisions of Articles 39 and 40 shall apply to the Court of Appeal.

Article 44
Judgments and Decisions

1. Article 41, paragraphs 1-3 shall apply *mutatis mutandis* to the Court of Appeal.

2. Judgments and decisions by the Court of Appeal shall be final.

Article 45
Revision of Judgments

1. An accused who has been found guilty may apply to the Court of Appeal for revision of the judgment.

2. An application for revision shall not be entertained unless the Court is satisfied:

(a) that a fact has been discovered of such a nature as to be a decisive factor; and

(b) that this fact was, when the judgment was given, unknown to the Court and the applicant.

3. The Rules of the Tribunal may lay down other grounds for revision.

4. Revision proceedings shall be opened by a judgment of the Court of Appeal expressly recording the existence of the new fact and recognizing that it is of such a character as to lay the case open to revision.

5. If revision proceedings are opened, the Court of Appeal may:

(a) decide to withhold execution of the judgment;

(b) re-open the case and vacate the judgment;

(c) re-open the case for a new trial before the Court of Appeal; or

(d) remand the case for a new trial before the Court of First Instance.

CHAPTER XII - ENFORCEMENT OF JUDGMENTS

Article 46
Enforcement

1. Penalties are to be enforced on behalf of the Court in a State party to this Convention which is a successor State to the former Yugoslavia.

2. A penalty can also be enforced in another State party to this Convention, if this State consents thereto.

3. The enforcement shall be under international supervision as provided for in Article 47 and the Rules of the Tribunal.

4. The Court may determine the way in which a sentence shall be dealt with subject to paragraphs 5 and 6.

5. The laws of the administering State party to this Convention as well as its administrative regulations concerning the enforcement and execution of the sentence shall apply, including conditional release or alternative measures provided under its laws, subject to the provisions of Article 47, paragraph 2.

6. The enforcement of a fine or a confiscatory measure shall be governed by the laws and regulations mentioned in paragraph 5. However, their proceeds shall go to the Tribunal.

Article 47
Supervision

1. The Plenary Court shall select one of the judges of the Court of First Instance to act as supervisor of the execution of judgments (Supervising Judge). An alternate Supervising Judge shall also be selected.

2. The Supervising Judge has the right to inspect any prison or other place of detention where sentences are served or persons are being kept under custody and to communicate with all sentenced persons in private. All national decisions on conditional release or alternative measures shall be subject to the approval of the Supervising Judge.

3. The provisions of this Article does not preclude the Court from suspending its judgment or place preconditions to its application in accordance with the Rules of the Tribunal.

CHAPTER XIII - CLEMENCY

Article 48
Board of Clemency

1. The States parties to this Convention shall designate a Board of Clemency. Every State party to this Convention shall be entitled to have one delegate on the Board.

2. The Board shall have the power of clemency with respect to persons sentenced by the Court in lieu of competent national organs of the States parties to this Convention.

3. Before deciding on a petition for clemency, the Board shall seek the advice of the Plenary Court.

4. The Board shall adopt its own rules of procedure.

CHAPTER XIV - ADMINISTRATIVE MATTERS

Article 49
Rules of the Tribunal

1. The Plenary Court shall draw up Rules of the Tribunal to regulate the functions and activities of the Court, the

Procuracy and the Secretariat. In doing so the Court should give due consideration to the Code of Criminal Procedure of the former Yugoslavia.

2. When the Rules of the Tribunal are being drawn up, the Procurator-General and the Secretary are entitled to participate but not to vote.

3. The Rules of the Tribunal shall be published. Rules pertaining to the security of the Tribunal and related provisions may, however, be kept confidential.

Article 50

Working Languages

1. The working language of the Tribunal shall be English.

2. The Court may decide to use any other language in a particular case.

Article 51

Privileges and Immunities

1. The privileges and immunities of judges are laid down in Article 10.

2. The Procurator-General, the Secretary and other officers and employees of the Tribunal shall enjoy, while performing their functions in the territory of the States parties to this Convention, the privileges and immunities accorded to persons connected with the International Court of Justice.

3. The Plenary Court may revoke the immunity of any person referred to in paragraph 2 with a two thirds vote, except for the immunity of the Procurator-General.

Article 52

Costs of the Tribunal

The costs of the Tribunal shall be met by the States parties to this Convention. The provisions for the calculation of the costs; for the drawing up and approval of the annual budget of the Tribunal; for the distribution of the costs among the States parties to this Convention; for the audit of the accounts of the

Tribunal; and for related matters, is contained in the Financial Protocol which appears in Annex 2. The Protocol constitutes an integral part of this Convention.

CHAPTER XV - INTERNATIONAL JUDICIAL ASSISTANCE AND OTHER FORMS OF COOPERATION

Article 53
General Provisions

1. The States parties to this Convention shall provide the Tribunal with all internationally recognized means of legal assistance. Assistance shall include, but not be limited to:

(a) ascertaining the whereabouts and addresses of persons;

(b) taking the testimony or statements of persons in the requested State or elsewhere;

(c) effecting the production or preservation of judicial and other documents, records, or articles of evidence;

(d) service of judicial and administrative documents; and

(e) authentication of documents.

2. The Tribunal is authorized to seek the co-operation of States non-parties to the Convention as appropriate.

Article 54
Communications and Requests

1. All communications in relation to this Convention shall be in writing and shall be between the competent national authority and the Secretariat of the Tribunal. The Procuracy may correspond directly with local authorities in the former Yugoslavia.

2. Whenever appropriate, communications may also be made through the International Criminal Police Organization (ICPO/Interpol), in conformity with arrangements which the Tribunal may make with this organization.

3. Documentation pertaining to judicial assistance and cooperation shall include the following:

(a) the basis and legal reasons for the request;

(b) information concerning the individual who is the subject of the request;

(c) information concerning the evidence sought to be seized, describing it with sufficient detail to identify it, and describing the reasons why, and the legal basis relied thereon;

(d) description of the basic facts underlying the request; and

(e) description of some evidence concerning the charges, accusations or conviction of the person who is the subject of the request.

4. All communications and requests made pursuant to this Convention shall be in any of the official languages of the Convention.

Article 55
Provisional Measures

In cases of urgency, the Tribunal may ask of the requested State party to the Convention any or all of the following:

(a) to provisionally arrest the person sought for surrender;

(b) to seize evidence needed in connection with any proceedings which shall be the object of a formal request under the provisions of this Chapter; or

(c) to undertake protective measures to prevent the escape of the person or destruction of the evidence sought.

Article 56
Delivery of Persons

Delivery of persons for any reason from a State to the Tribunal and vice versa shall be in accordance with established legal procedures under this Convention and the Rules of the Tribunal as well as the laws of the requested State.

Article 57

Rule of Speciality

1. A person delivered to the Tribunal shall not be subject to prosecution or punishment for any other crime than that for which he has been delivered.

2. Evidence delivered shall not be used for any other purpose than for the purpose for which it was delivered.

3. Waiver of the requirements of paragraphs 1 and 2 may be made by the requested State on the basis of a motivated request by the Tribunal.

Article 58

Costs

1. The costs for the delivery of persons to the Tribunal and for other judicial assistance and co-operation shall be borne by the Tribunal.

2. The costs for execution of sentences shall be borne by the State party to this Convention in which the execution takes place.

Article 59

Obligation to Try or Extradite

1. The States parties to this Convention undertake to surrender, extradite or transfer to the Tribunal on the basis of this Convention any person under investigation, charged, sought to be tried, or convicted by the Court in accordance with the jurisdiction of the Tribunal.

2. A State party to this Convention that decides to prosecute a person for a crime under the jurisdiction of the Tribunal does not have the obligation to surrender or extradite that person to the Tribunal.

3. A State party to this Convention may, as an alternative to prosecution and as an alternative to using the jurisdiction of the Tribunal, extradite a person to another state having jurisdiction and willing to prosecute.

4. Paragraphs 2 and 3 do not apply to any State in the territory of the former Yugoslavia.

CHAPTER XVI - TRANSFER OF PROCEEDINGS FROM THE TRIBUNAL TO NATIONAL JURISDICTION

Article 60
Transfer of Proceedings to States in the Territory of the Former Yugoslavia

1. When the Plenary Court is satisfied that a State party to this Convention in the territory of the former Yugoslavia has the appropriate means to adjudicate effectively and fairly cases falling under the jurisdiction of the Tribunal, it may authorize the Court of First Instance to transfer the proceedings in particular cases to the national courts of that State. Such transfer may not be made without the consent of the State to which the transfer is intended.

2. A decision by the Court of First Instance on transfer is final.

3. If transfer is decided, the case shall be dealt with in accordance with the national legislation of the receiving State.

CHAPTER XVII - FINAL PROVISIONS*

Article 61
Signature and Entry into Force

1. This Convention shall be open for signature with the Government of ..... by the CSCE participating States until ..... It shall be subject to ratification.

2. The CSCE participating States which have not signed this Convention may subsequently accede thereto.

3. This Convention shall enter into force two months after the date of deposit of the twelfth instrument of ratification or accession.

---

* The Rapporteurs have chosen to demonstrate a possible CSCE option. If the UN option is chosen, the provisions will naturally have to be elaborated in accordance with UN practice.

4. For every State which ratifies or accedes to this Convention after the deposit of the twelfth instrument of ratification or accession, the Convention shall enter into force two months after its instrument of ratification or accession has been deposited.

5. The Government of ..... shall serve as depositary of this Convention.

Article 62
Reservations

This Convention may not be the subject of any reservation.

Article 63
Amendments

1. Amendments to this Convention must be adopted in accordance with the following paragraphs.

2. Amendments to this Convention may be proposed by any State party thereto.

3. If the Standing Committee adopts the proposed text of the amendment, the text shall be forwarded by the Depositary to States parties to this Convention for acceptance in accordance with their respective constitutional requirements.

4. Any such amendment shall come into force on the thirtieth day after all States parties to this Convention have informed the Depositary of their acceptance thereof.

Article 64
Denunciation

1. Any State party to this Convention may, at any time, denounce this Convention by means of a notification addressed to the Depositary.

2. Such denunciation shall become effective one year after the date of receipt of the notification by the Depositary.

Article 65
Notifications and Communications

The notifications and communications to be made by the Depositary shall be transmitted to the Secretary of the Tribunal and to the States parties to this Convention.

Article 66
Transitional Provisions

Until a Secretary is appointed, the duties of the Secretary under Article 7, paragraph 5, and Article 18, paragraph 5 shall be performed by the Depositary.

Done at ...., on ....
in the English, French, German, Italian, Russian and Spanish languages, all six language versions being equally authentic.

Annex 1

(To draft Convention)

PROVISIONS FROM THE PENAL CODE OF THE FORMER YUGOSLAVIA TO BE APPLIED BY THE INTERNATIONAL WAR CRIMES TRIBUNAL FOR THE FORMER YUGOSLAVIA

Section A

Provisions from Chapter XVI of the Penal Code of the former Yugoslavia to be directly applied by the Tribunal

The following provisions from Chapter XVI of the Penal Code of the former Yugoslavia shall be applied*:

Article 141 - Genocide

Any person who, with the intent to destroy, in whole or in part, a national, ethnical, racial or regligious group, orders with respect to members of such a group their killing,

* Unofficial translation.

the infliction of serious physical injuries, the destruction of their mental or physical health, their forcible dispersal or deportation, the infliction of conditions of life which bring about the physical destruction of the group in whole or in part, the imposition of measures preventing births within the group or the forcible transfer of children to another group

or who commits, with the same intent, any of the acts mentioned,

is to be punished by a prison sentence of at least five years or by the death penalty.*

Article 142 - War crimes against the civilian population

(1) Any person who, in contravention of the provisions of international law, during a war, an armed conflict or an occupation, orders

an attack against the civilian population, a settlement, individual civilians or incapacitated persons hors combat causing the death, serious physical injuries or health defects,

an indiscriminate attack which affects the civilian population, the killing, torturing or inhuman treatment of the civilian population, its subjection to biological, medical or other scientific experiments, the taking out of tissues or organs for transplantation purposes, the infliction of serious suffering and damage to the physical integrity and health, the dispersal, deportation or forcible change of the national identity or conversion to another creed, forcible prostitution and rape, measures aiming at threatening and terrorising, the taking of hostages, collective punishment, illegal confinement of persons in concentration camps and other illegal prisons, the denial of the right of a lawful trial before an independent court, forced enrolment in hostile armed forces or in its

* According to Article 29, paragraph 2 of the Convention the Court shall not pass sentence of capital punishment.

communication services or administration, forced labour, the denial of food supplies to the population, the confiscation of property, pillage, the illegal and unauthorized destruction or appropriation of property on a large scale and unless justified by the necessities of warfare, illegal and disproportionately high contributions and requisitions, the devaluation of the local currency or the illegal circulation of money

or who commits any of the acts mentioned

is to be punished by a prison sentence of at least five years or by the death penalty.*

(2) The punishment according to para. 1 of this article is to be inflicted on any person who, in contravention of the provisions of international law, during a war, an armed conflict or an occupation, orders

an attack against objects which are under the special protection of international law as well as against potentially dangerous objects and installations like e.g. barrages, protective dams and nuclear power stations, and indiscriminate attack against civilian objects which are under the special protection of international law as well as unprotected places and demilitarized zones, an attack causing long-term and widespread destruction of the environment and prejudice to the health and the survival of the population

or who commits any of the acts mentioned.

(3) Any person who, in contravention of the provisions of international law, during a war, an armed conflict or an occupation, orders or executes, as part of the occupying force, the resettlement of parts of his civilian population to the occupied territory is to be punished by a prison sentence of at least five years.

* Cf. note to Article 141.

Article 144 - War crimes against prisoners of war

Any person who, in contravention of the provisions of international law, orders with respect to prisoners of war their killing, torturing or inhumane treatment, their subjection to biological, medical or other scientific experiments, the taking out of tissues or organs for transplantation purposes, the infliction of serious suffering and damage to the physical integrity and health, their forced enrolment in hostile armed forces or the denial of the right of a lawful trial before an independent court,

or who commits any of the acts mentioned

is to be punished by a prison sentence of at least five years or by the death penalty.*

Article 150 - Rude treatment of the wounded, sick or prisoners of war

Any person who, in contravention of the provision of international law, inflicts a rude treatment upon the wounded, sick or prisoners of war or who prevents that they avail themselves of their rights granted by international law is to be punished by a prison sentence of between six months and five years.

Article 151 - Destruction of cultural and historical monuments

(1) Any person who, in contravention of the provisions of international law, during a war or an armed conflict, destroys cultural or historical monuments and buildings or installations serving scientific, artistic, educational or humanitarian purposes is to be punished by a prison sentence of at least one year.

(2) If by an act falling under para. 1 of this article a clearly recognizable object is destroyed which is under the special protection of international law as belonging to the

* Cf. note to Article 141.

cultural or intellectual heritage of a people, the perpetrator is to be punished by a prison sentence of at least five years.

Section B

Provisions from the Penal Code of the former Yugoslavia to be applied by the Tribunal within the scope of the provisions enumerated in Section A

To support the application of the provisions enumerated in Section A the Tribunal may apply any provision of the Penal Code of the former Yugoslavia criminalizing acts, which are specifically mentioned in the provisions enumerated in that Section.

Annex 2

(To draft Convention)

FINANCIAL PROTOCOL
TO THE CONVENTION ON AN INTERNATIONAL WAR CRIMES TRIBUNAL FOR THE FORMER YUGOSLAVIA

Article 1
Contributions to the Budget of the Tribunal

1. Contributions to the budget of the Tribunal shall be divided among the States parties to the Convention according to the scale of distribution applicable within the CSCE, adjusted to take into account the difference in number between the CSCE participating States and the States parties to the Convention.

2. If a State ratifies or accedes to the Convention after its entry into force, its contribution shall be equal, for the current financial year, to one-twelfth of its portion of the adjusted scale, as established according to paragraph 1 of this Article, for each full month of that financial year which remains after the date on which the Convention enters into force in respect of it.

Article 2

Financial Year and Budget

1. The financial year shall be from 1 January to 31 December.

2. The Secretary, acting in accordance with Article 24 of the Convention, shall establish each year a budget proposal, which shall be submitted to the States parties to the Convention before 15 September.

3. The budget shall be approved by the Standing Committee by a two-thirds majority of the attending representatives. On approval of the budget for the financial year the Secretary shall request the States parties to the Convention to remit their contributions.

If the budget is not approved by 31 December the Tribunal will operate on the basis of the preceding budget and, without prejudice to later adjustments, the Secretary shall request the States parties to the Convention to remit their contributions in accordance with this budget.

The Secretary shall request States parties to the Convention to make fifty per cent of their contributions available on 1 January and the remaining fifty per cent on 1 April.

4. Barring a decision to the contrary by the Standing Committee, the budget shall be established in [currency of host State] and the contributions of the States shall be paid in this currency.

5. A State which ratifies or accedes to the Convention after its entry into force shall pay its first contribution to the budget within two months after the request by the Secretary.

6. The year the Convention enters into force, the States parties to the Convention shall pay their contribution to the budget within two months following the date of deposit of the twelfth instrument of ratification of the Convention. This budget is preliminary fixed at [amount in the currency of the host State].

Article 3
Obligations, Payments and Revised Budget

1. The approved budget shall constitute authorization to the Secretary to incur obligations and make payments up to the amounts and for the purposes approved.

2. The Secretary is authorized to make transfers between items and sub-items of up to 15 per cent of items/sub-items. All such transfers must be reported by the Secretary in connection with the financial statement mentioned in Article 7 of this Protocol.

3. Obligations remaining undischarged at the end of the financial year shall be carried over to the next financial year.

4. If so obliged by circumstances and following careful examination of available resources with a view to identifying savings, the Secretary is authorized to submit a revised budget, which may entail requests for supplementary appropriations. The approval by the Standing Committee shall be in accordance with Article 2, paragraph 3 of this Protocol.

5. Any surplus for a given financial year shall be deducted from the scheduled contributions for the financial year following the one in which the accounts have been approved by the Standing Committee. Any deficit shall be charged to the ensuing financial year unless the Standing Committee decides on supplementary contributions.

Article 4
Salaries, Nominal Retainers, Social Security and Pensions

1. Salaries shall be determined in accordance with the provisions of the Convention by the Standing Committee by a two-thirds majority of the attending representatives.

2. The President and the vice-President of the Plenary Court shall receive an annual nominal retainer in addition to their salaries. The annual nominal retainers shall be determined by the Standing Committee by a two-thirds majority of the attending representatives.

3. The Standing Committee shall ensure that the judges, the Procurator-General, the Secretary and other employees of the Tribunal are afforded a social security scheme and an adequate retirement pension.

Article 5

Travel Expenses

1. Travel expenses which are absolutely necessary for exercising their functions shall be paid to the judges, the Procurator-General, the Secretary and other employees of the Tribunal.

2. Travel expenses shall comprise actual transportation costs, including expenses normally incidental to transportation, and a daily travel allowance in lieu of subsistence expenses covering all charges of meals, lodging, fees and gratuities and other personal expenses. The daily travel allowance shall be determined by the Standing Committee by a two-thirds majority of the attending representatives.

Article 6*

Privileges and Immunities

1. Salaries, nominal retainers, pensions and travel expenses mentioned in Articles 4 and 5 of this Protocol are free from all taxation in the territory of the States parties to the Convention.

2. The privileges and immunities of the Tribunal, the judges, the Procurator-General, the Secretary and the staff of the Tribunal in the host State shall be regulated in the headquarters agreement to be concluded between the Tribunal and the host State.

* This Article has not been discussed in substance within the Financial Committee of the CSCE.

Article 7

Records and Accounts

1. The Secretary shall ensure that appropriate records and accounts are kept of the transactions and that all payments are properly authorized.

2. The Secretary shall submit to the Standing Committee not later than 1 March an annual financial statement showing, for the preceding financial year:

(a) the income and expenditures relating to all accounts;

(b) the situation with regard to budget provisions;

(c) the financial assets and liabilities at the end of the financial year.

Article 8

Audit

1. The accounts of the Tribunal shall be audited each year by two auditors, of different nationalities, appointed for renewable periods of three years by the Standing Committee. Judges and persons employed by the Tribunal may not be auditors.

2. Auditors shall annually conduct audits. They shall, in particular, check the accuracy of the books, the statement of assets and liabilities, and the accounts. The accounts shall be available for the annual auditing and inspection not later than 1 March.

3. Auditors shall perform such audits as they deem necessary to certify:

(a) that the annual financial statement submitted to them is correct and in accordance with the books and records of the Tribunal;

(b) that the financial transactions recorded in this statement have been effected in accordance with the relevant rules, the budgetary provisions and other directives which may be applicable; and

(c) that the funds on deposit and on hand have been verified by certificates received directly from the depositories or by actual count.

4. The Secretary shall give auditors such assistance and facilities as may be needed for the proper discharge of their duties. Auditors shall, in particular, have free access to the books of account, records and documents which, in their opinion, are necessary for the audit.

5. Auditors shall annually draw up a report certifying the accounts and setting forth the comments warranted by the audit. They may, in this context, also make such observations as they deem necessary regarding the efficiency of financial procedures, the accounting system and the internal financial control.

6. The report shall be submitted to the Standing Committee not later than four months after the end of the financial year to which the accounts refer. The report shall be transmitted to the Secretary beforehand, so that he will have at least fifteen days in which to furnish such explanations and justifications as he may consider necessary.

7. In addition to the annual auditing, auditors will at any time have free access to check the books, the statement of assets and liabilities, and accounts.

8. On the basis of the audit report, the Standing Committee shall signify its acceptance of the annual financial statement or take such other action as may be considered appropriate, according to the procudure determined in Article 2, paragraph 3 of this Protocol.

Article 9

Amendments

Amendments to this Protocol must be adopted in accordance with the provisions of Article 63 of the Convention.

* * *

B. LETTER DATED 9 FEBRUARY 1993 FROM THE SECRETARY-GENERAL ADDRESSED TO THE PRESIDENT OF THE SECURITY COUNCIL

S/25274, 10 February 1993.

By resolution 780 (1992) the Security Council requested me to establish a Commission of Experts with a view to providing me with its conclusions on the evidence of grave breaches of the Geneva Conventions and other violations of international humanitarian law committed in the territory of the former Yugoslavia. The Commission commenced its work early in November 1992 and held its third session in Geneva on 25 and 26 January 1993, following which it transmitted to me a first interim report, together with a number of ancillary documents, including a report of a preliminary site exploration of a mass grave near Vukovar.

The interim report provides a broad view of the Commission's work to date, its preliminary conclusions on the evidence examined and its views on a number of important legal issues, and describes a plan of work for the next stage of its activities.

I would particularly draw your attention to the following elements of the interim report:

(a) Grave breaches and other violations of international humanitarian law have been committed, including wilful killing, "ethnic cleansing" and mass killings, torture, rape, pillage and destruction of civilian property, destruction of cultural and religious property and arbitrary arrests;

(b) Because of the uneven value of much of the information provided, verification of facts is essential;

(c) The Commission has identified and proposes to carry out on-site investigations of alleged crimes in the Vukovar area, the mass grave near Vukovar, detention camps and the allegations of systematic sexual assaults.

In respect of the proposed investigations, the Commission has indicated that it intends to avail itself of offers of assistance from Governments and non-governmental organizations. It has also requested that I establish a trust fund to assist it in carrying out its mandate.

Finally, in its concluding remarks (para. 74) the Commission notes that should the Security Council or another international organ or body decide to establish an ad hoc war crimes tribunal, such an initiative would be consistent with the direction of its work.

I have examined the interim report carefully and I consider that the Commission has outlined a plan of work which will enable it to carry out its primary mandate, namely, to provide me with its conclusions on the evidence of grave breaches of the Geneva Conventions and other violations of international humanitarian law committed in the territory of the former Yugoslavia. I intend, therefore, to ask the Commission to continue its work on the database and to proceed as expeditiously as possible to the verification of facts through the programme outlined in its report. At the same time, I shall set in motion the necessary administrative steps for the establishment of a trust fund.

Given the evident importance of the contents of the interim report and the strong interest manifested by the Security Council in the work of the Commission, I am, therefore, forwarding a copy of the interim report (annex I) and the report of a preliminary site exploration of the mass grave near Vukovar (annex II) to you for the information of the Council. I felt it my duty to take this step at this stage even though the interim report is not the report foreseen in paragraph 4 of Security Council resolution 780 (1992).

(Signed) Boutros BOUTROS-GHALI

Annex I

[Original: English and French]

INTERIM REPORT OF THE COMMISSION OF EXPERTS ESTABLISHED PURSUANT TO SECURITY COUNCIL RESOLUTION 780 (1992)

CONTENTS

CONTENTS (continued)

INTRODUCTION

A. Mandate

1. The Commission of Experts which the Security Council requested the Secretary-General to establish by its resolution 780 (1992) is mandated, under paragraph 2 thereof, to examine and analyse the information submitted pursuant to resolutions 771 (1992) and 780 (1992), together with such further information as the Commission of Experts may obtain through its own investigations or efforts of other persons or bodies pursuant to resolution 771 (1992), with a view to providing the Secretary-General with its conclusions on the evidence of grave breaches of the Geneva Conventions and other violations of international humanitarian law committed in the territory of the former Yugoslavia.

B. Composition

2. The Commission, whose members sit in their personal capacity, consists of Professor Frits Kalshoven (Netherlands) as Chairman, Professor M. Cherif Bassiouni (Egypt), Mr. William J. Fenrick (Canada), Judge Kéba Mbaye (Senegal) and Professor Torkel Opsahl (Norway), as members.

C. Meetings

3. The Commission held its first two-day session in New York on 4 and 5 November 1992. During that session, it discussed organizational and procedural questions and began dealing with methodological and substantive issues related to its mandate. It also appointed Mr. Fenrick as Rapporteur on Issues of Law.

4. The Commission held its second and third sessions at Geneva from 14 to 16 December 1992 and on 25 and 26 January 1993, respectively. During those sessions, the Commission, adopted its rules of procedure (see appendix), appointed Mr. Bassiouni as Rapporteur on the Gathering and Analysis of Facts, and Mr. Fenrick as Rapporteur for On-site Investigations, and continued its consideration of the issues referred to in paragraph 3 above. At its third session, the Commission discussed and approved the present interim report.

D. References made to the Commission in other United Nations forums

5. At its second session, the Commission took note of the Security Council's request contained in resolution 787 (1992) that it "pursue actively its investigations with regard to grave breaches of the Geneva Conventions and other violations of international humanitarian law committed in the territory of the former Yugoslavia, in particular the practice of 'ethnic cleansing'".

6. The Commission furthermore noted that the Commission on Human Rights, in its resolution 1992/S-2/1 of 1 December 1992, had recommended that the Commission of Experts be granted the staff and resources necessary to enable it to act effectively and had requested the Commission to provide its conclusions to the Secretary-General in order to allow the Security Council to consider further appropriate steps towards bringing those accused to justice.

7. Also at its second session, the Commission noted that the Commission on Human Rights in the same resolution and the Third Committee of the General Assembly in a draft resolution adopted on 11 December 1992 a/ had reaffirmed that all persons who perpetrate or authorize crimes against humanity or other grave breaches of international humanitarian law are individually responsible for those breaches and that the international community will exert every effort to bring them to justice, and had called on all parties to provide all pertinent information to the Commission of Experts in accordance with Security Council resolution 780 (1992).

E. Information before the Commission

8. Further to the requests contained in Security Council resolutions 771 (1992) and 780 (1992) and to its own inquiries, the Commission has received several thousand pages of documentation containing allegations of grave breaches of the Geneva Conventions and other violations of international humanitarian law committed in the territory of the former Yugoslavia. The Commission also had access to video information.

9. As of 26 January 1993, reports containing such allegations b/ had been submitted by Austria, Bosnia and Herzegovina, Croatia, France, Germany, Norway, Slovenia, Ukraine, the United States of America and Yugoslavia. Some of these reports provide data relating to specific allegations which, if supported by evidence, constitute "grave breaches" and other violations of international humanitarian law. Others are of a general character. The Commission would be aided in its task if Governments would submit to it the files upon which these reports are based or more detailed information so that it can gather the data it needs to set up proper investigative files. Communications have also been received from Austria, Canada, Croatia, Denmark, Slovenia, Sweden and Switzerland expressing readiness to assist in the channelling to the Commission of information supplied to the competent national authorities by refugees and other persons having left the war zones. Such information, when received, will be passed on to the Rapporteur on the Gathering and Analysis of Facts. The material provided by Governments reveals that large-scale victimization has taken place.

10. The Commission also had before it reports containing allegations of the type referred to above, originating in various United Nations bodies, intergovernmental organizations, international non-governmental organizations, various national organizations and private sources.

11. The United Nations bodies and authorities concerned include the Special Rapporteur appointed under resolution 1992/S-1/1 of the Commission on Human Rights to investigate first hand the human rights situation in the territory of the former Yugoslavia, the Special Rapporteur of the Commission on Human Rights on Extrajudicial, Summary and Arbitrary Executions, the Office of the

a/ This draft resolution was adopted by the General Assembly on 18 December 1992 as resolution 47/147.

b/ Namely, allegations directly related to the situation in the territory of the former Yugoslavia.

United Nations High Commissioner for Refugees (UNHCR), the Human Rights Committee and the United Nations Protection Force (UNPROFOR). These reports also reveal or confirm the occurrence of large-scale victimization. Some of them contain indications of available evidence, others suggest the direction of future investigations.

12. The Conference on Security and Cooperation in Europe (CSCE) has submitted a number of reports, including the report of the CSCE Mission to the detention camps in Bosnia and Herzegovina, the report of the CSCE Human Rights Rapporteur Mission to Yugoslavia, and the report of the Mission to Bosnia and Herzegovina and to Croatia under the Moscow Human Dimension Mechanism of the CSCE. The third of these reports considers the practical implications of determining responsibility for "grave breaches" and other violations of international humanitarian law. Reports have also been received from the European Community, including information originating in the European Community Monitoring Missions and the initial findings of the EC Investigating Mission into the Treatment of Muslim Women in the former Yugoslavia.

13. As of 26 January 1993, communications expressing concern in general terms over events and violations of international humanitarian law had also been received from the following States: Australia, Austria, Belgium, Colombia, France, Iran (Islamic Republic of), Russian Federation and Slovenia. Communications of the same type had furthermore been received from the following intergovernmental forums: Group of Arab States within the United Nations, Conference of Foreign Ministers of the Balkan and Regional Countries, Council of Europe, Council of Ministers of the Western European Union, European Community, Organization of the Islamic Conference, Presidential Council of the Arab Maghreb Union, and Supreme Council of the Gulf Cooperation Council.

14. As of the same date, reports had also been received from a number of international non-governmental organizations. Those reports have proven helpful in enabling the Commission to gather important information. The accounts they contain are often detailed and most closely resemble the type of data that the Commission will require in attributing responsibility for "grave breaches" and other violations of international humanitarian law, subject to the ascertainment of the supporting evidence. The international non-governmental organizations concerned include: Amnesty International, International Committee of the Red Cross (ICRC), Médecins sans frontières, Helsinki Watch, International League for Human Rights, Union for Peace and Humanitarian Aid to Bosnia and Herzegovina and "World Campaign Save Humanity". The Commission would be aided in its task if it were to receive the relevant data that was not included in the reports in question.

15. The reports received vary in substance, nature, content and style. Mostly, as is understandable in view of their very nature, they lack specificity as to pertinent evidence that can be verified.

16. The Commission notes that the reports often show a marked similarity in the conduct of the various parties to the armed conflicts in the area and that such conduct is often of the most reprehensible character. The Commission emphasizes that reprehensible conduct by one party to a conflict is no excuse or justification for the commission of grave breaches or other violations by other parties to the conflict.

I. COORDINATION WITH OTHER BODIES AND ORGANIZATIONS

17. The Commission realizes the importance of coordinating its efforts with those of other United Nations bodies and intergovernmental organizations concerned with the situation in the territory of the former Yugoslavia. It has noted in particular the call contained in resolution 1992/S-2/1 of the Commission on Human Rights for the closest possible coordination with the Special Rapporteur appointed under resolution 1992/S-1/1 of the said Commission, Mr. Tadeusz Mazowiecki. The following arrangements have been made with Mr. Mazowiecki: as a general rule, the preliminary investigation of sites not visited so far that might be the scene, or contain evidence, of possible war crimes are to be carried out under the responsibility of the Special Rapporteur; whenever there appears to be sufficient ground to pursue the matter further, the relevant information will be passed on to the Commission for the action it deems appropriate.

18. Through its Chairman, the Commission has also been in touch with the Co-Chairmen of the International Conference on the former Yugoslavia.

19. The Commission is furthermore maintaining contacts with the CSCE. In a decision adopted on 7 November 1992, the Committee of Senior Officials of the CSCE stated that the Commission of Experts should give particular attention to the principle of personal responsibility for war crimes and re-examine how this principle could be put into practice by an ad hoc tribunal. At the Stockholm Council meeting on 15 December 1992, the Ministers agreed that the proposals on making the principle of formal accountability effective, including the possibility of the establishment of an ad hoc tribunal, should be refined "through continuing consultations with the Commission of Experts". The Commission, considering that its mandate empowered it to engage in consultations on the refinement of the principle of personal responsibility, has designated Mr. Bassiouni, to liaise with the CSCE on this particular aspect.

20. The Chairman, Mr. Bassiouni and Mr. Fenrick met on 24 January with the CSCE Committee, chaired by Mr. Corell, which comprises, in addition to its Chairman, Mr.Türk and Mrs. Thune, to exchange views, at the Committee's request, on the legal, evidentiary and practical problems relating to the establishment of an ad hoc international war crimes tribunal for the former Yugoslavia.

21. Through its Chairman, the Commission has also established contacts with ICRC and with UNHCR.

II. TASKS CARRIED OUT BY THE COMMISSION IN THE DISCHARGE OF ITS MANDATE

A. Examination and analysis of the information

22. The Commission considers that in order to discharge its mandate impartially and objectively, it must systematically analyse all the information before it. It has therefore undertaken the preparation of a database designed to provide a comprehensive, consistent and manageable record of all reported grave breaches of the Geneva Conventions and other violations of international humanitarian law being committed in the former Yugoslavia.

23. In creating the database, particular attention has been paid to securing detailed information by using a uniform reporting form. The database and uniform reporting system are necessitated by the volume of information received and the disparities in the contents and styles of the reports.

24. The Information Report Form which has been developed consists of eight separate sections. The first two sections are the Physical Harm form (1) and the Harm to Property form (2). The next three sections are the identification forms, relating respectively to Victim Identification (3), Perpetrator Identification (4) and Witness Identification (5). The next section is the Location Information form (6), which covers detailed information about the location of the incident being reported. The seventh section is the Evidence form (7), which provides a description of the evidence and its location. The final section is the War Crimes Information form (8), which asks for information specifically related to the qualification of the violation. The database computer entry system is designed to cross-reference data items or sets of items and to identify duplicate information. While each report is summarized during initial entry, provision has been made for entry of the complete document. As a result, it will be possible to conduct searches of documents in a manner which will result in a listing of every database entry which relates to a particular incident, person or location. Then, if necessary, the entire text of relevant documents can be printed. The information entered into the database is translated into tables generated according to the information sought. Cases can then be grouped into tables according to date, location, victim's name, perpetrator's name, etc. These tables will assist in establishing patterns relating to individual perpetrators, armed forces and locations.

25. As of 26 January 1993, approximately 70 per cent of the reports received by the Commission had been drawn into the database. The Commission wishes to

place on record its deep appreciation to the Rapporteur on the Gathering and Analysis of Facts for his invaluable contribution to this undertaking.

26. From the analysis carried out so far, the following tentative conclusions emerge.

27. The reported violations of international humanitarian law fall within the following categories: wilful killing; "ethnic cleansing" and mass killings; torture; rape; pillage and destruction of civilian property; destruction of cultural and religious property; arbitrary arrests, forcible deportation, detention and abuse during detention; discriminatory dismissal from employment and harassment; attacks on relief personnel and vehicles; attacks on journalists.

28. The database can only be as effective as the evidence received and the success of the Commission in bringing to light facts bearing upon the responsibility of individuals for grave breaches and other violations of international humanitarian law will first and foremost depend on the type of information submitted. Some reports appear to rely heavily on second-hand and media sources and many fail to provide important data (names of victims, perpetrators, date and specific location). In order for the Commission to conduct an effective investigation, access is required to the files on which reports are based. The Commission has taken note of offers which have been made by several Governments on the communication of files (see para. 9 above) and it intends to avail itself of these offers.

29. In a number of cases, the alleged facts seem to be attributable to groups operating in a disorganized and undisciplined manner under very limited command and control. In the absence of information on military operations (whereabouts of military units, order of battle, movements of militias and civil or military units), it is possible to identify massive victimization but extremely difficult to determine whether such victimization occurred in the context of an armed conflict and to establish chains of command and command responsibility.

30. Information on a single event is often contained in more than one report. Checking the database on such an event may show that the various sources complement each other, thus facilitating further investigation.

B. Identification of cases especially warranting in-depth investigation

31. The Commission understands that the purpose of the Security Council in requesting conclusions on the "evidence" of violations of international humanitarian law is not merely to establish the existence of certain patterns of criminality but also to obtain specific evidence such as an investigative body would need for prosecution purposes. Seen in this perspective, the Commission's task requires in-depth investigations, which, given the volume of the available information and existing practical constraints, can be carried out only on a selective basis. The Commission has identified the *prima facie* reliability of the source of information, the strength of the evidence, the number of victims, the identity and rank of the persons allegedly responsible and the gravity of the alleged violations as objective criteria it will apply in the conduct of the selection process. An important concern of the Commission in identifying the cases to be investigated in depth is to discern patterns of behaviour sufficiently consistent to reveal genocide, "ethnic cleansing" or systematic sexual assaults.

C. Verification of facts

32. The reports show that grave breaches and other violations of international humanitarian law have been committed. Tangible evidence of these violations must, however, be secured in the form of testimonies, written statements, identification of victims, pathological/forensic reports, films, photographs and maps of location and other forms of corroborating evidence. The Commission is aware of the difficulties which may arise in this context: evidence may be destroyed either wilfully or as a result of weather conditions and the victims and witnesses may be either difficult to locate or reluctant to supply information due to intimidation and fear of reprisals.

33. Rule 8 of the Commission's rules of procedure, entitled "Investigations", provides as follows:

> "1. The Commission may hear witnesses or experts, on its own initiative or upon proposal by States, international humanitarian organizations, or other persons or bodies. In such cases, the Commission shall determine the modalities for summoning witnesses and experts. States whose nationals have been summoned to appear before the Commission as witnesses or experts may be invited to be present when their nationals are heard.
>
> "2. The Commission may decide to request States to hear witnesses or experts.
>
> "3. The Commission may decide to visit the territory of one or more of the States that formed part of the former Yugoslavia, or any other State, upon invitation or on its own initiative with the consent of any such State. Visits may be carried out by the Commission in its entirety, by one or more of its members, or by staff of the Commission, as decided by the Commission."

34. As far as on-site investigations are concerned, the Commission has noted that some Governments have offered the services of teams of specialized investigators to perform certain functions under the Commission's control. The Commission intends to avail itself of these offers as appropriate.

35. Such missions of investigation, as well as visits of the Commission as are envisaged in paragraph 3 of rule 8 of the rules of procedure, will be preceded by a careful analysis of alleged facts and the gathering of as much corroborating evidence as can be obtained from credible sources, so that the investigative work can be properly focused and lead to concrete and substantial results.

D. Issues of law

1. Applicable rules of international law

36. The armed conflicts in the territory of the former Yugoslavia give rise to various legal issues. These relate to the law to be applied as well as to its interpretation in the light of the facts. The Commission has begun its examination of these issues and offers herein its preliminary views on some of them.

37. Paragraph 2 of Security Council resolution 780 (1992) specifies as the law the Commission is required to apply the Geneva Conventions of 1949, and "international humanitarian law". The Commission interprets the latter phrase to have the same meaning as "rules of international law applicable in armed conflict" as defined in article 2 (b) of Additional Protocol I to the Geneva Conventions, i.e., "rules applicable in armed conflict set forth in international agreements to which the Parties to the conflict are Parties and the generally recognized principles and rules of international law which are applicable to armed conflict".

38. Moreover, these rules are found, first, in the 1977 Additional Protocols to the Geneva Conventions. The former Yugoslavia was a party to these instruments. While the Federal Republic of Yugoslavia considers itself as the successor to that State and, hence, bound by these treaties, Croatia, Slovenia and Bosnia and Herzegovina have declared themselves similarly bound.

39. Other international agreements relevant to the armed conflicts in the territory of the former Yugoslavia include:

- The 1907 Hague Convention IV and the Regulations on the Laws and Customs of War on Land;

- The 1948 Convention on the Prevention and Punishment of the Crime of Genocide;

- The 1954 Hague Convention for the Protection of Cultural Property in the Event of Armed Conflict;

- The 1980 Convention on Prohibitions or Restrictions on the Use of Certain Conventional Weapons Which May Be Deemed to Be Excessively Injurious or to Have Indiscriminate Effects, with annexed Protocols;

as well as relevant human rights law applicable to the conflicts in the territory of the former Yugoslavia.

40. Apart from the above-mentioned international agreements, the conduct of hostilities in the territory of the former Yugoslavia is governed, as mentioned above, by "the generally recognized principles and rules of international law which are applicable to armed conflict", i.e., by the relevant rules of customary international law. The Commission notes that, while rules of customary international law may be found in the Geneva Conventions and certain other relevant instruments, some particularly important rules on the protection of civilian populations in armed conflicts are reflected in General Assembly resolutions 2444 (XXIII) and 2675 (XXV) entitled "Respect for human rights in armed conflict" and "Basic principles for the protection of civilian populations in armed conflicts", respectively. Special importance also attaches to the conventions and customary law on crimes against humanity.

2. Application of the rules relating to international armed conflict to the conflicts in the former Yugoslavia

41. Since 1949, the law has distinguished between international armed conflicts and non-international armed conflicts occurring in the territory of a single State (hereinafter, internal armed conflicts). Generally speaking, the rules for internal armed conflict are fewer and less detailed than those applicable to international armed conflicts. In the 1949 Geneva Conventions, the rules for internal conflicts are found in one single article, common article 3. The 1954 Hague Convention on Cultural Property likewise contains one article (article 19) relating to internal armed conflicts.

42. As for the two Additional Protocols adopted in 1977, one (Protocol I) is applicable to international armed conflicts and the other (Protocol II) to internal armed conflicts.

43. Both the 1949 Geneva Conventions and the 1954 Hague Convention leave open the possibility for parties to an internal armed conflict to bring into force, by means of special agreements, all or part of the provisions of these Conventions. The various parties to the successive armed conflicts in the former Yugoslavia have concluded a series of such special agreements.

44. Under existing treaty law, for the Commission to classify the various armed conflicts in the territory of the former Yugoslavia as international or internal ones would require it to determine whether a given situation amounts to an armed conflict at all and, if so, one between two or more States or one being waged in the territory of one State. Further determinant factors would be the dates on which the several States in the region are deemed to have acquired statehood and the dates from which the treaties in question are regarded as applicable to each of them.

45. The Commission is of the opinion, however, that the character and complexity of the armed conflicts concerned, combined with the web of agreements on humanitarian issues the parties have concluded among themselves, justify an approach whereby it applies the law applicable in international armed conflicts to the entirety of the armed conflicts in the territory of the former Yugoslavia.

46. The Commission emphasizes that the applicable rules include the prohibition of genocide, as codified in the Genocide Convention, as well as fundamental norms of human rights law. While the latter have been embodied, and elaborated, in treaties to which the former Yugoslavia was a party, their applicability to the parties to the various armed conflicts in the region may be deemed to derive from their character as peremptory norms of international law.

3. Grave breaches, war crimes, crimes against humanity

47. The Geneva Conventions and Additional Protocol I contain rules on the treatment of grave breaches. While "grave breaches" are carefully defined in each of these instruments, they fall under the general heading of war crimes. The Commission understands the general notion of war crimes as comprising any violation of the law of international armed conflicts, sufficiently serious and committed with the requisite intent to be regarded as a crime.

48. A war crime is usually a crime committed by a person demonstrably linked to one side of an armed conflict against persons or property on the other side. The perpetrator may be a member of the armed forces (as defined in article 43 of Protocol I) or a civilian. The issue of a demonstrable link is of particular relevance where victims and offenders are of the same nationality or from countries which are on the same side of a conflict. The Commission intends to address this issue in due course.

49. The notion of crimes against humanity as defined in conventional international law and as applied in customary international law is considered by the Commission to be applicable to these conflicts. The Commission regards as crimes against humanity gross violations of fundamental rules of humanitarian and human rights law committed by persons demonstrably linked to a party to the conflict, as part of an official policy based on discrimination against an identifiable group of persons, irrespective of war and the nationality of the victim.

50. The Commission notes that fundamental rules of human rights law often are materially identical to rules of the law of armed conflict. It is therefore possible for the same act to be a war crime and a crime against humanity.

4. Command responsibility

51. A person who gives the order to commit a war crime or crime against humanity is equally guilty of the offence with the person actually committing it. This principle, expressed already in the Geneva Conventions of 1949, applies both to military superiors, whether of regular or irregular armed forces, and to civilian authorities.

52. Superiors are moreover individually responsible for a war crime or crime against humanity committed by a subordinate if they knew, or had information which should have enabled them to conclude, in the circumstances at the time, that the subordinate was committing or was going to commit such an act and they did not take all feasible measures within their power to prevent or repress the act.

53. Military commanders are under a special obligation, with respect to members of the armed forces under their command or other persons under their control, to prevent and, where necessary, to suppress such acts and to report them to competent authorities.

5. Superior orders

54. A subordinate who has carried out an order of a superior or acted under government instructions and thereby has committed a war crime or a crime against humanity, may raise the so-called defence of superior orders, claiming that he cannot be held criminally liable for an act he was ordered to commit.

The Commission notes that the applicable treaties unfortunately are silent on the matter. The Commission's interpretation of the customary international law, particularly as stated in the Nuremberg principles, is that the fact that a person acted pursuant to an order of his Government or of a superior does not relieve him from responsibility under international law, provided a moral choice was in fact available to him.

6. "Ethnic cleansing"

55. The expression "ethnic cleansing" is relatively new. Considered in the context of the conflicts in the former Yugoslavia, "ethnic cleansing" means rendering an area ethnically homogeneous by using force or intimidation to remove persons of given groups from the area. "Ethnic cleansing" is contrary to international law.

56. Based on the many reports describing the policy and practices conducted in the former Yugoslavia, "ethnic cleansing" has been carried out by means of murder, torture, arbitrary arrest and detention, extra-judicial executions, rape and sexual assault, confinement of civilian population in ghetto areas, forcible removal, displacement and deportation of civilian population, deliberate military attacks or threats of attacks on civilians and civilian areas, and wanton destruction of property. Those practices constitute crimes against humanity and can be assimilated to specific war crimes. Furthermore, such acts could also fall within the meaning of the Genocide Convention.

57. The Commission is mindful of these considerations in the examination of reported allegations.

7. Rape and other forms of sexual assault

58. Throughout the various phases of the armed conflicts in the former Yugoslavia, reports have referred to allegations of widespread and systematic rape and other forms of sexual assault. Such reports have become more frequent, raising urgent concerns, and have led to several specific investigations into these allegations.

59. Acts such as rape, enforced prostitution or any form of sexual assault against women are explicitly prohibited in the relevant treaties in force. Superiors who authorize or tolerate the commission of such acts or who fail to take all practicable measures to prevent or suppress them are also culpable.

60. The Commission will examine the question whether the systematic commission of such acts, or the development and encouragement of a policy encouraging such acts, should be regarded as crimes in themselves and, if so, as war crimes or crimes against humanity.

III. INVESTIGATION OF MASS GRAVE SITES

61. The Commission has not awaited the completion of the database to undertake verification of particularly disturbing allegations. Responding to urgent and repeated calls in particular from Mr. Vance, Co-Chairman of the International Conference on the former Yugoslavia, and from the Commission on Human Rights in paragraph 13 of its resolution 1992/S-2/1, the Commission has arranged for an immediate investigation by a team of forensic experts of the mass grave of Ovcara, near Vukovar, in United Nations Protected Area (UNPA) East which was discovered during Mr. Mazowiecki's second mission to the area. To that end, the Commission engaged the services of Physicians for Human Rights, a non-governmental organization. Under the Cooperation Service Agreement concluded between the United Nations and Physicians for Human Rights, a team of forensic experts is to carry out the investigation of mass graves, under the control and supervision of the Commission. Although no direct contractual link exists between the Organization and the experts, the latter are accorded the status of expert on mission, which, given the nature of their mission, affords them the necessary protection. In this respect, the

Cooperation Service Agreement is consistent with the existing procedures for obtaining the use of civilian personnel provided by Governments in peace-keeping operations,, whereby civilian personnel so provided are accorded the status of expert on mission for the United Nations, under article VI of the Convention on the Privileges and Immunities of the United Nations, notwithstanding the absence of a direct contractual link between them and the United Nations (see report of the Secretary-General, A/45/502, of 18 September 1990). The services are provided at no cost to the Organization, and Physicians for Human Rights is made responsible for payment of all salaries and benefits, including, in particular, adequate life and medical insurance coverage to the experts.

62. The report on the first phase of the investigation conducted on the site by Physicians for Human Rights was before the Commission at its third session. The conclusions of the report include the following:

(1) A mass execution took place at the grave site;

(2) The grave is a mass grave, containing perhaps as many as 200 bodies;

(3) The remote location of the grave suggests that the executioners sought to bury their victims secretly;

(4) There is no indication that the grave has been disturbed since the time of execution and interment;

(5) The grave appears to be consistent with witness testimony that purports that the site is the place of execution and interment of the patients and medical staff members who disappeared during the evacuation of Vukovar Hospital on 20 November 1991. However, before that determination can be made with scientific certainty, the grave will need to be excavated and a number of bodies will need to be identified using forensic methods and procedures;

(6) There are indications that at least some of the bodies are those of Croatians.

63. The Commission of Experts has noted that, pursuant to Commission on Human Rights resolution 1992/S-1/1, and at the request of the Special Rapporteur on the human rights situation in the territory of the former Yugoslavia, the Special Rapporteur on Extrajudicial, Summary or Arbitrary Executions has conducted preliminary investigations into allegations of burial of victims of war crimes in various mass graves in the former Yugoslavia, especially in Croatia. The objective is to determine to what extent these allegations can be considered prima facie reliable. If, as a result of these investigations, it could be reasonably assumed that some or all of these sites contain the remains of persons who were victims of war crimes, the findings of the Special Rapporteur would be forwarded to the Commission of Experts.

64. The mission of the Special Rapporteur on Extrajudicial, Summary or Arbitrary Executions was conducted from 15 to 20 December 1992. In the preliminary investigation and assessment of the sites visited, the Special Rapporteur was assisted by one member of the team of forensic experts referred to in paragraph 61 above. The findings will form part of the report of the Special Rapporteur on the situation of human rights in the former Yugoslavia to the Commission on Human Rights at its forty-ninth session.

IV. PROJECTED PLAN OF WORK

65. The Commission intends to complete the database as fast as possible since this alone can provide the foundation for the formulation of conclusions on the evidence of grave breaches of the Geneva Conventions and other violations of international humanitarian law.

66. For the reasons given in paragraph 31 above, the Commission intends to engage in selective in-depth investigations in the following general areas:

(a) Mass killings and destruction of property;

(b) Treatment of prisoners and detainees;

(c) Systematic sexual assaults;

(d) "Ethnic cleansing".

67. As short-term objectives the Commission intends:

(a) To conduct further investigations into mass killings and destruction of property in the Vukovar area by expanding the scope of the various investigations conducted by forensic experts from Physicians for Human Rights and by deploying a team of military lawyers, police investigators, and necessary support personnel to the Vukovar area;

(b) To conduct an on-site investigation into the treatment of prisoners and detainees at two or more camps or detention centres at places in Bosnia and Herzegovina yet to be specified;

(c) To study all available reports on systematic sexual assaults and determine as soon as possible the most effective way to approach the problem and whether on-site investigations should be undertaken;

(d) To study all available reports on "ethnic cleansing" and determine as soon as possible the most effective way to approach the problem and whether on-site investigations should be undertaken.

68. The Commission intends to avail itself of the offer of the Canadian Government to provide an investigative team and to use that team to commence the investigation of offences in the Vukovar area as soon as possible. The Commission does not, at present, have investigative teams at its disposal to conduct the investigations referred to in subparagraph 67 (b) or to conduct the potential on-site investigations referred to in subparagraphs 67 (c) and (d) above.

V. RESOURCES AND BUDGETARY REQUIREMENTS

69. The Commission has been provided with a budget for a period of nine months from 1 December 1992. It covers the compensation and travel of the members, as well as the travel and subsistence of two staff members sent over from the Office of Legal Affairs at Headquarters. It also provides for general temporary assistance, the latter object permitting only the recruitment of two secretaries. Any other costs have thus been left for absorption by the ordinary budget of the Organization.

70. To carry out its task, including the work on the database and in-depth investigations, additional means are required. As noted in paragraphs 34 and 68 above, the Commission intends to avail itself of the offers some Governments have already made. More will be needed, however, in terms of financial and personnel resources.

71. The Commission will make every effort to obtain such additional resources and it will, in particular, request the establishment of a trust fund to receive voluntary contributions intended to help the Commission carry out its mandate.

VI. CONCLUDING REMARKS

72. Jurisdiction for war crimes is governed by the universality principle and, hence, is vested in all States, whether parties to the conflict or not. Although the Genocide Convention emphasizes territorial jurisdiction, it also establishes the jurisdictional basis for an international tribunal. It is well recognized that the principle of universality can also apply to genocide as well as to other crimes against humanity.

73. States may choose to combine their jurisdictions under the universality principle and vest this combined jurisdiction in an international tribunal. The Nuremberg International Military Tribunal may be said to have derived its jurisdiction from such a combination of national jurisdictions of the States parties to the London Agreement setting up that Tribunal.

74. The Commission was led to discuss the idea of the establishment of an ad hoc international tribunal. In its opinion, it would be for the Security Council or another competent organ of the United Nations to establish such a tribunal in relation to events in the territory of the former Yugoslavia. The Commission observes that such a decision would be consistent with the direction of its work.

Appendix

Rules of procedure of the Commission

Rule 1. Mandate

The Commission shall examine and analyse the information submitted by States, international humanitarian organizations, or other persons or bodies pursuant to Security Council resolutions 771 (1992) and 780 (1992), as well as such further information as the Commission may obtain through its own investigations or efforts, with a view to providing the Secretary-General with its conclusions on the evidence of grave breaches of the Geneva Conventions of 12 August 1949 and other violations of international humanitarian law committed in the territory of the former Yugoslavia.

Rule 2. Meetings and quorum

1. The Commission shall hold its meetings in private but may open them to the public as and when it deems it necessary for the enhancement of the effectiveness of its work.

2. The Commission shall meet at such times as it may designate; meetings may otherwise be called by the Chairman, as a rule with at least one week's notice.

3. The Chairman may declare a meeting open when at least a majority of the members of the Commission are present. The presence of a majority of the members shall be required for any decision to be taken.

Rule 3. Restraint in the disclosure of information

Members of the Commission shall exercise restraint in disclosing information. They shall refrain from taking a stand in public on any confidential question under discussion in the Commission. The Chairman will make information on the work of the Commission available to the extent he deems it appropriate.

Rule 4. Powers of the Chairman

The Chairman shall declare the opening and closing of each meeting of the Commission and, at such meetings, shall direct the discussions, accord the right to speak, put questions to the vote, announce decisions, rule on points of order and have complete control of the proceedings.

Rule 5. Secretariat

The Secretary of the Commission shall be responsible for making all arrangements connected with the work of the Commission including arrangements for the meetings of the Commission. He or she shall distribute documents and materials to the members of the Commission as requested by the Commission, its Chairman or any member thereof, and shall be responsible for the preparation of the records of the meetings of the Commission.

Rule 6. Records

1. The Commission will be provided with records of its meetings in English and French.

2. The Commission will arrange for the safe keeping and conservation of its records and files. After the conclusion of its work, the Commission will transmit its records and files to the Secretary-General of the United Nations.

Rule 7. Participation of States, international humanitarian organizations, or other persons or bodies

The Commission may invite States, international humanitarian organizations, or other persons or bodies to participate in its discussions, when the Commission deems it necessary for the enhancement of the effectiveness of its work.

Rule 8. Investigations

1. The Commission may hear witnesses or experts, on its own initiative or upon proposal by States, international humanitarian organizations, or other persons or bodies. In such cases, the Commission shall determine the modalities for summoning witnesses and experts. States whose nationals have been summoned to appear before the Commission as witnesses or experts may be invited to be present when their nationals are heard.

2. The Commission may decide to request States to hear witnesses or experts.

3. The Commission may decide to visit the territory of one or more of the States that formed part of the former Yugoslavia, or any other State, upon invitation or on its own initiative with the consent of any such State. Visits may be carried out by the Commission in its entirety, by one or more of its members, or by staff of the Commission, as decided by the Commission.

Rule 9. Decisions

The Commission will make every effort to take its decisions by consensus. In the absence of consensus, decisions of the Commission will be taken by a majority of the members present and voting.

Rule 10. Reports

1. The Commission may designate a rapporteur for any question of a general or specific nature.

2. The Commission shall report its conclusions to the Secretary-General in accordance with Security Council resolution 780 (1992).

3. Members of the Commission who wish to make a separate statement may have such a statement appended to the report.

Rule 11. Other procedural matters

Any procedural matters arising at a meeting which are not covered by these rules shall be dealt with by the Chairman in the light of the rules of procedure applicable to Committees of the General Assembly.

C. LETTER DATED 10 FEBRUARY 1993 FROM THE PERMANENT REPRESENTATIVE OF FRANCE TO THE UNITED NATIONS ADDRESSED TO THE SECRETARY-GENERAL

S/25266, 10 February 1993.

Please find attached the report of the Committee of French Jurists set up by Mr. Roland Dumas, Minister of State and Minister for Foreign Affairs, to study the establishment of an International Criminal Tribunal to judge the crimes committed in the former Yugoslavia.

I should be grateful if you would have this report distributed as a document of the Security Council.

(*Signed*) Jean-Bernard MERIMEE

CONTENTS

CONTENTS (continued)

CONTENTS (continued)

INTRODUCTION

1. An end was put to Hitler's atrocities by force of arms, not arguments. 1/ Despite the Allies' solemn declarations promising punishment for those responsible for atrocities, these actually increased up until the end of the Second World War, as if the prospect of punishment, far from restoring respect for the laws of humanity, prompted still greater excesses.

2. Breaches of the laws of war and of humanity are, alas, now taking place in the territory of the former Yugoslavia, but conditions have changed since the Second World War.

3. The Nürnberg and Tokyo Judgments showed that leaders who organize atrocities are no longer immune from the severest penalties.

4. The United Nations has a special role to play in the conflict by virtue of several resolutions.

5. A well-informed international public opinion expects effective action to be taken to put an end to the present situation.

6. In addition to such conventional means as the use of armed force or negotiations to put an end to an unacceptable situation, the use of judicial means while the conflict is still going on, rather than after it has ended, can, through the speedy prosecution of those responsible for atrocities, help put an end to such excesses or at least discourage some subordinates from collaborating therein. Such an approach is also comforting for the victims, in that they can be sure that everything possible will be done to punish the guilty. Lastly, this approach, if successful, could lead to the establishment of a permanent international court with the authority to intervene swiftly in new conflicts.

1/ Pierre Legendre, Le Crime du caporal Lortie, Fayard, 1989.

7. It was with these considerations in mind that the Committee of Jurists established on 15 January 1992 2/ by Mr. Roland Dumas, Minister of State and Minister for Foreign Affairs, sought to fulfil its mandate.

8. This mandate was established in the letter which Mr. Dumas sent on 16 January to Mr. Pierre Truche, Procurator-General of the Court of Cassation and Chairman of the Committee, 3/ in which he expressed the hope that the Committee would be able, on the basis of existing studies and work, to consider precisely and speedily the various issues raised by the establishment of an International Criminal Tribunal that would be competent to judge the war crimes, crimes against humanity or serious violations of certain international conventions being committed in the territory of the former Yugoslavia, and would submit to him a proposal concerning its possible Statute.

9. The Minister added that the Committee would be able to make all the proposals it deemed appropriate with regard to the procedure to be followed in establishing the Tribunal and all other points that might be relevant to the end for which the Committee had been established. For the purpose of performing its mission, the Committee could, should it deem necessary, proceed to hear competent individuals.

10. The Committee held five meetings between 18 January and 6 February 1993 at the Ministry of Foreign Affairs, 4/ and was assisted in its work by several members of the staff of the Department's Division of Legal Affairs. Professor Alain Pellet acted as Rapporteur.

11. After making a selective inventory of the copious documentation that exists on the subject of the establishment of an international criminal court, 5/ members of the Committee drew up a list of the problems raised by the creation of an International Tribunal and shared out the issues to be studied, each of them drafting a note on the issues most closely related to his or her sphere of competence.

12. These notes and the report drafted by the Rapporteur were discussed by the full Committee. The Committee's conclusions were adopted unanimously.

13. Because it had only a very short time in which to complete its work, the Committee was unable to hold formal hearings with competent individuals. However, it was kept informed of deliberations taking place in other countries, or in some international bodies, concerning the establishment of an International Criminal Tribunal to judge the crimes committed in the former Yugoslavia, or of a permanent international criminal court. Some members of the Committee also contacted competent French or foreign individuals and reported on these contacts to the full Committee.

14. Although the Committee tried to make as thorough a study as possible, time constraints prevented it from going into all the details that it probably should have considered on some points. The study which follows is therefore necessarily brief.

15. In particular, the Committee felt that it should not include in its report a comprehensive, definitive proposal for the possible Statute of the Tribunal. For purposes of illustration, however, annex V gives an idea of the provisions which such a Statute could comprise, while annex IV outlines in more general terms the principles which the Committee believes could guide the establishment of an International Criminal Tribunal to judge the crimes committed in the territory of the former Yugoslavia.

2/ The composition of the Committee is indicated in annex I.

3/ The full text of the letter from the Minister to the Chairman of the Committee is reproduced in annex II.

4/ On 18, 21 and 27 January and 1 and 6 February 1993.

5/ The list of the proposals for the establishment of an international criminal court of which the Committee was seized is reproduced in annex III.

16. For the same reasons, in some cases the Committee chose to emphasize that several possibilities exist and that choosing between them will depend on further study or on considerations of political expediency which do not fall within its mandate.

17. Having made these general remarks, the report is divided into five parts dealing with:

- The nature of the Tribunal and the procedure that could be followed in establishing it (Part I);
- The competence of the Tribunal (Part II);
- Prosecutions and proceedings (Part III);
- Sentencing and penalties (Part IV); and
- Institutional aspects (Part V).

18. To avoid making the Committee's report unduly cumbersome, five documents are annexed to it:

Annex I: Composition of the Committee

Annex II: Mandate of the Committee (letter dated 16 January 1993 from Mr. Roland Dumas, Minister of State and Minister for Foreign Affairs, to Mr. Pierre Truche, Procurator-General of the Court of Cassation and Chairman of the Committee)

Annex III: Basic documentation used by the Committee

Annex IV: Principal recommendations of the Committee - applicable principles

Annex V: Possible provisions for the Statute of the Tribunal.

I. THE NATURE OF THE TRIBUNAL AND THE PROCEDURE THAT COULD BE FOLLOWED IN ESTABLISHING IT

A. Legitimacy of establishing a Tribunal

19. As the Minister of State indicates in his letter of 16 January 1993 to the Chairman of the Committee, "Unfortunately, there is no longer any doubt that particularly serious crimes are being committed in the territory of the former Yugoslavia that constitute war crimes, crimes against humanity or serious violations of certain international conventions.

> "Such actions cannot go unpunished, and the absence of real penalties, in addition to being an affront to public conscience, could encourage the perpetrators of these crimes to pursue their regrettable course of action".

20. The Committee agrees entirely with this assessment and has no doubt as to the advisability of proceeding swiftly to the establishment of an International Criminal Tribunal that would be competent to judge these crimes committed in the former Yugoslavia.

21. The legitimacy of creating such a Tribunal would seem to be all the more clearly established in that it would not be open to two charges sometimes levelled at the Nürnberg and Tokyo International Military Tribunals:

(a) While, at the time, there may have been doubts about due respect for the principle whereby a crime is not punishable unless it has *a priori* been defined by law (*nullum crimen sin lege*), this is no longer true today: punishment of the crimes and atrocities committed by the Nazis was required by the "dictates of the public conscience" 6/ but was justified legally only by the general principles of law recognized by all nations. Nowadays, such punishment is also justified by indisputable norms of international customary law, thanks to the development of international law that has since taken place as a result of both domestic and international case-law, treaty practice and United Nations resolutions;

(b) Furthermore, while the Tribunals established at the end of the War could have been accused of dispensing the justice of those who won the War, such a criticism could in no circumstances be levelled at the Tribunal whose establishment is now envisaged; quite the contrary, since the internationalization of the prosecutions and the judgement would, for both the victims and the accused, be a guarantee of impartial justice rendered without any intervention of the parties concerned.

B. "Profile" of the Tribunal - an ad hoc court

22. In the Committee's view, the above general considerations would seem to dictate the "profile" of the proposed Tribunal.

23. Such a Tribunal:

(a) Must be international, both in its manner of establishment, its composition and its powers;

(b) Must be universal, because the crimes it is to punish are an affront to the conscience of all humanity;

(c) Must offer the utmost guarantees of impartiality in respecting the rights of the defence and due consideration for the victims;

(d) Should not become another international bureaucracy divorced from reality, as this would deprive it of any deterrent effect.

24. To this end, as the letter dated 16 January 1993 from the Minister of State indicates, it is essential to proceed swiftly to the establishment of the Tribunal.

25. This latter requirement, in and of itself, demands that we lean towards the creation not of a permanent international criminal court, to which the Tribunal could none the less be the prelude, but of an ad hoc Tribunal whose powers would be clearly delimited. Experience has shown that the creation of a permanent international court with general and diversified powers, while not impossible, would encounter numerous obstacles, and it seems unrealistic to believe that such a court could be established within the necessary time-frame. 7/

6/ To use the wording of article 158 of the fourth Geneva Convention relative to the Protection of Civilian Persons in Time of War of 12 August 1949; see also article 63 of the first Convention, article 62 of the second Convention and article 142 of the third Convention.

7/ See, however, resolution 47/33 adopted by the General Assembly on 25 November 1992, which gives the International Law Commission a mandate to "continue its work". Without wishing to question the determination of Member States successfully to complete that work, we should however recall the adoption by the General Assembly on 12 September 1950 of resolution 489 (V) setting up a Committee responsible for preparing "proposals relating to the establishment and the statute of an international criminal court". Draft statutes submitted in 1951 and 1953 went nowhere and consideration of the 1953 draft was suspended in 1957. It was only in 1990 that the General Assembly requested the International Law Commission to resume consideration of the question.

C. Drawbacks of the treaty approach

26. The Committee discussed the procedures for establishing the Tribunal and, therefore, the nature of the legal document which could bring it into being and the procedure whereby such a document could be prepared and then adopted.

27. Establishing the Tribunal through the conclusion of an international treaty among States is one of the approaches which automatically come to mind for several reasons: first of all, this was the course followed in the case of the main precedent which we can really invoke, the London Agreement of 8 August 1945 for the prosecution and punishment of the major war criminals of the European Axis, which established the Nürnberg Tribunal. 8/ Secondly, the establishment of a court affects the sovereignty of States very closely. In this connection, we might note that in all the discussions that have taken place within the United Nations, particularly over the past two years, on the establishment of a universal international criminal court, the conclusion of a treaty has been viewed as the normal approach.

28. It is clear, however, that the establishment of an ad hoc Criminal Tribunal by means of a treaty among States would encounter difficulties so serious that they can probably be considered diriment.

(a) The idea of using a treaty first raises the issue of which States could or should sign and ratify the treaty in question. Quite apart from the fact that it is totally unrealistic to assume that the Tribunal would be established following ratification of the treaty by the entire membership of the United Nations, the question of signatory States also raises a philosophical and legal issue, namely, who, and in the name of what principle, can be given or can take upon himself the power to establish a Tribunal responsible for trying crimes, however odious, committed in certain countries, several of which would in all likelihood refuse to sign and ratify the treaty in question.

(b) No matter how many States were given the right to establish an International Criminal Tribunal and no matter what their geographical location, it would be unrealistic to expect all of them to ratify the agreement that we assume would be concluded. The number of States whose agreement was indispensable or, to put it technically, the number of States that would have to ratify the treaty in order for it to enter into force, would therefore have to be determined.

(c) Lastly, the international negotiations and the diplomatic conference that would be required in order for an agreement to be reached that could be opened for signature by States with any real chances of success could be expected to take a long time, and the time required for its ratification would further delay its entry into force.

D. Lack of competence of the United Nations to establish, by binding decision, a permanent universal criminal court

29. The approach of concluding an agreement among States thus appears to be fraught with difficulties of principle and technical hurdles. However, another solution, that of the United Nations, is conceivable.

30. By virtue of the Charter, 9/ the United Nations clearly has competence in the field of human rights and protection of the fundamental rights of the human person.

31. Moreover, this would not be the first time - far from it - that the question of an international criminal court was studied within the United

---

8/ By contrast, the Charter of the International Military Tribunal for the Far East was "approved" on 19 January 1946 by the Supreme Allied Commander.

9/ Cf. Articles 1 (3), 13 (1) (b), 55 (c) or 62 (2).

Nations. Although the proposals so far considered have not gone anywhere, 10/ they at least establish, if need be, the legitimacy of United Nations intervention in this field.

32. Some passages of the London Agreement establishing the Nürnberg Tribunal also reflect this legitimacy: the Agreement affirms that the "Four" were acting "in the interest of all the United Nations". 11/

33. If it was a matter of establishing a jurisdiction with universal competence, however, the Committee would be very reluctant to consider the United Nations as being competent to establish an international criminal court with binding force. There are no provisions in the Charter that could be invoked as giving the Security Council or the General Assembly such powers.

E. Competence of the Security Council to establish an ad hoc Criminal Tribunal under Chapter VII of the Charter

34. The nature of the problem changes, however, when what is to be established is not a universal international criminal court, but rather an ad hoc Tribunal designed specifically to punish the perpetrators of abominable crimes committed in an ongoing conflict. In line with the trend towards interpreting the Charter dynamically and teleologically, the Committee believes that the Security Council could, if necessary, establish such a Tribunal by virtue of the powers conferred on it by Chapter VII of the Charter "with respect to threats to the peace, breaches of the peace, and acts of aggression".

35. By virtue of these provisions, should the Security Council determine the existence of a threat to the peace or a breach of the peace, it has the power to decide what measures shall be taken to maintain or restore international peace and security.

36. Now, one of the justifications most frequently advanced for the establishment of an ad hoc Tribunal is the fact that, setting aside any moral considerations, establishing such a Tribunal would put an end to the de facto impunity which the authors of the crimes taking place in the former Yugoslavia believe they enjoy. No doubt the former Yugoslavia and the States that have replaced it were, or still are theoretically bound by such fundamental international instruments as the Convention on the Prevention and Punishment of the Crime of Genocide or the Geneva Conventions of 1949. No doubt even these States, in theory, have the necessary means, under their domestic law to punish such crimes judicially. However, the current state of the institutions of some of the countries concerned and the situation of all-out or avowed war prevailing in their territories rules out any possibility of effective prosecution. The establishment of a credible international court, even if it were to prosecute and punish only a limited number of those guilty of crimes, can therefore be considered likely to help restore the peace and security of those countries and, hence, international peace and security.

37. Moreover, the Security Council has already embarked on such a course, albeit cautiously. Invoking Chapter VII, it has demanded "that all parties and others concerned in the former Yugoslavia ... immediately cease and desist from all breaches of international humanitarian law ... including those involved in the practice of 'ethnic cleansing'" and has requested States, international humanitarian organizations and the Secretary-General to collate substantiated information on such violations. 12/ It has also requested the Secretary-General to establish an impartial Commission of Experts to examine and analyse such information. 13/ There would seem to be little point in collating such information if the Security Council cannot act on the findings of these investigations.

10/ See footnote 7 above.

11/ Fourth preambular paragraph.

12/ Resolution 771 (1992) of 13 August 1992.

13/ Resolution 780 (1992) of 6 October 1992. Pursuant to this resolution, the Secretary-General has established a five-member Commission (see document S/24657).

F. Scope of Article 41 of the Charter

38. It may well be asked, however, whether the establishment of a Tribunal, owing to its very special nature, is among the measures which the Security Council has the power to take under Chapter VII.

39. In that connection, Article 39 refers back to Articles 41 and 42. 14/ The first-mentioned of these provisions lists certain measures which the Members of the United Nations may be called upon to implement other than measures involving the use of armed force (which come under Article 42). The measures referred to in Article 41, which are primarily economic in nature, 15/ may appear to be very far from the establishment of a Tribunal. However, this list is merely illustrative and should not be interpreted as ruling out other measures should they prove necessary. The criterion for a contemporary interpretation of Article 41 is commensurability to the objective that is sought. From this perspective, the establishment of a Tribunal would be an appropriate measure if, in the circumstances obtaining at the time, it seems likely to attain or facilitate the objective of restoring international peace and security.

40. While this reasoning holds up if the decision to establish the Tribunal is taken while hostilities are in progress, does it remain valid once hostilities have ceased? The Committee is of the view that this question should be answered in the affirmative. In the first place, Chapter VII is concerned not only with the restoration of peace, but also with its maintenance. Secondly, the effective functioning of the Tribunal after the end of hostilities is a key factor affecting its credibility and hence its ability to achieve its purposes. This does not, moreover, mean that that Tribunal should be a permanent body. It would be for the Security Council to terminate the Tribunal if it determined that the latter was no longer serving the purposes for which it had been created.

G. Possible role of the General Assembly

41. The Committee believes that it is not within its purview to take a position on whether a resolution of the Security Council should be used for the purpose of establishing the proposed Tribunal. That is a matter of judgement that is exclusively political in nature. However, the Committee maintains that such a step is juridically possible provided that the Council acts under Chapter VII of the Charter of the United Nations and that the body set up has ad hoc jurisdiction, limited to what the Council deems necessary to restore and maintain international peace and security.

42. The Committee does not believe, however, that the General Assembly, acting in the absence of any consideration of the matter by the Security Council, could, by means of a resolution, establish an ad hoc international jurisdiction.

43. While the Charter vests in the Council "primary responsibility for the maintenance of international peace and security", 16/ it does not give the General Assembly the authority to adopt mandatory resolutions. The Assembly's powers are limited to making recommendations in accordance with the provisions of Article 10 and, as appropriate, Articles 11, 13 and 14.

14/ Article 39: "The Security Council shall determine the existence of any threat to the peace, breach of the peace, or act of aggression and shall make recommendations, or decide what measures shall be taken in accordance with Articles 41 and 42, to maintain or restore international peace and security."

15/ But not exclusively: Article 41 also envisages the severance of diplomatic relations.

16/ Art. 24, para. 1.

44. It does not follow, however, that the General Assembly can play no role in the process of establishing an ad hoc Criminal Tribunal. It could become involved if the Security Council deems it useful to refer certain issues raised by the drafting of a statute for the Tribunal to the Assembly for its consideration.

H. Alternative solutions

45. Although the Committee maintains the establishment of an ad hoc Tribunal by a resolution of the Security Council adopted under Chapter VII is a juridically possible response to the crimes committed in the territory of the former Yugoslavia, the Committee considered whether "mixed" solutions combining United Nations involvement and the involvement of certain individual States might not be conceivable.

46. If an international criminal jurisdiction is not established, the following measures could be explored:

(a) Still acting under Chapter VII, and hence by means of decisions that are binding on those to whom they are addressed, the Security Council could invite States in whose territory crimes are committed to bring the perpetrators to trial;

(b) Along the lines of discussions that are under way within the Council of Europe, 17/ tribunals whose members would include a specific number, to be determined, of both national judges and prominent individuals from other countries appointed by an international body could be set up under the national laws of the States which have come into existence as a result of the breakup of the former Yugoslavia or of some of those States for the purpose of trying the perpetrators of war crimes and crimes against humanity;

(c) Another possible solution would be a single international Tribunal having a basis in the domestic laws of the States which have emerged from the former Yugoslavia. In this case, the States would enact legislative provisions relating to the establishment of the Tribunal, recognizing the legitimacy of its involvement and referring to the rules adopted by international agreement to settle matters relating to jurisdiction, penalties, prosecution and so forth. The Tribunal itself would be set up either directly by a resolution of the Security Council or by a Convention concluded between the States to which authority has been delegated by the Security Council for that purpose;

(d) A final possibility would be for the Security Council to set forth the principle of establishing an International Criminal Tribunal and to entrust to some States or a group of States the task of seeing to it that this is done by means of a treaty to be concluded by them.

47. However, even when the so-called principle of "universal competence" applies, according to which States holding individuals suspected of war crimes and crimes against humanity have a duty, under many international conventions, to punish or extradite them, most of these solutions have one obvious drawback: implementation of these solutions is dependent on the goodwill of the States concerned, and this casts much doubt on their effectiveness, at least in the present circumstances.

48. None the less, the last-mentioned possibility does not have this disadvantage. On the contrary, it presents the advantage of solving the problem of the legitimacy of intervention by a limited number of States. In addition, it would be consistent with the spirit of the Charter, in particular Article 41, in that the Security Council, instead of taking all necessary action itself, would invite some Members of the United Nations to implement

---

17/ These discussions, however, are focusing more on the possible establishment of new judicial bodies having jurisdiction for human rights than on the establishment of criminal tribunals.

the measures that are needed. Nevertheless, even though the drafting and ratification of a treaty concluded between a limited number of States is likely to take less time and pose fewer problems than the conclusion of a universal treaty, such a procedure, which would be set in motion following a decision by the Security Council, would probably not come off very quickly.

II. THE COMPETENCE OF THE TRIBUNAL

A. Necessary balance between different considerations

49. The Committee dwelled at great length on questions relating to the competence of the Tribunal and the applicable law. It became apparent that these problems are the most difficult to resolve from the technical point of view and that, politically, they are the most sensitive.

50. A satisfactory balance must be found between the following considerations:

(a) Limiting the powers of the Tribunal to the purpose for which it is created, which can only be, at least if the Tribunal is established pursuant to a resolution of the Security Council adopted under Chapter VII of the Charter (see part I, sect. E, above), the restoration of international peace and security, on the one hand, and the concern not to establish a "one-off" jurisdiction, on the other;

(b) A credible jurisdictional mechanism serving as a deterrent to the perpetrators of atrocities at all levels, on the one hand, and the necessity of avoiding the establishment of very cumbersome and bureaucratic judicial machinery, on the other;

(c) The international character of the crimes to be punished, on the one hand, and the fact that the Tribunal's jurisdiction would be limited to trying crimes committed during a specific time-period in a given territory, on the other;

(d) The principles of public international law, on the one hand, and the principles of criminal law and criminal procedure, on the other.

51. These requirements are not contradictory. The proposals adopted by the Committee respond to the concern to reconcile the various considerations with respect to the Tribunal's jurisdiction *ratione materiae*, *ratione loci*, *ratione temporis* and *ratione personae*, and the related, but essential problem of the applicable law.

B. Necessarily limited role of domestic laws

52. In this regard, the essential starting-point would seem to be the international character both of the crimes themselves and the institution which will be entrusted with the task of judging them. Accordingly, unlike the possibilities that would exist if certain alternative models were to be adopted, 18/ it is unthinkable that the Tribunal should apply, both as regards procedure and as regards law, national rules that are specific to a given State or States.

53. In no way does this mean that the domestic law of the States is of no relevance to either of those two areas. Firstly, there is common ground in the laws of all nations both with respect to the protection of basic human rights and with respect to criminal procedure. The recognition of this fact was, moreover, the starting-point and the justification for the establishment of the Nürnberg Tribunal. Secondly, this consideration is all the more cogent in the present case in that the States most directly concerned by the establishment of the Tribunal have emerged from the breakup of a single State, the former Yugoslavia, and appear to have preserved, at least as a transitional measure, many of the juridical institutions of the former State, particularly in the area of penal law.

18/ See, for example, para. 46 (a), (b) and, perhaps, (c).

54. It is particularly significant that the national Penal Code of the former Socialist Federal Republic of Yugoslavia (art. 125) contains provisions incorporating into domestic law all the grave breaches enumerated in the four Geneva Conventions and also other crimes as defined in other international conventions, including: "forced conversion to another religion, compelling an individual to engage in prostitution, the use of measures of intimidation and terrorism, collective penalties, unlawful internment in a concentration camp, forcible recruitment into the intelligence services or administration of the occupying Power, actions aimed at starving the population, and the levying of unlawful or excessive contributions or requisitions ...".

55. Moreover, the Socialist Federal Republic of Yugoslavia was a party to nearly all the existing international conventions on the protection of human rights 19/ and some of the successor States have made declarations concerning succession to some, if not all 20/ of these conventions, which may therefore be invoked against them. 21/ The "Federal Republic of Yugoslavia (Serbia and Montenegro)", for its part, considers itself to be the continuation of the former Socialist Federal Republic of Yugoslavia.

56. These facts establish beyond all question that, under the domestic law of the States which have come into existence following the breakup of the former Yugoslavia, the violation of these Conventions is subject to criminal charges; that the perpetrators of such violations cannot legitimately claim to have acted in accordance with national law; and that, from this point of view alone, punishment for the abominable deeds they have committed is indisputably consistent with the principle nullum crimen sine lege (see part I, sect. A, above).

C. International characterization of crimes

57. These considerations do not, however, exhaust the question of the applicable law, for an international judicial body cannot render a judgement on the basis of domestic law, even though that law may recapitulate the rules of general international law.

58. As the United Nations International Law Commission has rightly emphasized, "the characterization of an act or omission as a crime against the peace and security of mankind 22/ is independent of internal law. The fact

---

19/ In particular the four Geneva Conventions of 1949 and the additional protocols thereto of 1977, the 1948 Convention on the Prevention and Punishment of the Crime of Genocide, the 1984 Convention against Torture and Other Cruel, Inhuman or Degrading Treatment or Punishment, the two International Covenants on Human Rights of 1966 and the two Conventions against slavery, of 1926 (as amended in 1953) and 1956, International Labour Organisation Convention No. 29 concerning forced labour of 1930, the 1950 Convention for the Suppression of the Traffic in Persons and of the Exploitation of the Prostitution of Others, the 1965 Convention on the Elimination of All Forms of Racial Discrimination, the 1968 Convention on the Non-Applicability of Statutory Limitations to War Crimes and Crimes against Humanity and the 1989 Convention on the Rights of the Child.

20/ Within the time allotted to it, the Committee was unable to gather complete information on this point.

21/ On 11 May 1992, Croatia made a declaration of succession to the four Geneva Conventions of 1949 and the two Protocols of 1977. Bosnia and Herzegovina and Slovenia made similar declarations, the former on 31 December 1992 and the latter on 25 June 1991 (as regards the Conventions) and 26 March 1992 (as regards the Protocols).

22/ This applies, in general, to all international crimes.

that an act or omission is or is not punishable under internal law does not affect this characterization". 23/

59. In international law, this characterization has several bases and is derived from a number of "sources" (in most cases, more than one at the same time):

(a) The general principles of law recognized by the community of nations, which formed the legal basis for prosecution before the Nürnberg Tribunal (see part I, sect. A, above) and to which reference is made in article 15, paragraph 2, of the International Covenant on Civil and Political Rights of 1966 and article 7, paragraph 2, of the European Convention on Human Rights;

(b) The large number of international conventions in existence today which have codified and spelt out these principles; 24/

(c) Well-established general rules of customary law which, for the most part, are merely set forth in these conventions. 25/

60. The Committee considered the matter of the basis to be adopted for the Tribunal's competence in the present instance. There are two alternatives:

(a) Either its Statute would refer to existing conventions, which would be expressly mentioned in the Statute;

(b) Or it would enumerate the crimes which the Tribunal would be called upon to punish without making reference to any specific convention or conventions.

61. The practical result would be the same, since, clearly, the list of crimes in the second alternative would be drawn up mainly by reference to existing conventions. But the implications of the two approaches are very different:

(a) Specific reference to certain conventions would supplement the mere listing of crimes with an additional factor of legitimacy in that the most important conventions have been broadly ratified; in addition, in the present case, the States concerned are bound by nearly all of the relevant treaties;

(b) Conversely, however, this approach may obscure the fundamental fact that the crimes in question are punishable whether or not the States in question have ratified the relevant convention. 26/ It is, furthermore, questionable whether a tribunal established by means other than a convention should be asked to punish the violation of rules set forth in one or more conventions, some of which, moreover, provide for their own monitoring procedures.

23/ Article 2 of the draft Code of Crimes against the Peace and Security of Mankind, adopted on first reading by the International Law Commission in 1991.

24/ See the non-exhaustive enumeration in footnote 19.

25/ Cf. the articles common to the Geneva Conventions of 1949, which refer to the "principles of the law of nations".

26/ The prohibition of genocide is no less binding on Angola, which has not ratified the 1948 Convention on the Prevention and Suppression of the Crime of Genocide, than on France, which has. Cf. the advisory opinion of the International Court of Justice of 28 May 1951, rendered on the subject of reservations to the Convention: "The principles underlying the Convention are principles which are recognized by civilized nations as binding on States, even without any conventional obligation" (ICJ Reports 1959, p. 23; see also ICJ Reports 1986, p. 114).

62. A middle ground would be to enumerate the crimes envisaged while specifying that what is involved is crimes "specified, inter alia," in one or another international convention. The Committee, however, is of the view that considerations of principle militate in favour of the technique of enumeration.

D. Competence ratione materiae - punishable crimes

63. Whichever approach is adopted - enumeration or reference - the question of the Tribunal's competence ratione materiae remains unresolved.

64. The Committee considers that a basis for resolving this question should be sought in the four Geneva Conventions of 1949, which have been ratified by nearly every State in the world 27/ and which have been referred to in several Security Council resolutions dealing with the Yugoslav crisis, 28/ in particular the fourth Geneva Convention Relative to the Protection of Civilian Persons in Time of War, article 147 of which defines the "grave breaches" which States parties are required to punish. This list is more or less coterminous with that contained in article 3, which is common to the four Conventions and which prescribes the minimum rules that are also applicable in the case of armed conflict not of an international character.

65. One might have considered going no further than this list out of a concern for "readability", pointing out that these Conventions enjoy the unanimous support of States and that, what is more, all the crimes that are currently being committed in the former Yugoslavia can be related to that list. Such a limitation would, however, have serious drawbacks:

(a) It would seem paradoxical in the context of the former Yugoslavia not to mention genocide as such or, in any event, the factors that constitute genocide, or indeed "ethnic cleansing" directly, and not to refer to the persecution directed against members of "a national, ethnical, racial or religious group, as such"; 29/

(b) The 1949 Conventions are old and it seems difficult not to take into account subsequent developments in the law, as reflected, inter alia, in the two Protocols of 1977. 30/

E. Categories of punishable crimes

66. If the Statute of the Tribunal were to refer solely to the Geneva Conventions, it would be impossible to make a distinction between the different "grave breaches" enumerated therein without differentiating among such breaches according to whether or not they are of a mass and systematic nature. 31/

27/ Ratifications as at 31 January 1993: first Geneva Convention: 170 - second Geneva Convention: 168 - third Geneva Convention: 174 - fourth Geneva Convention: 164.

28/ Cf. resolutions 764 (1992) of 13 July 1992; 771 (1992) of 13 August 1992; and 780 (1992) of 6 October 1992.

29/ Cf. art. II of the 1948 Genocide Convention.

30/ Certain States have not ratified some of these instruments, for reasons unrelated to the problem under consideration. The difficulty that might result from this situation if the Statute of the Tribunal contained express references to the Conventions or Protocols would be overcome if the Statute recapitulated the list of crimes enumerated in those instruments without making express reference to them.

31/ See article 147 of the fourth Geneva Convention.

67. However, if, instead of simply referring to the 1949 Conventions, the Statute of the Tribunal recapitulates the enumeration of grave breaches contained therein and the list of crimes set out in article 3, common to the four Conventions, which is applicable in the case of armed conflict not of an international character as well as in the event of a war (see part II, sect. D, above), the competence of the Tribunal may be limited to the most heinous crimes.

68. Such was the position taken in the London Agreement of 8 August 1945, which restricted the competence of the Nürnberg Tribunal to "major criminals whose offences have no particular geographical location", all other criminals being "sent back to the countries in which their abominable deeds were done in order that they may be judged and punished according to the laws of these liberated countries and of the free Governments that will be created therein". 32/ Transposing this provision to the present case would be difficult. Firstly the crimes to be prosecuted seem, for the most part, to have a rather precise geographical location. Secondly, the places in question are not, unfortunately, "liberated" and this circumstance is one of the justifications for the establishment of an international Tribunal.

69. Nevertheless, in the Committee's opinion, the competence of the Tribunal should be limited to the most serious war crimes, those committed on a mass and systematic scale, causing particular revulsion and calling for an international response. That limitation, which is also motivated by the concern not to encumber the Tribunal with cases that are less representative, would in no way let the perpetrators of crimes not in this category go unpunished: they would remain subject to the enforcement system of the Geneva Conventions.

70. On the other hand, the Committee believes that this limitation should not apply to crimes against humanity, especially those which target groups as such, which are by nature collective and which form part of a deliberate criminal policy.

F. Competence *ratione loci*

71. The problems raised by the competence *ratione loci* of the Tribunal are infinitely less difficult, if only because the letter dated 16 January 1993 from the Minister of State (see annex II), constituting the mandate of the Committee, refers exclusively to crimes "committed in the territory of the former Yugoslavia".

72. That also applies to the relevant resolutions of the Security Council, 33/ and it is quite clear that since the legal basis for the establishment of any ad hoc tribunal by the Council derives exclusively from the latter's competence under Chapter VII of the Charter, the Council can act only in the context of what is strictly necessary to restore and maintain peace. The Council therefore cannot vest in the Tribunal - which under Article 29 of the Charter would be one of its subsidiary organs - geographical competence that the Council itself does not enjoy.

73. On the other hand, the Council might, by strictly applying the law, limit the competence of the Tribunal to crimes committed only in certain parts of the territory of the former Yugoslavia. The Committee takes the view that such a limitation would have a disastrous effect in that it would prejudge the guilt of some and the innocence of others - innocence to be protected by the strict principles suggested with regard to prosecution (see part III below).

32/ Second preambular paragraph; see also article 1.

33/ See footnote 28 above.

G. Competence ratione temporis

74. The same caution is called for in connection with the competence of the Tribunal ratione temporis.

75. Among the crimes that the Tribunal would be responsible for trying are crimes against humanity, to which statutory limitations do not apply. The first question, therefore, is whether the Tribunal should be given competence in regard to such crimes, irrespective of when they were committed.

76. On this point, the Committee takes the view that it would not be reasonable to extend the competence of the Tribunal to crimes predating the dissolution of the former Yugoslavia and the outbreak of the current conflicts. Such competence could hardly be justified by reference to Chapter VII of the United Nations Charter, under which the establishment of a tribunal would be authorized only for the purpose of maintaining or restoring peace, not in order to punish earlier crimes. Lastly, it should be noted that not attributing competence to the Tribunal in regard to such crimes would in no way preclude prosecution in the ordinary courts.

77. It therefore appears appropriate to attribute competence to the Tribunal only in respect of crimes committed during the period beginning with the dissolution of the former Yugoslavia.

78. It is admittedly difficult to pinpoint the moment of that dissolution.

79. It might be the date of resolution 713 (1991) - 25 September 1991 - the first of 26 resolutions on the situation in Yugoslavia adopted by the Security Council in the past 18 months. While, however, the mere fact of its adoption confirms that a threat to peace existed on that date, as duly noted by the international community, it can be assumed that adoption came after the outbreak of hostilities. There would be even more justification for the same objection with regard to the later resolutions. In terms of the principles involved, there would be no reason to authorize the punishment of crimes against humanity only from the date of Security Council action.

80. It is therefore appropriate to go back to the beginning of the process of dissolution of the former Yugoslavia. The most significant dates in that respect are:

(a) 25 June 1991 - Proclamation of independence by Croatia and Slovenia;

(b) 27 June 1991 - Federal Army intervention in Slovenia;

(c) 3 July 1991 - Outbreak of clashes between Serbian and Croatian militias;

(d) 1 April 1992 - Outbreak of clashes between Serbian and Muslim militias, and beginning of the siege of Sarajevo, one month after the referendum on the independence of Bosnia and Herzegovina.

81. In considering this chronology, the Committee took the view that while the outbreak of hostilities could be traced back to 27 June 1991, the choice of that date might give rise to misinterpretation and reflect some prejudice. It believes that 25 June, the date of the first legal move towards dissolution of the Socialist Federal Republic of Yugoslavia, is a more neutral date, and consequently more appropriate.

H. Competence ratione personae

82. Determination of the competence of the Tribunal ratione materiae (see part II, sects. D and E, above) will largely influence determination of its competence ratione personae: the perpetrators of crimes listed in the Statute of the Tribunal or in instruments referred to therein may be brought before the Tribunal.

83. The Committee is aware, however, that the concept of "perpetrator" covers very different situations. It believes that a distinction should be drawn between three levels of responsibility.

84. The highest level is occupied by the policy makers, those who turned the violation of basic human rights and the laws of war into a permanent system for attaining political objectives.

85. Yet when it comes to prosecuting them, one difficulty arises: the traditional concepts of incitement to commit offences and of criminal intent do indeed cover the hypothesis, but do not allow for effective action. On the basis of those concepts, the specific criminal role of leaders would be identified only when those who actually committed the offences are being tried, and in most cases it would be very difficult to show the link between each offence and general directives from afar. Such a criminal role would thus remain unpunished.

86. It would be another matter if, as in the case of the Nürnberg trials, "formulation or execution of a common plan or conspiracy to commit any of the ... crimes" coming within the jurisdiction of the Tribunal (crime of "conspiracy"), 34/ were to be treated as a separate offence. This is the solution to be adopted.

87. At the intermediate level, the orders of superiors are issued. Unlike the general directives, the purpose of which is to establish a political system dependent on the necessary commission of crimes (see paragraph 84 above), these orders lead to acts that are the constituent elements of crimes.

88. Yet here again, the concept of complicity does not seem adequate:

(a) The content of the orders is not always precise enough for complicity to be established;

(b) No sanctions would be available in the case of orders that were not followed up.

89. It therefore seems legitimate to define as an offence in itself the decision to use authority in a criminal fashion, instead of viewing it as mere complicity in the offence of the actual perpetrator. Psychologically, that restores the balance of responsibilities.

90. Nevertheless, in the Committee's opinion, the deeds done at the subordinate level should also be liable to prosecution. The reminder to the actual perpetrators that they are individually responsible for their own actions is a necessary measure of preventive intimidation, and is probably more effective among the rank and file than at the top.

91. It is all the more essential that the Tribunal should be competent in respect of - and only in respect of - crimes committed on a mass and systematic scale. That would substantially reduce the risk of submerging the international jurisdiction in so many cases that it would be unable to function effectively (see part II, sect. E, above).

I. "Criminal groups"

92. In addition, membership in a de jure or de facto group whose primary or subordinate goal is to commit crimes coming within the jurisdiction of the Tribunal would constitute a specific offence.

34/ Article 6, third paragraph, of the Charter of the Nürnberg Tribunal.

93. That was the solution adopted in articles 9 and 10 of the Charter of the Nürnberg Tribunal, and it can be related to well-known concepts in penal law, such as criminal association or conspiracy.

94. Two precautions should, however, be taken so as to avoid any shift towards an unacceptable form of collective responsibility. The first would be to confer on the Tribunal competence to declare a group to be criminal in a separate decision. 35/ The second would be to allow as a defence - retroactively, if need be - any spontaneous withdrawal by an individual from such a group.

J. Defence of obeying the orders of a superior or performing official duties

95. If it is logical to divorce the actual carrying out of the act from its remote source (directives) or its proximate source (orders of superiors), by the same token, the carrying out of the act should in turn be examined *per se*. The order of a superior, in itself, cannot serve as a defence. The possibility that, in the circumstances, the subordinate had no choice but to carry out the order cannot, however, be ruled out. It therefore seems reasonable to rely on the Nürnberg precedent 36/ followed in national judicial practice, and take the view that the fact that an individual charged with a crime before the Tribunal obeyed an order of a superior "does not relieve him of ... responsibility if, in the circumstances at the time, it was possible for him not to comply with that order". 37/ That leaves room for mitigation of responsibility.

96. Conversely - and here again in keeping with the Nürnberg precedent - it should be reaffirmed that the fact that a person was performing official duties in no way constitutes a factor relieving him of responsibility. "Act of State" does not exist.

III. PROSECUTIONS AND PROCEEDINGS

A. General principles applicable to prosecutions

97. The options in regard to investigations and prosecutions may seem to be more exclusively of a technical nature. Nevertheless, they do affect the credibility of the whole institution.

98. If the precise operating procedures of the Tribunal at this level are established on the basis of purely abstract considerations in terms of what would be an ideal solution, without regard for the international realities and the situation on the ground in the former Yugoslavia, the project will not see the light of day, and, at best, the Tribunal's work will remain purely symbolic. If, on the other hand, the solutions are prompted by the concern to establish effective mechanisms without sacrificing the fundamental principles of criminal procedure and the humanist values that are to be defended, Utopia may turn into reality and the Tribunal may be able to function effectively.

99. On that basis, the Committee considers, first of all, that the prosecuting authority should enjoy some leeway, either in waiving or in discontinuing proceedings. That would introduce a useful element of

---

35/ Cf. article 9 of the Charter of the Nürnberg Tribunal.

36/ Cf. article 8 of the Charter of the Nürnberg Tribunal.

37/ Article 11 of the draft Code of Crimes against the Peace and Security of Mankind, prepared by the International Law Commission.

flexibility in enforcement, provided that the principle of equality before the law is not called in question. [38] With a view to ensuring respect and avoiding arbitrary action in this area, the decision on discretionary prosecution should be taken only by a collegial body (see part V, sect. E, below), should state the grounds on which it is based, should be inspired by the principle of individualization, and should fully respect the rights of victims.

100. Secondly, it does not seem reasonable to admit civil actions before the Tribunal. That would lead to a flood of claims, which the international court would not be in a position to process effectively. It seems preferable to proceed from the principle that it will be for the national courts to rule on claims for reparation by victims or their beneficiaries.

101. Lastly, the Committee takes the view that a single commission should be instructed to conduct investigations, to decide, on a collegial basis, whether to prosecute offences before the Tribunal, and if it so decides, to argue the case for the prosecution before the Tribunal.

B. Referral to the Commission for Investigation and Prosecution

102. As the Committee has indicated (see part I, sect. E, above), the establishment of an international Tribunal to prosecute crimes committed in the former Yugoslavia would not happen *ex nihilo*. It would come as the logical follow-up to initiatives already taken within the United Nations, two of which are particularly significant:

(a) In resolution 1992/S-1/1, adopted on 14 August 1992, the United Nations Commission on Human Rights requested:

> "its Chairman to appoint a special rapporteur to investigate first-hand the human rights situation in the territory of the former Yugoslavia, in particular within Bosnia and Herzegovina, and to receive relevant, credible information on the human rights situation there from Governments, individuals, intergovernmental and non-governmental organizations, on a continuing basis, and to avail himself or herself of the assistance of existing mechanisms of the Commission on Human Rights".

Having been appointed Special Rapporteur, Mr. Tadeusz Mazowiecki made several visits to the former Yugoslavia, accompanied by four thematic rapporteurs, and in accordance with his mandate, gathered and compiled "systematically information on possible violations of human rights in the territory of the former Yugoslavia, including those which may constitute ... crimes". As the Commission on Human Rights noted, such information (presented in three reports) "could be of possible future use in prosecuting violators of international humanitarian law";

(b) For its part, the Security Council in resolutions 771 (1992) of 13 August 1992 and 780 (1992) of 6 October 1992, called upon States and humanitarian organizations to collate and make available to it:

> "substantiated information in their possession or submitted to them relating to the violations of humanitarian law, including grave breaches of the Geneva Conventions, being committed in the territory of the former Yugoslavia".

In addition, resolution 780 (1992):

> "Requests the Secretary-General to establish, as a matter of urgency, an impartial Commission of Experts to examine and analyse the information submitted pursuant to resolution 771 (1992) and the present resolution, together with such further information as the Commission of

---

38/ The principle of discretionary prosecution was set forth in recommendation No. R (87) 18, adopted by the Committee of Ministers of the Council of Europe on 17 September 1987.

Experts may obtain through its own investigations or efforts, of other persons or bodies pursuant to resolution 771 (1992), with a view to providing the Secretary-General with its conclusions on the evidence of grave breaches of the Geneva Conventions and other violations of international humanitarian law committed in the territory of the former Yugoslavia."

This five-member Commission, with Mr. F. Kalshoven as Chairman and Mr. C. Bassiouni as Rapporteur, began its work in October 1992.

103. Thus, abundant documentation on crimes committed in the territory of the former Yugoslavia has already been gathered by impartial and competent experts, and could be made available to the Commission for Investigation and Prosecution as soon as it is established. It would also be useful for such collaboration between the Tribunal and the Mazowiecki and Kalshoven Commissions to continue - according to procedures to be worked out - after the Tribunal begins its work. Consideration might be given to the possibility of having those bodies refer matters to the Commission for Investigation and Prosecution.

104. That right of referral may also be extended to certain humanitarian organizations, a list of which might be drawn up by the Security Council. In any event, the Commission for Investigation and Prosecution should also be able to intervene ex officio.

C. The investigation - gathering of evidence

105. When it takes that decision, it will be for the Commission to confirm the evidence already gathered and to seek further evidence for and against the accused, strictly respecting the rights of the defence (see part III, sect. F, below) as it undertakes all useful investigatory measures, such as:

(a) Questioning of the accused;

(b) Hearing of victims and witnesses;

(c) Confrontation of witnesses;

(d) Commission of experts;

(e) Character checks;

(f) Compilation of pertinent written and audio-visual material;

(g) Visits to the scene.

106. The Statute of the Tribunal should contain a provision whereby States would be obliged to extend cooperation, in particular that of their judicial investigation services to the Commission. However, there is probably no reason for this provision to be very detailed, especially if the Tribunal is to be established by a Security Council resolution adopted within the framework of Chapter VII of the Charter, Article 48 of which makes it an obligation for the Members of the United Nations to take "the action required to carry out the decisions of the Security Council for the maintenance of international peace and security".

D. "Transfer" of prosecuted persons - extradition - imprisonment

107. At least from the legal standpoint, this should also facilitate the transfer of accused persons to the Tribunal, where appropriate.

108. The Committee does not exclude the possibility of taking proceedings against defendants in their absence - a solution clearly dictated by realism. The details of the proceedings would have to be laid down in the Tribunal's

rules, which should indicate that, since the trial is being conducted in the absence of the defendant, he cannot be represented by counsel and no one can put questions to witnesses and experts on his behalf. In accordance with the general principles of criminal law, the judgement would be annulled if the accused person is arrested or gives himself up. In the case of either of these occurrences during proceedings conducted in the defendant's absence, the trial must be discontinued; in either event, the Tribunal should refer the case to the Commission for Investigation and Prosecution so that proceedings may be started once again. However, judgement in the defendant's absence must be a last resort, and every effort must be made to ensure that the defendant effectively appears, so that the judgement cannot be challenged and the trial is of an exemplary nature.

109. It should be stressed that the issue of the transfer of accused persons to the Tribunal would arise in a form that differs from that of classic extradition problems:

(a) Firstly, subject to a hypothetical examination of the lawfulness thereof, 39/ the obligation to transfer the accused person that would be laid down in the Statute would be derived not from a treaty-based obligation but from the duty of States Members of the United Nations to implement the decisions of the Security Council;

(b) Secondly, the beneficiary of the obligation to transfer the accused person would not be another State but an international court, which would facilitate the transfer to the Tribunal for requested States, without any need to conduct the proceedings and invoke the substantive requirements often specified by domestic laws on extradition. 40/

110. Similarly, it is interesting to note that, although it is entitled "Extradition and punishment of war criminals", General Assembly resolution 3 (I), of 13 February 1946, recommended that States should "take all the necessary measures" to send back to the countries in which their abominable deeds had been done those responsible for the crimes set forth in the London Agreement, without specifically mentioning extradition as such a measure. Moreover, Jean Pictet, in his authoritative commentary on the 1949 Geneva Conventions, emphasizes that the principle of universal jurisdiction laid down in the Conventions in no way precludes the transfer of accused persons to an international tribunal. 41/

111. Furthermore, article 1.F of the Geneva Convention of 28 July 1951 relating to the Status of Refugees, ratified by 111 States (including the former Yugoslavia), prohibits States parties from granting refugee status to any person with respect to whom there are serious reasons for considering that:

> "(a) He has committed a crime against peace, a war crime, or a crime against humanity, as defined in the international instruments drawn up to make provision in respect of such crimes;
>
> "...
>
> "(c) He has been guilty of acts contrary to the purposes and principles of the United Nations."

39/ Cf. ICJ, order of 14 April 1992, Case concerning questions of interpretation and application of the 1971 Montreal Convention arising from the aerial incident at Lockerbie, Reports, 1992, p. 3; see p. 15 in particular.

40/ For the same reasons, it can be assumed that a request by the Tribunal for the transfer of an accused person would have priority over a request for extradition made by a State.

41/ See Jean Pictet, Director, Commentaires de la Convention de Genève relative à la protection des personnes civiles en temps de guerre, International Committee of the Red Cross, Geneva, 1956, p. 635.

112. Naturally, these principles do not, in and of themselves, guarantee the effective transfer to the Tribunal of persons accused of having committed war crimes or crimes against humanity; however, there are no insurmountable legal objections to the transfer of accused persons if the requested States have the political will to effect the transfer.

113. Assuming that that is the case, it would be for the Commission for Investigation and Prosecution to decide on the imprisonment of a person in respect of whom there may be charges where imprisonment is required for the purposes of the investigation, or where there is a serious risk that the accused person will abscond. However, in accordance with the fundamental principles of the law of criminal procedure, 42/ the defendant must be able to take proceedings before one of the Judges of the Tribunal in respect of a detention measure.

E. Referral to the Tribunal

114. When the Commission believes that the investigation has been completed, it could take one of the following - reasoned - decisions:

(a) Simple dismissal, if the charges are insufficient; 43/

(b) Transfer to an independent, impartial national tribunal if the offences, although flagrant, have not been committed in a mass and systematic manner. 44/ In this event the national tribunal to which the case would be transferred would be obliged to be seized of the matter and render a decision on it;

(c) Referral to the Tribunal by means of an indictment setting forth the facts and listing the charges.

F. The rights of the defence

115. The Committee believes that the question of respect for the rights of the defence does not give rise to any particularly difficult technical problems. It noted that the rights in question were safeguarded - if not in the same terms, at least in accordance with the same principles - both by the Charters of the International Military Tribunals set up following the Second World War 45/ and by the various proposals setting up international criminal courts that it consulted.

116. Naturally, it is of the greatest importance that the defendants should benefit fully from all the guarantees provided by contemporary criminal procedure systems. The guarantees in question are felicitously and precisely summarized in article 14 of the International Covenant on Civil and Political Rights of 16 December 1966, which as at 31 January 1993 had been ratified by 112 countries, including the former Yugoslavia.

42/ See article 9, para. 4, of the 1966 International Covenant on Civil and Political Rights.

43/ In such a case, it might be appropriate for the Commission to be able, if it believes circumstances so dictate, to grant compensation to the person discharged. Cf. ibid., para. 5.

44/ This possibility would be excluded if the Statute of the Tribunal confined itself to referring to the 1949 Geneva Conventions with respect to competence *ratione materiae* (see part II, sect. D, above). It should not be confused with the power that could be given to the Tribunal itself to relinquish jurisdiction, where appropriate, for the benefit of a national court, even though the requirements for the Tribunal to exercise competence might be met (see part IV, sect. C, below).

45/ See article 16 of the Charter of the Nürnberg Tribunal and art. 9 of the Charter of the International Military Tribunal for the Far East.

117. In the Committee's view, the Statute of the Tribunal should reproduce, with appropriate drafting changes, the provisions on criminal procedure set out in paragraphs 2 and 3 of article 14 of the Covenant, which, as stressed by the United Nations Human Rights Committee, must apply to "all courts and tribunals ... whether ordinary or specialized" and whose requirements "are essential for the effective protection of human rights". 46/

118. It would also be helpful to include in the Statute a provision guaranteeing the defendant's right to have the assistance of counsel.

119. It should be noted, on the other hand, that other provisions of the 1966 Covenant applicable to national criminal procedure are not transferable to the international order. This is so particularly in the case of article 15, which - after enunciating the nullum crimen sine lege principle, which is applicable to both international and domestic law (see part I, sect. A, and part II, sect. C, above) - adds that:

> "Nothing in this article shall prejudice the trial and punishment of any person for any act or omission which, at the time when it was committed, was criminal according to the general principles of law recognized by the community of nations."

120. This is the fundamental justification for putting on trial those responsible for international crimes.

G. Reference to the rules of procedure

121. Without prejudice to the rights of the defence, which must be safeguarded by the Statute of the Tribunal itself, the Committee believes that procedural details should be laid down by the Rules of the Tribunal, and that they should be in keeping with the provisions of the Statute itself and general principles governing the law of criminal procedure.

122. It is important that the text of the Rules be limited to what is strictly necessary. Only a brief, comprehensible Statute can be drafted and adopted within a reasonable period of time, and it is essential that it be concise and "readable" so as to interest the public at large and gain public support, both of which are so necessary.

IV. JUDGEMENT AND SENTENCE

A. Pronouncement of judgement

123. As in the case of all preceding courts, the very idea of a collegiate court means that the judgement must be rendered by a majority of the members of the Chamber. If the Chamber is made up of five Judges, as suggested by the Committee (see part V, sect. B, below), it is not helpful to provide that the vote of the President should be decisive, because the principle that alternates should attend hearings from start to finish and be able to replace any member of the Tribunal who is unable to be present would provide virtually total assurance that the membership of the Chamber could be completed (see part V, sect. B, below).

124. It is clearly essential that the reasons on which the judgement is based be given, in accordance with the general principles of law recognized by all nations and all precedents. 47/ Any revision proceedings (procédure de réformation) for which provision would appear to need to be made (see part IV,

---

46/ Official Records of the General Assembly, Thirty-ninth Session, Supplement No. 40 (A/39/40), p. 144.

47/ See article 26 of the Charter of the Nürnberg Tribunal, in particular.

sect. F, below) would be made impossible if the reasons on which the judgement is based are not given. The Tribunal's considerable freedom with respect to the scale of penalties is a further reason for making the statement of reasons a strict obligation (see part IV, sect. B, below).

125. On the other hand, despite the actual practice of the Nürnberg Tribunal, for which no provision was made in its Charter, the Committee does not consider it legitimate that the Judges should be able, in criminal matters, to combine the statements of their individual or dissenting opinions.

126. In accordance with the universally accepted principles reflected in article 14, paragraph 1, of the 1966 International Covenant on Civil and Political Rights, judgement should be rendered in public. However, it would appear to be desirable to leave it to the Tribunal to decide whether or not to make public the names of some witnesses or victims, if the persons in question need protection from reprisals or unjustifiable social opprobrium (particularly in the case of rape).

B. Sentence

127. In the Committee's view, there are a number of reasons for having a broad range of sentences to be handed down by the Tribunal:

(a) The particularly heinous nature of crimes in respect of which perpetrators are to be prosecuted precludes limiting the penalties to those of a pecuniary or symbolic nature;

(b) On the other hand, the Committee strongly opposes the death penalty; however abominable the offences in question may be, "if a democracy applies to terrorists the logic of death applied by them, it is endorsing the values of the terrorists themselves"; 48/

(c) By process of elimination only rigorous imprisonment remains.

128. The Committee considered establishing a scale of penalties. It concluded, however, that such an approach would introduce excessive inflexibility: *a priori* and by definition, the Tribunal would have jurisdiction over extremely serious crimes (see part II, sects. D and E, above), but justice becomes injustice if it is blind, and it would be unacceptable for the Judges not to be able to take into account, in setting the length of the sentence, the circumstances in which the offence was perpetrated and the personality of the offender.

129. With regard to the circumstances in which the offence was committed, the sentence should reflect, in particular:

(a) The gravity of the offence (intention, premeditation, motives and goals of the perpetrator, state of mind that led to the criminal act, etc.);

(b) The values safeguarded by treating the act as a serious crime (human dignity, right to life, right to physical and/or moral integrity, and right to own property);

(c) The extent of the harm caused (either harm actually caused or the threat to cause harm, number of persons involved, and value of the property affected).

130. With regard to the personality of the perpetrator, the Tribunal could, for example, take account of his background and personal situation, as well as his conduct following the offence.

48/ Address by Mr. Robert Badinter, Minister of Justice, to the Senate on 28 September 1981 (*J.O.R.F*, Débats parlementaires, Sénat, 29 September 1981, p. 1665).

131. The fundamental principles of proportionality and individualization of the sentence would thus be safeguarded; it must be stressed that it is essential that the sentence indicate, possibly briefly but precisely, the grounds for the Tribunal's decision.

C. Non bis in idem - concurrence of international and national jurisdictions

132. The concurrence of international and national jurisdictions, made possible through the establishment of the Tribunal, gives rise to great problems.

133. The difficulties in question cannot be solved by means of mechanical implementation of the *non bis in idem* principle. As set forth in article 14, paragraph 7, of the 1966 Covenant, this principle has the purpose of avoiding the irrational and unjust consequences of the accumulation of national criminal competences, if such accumulation were to lead to an accumulation of sentences and penalties. 49/ However, once a competent international court has been established, this principle must be combined with the principle of giving priority to the international decision. 50/

134. There is, however, a third factor to take into account: a national jurisdiction should not be deprived of its powers if it is likely to prove more effective than the international jurisdiction.

135. Implementation of the following rules would reconcile these requirements:

(a) It is not helpful to lay down the principle of any *lis alibi pendens* exception: it is only once the Tribunal has rendered a final judgement, whether such judgement constitutes a conviction or an acquittal, that the principle of international priority comes into play: the taking of such a decision would mean that a domestic judgement in respect of the same acts, even if rendered prior to the Tribunal's decision, would be without effect;

(b) With regard to implementation, the hypothesis that two irrevocable decisions - one domestic and the other international - would only partly cover the same acts should be left aside; 51/

(c) It would seem, lastly, that there would only be advantages in the international court being able to relinquish its own jurisdiction to national courts, fairly exercising jurisdiction, particularly as regards the judgement of crimes perpetrated by persons who are merely executants (see part II, sect. H, above).

136. The possibility of relinquishing jurisdiction is recommendable both for practical reasons (decongesting the international court) and for political reasons. It would seem desirable, in fact, to restore as quickly as possible the exercise of normal jurisdiction to the courts of the States resulting from the breakup of the Socialist Federal Republic of Yugoslavia, and thus help to re-establish the normal operation of judicial authority in the countries in question.

49/ It can, moreover, be noted that, in its report on communication 204/1986, *X v. Italy*, 2 November 1987, the Human Rights Committee expressed the view that article 14 of the Covenant "[prohibited] double jeopardy only with regard to an offence adjudicated in a given State". Selected decisions of the Human Rights Committee. October 1982 - April 1988, volume II.

50/ The drafting of article 15 of the Covenant is based, *mutatis mutandis*, on such considerations where the implementation of the *non bis in idem* principle and its reconciliation with the possible existence of an international indictment are concerned.

51/ This should be done by means of a method of imputation giving due priority to the international decision.

137. Such a decision could be taken only by a chamber of the Tribunal, on the initiative, where appropriate, of the Commission for Investigation and Prosecution, and the reasons on which the decision is based would have to be given. In such an event, the case would be transferred to the competent national jurisdiction.

D. Effect of judgements - the question of appeals

138. Article 14, paragraph 5, of the 1966 Covenant on Civil and Political Rights provides as follows:

> "Everyone convicted of a crime shall have the right to his conviction and sentence being reviewed by a higher tribunal according to the law."

139. However, as normally interpreted, this provision is regarded as implying that a remedy of judicial review (recours en cassation) at least exists, but not as laying down the principle of a right of appeal. 52/ Furthermore, the Nürnberg and Tokyo precedents and most proposals for the establishment of an international criminal court considered by the Committee provide no opportunity to appeal against the judgements of the Tribunals or the court. 53/

140. The Committee believes that the practical difficulty of establishing appeals proceedings indicates that it is in fact not desirable that such proceedings be instituted. Moreover, the great formality of the trial and the publicity attracted by it would constitute major safeguards for the defendant, and the existence of revision proceedings (procédure de réformation) and review proceedings (procédure de révision) and the possibility of a pardon reduce yet further the need to establish appeals proceedings.

E. Review proceedings (recours en révision)

141. Providing no possibility for review in the event of the discovery of a new fact likely to have a decisive impact on the judgement that was unknown to the Tribunal at the time when it rendered its judgement, would be most unjust. Furthermore, virtually all proposals for the establishment of an international criminal jurisdiction provide for and make arrangements for such proceedings.

142. Article 29 of the Charter of the Nürnberg International Military Tribunal gave the prosecution the initiative. Whatever the Nürnberg Tribunal's reasons were at the time, such an imbalance would be difficult to justify now and the Committee is convinced that a review should potentially benefit either the prosecution or the defence.

143. Accordingly, it should be possible for the proceedings to be instituted either by the person convicted or by the Commission for Investigation and Prosecution, which in this case would have to follow the same procedure as in the case of an initial referral, the investigation stricto sensu being entrusted to a different member of the Commission.

52/ Moreover, France, whose criminal law does not provide for appeals in criminal matters, made an interpretive statement to that effect, accompanying its ratification of the Covenant.

53/ Some recent proposals, however, contemplate the institution of appeal proceedings (see, e.g. Mr. Cherif Bassiouni, "Draft statute of an International Criminal Tribunal", Nouvelle études penales, Erès, 1992, art. XXVIII).

F. Revision proceedings (*procédure de réformation*)

144. Moreover, review does not meet the requirements of article 14, paragraph 5, of the 1966 Covenant (see part IV, sect. D, above), which provides, in criminal matters, for a possibility of review (*voie de cassation*) or equivalent proceedings.

145. *Prima facie*, this approach gives rise to the same practical objections as those that arise in respect of an appeal and presupposes the establishment of extremely cumbersome judicial machinery. However, this obstacle would disappear if consideration of a request for revision (*demande en réformation*) 54/ could be entrusted to an already existing court.

146. The Committee therefore considered which court could be entrusted with such a task. The European Court of Human Rights comes to mind, but only a treaty-based approach would make it possible to overcome the numerous legal problems that would arise. However, it would be somewhat paradoxical to ask a regional court, however high its standing, to revise, where appropriate, judgements rendered by a tribunal established in a universal context and with a universal perspective.

147. It would be more natural to have recourse to the International Court of Justice, as the "principal judicial organ of the United Nations". 55/

148. However, one should not overlook the difficulties of instituting revision proceedings before the world Court:

(a) The judgements resulting therefrom would not apply, for the most part, to disputes between States, whereas only States may refer cases to the Court; 56/

(b) United Nations organs may, with regard to matters concerning them, apply to the Court only with requests for advisory opinions. 57/

149. These objections could probably be overcome by having recourse to the "binding advisory jurisdiction" of the Court. 58/ However, while the possibility of entrusting revision proceedings to the Court does not seem far-fetched, such a step would undoubtedly give rise to fairly difficult technical problems concerning, in particular, the initiation of the proceedings and the choice of organ called upon to formulate the application for an opinion.

150. Consequently, it would probably be better to envisage the establishment of a special court for the revision of judgements of the Tribunal (Court of Revision), which could be composed of:

(a) The President or Vice-President of the International Court of Justice;

54/ The term "revision" ("*réformation*") would seem to be more neutral, from a technical point of view, than the word "review" ("*cassation*"). It basically represents the same reality, however.

55/ Art. 92 of the United Nations Charter.

56/ Art. 36 of the Statute of ICJ.

57/ Art. 96 of the Charter and Art. 65 of the Statute.

58/ ICJ has always acknowledged that "the fact that the Opinion of the Court is accepted as binding provides no reason why the Request for an Opinion should not be complied with" (cf. ICJ advisory opinion of 23 October 1956, *Judgments of the Administrative Tribunal of ILO upon Complaints Made against UNESCO*, *Reports*, 1956, p. 84).

(b) The President of the European Court of Human Rights;

(c) The President of the Inter-American Court of Human Rights; and

(d) The President of the African Commission on Human and Peoples' Rights;

or their representatives, selected from among those organs, which the Committee considers should play a prominent role in the procedure for nominating the members of the Tribunal (see part V, sect. B, below).

151. In order to avoid improper applications, it would be appropriate either to institute a screening process - which might render the machinery cumbersome - or, which is undoubtedly preferable, to empower the Court of Revision to reject applications for revision, whether made by the convicted person or by the Commission for Investigation and Prosecution, if they are clearly without substance, by following a summary procedure.

152. The supervision exercised by the Court of Revision should apply only to points of law, to the exclusion of all questions of fact. 59/

153. Unlike ICJ, a Court of Revision could hand down a decision which would be binding on the Tribunal. If the Court criticized the legal reasoning followed by the Tribunal, it would be left to another chamber to award a new judgement that would conform to the decision of the Court.

G. Execution of sentences

154. Once the judgement has become final, the question arises as to the means of execution of the term of rigorous imprisonment (see part IV, sect. B, above) that might eventually be imposed.

155. In this respect, there is a choice between international execution - along the lines of the solution adopted following the Nürnberg trials - or execution through the intermediary of a State - as provided for in article 40 of the League of Nations Convention for the Creation of an International Criminal Court of 16 November 1937. The precedent - which is not very persuasive in this respect - based on the unique experience of international execution, with its high cost and the considerable difficulties of implementation, leads the Committee to declare itself clearly in favour of handing over the convicted person to a State, designated by the Tribunal, for the sentence to be served under the conditions laid down by the national law of that State.

156. It goes without saying that:

(a) The State entrusted with execution of the sentence must already have accepted that responsibility (the list of countries that "volunteer" could be prepared by the Security Council or by the Tribunal);

(b) The law of that State must respect in all points the rights guaranteed to persons deprived of liberty; 60/

59/ This could be based on art. 11 of the Statute of the United Nations Administrative Tribunal, under which judgements rendered by that body may be contested by means of a "binding advisory opinion", "on the ground that the Tribunal has exceeded its jurisdiction or competence or that the Tribunal has failed to exercise jurisdiction vested in it, or has erred on a question of law relating to the provisions of the Charter of the United Nations, or has committed a fundamental error in procedure which has occasioned a failure of justice".

60/ Cf. art. 10 of the 1966 Covenant on Civil and Political Rights.

(c) A mechanism must be devised in order to enable the costs entailed by the deprivation of liberty to be borne at the international level. 61/

H. Pardon and remission of sentence

157. Even though the death sentence could not be pronounced (see part IV, sect. B, above), there are obvious considerations, both human and political, that seem to require that provision be made for the possibility of a pardon or a remission of the sentence. That possibility, which was ruled out neither by the Charter of the Nürnberg Tribunal 62/ nor by that of the Tokyo Tribunal, 63/ is, moreover, envisaged by most of the proposals for creating an international criminal court.

158. In specific terms, a pardon could be granted either by the Tribunal itself - but that would confuse the functions somewhat and might cause the existence of that body to be unduly prolonged - or by the Security Council, or by the State entrusted with execution. The last two solutions both have their merits: the State of execution is "closer to the convicted person" and is aware of the real personal situation of that individual (illness, remorse); while the Security Council is in a better position to take into account the political risks and advantages of a grant of pardon or a remission of the sentence.

159. In the view of the Committee, there is a satisfactory means of combining these two procedures by deciding that the State entrusted with execution of the sentence may pardon the convicted person or reduce the sentence if the Security Council does not object within a specific period following notification by the authorities of that State of their intention.

V. INSTITUTIONAL ASPECTS

A. Composition of the Tribunal - general problems

160. The problem of the composition of the Tribunal covers a number of varied points:

(a) The total number of judges and possible alternates;

(b) The qualifications required;

(c) The manner of their appointment;

(d) The term of their functions;

(e) The number of members constituting a chamber;

(f) The manner of their appointment;

(g) Possible challenge of their appointment; etc.

61/ The costs to be borne by the United Nations budget or by a fund based on voluntary contributions. The execution of sentences does not necessarily have to be financed in the same way as the functioning of the Tribunal (see part V, sect. I, below).

62/ Art. 29.

63/ Art. 17.

161. On all these questions, of very unequal importance, a comparison of the systems adopted under the principal instruments or draft instruments for setting up an international criminal court 64/ indicates considerable uniformity except for the number of judges, which varies considerably from case to case: members representing each type of jurisdiction are elected from among the candidates nominated by the States parties. They must be qualified in criminal law and international law and/or in international criminal law, less often in human rights, and, in accordance with the precedent set by Article 9 of the Statute of ICJ, should represent the main forms of civilization and the principal legal systems of the world.

162. It does not follow, however, that this standard model must or can be copied exactly:

(a) The Tribunal to be set up would be ad hoc, whereas most of the reference models concern proposals for permanent courts;

(b) Except for the Tokyo International Military Tribunal, these bodies were set up (Nürnberg Tribunal) or were to be set up under legal instruments, whereas in the present instance the establishment of such a body by the United Nations Security Council appears to be the most feasible means (see part I, sect. E, above);

(c) It would, moreover, be set up within a specific historical and geographical context, which should be borne in mind.

163. The Committee considers that there is no "ready-made" or obvious solution in this field. The one it suggests is based on the desire to guarantee that the Tribunal will function effectively while ensuring the legitimacy of the members composing it.

B. Number of judges - chambers

164. As far as their number is concerned, the overriding consideration should be that the number of judges be as limited as is compatible with their functions.

165. If a chamber is composed of five judges, which would appear to be necessary in order to ensure minimal representation of the main legal systems of the world and a desirable balance between the qualifications of its members (criminal law, international law, human rights), and if it is understood that a chamber having a different composition might re-examine the matter in the case of revision of the judgement (see part IV, sect. F, above), the minimum number of judges is 10. 65/

166. This figure should be augmented by at least one judge competent to rule on applications for release of the accused, and another responsible for enforcing the sentences.

167. Moreover, in order to avoid a complete retrial if a judge becomes incapacitated during the proceedings, it would no doubt be useful to draw on the Charter of the Nürnberg Tribunal, which provided for the presence at the proceedings of alternates capable of replacing the members if the latter were no longer able to perform their functions. 66/

64/ See annex III.

65/ The need to ensure that the revision proceedings are carried out by a chamber that is different from the one which awarded the first judgement has led the Committee to abandon, with regret, a suggestion that the "major criminals" (see paras. 84-86 above) should be the subject of a judgement by the Tribunal meeting in plenary session.

66/ Cf. Art. 2 of the Charter of the Nürnberg Tribunal.

168. It does not seem to be necessary to have as many alternates as members, or even to envisage the special status of alternate judge: it is simpler and probably more equitable for each judge to perform the functions, in turn, of member and alternate in the various chambers.

169. In these circumstances, a total of 15 judges, with the addition of the members of the Commission for Investigation and Prosecution, does not appear to be excessive.

C. Appointment and qualifications of judges

170. Several mechanisms may be envisaged with regard to their appointment, but it is essential that they enjoy undisputed legitimacy.

171. This result could be achieved if existing international jurisdictions were entrusted with the task of electing the judges to the Tribunal from among their existing or former members. The International Court of Justice, the European Court of Human Rights, the Inter-American Court of Human Rights and the African Commission on Human and Peoples' Rights could be called upon to constitute the Tribunal; such a procedure would obviously offer the greatest guarantees of impartiality.

172. Apart from possible political resistance on the part of States, which would thereby be deprived of their traditional competence either to nominate or to appoint members of international jurisdictions, such a system could meet with two objections:

(a) On the one hand, existing jurisdictions do not necessarily include in their midst specialists in criminal law;

(b) On the other hand, and more importantly, some of those jurisdictions might find themselves in the awkward position of being under an obligation to nominate certain of their members to the Tribunal; such members would no longer be able to participate in the consideration of cases which they may have had to consider in their original jurisdiction, 67/ which might have to deal with such cases in another context; this could apply in particular to ICJ and the European Court of Human Rights.

173. Such obstacles could be avoided if those jurisdictions were to appoint members of the Tribunal not from among their own members but from among outside persons possessing well-known competence:

(a) In international law;

(b) In criminal law and, particularly, in international criminal law;

(c) In human rights, with the proviso that the composition of the Tribunal should represent a balance among those different qualifications and among the main legal systems of the world.

174. Under such a system, ICJ could be called upon to appoint six judges, while the European Court of Human Rights, the Inter-American Court of Human Rights and the African Commission on Human and Peoples' Rights could each appoint three.

175. If such a procedure were to encounter political difficulties, the Committee is of the view that the Security Council could be called upon to elect the members of the Tribunal from lists of candidates submitted by these four bodies.

67/ Cf. Art. 17, para. 2, of the Statute of ICJ.

D. Officers of the Tribunal

176. It would rest with the Tribunal thus constituted to elect from among its members a President and a Vice-President, who would be called upon to preside alternately over the chambers formed to try cases, the composition of which would be decided by the Tribunal meeting in plenary session.

E. Composition of the Commission for Investigation and Prosecution

177. The composition of the investigation and prosecution body is of equal importance to that of the Tribunal itself: it would in fact be invested with absolutely essential functions and would perform a screening role with regard to cases brought to its attention. It is the body which would decide on whether or not to institute proceedings, decide on measures of detention and issue warrants, institute an investigation, decide on the existence of charges and on whether to submit the case to the Tribunal, and present the case for the prosecution (see part III, sects. B to E, above).

178. While some of these tasks are necessarily of an individual nature (for example, the examination and hearing of witnesses, the appointment of experts, the preparation and presentation of the case for the prosecution), many decisions should, in the Committee's view, be taken collectively, bearing in mind both their gravity and the international character both of the crimes being prosecuted and of the Tribunal. This implies that they must be carefully weighed in terms of a wide range of sensibilities.

179. Application of the modified principle of discretionary prosecution put forward by the Committee (see part III, sect. A, above) further accentuates the need to set up a collegiate body composed of nationals of several States which alone would be able, on an acceptable basis, to choose persons to be brought before the Tribunal. That, moreover, was the solution adopted in articles 14 and 15 of the Charter of the Nürnberg Tribunal. 68/

180. The Committee therefore considers that it would be appropriate to establish a Commission for Investigation and Prosecution, the five members of which could be appointed, like the judges of the Tribunal, from among persons possessing recognized competence in criminal procedure, two of them being appointed by ICJ and one each by the European Court of Human Rights, the Inter-American Court of Human Rights and the African Commission on Human and Peoples' Rights, or, failing that, elected by the Security Council from lists of candidates submitted by those bodies.

F. The Registry

181. The Tribunal and the Commission for Investigation and Prosecution should be assisted in their respective tasks by a Registry with a composition as limited as possible, under a Registrar appointed by the Tribunal.

182. Should the Tribunal be established by a decision of the Security Council, the initial staff of the Registry should, firstly, be placed at the disposal of the Tribunal by the Secretary-General - and augmented subsequently by recruitment conducted by the Registrar under the Tribunal's supervision - and, secondly, should be subject, as appropriate, to the Charter and the Staff Rules of the United Nations or to the Staff Rules of ICJ.

68/ Similarly, article 33 of the draft statute for an international criminal court drawn up in 1953 by the United Nations entrusted a special chamber with the functions of investigation and committal.

G. Privileges and immunities

183. Along the lines of that provided for in Articles 19, 32, paragraph 8, and 42, paragraph 3, of the Statute of ICJ, the judges, the members of the Commission for Investigation and Prosecution and the Registrar should enjoy diplomatic privileges and immunities; and the other officials of the Registry, the defence counsel and all other persons called upon to participate in the proceedings (experts, witnesses), should enjoy the privileges and immunities they needed for the performance of their duties.

184. This should not pose any major problems if the Tribunal is established and functions within the framework of the United Nations, since Article 105 of the Charter would apply to all the officials of the Court and the benefits of the Convention on the Privileges and Immunities of the United Nations could, without great difficulty, be extended to persons participating in the proceedings. 69/

H. Working languages of the Tribunal

185. If the Tribunal is to be established by the Security Council, the working languages should no doubt be the official languages of the United Nations. On the other hand, if it is established by other means, it should be borne in mind that the working languages of international jurisdictions have traditionally been French and English. For reasons of economy, limitation to these two languages could, moreover, be proposed: they are also the two sole official languages of ICJ. 70/

186. In all cases, the fundamental principles of respect for the rights of the defence must be observed (see part III, sect. E, above), which implies that the accused should, where necessary, have the assistance of an interpreter during the investigation and the trial, and that all court documents should be translated into his language. 71/

I. Funding

187. If the Tribunal were to be a subsidiary organ of the Security Council, established under Article 29 of the Charter, it would seem legitimate for such an organ to be financed out of the United Nations regular budget. Admittedly, the regular budget normally covers expenditure relating to the perennial administrative activities of the Organization. In the past, however, other expenses have been charged to that budget, as in the case of the mission of the Secretary-General pursuant to Security Council resolution 309 (1972), relating to Namibia. Even if the Tribunal is not set up formally as a subsidiary organ within the meaning of Article 29, that solution could possibly be adopted.

188. It is true that, during the vote on the budget, the General Assembly could in principle impede the functioning of the Tribunal by refusing to appropriate the necessary funds, or by reducing their amount. However, such an attitude could be considered as not being in conformity with the Charter, bearing in mind the advisory opinion given by ICJ on 13 July 1954: "The function of approving the budget does not mean that the General Assembly has an absolute power to approve or disapprove the expenditure proposed to it; for

---

69/ See, in this connection, General Assembly resolution 90 (I) of 11 December 1946, which recommends that the benefits of article IV, sects. 11, 12 and 13, of that Convention should be extended to the agents, counsel and advocates appearing before the Court.

70/ Cf. Art. 39 of the Statute.

71/ Cf. Art. 14, para. 3 (f), of the 1966 Covenant on Civil and Political Rights.

some part of that expenditure arises out of obligations already incurred by the Organization, and to this extent the General Assembly has no alternative but to honour these engagements." 72/

189. If, however, the Tribunal is established by the Security Council under Chapter VII of the Charter and if its establishment is thus equated with a peace-keeping operation, it would be possible to devise a weighted scale for the apportionment of contributions (in other words, in all probability by increasing the assessment of the permanent members of the Council and reducing the normal contribution of the developing countries). The negotiation of such a schedule might well prove to be complicated, however, as shown by the discussions which are continuing at the present time, in view of the considerable number of ongoing peace-keeping operations.

190. A further idea would be to call for voluntary contributions, as in the case of the operations of the United Nations Peace-keeping Force in Cyprus or, in certain respects, as in the case of the Organization's current intervention in Yugoslavia. That solution, too, would be complicated. The Tribunal could not be set up and commence its work until the total financing of its activities was guaranteed for a period judged reasonably necessary for the performance of its functions.

191. That requirement would not dovetail easily with national budgetary rules (annual nature of budgets) and it would not be easy to make a sufficiently precise assessment of the foreseeable costs of the institution. The objection might also be raised that a mechanism for voluntary contributions would not conform with the spirit of the establishment of a Tribunal by the Security Council.

VI. CONCLUSIONS

192. After as detailed a study as possible, taking into account the extremely short notice given to it, the Committee of Jurists has become convinced that the establishment of an Ad Hoc International Tribunal set up to judge war crimes and crimes against humanity committed in the territory of the former Yugoslavia is possible in law. Without underestimating the problems of a legal and technical nature arising from such a proposal, the Committee considers that they are far from insurmountable and that there are means available to States to take swift action to set up the International Criminal Tribunal - action which the Committee was mandated to consider - if the international community demonstrates a clear political will to that end.

193. The Committee is aware that it does not have the mandate to take a decision on the appropriateness of such a proposal.

194. In conclusion, however, it wishes to emphasize that, in the opinion of all its members, such action would constitute a very important step towards building an international society more concerned about respect for law.

195. In addition to its immediate, law-enforcement function in the strict sense, such a Tribunal could in fact play a not inconsiderable preventive role by deterring the authors of crimes that are being committed daily just a few hundred kilometres from our country from pursuing their deeds, and its

---

72/ Effect of Awards of Compensation Made by the United Nations Administrative Tribunal, Reports 1954.

creation would, in the long term, constitute an invaluable symbol of the genuine will of the international community to uphold the rule of international law.

Pierre TRUCHE
President

Bernard de BIGAULT du GRANRUT

Paul BOUCHET

Mireille DELMAS-MARTY

Louis JOINET

Claude LOMBOIS

Alain PELLET
Rapporteur

Jean-Pierre PUISSOCHET

ANNEX I

Composition of the Committee

Mr. Pierre Truche, Procurator-General of the Court of Cassation, Chairman

Mr. Bernard de Bigault du Granrut, lawyer at the Paris Bar, former President of the Bar

Mr. Paul Bouchet, Honorary State Counsellor, President of the National Consultative Commission on Human Rights

Madame Mireille Delmas-Marty, Professor at the University of Paris I (Panthéon-Sorbonne)

Mr. Louis Joinet, Advocate-General of the Court of Cassation, Chairman-Rapporteur of the Working Group on Arbitrary Detention (United Nations)

Mr. Claude Lombois, Director of Education, Professor at the University of Paris II (Panthéon-Assas)

Mr. Alain Pellet, Professor at the University of Paris X (Nanterre) and at the Institute of Political Studies of Paris, member of the United Nations International Law Commission, Rapporteur

Mr. Jean-Pierre Puissochet, State Counsel, Director of Legal Affairs at the Ministry of Foreign Affairs

The Committee wishes to express its appreciation to Mr. Terry Olsen, Mr. Michel Raineri and Mrs. François Rouchereau and to the staff of the Division of Legal Affairs of the Ministry of Foreign Affairs who provided secretariat services with great devotion and efficiency.

ANNEX II

Letter dated 16 January 1993 from Mr. Roland Dumas, Minister of State and Minister for Foreign Affairs, to Mr. Pierre Truche, Procurator-General of the Court of Cassation and Chairman of the Committee

Sir,

Unfortunately, there is no longer any doubt that particularly serious crimes are being committed in the territory of the former Yugoslavia that constitute war crimes, crimes against humanity or serious violations of certain international conventions.

Such actions cannot go unpunished, and the absence of real penalties, in addition to being an affront to public conscience, could encourage the perpetrators of these crimes to pursue their regrettable course of action. For that reason, France believes that it is essential to proceed swiftly to the establishment of an International Criminal Tribunal that would be competent to judge these crimes committed in the former Yugoslavia.

France hopes that its establishment may enable the 12 States members of the European Community to give concrete follow-up to the decision that they have just adopted in Paris and that, in addition, this work will permit the speedy establishment of the Tribunal under United Nations auspices.

That is the reason why I have established a Committee of Jurists, composed of a limited number of eminent persons. I should be particularly gratified if you would agree to preside over and guide its work.

I hope that the Committee will be able, on the basis of existing studies and work, to consider precisely and speedily all the various issues raised by the establishment of such a Tribunal and to submit to me a proposal concerning its possible Statute. The Committee will be able to make all the proposals it deems appropriate with regard to the procedure to be followed in establishing the Tribunal and all other points that may be relevant to the end for which the Committee is established. For the purpose of performing its mission, the Committee may, should it deem it necessary, proceed to hear competent individuals.

In view of the urgency of the matter and being aware of the importance of the effort that I am requesting of the members of the Committee, I should be glad if a report on this work could be sent to me by the end of January 1993.

Accept, Sir, the assurances of my highest consideration.

(Signed) Roland DUMAS

ANNEX III

Basic documentation used by the Committee

1. International Law Association (Committee on the Permanent International Penal Court): Draft Statute of the International Penal Court (1926)

2. International Association for Penal Law: Draft Statute for the Creation of a Penal Chamber of the International Court of Justice (1928 - revised in 1946)

3. Convention for the Creation of an International Criminal Court (Geneva, 16 November 1937)

4. London International Assembly (established under the auspices of the League of Nations): Draft Convention for the Creation of an International Criminal Court (London, 1943)

5. United Nations Commission on War Crimes: Draft Convention Establishing a United Nations Tribunal on War Crimes (1944)

6. London Agreement for the Prosecution and Punishment of the Major War Criminals of the European Axis (London, 8 August 1945)

7. Special proclamation of the Supreme Allied Commander at Tokyo: Charter of the International Military Tribunal for the Far East (19 January 1946)

8. Memorandum from the representative of France to the General Assembly Committee to study the progressive development and codification of international law: proposal for the establishment of an International Criminal Court (1947 - A/AC.10/21)

9. Establishment of a Permanent International Criminal Court for the Punishment of Acts of Genocide, Economic and Social Council resolution 77 (V), annex I

10. Establishment of an Ad Hoc International Criminal Court for the Punishment of Acts of Genocide, ibid., annex II

11. French delegation to the Sixth Committee of the United Nations: Draft Convention on Genocide (containing provisions relating to an International Criminal Court) (1948 - A/C.6/211)

12. United Nations Committee on International Criminal Jurisdiction: revised draft statute for an International Criminal Court (1953)

13. Foundation for the Establishment of an International Criminal Court and International Criminal Law Commission: Draft statute for an International Criminal Court (Bellagio and Wingspread, 1972)

14. United Nations Draft Convention on the Establishment of an International Penal Tribunal for the Suppression and Punishment of the Crime of Apartheid and Other International Crimes (1981)

15. International Law Association: Draft statute for an International Criminal Court and draft Protocol I concerning applicable penalties (Paris, 1984)

16. Ibid.: Draft Protocol II concerning exonerating causes and draft Protocol III concerning forms of commission of infractions (preparatory acts, attempts, perpetration, incitement, assistance, conspiracy, etc.) (1988)

17. Committee of Experts on International Criminal Policy for the Prevention and Control of Transnational and International Crime and for the Establishment of an International Criminal Court: Draft Convention Establishing an International Criminal Court (Havana, 1990)

18. Center for United Nations Reform Education, B. F. MacPherson: Draft statute for an International Criminal Court (1992)

19. International Association for Penal Law, Mr. Cherif Bassiouni: Draft Statute of the International Criminal Tribunal (1992)

ANNEX IV

Principal recommendations of the Committee - applicable principles

The Committee considers that the establishment of a Tribunal for the trial of the crimes against humanity and war crimes committed in the territory of the former Yugoslavia is legally possible and may be effected speedily if States have the political will to do so.

In the view of the Committee, the following principles should be applied:

Nature of the Tribunal

1. The Criminal Tribunal for the former Yugoslavia should be an ad hoc jurisdiction established on a universal basis (introduction, paras. 1-6; part I, sects. A and B; annex V, art. I, para. 1).

Establishment of the Tribunal

2. The establishment of a Tribunal by means of a treaty would take considerable time and would raise more legal problems than it would resolve (part I, sect. C).

3. The most appropriate mode of establishment would be by a resolution of the United Nations Security Council, acting under Chapter VII of the Charter with a view to the restoration and maintenance of international peace and security (part I, sects. D to G).

4. Failing that, "mixed" solutions might also be envisaged combining the intervention of the Security Council and that of certain States, either by the countries which have come into existence as a result of the dissolution of the former Yugoslavia being invited by the Council to take certain initiatives with the view to the trial of the criminals or by the Council entrusting the task of constituting an International Tribunal to a group of States (part I, sect. H).

Term of existence of the Tribunal

5. The Tribunal might be dissolved by the Security Council when the Council considered its existence to be no longer necessary to the restoration and maintenance of international peace and security (part I, sect. F; annex V, art. I, para. 2, and art. II, para. 2).

Composition of the Tribunal

6. The Tribunal might be composed of 15 Judges presenting guarantees of extensive competence in international law, criminal law and, in particular, international criminal law and human rights. Its composition should be balanced both as regards the areas of competence of the Judges and at the geographical levels (part V, sects. A to C; annex V, art. II, para. 1).

7. The mode of appointment of the Judges should guarantee their legitimacy. It might be guaranteed by their appointment by the International Court of Justice, the European and the Inter-American Courts of Human Rights and the African Commission on Human and Peoples' Rights or by the establishment by them of a list of candidates from which the Security Council would elect the Judges (part V, sect. C; annex V, art. II, para. 1).

8. The Tribunal will establish its bureau (part V, sect. D; annex V, art. II, para. 3).

Competence of the Tribunal

9. Ratione materiae, the Tribunal should be competent to try cases involving grave breaches of the Geneva Conventions of 1949 - a list of which should be reproduced in the text of the Statute - where they present a

systematic and mass character, and crimes against humanity committed with intent to destroy, in whole or in part, a national, ethnic, racial or religious group, as such (part II, sects. A to E; annex V, art. VI).

10. The Committee emphasizes that the above-mentioned crimes already constitute international crimes according to existing customary and conventional rules of international law and general principles of law recognized by all nations. Conviction of the perpetrators thereof by an international court does not have retroactive effect and could in no way violate the principle of _nullum crimen sine lege_. The establishment of the Tribunal would, on the contrary, make it possible to guarantee impartial justice without any spirit of revenge (part I, sect. A, and part II, sects. B and C).

11. _Ratione loci_, the competence of the Tribunal should extend to crimes defined as such committed anywhere in the territory of the former Yugoslavia (part II, sect. F; annex V, art. I, para. 1).

12. _Ratione temporis_, the competence of the Tribunal should be restricted to the period beginning on 25 June 1991, which marks the beginning of the process of the dissolution of the former Yugoslavia (part II, sect. G; annex V, art. I, para. 1).

13. _Ratione personae_, political decision-makers, those giving orders and those executing them and individuals participating in a group constituted with a view to committing the crimes coming within the competence of the Tribunal may be prosecuted. Neither the official capacity of the perpetrators of those crimes nor the orders received will relieve the individuals in question of criminal responsibility (part II, sects. H to J; annex V, art. VII).

Investigation and prosecution

14. Investigation and prosecution should be entrusted to a Commission that will take the most serious decisions on the matter on a collegial basis (part III, sect. A, and part V, sect. E; annex V, art. III).

15. The Commission for Investigation and Prosecution might be composed of five members appointed in the same way as the Judges of the Tribunal and selected from among persons competent with regard to criminal proceedings (part V, sect. E; annex V, art. III).

16. The Committee declares itself in favour of the principle of discretionary prosecution, provided that the decisions taken respect the principle of equality before the law, are taken on a collegial basis and are well-founded (part III, sects. A, B and E and part IV, sect. C; annex V, art. IX, para. 4, and art. XI, para. 2).

17. The Commission for Investigation and Prosecution might be seized _ex officio_ or be seized by one of the bodies already established within the United Nations to gather information on war crimes and crimes against humanity committed in the territory of the former Yugoslavia ("Mazowiecki Commission" and "Kalshoven Commission") and also by humanitarian organizations to be listed by the Security Council. No civil actions shall be admitted (part III, sects. A and B; annex V, art. XI, para. 1).

18. The Commission for Investigation and Prosecution will conduct the investigation in accordance with the general principles of law in the matter and with full respect for the rights of the defence (part III, sects. B and F; annex V, art. XII).

19. States, both parties to the conflicts that divide the former Yugoslavia and others, should be required to cooperate fully with the Commission and, in particular, to deliver the prosecuted persons to the Tribunal. In the view of the Committee, the existing traditional rules on the question of extradition would not oppose such delivery (part III, sects. B and C; annex V, art. XIII).

20. Once the investigation is terminated, the Commission may, by a collegial and well-founded decision, either decide that there no grounds for prosecution or commit the defendant to the Tribunal or to a national court, if there are certain charges against him that do not, however, appear to constitute crimes within the meaning of the Statute of the Tribunal (part III, sect. F; annex V, art. XIV).

Proceedings before the Tribunal

21. Proceedings before the Tribunal must scrupulously respect the fundamental principles of criminal procedure recognized by all nations and, in particular, the rights of the defence (part III, sects. E to G; annex V, art. XV).

22. The proceedings may take place before a Chamber composed of five Judges and two surrogate Judges (part V, sect. B; annex V, art. II, para. 4, and art. XV, para. 1).

Sentencing and penalties

23. Judgements shall be adopted by a majority of the members of the Chamber and shall state the grounds on which they are based (part IV, sect. A; annex V, art. XVI, para. 1).

24. The Tribunal may either release the defendant, or relinquish jurisdiction in favour of a national court (with a view, principally, to contributing to the re-establishment of the normal functioning of the judicial authority in the States arising out of the dissolution of the former Yugoslavia), or convict the defendant (part IV, sects. A and C; annex V, art. VIII, para. 1, and art. IX, para. 4).

25. A defendant found guilty may be sentenced to rigorous criminal imprisonment, the duration of which shall be determined on the basis of the principles of proportionality and individualization (part IV, sect. B; annex V, art. VIII, para. 2).

26. Machinery should be envisaged for settling the problems that might arise from the concurrence of national and international jurisdictions in favour of the latter (part IV, sect. C; annex V, art. IX, paras. 1 to 3).

27. Sentences may be served in the territory of a State which has been designated for that purpose by the Tribunal and which has agreed to discharge such commission in cooperation with the Judge enforcing the sentence (part IV, sect. G; annex V, art. XIX, para. 1).

28. The State entrusted with the execution of sentence should be able, under the supervision of the Security Council, to pardon the convicted person or to mitigate the sentence (part V, sect. A; annex V, art. XIX, para. 2).

Judicial remedies

29. While an appeal against judgements appears to be ruled out, a revision procedure based exclusively on points of law should nevertheless be envisaged (part IV, sects. D and F; annex V, art. XVIII).

30. If new facts come to light, the convicted person or the Commission for Investigation and Prosecution should apply for review of the judgement (part IV, sect. E; annex V, art. XVII).

ANNEX V

Possible provisions for the Statute of the Tribunal

Several reasons prompted the Committee not to prepare a draft Statute, in the strict sense of the term, for the International Tribunal to try the crimes against humanity and the war crimes committed in the former Yugoslavia. In the first place, the exact wording of the articles depends on very diverse considerations, some of which, particularly the means of its establishment, are unknown to the Committee. In the second place, whatever method is selected, it seemed to the Committee that this Statute must be worked out in an international forum and that any proposal which France might make would necessarily be modified and probably enriched through confrontation with the ideas on the same subject produced in parallel by other bodies. Lastly, in the brief period allotted to it, the Committee would not in any event have had the time to work out the provisions of such a Statute in every detail.

The present annex therefore must be regarded as but one example, incomplete and capable of improvement, of possible provisions for the Statute of the Tribunal.

In drawing up these provisions, the Committee assumed that the Tribunal would be established by a resolution of the United Nations Security Council in the context of the powers conferred on the Council under Chapter VII of the Charter with a view to the maintenance of international peace and security. It wishes to repeat, however, that other assumptions are possible.

ARTICLE I

Establishment of the Tribunal

1. There is hereby established an International Tribunal for the trial of persons responsible for the crimes referred to in article VI which are committed in the territory of the former Yugoslavia subsequent to 25 June 1991.

2. The Security Council shall terminate the existence of the Tribunal when it considers that the Tribunal is no longer necessary to the restoration and maintenance of peace.

ARTICLE II

Composition and organization of the Tribunal

1. The Tribunal shall be composed of a body of independent judges appointed from among persons of recognized competence in

international law,

criminal law, especially international criminal law,

human rights.

The 15 Judges who make up the Tribunal shall be appointed [by the Security Council] as follows

Six [from a list of 18 names drawn up] by the International Court of Justice, and

Three [from lists of 9 names drawn up] respectively by the European Court of Human Rights, the Inter-American Court of Human Rights and the African Commission on Human and Peoples' Rights.

[The Security Council] [The nominating authorities] shall bear in mind not only that the persons to be appointed to the Tribunal should individually possess the qualifications required, but also that in the body as a whole the representation of the principal legal systems of the world should be assured and that the qualifications of the candidates should be sufficiently diversified and balanced.

No two members of the Tribunal may be nationals of the same State.

2. Should the Tribunal be required to continue its work beyond 31 December [1998], the Security Council shall take the necessary measures to ensure the renewal by rotation of the Judges and of the Commission for Investigation and Prosecution.

3. The Tribunal shall elect from among its members a President and a Vice-President, together with a Judge to hear appeals from decisions to place a person in custody taken by the Commission for Investigation and Prosecution and a Judge responsible for the enforcement of sentences.

4. The composition of the Chambers of five Judges which try the cases or which issue the final decisions following proceedings for revision shall be determined by the plenary Tribunal.

Either the President or the Vice-President of the Tribunal shall preside over the Chambers; in addition two alternate members shall be selected from among the Judges who follow the entire proceedings for the purpose of replacing a full member who is absent.

No judge may participate in the adoption of a judgement if he has been required previously to take cognizance of the facts of the case in any way that might give rise to doubt as to his impartiality.

ARTICLE III

Commission for Investigation and Prosecution

The Commission for Investigation and Prosecution shall be an independent body whose members shall be appointed from among persons with the necessary qualifications in criminal procedure.

The five members who make up the Commission shall be appointed [by the Security Council] as follows:

Two [from a list of six names drawn up] by the International Court of Justice, and

One [from lists of three names drawn up] respectively by the European Court of Human Rights, the Inter-American Court of Human Rights and the African Commission on Human and Peoples' Rights.

No two members of the Commission may be nationals of the same State.

ARTICLE IV

The Registry

The Tribunal and the Commission for Investigation and Prosecution shall be assisted in their respective work by a Registry, which shall be headed by a Registrar appointed by the Tribunal.

The Regulations [and Rules of the staff of the United Nations] [of the staff of the International Court of Justice] shall apply mutatis mutandis to the staff of the Registry.

ARTICLE V

Privileges and immunities

The members of the Tribunal, the members of the Commission for Investigation and Prosecution and the Registrar shall enjoy diplomatic privileges and immunities in the exercise of their duties.

The counsel of the defendants, the experts and the witnesses shall enjoy such privileges and immunities as are required for the independent exercise of their duties and for their participation in the activities of the Tribunal.

ARTICLE VI

Definition of the crimes within the jurisdiction of the Tribunal

1. The Tribunal shall be competent to try persons who are suspected of committing one or more of the following crimes:

(a) Any of the following acts committed with intent to destroy, in whole or in part, a national, ethnic, racial or religious group, as such:

(i) Killing members of the group;

(ii) Causing serious bodily or mental harm to members of the group;

(iii) Deliberately inflicting on the group conditions of life calculated to bring about its physical destruction in whole or in part;

(iv) Imposing measures intended to prevent births within the group;

(v) Forcibly transferring children of the group to another group;

(b) And, when they are mass and systematic, any of the following acts:

(i) Violence to life and person, in particular murder of all kinds, and cruel treatment such as torture, mutilation or any kind of corporal punishment;

(ii) Collective punishment;

(iii) Taking of hostages;

(iv) Outrages upon personal dignity, in particular humiliating and degrading treatment, rape, forced prostitution and indecent assault;

(v) The passing of sentences and the carrying out of executions without previous judgement pronounced by a regularly constituted court, and affording all the judicial guarantees which are recognized as indispensable by all nations;

(vi) Extensive destruction and appropriation of property, not justified by military necessity and carried out unlawfully and wantonly;

(vii) Plunder.

2. The characterization of an act or omission as an international crime within the jurisdiction of the Tribunal is independent of internal law. The fact that an act or omission is or is not punishable under internal law does not affect this characterization.

ARTICLE VII

Persons responsible

1. The crimes referred to in article VI shall be deemed to have been committed by any individual who:

(a) Participated in drawing up a common plan to commit the crime or have it committed, was associated in some way with its implementation or its transmission to persons called upon to execute it or gave general or specific instructions for its execution, even in part;

(b) Gave orders for the commission of one or more of the said crimes;

(c) Committed, tried to commit, knowingly helped to commit or knowingly allowed to be committed even though he could have prevented one or more of the said crimes.

2. The crimes referred to in article VI shall be deemed to have been committed by any individual who was a member of an organization or a de facto group, at any level whatsoever, having as its objective, even secondary, the commission of one or more of the said crimes.

Any individual who, of his own accord and prior to any proceedings, ceased to belong to the organization or the group and since that time has consistently refrained from participating in its activities shall be absolved of responsibility for the offence provided for in the present paragraph.

Prior to any formal conviction on this ground, the Tribunal shall determine by a separate decision the criminal character of an organization or a group.

3. The fact that the perpetrator of a crime acted pursuant to an order of a Government or a superior does not relieve him of criminal responsibility if, in the circumstances at the time, it was possible for him not to comply with that order.

4. The official position of the perpetrator of a crime does not relieve him of responsibility in criminal matters.

ARTICLE VIII

Penalties

1. A defendant found guilty of one or more of the crimes referred to in article VI shall be sentenced to rigorous imprisonment.

2. The length of the penalty shall be determined by applying the principles of proportionality and individualization. In setting the length of the penalty, the Tribunal shall take account of the favourable or unfavourable circumstances that determined its decision, which shall spell out the reasons on which it is based.

ARTICLE IX

Non bis in idem; concurrence of jurisdictions

1. The jurisdiction of any national criminal court under internal law shall not prejudice the jurisdiction of the Tribunal.

2. No proceedings can be instituted or continued before a national court for any act, even if characterized differently, which has been irrevocably pronounced on by the Tribunal once the defendant substantiates, in the event of sentencing by the Tribunal, that the penalty has been carried out or is being carried out.

3. Any sentence by the Tribunal shall annul a national judgement handed down with respect to the same acts, even if characterized differently, since a convicted person cannot evade the execution of a penalty.

The sentence handed down by a national court for a number of offences only some of which have been penalized by the Tribunal shall be absorbed by the penalty imposed by the Tribunal if such penalty is heavier.

If the penalty imposed by the Tribunal is lighter than the sentence handed down by the national court, the two shall be merged if they are of the same nature. If this is not the case, they shall be cumulative, the penalty imposed by the Tribunal always being carried out first.

4. The Tribunal may, of its own accord or at the request of the Commission for Investigation and Prosecution, relinquish jurisdiction in favour of a criminal court of the State in whose territory the crime was committed or of which the perpetrator or the victim is a national, if it considers that the conditions for independent and impartial justice are present.

The decision by which the Tribunal relinquishes jurisdiction shall state the reasons on which it is based. The records of the case shall then be transmitted to the competent national court.

ARTICLE X

Rights of the defence

1. The accused shall be presumed innocent until proved guilty by the Tribunal.

2. The accused must be tried impartially; in particular, he has:

(a) The right to a fair and public hearing;

(b) The right to be informed promptly and in detail in a language which he understands of the nature and cause of the charge against him;

(c) The right to legal assistance of his own choosing in the preliminary examination and to be informed, if he does not have legal assistance, of this right; the right to have legal assistance assigned to him, in any case where the interests of justice so require, and without payment by him in any such case if he does not have sufficient means to pay for it;

(d) The right to have adequate time and facilities for the preparation of his defence and to communicate with counsel of his own choosing;

(e) The right to be tried without undue delay;

(f) The right to be tried in his presence, and to defend himself in person or through legal assistance of his own choosing;

(g) The right to examine, or have examined, the witnesses against him and to obtain the attendance and examination of witnesses on his behalf under the same conditions as witnesses against him;

(h) The right to have the free assistance of an interpreter if he cannot understand or speak the language used in the preliminary examination or the hearing;

(i) The right not to be compelled to testify against himself or to confess guilt.

ARTICLE XI

Referral to the Commission for Investigation and Prosecution

1. The Commission for Investigation and Prosecution may be seized *ex officio*.

2. The Special Rapporteur appointed pursuant to resolution 1992/S-1/1, of 14 August 1992, of the United Nations Commission on Human Rights and the impartial Commission of Experts constituted pursuant to resolution 780 (1992) of the Security Council shall refer to the Commission for Investigation and Prosecution information known to them about acts which might constitute the crimes referred to in article VI of the present Statute.

The humanitarian organizations listed in an annex to the present Statute may also refer information about such acts to the Commission.

3. The Commission for Investigation and Prosecution shall decide, by a decision of the majority of its members, whether or not to institute proceedings.

ARTICLE XII

Investigation

1. The Commission for Investigation and Prosecution shall have all the necessary powers to confirm the evidence already gathered and to seek further evidence, both for and against the accused.

2. These powers and the investigation proceedings shall be laid down in the Rules of the Tribunal.

ARTICLE XIII

Judicial cooperation; handing over of the accused; placing the accused in custody

1. Every State shall be required to extend to the Commission for Investigation and Prosecution the assistance of its judicial bodies and police in the investigational measures decided on by the Commission and to facilitate, by every means available, the process of tracking down, arresting and transferring any person accused of one of the crimes referred to in article VI so that he can appear before the Tribunal.

2. The Commission for Investigation and Prosecution may decide to place in custody a person accused of such a crime if the circumstances of the investigation so require or if there is a real danger that the accused may evade justice.

The accused may institute an appeal against any detention measure before one of the judges of the Tribunal designated for this purpose.

ARTICLE XIV

Referral to the Tribunal

When it considers that the investigation is terminated, the Commission for Investigation and Prosecution shall, by a decision of the majority of its members which is public and states the reasons on which it is based,

(a) Either decide that the charges are insufficient and that there are no grounds for prosecution;

(b) Or transfer the accused to an independent and impartial national court if the offences, although characterized, do not conform to the definition of the crimes that are within the jurisdiction of the Tribunal according to article VI of the present Statute; the competent national court shall, in such instance, be seized of the matter and shall try the accused;

(c) Or refer to the Tribunal an indictment describing the facts and detailing the counts.

ARTICLE XV

Proceedings

1. The proceedings shall be held in public before a Chamber of the Tribunal.

The Chamber may order the court to be cleared and closed during all or part of the trial in the interests of law and order or where the interests of privacy or the safety of the victim, the defendant or the witnesses so require, or to the extent that it deems that the special circumstances of the case so require.

2. A defendant may be subject to a contumacious judgement.

3. The Rules of the Tribunal, to be adopted by it and by the Commission for Investigation and Prosecution sitting in full session, shall establish the details of the proceedings on the basis of respect for basic human rights, the general principles of the law of criminal procedure which are recognized by all nations, and the provisions of this Statute.

ARTICLE XVI

Consideration and judgement

1. Judgements shall be adopted by a majority vote of the Judges who are members of the Chamber. Judgements shall state the grounds on which they are based and shall not include the individual or dissenting opinions of the Judges. They shall be read out at a public hearing.

2. Judgements shall be enforceable.

ARTICLE XVII

Review

If one or more new facts come to light which are likely to have a decisive influence on the judgement and of which the Tribunal was unaware at the time that judgement was rendered, the Commission for Investigation and Prosecution or the convicted person may submit to the Tribunal an application for review of the judgement.

ARTICLE XVIII

Revision

1. There shall be established a Court of Revision of Judgements of the Tribunal, consisting of the President and Vice-President of the International Court of Justice and the Presidents of the European Court of Human Rights, the Inter-American Court of Human Rights and the African Commission on Human and Peoples' Rights, or their representatives designated from within these bodies.

An application may be submitted to the Court of Revision by the Commission for Investigation and Prosecution or the convicted person, claiming that the Tribunal, in rendering its judgement, has exceeded its competence or has failed to exercise competence vested in it, or has erred on a question of law, thus vitiating the judgement, or has committed a fundamental error in procedure which has occasioned a failure of justice.

2. The Court of Revision shall, following a summary procedure, reject applications which are clearly unfounded.

3. Should the Court of Revision decide that the judgement has been vitiated by one of the flaws enumerated in the preceding paragraph, a Chamber of the Tribunal, being composed of members other than those who rendered the initial judgement, shall render a new judgement pursuant to the Court's decision.

ARTICLE XIX

Execution of sentences; pardon

1. Sentences shall be served in a State designated by the Tribunal on the basis of a list drawn up by the Security Council of States Members of the United Nations which have expressed their willingness to accept convicted persons. Imprisonment shall be subject to the national rules of the State in which the sentence is executed and shall be imposed under the supervision of

the Judge appointed by the Tribunal from among its members to enforce the sentences.

2. If it deems that circumstances so require, the State in which the sentence is executed may submit to the Security Council a report stating the grounds for the pardon or the measure mitigating the sentence pronounced which it proposes to implement. The opinion of the Judge overseeing the execution of sentences shall be annexed to this report.

If the Security Council does not object to such a measure within a period of one month, the State in which the sentence is executed shall grant the pardon or mitigate the sentence as envisaged in its report.

ARTICLE XX

Languages

[To be inserted]

ARTICLE XXI

Funding; seat

[To be inserted]

D. LETTER DATED 16 FEBRUARY 1993 FROM THE PERMANENT REPRESENTATIVE OF ITALY TO THE UNITED NATIONS ADDRESSED TO THE SECRETARY-GENERAL

S/25300, 17 February 1993.

I have the honour to forward herewith a draft statute of a Tribunal for War Crimes and Crimes against Humanity Committed in the Territory of the Former Yugoslavia, together with some explanatory notes.

The said documents are the result of a study carried out by a Commission of Italian jurists, chaired by Professor Giovanni Conso, former President of our Constitutional Court, and currently Minister of Justice, which was set up by the Italian Government for the purpose.

The Italian project is intended as a contribution to the present debate concerning the establishment of an international penal jurisdiction for crimes committed in the former Yugoslavia.

I would, therefore, be grateful if you could have the project circulated as a document of the Security Council.

(Signed) Vieri TRAXLER
Ambassador

Annex I

[Original: English and French]

Commission on War Crimes and Crimes against Humanity Committed in the Former Yugoslavia: Statute of the Tribunal for War Crimes and Crimes against Humanity Committed in the Territory of the Former Yugoslavia

Article 1

Jurisdiction of the Tribunal

1. The Tribunal shall have jurisdiction on crimes referred to in article 4 committed in the territory of the former Yugoslavia after 25 June 1991.

2. The Tribunal shall also have jurisdiction on the same crimes when committed in places not subject to the sovereignty of any State, when the offender or the victim is a national of one of the States born from the dissolution of the former Yugoslavia.

Article 2

Structure of the Tribunal

The Tribunal shall comprise the following bodies:

(a) The Court;

(b) The Prosecutor's Office;

(c) The Registry.

Article 3

Concurrence of jurisdiction (Ne bis in idem)

1. The Tribunal's jurisdiction is not precluded by any criminal proceedings pending for the same acts before a national judicial authority. However, the Court, meeting in plenary session, can, upon request of the Prosecutor's Office or of the defender of the accused, waive its own jurisdiction in favour of the judicial authority of the State in whose territory the act has been committed or of the State of which the author of the crime or the victim has the nationality, when it considers that such authority guarantees acceptable conditions for an independent and impartial justice, and that waiver of jurisdiction is in the interest of justice.

2. When a final judgement has been delivered by the Court, an accused person shall not be submitted to another trial by a national judicial authority for the same acts, however differently qualified, provided that, in case of condemnation, the penalty has been purged or its purging is under way or the penalty has been extinguished.

3. When enforcing penalties imposed by the Court, the relevant authority shall take into account penalties that have been imposed for the same acts by a national judicial authority and which have already been executed.

Article 4

Crimes subject to the jurisdiction of the Tribunal

The following crimes are subject to the jurisdiction of the Tribunal:

(a) War crimes, such as violations of the Geneva Conventions of 12 August 1949 and of the Additional Protocols of 10 June 1977, as well as any other war crime as defined by international customary law or by international treaties;

(b) Crimes of genocide, in violation of the Convention on the Prevention and Punishment of the Crime of Genocide, opened for signature in New York on 9 December 1948;

(c) Crimes against humanity consisting of systematic or repeated violations of human rights, such as wilful murder and deliberate mutilation, rape, reducing or keeping persons in a state of slavery, servitude or forced labour, or persecuting or heavily discriminating against them on social, political, racial, religious or cultural grounds; or deporting or forcibly transferring populations;

(d) Acts of torture, in violation of the Convention against Torture and Other Cruel, Inhuman or Degrading Treatment or Punishment signed in New York on 10 December 1984.

Article 5

Principles of criminal liability

1. The official status of the author of any of the crimes referred to in article 4, and particularly the fact of having acted in the capacity of head of State or member of the Government, does not exclude criminal liability.

2. The fact that the author of one of the crimes referred to in article 4 may have acted on the orders of a Government or of a hierarchical superior does not exclude criminal liability if, given the circumstances at the time of the offence, the offender had the possibility to disregard such orders.

3. The fact that one of the crimes referred to in article 4 is committed by a subordinate does not exclude the hierarchical superiors from criminal liability, if they knew, or were in possession of information which would have enabled them to conclude, in the circumstances of the moment, that the subordinate was committing, or was about to commit, the crime or if they had failed to take every possible measure to prevent its commission.

Article 6

Plurality of offenders

The fact of instigating the commission of any of the crimes referred to article 4 or of being an accomplice thereto or of agreeing to the commission of the crimes, shall be punished according to the provisions of article 7.

Article 7

Penalties

1. For the crimes referred to in article 4, the Court shall apply the penalties provided for by the criminal law in force at the time of commission in the State in whose territory the crime was committed.

2. If the crime is committed in a place not subject to the sovereignty of any State, the Court shall apply the penalties provided for by the criminal law in force at the moment of its commission in the State born from the dissolution of the former Yugoslavia of which the offender is a national or, subordinately, of which the victim is a national.

3. In no case, however, may the death penalty be inflicted.

Article 8

The Court

1. The Court shall examine the substance of the charges made by the Prosecutor and ascertain the guilt or the innocence of the accused person. In case of a conviction, the Court shall inflict the relevant penalties.

2. The Court shall consist of eighteen members, two each being appointed by the Presidents or Chairmen of the International Court of Justice, the European Court of Human Rights, the Human Rights Committee (Civil and Political), the Committee on the Elimination of Racial Discrimination, the Committee against Torture, the European Committee for the Prevention of Torture, the Committee on the Elimination of Discrimination against Women, the Committee on the Rights of the Child.

3. The members of the Court shall be persons of recognized competence in the field of international criminal law and human rights, offering guarantees of full independence. The Court cannot include more than one member having the same nationality.

4. In its first session, the Court elects its President. In case of a tied vote, the senior candidate shall be elected.

5. The Court shall comprise at least three Chambers, one of which as a Chamber of guarantee (Chambre d'accusation) and another one as a Judge of appeal. Each Chamber shall consist of three members. In plenary session the Court sits in a Chamber of seven members. The Chamber of guarantee meets to confirm measures of precuationary detention. It holds also the preliminary hearing whose function is to verify whether the Prosecutor's request for dismissing the charges or for prosecuting are adequately motivated.

6. The Court has its seat at ...

Article 9

The Prosecutor's Office

1. The Prosecutor's Office is responsible for investigating the information on crimes which it has received or acquired ex officio or on denunciation. It avails itself of the police forces of the State in which inquiries are being conducted or of any other structures as provided for in article 14.2. At the end of the investigations, the Prosecutor's Office shall request the Tribunal to dismiss the charges or shall proceed to prosecute, pursuant to article 8.5.

2. Non-governmental organizations working in the humanitarian field or in the field of human rights, having a consultative status or being accredited with the United Nations or the Council of Europe can submit documented denunciations to the Prosecutor's Office.

3. Any request to dismiss charges together with its grounds shall be communicated to the organization which has submitted the denunciation. The organization can submit to the Chamber of guarantee of the Court its observations thereon.

4. The Prosecutor's Office consists of thirty-six members, four each to be appointed by the persons referred to in article 8.2 and under the conditions provided by article 8.3. No more than two members of the Prosecutor's Office may be of the same nationality.

5. The members of the Prosecutor's Office shall elect the General Prosecutor from among them, who shall be responsible for the Office. In the case of a tied vote, the senior candidate shall be elected.

6. The Prosecutor's Office has its principal seat in the place where the Court has its seat. Sub-offices may be established in the countries where inquiries are held.

Article 10

The Registry

1. The Registry is responsible for the administration, financial affairs and organization of the Tribunal, with separate offices in the Court and the Prosecutor's Offices.

2. The Registry is located in the place where the Court has its seat.

Article 11

Principles of proceedings

1. Every person who is charged with a crime under article 4 has the right:

(a) To be presumed innocent until found guilty by the Court, excluding therefore any restraint of personal freedom not justified by needs of precaution; should this be the case, the Prosecutor's Office shall immediately ask a confirmation to the relevant Chamber of the Court;

(b) To be immediately informed, in a language he understands and with full explanations, of the nature and grounds of charges addressed against him and in case of precautionary measures, of the reasons for his seizure;

(c) To have sufficient time and to benefit from the resources, for preparing his defence, with the right to communicate with a lawyer of his choice, all the costs of which shall be paid in the event that the accused is unable to meet them;

(d) To be judged within a reasonable period of time at a public hearing, appearing personally and being represented by a counsel chosen by him as provided for by (c) above or by a defence counsel appointed by the Court;

(e) To be assisted free of charge, when he does not know the language used at the trial, by an interpreter to enable him to understand the proceedings in which he is personally involved, all the written trial documents being translated in advance;

(f) To question or to have questioned all the witnesses for the prosecution, requesting a confrontation with them if necessary, and to request witnesses for the defence to be cross-examined and to appear and be questioned under the same conditions as the witnesses for the prosecution;

(g) To avail himself of the right to remain silent after having been duly informed of this right;

(h) Not to have any evidence acquired unlawfully, whether directly or indirectly, used against him.

2. In any case adequate protection shall be ensured for witnesses and persons injured by the crime against any form of intimidation or pressure.

3. The Court, in its General Assembly, having heard the Prosecutor, when adopting the Tribunal's rules, shall also dictate rules necessary in order to implement in the various phases of proceedings the principles under numbers 1 and 2.

Article 12

Appeals

Appeals against judgements delivered by any Chamber of the Court may be lodged before the Appeals Chamber of the same Court. The judges who were members of the bench during the previous proceedings may not hear the appeal.

Article 13

Res judicata and revision

1. Judgements against which no appeal is lodged and judgements delivered on appeal shall be considered final, and become enforceable. However, if evidence unknown at the time of the judgement comes to light, the Court may decide, on request, whether the new evidence justifies acquitting the convicted person or shows that the offence was not a crime pursuant to article 4. When ascertaining one or the other occurrence the enforcement of the penalty shall be suspended and the conviction quashed.

2. At the revision hearing, the Court judges in plenary session and none of the judges on the bench which have intervened in previous proceedings may hear the appeal.

Article 14

Enforcement

1. The enforcement of the sentences of the Court shall be the responsibility of the Prosecutor's Office.

2. Unless the Court decides otherwise, it is primarily the responsibility of the competent organs of the State in whose territory the crimes are committed to enforce precautionary measures and penalties inflicted by the Court. The modalities of the supervision of the enforcement are indicated by the rules referred to in article 11.3.

3. The Security Council of the United Nations adopts any appropriate measures for the effective implementation of the provisions of the present statute.

Annex II

[Original: English and French]

Explanatory notes to the draft statute of an international Tribunal

This draft is based on the assumption that the Tribunal is set up by a resolution of the Security Council, adopted under Chapter VII of the Charter of the United Nations, as an independent and autonomous United Nations body, governed by a statute which would take the form of an annex to the Council's resolution.

Due to the independence and autonomy of the Tribunal, it is up to it to equip itself with the necessary rules of procedure.

On the other hand, it is up to the Security Council, possibly within the scope of the same resolution, to request States Members or not members of the United Nations to make the necessary provisions for the concrete operation of the Tribunal. Reference is made here to provisions in the field of extradition and legal assistance to the Tribunal; detention of people under investigation; means for enforcement of penalties as well as precautionary measures, etc. Reference is also made to financial provisions.

Article 1

Jurisdiction of the Tribunal

The Tribunal shall have jurisdiction over the crimes envisaged under article 4, where committed in former Yugoslavia. On the basis of the principle of territorial jurisdiction, any crime committed outside the territory of the former Yugoslavia shall be judged by the State of the locus commissi delicti. In fact, crimes indicated under article 4 and related to the present conflict can hardly be perpetrated outside the former Yugoslavia.

Relevance shall be given to the nationality of the offender or of the victim to decide upon the court jurisdiction, when the act is committed in an area which is not subject to the sovereignty of any State.

The Tribunal shall have jurisdiction only over the crimes committed after 25 June 1991, the date on which Croatia and Slovenia were proclaimed independent.

Article 2

Structure of the Tribunal

The Tribunal shall be organized in three entities, in charge respectively of judging, prosecuting and supporting the proceedings; for further details see articles 8, 9 and 10.

Article 3

Concurrence of jurisdiction (Ne bis in idem)

According to the Commission, there must be a trade-off between the "ne bis in idem" principle (which is the expression of a fundamental human right) and the need to give priority to the international Tribunal.

As a result, the following decision has been reached:

(a) The jurisdiction of the Court shall not be questioned by pending criminal proceedings for the same facts before a national jurisdiction;

(b) The Court, in joint session (see art. 8), shall be able to waive its jurisdiction in favour of a national judicial authority competent on the basis of the principle of territoriality, or of those of active or passive personality, provided that such jurisdiction be independent and impartial and that this waiver be desirable in the interest of justice. This will allow the Court to take a discretional decision and to transfer to the national judicial authority the cases that do not need to be dealt with by an international jurisdiction because they are of modest dimension or because, in general, the national authority can best judge them;

(c) The irrevocable judgement of the Court shall produce a preclusive effect _vis-à-vis_ any domestic criminal case;

(d) For equity's sake, one shall take into consideration penalties inflicted by a national jurisdiction for the same crime and already served; this is a solution based on the principle of "proportionality" as applied by the European Community Court of Justice (see, for example: _Wilhem vs Bundeskartellamt_).

Article 4

Crimes subject to the jurisdiction of the Tribunal

In determining war crimes and those against humanity falling within the jurisdiction of the Tribunal, reference has been made to the international crimes on which there is a general consensus, as reflected by widely acknowledged principles of international law (e.g. the Nürnberg principles) or in universally accepted conventions.

Among war crimes under the jurisdiction of the Court (subpara. (a)) the serious violations of the 1949 Geneva Conventions and of the Additional Protocols were included as the historically most significant part of humanitarian law.

It was also deemed appropriate to add a reference to war crimes stemming from other provisions of international customary and conventional law so as to take into account further kinds of violations, on the basis of the most recent developments of humanitarian law (suffice it to recall the violations of the Hague Convention of 14 May 1954 on the Protection of Cultural Heritage in the Event of Armed Conflict).

Subparagraph (b) considers genocide according to the definition set forth in the United Nations Convention of 1948; in fact, genocide is the most heinous among crimes against humanity; it was given specific attention and defined as a "crime under international law" in General Assembly resolution 96 (I) of 11 December 1946 and subjected to the jurisdiction of an international criminal Court (never implemented by the way) by the 1948 Convention.

Subparagraph (c) concerns the most serious human rights' violations, according to the wording of article 21 of the Draft Code of Crimes against the Peace and Security of Mankind; moreover, it was deemed necessary to add maiming and rape to the crimes envisaged in the above-mentioned article, because these are crimes very frequently committed in the present conflict, causing a public outcry. Also serious discriminations out of social, political, racial, religious or cultural reasons were added since they are violations of the United Nations Convention on the Elimination of All Forms of Racial Discrimination, opened to signature in New York on 7 March 1966. Instead, the reference to "crimes against mankind" in the wording of the Nürnberg Tribunal statute was considered obsolete, in that it envisaged a link with a war crime, thus largely restricting the scope of action of the Court to be set up.

Subparagraph (d) considers torture according to the definitions provided by the United Nations Convention. These offences are already included among war crimes; in particular, torture is mentioned under article 147 of the Fourth Geneva Convention.

Further reference to other international crimes should be carefully assessed, in order not to mention crimes on which no general consensus exists.

Article 5

Principles of criminal liability

Article 5 envisages some important principles governing criminal liability for international crimes that have been universally transposed into international criminal law, like the Nürnberg principles and some of the most recent international conventions.

The first section rules out any form of immunity for the act of State; it is a principle which has a precedent in the Convention on the Prevention and Punishment of the Crime of Genocide and which is by now accepted by the most recent trends in international criminal law.

The exclusion of the exception related to orders by hierarchical superiors, envisaged under paragraph 2 is applicable only when the subordinate has concretely had the possibility not to obey them.

The principle of hierarchical superiors' liability for war crimes or crimes against humanity - explicitly provided for under paragraph 3 - is also found in the international case law and transposed into article 86 of the First Additional Protocol to the Geneva Conventions.

Article 6

Conspiracy to commit the crime

All international criminal law texts explicitly refer to penalties for certain forms of complicity in committing the crime. As a result, the draft statute includes a provision punishing complicity, instigation and conspiracy to commit the crime.

Article 7

Penalties

All war crimes and those against humanity provided for under article 4 are considered international crimes as set forth by international law or far-ranging conventions. However, these international law sources do not envisage any penalties for such crimes; the need to respect the principle "nullum crimen, nulla poena sine lege", the basis of fundamental human rights, has induced the Italian Commission to decide in favour of the penalties set forth by the criminal law of the State of the locus commissi delicti (according to paragraph 1 of article 1, reference is inevitably to one of the States resulting from the dissolution of the former Yugoslavia).

If the principle is inapplicable (because the crime has been committed in a place which is not subject to the sovereignty of any State), recourse shall be made to the principle of active or passive personality in order to determine the law to be enforced.

Nevertheless, the death penalty has been excluded, in line with a principle that is by now part of the European legal heritage, as shown by Additional Protocol No. 6 to the European Convention on Human Rights.

Article 8

The Court

After a brief indication, in paragraph 1 of the main competence of the Court, its composition is spelled out hereinafter so as to:

(a) Use or enhance the existing ad hoc international bodies designed legally and politically to safeguard human rights world wide and in the European region (i.e. the United Nations and the European regional subsystem of human rights);

(b) Create synergy between these agencies to ensure impartiality and, at the same time, effectiveness of the Tribunal.

The bodies referred to are all "composed by individuals" and, therefore, this makes them supranational and independent.

In accordance with the deontology of human rights, the particular nature of crimes committed in the former Yugoslavia and the requests coming from various associations, a high number of women will probably be included in the membership of the Court.

Even if targeted, the role of the various United Nations agencies in the criminal jurisdiction is such that the very United Nations supranational authority will be strengthened, and so too its democratic vocation, thus paving the way for a "high-profile" international criminal court.

The concurrent involvement of bodies operating within the framework of the Council of Europe will set the stage for a functional coordination with the United Nations and accelerate the process to push the latter towards the model of a genuine jurisdictional authority.

Paragraph 3 lists the criteria to be complied with by the entities that have to choose the 18 judges composing the Court, in order to ensure professionalism, impartiality and effective representation. While paragraph 4 deals with the election of the President, paragraph 5 explains how the Court will be organized in Chambers, in that a unified structure is not feasible. There will be a minimum number of Chambers (three), but the upper limit has not been decided yet and will depend on the amount of work to be concretely conducted.

The lower limit stems from the need to have at least a Chamber for preliminary inquiries, at least another Chamber for judgements of the first instance and at least a third one for appeals. To keep the structure as streamlined as possible, there will be three members when the case has to be judged by a single Chamber and seven when the Chambers join, as in the exceptional instances specified under articles 8 and 13.

Of course, in order for the Court to function, the United Nations should resort to special contributions by member States or by a group of member States (such as those belonging to the Conference on Security and Cooperation in Europe).

Article 9

The Prosecutor's Office

Paragraph 1 indicates the Prosecutor's Office's functions and paragraph 2 its organization and structure, which are similar to those indicated in the previous article, except for the number of attorneys that is two times as high. This is due to the need for them to work not only in the Court but also in the field for investigative purposes.

The role of non-governmental organizations in starting legal action is outlined in paragraphs 2 and 3.

Article 10

The Registry

The Registry is designed to support the Court and the Prosecutor's Office and therefore is organized into different offices and branches.

Article 11

Principles of proceedings

The procedural principles are designed to safeguard the defendant. Paragraph 1 lists the established principles set forth under article 6, section 3, of the European Convention on Human Rights and under article 14, section 3, of the United Nations Covenant on Civil and Political Rights of 1966. Subparagraph (a) also considers the problem of preventive detention; while the important right to have counsel is mentioned under subparagraph (e). Subparagraph (d) refers to the right to be present in court of the accused person hence the exclusion of judgements in default unless specifically accepted. Subparagraph (f) spells the right to have a skilled interpreter.

Paragraph 2 emphasizes the need to protect witnesses and victims against any form of intimidation and physical or psychological pressure.

Paragraph 3 entrusts the Court with the task of setting its own rules and of defining the procedure that will be followed by the judge and the parties throughout the proceedings, in line with the principles mentioned in the previous articles.

Article 12

Appeals

In compliance with a provision contained in article 14, section 5, of the United Nations Covenant on Civil and Political Rights of 1966, the defendant shall be entitled to lodge an appeal. This same right shall also be granted to the Prosecutor. Given the difficulties in creating an ad hoc Court of Appeal, the final judgement shall be made by a separate Chamber of the Court, other than those which acted at the first hearing.

Article 13

Res judicata and revision

Judgements against which no appeal is lodged and judgements delivered on appeal shall be considered final and become enforceable. They can however be challenged (revision) in the exceptional case in which some new evidence previously unknown at the time of the hearing comes to light and could acquit the defendant or could turn the crime into an offence not envisaged under articles 1 and 4. Under these circumstances, the judgement shall be made by the unified Chambers of the Court.

Article 14

Enforcement

For enforcement and precautionary measures, reference should be made to locus commissi delicti. Any possible different provision other than the ordinary ones falls within the competence of the Tribunal. In line with what is laid down in the preamble, it is up to the United Nations Security Council to ensure the best enforcement of the provisions laid down in this statute and particularly to enforce the sentences imposed by the Court when the State involved rejects the enforcement and tries to hamper the work of the enforcement bodies.

Needless to say, the nature of the measures adopted by the United Nations will have to be in line with the goals and principles of its Charter, as interpreted in the light of the international code of human rights.

Annex III

Composition of the Commission on War Crimes and Crimes against Humanity Committed in the Former Yugoslavia

- Prof. Giovanni Conso, Chairman, former President of the Italian Constitutional Court, Minister of Justice
- The Hon. Judge Carlo Russo, member of the European Court of Human Rights
- Ambassador Walter Gardini, former Director General for Political Affairs, member of the Board of Advisers, Legal Department, Ministry of Foreign Affairs
- Dr. Liliana Ferraro, Director General, Department for Criminal Law, Ministry of Justice
- Prof. Luigi Ferrari Bravo, Professor of European Communities Law at the University of Rome, Head of the Legal Department, Ministry of Foreign Affairs
- Prof. Paolo Ungari, Professor of History of Modern and Contemporary Law at LUISS University of Rome, and President of the Italian Commission on Human Rights
- Prof. Antonio Papisca, Professor of International Relations, University of Padua
- Prof. Giovanni Grasso, Professor of Criminal Law, University of Catania
- Prof. Cherif Bassiouni, Professor of Law, De Paul University of Chicago, President of the International Institute of Criminal Law, Siracuse

E. NOTE VERBALE DATED 12 MARCH 1993 FROM THE PERMANENT MISSION OF MEXICO TO THE UNITED NATIONS ADDRESSED TO THE SECRETARY-GENERAL

S/25417, 16 March 1993.

The Permanent Mission of Mexico to the United Nations presents its compliments to the Secretary-General and has the honour to transmit to him herewith the text of the views of the Government of Mexico, supplied pursuant to paragraph 2 of Security Council resolution 808 (1993) on the establishment of an international tribunal for the prosecution of persons responsible for serious violations of international humanitarian law committed in the territory of the former Yugoslavia since 1991.

The Permanent Mission of Mexico to the United Nations would be grateful if the Secretary-General would have this letter and its annex distributed as a document of the Security Council.

Annex

Views of the Government of Mexico supplied pursuant to paragraph 2 of Security Council resolution 808 (1993)

Introduction

1. The Government of Mexico wishes to place on record its satisfaction at the determination shown by the Security Council to promote respect for international humanitarian law in the States of the former Socialist Federal Republic of Yugoslavia. Accordingly, Mexico reaffirms its support for Security Council resolutions, including resolution 808 (1993), demanding an immediate end to all violations of international humanitarian law, particularly those occurring in the territory of Bosnia and Herzegovina.

2. However, Mexico wishes to express its concern at some aspects of the procedure that was followed in deciding to establish an international tribunal to prosecute persons responsible for serious violations of international humanitarian law committed in the territory of the former Yugoslavia since 1991. The Mexican Government also wishes to give its views on the jurisdiction and rules of procedure of the tribunal that is ultimately established.

Establishment of an international criminal court

3. It is clear that Security Council resolution 808 (1993) raises issues on which there is as yet no widely-shared opinion within the international community. First of all, the establishment of an international criminal court is closely linked to the exercise of State sovereignty, both from the standpoint of territorial jurisdiction and from that of personal jurisdiction. This explains why the General Assembly, acting through the International Law Commission, has yet to complete the mandate entrusted to it with regard to the draft Code of Crimes against the Peace and Security of Mankind, to which the question of the establishment of an international criminal court is related. This delay can be attributed to lack of political will on the part of Member States. However, it cannot be denied that lacunae in the progressive development of international law, such as the absence of a definition of aggression for almost two decades, prevented progress from being made in the consideration of this topic.

4. The decision taken by the Security Council has no precedent in the annals of the United Nations. Although we have the historic precedent of the 1945 London Agreement establishing the Nürnberg Tribunal and the subsequent formulation of the principles contained in General Assembly resolution 95 (I) which establish individual responsibility for violations of humanitarian law,

this is the first time that the establishment of an international criminal court has not been brought about by the action of a group of victorious Powers. There is no express provision in the Charter of the United Nations which can be invoked as giving the Security Council or the General Assembly the power to establish a special criminal court with binding jurisdiction.

5. Now, in the present case, it must be recognized that the situation in the former Yugoslavia is a threat to the maintenance of international peace and security, so that intervention by the Security Council under Chapter VII of the Charter is fully justified. Accordingly, the establishment of an international criminal court such as that referred to in resolution 808 (1993) must be understood as a measure designed to put an end to the conflict taking place in the former Yugoslavia.

6. Given the extraordinary circumstances which prompted the decision to establish the tribunal, this tribunal is special and does not therefore create any precedent for the future establishment of a universal, permanent international criminal court with binding jurisdiction. Any such future tribunal will have to have optional jurisdiction and will have to be established as a result of a convention or international treaty freely signed by States, on the basis of the corresponding recommendations made by the International Law Commission to the General Assembly.

7. In this context, it is extremely important to emphasize that the General Assembly is, by virtue of Articles 10, 11, 13, 14, 34 and 35 of the Charter of the United Nations, vested with responsibilities in the maintenance of international peace and security. By virtue of those Articles, and notwithstanding the provisions of Article 12 of the Charter, the General Assembly has the power to make recommendations for the maintenance of international peace and security and, in the absence of action by the Council, could even take whatever measures it deems appropriate.

8. In this particular case, the General Assembly could have played an important and valuable role in supporting and advising the Security Council, especially since this is a matter related to the issue of the establishment of a universal international criminal court, an issue on which significant progress has been made in the International Law Commission since 1990.

9. The Government of Mexico has always believed it vitally important to ensure a proper balance between the principal organs of the United Nations. To this end, Mexico has advocated the need to adapt the Organization's working methods and, in particular, to strengthen the role of the General Assembly.

10. At the same time, the Government of Mexico believes it is essential, in order to guarantee that Member States adhere fully to the decisions of the Security Council, that the Council's actions should at all times respect the sovereign rights of States and that its decisions should be taken in a context of transparency which reflects the interests and aspirations of all States Members of the United Nations.

11. Mexico reiterates that the dialogue between the Security Council and the General Assembly must be reinforced, so that the Assembly can make full use of its powers and can take a position on situations which could threaten international peace and security, without prejudice to the primary responsibility vested in the Security Council.

12. With this idea in mind, the Government of Mexico believes that the basis for the Security Council's decision could be found, as was done in the report of the committee of jurists submitted by France (S/25266), in the powers conferred on it by Article 41 of the Charter, since the list of measures in that Article is not exhaustive. However, it must be made clear that as early as the San Francisco Conference, Mexico and other countries proposed that decisions taken by the Council under Article 41 should have the prior approval of the General Assembly (see UNCIO, IV, p. 223). This shows that Mexico has always been concerned to secure the establishment of a system of collective security which takes the rights and legitimate aspirations of the entire international community into account.

Principles governing the functioning of the international tribunal

13. The Government of Mexico believes that, in order for the tribunal established by resolution 808 (1993) to have the necessary legitimacy, its main attribute must be its total independence from any State or international, governmental or non-governmental political organ, and the impartiality of its proceedings and members.

14. In this connection, Mexico believes that neither the Security Council nor any other organ should interfere in the performance of the functions entrusted to the tribunal once the tribunal has been established and has been provided with a statute.

15. The judicial proceedings carried out by the tribunal will have to adhere strictly to the general principles of law, such as the need to guarantee the right of due process and the protection of the individual rights of the accused.

16. Furthermore, the members of the tribunal will have to be individuals of recognized legal competence, impartiality and integrity, in order to guarantee the objectivity of trials. Judges will have to be unremovable to safeguard their independence.

17. Mexico believes that the tribunal, like any other court, should decide for itself whether it is competent to hear a given case that is submitted to it. However, its statute will have to delimit very clearly and precisely its material sphere of competence, which will have to be restricted to crimes typified by international law, and its territorial sphere, which will have to be limited to the territory of the former Yugoslavia.

F. SOME PRELIMINARY REMARKS BY THE INTERNATIONAL COMMITTEE OF THE RED CROSS ON THE SETTING-UP OF AN INTERNATIONAL TRIBUNAL FOR THE PROSECUTION OF PERSONS RESPONSIBLE FOR SERIOUS VIOLATIONS OF INTERNATIONAL HUMANITARIAN LAW COMMITTED ON THE TERRITORY OF THE FORMER YUGOSLAVIA

(United Nations Security Council Resolution 808 (1993) Adopted on 22 February 1993)

DDM/JUR/422b, 25 March 1993.

1. The ICRC considers as a positive development all efforts aimed at ensuring respect for International Humanitarian Law and preventing as well as repressing violations of this law. It therefore welcomes the decision of the Security Council, as embodied in Resolution 808 (22 February 1993), to create an international tribunal to prosecute persons responsible for serious violations of International Humanitarian Law committed in the territory of the former Yugoslavia since 1991. This decision is particularly important as it constitutes a follow up to preceding resolutions of the Council (764 of 30 July and 771 of 30 August 1992) reaffirming that all parties are bound to comply with their obligations under International Humanitarian Law, in particular the Geneva Conventions of 12 August 1949, that persons who commit or order the commission of grave breaches of these Conventions are individually responsible in respect of such breaches, and demanding that all parties and other concerned in former Yugoslavia, and all military forces in Bosnia and Herzegovina, immediately cease and desist from all breaches of International Humanitarian Law.

2. The ICRC equally considers the Council's decision particularly heartening as it represents a concrete expression of the general commitment formulated as a legal obligation in common Article 1 of the Geneva Conventions and in Article 1 of Additional Protocol I, in terms of which all High Contracting Parties undertake to ensure respect for these instruments.

3. International Humanitarian Law as embodied in the four Geneva Conventions and Additional Protocol I does contain an obligation incumbent upon the parties to a conflict as well as other contracting parties to repress grave breaches of this law, which are thus submitted to universal jurisdiction. However, it does not provide for any international jurisdiction, although, at the same time, in no way does it prohibit such jurisdiction. Consequently, the competence to create an international tribunal cannot be based upon existing International Humanitarian Law itself but, in the present case, upon Resolution 808.

4. The ICRC has the mandate to protect and assist victims of armed conflicts and to look for the faithful application of International Humanitarian Law. It is not up to the ICRC to decide, on behalf of the international community, which aspects of the different past and present armed conflicts in the former Yugoslavia are not covered by the law of international armed conflicts. However, with regard to such qualification, the ICRC wishes to underline the fact that, according to International Humanitarian Law as its stands today, the notion of war crimes is limited to situations of international armed conflict.

5. The ICRC is indeed aware of the draft code of crimes against the peace and security of mankind which is being elaborated by the International Law Commission, Article 22 of which sets forth a list of exceptionally serious war crimes : this list is not identical to the list of war crimes (grave breaches) under International Humanitarian Law, on the one hand, and it applies to both international and non-international conflicts on the other hand.

6. The ICRC also considers important to note that the web of agreements on humanitarian questions that the parties to the conflicts in the former Yugoslavia have concluded among themselves do entail the applicability of a great majority, although not the entirety, of the law applicable in international armed conflicts.

7. Since the proposed tribunal will be the first of its kind since those set up immediately after the Second World War, its precedent setting value will presumably be very high. The ICRC therefore considers it of the utmost importance that the tribunal's credibility not be subject to the slightest doubt. Towards this end, the ICRC suggests that, both in the setting up of such a tribunal and in its proceedings, be taken duly into consideration the fundamental guarantees, guarantees relating to judicial procedure, provisions concerning applicable law and penalties, as laid down in the Geneva Conventions and Protocol I.

   a) **Applicable legislation**

   Under the terms of common Article 49/50/129/146 of the four Geneva Conventions, respectively, and of Article 85(1) of Protocol I, which concern grave breaches, there is an explicit obligation upon States to both, enact any legislation necessary to provide effective penal sanctions, and to repress grave breaches.

   The Geneva Conventions hold that the applicable legislation in penal and disciplinary matters is internal law, that is, *inter alia*, the law of the Detaining Power for the prisoners of war (Third Convention, Article 82(1)), for civilian internees (Fourth Convention, Article 117(1)), the penal laws of the occupied territory for all members of the population of these territories, subject to certain exceptions only (Fourth Convention, Article 64), and the law of the requested Party in case of mutual assistance in criminal matters.

b) **Penalties**

Prisoners of war shall only be sentenced to penalties which are provided for members of the Detaining Power who have committed the same act (Third Convention, Article 87(1)). The same principle applies to the execution of penalties; prisoners of war shall not be subjected to more severe treatment than would undergo members of the armed forces of the Detaining Power of equivalent rank or category (Third Convention, Article 88).

The courts or authorities shall not have the right to impose a heavier penalty than that which was applicable when the offence was committed. If the law has changed after the commission of the offence and provides a lighter penalty, the offender shall benefit from this new rule (Protocol I, Article 75(4)(*c*)).

When fixing the penalty against a prisoner of war, a civilian internee, or a member of the population of an occupied territory, the courts or authorities shall take into account the fact that these persons are not nationals of the Detaining Power.

In any case, all forms of cruelty are forbidden (Third Convention, Article 87(3), Fourth Convention, Article 118(2), Protocol I, Article 75(2)(*a*) and (*b*)).

c) **Judicial guarantees**

The main judicial guarantees provided by the Geneva Conventions and Protocol I are:

* The right to be tried by an independent and impartial tribunal (Third Convention, Article 84(2), Protocol I, Article 75(4)).

* The right to be informed of the charges (Third Convention, Article 104(2), Fourth Convention, Article 71(2), Protocol I, Article 75(4)(*a*)).

* The rights and means of defence (Third Convention, Articles 99 and 105, Fourth Convention, Articles 72 and 74, Protocol I, Article 75(4)(*a*) and (*g*)). For example: the rights to present evidence, to be assisted by a qualified and freely chosen advocate, to call witnesses and to be helped by a competent interpreter.

* The principle of individual penal responsibility (Protocol I, Article 75(4)(*b*)).

* The "*nullum crimen sine lege*" principle (Third Convention, Article 99(1), Protocol I, Article 75(4)(*c*)).

* The presumption of innocence (Protocol I, Article 75(4)(*d*)).

* The right to be present at one's trial (Protocol I, Article 75(4)(*e*)).

* The right not to testify against oneself or to confess guilt (Protocol I, Article 75(4)*(f)*).

* The *"non bis in idem"* principle (Third Convention, Article 86, Fourth Convention, Article 117(3), Protocol I, Article 75(4)*(h)*).

* The right to have the judgment pronounced publicly (Protocol I, Article 75(4)*(i)*).

* The right of appeal (Third Convention, Article 106, Fourth Convention, Article 73, Protocol I, Article 75(4)*(j)*).

8. As the Interim Report of the Commission of Experts established pursuant to Security Council Resolution 780 (1992) (S/25274, 26 January 1993) and the Council's Resolution calling for the creation of an international tribunal (Resolution 808, 22 February 1993) both refer to grave breaches and serious violations of International Humanitarian Law, the ICRC, in its capacity as guardian of this law, deems it necessary to draw attention to certain clarifications that these notions necessitate.

9. Grave breaches are specifically enumerated in the Conventions and Protocol I (common Article 50/51/130/147 of the four Geneva Conventions respectively and Articles 11 and 85 of Protocol I - see annex) whilst other violations of International Humanitarian Law are not. Under the same articles, there is an explicit obligation upon States to both, enact any legislation necessary to provide effective penal sanctions, and to repress grave breaches, whilst, with regard to other violations, there exists only the obligation to suppress them. It is true that Articles 89 (co-operation) and 90 (International Fact-Finding Commission, at paragraph 2*(c)*(i)) do contain the term "serious violations". However, neither do they enumerate these violations nor do they impose an obligation upon States to repress them but, for its part, Article 89, requires the Contracting Parties to act jointly or individually, in co-operation with the United Nations and in conformity with the Charter.

10. To give a general idea of what these serious wiolations other than the graves breaches may be, here is an excerpt of the relevant passage, in relation to Article 98, of the Commentary on the Protocols published by the ICRC (paras. 3591 and 3592) :

   "[The term "other serious violations"] refers to conduct contrary to these instruments which is of a serious nature but which is not included as such in the list of "grave breaches".

   We do not need to have in mind exactly what conduct could fall under this definition, to be able nevertheless to distinguish three categories that qualify :
   - isolated instances of conduct, not included amongst the grave breaches, but nevertheless of a serious nature;
   - conduct which is not included amongst the grave breaches, but which takes on a serious nature because of the frequency of the individual acts committed or because of the systematic repetition thereof or because of circumstances;

- "global" violations, for example, acts whereby a particular situation, a territory or a whole category of persons or objects is withdrawn from the application of the Conventions or the Protocol".

11. Under Article 85(5) of Protocol I, grave breaches of International Humanitarian Law are considered as war crimes. It ought to be noted that grave breaches as enumerated in the Conventions and Protocol I cover practically all of the breaches, with the exception of those coming rather within the purview of *jus ad bellum*, contained in prior legal instruments, in particular the list established in 1919 by the Preliminary Peace Conference's Commission of Jurists and extended by the United Nations War Crimes Commission.

    However, nothing prevents the international community from deciding that other violations not considered grave breaches under the Conventions and Protocol I equally constitute war crimes.

    In this context, the ICRC would like the following point to be made clear. The Fourth Geneva Convention clearly lists as war crimes any crimes against humanity as defined in the implementation law of the London Agreement creating the Nuremberg Tribunal, i.e. breaches committed against civilians of the adverse Party living on a belligerent's own territory or civilians living under occupation. On the other hand, although a government's acts against its own citizens are also partly covered by Protocol I, the participants in the 1974-1977 Diplomatic Conference continued to refuse to call them war crimes. This means that the acts committed by Germany against Polish Jews during the Second World War were considered *war crimes*, whereas those committed against German Jews remained *crimes against humanity*.

    This distinction obviously does not imply a scale of degrees of horror. Whether war crimes or crimes against humanity, both categories of breaches fall under international penal law. The latter are not considered to be war crimes simply because, unlike the former, they can be committed independently of an armed conflict and, even when committed during a conflict, are not necessarily related to it.

12. Finally, the ICRC fervently hopes that the creation of an international tribunal to judge war crimes committed within the territory of the former Yugoslavia will only be a first step towards the rapid establishment of a permanent international tribunal to try war criminals that might exist within all parties involved in every conflict in the world. Indeed, the impression that there is a selective approach of such problems would be very detrimental to the credibility of the will of the international community to progress towards justice. It equally hopes that any international tribunal, to be created pursuant to Resolution 808 of the Security Council or later on, will take into account the legal provisions of International Humanitarian Law, referred to earlier.

ICRC involvement in war-crimes proceedings

1. The 1949 Geneva Conventions confer on the ICRC a functional international legal personality which encompasses the protection and the immunities required for the institution to discharge its mandate under the said Conventions (see, for example, Article 126, paragraph 4, of the Third Geneva Convention and Article 143, paragraph 5 of the Fourth Geneva Convention).

   Persons carrying out activities under the ICRC's responsibility should therefore not be compelled to provide information or give testimony relating to any situation covered by the Geneva Conventions, namely international and non-international armed conflicts.

   With the adoption of the Geneva Conventions and their Additional Protocols, the ICRC was mandated as a neutral and impartial body to provide, in times of armed conflict of an international or non-international character, protection and assistance for military and civilian victims of such situations and their direct consequences. To this end, the treaties assign the ICRC a number of specific tasks (for example, visiting prisoners) and give it the right to take action.

   The ICRC's specific role as a neutral intermediary between warring parties is thus essentially an operational one and presupposes access to the victims while hostilities are still going on.

   In order to be able to carry out its humanitarian mission, the ICRC must at all times be seen to be reliable and enjoy the confidence of governments, all the parties to the conflicts concerned and the victims themselves. This credibility and confidence are founded upon the institution's neutrality and impartiality and upon its commitment to the governments and the belligerents not to divulge information that comes into its possession in the course of its delegates' work. Only strict observance of this rule can ensure that the ICRC is given access to victims of present and future conflicts.

   The ICRC's mission is to protect and assist conflict victims, and thus is both preventive and curative in nature. The delegates in the field focus their attention on the victims' needs, so they often have only scanty information, based on hearsay, about acts amounting to grave violations of international humanitarian law.

   Any participation by the ICRC in war-crimes proceedings involving providing information or giving testimony would therefore place the institution's work at serious risk.

   - It would violate the ICRC's pledge of discretion and confidentiality vis-à-vis both the victims and the parties to conflicts.

   - It would undermine the confidence of both the authorities (parties to a conflict) and the victims;

   - It would consequently threaten the safety of the victims (prisoners visited, civilians assisted, etc.) and possibly expose them to reprisals; as a result the ICRC could be denied access to victims of the conflicts concerned and of other present or future situations.

- It might also threaten the safety of delegates and other staff working under ICRC responsibility in the field.

2. The position of the other components of the International Red Cross and Red Crescent Movement, that is, the National Red Cross or Red Crescent Societies and the International Federation of Red Cross and Red Crescent Societies, is somewhat different but also worth considering.

   The primary function of the National Societies is to help the armed forces medical services care for the war-wounded, whichever side they are on. The International Federation may also take action to help the victims of war.

   If members of National Societies or delegates of the International Federation were obliged to testify, their own activities could also be adversely affected. Indeed, their activities are, like those of the ICRC itself, based on the Movement's fundamental principles, in particular, humanity, neutrality and impartiality.

   Furthermore the resulting loss of confidence would certainly have serious repercussions on the work of the ICRC.

Annex

1. *Breaches specified in all four Geneva Conventions*:

   - wilful killing,
   - torture,
   - inhuman treatment,
   - biological experiments,
   - wilfully causing great suffering,
   - causing serious injury to body or health,
   - destruction and appropriation of property not justified by military necessity and carried out unlawfully and want only.

2. *Breaches specified in both the Third and Fourth Geneva Conventions*:

   - compelling a prisoner of war or a civilian protected by the Fourth Geneva Convention to serve in the armed forces of the hostile Power,

   - wilfully depriving a prisoner of war or a civilian protected by the Fourth Geneva Convention of the right to fair and regular trial, prescribed in the Third and Fourth Geneva Conventions.

3. *Breaches specified in the Fourth Geneva Convention*:

   - unlawful deportation or transfer [see also Protocol I, Article 85(4)(*a*)],
   - unlawful confinement,
   - taking of hostages.

4. *Grave breaches under Article 85 of Protocol I*

   4.1. *The following acts, when committed wilfully and causing death or serious injury to body or health*:

- making the civilian population the object of attack,

- launching an indiscriminate attack, or an attack against works or installations containing dangerous forces in the knowledge that such an attack will cause excessive damage to civilian objects in relation to the military advantage anticipated,

- making non-defended localities and demilitarized zones the object of attack,

- making a person the object of attack in the knowledge that he is *hors de combat*,

- making perfidious use of the protective emblem of the red cross or red crescent.

4.2. *The following acts, when they are committed wilfully and in violation of the Conventions or the Protocol*:

- the transfer by the Occupying Power of parts of its own civilian population into the territory it occupies, or the deportation or transfer of all or parts of the population of the occupied territory within or outside this territory,

- any unjustifiable delay in the repatriation of prisoners of war or civilians,

- practices of *apartheid* and other inhuman and degrading practices based on racial discrimination,

- attacking and causing large-scale destruction of clearly recognized historic monuments, works of art or places of worship which constitute the cultural or spiritual heritage of peoples and which are under special protection.

4.3. *Acts constituting grave breaches of the Geneva Conventions when committed against*:

- persons in the power of an adverse Party, protected under Articles 44, 45 and 73 of the Protocol,

- the wounded, sick or aliens belonging to the adverse Party who are protected by the Protocol,

- medical or religious personnel, medical units or medical transports which are under the control of the adverse Party and are protected by the Protocol.

G. THE NATIONAL ALLIANCE OF WOMEN'S ORGANZATIONS

31 March 1993.

To:

The Secretary General of the United Nations
The United Nations Commission of Experts
The Members of the Security Council
The United Nations Office of Legal Counsel

RE: GENDER JUSTICE AND THE CONSTITUTION OF THE WAR CRIMES TRIBUNAL PURSUANT TO SECURITY COUNCIL RESOLUTION 808.

The undersigned fully endorse Security Council Resolution 808 calling for the establishment of a war crimes tribunal to prosecute "persons responsible for serious violations of international humanitarian law committed in the territory of the former Yugoslavia since 1991" and calling for a report recommending the "effective and expeditious implementation" of a tribunal by April 22, 1993. We condemn all the atrocities committed by all sides in this war and note the particularly systematic and mass nature of those committed by Serbian forces.

Having studied the latest Report of the Commission of Experts and the proposals submitted to date, we are concerned, however, that the effective condemnation, prosecution and redress of gender-specific crimes, -- particularly rape, forced prostitution, and forced pregnancy -- requires more considered attention as well as the equal participation of women in every aspect of the process. We note that despite the fact that rape and forced prostitution have been previously recognized as war crimes, they have rarely been effectively prosecuted. This results, in part, from the fact that the rape and sexual abuse of women are so characteristic of war that nations are loathe to condemn them for fear of condemning their own troops. It also results from the tendency, despite explicit sanction and short-lived outrage, not to view rape as among the gravest offenses against human rights and humanitarian law. Thus we are concerned that in establishing the jurisdiction of the tribunal to prosecute war crimes and crimes against humanity arising out of the conflict in the former Yugoslavia, that rape be identified in its two-fold aspects--as a crime against women and as a tactic of ethnic cleansing.

The establishment of an ad hoc war crimes tribunal to try violations committed in the former Yugoslavia is thus an occasion not only to assure full justice to women in the former Yugoslavia who have been and continue to be brutalized in sex-specific ways, but also to correct the historic trivialization of the abuse of women in war.

To this end, we specifically call upon all relevant parties to embody the following principles and concerns in the constitution of the war crimes tribunal:

1. That rape, forced prostitution and forced pregnancy be viewed as crimes against humanity and grave breaches of the laws of war *whether or not* they are associated with the abominable practice of "ethnic cleansing." Where rape, forced prostitution and forced pregnancy are vehicles of ethnic cleansing, they are genocidal crimes and, as such, constitute the "grave breaches" of humanitarian law as well as crimes against humanity. But it must be likewise recognized and charged that apart from ethnic cleansing, rape, forced prostitution and forced pregnancy constitute war crimes and crimes against humanity because they are crimes of gender hatred, violence, discrimination, and dehumanization perpetrated against women as a class.

-- Within the framework of "grave breaches" against the civilian population recognized by the Fourth Geneva Convention, rape, forced prostitution and forced pregnancy are not simply crimes against "honor," but also crimes of violence. They constitute forms of "willful torture and inhuman treatment" and they "willfully caus[e] great suffering or serious injury to body or health." Rape in detention has been recognized as a form of torture, often among the most debilitating. Moreover, these abuses are intended to be and frequently are devastating to women's physical and mental health as well as life-threatening. They cause physical suffering, injury, incapacitation, infection with HIV and sexually transmitted diseases, sterility, and involuntary pregnancy and maternity, all of which produce profound emotional suffering and trauma as well as terrible economic and social dislocation and hardship. Every act of rape in war -- whether a consequence of indiscipline, retaliation, or genocidal policies -- is a "grave breach," a principle that has been recently reaffirmed by international scholars and the International Committee of the Red Cross.

--Sexual and reproductive abuses of women, when they are mass and systematic, should also be prosecuted as "crimes against humanity." They qualify, on the one hand, as egregious crimes of violence against women as members of the civilian population, as recognized in Allied Control Council Law No. 10. On the other hand, they qualify as persecution-based offenses because they constitute discrimination on the basis of gender. The concept of "crimes against humanity" is an evolving one. The previous lack of regard for women as suffering wrongs and having rights as a group explains the failure heretofore to mention sex along with religious, ethnic, racial and other identifiable groups in the standard definition of persecution-based "crimes against humanity." The inhumanity of sexual and reproductive abuse and their potentially life-long effect on women does not depend on their being an aspect of ethnic cleansing as the experience of the "comfort" women forced into prostitution by the Japanese and other women raped as part of the plunder of war demonstrate.

2. That rape and forced prostitution be separately identified as crimes to be investigated and prosecuted by the tribunal. Although crimes involving the sexual abuse of women are implicit in the more general categories of "grave breach" and "crimes against humanity," they should also be identified separately in the statement of the substantive jurisdiction of the war crimes tribunal. The explicit recognition of these crimes is essential to assuring their full prosecution as well as to undoing the legacy of disregard.

3. The offense of forced pregnancy should also be separately identified in order to assure its full investigation and separate condemnation both as a crime of gender and a crime of genocide. Forced pregnancy is always a potential and foreseeable consequence and, is, therefore, an ever-present aspect of the crime of rape. In the instant conflict, there are reports that rape, particularly of Muslim women in Bosnia, has been committed with the expressed intent to impregnate the women, to force them to suffer pregnancy and/or childbirth, to bear part-Serbian babies, and to further humiliate them and threaten their capacity to remain in their communities and bear children voluntarily in the future. This must be recognized as a distinct or aggravated offense against the lives, integrity and dignity of women as humans at the same time as it is a tactic of ethnic cleansing.

4. That at least 50% of the personnel involved at every level and in every aspect of the Tribunal's functions be women. The Secretary General has recognized the importance of gender parity at every level of UN functioning. The creation of a War Crimes Tribunal provides a fresh occasion to put that principle into operation. Moreover, the nature of the Tribunal's function, the prevalence of gender-specific violations in this war, and the pervasiveness and subtlety of the gender-specific issues presented (as only partially illustrated by this list of concerns) adds urgency to the implementation of gender parity. Most immediately, given their significance in the process of establishing the tribunal, the presently all-male Commission of Experts must have its membership supplemented by an equal number of women and the Office of Legal Counsel, and the Security Council, should likewise assure the equal participation of women at all phases of the shaping of their proposal for the Tribunal.

5. To encourage victims of sexual and reproductive violence to lodge and pursue claims and to ensure the sensitivity of their treatment, all investigatory, prosecutorial and judicial personnel should have gender-sensitivity training and there should be established a special sex crimes unit staffed primarily by women experienced in the particularities of proving these offenses and mitigating trauma to the victims. Experience in many countries throughout the world has made it clear that without a receptive, sensitive process, women and other victims of sexual abuse will not come forward, and, if they do, they may be further traumatized by the experience. Given the prevalence of rape and sexual abuse in the present conflict, it is critical that all personnel involved in the effort to bring perpetrators to justice be trained in understanding these crimes and their effects from the perspective of women affected. This requires both gender and culturally specific sensitization. In addition, the establishment of women's police precincts in Brazil and of special multi-disciplinary sex-crimes units in prosecutor's offices in a number of countries suggest models for minimizing harm and assisting victims to reconstruct their lives. These approaches have been endorsed, *inter alia,* in the proposed UN Declaration on Violence Against Women and should be explicitly provided for in this context.

The necessity of establishing immediately an adequately resourced as well as gender-balanced and gender/culturally-sensitive prosecutorial agency to do the necessary fact-finding and preparation of cases for prosecution cannot be under emphasized.

6. In accordance with the Covenant on Political and Civil Rights, the procedures of the tribunal must strike a balance between the rights of the accused and respect for the integrity of the victims. It is important that the procedures and evidentiary rules devised for prosecuting these offenses be constructed with the specific context in mind. Use of existing penal statutes--such as those applicable in the former Socialist Republic of Yugoslavia--are an instructive source for the jurisdiction of the Tribunal particularly to the extent that they recognize international law and preclude claims that persons will be tried for conduct which was not previously criminal. But most domestic legislation is defective in significant respects where issues of gender-specific violence and particularly rape and sexual abuse is concerned. For this reason, it is crucial that the substantive jurisdiction and procedures of this Tribunal be constructed in light of international principles, taking into account the recent international work designed to improve the effectiveness of state responses to gender-based violence.

Many of those participating as prosecuting or supporting witnesses have been recently and grossly traumatized by the conduct of those accused, and rape and sexual abuse (whether of women or men) are particularly shattering events. While for some, public accusation of the aggressor will be an important and empowering event, for others it will be impossible or exacerbate the trauma suffered. Accordingly, certain measures, consistent with the rights of the accused, are in order to minimize the possibility of further traumatization. For example,

--victims should not be publicly identified without their consent.

--where it is impossible to shield the victims' identity, or where the victims are not able to appear in public, the proceedings should be held *in camera* with safeguards to prevent abuse.

--victims should be able to testify without face-to-face confrontation with the defendant, while preserving the defendant's rights through video and one-way observation methods.

--the inherently coercive circumstances of the crimes, the tenacity of sexist assumptions, and the need to safeguard the mental integrity and privacy of victims of rape and sexual abuse should be recognized in developing appropriate evidentiary rules, including but not limited to rules forbidding the introduction of evidence of the victim's prior sexual conduct or reputation, and controlling cross-examination to prevent abuse of the witnesses as well as misleading and inflammatory innuendo.

--expert testimony on the traumatic effects of rape and sexual abuse should be permitted but not required.

7. The structure of the War Crimes Tribunal should accommodate prosecution of both those who directly perpetrate the crimes and those who are guilty though command or political responsibility. As in the post-World War II tribunals, it is critical to provide for the prosecution of both the direct actors and those with overall responsibility for the atrocities, i.e. of those who ordered, encouraged, assisted, condoned or failed to take effective measures to prevent them. Notwithstanding the difficulty of bringing both classes of perpetrators to justice, the issuance and pendency of indictments is important to vindicate victims and to, at the least, constrict the lives and liberty of the accused who evade the Tribunal's process.

8. The War Crimes Tribunal must be established consistent with the principle that there is no statute of limitations for war crimes and crimes against humanity. Statutes of limitations are precluded with respect to offenses of this dimension in order to prevent wrongdoers from escaping justice. With crimes of this nature, the traumatization of the victims may also delay the very bringing of charges, as it can take years, if not decades, for women to be able to remember such events or to overcome the shame that they inflict. Thus, it is critical to provide that the War

Crimes Tribunal and its subsidiaries must continue for a substantial period of years and that a continuing mechanism for receiving and prosecuting complaints or referring them and, thereafter, be empowered to refer cases to appropriate national tribunals under circumstances that guarantee fair and just implementation of international law.

9. That the war crimes tribunal be mandated to consider claims for compensation, including rehabilitation, of victims. International law guarantees compensation to victims, yet the same problem that requires establishment of an international body to prosecute criminally--the hostility and unreliability of national tribunals--also requires that the system established by the tribunal provide for the award of compensation to victims. This does not mean that the Tribunal itself must consider claims for compensation, but rather that auxiliary mechanisms be explicitly created to fulfill this function.

10. That the Security Council establish a fund for the benefit and compensation of victims of war crimes and crimes against humanity through seizing the assets of the aggressor governments and political entities and empowering the Tribunal to order the forfeiture of property and payment of fines. Adequate compensation to victims to enable them to reconstruct their lives is a key aspect of doing justice. Funds for this purpose can be acquired through different means, drawing upon the precedents established in the post-World War proceedings and the recently constituted Compensation Commission set up by the United Nations to compensate victims of the aggression against Kuwait.

H. LETTER DATED 31 MARCH 1993 FROM THE REPRESENTATIVES OF EGYPT, THE ISLAMIC REPUBLIC OF IRAN, MALAYSIA, PAKISTAN, SAUDI ARABIA, SENEGAL AND TURKEY TO THE UNITED NATIONS ADDRESSED TO THE SECRETARY-GENERAL

A/47/920*, S/25512*, 5 April 1993.

On behalf of the members of the Organization of the Islamic Conference, and in our capacity as members of the Contact Group of OIC on Bosnia and Herzegovina, and pursuant to paragraph 2 of Security Council resolution 808 (1993) of 22 February 1993, we have the honour to submit, attached to the present letter, the text of the recommendations of OIC on the establishment of an ad hoc international war crimes tribunal for the territory of the former Yugoslavia (see annex).

We would be grateful if the present letter and its annex could be circulated as a document of the General Assembly, under agenda item 143, and of the Security Council.

(Signed) Nabil A. ELARABY
Ambassador
Permanent Representative of Egypt

(Signed) REDZUAN M. Kushairi
Minister
Chargé d'affaires a.i.
Deputy Permanent Representative
of Malaysia

(Signed) Gaafar M. ALLAGANY
Ambassador
Chargé d'affaires a.i.
Deputy Permanent Representative
of Saudi Arabia

(Signed) Mustafa AKŞIN
Ambassador
Permanent Representative of Turkey

(Signed) Kamal KHARRAZI
Ambassador
Permanent Representative of the
Islamic Republic of Iran

(Signed) Jamsheed K. A. MARKER
Ambassador
Permanent Representative of Pakistan

(Signed) Kéba Birane CISSE
Ambassador
Permanent Representative of the
Republic of Senegal

ANNEX

Recommendations of the Organization of the Islamic Conference on the establishment of an ad hoc International War Crimes Tribunal for the territory of the former Yugoslavia

I. AUTHORITY, JURISDICTION AND COMPETENCE OF THE TRIBUNAL

1. An ad hoc Tribunal shall be established pursuant to a Security Council resolution under Chapter VII of the Charter of the United Nations to prosecute war crimes and crimes against humanity committed in the territory of the former Yugoslavia on or after 1 January 1991.

2. The Statute of the Tribunal shall be approved by the General Assembly within 30 days of the date of adoption of a resolution by the Security Council establishing the Tribunal, under Chapter VII.

3. Funding of the Tribunal should be authorized by the General Assembly.

4. All Member States are obliged to cooperate with and support the Tribunal and its various organs and to enforce its orders and decisions, and to arrest and transfer indicted persons to the jurisdiction of the Tribunal.

---

* Reissued for technical reasons.

5. No State or individual shall have the right to challenge the Tribunal's establishment, its applicable law, judicial composition, organizational structure, jurisdiction or competence. Any challenge of a procedural nature shall be exclusively heard and decided by the Tribunal in accordance with its procedures and rules.

6. The Tribunal's jurisdiction over individuals is exclusive and cannot be defeated by any national exercise of jurisdiction. Subject to the primary jurisdiction, any Member State can exercise its jurisdiction on the basis of the theory of universality.

II. APPLICABLE LAW

1. The crimes over which the Tribunal shall exercise its jurisdiction and the applicable law shall be as follows:

(a) War crimes, violations of the Geneva Conventions of 12 August 1949 and of the Additional Protocols of 10 June 1977, as well as any other war crime under customary international law and other relevant treaties;

(b) Genocide, violations of the Convention on the Prevention and Punishment of the Crime of Genocide of 9 December 1948;

(c) Crimes against humanity, as defined in articles 6 (c) and 5 (c) of the London and Tokyo Charters, respectively, and as further developed by customary international law, which includes: murder, torture, mutilation, rape, reducing or keeping a person in a state of slavery, servitude or forced labour, deporting or forcibly transferring populations, systematic pillage and looting, systematic destruction of public and private property, when committed as part of a policy of persecution on social, political, racial, religious or cultural grounds;

(d) Torture, in violation of the Convention against Torture and Other Cruel, Inhuman or Degrading Treatment or Punishment, of 10 December 1984.

2. The Tribunal shall be competent to try persons accused of responsibility for such crimes at any level, whether as leaders, intermediaries or subordinates, and no form of immunity shall be deemed a bar to prosecution.

3. The fact that an individual is performing official duties shall not be a defence.

4. The order of a superior shall not be a defence.

III. GUIDING PRINCIPLES ON PENALTIES, PROCEDURES AND EVIDENCE

1. The Tribunal shall investigate, prosecute, judge and impose penalties on those individuals found guilty in accordance with the applicable law and procedures of the Tribunal based on respect of the rights of the victims and the accused.

2. Basic principles, norms and standards of due process and procedural fairness recognized by international human rights and international humanitarian law shall be established in the Statute. The Tribunal shall, in accordance with those principles, promulgate detailed rules of procedure and evidence before it commences operations.

3. The Statute shall set forth provisions for the Tribunal with respect to evidentiary matters, including in particular those necessary for the protection of victims and witnesses from reprisals and embarrassment, the more so with respect to victims of torture and rape.

4. There shall be a victim compensation scheme.

5. Governments found responsible for crimes committed by individuals in the service of such Governments or acting for and on behalf of such Governments should be required under principles of State responsibility to pay such compensation.

6. Penalties shall be promulgated by the Tribunal before it starts adjudicating cases but on the basis of provisions established in the Statute. Penalties shall be based on "general principles" of law as they exist in the world's major legal systems.

7. Accused persons who refuse to appear before the Court or are not surrendered to the Tribunal shall be the subject of a public indictment accompanied by an internationally valid warrant for their arrest to be executed by all Member States.

8. All Member States shall have jurisdiction to prosecute a person charged with a crime by the Tribunal if the Tribunal is no longer in existence.

9. The principle ne bis in idem shall apply to the Tribunal's judgements. The Tribunal, however, shall not be bound by the exercise of jurisdiction of any State if it deems that the national proceedings were conducted for the purposes of defeating the Tribunal's jurisdiction or that the proceedings were designed to shield the accused from criminal responsibility.

IV. COMPOSITION OF THE TRIBUNAL

1. The Tribunal's organs shall be composed of:

(a) The Court;

(b) The Procurator-General;

(c) The Secretariat.

2. The Court shall consist of seventeen judges, one of whom shall be elected by them to be the President, and an equal number of alternate judges to serve as alternate for any judge unable to fulfil his or her judicial functions.

3. The judges shall be persons of high competence in international criminal law and human rights law, of high moral integrity, impartiality and independence. They shall represent, on an equitable geographic basis, the world's major legal systems, with particular representation from the Islamic countries and with due regard to gender representation.

4. The General Assembly and Security Council shall elect the judges along the lines of the procedure for the election of judges to the International Court of Justice.

5. The Court shall be divided in three adjudicating chambers, one indicting chamber and one appellate chamber. All chambers except the latter shall consist of three judges, the appellate chamber of five judges.

6. The appointment of judges to the chambers shall be done by a random system established by the rules of the Court.

7. The Secretary-General of the United Nations shall appoint an independent Chief Prosecutor with demonstrated expertise and commitment, on the basis of recommendations by Member States.

8. The Chief Prosecutor shall appoint, direct and supervise a staff of deputy and assistant Prosecutors, as well as a staff of investigators. The deputy and assistant Prosecutors shall include representatives on an equitable geographic basis, from the world's major legal systems, with particular representation from the Islamic countries and with due regard to gender representation.

9. The Chief Prosecutor shall publicize all indictments, alerting all Member States to apprehend any indicted persons within their borders and to submit them to the jurisdiction of the Tribunal.

10. The Prosecutors shall have the duty to prosecute all cases where substantiated charges are made.

11. The Chief Prosecutor shall not have the authority to grant immunity from prosecution without the consent of the indicting chamber and only in cases where it is demonstrated to be in the best interest of justice.

12. The Prosecutors shall receive full cooperation from Member States, including the cooperation of law enforcement agencies.

13. The Prosecutor's office shall be properly funded and shall have sufficient resources to conduct investigations, secure credible evidence, hire appropriate experts, store and organize evidence, engage the participation of witnesses and victims, and provide appropriate protection to witnesses and victims.

V. ADJUDICATION

1. The Tribunal shall respect the rights of victims and witnesses and shall, where appropriate, provide for:

(a) Protection of the identities of witnesses and victims;

(b) Hearing of evidence in camera;

(c) Reception of evidence by means of affidavits, video tape and recordings, provided that the Tribunal may, at its discretion, require affiants to appear for cross-examination; and

(d) Conduct special hearings at locations within the territory of the former Yugoslavia.

2. Defendants shall have the right to apply to the Tribunal for release pending trial or modification of detention measures. The Tribunal shall permit release only upon being satisfied that the defendant is not likely to flee, not likely to constitute a threat to international peace and security, and not likely to intimidate or endanger potential witnesses. In such cases, the Tribunal shall require the posting of an appropriate bond to secure the appearance of the defendant at the trial.

3. Defendants who are unable to pay for legal assistance shall have the right to have counsel appointed.

4. Each trial before the Tribunal shall be heard by at least three judges and at least one alternate in the event a judge becomes incapacitated.

5. Judgements shall be rendered by a majority and each judgement shall state the findings of fact and conclusions of law made by the Tribunal.

VI. SENTENCING, PENALTIES AND APPEALS

1. Upon determination of guilt, a separate hearing shall be held on sentencing. At the sentencing hearing, the prosecution and defence may present evidence of aggravation or mitigation, and witnesses and victims shall be permitted to present relevant testimony.

2. Considering the gravity of the crimes alleged, the Tribunal shall have authority to render all appropriate penalties and to supervise their execution.

3. The Tribunal shall have authority to order confiscation and/or restitution of the proceeds of the criminal conduct and to order damages to compensate victims for their injuries and losses arising from the criminal conduct.

4. The prosecution and the defence may appeal a judgement where it is shown that:

(a) There is newly discovered evidence which would probably alter the judgement and which by due diligence could not have been discovered at the time the judgement was entered;

(b) A fraud upon the Tribunal was committed which substantially affected the judgement; or

(c) The facts proved do not constitute a crime within the jurisdiction of the Tribunal;

(d) The judgement is in error as to the law or facts.

5. Pardons shall not be granted and sentences shall not be reduced, except by a pardon board established by the Security Council.

I. AMNESTY INTERNATIONAL
Memorandum to the United Nations: The Question of Justice and Fairness in the International War Crimes Tribunal for the Former Yugoslavia

Distr: SC/CO/PG/PO, AI Index: Eur 48/02/93, April 1993.

TABLE OF CONTENTS

Memorandum to the United Nations: The question of justice and fairness in the international war crimes tribunal for the former Yugoslavia

[A] OVERVIEW AND SUMMARY OF RECOMMENDATIONS

1. INTRODUCTION

The decision by the United Nations (UN) Security Council to establish an *ad hoc* international war crimes tribunal for the former Yugoslavia (the Tribunal) could be a first step towards breaking the cycle of impunity and gross human rights violations in the former Yugoslavia. Unfortunately, however, experience has shown that *ad hoc* judicial tribunals are too often created and manipulated to serve political interests of particular states. They often lack real independence and impartiality and fail the basic tests of justice and fairness which are well established in international law.

Amnesty International has consistently called for full and impartial investigations into all allegations of gross violations of human rights and humanitarian law in the former Yugoslavia and for all those responsible to be brought to justice. Amnesty International does not take a position on questions of statehood or territorial control. It does insist that bringing to justice those who violate basic rules of minimum civilised conduct is as essential in war as in peacetime. Military and civilian authorities must send a clear message that violations of basic human rights will not be tolerated and that those who commit such acts will be held personally accountable. This was the message reaffirmed in Nuremberg and Tokyo after the Second World War and which the international community has failed to enforce consistently. Sweeping aside the question of responsibility only leads to renewed cycles of violence and violations of human rights. The UN will be discredited if the Tribunal is not given the wide powers it needs and if it fails successfully to prosecute and convict those perpetrators it finds responsible.

Furthermore, the Security Council has already been subject to accusations of double standards in selectively enforcing universal human rights and humanitarian law. Universal principles must be implemented in all countries throughout the world. Amnesty International has therefore called on the UN expressly to recognise that the *ad hoc* Tribunal for the former Yugoslavia is only the first step in establishing a permanent, international criminal court competent to try cases involving gross violations of humanitarian and human rights law. While some aspects of the law and practice of this *ad hoc* Tribunal should be a model of high standards for the future, on some issues different solutions will be more appropriate for a permanent institution.

Several of the issues raised in this Memorandum respond directly to the concrete proposals which have been made about how to establish this Tribunal, especially those submitted to the Security Council by France[1] (the French proposal), Italy[2] (the Italian proposal), Sweden on behalf of the Conference on Security and Co-operation in Europe[3] (the CSCE proposal), USA[4] and Egypt, Iran, Malaysia, Pakistan, Saudi Arabia, Senegal and Turkey on behalf of the Organization of Islamic Conference[5]. Some issues have been raised by Amnesty International because the organization considers they have not been dealt with at all, or adequately, in existing proposals.

2. SUMMARY OF AMNESTY INTERNATIONAL'S RECOMMENDATIONS

For many years Amnesty International has consistently worked both for fair trial of political prisoners and against the impunity of human rights violators, throughout the world. On the basis of this experience we offer a number of recommendations about practices and safeguards which we consider would help to make the Tribunal more fair, just and effective, in accordance with internationally accepted standards. This Memorandum does not set out a blueprint for the Tribunal; it addresses a number of issues which are within the specific mandate of Amnesty International[6]. Our recommendations also arise out of our continuing research of human rights violations in the former Yugoslavia[7].

---

[1]. Report of the Committee of French Jurists set up by Mr. Roland Dumas, Minister of State and Minister for Foreign Affairs, to study the establishment of an International Criminal Tribunal to judge crimes in the former Yugoslavia, reproduced in UN Doc.S/25266, 10 February 1993.

[2]. Study carried out by a Commission of Italian Jurists, set up by the Italian Government, reproduced in UN Doc.S/25300, 17 February 1993.

[3]. Proposal for an International War Crimes Tribunal for the Former Yugoslavia by Rapporteurs (Corell-Türk-Thune) under the CSCE Moscow Human Dimension Mechanism to Bosnia-Herzegovina and Croatia, 9 February 1993, only the contents reproduced in UN Doc.S/25307, 18 February 1993.

[4]. Attached to Letter dated March 1993 from the Permanent Representative of the USA to the UN addressed to the Secretary-General.

[5]. See UN Doc: A/47/920, S/25512, 5 April 1993.

[6]. Amnesty International works for the release of prisoners of conscience (those detained by reason of their political, religious or other conscientiously held beliefs or by reason of their colour, sex, ethnic origin or language, provided they have not used or advocated violence) fair trials for political prisoners, an end to the death penalty, torture and other cruel treatment, and a stop to extrajudicial executions and "disappearances".

[7]. See Bosnia-Herzegovina: Gross abuses of basic human rights, AI Index: EUR 63/01/92, October 1992; Bosnia-Herzegovina: Rana u duši - A wound to the soul, AI Index: EUR 63/03/93, January 1993; Bosnia-Herzegovina: Rape and sexual abuse by armed forces, AI Index: EUR 63/01/93, January 1993; Yugoslavia: Torture and deliberate and arbitrary killings in war zones, AI Index: EUR 48/26/91, November 1991; Yugoslavia: Further reports of torture and deliberate and arbitrary killings in war zones, AI Index: EUR 48/13/92, March 1992; Yugoslavia: Ethnic Albanians - Victims of torture and ill-treatment by police in Kosovo province, AI Index: EUR 48/18/92, June 1992.

I. Creation of Tribunal (see section 3 below)

A Security Council resolution under Chapter VII of the UN Charter would be a quick and effective method of establishing the Tribunal. However, the life of the Tribunal should not be determined by political considerations, such as the conclusion of a peace settlement, but be based on an objective, professional judgment by the Tribunal's lawyers and judges that its work is completed:

1. The Security Council should expressly recognise that the Tribunal will continue to operate as long as is necessary to bring to justice gross violators of human rights and humanitarian law in the conflicts in the former Yugoslavia.

2. The Tribunal should be in operation and investigating cases as soon as possible.

II. Independence and qualification of judges (see section 4)

Judges must have proven competence, independence and impartiality and be free to carry out their duties without external interference. If states are to appoint judges, as many states should be involved as possible, in order to enhance the Tribunal's legitimacy and to ensure a broad cross-section of different legal systems and regional experience on the bench:

1. The majority of judges should have proven competence as criminal trial judges or criminal lawyers. Some judges should have experience in international criminal law, humanitarian law and human rights law.

2. The Security Council and the Generaly Assembly should jointly appoint judges, in the way appointments are made to the International Court of Justice (ICJ), except that the ICJ and/or other international judicial bodies should nominate candidates.

3. The Statute should incorporate by reference the UN Basic Principles on the Independence of the Judiciary.

III. Competence of the Tribunal (see section 5)

The Tribunal should have jurisdiction over a broad enough range of crimes to cover all the gross human rights and humanitarian law violations committed in the conflicts, without violating the principle that criminal law must not have retroactive effect. The starting point for Amnesty International will be to study whether the jurisdiction is wide enough to cover acts which violate people's rights to be free from arbitrary deprivation of life, torture and cruel, inhuman or degrading treatment or punishment, arbitrary detention and enforced disappearance and the right of political prisoners to receive a fair trial:

1. The punishable crimes should not be limited to crimes of a mass or systematic nature.

2. The Tribunal should at least have competence over acts which amount to violations of the laws and customs of war, crimes against humanity, genocide, torture and other relevant crimes under domestic law in force at the time in the former Yugoslavia.

3. Crimes against humanity will be a particularly important category of crimes for the Tribunal to ensure the prosecution of gross human rights violations committed against any civilian population. In International law people can be tried for crimes against humanity independently of war crimes. The use of crimes against humanity avoids the unresolved controversy about whether the various conflicts are international or non-international (torture and genocide also avoid this question).

IV. Membership of a "criminal" organization (see section5.2)

The imposition of collective punishment has no place in criminal trials which must determine individual criminal responsibility:

1. No one should be deemed to have committed specific criminal acts merely by being a member of an organization that had as its object the commission of these crimes.

2. Nor should past membership of a "criminal" organization be a crime by itself if the organization was not criminal under national or international law at the time.

V. People over whom the Tribunal should have competence (see section 5.3)

1. Justice will not be done - nor seen to be done - unless both leaders and subordinates are prosecuted. Those who have committed or ordered or acquiesced in gross human rights violations should be brought to justice. Superior orders cannot be invoked as a defence.

2. Perpetrators from all parties to the conflict should be brought to justice.

VI. Investigations (see section 6)

1. There should be no restrictions on who can provide information to the investigation and prosecution body. This body should have the duty to assess all information received, including from victims, non-governmental organizations, governments and intergovernmental organizations.

2. Investigators and prosecutors will need wide powers to act quickly and effectively, including summoning witnesses for questioning and carrying out thorough investigations within the former Yugoslavia, including the power to search and seize evidence.

3. The Security Council must take the steps necessary to ensure that national authorities are obliged actively to cooperate with the Tribunal, including helping to investigate cases, arresting suspects and transferring them to the Tribunal, in accordance with the Principles of international co-operation in the detection, arrest, extradition and punishment of persons guilty of war crimes and crimes against humanity, adopted by the UN General Assembly in 1973.

4. All pre-trial measures, including pre-trial detention, search warrants and seizures, should be subject to supervision or review by judges of the Tribunal.

VII. Prosecution (see section 7)

Any suggestion that a person has not been indicted by the prosecution office for reasons of international politics or the wishes of states, would seriously damage the authority of the Tribunal:

1. There should be a method to seek review of a decision not to proceed with a prosecution, which should include the right of victims to make a complaint.

VII. Trials in absentia (see section 8)

1. Trials *in absentia* should be prohibited.

2. If an accused wilfully refuses to appear, the Tribunal may hold a preliminary hearing to establish basic facts about the crime, without determining the guilt or innocence of the accused.

IX. Protection of the accused (see section 9)

It would be unthinkable for the Tribunal to fall below internationally accepted standards for fair trial, particularly those adopted by the UN, which apply from the time of arrest until the exhaustion of all judicial and other remedies:

1. The Statute should incorporate by reference, and require all Tribunal organs to observe, at least the guarantees provided in Articles 9, 10, 14 and 15(1), International Covenant on Civil and Political Rights, the UN Body of Principles for the Protection of All Persons under Any Form of Detention or Imprisonment, and the UN Standard Minimum Rules for the Treatment of Prisoners.

2. The Statute should guarantee that every accused who cannot afford to pay will automatically receive free legal assistance.

3. A separate public defender's office should be created, with branch offices located in the former Yugoslavia.

X. Protection of victims (see section 10)

1. Victims or their families should be able to be represented at the trial to protect their interests, particularly relating to compensation, without prejudicing the rights of the accused.

2. The Tribunal should be given wide powers to protect victims, their families and witnesses, from reprisals and unnecessary mental anguish, including obtaining expert advice about how to minimise the psychological impact of the proceedings; excluding public and the press in exceptional circumstances, and ordering extraordinary measures to protect the identity of witnesses from the accused. In all cases the interests of the witnesses should be balanced against the right of the accused to hear all the prosecution evidence and to cross-examine witnesses.

3. A special unit should be set up to deal with such protection issues at every stage of the proceedings.

XI. Rights to compensation, restitution and rehabilitation (see section 11)

1. The Tribunal should have the power to order a convicted person to provide compensation and restitution to a victim or dependents, for injury caused by the criminal act, in accordance with the UN Declaration of Basic Principles of Justice for Victims of Crime and Abuse of Power.

2. The Security Council should indicate what mechanism will be established to protect the civil rights of victims and their dependents, including the establishment of a separate international commission to process compensation claims against individuals as well as claims against states.

XII. Special considerations in cases involving violence against women (see sec 10.3)

1. Rape, sexual abuse and forced prostitution should be separate indictable offences.

2. The investigation and prosecution body should specifically include people with experience and sensitivity in collecting evidence in cases involving violence against women and in prosecuting such cases.

3. The Tribunal should include female investigators, prosecutors and judges with such experience.

4. Creative use of the Tribunal's powers to protect victims and witnesses will be particularly important to deal with cases of violence against women.

XIII. Relationship between international and national jurisdictions (see section 12)

1. The Tribunal should retry a person who has been convicted or acquitted in a trial at the national level which was manifestly unfair or a sham.

2. National authorities should be prohibited from retrying a person who has been convicted or acquitted by the Tribunal for the same acts.

3. The Tribunal should be permitted to transfer a case to a national court, but only if it is satisfied that the trial will be just, fair and effective, carried out by a court which is manifestly independent and impartial, and provided that the national court cannot impose the death penalty and the accused would not face a genuine risk of his or her fundamental human rights being violated.

XIV. Rights of appeal (see section 13)

1. A convicted person should have the right to challenge a manifestly unfounded finding of fact by the Tribunal.

2. Both the convicted person and the prosecution should be able to appeal on questions of law or against sentence or seek a revision if decisive new evidence comes to light.

XV. Penalties and supervision of sentences (see section 14)

1. The death penalty must be expressly excluded.

2. Decisions about post-conviction pardons, compassionate release and remission of sentences should be supervised by an international, impartial and independent body.

3. Convicted persons serving sentences should have the right ultimately to complain to an international, independent and impartial judicial body about conditions of imprisonment.

XVI. Adequate resources (see section 15)

The tribunal should be provided with the considerable resources and powers it will need to properly investigate all complaints and to ensure that those suspected of violations are brought before the court and prosecuted fairly and without delay:

1. The Tribunal should have the flexibility to increase the number of judges, prosecutors and investigators in light of the caseload.

2. The Tribunal will need enough resources to employ, or seek the advice of, experts at every stage of the proceedings.

XVII. Towards a permanent international court (see section 1 above)

The UN should expressly recognise that this *ad hoc* Tribunal is only the first step in establishing a permanent, international criminal court competent to try cases involving gross violations of humanitarian and human rights law.

[B] DETAILED DISCUSSION OF RECOMMENDATIONS

3. CREATION OF THE TRIBUNAL

It appears likely that the Tribunal will be established by a resolution of the Security Council acting under Chapter VII of the UN Charter, though the possibility of a treaty based body has not been ruled out. Whatever method is used, certain principles should guide how it is set up. The Tribunal must be in operation and investigating cases as soon as possible, before evidence is destroyed and offenders flee. The Tribunal must be created in such a way that it is widely acknowledged as being legitimate, independent and impartial. Every effort must be made to demonstrate that this Tribunal is an expression of a collective, global responsibility for the enforcement of universal human rights principles. The General Assembly, which last year urged the Security Council to establish such an institution[8], should help to build this consensus by showing its support for steps taken to create the Tribunal.

A Security Council resolution under Chapter VII would be a quick and effective method of establishing the Tribunal. However, the full scope of measures which may be taken under Chapter VII "to maintain or restore international peace and security" (Article 39, UN Charter) is unknown and the Tribunal could be dissolved by the Security Council for political reasons as swiftly as it is created. Amnesty International therefore urges the Security Council expressly to recognise that the Tribunal will continue to operate as long as is necessary to bring to justice gross violators of human rights and humanitarian law in the conflicts in the former Yugoslavia and that this is a necessary measure to maintain international peace and security.

The Tribunal may even have to exist long after the last trial in order to supervise the execution of sentences. On the other hand, the jurisdiction of the Tribunal could be ceded to a future permanent international criminal court. In any case, the life of the Tribunal should not be determined by political considerations, such as the conclusion of a peace settlement, but be based on an objective, professional judgment that its work is completed. This assessment could be made by the Tribunal's lawyers and judges.

4. INDEPENDENCE AND QUALIFICATION OF JUDGES

In this highly politicised environment, particular efforts must be made to ensure that the Tribunal is able to carry out its work without any direct or indirect interference or improper influence and that judges (as well as prosecutors and investigators) are acknowledged as being independent, impartial and suitably qualified.

---

[8]. UNGA Resolution 47/121, 18 December 1992, para. 10.

The main function of the Tribunal will be to assess complex and confusing facts in order to determine the guilt or innocence of individuals. Amnesty International considers that the majority of the judges should therefore have proven expertise as criminal trial judges or criminal lawyers. Depending on the way the Statute is drafted, the Tribunal will also have to decide questions of international law. Some judges should therefore also have competence in international criminal law, humanitarian law or human rights law, though such expertise could also be provided by specially appointed advisers.

To ensure absolute impartiality, any person who has formulated or implemented a government's policy in relation to the former Yugoslavia or who has otherwise been involved in activities which might put into doubt his or her impartiality on issues which the Tribunal may consider, should be disqualified as a candidate. The criteria for determining impartiality should be agreed before candidates are nominated. Furthermore, to ensure maximum independence and impartiality, Amnesty International does not consider that parties to the conflict in the former Yugoslavia should have a right to appoint judges.

If states are to appoint judges, the selection process should involve as many states as possible, in order to enhance the Tribunal's legitimacy and reflect a broad cross-section of different legal systems and regional experience. Both the Security Council and the General Assembly should participate along the lines used for appointing judges to the International Court of Justice. However, rather than involving the Permanent Court of Arbitration, it would be more appropriate for candidates to be nominated by the International Court of Justice and/or the international judicial institutions mentioned below.

The Italian proposal suggests that various UN treaty monitoring bodies should each appoint two judges. These committees, however, are not primarily judicial bodies and include many experts in fields such as medicine, journalism, and even law, who have little experience in criminal law. Nevertheless, some members, with the relevant expertise, could perhaps be consulted on this question.

The French proposal suggests that the ICJ and the highest regional human rights bodies in Europe, Africa and the Americas, should each select a number of judges. If this method is adopted, Amnesty International considers that only existing international courts should be involved in the selection, as these are most likely to have the judicial experience and independence to select other appropriate judges. This would limit participation to the: ICJ, Inter-American Court of Human Rights and European Court of Human Rights. It is unfortunate that there is no comparable court in Asia or Africa. However, the selecting institutions could appoint judges who reflect the major legal traditions in the Asian and African regions. Indeed, the ICJ, as the only global court, could be given a leading role in selecting a properly balanced bench.

Guarantees for the independence and impartiality of the Tribunal's judges will depend partly on factors already articulated in the UN Basic Principles on the Independence of the Judiciary (Basic Principles) which have been approved by the UN General Assembly[9]. They relate to matters such as tenure, conditions of office, court administration and procedure for suspending or removing judges. These standards represents an international consensus on guarantees for an independent judiciary and Amnesty International urges that the Basic Principles be incorporated by reference in the Statute.

The French and Italian proposals both provide for a fixed number of judges, 15 and 18 respectively. No one yet knows what will be the workload of the court and any *a priori* decision on the number of judges is necessarily arbitrary. Amnesty International believes the Statute should allow for more judges to be selected on the recommendation of the judges and/or prosecution organ, if needed in light of the caseload. However, to prevent political interference, such new judges should not be assigned to cases in which proceedings have already begun.

5. COMPETENCE OF THE TRIBUNAL

5.1. Jurisdiction & applicable law

The creation of this ad hoc international Tribunal embodies the principle clarified at the Nuremberg and Tokyo war crimes tribunals, reaffirmed in many UN General Assembly resolutions, repeated by the UN International Law Commission (ILC) and embodied in many UN conventions, that individuals are criminally responsible for any act which constitutes a crime under international law, even if internal law does not criminalize the same act or even authorises it. The Tribunal will be an expression of the collective responsibility of states to enforce international law. The primary source for the Tribunal's jurisdiction should be international law, independent of domestic law.

The principle of legality, or non-retroactive application of criminal law, will not be violated if the Tribunal is given competence over acts which violate clear rules of conventional or customary international criminal law at the time they were committed[10]. The ICCPR reaffirms this principle by providing firstly, that a person can be charged with a crime if it was an offence under either national or international law at the time it was committed (Article 15(1)) and, secondly, that the principle of legality does not prevent anyone being tried for an act which was "criminal according to the general principles of law recognised by the community of nations" (Article 15(2)). It is equally clear that procedural rules are not affected by the legality principle[11]. International law, however, does not set down penalties for crimes under international law, leaving this for states to decide. The principle would be violated if the Tribunal imposed sentences based on rules which were not sufficiently certain at the time the crimes were committed.

There is, however, a useful interplay between international law and national law. The former Socialist Federative Republic of Yugoslavia (SFRY) ratified all major human rights and humanitarian law conventions[12]. The Republic of Yugoslavia claims to be the successor state to the SFRY and has therefore succeeded to its international obligations. Under Article 210 of the 1974 Constitution of the SFRY, properly ratified international treaties can be applied directly by national courts. Furthermore, the Criminal Code of the

---

[9]. Adopted unanimously by the Seventh UN Congress on the Prevention of Crime and the Treatment of Offenders in September 1985. Subsequently endorsed by UNGA Resolution 40/32 of 29 November 1985 and Resolution, 40/146 of 13 December 1985.

[10]. The ILC, in its latest report, reaffirmed that there are rules of both conventional and customary international law which bind individuals. It did recommend that the jurisdiction of a permanent criminal court should be limited to offences defined in treaties in force but this has more to do with practical concerns about whether states would accept an open-ended jurisdiction in advance which extended to crimes against general international law not yet defined. It also assumed that the draft Code of Crimes against the Peace and Security of Mankind would be included in the jurisdiction once completed and adopted. See Report of the International Law Commission on the work of its 44th session, 4 May - 24 July 1992, UN Doc: A/47/10 (hereafter ILC 1992 Report), paras. 449-451 and 492.

[11]. ILC 1992 report, para.500.

[12]. The former Yugoslav Republic had ratified the four 1949 Geneva Conventions and two 1977 Additional Protocols; the Genocide Convention; the Convention against Torture; International Covenant on Civil and Political Rights (ICCPR); International Covenant on Economic, Social and Cultural Rights (ICESCR), the two UN Conventions against Slavery; ILO Convention No.29 concerning forced labour; the Convention for the Suppression of the Traffic in Persons and of the Exploitation of the Prostitution of Others; Convention on the Elimination of All Forms of Racial Discrimination (CERD); Convention on the Rights of the Child and the Convention on the Non-Applicability of Statutory Limitations to War Crimes and Crimes against Humanity. Croatia and Bosnia-Herzegovina, as states which have emerged from the former Yugoslavia are bound by the conventions which the former Yugoslavia had ratified. In addition, Croatia, Slovenia and Bosnia-Herzegovina have all formally succeeded to a number of conventions: In 1992 Croatia formally succeeded to the ICCPR, ICESCR, Convention against Torture, CERD, the Geneva Conventions and two Additional Protocols, the Genocide Convention, the Convention on the Rights of the Child, the Convention relating to the status of refugees and Protocol, and the Convention relating to the Status of Stateless Persons. Bosnia-Herzegovina formally succeeded in 1992 to the Geneva Conventions and Additional Protocols and the Genocide Convention.

former Socialist Federative Republic of Yugoslav (the former Yugoslav Penal Code)[13], gave domestic effect to many of these international norms, particularly Chapter XVI which incorporated rules from the 1949 Geneva Conventions[14] and the Convention on the Prevention and Punishment of the Crime of Genocide (the Genocide Convention)[15]. This domestic enforcement of international crimes parallels the more direct, international jurisdiction. Indeed, the Tribunal will largely do what the national courts in the former Yugoslavia could, but are unwilling or unable, to do. There is no reason why it could not draw on domestic Yugoslav law to support and strengthen its international jurisdiction in several ways:

1. Where crimes found in customary international law are so ill-defined that to incorporate them in the Tribunal's jurisdiction would have a retroactive effect, such crimes could be included in the Statute if they were also criminalized in the former Yugoslavia at the time the act was committed.

2. Conversely, because of the specific geographic focus, there is no reason why the Tribunal should not also have competence over crimes which are prohibited by Yugoslav law but are not crimes in international law, as long as the domestic law is not otherwise inconsistent with international law.

3. Former Yugoslav law could be used as a guide to decide penalties, except that the death penalty should not be imposed[16].

In this way the jurisdiction of the Tribunal should be broad enough to cover all gross human rights violations, without having retroactive effect.

What acts constitute crimes under international law has more to do with the haphazard influence of history and politics than with the reality of what acts should be criminalized. Because of the specific mandate of the organization, the starting point for Amnesty International will be to study whether the Tribunal has competence over crimes which violate people's rights to be free from arbitrary deprivation of life, torture and cruel, inhuman or degrading treatment or punishment, arbitrary detention and enforced disappearance and the right of political prisoners to receive a fair trial.

---

[13]. The whole former Yugoslav Penal Code has been incorporated into Bosnia-Herzegovina law and the new Croatian Penal Code expressly retains Chapter XVI of the code.

[14].Hereafter the four 1949 Geneva Conventions referred to as Geneva I, II, III or IV; the two 1977 Additional Protocols hereafter referred to as Protocol I and Protocol II.

[15]. See for example, Articles 141 (Genocide), 142 (War crimes against civilian population), 143 (war crimes against the wounded and sick), 144 (war crimes against prisoners of war), 146 (unlawful killing and wounded of the enemy), 150 (brutal treatment of the wounded, sick or prisoners of war), and 151 (destruction of cultural and historical monuments), 152 (incitement to aggressive war), 154 (racial and other discrimination) of the former Yugoslav Penal Code.

[16]. The ILC has recommended that a future permanent criminal court will need a residual power to refer to penalties imposed under national law in the absence of international penalties. See ILC 1992 Report, para. 502.

Amnesty International does not believe that the Statute should include a general restriction that only crimes of a mass or systematic nature can be prosecuted[17]. By basing its jurisdiction on crimes under international law, and possibly Chapter XVI of the former Yugoslav Penal Code, the competence of the Tribunal will necessarily be limited to the most serious crimes. Some categories of crimes under international law, such as crimes against humanity, are limited by definition to acts of a mass or systematic nature. But to place such a limitation on other crimes is arbitrarily to change the definition of these crimes. One act of torture is just as much a crime under international law as a pattern of torture. Finally, terms such as "mass or systematic" are inherently ambiguous and it would be difficult for the prosecution to decide whether some cases qualify.

Amnesty International urges the drafters of the Statute to ensure that interpretation of what acts are within the Tribunal's competence is not complicated by the unresolved question of whether the various conflicts are international or non-international. This controversy is a result of the undeveloped nature of international law, will not help to make the trials more just and fair and will present yet another legal hurdle for the prosecution.

There may be several ways to avoid this controversy. It may be necessary only to incorporate provisions from the Geneva Conventions and Protocols regulating non-international conflicts. The Tribunal's jurisdiction could then be supplemented by categories of crimes, such as crimes against humanity, genocide and torture, where the international-internal conflict distinction is irrelevant.

The former Yugoslav Penal Code could be another important source of crimes. Chapter XVI incorporates, *inter-alia*, rules relating to international armed conflict found in the grave breach provisions of the Geneva Conventions and the Hague Regulations of 1907. As they appear in Chapter XVI these provisions apply to such acts committed "in violation of the rules of international law" during "wartime or armed conflict". Although it is not clear, these articles may apply to both international and non-international armed conflict.

It is significant that in a series of written agreements, signed under the auspices of the International Committee of the Red Cross, the parties to the Croatian-Serbian conflict and the conflict in Bosnia-Herzegovina committed themselves to respecting various provisions in the Geneva Conventions and Protocol I relating to the protection of civilians, captured combatants and the wounded and sick[18]. Although the agreements are stated to be without prejudice to the legal status of the parties, this *de facto* recognition of provisions for international conflicts could justify applying rules for international conflict to the conflicts in the former Yugoslavia, at least from the date of the agreements, in relation to the parties to those agreements.

---

[17]. The French proposal limits jurisdiction to crimes "committed on a mass and systematic scale, causing particular revulsion and calling for an international response" - art. VI of draft statute in French proposal. What is meant by "mass" and "systematic" is not clear. The ILC, in its 1991 draft Code of Crimes against the Peace and Security of Mankind, took "the mass-scale element [to] relate to the number of people affected by such violations or the entity that has been affected". It defined "systematic" as relating to "a constant practice or to a methodical plan to carry out such violations".

[18]. See, (i) Statement on respect of humanitarian principles made by the Presidents of the six republics in the Hague on 5 November 1991; (ii) Memorandum of Understanding, dated 27 November 1991, signed in Geneva by representatives of the Republic of Croatia, Federal Republic of Yugoslavia and Republic of Serbia; (iii) Addendum to the Memorandum of Understanding of 27 November 1991, signed by representatives of the Federal Republic of Yugoslavia and the Republic of Croatia; (iv) Agreement reached under ICRC auspices on 28 & 29 July 1992, signed by Prime Minister of Federal Republic of Yugoslavia and Vice-Prime Minister of Republic of Croatia; (v) Agreement signed on 22 May 1992 by representatives of the Presidency of the Republic of Bosnia-Herzegovina, the Serbian Democratic Party, the Party of Democratic Action and the Croatian Democratic Community.

If use of the Geneva Convention and Protocols is limited to provisions on non-international conflict, Common Article 3 and Protocol I will still be a vital source of relevant crimes. Protocol II, Article 14, for example, prohibits the starvation of civilians as a method of combat and Protocol II, Article 13(2), provides that civilians "shall not be the object of attack". Article 13(2) prohibits "acts or threats of violence the primary purpose of which is to spread terror among the civilian population" and in Article 4(2)(d), "acts of terrorism" are prohibited. Such tactics which spread a climate of fear and result in the civilian population having no option but to flee, have been an integral part of violations committed in the course of "ethnic cleansing". Protocol II also prohibits unlawful deportation or transfer of civilians[19]. Hostage taking, another widespread abuse in the conflicts, is prohibited regardless of whether the conflict is international or internal[20].

It is not clear whether atrocities committed in the former Yugoslavia amount to genocide, as defined by the Genocide Convention. The devastating effect on whole national, ethnic or religious groups of violations committed in the context of "ethnic cleansing" clearly raises this issue and Amnesty International would welcome the Tribunal being given an opportunity to make its own assessment.

In light of these comments Amnesty International considers the Tribunal should at least have competence over acts which amount to violations of:

♦ the **laws and customs of war** (drawing on conventional and customary rules regulating internal conflict and/or rules regulating international conflict), particularly those found in the Geneva Conventions and Additional Protocols;
♦ **crimes against humanity** (see the discussion below);
♦ **genocide** as defined in the Genocide Convention;
♦ **torture** as defined in the Convention against Torture and Other Cruel, Inhuman Degrading Treatment or Punishment, and
♦ other relevant acts criminalized at the time they were committed by **laws in force in the former Yugoslavia.**

In light of the scale of allegations[21] of rape, forced prostitution and indecent assault in the conflicts in the former Yugoslavia, Amnesty International considers it should be unambiguous in the Tribunal's Statute that these acts are separate indictable crimes, although they are also clearly included within the meaning of provisions in the Geneva Conventions and Additional Protocols[22].

---

[19]. See Protocol II, art.17, as well as Geneva IV, art.147, and Protocol I, art.85(4)(a).

[20]. See Geneva Conventions, Common Article 3, Protocol I, Article 75(2)(c), and Protocol II, Article 4(2)(c).

[21]. See Amnesty International, **Bosnia-Herzegovina: Rape and sexual abuse by armed forces**, AI Index: EUR 63/01/93, January 1993; European Community Investigative mission into the treatment of Muslim women in the former Yugoslavia (headed by Dame Ann Warburton), Report to European Community Foreign Ministers, January 1993; UN Commission on Human Rights Special Rapporteur on the former Yugoslavia, report to 49th session of Commission on Human Rights, Annex II, UN Doc: E/CN.4/1993/50.

[22]. Viz. within the meaning of Common Article 3, Protocol II, Article 4 and the grave breach provisions such as Geneva IV, Article 147 which prohibits "wilfully causing great suffering or serious injury or to body or health". The exploitation of others for the purposes of prostitution has also been prohibited by the Convention for the Suppression of the Traffic in Persons and of the Exploitation of the Prostitution of Others, approved by the UNGA resolution 317(IV), 2 December 1949, although it is declared criminal only to the extent permitted by domestic law (art.3).

Crimes against humanity

It was mentioned above that crimes against humanity is one useful category of offences to avoid a debilitating debate about whether the conflicts are international or non-international. It also avoids the need to determine whether the crime was committed against a belligerent party in war or against one's own civilian population. Crimes against humanity is a vigorous and well established category of crime, well suited to the needs of this Tribunal. Civilian and military authorities who have committed gross human rights violations against civilian populations under their administrative control could be prosecuted under this head. Many of these violations have led to the forcible expulsion of thousands of people. Existing international law requires states to cooperate in the detection, arrest, and bringing to trial of people suspected of crimes against humanity[23]. There is universal jurisdiction over crimes against humanity and every state must prosecute or extradite alleged offenders found in their territory. A state must also refuse asylum to anyone who may have committed such crimes. These international obligations will be important to help ensure perpetrators from the former Yugoslavia are brought to trial.

In the Nuremberg Charter crimes against humanity was established as a separate category of offences to enable Nazis to be tried for crimes committed against German citizens. However, such acts could not be prosecuted unless they were committed in execution of or in connection with a crime against peace or a war crime. Since then, however, crimes against humanity have developed into an independent category of international crimes. In other words, it is no longer necessary to show that the crime was committed in the execution of or in connection with a war crime or crime against peace.

Only months after signing of the Nuremberg Charter, Allied Control Council Law No.10 (20 December 1945) which formed the jurisdictional basis for war crimes trials in Germany after the Nuremberg tribunal, defined crimes against humanity without the limitation imposed by the Nuremberg Charter:

> "Atrocities and offences, including but not limited to murder, extermination, enslavement, deportation, imprisonment, torture, rape, or other inhumane acts *committed against any civilian population* [emphasis added] or persecutions on political, racial or religious grounds ..."

Although the UN General Assembly in 1946 retained the Nuremberg Charter formulation of crimes against humanity[24], the 1954 version of the ILC draft Code of Offences against the Peace and Security of Mankind (which largely followed the Nuremberg definition of crimes against humanity) did not require that the acts had to be committed in connection with war crimes or crimes against peace.

International law has continued to expand the category of crimes against humanity to include *apartheid*[25] and genocide[26]. Most recently, the UN General Assembly has recognised the systematic practice of enforced disappearance to be in the nature of a crime

---

[23]. See section 6.2 below.

[24]. UNGA Resolution 95 (1), 11 December 1946.

[25] **See art. 1, International Convention on the Suppression and Punishment of the Crime of *Apartheid*, adopted by UNGA 30 November 1973.**

against humanity[27]. The ILC has included in its 1991 draft Code of Offences against the Peace and Security of Mankind an updated version of its 1954 description of crimes against humanity which reflects the enduring nature of this category of offences without the acts being dependent on any other crime[28].

5.2. *Membership of a "criminal" organization*

Amnesty International is concerned about the provisions in the French proposal, based on the Nuremberg Charter, that crimes within the jurisdiction of the Tribunal "shall be deemed to have been committed" by any individual who was a member of an organization which had as its primary or secondary objective the commission of one or more such crimes. The imposition of this form of collective guilt should have no place in a criminal trial which must determine whether an individual has committed specific criminal acts in a particular place at a particular time, with the requisite criminal intent. Membership of an organization which had as its objective the commission of one or more of the crimes may be evidence towards proving that the accused participated in acts sponsored by the organization. But membership alone is not sufficient to prove individual guilt. It is ironic that such a crime is being contemplated, when the Geneva Conventions and Protocols expressly prohibit collective punishment [29] and require that no one can be convicted of an offence "except on the basis of individual penal responsibility"[30].

Amnesty International would also be concerned if the Statute included past membership of an organization declared to be "criminal" as a separate offence. If such organizations were not "criminal" under national or international law at the time an accused joined, such an *ex post facto* declaration with criminal consequences would amount to a retroactive application of the law.

What is not prohibited by criminal law principles is the indictment, as a separate criminal act, of anyone who has set up or helped to set up a formal or informal group of people for the purpose of committing crimes within the jurisdiction of the Tribunal. The prosecution would still have to establish, however, that the individual accused participated in the creation of the group with the necessary intent to create a group with such aims.

5.3. People over whom Tribunal should have competence

Justice will not be done - nor seen to be done - unless both leaders and subordinates are prosecuted. Those who have committed or ordered or acquiesced in gross human rights violations should be brought to justice. Superior orders cannot be invoked as a defence. Furthermore, perpetrators from all parties to the conflict should be brought to justice.

---

27. Preamble to UN Declaration on the Protection of All Persons from Enforced Disappearance, adopted by UNGA Resolution 47/133, 18 December 1992.

28 Article 21 of the 1991 draft, entitled "systematic or mass violations of human rights" and is expressed to cover crimes against humanity, provides that: "An individual who commits or orders the commission of any of the following violations of human rights: murder, torture, establishing or maintaining over persons a status of slavery, servitude of forced labour, persecution on social, political, racial, religious or cultural grounds in a systematic manner or on a mass scale; or deportation or forcible transfer of population shall, on conviction thereof, be sentenced to ..."

29 Geneva IV, art.33, Protocol I, art.75(2)(d).

30 Protocol I, art.75(4)(b) & Protocol II, art.6(2)(b).

6. INVESTIGATIONS

6.1. Initiating investigations: the role of victims and NGOs

The investigation and prosecution organ should be free to seek and receive unsolicited information from the widest possible range of sources, including victims and their families, other individuals, non-governmental organizations, governments and inter-governmental organizations. There should be no restriction on who can provide information. It will then be up to the investigators and prosecutors to assess the weight of the information and whether it warrants further investigation and possible prosecution. The investigation and prosecution body should also be able to begin an investigation on its own initiative.

Amnesty International is concerned that if the Statute recognises specific organizations or categories such as "humanitarian organizations" which may submit denunciations, the implication is that the investigation and prosecution organ has no duty to take note of information submitted by other organizations and individuals. The reality is that an organization's size, or whether or not it has consultative status with intergovernmental organizations, bears little relationship to the importance or relevance of information submitted to the Tribunal. Some non-governmental organizations as well as bodies such as the UN Commission of Experts established pursuant to Security Council resolution 780 (1992) and the UN Commission on Human Rights Special Rapporteur on the former Yugoslavia, are systematically collecting evidence from a wide variety of sources which may be of considerable help to the Tribunal. However, no *a priori* assumption should be made in the Statute about the relevance or reliability of information from particular sources.

6.2. Rights and powers during pre-trial investigation

In the absence of an international police force, the investigators must be given wide powers to act quickly and effectively, including summoning witnesses for questioning and carrying out searches and seizure of evidence and full on-site investigations within the former Yugoslavia. Investigators will need unrestricted freedom to enter and travel within the territory of states. The Security Council must take the steps necessary to ensure that national authorities are obliged actively to cooperate with the Tribunal, including helping to investigate cases, arresting suspects and delivering them to the Tribunal. Indeed, in relation to war crimes and crimes against humanity, states are already obliged to provide such assistance, in accordance with the 1973 UN General Assembly's Principles of international co-operation in the detection, arrest, extradition and punishment of persons guilty of war crimes and crimes against humanity[31].

The wide powers of the investigators, however, will have to be balanced against the right of any person whose freedom, privacy or property is affected by such intrusive powers to be treated fairly and justly. There is some divergence of opinion about whether the investigation and prosecution body should be quasi-judicial with autonomy to decide pre-trial measures, as in the civil law system, or an administrative body which should apply to a judge for intrusive, pre-trial orders.

Regardless of which system is chosen, all pre-trial procedures should at least be subject to supervision or review after the fact by an independent judicial authority. The French proposal gives a right of complaint to the prosecution body sitting collectively. This is not entirely satisfactory as this body would consist of colleagues of the prosecutor whose actions are being appealed. There should therefore be an ultimate right of appeal to a judge.

---

[31]. Adopted by the UNGA Resolution 3074 (XXVIII), 3 December 1973. See also the UN Convention on the Non-Applicability of Statutory Limitations to War Crimes and Crimes against Humanity, adopted by UNGA Resolution 2391 (XXIII), 26 November 1968.

Specifically, Article 9(3) of the International Covenant on Civil and Political Rights (the ICCPR) requires that anyone arrested or detained on a criminal charge should be brought promptly before an authority exercising judicial power. Under Article 9(4), any detainee should be entitled to bring proceedings before a court to challenge the lawfulness of the detention. The judicial authority should exercise effective and continuing supervision throughout the detention. Anyone affected by pre-trial measures such as searches, seizures or orders to appear for questioning, should have the right to challenge their lawfulness before an independent judicial authority. In addition, law enforcement officials acting on behalf of the Tribunal should observe minimum standards on the use of force, as laid out in the UN Basic Principles on the use of force and firearms by law enforcement officials[32] and the Code of Conduct for Law Enforcement Officials[33].

Because of the turmoil of war and the fact that the Tribunal will probably sit outside the former Yugoslavia, access to the court will not be quick or easy. The Tribunal should take whatever steps are necessary to facilitate the exercise of the right to judicial review of pre-trial measures. This may include locating 'public defenders' in the region who can offer their services free of charge to those who cannot pay. Their existence would have to be widely publicised. Furthermore, at least one judge should be available to hear pre-trial matters as soon as the first investigation is launched, even if other trial judges are not convened until a case has been referred to the Tribunal.

7. PROSECUTION

Any suggestion that the prosecution has not proceeded with a case for reasons of international politics or the wishes of one or more states, would seriously damage the authority of the Tribunal. There should therefore be some method for seeking a review of a decision not to proceed with a prosecution. Victims are most affected by such a decision and Amnesty International supports the CSCE recommendation that they be able to make a complaint. Depending on the structure of the Tribunal, this application would be made either to a judge or the prosecution body sitting as a collective, quasi-judicial organ.

If the prosecution body decides to proceed with the prosecution, should there be a preliminary hearing in which a judicial body decides whether there is sufficient evidence to indict the suspect? Different legal traditions give different answers, but Amnesty International would highlight two factors which it considers should be taken into account in making this choice.

Firstly, many witnesses are likely to have to endure great trauma in recounting horrific events several times, for investigators, prosecution lawyers and in the trial. They should not be made to repeat their testimony at a preliminary hearing as well as at a trial unless absolutely necessary to ensure justice and fairness. Witnesses at preliminary hearings will need the same protection against reprisals and mental anguish which is provided at the trial (see section 10 below).

Secondly, the preliminary hearing is likely to attract considerable publicity which could prejudice the interests of the accused. The accused should therefore enjoy basic guarantees of fairness, including the right to be represented by a lawyer, to cross-examine witnesses and to obtain copies of all documents tendered during the hearing. Any preliminary hearing, like the trial, should in principle always be open to the public.

---

[32]. Adopted by consensus by the Eighth UN Congress on the Prevention of Crime and Treatment of Offenders, 7 September 1990.

[33]. Adopted by UNGA Resolution 34/169, 17 December 1979.

8. TRIALS *IN ABSENTIA*

A difficult legal and policy question is whether the Tribunal should be able to try accused *in absentia*. The function of a criminal trial is objectively to determine the innocence or guilt of individual accused and the burden of establishing this guilt rests on the prosecution. Anything which fundamentally prejudices the ability of the Tribunal to make this decision should, in principle, be avoided[34]. Amnesty International believes that because of the likely complexity and confusion surrounding the alleged facts, exacerbated by the chaos of war and deliberate or unintentional misinformation, the accused should be present to hear the full prosecution case, to cross examine witnesses, refute facts and present a full defence. With anything less the reliability of the verdict will always be in doubt and justice will not be seen to be done.

Trials *in absentia* would seem to be excluded by the unambiguous words of ICCPR, Article 14(3)(d) which guarantees the right of an accused "to be tried in his presence". The UN Human Rights Committee has held that trials *in absentia* are justified in exceptional circumstances[35] and the European Court of Human Rights has interpreted the equivalent article[36] in the European Convention on Human Rights in a similar way. The ILC Working Group on the question of an international criminal jurisdiction, however, has expressly recommended against trials *in absentia* in any permanent international criminal court[37].

The creation of this Tribunal is already a highly politicised issue and every effort must be made to ensure that it fulfils its role objectively, and does not become a token, political gesture. Amnesty International is concerned that trials *in absentia* could be more like political show trials. Justice will not be done, particularly if, because of the difficulty of arresting accused, trials *in absentia* became the norm and not the exception. The French proposal provides that if the accused is subsequently arrested or voluntarily gives him or herself up, the conviction *in absentia* would be annulled and the case would be considered afresh by the prosecution body. Amnesty International does not consider that such safeguards would adequately balance the inherent dangers of trials *in absentia* in this forum.

There may, however, be another alternative. If the accused has been properly notified of the date and place of the trial and he or she wilfully refuses to appear, the Tribunal could hold a preliminary hearing. By establishing the basic facts of where, how and when a particular incident occurred, this hearing could begin to reveal the truth, for the benefit of victims and the community. It could also record evidence which is in danger of being lost. The determination of guilt or innocence of an individual, however, would be left to a subsequent trial in the presence of the accused.

---

[34]. In a 1975 resolution of the Committee of Ministers of the Council of Europe it is provided that where an accused has been served with a summons, the court "must order an adjournment if it considers personal appearance of the accused to be indispensable"; Resolution (75)11 of the Council of Europe Committee of Ministers, "on the criteria governing procedures held in the absence of the accused", adopted 21 May 1975.

[35]. See Human Rights Committee, General Comment 13(21), under article 40(4) ICCPR, as well as *Monguya Mbenge et al.* v. *Zaire* (16/1977), Report of the Human Rights Committee, GAOR, 38th Session, Supplement No.40, Annex X, in which the Committee said that a trial *in absentia* at least requires that "all due notification has been made to inform him [the accused] of the date and place of his trial and to request his attendance".

[36]. Art.6(3)(c) is not as strong as the ICCPR, as it only guarantees the right of an accused "to defend himself in person" and not the right to be "tried in his presence".

[37]. ILC 1992 report, para.504.

If trials *in absentia* are permitted, additional guarantees will be needed to ensure that the prosecution evidence is tested as far as possible. In contrast to the French proposal, Amnesty International considers that a lawyer must be appointed by the Tribunal to represent the interests of an accused who is not present in court. The resolution of the Council of Europe Committee of Ministers referred to above also provides that when the accused is tried in his absence, "evidence must be taken in the usual manner and the defence must have the right to intervene"[38].

9. PROTECTION OF THE ACCUSED

9.1. Incorporating fair trial guarantees

There is a general international consensus on the minimum standards for a fair trial covering the period from arrest until the exhaustion of all judicial and other remedies. This consensus is expressed in international human rights and humanitarian law treaties and is also reflected in general principles of law.

The Universal Declaration of Human Rights and the ICCPR give broad guidance to the drafters of the Statute, but many of the rights are not detailed enough to help solve practical problems[39]. Amnesty International considers that the Statute should, at the very least, expressly incorporate by reference, and require all organs of the Tribunal to comply with:

♦ ICCPR Articles 9, 10, 14[40] and 15(1);
♦ the UN Body of Principles for the Protection of All Persons under Any Form of Detention or Imprisonment (Body of Principles)[41], and
♦ the UN Standard Minimum Rules for the Treatment of Prisoners (the Standard Minimum Rules)[42].

Although these instruments - except for the ICCPR - are not in the form of treaties, they represent an international consensus on minimum standards for the treatment of anyone detained or imprisoned, including those awaiting trial and those imprisoned under sentence. They will be particularly important in regulating aspects of detention on which there is a wide divergence of national practice, such as limiting incommunicado detention by ensuring regular access to family, doctors and lawyers[43].

---

[38]. See para. 5 of resolution cited footnote 34 above.

[39]. The General Comments of the Human Rights Committee give some guidance to the meaning of the broad rights guaranteed in the ICCPR.

[40]. Most of the guarantees in ICCPR Article 14 are also found in Protocol I, Article 75(4) and Protocol II, Article 6. See more detailed guarantees for prisoners of war, in Geneva III, Articles 99-108.

[41]. Adopted by UNGA Resolution 43/173, 9 December 1988, without a vote.

[42]. Adopted by First UN Congress on the Prevention of Crime and the Treatment of Offenders, 1955, approved by ECOSOC resolutions 663 C (XXIV) 31 July 1957 and 2076 (LXII) 13 May 1977. In 1984 UNGA endorsed the ECOSOC Procedures for the Effective Implementation of the Standards Minimum Rules for the Treatment of Prisoners, in Resolution 39/118, 14 December 1984.

[43]. See especially Principles 15-19, 24 and 25, Body of Principles.

In addition, Amnesty International would recommend that the Statute incorporate the UN Guidelines on the Role of Prosecutors[44] and the UN Basic Principles on the Role of Lawyers[45], which set out minimum rights and duties of lawyers in general and prosecutors in particular.

It would unthinkable for an institution created by the UN to fall below such standards approved by the General Assembly. The Tribunal has on opportunity to be a model of high standards by expressly adhering to minimum standards which had not been codified at the time of the Nuremberg tribunal.

In regard to rules of evidence, Amnesty International would urge that the Tribunal be required to comply with the well established rule, reaffirmed in the UN Convention against Torture and Other Cruel, Inhuman or Degrading Treatment or Punishment, that evidence made as a result of torture cannot be invoked in any proceedings (Article 15). Amnesty International would urge that this rule be extended to include evidence extracted through the use of cruel, inhuman or degrading treatment or punishment[46]. We would also recommend that the Tribunal be required to observe the provision in Body of Principles, Principle 27, that the failure to comply with that instrument must be taken into account when determining the admissibility of evidence against the accused. Amnesty International would also be concerned if the Tribunal was able to convict solely on the basis of contested, uncorroborated confessions.

9.2. Access to legal assistance

The Statute should expressly require that all detainees have the right of legal assistance of their choice, not only for the trial, but promptly after arrest and throughout every stage of the proceedings, including any preliminary hearing. Counsel should have access to their clients on the conditions guaranteed by Principles 15, 17 and 18 in the Body of Principles and by the Standard Minimum Rules and the Basic Principles on the Role of Lawyers.

Free legal assistance is required to be provided by Article 14(3)(d) if the accused cannot pay, "where the interests of justice so require". Amnesty International considers that because of the seriousness and consequences of crimes being tried, the interests of justice demand that every accused who cannot afford to pay should automatically receive free legal assistance and that this should be expressly guaranteed in the Statute. The detainee must, of course, be informed of his or her right to legal assistance as well as other rights[47].

It may be difficult to ensure that defence lawyers with the necessary expertise and even language skills are available quickly. Amnesty International would recommend that a separate public defender's office be established, independent of other organs of the

---

[44]. Adopted by consensus by the Eighth UN Congress on the Prevention of Crime and the Treatment of Offenders on 7 September 1990 and welcomed by the UNGA Resolution 45/121 of 14 December 1990.

[45]. Adopted by the Eighth UN Congress on the Prevention of Crime and the Treatment of Offenders by consensus on 7 September 1990 and welcomed by the UNGA Resolution 45/121 on 14 December 1990.

[46]. See the much broader prohibition on interrogation methods which use "violence, threats or methods of interrogation which impair his [the detained person's] capacity of decision or his judgment", Principle 21, Body of Principles which would apply if the Body of Principles was incorporated.

[47]. ICCPR, Art.14(3)(d) & Body of Principles, Principle 13.

Tribunal but created by the Tribunal's Statute. Just like the prosecutors, the defence lawyers in this office would build up considerable experience in operating in this unique jurisdiction. It could provide free legal assistance for those who cannot afford to pay and who would be unlikely to know how to find appropriate counsel. The public defender's office could be responsible for basing some lawyers in the former Yugoslavia, as recommended above in relation to pre-trial measures. Defence lawyers should at all times comply with the principles and enjoy the rights set out in the UN Basic Principles on the Role of Lawyers[48].

10. PROTECTION OF VICTIMS

Victims and their families have a vital interest in knowing the truth about past human rights violations, in seeing that justice is done and in protecting their own civil interests. Yet victims, witnesses and families also remain vulnerable to intimidation and retaliation as a result of a trial, often long after the accused has been convicted or acquitted. Amnesty International believes that careful and detailed consideration must be given to the right of victims to participate in the judicial process and to ensure that they, their families and witnesses on their behalf are properly protected.

It has already been recommended in section 6.1 that victims and their families, like any other individual or organization should be able to give information to the investigation and prosecution body, who will assess its weight. It has also been suggested in section 7 that alleged victims or their families should have standing to challenge a decision not to prosecute an individual.

10.1. Participation in the trial

International standards, as well as some civil law jurisdictions, recognise that victims may have a right to participate in the criminal trial. The UN Declaration of Basic Principles of Justice for Victims of Crime and Abuse of Power (the Declaration on Victims)[49], provides in para.6(b) that the judicial process should allow:

> " ... the views and concerns of victims to be presented and considered at appropriate stages of the proceedings where their personal interests are affected, without prejudice to the accused ..."

Amnesty International would urge the drafters of the Statute to consider how this provision could be implemented, for example, by permitting a victim to be represented during the trial. Victims should also be able to request information from the prosecutor's office about the progress of proceedings in which they have an interest.

10.2. Protection of victims, their families and witnesses

The hostility between national groups in the former Yugoslavia has been so intense that the Tribunal will need wide powers to protect victims, their families and witnesses on their behalf. Furthermore, witnesses could suffer considerable mental anguish by having repeatedly to relive horrific events before investigators, prosecutors and judges.

---

[48]. Adopted by consensus by the Eighth UN Congress on the Prevention of Crime and Treatment of Offenders, 7 September 1990.

[49]. Adopted by the UN General Assembly on 29 November 1985 (Resolution 40/34).

The Declaration on Victims emphasises that "victims should be treated with compassion and respect for their dignity" (para.4). It also provides in para.6(d) that the judicial system should take:

> " ... measures to minimize inconvenience to victims, protect their privacy, when necessary, and ensure their safety, as well as that of their families and witnesses on their behalf, from intimidation and retaliation".

The Tribunal will also need to interpret sensitively the authority given in ICCPR Article 14(1) to exclude the press and public from trials in exceptional circumstances, "to the extent strictly necessary in the opinion of the court in special circumstances where publicity would prejudice the interests of justice".

In addition to suppressing names of witnesses, the Tribunal should have the power to order extraordinary measures to protect the identity of witnesses from the accused. Amnesty International recognises that in all cases the interests of the witnesses will have to be balanced against the right of the accused to hear all the prosecution evidence and to cross-examine witnesses. Methods will have to be found to ensure that while all witnesses can be cross-examined, they can also receive adequate protection. At least defence lawyers from the Tribunal's public defenders' office as well as judges, should always be able to confront and cross-examine witnesses. In some cases the prosecution will need great care in selecting the evidence to present which will be sufficient to secure a conviction without unnecessarily endangering witnesses.

Protection also means actively supporting and caring for victims and witnesses who participate in the judicial process. If children give information to investigators or testimony to the court, the prosecution and the trial court should consult with psychologists on ways in which the potential psychological damage of the investigatory and court process could be minimized. A special unit should be set up to deal with all the protection issues which arise at each stage of the proceedings.

Witnesses and victims who fear the consequences of making a complaint or giving evidence should be able to seek protection, not only from officers of the Tribunal, but also from peace-keeping forces including civilian police monitors, as well as any human rights monitoring mission which may be established in the former Yugoslavia. Investigators, prosecutors and judges of the international Tribunal should all have a duty actively to refer witnesses and victims at risk to these other bodies as appropriate.

10.3. Special considerations in cases involving violence against women

The type of special measures described above should be used to deal with the particular demands of investigating, prosecuting and judging crimes involving violence against women, including rape and other sexual abuse and forced prostitution.

Several non-governmental organizations, including Amnesty International, have reported that women in the former Yugoslavia are very reluctant to come forward with testimony about

---

[50]. See Amnesty International, **Bosnia-Herzegovina: Rape and sexual abuse by armed forces**, cited footnote 21 above; Report of UN Special Rapporteur on the former Yugoslavia cited in footnote 21 above; Ecumenical Women's Team Visit, **Rape of Women in War**, World Council of Churches, Zagreb, December 1992.

violence against women[50]. Some women feel they must obliterate the experience from their memory; others feel degraded and ashamed or fear they will suffer social stigma should they disclose what has happened to them[51]. The trauma and stress has been exacerbated by the pressure to repeatedly give statements to fact-finding missions or press interviews. An expert mission of the UN Special Rapporteur on the former Yugoslavia has commented that:

> " ... Fear of reprisals against themselves and their families, some of whom may still be in the areas affected by the conflict, also makes victims unwilling to speak ... Some of the women met by the team of experts felt exploited by the media and the many missions 'studying' rape in the former Yugoslavia. Furthermore, health care providers were concerned about the effects on women of repeatedly recounting their experiences without adequate psychological and social support systems in place.[52]

Creative use by the Tribunal of wide powers to protect witnesses and victims will be particularly important to tackle these problems. A woman, for example, may be willing to testify or otherwise provide information against a suspect even though her husband and family do not know she was sexually attacked. Prevailing cultural and religious mores, the mental anguish and consequences for her family life if the woman's family discovered the truth, could justify the Tribunal suppressing her identity. In some cases such guarantees may be the only way to convince women to give evidence.

The fact-finders must have a particular awareness of cultural and religious mores and expertise in collecting such evidence with sensitivity. The Tribunal should specifically hire investigators and prosecutors with this type of experience and sensitivity if cases involving rape, sexual abuse and forced prostitution are to be successfully prosecuted without causing unnecessary trauma for the victims and their families. Experience shows that victims and witnesses in such cases are often more likely to confide in and trust other women. Female investigators and prosecutors with the necessary expertise should be available for these cases. Particularly if trial judges are given a more inquisitorial role akin to the practice in some civil law jurisdictions, it will be essential for female judges to be involved in these cases.

11. RIGHTS TO COMPENSATION, RESTITUTION AND REHABILITATION

Victims or their dependents have an enforceable right in international law to claim restitution, compensation and rehabilitation from those responsible for violations of their human rights[53]. The Tribunal should have the power to order a convicted person to

---

[51]. See generally, Amnesty International, **Women in the Frontline**, AI Index: ACT 77/01/91, March 1991, esp. pp.18-24.

[52]. Report of UN Special Rapporteur on the former Yugoslavia to the 49th session of the UN Commission on Human Rights, cited in footnote 21 above, paras.51 & 52.

[53]. Last year the UN General Assembly reaffirmed the "right of victims of 'ethnic cleansing' to receive reparation for their losses", UNGA Resolution 47/147, 18 December 1992, para. 11. The Sub-Commission on Prevention of Discrimination and Protection of Minorities also recognised on 13 August 1992 the right to full reparation for losses suffered as a result of "displacement", E/CN.4/Sub.2/1992/52, 18 August 1992.

provide compensation and restitution to a victim or dependents, for injury caused by the criminal act, in accordance with the UN Declaration on Victims[54]. This would be especially appropriate where the crime was clearly the cause of the victim's loss and the accused retains property which he or she could be ordered to return to the victim.

In addition, however, Amnesty International urges the Security Council to indicate in detail, at the same time as it creates the Tribunal, what mechanism will be established to protect the civil rights of victims and their dependents to compensation, restitution and rehabilitation for gross violations of human rights and humanitarian law. This could include the establishment of a separate international commission to process claims against individuals as well as claims against states, similar to the fund and commission established following the 1991 Gulf War[55].

The Security Council should also expressly provide that facts established during a criminal trial are deemed to be proved for the purposes of subsequent civil proceedings at the national or international level. Subsequent civil proceedings could then focus on assessing the injury and appropriate remedies. Acquittal of an accused in the criminal trial, however, should not prejudice the success of subsequent civil proceedings relating to similar facts, as the standard of proof and procedural rules will be different in a civil case.

12. RELATIONSHIP BETWEEN INTERNATIONAL AND NATIONAL JURISDICTIONS

National authorities have the primary obligation to bring perpetrators of human rights violations to justice. If such trials are fair and just there is no reason for the verdict to be disturbed. Recent trials in the former Yugoslavia, however, amply demonstrate the real doubts about the fairness of many such trials. If a person has been convicted at the national level in a trial which was unfair, or if the trial was a sham, perhaps in an attempt to avoid justice, the international Tribunal could and should retry that person if the crimes are within its jurisdiction[56]. The conviction and punishment imposed by a national court would have no effect if the Tribunal is seized with the case. The Statute should set out the criteria on which the Tribunal may determine that a national trial was unfair or a sham and that a person could be retried.

Conversely, on the assumption that a trial before the International Tribunal will be fair and just, the Statute should expressly prohibit the retrial of that person by a national court. This is necessary to help prevent the staging of subsequent trials for purely political motives.

Because of the primary role of national courts, Amnesty International supports the proposal that the Tribunal should be able to transfer cases down to the national authorities. However, the Statute should enumerate several conditions which should be satisfied before

---

[54]. This could include, for example, compensation to cover the cost of bringing up children resulting from rape.

[55]. Pursuant to Security Council Resolution 687 (1991), paras 16 & 18. Reference should also be made to the Council of Europe, 1983 Convention on the Compensation of Victims of Violent Crimes, which came into force on 1 February 1988. In the context of the Yugoslav conflicts, the Commission on Human Rights and the General Assembly have reaffirmed that states are to be held accountable for violations of human rights which their agents commit upon the territory of another State, see UN Commission on Human Rights Resolution 1992/s-1/1, 14 August 1992, UNGA Resolution 47/147, 18 December 1992, para. 10.

[56] The rule against double jeopardy, embodied in ICCPR Article 14(7), does not prohibit the trial in different jurisdictions of the same person in relation to the same facts. It therefore does not present the Tribunal from trying a person who has been already convicted or acquitted by a national court.

the transfer is approved, only some of which are provided for in the various proposals. Clearly, the international Tribunal should consider whether the trial at the national level will be just and effective, comply with all international fair trial guarantees, and be carried out by a court which is manifestly independent and impartial. In addition, Amnesty International would oppose transfer of the accused if the national court could impose the death penalty, or if the accused faced a genuine risk that his or her fundamental human rights would be violated. The accused should have a right to appeal against a decision to transfer to the national court.

13. RIGHTS OF APPEAL

There is considerable divergence between civil law and common law systems on the scope of the right of appeal. The starting point for Amnesty International is the guarantee in ICCPR Article 14(5) that "everyone convicted of a crime shall have the right to his conviction and sentence being reviewed by a higher tribunal according to law". There is general agreement that in relation to the Tribunal both the convicted person and the prosecutor should be able to appeal on questions of law.

There is disagreement about whether to allow any appeal on questions of fact. Amnesty International does not consider it is sufficient merely to reject the right to appeal on the facts, as the French proposal concludes, on the assumption that "the great formality of the trial and the publicity attracted by it would constitute major safeguards for the defendant"[57] On the contrary, the highly politicised nature of these trials may jeopardize the fairness of the trials. What ICCPR, Article 14(5) primarily demands is that the convicted person must be able to rectify a miscarriage of justice, regardless whether the mistake is described as one of fact or law. The Statute should therefore allow a convicted person to challenge a manifestly unfounded finding of fact by the trial court. It does not matter in substance whether this amounts to an appeal on the facts or a claim that the manifestly unfounded finding of fact resulted from a misapplication of substantive or procedural law.

In addition, both the convicted person and the prosecution should be able to appeal against the sentence imposed and also seek a revision of the judgment if decisive new evidence comes to light. The Statute will have to set out the procedure if a revision of the judgment is sought after the Tribunal has been dissolved.

In all cases it will be for the appeal court to determine the appropriate remedy, whether to acquit the convicted person or to return the case for retrial according to law or to substitute another judgment for the lower court judgment or to alter the sentence.

To guarantee impartial and objective justice, the appeal court should be clearly separate from the trial court, either through an independent chamber of the trial court or by creating a different institution. The appeal proceedings should follow the same fair trial standards guaranteed at the trial.

14. PENALTIES AND SUPERVISION OF SENTENCES

Amnesty International unconditionally opposes the imposition of the death penalty and welcomes the fact that the French, CSCE and Italian proposals all exclude capital

---

[57]. French proposal, *opcit* para.140.

punishment. Amnesty International takes no position on the imposition of other appropriate penalties, except that it would oppose the systematic imposition of penalties that bear little relationship to the seriousness of the offences.

It is not clear where convicted persons will be imprisoned and wether they will be under the control of national or international authorities. If specific national authorities are to be responsible, Amnesty International considers that decisions about pardons, compassionate release and remission of sentences should not be left to the sole discretion of the national authorities. Any review or supervision of such decisions should be carried out by an international body which is impartial and independent.

Regardless of where prisoners are located and who is responsible for them, the conditions of their imprisonment should never fall below minimum international standards. Amnesty International has already recommended above that the Body of Principles and the Standard Minimum Rules should be incorporated as binding obligations in the Statute.

In line with Principles 32 and 33 of the Body of Principles, detainees should have a continuing right to complain about their treatment, ultimately to a judicial authority. Amnesty International considers that either the *ad hoc* Tribunal or some other independent and impartial international body should continue to supervise the imprisonment by having the authority to hear applications from the imprisoned person or his or her family.

15. RESOURCES

All of the Tribunal's powers and safeguards will be of little use unless it is given adequate human and financial resources. Even with a generous allocation of investigators, prosecutors, judges, experts and support staff, the size of the whole institution would probably number in the hundreds rather than the thousands. In comparison, UNPROFOR has more than 23,000 personnel and costs more than US $40 million every month. If the Tribunal is starved of resources, members of the UN, and the Security Council in particular, will be guilty of turning the whole process into a political gesture.

At this stage no one knows how many cases should be investigated and how many will be brought to trial. While the Tribunal could begin as a relatively modest exercise, it must be flexible from the outset to be able to increase the staff and resources rapidly to meet demand. An arbitrary, maximum number of judges, investigators and prosecutors should not be rigidly fixed in the Statute.

Investigators, prosecutors and judges will need the resources to hire expert advice, including in the fields of forensic science, medicine, psychology, law, fact-finding and research, information technology, translation and military affairs. The protection of victims, their families and witnesses on their behalf will need special attention. Mention has already been made of the need to employ specialists at all stages of the process to deal with particular crimes such as rape and sexual abuse, or those committed against children.

J. LETTER DATED 6 APRIL 1993 FROM THE PERMANENT REPRESENTATIVE OF BRAZIL TO THE UNITED NATIONS ADDRESSED TO THE SECRETARY-GENERAL

A/47/922, S/25540, 6 April 1993.

Upon instructions, I have the honour to forward herewith the text of a memorandum by the Government of Brazil on aspects related to the implementation of Security Council resolution 808 (1993), of 22 February 1993, regarding the establishment of an international tribunal for the prosecution of persons responsible for serious violations of international humanitarian law committed in the territory of the former Yugoslavia since 1991.

I should be grateful if you would have the present letter and its annex circulated as a document of the General Assembly, under agenda items 91, 97 (c), 129 and 143, and of the Security Council.

(Signed) Ronaldo Mota SARDENBERG
Ambassador
Permanent Representative of Brazil
to the United Nations

ANNEX

Memorandum dated 31 March 1993 by the Government of Brazil on aspects related to the implementation of Security Council resolution 808 (1993)

1. Brazil has condemned in the strongest terms the serious war crimes and crimes against humanity committed in the ongoing conflict in the territory of the former Socialist Federal Republic of Yugoslavia. Those horrendous acts have shocked and outraged the Government of Brazil and Brazilian society. They call for strong action by the international community, including through the United Nations, to uphold the fundamental values of justice and the dignity of the human person. There can be no doubt that the perpetrators of such crimes must be held personally accountable for their acts and must be brought to justice.

2. To that end, the Government of Brazil favours the establishment of an international tribunal to prosecute and try persons found to be responsible for serious violations of international humanitarian law committed in the territory of the former Socialist Federal Republic of Yugoslavia since the outbreak of conflict in 1991. In that spirit, Brazil voted in favour of Security Council resolution 808 (1993) of 22 February 1993 and attaches great importance to the work now being carried out by the Secretary-General in preparing the report to be submitted to the Security Council in accordance with paragraph 2 of that resolution.

3. The discussions and studies carried out for some time by the International Law Commission concerning the possibility of an international criminal jurisdiction and the related subject of a draft code of crimes against the peace and security of mankind are indicative of the legal and practical difficulties involved in the structuring and the operation of any such international jurisdiction. Not only are those difficulties of a technical nature, but they also relate to the problem of ensuring the political support that is required for an international court to be a meaningful institution.

4. The creation of an international criminal tribunal ought to reflect a careful and comprehensive examination of the extremely complex issues involved in this initiative. To that end, a wide spectrum of consultations with legal experts from different countries and different legal systems should prove to be extremely useful. Prior studies undertaken on this and related subjects, as

well as the records of intergovernmental discussions and deliberations, such as those undertaken in the Sixth Committee of the General Assembly, can also provide valuable elements for the success of the endeavours resulting from resolution 808 (1993).

5. The Government of Brazil has carefully considered the suggestions submitted by other Member States, notably those contained in the documents recently presented to the Security Council by France (S/25266), Italy (S/25300) and Sweden, on behalf of the Chairman-in-Office of the Conference on Security and Cooperation in Europe (CSCE) (S/25307). Brazil expresses its appreciation for the suggestions set out in those documents, which can constitute, in many aspects, important inputs for the work to be carried out by the Secretariat.

6. The general position of the Government of Brazil on this question was expressed in the statement made in the Security Council by the delegation of Brazil on the occasion of the adoption of resolution 808 (1993) (see S/PV.3175, pp. 4-7). The following additional comments refer to specific aspects related to the implementation of that resolution. The Government of Brazil deems it important that these points be duly taken into account in the deliberations relating to the implementation of resolution 808 (1993).

7. The international tribunal referred to in paragraph 1 of resolution 808 (1993) should be an ad hoc independent non-political body. It should be impartial and effective in its work. All stages and aspects of its work must be accomplished in strict observance of the due process of law.

8. The international tribunal should be based on a solid legal foundation that ensures, in a transparent and unobjectionable manner, the legitimacy of its decisions. Legitimacy is required, first and foremost, as an essential element inherent in the idea of justice, but also as an important factor for the effectiveness of the work of the tribunal.

9. The question of the method by which the tribunal is to be established calls for particular attention.

10. It should be established in such a way as to allow it to have jurisdiction over all cases of serious violations of international humanitarian law committed in the territory of the former Yugoslavia by any of the parties to the conflict during an agreed period of time.

11. The international system is based on the existence of a plurality of equally sovereign States. In such a system, which lies at the very foundation of the United Nations, the assertion and the exercise of criminal jurisdiction are essential attributes of national statehood. As a result, criminal jurisdiction cannot be presumed to exist, virtually or in actuality, at the international level.

12. Except under very special circumstances, such as those which prevailed at the end of the Second World War and which made possible the establishment of the Nuremberg and Tokyo International Military Tribunals, criminal jurisdiction can only exist, and be exercised, at the international level if and when it is conferred upon an international body by the State or States concerned.

13. In the light of the above, the most appropriate and effective method for establishing the international tribunal referred to in resolution 808 (1993) would appear to be along the lines suggested in the proposal for an international war crimes tribunal for the former Yugoslavia prepared by the CSCE rapporteurs (S/25307). That method would include the conclusion of a convention setting up an ad hoc international jurisdiction and containing the terms of reference for its exercise, including the text of the statute of the international tribunal.

14. Reference should also be made in this regard to the report of the committee of jurists presented by France, in which, although preference is expressed by the authors for the establishment of an ad hoc tribunal by a resolution of the Security Council adopted under Chapter VII of the Charter of the United Nations, possible alternative solutions are also discussed (S/25266).

15. The role of the Security Council regarding the establishment and functioning of the tribunal should remain within the limits of the very considerable powers expressly entrusted to it by the Members of the United Nations in accordance with the Charter. The Government of Brazil is not convinced that the competence to establish and/or exercise a criminal jurisdiction is among the constitutional powers of the Security Council.

16. If the tribunal were to be established as a subsidiary organ of the Security Council or as an organ otherwise subordinated to the Council, its independence and impartiality could be questioned.

17. There is a need for a clear and unambiguous definition of the law to be applied by the tribunal, not least as regards the characterization of the crimes to be punished. The relevant international instruments in force in the territory of the former Socialist Federal Republic of Yugoslavia provide an important basis in this regard.

18. The work of the tribunal must be carried out with full respect for the human rights and fundamental freedoms of the defendants. International legal instruments in the field of human rights, especially the International Covenant on Civil and Political Rights, and generally accepted principles of criminal law must be fully respected.

19. This consideration is valid for all aspects of the work of the tribunal, including the assessment of penalties, one of the most sensitive questions related to the establishment of an ad hoc international criminal jurisdiction. In particular, it is essential that no form of cruel, inhuman or degrading punishment be included among the penalties to be imposed by the tribunal.

20. If the members of the Security Council do decide to create the tribunal by a resolution of the Council, consideration should be given to the adoption of measures that would ensure the participation and involvement in this process, through the General Assembly, of the whole membership of the United Nations. In particular, it should be provided that the members of the tribunal be elected by the General Assembly and the Security Council, in a procedure analogous to that applicable to the election of the members of the International Court of Justice, so as to ensure that the body as a whole is based on equitable geographical representation and adequately represents the principal legal systems of the world.

21. Consideration could also be given to other suggestions for involving the General Assembly in the process of establishing the tribunal, such as that contained in paragraph 44 of the document submitted by France (S/25266).

22. It is the hope of the Government of Brazil that an effective international tribunal will be established, on a solid legal basis, to prosecute and try the persons responsible for the heinous war crimes and crimes against humanity committed in the territory of the former Socialist Federal Republic of Yugoslavia. Brazil stands ready to participate in deliberations to that end, on the basis of the report to be submitted to the Security Council by the Secretary-General.

K. LETTER DATED 5 APRIL 1993 FROM THE PERMANENT REPRESENTATIVE OF THE RUSSIAN FEDERATION TO THE UNITED NATIONS ADDRESSED TO THE SECRETARY-GENERAL

S/25537, 6 April 1993.

I have the honour to transmit to you, pursuant to paragraph 2 of Security Council resolution 808 (1993), a draft statute of the international tribunal to hear cases relating to crimes committed in the territory of the former Yugoslavia, with the relevant explanatory notes.

I should be grateful if you would have the text of this letter and the draft statute, together with the explanations, distributed as a document of the Security Council.

(Signed) Y. VORONTSOV

Annex I

Statute of the International Tribunal to hear cases relating to crimes committed in the territory of the former Yugoslavia

Article 1. Establishment of the Tribunal

An International Tribunal (hereinafter called "the Tribunal") is hereby established to hear cases relating to crimes falling within its jurisdiction under this Statute committed in the territory of the former Yugoslavia.

Article 2. Organs of the Tribunal

The organs of the Tribunal shall be:

(a) The Judicial Branch of the Tribunal (hereinafter called "the Judicial Branch"), composed of:

- The Court of First Instance;

- The Appellate Court;

- The Plenum of the Judicial Branch;

(b) The Bureau of the Tribunal for investigation and prosecution (hereinafter called "the Bureau");

(c) The Registry of the Tribunal (hereinafter called "the Registry");

[(d) The Special Committee on crimes in the former Yugoslavia (hereinafter called "the Committee")].

Article 3. The Court of First Instance

1. The Court of First Instance shall be composed of 15 judges elected by the Committee from among candidates nominated by States participating in the Conference on Security and Cooperation in Europe (CSCE). Each State shall nominate one candidate.

[1. The Court of First Instance shall be composed of 15 judges elected according to the procedure established for the election of members of the International Court of Justice [, mutatis mutandis].]

2. To try each case in the Court of First Instance, a chamber composed of three judges shall be established.

Article 4. The Appellate Court

1. The Appellate Court shall be composed of nine judges elected from among candidates nominated by States represented in the Committee. Each State shall nominate one candidate.

2. To try each case in the Appellate Court, a chamber composed of three judges shall be established.

Article 5. Judges

Judges shall be elected from among persons of high moral character, who possess the qualifications required in their country of nationality for appointment to the highest judicial offices. No two members of the Judicial Court may be nationals of the same State.

Article 6. Plenum of the Judicial Branch

1. The Plenum of the Judicial Branch shall be composed of the judges of the Court of First Instance and the judges of the Appellate Court.

2. The Plenum of the Judicial Branch shall elect a President from among the judges of the Appellate Court and a Vice-President from among the judges of the Court of First Instance.

Article 7. Rules of the Tribunal

1. The Plenum of the Judicial Branch shall adopt the Rules of the Tribunal, subject to approval by the Committee.

2. The Rules of the Tribunal shall contain, inter alia, the rules of procedure of the Court of First Instance, the Appellate Court, the Plenum of the Judicial Branch and the Bureau.

Article 8. Procedure for the adoption of decisions in the Judicial Branch

1. Decisions of the Plenum of the Judicial Branch shall be adopted by a majority of votes of the total number of judges.

In the event of an equality of votes, the President shall have a casting vote.

2. Decisions of the Court of First Instance and of the Appellate Court in chambers shall be adopted by a majority of votes of the members, who may not abstain in the vote.

Article 9. The Bureau

1. The Bureau shall be composed of 35 members elected by the Committee from among candidates nominated by States represented in the Committee. Each State shall nominate two candidates.

2. The requirements specified in article 5 of this Statute shall apply to members of the Bureau.

3. The Committee shall appoint from among the members of the Bureau a Chief Prosecutor and a Deputy Prosecutor, who shall not be nationals of the same State.

4. The members of the Bureau shall not include more than two nationals of the same State.

Article 10. The Registry

1. The Registry shall perform administrative, technical and organizational duties to ensure the smooth functioning of the Tribunal.

2. The Committee shall appoint a Registrar of the Tribunal to head the Registry of the Tribunal.

3. The Registrar of the Tribunal shall recruit and appoint the staff required for the performance of the Registry's functions.

Article 11. The Committee

1. The Committee shall be composed of representatives of the founding States of the Tribunal and representatives of States which have applied to participate in the Tribunal in accordance with the procedure provided for in article 35 of this Statute.

2. The founding States of the Tribunal shall be the States members of the Security Council and the States formed on the territory of the former Yugoslavia.

3. Each of the States referred to in paragraph 1 shall appoint a representative to the Committee.

4. The Committee shall elect a President and a Vice-President.

5. In addition to the functions specified in other articles of this Statute, the Committee shall adopt the budget of the Tribunal and the Financial Regulations of the Tribunal and shall establish the Staff Regulations for the staff of the Registry.

6. The Committee shall adopt its own rules of procedure.

7. With the exception of decisions relating to the election of judges and members of the Bureau, the decisions of the Committee shall be adopted by consensus. If a consensus cannot be achieved, the President shall suspend the meeting for 24 hours for consultations. If at the end of 24 hours a consensus has not been achieved, a decision shall be taken by a two-thirds majority of the representatives of States present and voting, including the concurring votes of representatives of all the permanent members of the Security Council.

8. A quorum of the Committee shall consist of two thirds of the representatives of the founding States of the Tribunal and of States which have applied to participate in the Tribunal in accordance with the procedure provided for in article 35 of this Statute.

Article 12. Crimes within the jurisdiction of the Tribunal

1. The following crimes shall be within the jurisdiction of the Tribunal:

(a) Military crimes such as serious violations of the Geneva Conventions for the protection of war victims of 12 August 1949 or the Protocols Additional thereto of 8 June 1977, or legislation which is not contrary to international law and which, at the time the crime was committed, was in force in the State formed on the territory of the former Yugoslavia in which the crime was committed, and any other military crime characterized as such under the generally recognized rules of international law;

(b) The crime of genocide, as defined in the provisions of the Convention on the Prevention and Punishment of the Crime of Genocide of 9 December 1948 or in legislation which is not contrary to international law and which, at the time the crime was committed, was in force in the State formed on the territory of the former Yugoslavia in which the crime was committed;

(c) Crimes against mankind, as defined under the generally recognized rules of international law and as reflected, in particular, in the Charter of the International Military Tribunal and the relevant resolutions of the General

Assembly of the United Nations or in legislation which is not contrary to international law and which, at the time the crime was committed, was in force in the State formed on the territory of the former Yugoslavia in which the crime was committed;

(d) Acts of torture, as defined in the relevant provisions of the Convention against Torture and Other Cruel, Inhuman or Degrading Treatment or Punishment of 10 December 1984 or in legislation which is not contrary to international law and which, at the time the crime was committed, was in force in the State formed on the territory of the former Yugoslavia in which the crime was committed.

2. The fact that an act or omission is or is not punishable under internal law does not affect the characterization of the act or omission as a crime falling within the jurisdiction of the Tribunal.

3. The crimes specified in paragraph 1 shall fall within the jurisdiction of the Tribunal if they were committed since 1 January 1991:

(a) In the territory of the former Yugoslavia;

(b) In places which are not under the sovereignty of any State if the perpetrator or the victim is a national of one of the States formed on the territory of the former Yugoslavia.

Article 13. Individuals subject to the jurisdiction of the Tribunal

Individuals accused of the crimes specified in article 12 of this Statute shall be subject to the jurisdiction of the Tribunal, irrespective of their nationality.

Article 14. Principles of criminal responsibility

1. The crimes specified in article 12 of this Statute shall be deemed to have been committed by any individual who:

(a) Committed such a crime directly; and/or

(b) Organized or directed the commission of such a crime; and/or

(c) Attempted to commit such a crime or was associated in some way with the commission of such a crime, or incited others to commit such a crime, or deliberately assisted others in the commission of such a crime.

2. An individual who, of his own accord and prior to any proceedings, has refused to carry out to its conclusion any crime specified in article 12 of this Statute shall be subject to the jurisdiction of the Tribunal only if the act actually committed by him constitutes another crime under article 12 of this Statute.

3. The official position of an individual who commits a crime specified in article 12 of this Statute and, in particular, his position as head of State or the responsible official of any Government department shall not be regarded as grounds for relieving him of responsibility or mitigating the penalty.

4. The fact that an individual who has committed a crime specified in article 12 of this Statute acted pursuant to an order of a Government or a superior does not relieve him of criminal responsibility if the Tribunal deems that, in the circumstances which existed at the time the crime was committed, it was possible for him not to comply with that order.

[Article 15. Non-applicability of statutory limitations

No statutory limitations shall apply to the crimes specified in article 12 of this Statute.]

Article 16. Non bis in idem

1. No one shall be tried or punished for a crime under this Statute for which he has already been convicted or acquitted by the Tribunal.

2. Subject to the provisions of paragraph 3, no one shall be tried or punished by the Tribunal for a crime under this Statute in respect of an act for which he has already been convicted or acquitted by a national court, provided that, if a penalty was imposed, it has been enforced or is in the process of being enforced.

3. Notwithstanding the provisions of paragraph 2, an individual may be tried and punished by the Tribunal for a crime under this Statute if the act which was the subject of a trial and judgement as an ordinary crime corresponds to one of the crimes specified in this Statute.

4. In handing down its judgement, the Court shall take into account any penalty imposed and enforced under a judgement previously handed down in respect of the commission of the same act.

Article 17. Judicial guarantees

An individual charged with a crime under this Statute shall be entitled without discrimination to the guarantees recognized under the generally accepted rules of international law and the general principles of law. In particular, he shall be presumed innocent until proved guilty and, inter alia, have the rights:

(a) To a fair and public hearing;

(b) To be informed promptly and in detail in a language which he understands of the nature and cause of the charge against him;

(c) To have adequate time and facilities for the preparation of his defence and to communicate with counsel of his own choosing;

(d) To have legal assistance of his own choosing during the preliminary examination;

(e) To be tried without undue delay;

(f) To be tried in his presence and to defend himself in person or through legal assistance of his own choosing;

(g) To be informed, if he does not have legal assistance, of this right, and to have legal assistance assigned to him and, without payment by him in any such case if he does not have sufficient means to pay for it;

(h) To examine, or have examined, the witnesses against him and obtain the attendance and examination of witnesses on his behalf under the same conditions as witnesses against him;

(i) To have the free assistance of an interpreter if he cannot understand or speak the language used during the preliminary examination or the hearing;

(j) Not to be compelled to testify against himself or to confess guilt.

Article 18. Organization of the work of the Bureau

1. The Bureau shall carry out an investigation upon the receipt of the relevant information concerning acts which may be categorized as crimes under this Statute.

2. The Special Rapporteur appointed pursuant to resolution 1992/S-1/1 of 14 August 1992 of the United Nations Commission on Human Rights and the impartial Commission of Experts established pursuant to Security Council resolution 780 (1992) of 6 October 1992 shall provide the Bureau with the information referred to in paragraph 1.

The information referred to in paragraph 1 may be provided to the Bureau by the Fact-Finding Commission established pursuant to article 90 of Protocol 1 of 1977 Additional to the Geneva Conventions on the protection of war victims of 1949 and also by non-governmental humanitarian organizations.

3. The Bureau may ex officio collect the information referred to in paragraph 1.

4. A decision to carry out an investigation shall be taken by a majority of the members of the Bureau. In the event of an equality of votes, the Chief Prosecutor shall have a casting vote.

5. In the event that a decision to carry out an investigation is not taken, the organization which provided the information referred to in paragraph 1 shall be notified. That organization may present its comments in that connection to the Bureau.

6. The competence of the Bureau to carry out an investigation, the procedure for carrying out an investigation and the rights of the individual under investigation shall be defined in the Rules of the Tribunal in accordance with the generally recognized rules of international law, the general principles of law recognized by the world community and this Statute.

The Bureau, in particular, shall have the right to call and examine witnesses, to ask for and receive evidence, to call experts and to receive their findings.

Article 19. Referral to the Court of First Instance

1. Upon conclusion of its investigation, the Bureau shall take a decision, stating the reasons on which it is based:

(a) To close the case; or

(b) To refer the case to the court of the State in whose territory the acts characterized by the Bureau as crimes, were committed or in which the individual who committed those acts or the victim of those acts is resident, if those acts, albeit characterized by the Bureau as crimes, cannot, in the Bureau's opinion, be characterized as crimes defined in this Statute; or

(c) To refer the case to the Court of First Instance.

2. In the cases referred to in paragraph 1 (c), an indictment shall be drawn up and referred to the Court of First Instance.

The indictment shall contain, in particular, an indication of the place and time of commission of the acts characterized by the Bureau as a crime under this Statute; a description of these acts, the means by which they were committed and their motives and consequences; evidence attesting to the commission of a crime and to the guilt of the defendant; arguments adduced by the defendant in his defence and the results of the verification of those arguments; the exact wording of the charge and an indication of the points of law on which it is based; and, where necessary, other elements.

Article 20. Proceedings in the Court of First Instance

1. The proceedings shall be conducted in accordance with the Rules of the Tribunal.

2. The proceedings shall be conducted in public in one of the chambers of the Court of First Instance, unless the chamber decides to conduct the proceedings in camera in the interests of law and order or for considerations related to the privacy or safety of the victim, the defendant or the witness, or where the special circumstances of the case are such that public proceedings might prejudice the interests of justice.

3. Without prejudice to the rights of the defendant established by article 17, paragraph (f), of this Statute, the case may be considered in his absence.

Article 21. Judgements of the Court of First Instance

1. Judgements of the Court of First Instance shall be adopted by a majority of the votes of the judges constituting the chamber and shall be delivered in public.

2. Judgements of the Court of First Instance shall be drawn up in accordance with the Rules of the Tribunal. [Dissenting opinions by the judges shall be annexed to the judgement.]

3. A judgement of the Court of First Instance shall enter into force, shall be considered final and shall be enforceable upon the expiry of the appeal period established by article 23 of this Statute, if no appeal has been lodged against it during that period.

Article 22. Penalties

1. Subject to the provisions of paragraph 3, for the crimes in article 12 of this Statute, the Court shall designate the penalties established under the legislation of the State in which the crime was committed which was in force at the time the crime was committed.

2. If a crime has been committed in a place which is not under the sovereignty of any State, the Court shall designate a penalty provided for under the legislation of the State of which the perpetrator is a national or the State of which the victim is a national, which was in force at the time the crime was committed.

3. Sentence of death shall not be imposed. When determining the penalty, the Court shall take into account any extenuating or aggravating circumstances.

Article 23. Appeal

1. An appeal against a judgement of the Court of First Instance may be lodged with the Appellate Court within a period of 30 days from the date on which a copy of the judgement is handed to the convicted person.

2. An appeal may be lodged by the convicted person or, at his request, by his counsel, or by the prosecutor in the given case, or by the Chief Prosecutor. An appeal may be concerned only with points of law.

Article 24. Proceedings in the Appellate Court

Proceedings in the Appellate Court shall be conducted in accordance with the provisions of article 20 of this Statute, mutatis mutandis.

Article 25. Decision of the Appellate Court

1. The provisions of article 21, paragraphs 1 and 2, of this Statute shall apply, mutatis mutandis, to decisions of the Appellate Court.

2. A decision of the Appellate Court shall be final and enforceable.

Article 26. Review of the judgement

1. A judgement which has entered into force may be contested in the Appellate Court by the Bureau or by the convicted person, if, after the judgement is rendered, one or more circumstances come to light which could have a decisive influence on the judgement.

2. An appeal against a judgement shall be considered by a chamber of the Appellate Court. Judges who participated in the consideration of the case in question may not form part of this chamber.

3. If a chamber of the Appellate Court determines that there are grounds to conduct proceedings with a view to revising the judgement, it may adopt a decision:

(a) To grant a stay of execution;

(b) To take the case under its own consideration and to set aside the finding of guilt;

(c) To refer the case to the Court of First Instance for a new hearing.

Article 27. Execution of judgements

1. At the discretion of the Court and subject to the provisions of paragraph 3, a judgement shall be executed in the State in whose territory the crime was committed, or in the State of which the perpetrator is a national.

2. Execution of the judgement shall be effected in accordance with the legislation of the State in which the judgement is to be executed just as if it had been rendered by a court of that State, regardless of the fact that the acts in respect of which the judgement has been rendered may not be considered crimes under the legislation of that State or that, if they are considered crimes, different penalties are prescribed for them than that prescribed in the judgement.

3. If, having rendered a judgement, the Court should consider that due execution of the judgement cannot be ensured in the State designated in paragraph 1, it may decide that the judgement shall be executed in one of the States which have expressed their willingness to accept convicted persons.

4. The execution of sentences shall be monitored by the Bureau in accordance with the Rules of the Tribunal.

Article 28. Pardon

The State in which the judgement is executed may approach the Committee regarding a pardon or the mitigation of a penalty. In that event, it shall address to the Committee a duly substantiated request for a pardon or the mitigation of a penalty. The Committee shall adopt a decision within 30 days from the date of receipt of such request. The pardon shall be granted or the penalty mitigated by the State in which the judgement is executed.

Article 29. Competence of the Tribunal and the obligation of States to provide assistance

1. The Judicial Branch or the Bureau may request any State to provide assistance in the exercise of its functions, including, inter alia, the conduct of appropriate judicial procedures and the production of the corresponding information.

The Judicial Branch or the Bureau may adopt a decision to take into custody an individual who is charged with or suspected of the commission of a crime specified in this Statute, if such action is necessary for the investigation or for the administration of justice.

2. Each State shall render assistance to the Tribunal in the exercise of its functions, including, inter alia, the conduct of appropriate judicial procedures and the production of the corresponding information.

Each State shall render assistance to the Tribunal by tracking down, arresting and handing over to the Tribunal an accused or suspected person.

For the purposes of handing over such persons, the Tribunal shall not be regarded as a court of a foreign State.

Article 30. Ensuring the execution of the decisions of the Tribunal

1. The Plenum of the Judicial Branch or the Bureau may determine that any decision of the Court or the Bureau, as the case may be, is not being executed by a particular State. In that case, the Plenum of the Judicial Branch or the Bureau, as the case may be, shall notify the Committee of the situation that has arisen.

2. On the basis of the notification referred to in paragraph 1, the Committee may draw the attention of the State concerned to the failure to execute the decision of the Tribunal and may insist on execution within the prescribed period.

3. If, in the view of the Committee, its request is not being complied with, it may request the Security Council to adopt measures to ensure that the Tribunal's judgement is executed.

4. Upon receipt of the Committee's request, the Security Council may adopt a decision to take such measures under the Charter of the United Nations as it deems essential to ensure execution of the Tribunal's judgement.

Article 31. Privileges and immunities

1. Judges, members of the Bureau and the Registrar shall enjoy diplomatic privileges and immunities in the exercise of their duties.

2. The staff of the Registry, the counsel of the defendants, the experts and the witnesses shall enjoy such privileges and immunities as are accorded to persons of comparable status associated with the International Court of Justice.

3. The Committee may adopt a decision to withdraw the immunity of members of the Bureau.

4. The Plenum of the Judicial Branch may adopt a decision to withdraw the immunity of the Registrar, the counsel of the defendants, the experts and the witnesses.

Article 32. Seat of the Tribunal

The seat of the Tribunal shall be established at ...

Article 33. Financial questions

Financial questions relating to the work of the Tribunal shall be governed by the Financial Regulations of the Tribunal, which shall be adopted by the Committee and approved by the Security Council of the United Nations.

Article 34. Languages

1. The official and working language of the Tribunal shall be English.

2. The Court may adopt a decision to use another language in the consideration of any case.

Article 35. Participation in the Tribunal

1. After the adoption of this Statute, States which are not founding States of the Tribunal may submit an application to participate in the Tribunal.

2. The application referred to in paragraph 1 shall be addressed to the Registry of the Tribunal.

3. The Registrar shall notify all the States specified in article 11, paragraph 1, of this Statute of the receipt of an application referred to in paragraph 1.

4. Thirty days after the date of notification referred to in paragraph 3, the State submitting the application referred to in paragraph 1 shall become a participant in the Tribunal.

Annex II

Explanatory notes on the draft Statute of the International Tribunal to hear cases relating to crimes committed in the territory of the former Yugoslavia

The Russian draft Statute of the International Tribunal to hear cases relating to crimes committed in the territory of the former Yugoslavia has been prepared by a group of lawyers under the auspices of the Legal Department of the Ministry of Foreign Affairs of the Russian Federation. The group comprised, in addition to a number of members of the Legal Department: G. Tunkin, Corresponding Member of the Russian Academy of Sciences, President of the Russian Association of International Law, Head of the Faculty of International Law of Moscow State University; V. Vereshchetin, Professor, member of the United Nations International Law Commission, Deputy Director of the Institute of State and Law of the Russian Academy of Sciences; K. Gutsenko, Professor, Head of the Faculty of Criminal Procedure of Moscow State University; and S. Kelin, Professor, Senior Fellow of the Institute of State and Law of the Russian Academy of Sciences.

The draft is based on the possibility that a Tribunal might be established and its Statute adopted by a decision of the Security Council of the United Nations taken in accordance with Articles 24, 29, 39 and 41 of the Charter.

In this context, for the preparation of the constituent instrument of the Tribunal, it is proposed that a subsidiary organ of the Security Council should be established - a Special Committee on crimes in the former Yugoslavia - to be composed of representatives of the States members of the Security Council and the States formed on the territory of the former Yugoslavia. After the adoption of the Statute, the Committee will exercise important functions in expediting the work of the Tribunal. For this purpose, the Committee could become one of the organs of the Tribunal or could operate outside the framework of its structure, but in close liaison with it (articles 2, 7, 9, 11, 28 and 30 of the draft Statute).

With a view to promoting the universal nature of the Tribunal, the draft establishes (in article 35) a procedure whereby, once the Statute has been adopted, any State may apply to participate in the Tribunal and, accordingly, become part of the Committee, which will thus consist of the founding States and States which have availed themselves of the aforementioned procedure (article 11).

Under the draft Statute, the Tribunal will hear cases relating to military crimes, crimes against mankind, the crime of genocide and acts of torture, committed in the territory of the former Yugoslavia. The crimes in question will be those committed since 1 January 1991 (article 12), since Security Council resolution 808 (1993) refers to crimes committed since 1991. At the same time, there are grounds for considering another date, namely, 25 June 1991, since, from a legal standpoint, it was from that date that the new States of the territory of the former Socialist Federal Republic of Yugoslavia started to emerge.

In view of the importance which the situation in the territory of the former Yugoslavia has for the continent of Europe, a procedure has been established by which the candidature of judges would be submitted by the States participating in the Conference on Security and Cooperation in Europe (CSCE) (article 3). At the same time, bearing in mind that the Tribunal is to be established within the framework of the United Nations, the procedure established for the election of judges to the International Court of Justice could be used, _mutatis mutandis_, for the formation of the Court of First

Instance. A different procedure is provided for the formation of the Appellate Court: the election of judges by the above-mentioned Committee (article 4). For the characterization of crimes, it is proposed that the Court should apply international law and - provided that it is not contrary to international law - internal law (article 12), and in the handing down and execution of penalties, the law of the State in which the crime was committed and in which the judgement is to be executed, as appropriate (articles 22 and 27).

The draft Statute establishes the generally recognized right of the defendant to be tried in his presence and, at the same time, without prejudice to this right, provides for the possibility of considering a case in the absence of the defendant (in the event, for example, of the defendant's failure to appear) (article 20).

In the draft Statute, the death sentence is not permitted (article 22).

The draft Statute is based on the obligation of all States to render every assistance to the Tribunal, including the obligation to hand over the persons concerned at its request. The provision that, for the purposes of handing over such persons, in accordance with the Statute, the Tribunal shall not be viewed as a court of a foreign State (article 29) is particularly important.

In so far as the Tribunal, in the event that it is established as a subsidiary organ of the Security Council, will be set up within the framework of Articles 39 and 41 of the Charter of the United Nations, a mechanism is proposed which involves the participation of the Security Council in ensuring the execution of the decisions of the Tribunal (article 30).

The draft Statute is provisional in nature and contains certain alternative texts in square brackets.

In the event that the Statute of the Tribunal is adopted (or confirmed) by a resolution of the Security Council, it would be advisable to provide for its entry into force within a specified period, for example, 60 days, and to invite the States which have been formed on the territory of the former Yugoslavia to convey their agreement with the statute within this period. Agreement could be explicit or tacit (no objection). If no agreement is reached, the Security Council, upon expiry of the specified period, would reconsider the situation as it then stood.

L. LETTER DATED 5 APRIL 1993 FROM THE PERMANENT REPRESENTATIVE OF THE UNITED STATES OF AMERICA TO THE UNITED NATIONS ADDRESSED TO THE SECRETARY-GENERAL

S/25575, 12 April 1993.

Resolution 808 (1993) requested the Secretary-General to submit a report to the Security Council containing options for the charter of an international tribunal for prosecution of persons responsible for violations of international humanitarian law in the former Yugoslavia, taking into account suggestions put forward by Member States.

Following consultations with your office, I have the honour to forward herewith for consideration by you in the preparation of this report, the United States Government's views and proposals. We hope that our submission proves helpful to you.

I would appreciate it if you would have this paper circulated as a document of the Security Council.

(Signed) Madeleine K. ALBRIGHT

Annex I

Creation of an international tribunal for violations of international humanitarian law in the former Yugoslavia

Pursuant to Security Council resolution 808 (1993), the United States offers the following views and proposals for the creation of an international tribunal for the prosecution of persons responsible for violations of international humanitarian law in the former Yugoslavia.

In our view, the Tribunal should be established by the international community to enforce international standards. The Security Council has the authority under Chapter VII of the Charter of the United Nations to create such a tribunal, and is the appropriate body to do so. The process should not be limited to a single regional group. The Tribunal should apply substantive and procedural law that is internationally accepted.

The Tribunal must be fair and be seen as fair. It must therefore respect basic norms of due process, including: an impartial and independent trial court; a prosecutorial authority independent from the trial court; the participation of defendants in their own defence; the right to appeal to an independent appellate panel; and the observance of fundamental rights of defendants, including the right to counsel, to public proceedings, to cross-examine witnesses and to present evidence.

Finally, the process for establishing the tribunal should be designed to bring it into existence at an early date. The Security Council is in a position to do so in accordance with the procedure set forth in resolution 808 (1993). The alternative of establishing a tribunal by treaty would, in our view, be much less effective and take much more time. This alternative would require a lengthy process of negotiation, conclusion and ratification; and it might lead to the absence of important States at the time the tribunal begins its work.

Accordingly, we propose that the following specific steps be taken in establishing the tribunal:

1. The Security Council should consider the recommendations to be made by the Secretary-General pursuant to resolution 808 (1993). It should adopt a

resolution under Chapter VII that would formally establish the tribunal and approve its charter.

2. The charter should contain the essential elements of the organization and operation of the tribunal, such as: its composition; the scope of its jurisdiction; the basic procedure for indictment, trial and appeal; the rights of defendants; and the enforcement of its decisions. (A proposed draft charter is attached.) Procedural details would be left to a set of rules to be adopted at a later date. It would be important to develop rules that are fair and that provide appropriate protection for victims who are providing evidence to the tribunal.

3. The Security Council resolution establishing the tribunal should require that States endeavour to take any necessary measures, including the adoption of domestic legislation or the conclusion of subsidiary treaty arrangements, to permit them to comply fully with orders of the tribunal, including those for the surrender of accused persons, the production of evidence and the taking of testimony. The resolution should also require States to provide reasonable assistance to other States in complying with orders of the tribunal.

4. The Security Council should create a subordinate body, comprised of the members of the Security Council, to be known as the Administrative Council. This body would, among other things, exercise general administrative control over the staffing and operations of the Chief Prosecutor and the tribunal, and approve recommendations for financing the tribunal's operations. Such financing should be provided through regular United Nations assessments.

Annex II

Draft charter of the international tribunal for violations of international humanitarian law in the former Yugoslavia

I

ORGANIZATION

A. Tribunal

Article 1. The International Tribunal for Violations of International Humanitarian Law in the Former Yugoslavia (hereinafter referred to as the "Tribunal") is established for the purpose of the just and prompt trial of persons accused of violations of international humanitarian law, as set forth in article 10, committed in the territory of the former Yugoslavia on or after 1 January 1991.

Article 2. The Tribunal shall consist of a Trial Court and an Appeals Court.

(a) The Trial Court shall consist of nine members, who shall preside over trials in panels of three members each. The members of the Trial Court shall by majority vote select from among themselves a Chief Judge of the Trial Court, who shall be an experienced jurist. He or she shall have such administrative responsibilities as the members of the Trial Court shall decide.

(b) The Appeals Court shall consist of nine members, who shall preside over appeals in panels of three judges each. The Appeals Court may consider particular appeals in panels of more than three judges where it determines that this is warranted by the importance of the issues involved or other special circumstances. The members of the Appeals Court shall by majority vote select a Chief Judge of the Appeals Court and the Tribunal from among themselves, who shall be an experienced jurist. He or she shall have such administrative responsibilities as the members of the Appeals Court shall decide.

Article 3

(a) Each member of the Tribunal shall be a person of high moral character and shall have the legal competence and qualifications required for appointment to a criminal court of the State in which that member is resident or of which that member is a national, including preferably experience in the conduct of criminal trials or appeals.

(b) Members of the Tribunal shall be appointed for a term of ___ years, and may only be removed for appropriate cause by the Security Council, which may also appoint alternate Trial Court and Appeals Court judges to serve in the event of disability, recusal or removal of a member of the Tribunal.

(c) The Rules to be adopted pursuant to article 6 shall make provision for the recusal or removal of Tribunal members in particular cases, and for their replacement by alternates, when appropriate.

(d) Except where otherwise provided herein, decisions of the Tribunal shall be made by majority vote of the panel presiding over a trial or appeal.

Article 4. The Tribunal is authorized to establish a Registry and other subsidiary bodies and appoint personnel as it deems necessary to assist it in the performance of its functions.

Article 5. The Tribunal shall have such powers as are necessary and appropriate for the conduct of criminal trials and appeals, including the power:

(a) To issue arrest warrants;

(b) To summon witnesses, to require their attendance and testimony and to put questions to any witness, including the accused person should he testify;

(c) To require the production of documents and other evidentiary materials;

(d) To administer oaths to witnesses;

(e) To conduct or authorize appropriate proceedings, including the taking of evidence on commission.

Article 6. The Tribunal shall, with the approval of the Security Council, adopt Rules of Procedure for the conduct of trials and appeals, the admission of evidence, the protection of witnesses and other sources of information, and other appropriate matters, as well as sentencing guidelines.

Article 7. The Tribunal shall have its seat at _______. This shall not prevent the Tribunal from sitting and exercising its powers elsewhere if it deems appropriate. Subject to the approval of the Security Council, the Secretary-General shall conclude at the earliest possible date an agreement with the Government of __________, and other States as appropriate, concerning the location and operation of Tribunal headquarters; privileges and immunities appropriate for their functions to be accorded to members and personnel of the Tribunal, the Registry and the Office of the Chief Prosecutor, and to counsel of accused persons; the incarceration of accused persons; the protection of witnesses during proceedings, and other relevant matters.

B. The Office of the Chief Prosecutor

Article 8. The Office of the Chief Prosecutor shall be responsible for the investigation and prosecution of defendants before the Tribunal. The Chief Prosecutor:

(a) Shall be a person qualified to perform, and with significant experience in the conduct of, investigations and prosecutions of major criminal cases in the State in which he or she is resident or of which he or she is a national;

(b) Shall be appointed by, report to, and be removable at the discretion of, the Security Council.

Article 9. The Chief Prosecutor is authorized to:

(a) Investigate allegations of violations set forth in article 10 and to collect and preserve evidence relating to those violations;

(b) Request warrants of arrest pursuant to article 14;

(c) Request States to arrest, detain and transfer accused persons pursuant to article 15;

(d) Request assistance from States, including but not limited to the provision of evidence, the identification and location of persons, the taking of testimony and the serving of Tribunal documents;

(e) Issue indictments and accompanying documents. The indictment shall include full particulars specifying in detail the charges against the accused person. A copy of the indictment and of all the documents lodged with the indictment, translated into a language that he or she understands, shall be furnished to the accused person as provided in article 17;

(f) Conduct examinations of witnesses and accused persons, consistent with the rights contained in article 20;

(g) Prosecute individuals against whom indictments have been issued;

(h) Appoint subordinates to carry out such duties as may be assigned to them;

(i) Perform such other acts and functions as may be necessary and appropriate for the purposes of investigation, indictment and prosecution in accordance with this Charter.

II

JURISDICTION AND GENERAL PRINCIPLES

Article 10. The Tribunal shall have the power to try and to punish persons for any of the following violations of international law arising out of the conflict in the former Yugoslavia on or after 1 January 1991:

(a) Violations of the laws or customs of war, including the regulations annexed to the Hague Convention IV of 1907 and grave breaches of the Geneva Conventions of 12 August 1949. For this purpose, the conflict in the former Yugoslavia on or after 25 June 1991 shall be deemed to be of an international character;

(b) (i) Acts of murder, torture, extrajudicial and summary execution, illegal detention and rape that are part of a campaign or attack against any civilian population in the former Yugoslavia on national, racial, ethnic or religious grounds;

(ii) Acts that violate the Convention on the Prevention and Punishment of the Crime of Genocide of 9 December 1948.

Article 11. There shall be individual responsibility for the violations set forth in article 10.

(a) The fact that an accused person acted pursuant to order of his or her Government or of a superior shall not free him or her from responsibility, unless the accused person did not know and could not reasonably have been expected to know that the act ordered was unlawful. In all cases where the order is held not to constitute a defence, the fact that the individual was acting pursuant to orders may be considered in mitigation of punishment if the Tribunal determines that justice so requires.

(b) An accused person with military or political authority or responsibility is individually responsible if violations described in article 10 were committed in pursuance of his or her order, directive or policy. An accused person is also individually responsible if he or she had actual knowledge, or had reason to know, through reports to the accused person or through other means, that troops or other persons subject to his or her control were about to commit or had committed such violations, and the accused person failed to take necessary and reasonable steps to prevent such violations or to punish those committing such violations.

(c) The official position of an accused person, including as a Head of State or a responsible official in a Government, shall not be considered as freeing him or her from responsibility or grounds for mitigating punishment.

(d) Those who conspired to commit or who were accomplices to any of the violations in article 10 are individually responsible for such violations.

Article 12

(a) The fact that a person has been detained, tried, acquitted or punished by a State or States shall not preclude the detention, trial or punishment of that person by the Tribunal for the same acts if the Tribunal determines that there were violations of this Charter not comprehended in the prior prosecution or that the prior prosecution was not diligently prosecuted before an impartial tribunal. In considering the punishment of such a person, the Tribunal shall take fully into account any punishment of that person by a national court for the same acts.

(b) The Tribunal may, at its discretion, defer to the prosecution of an accused person by a State or States, when it is satisfied that such trial will be in the interests of justice and without prejudice to its authority under paragraph (a). The Office of the Chief Prosecutor may also assist in the investigation and prosecution of persons by a State or States.

Article 13. The Tribunal shall not initiate the trial of a person charged with violations under this Charter in his or her absence.

III

APPREHENSION AND DETENTION OF ACCUSED PERSONS AND LEGAL ASSISTANCE

Article 14

(a) At the request of the Chief Prosecutor, the Trial Court shall issue warrants of arrest for an accused person, upon a finding that there is a reasonable basis to believe that he or she has committed a violation as set forth in article 10.

(b) From the time of coming into the custody of the Tribunal, accused persons shall have the right, which they may waive:

- Not to be compelled to testify against themselves or to confess guilt and to be informed of this right;

- To legal assistance; to have legal assistance assigned to them, without payment by them in any such case if they do not have sufficient means to pay for it; and to be informed of this right.

Article 15. Upon presentation of a warrant of arrest and supporting documentation by the Chief Prosecutor that there is a reasonable basis to believe that he or she has committed a violation as set forth in article 10, a State shall arrest, detain and transfer persons identified in the warrant and in its custody or found within its territory to the custody of the Tribunal.

Article 16

(a) Upon receiving an order of the Tribunal pursuant to article 5 for the production of evidence, the identification and location of persons, the taking of testimony and the service of Tribunal documents, a State shall provide the assistance ordered by the Tribunal.

(b) States shall give prompt consideration to other requests for assistance by the Chief Prosecutor pursuant to article 9.

Article 17

(a) Without delay after an accused person comes into the custody of the Tribunal, there shall be a hearing at which an indictment shall be presented to the Trial Court and to the accused person.

(b) The accused person shall have the right to give an explanation relevant to the charges made against him or her and to enter a plea.

(c) After this hearing, the Trial Court shall decide whether there is reasonable cause to hold the accused person over for trial.

Article 18. The Trial Court has the authority to order pre-trial detention or to grant conditional release. Any such detention shall be in a State chosen by the Tribunal from a list of States that have agreed to detain persons for this purpose.

Article 19. The Trial Court shall ensure fair and expeditious hearings of all matters before it. To that end, it shall:

(a) Confine the trial to the issues raised by the indictment;

(b) Impose appropriate restrictions or punishment on participants in proceedings before the Trial Court for violation of decorum or refusal to comply with the rules and orders of the Trial Court.

IV

RIGHTS OF THE ACCUSED PERSON AFTER PRELIMINARY HEARING

Article 20. Accused persons shall be presumed innocent until proved guilty beyond a reasonable doubt in a public trial. From the time of the Trial Court's decision to hold the accused person over for trial under article 17 (c), each accused person shall have the rights guaranteed under international law and by this Charter, including the right:

(a) To be informed promptly and in detail, in a language which the accused person understands, of the nature and cause of the accusation against him or her;

(b) To be informed of the evidence supporting the accusation against him or her, and to be provided any exculpatory evidence in the possession of the Chief Prosecutor;

(c) To have adequate time and facilities for the preparation of a defence and communication with defence counsel;

(d) To be tried without undue delay;

(e) To be tried in his or her presence, and to defend him- or herself in person or through legal assistance of his or her own choosing; to be informed, if he or she does not have legal assistance, of this right; and to have legal assistance assigned to him or her, without payment by him or her in any such case if he or she does not have sufficient means to pay for it;

(f) To examine or have examined witnesses against the accused person and to obtain the attendance and examination of witnesses on his or her behalf under the same conditions as witnesses against him or her;

(g) To have the free assistance of an interpreter at all phases of the proceedings against him or her if the accused person cannot understand or speak the language used in court;

(h) Not to be compelled to testify against him- or herself or to confess guilt and not to have his or her failure to make any statement or explanation used against him or her;

(i) To appeal the judgement and sentence of the Trial Court in accordance with article 24 of this Charter.

V

JUDGEMENT AND SENTENCING

Article 21. The Trial Court shall have the power to sentence convicted persons to imprisonment or other appropriate punishment.

Article 22. Imprisonment shall be in a State chosen by the Trial Court from a list of States that have agreed to imprison persons for this purpose.

Article 23. Complaints about the conditions of imprisonment shall be made to national authorities or to the Tribunal and, after it has ceased operations, to the Security Council.

VI

APPEALS

Article 24

(a) Upon written notice filed within 30 days of the date of entry of judgement, a convicted person shall have the right to appeal to the Appeals Court a conviction on the grounds that the Trial Court committed an error of law invalidating the decision, or an error of fact that caused a manifest miscarriage of justice.

(b) An application for reversal of a conviction may also be made to the Appeals Court, or, if the Tribunal has ceased operating, to the Security Council, upon discovery of some fact of such a nature as to be a decisive factor, which fact was, when the judgement was given, unknown to the Court and to the convicted person. The application for reversal of conviction must be made within six months of discovery of the new fact.

(c) The Rules adopted pursuant to article 6 may also provide for interlocutory appeals by the accused person or Chief Prosecutor of other matters.

Article 25. After the convicted person's appeal is exhausted, or if the convicted person elects not to exercise the right to appeal, the convicted person may seek clemency or commutation of his sentence from the Security Council.

M. LETTER DATED 13 APRIL 1993 FROM THE PERMANENT REPRESENTATIVE OF CANADA TO THE UNITED NATIONS ADDRESSED TO THE SECRETARY-GENERAL

S/25594, 14 April 1993.

I enclose comments prepared by the Government of Canada with respect to United Nations Security Council resolution 808 (1993) and the creation of an ad hoc tribunal to try charges of war crimes in the former Yugoslavia.

I should be grateful if you would have this letter and the enclosed comments circulated as a document of the Security Council.

(Signed) Louise FRÉCHETTE
Ambassador
Permanent Representative

Annex

Canadian comments with respect to United Nations Security Council resolution 808 (1993) and the creation of an ad hoc tribunal to try charges of war crimes in the former Yugoslavia

1. Canada supports the recent decision of the United Nations Security Council to establish an international criminal tribunal to prosecute individuals responsible for serious violations of international humanitarian law committed in the territory of the former Yugoslavia since 1991. We believe that there is authority, under Chapter VII of the Charter of the United Nations, for the Security Council to adopt a resolution to create an ad hoc tribunal designed specifically to restore and maintain peace and security in the former Yugoslavia.

Concurrent jurisdiction

2. Canada believes that the jurisdiction of the tribunal should be concurrent with that of national courts. Given that there may, in some circumstances, be concern that national courts might not comply with international standards, where the ad hoc tribunal chooses to exercise its jurisdiction in a particular case it should have preferential jurisdiction over national courts.

3. Canada takes the position that no one shall be liable to be tried or punished again for an offence for which he or she has already been finally convicted or acquitted, as set out in article 14 of the International Covenant on Civil and Political Rights, except where the matter was not diligently prosecuted in the national courts or international standards for the protection of human rights were not met.

Structure of the tribunal

4. While Canada supports the view that the Security Council define the structure of the tribunal and the extent of its jurisdiction by resolution, for practical reasons we believe that the tribunal should be given authority to establish detailed rules of procedure and admissibility of evidence on a priority basis once the tribunal is created and before prosecutions begin.

5. With respect to the appointment of officials to the ad hoc tribunal, Canada favours a system similar to that provided for in the Conference on Security and Cooperation in Europe (CSCE) draft proposal. Each State Member of the United Nations should be encouraged to nominate judges, prosecutors or other court officials with appropriate backgrounds and criminal law experience. The Secretary-General or the Security Council could then draw on the list of nominees to make appointments as required.

6. The continued contribution of the United Nations Commission of Experts to investigate war crimes in the former Yugoslavia, created by Security Council resolution, and the Commission's role in ongoing investigations, should also be ensured by specific reference in the Security Council resolution establishing the ad hoc tribunal.

Jurisdiction

7. With respect to the subject-matter jurisdiction of the ad hoc tribunal, it is essential that the principle of nullem crimen sine lege, nulla poena sine lege (there should be no crime except according to predetermined fixed law; there should be no crime without penalty) be applied.

8. Canada takes the position that serious violations of both customary and conventional international humanitarian law which fall within the competence of the ad hoc tribunal should be clearly articulated by the United Nations Security Council rather than merely incorporated by reference. The conduct prohibited and the required accompanying mental state should be expressly stated.

9. Security Council resolution 808 (1993) decided to establish a tribunal for the prosecution of "persons responsible for serious violations of international humanitarian law". Canada interprets serious violations of international humanitarian law to include:

(a) Violations of the laws or customs of war, including grave breaches of the Geneva Conventions and Additional Protocol I;

(b) Crimes against humanity under customary or conventional law including such acts as wilful killing and deliberate mutilation, extrajudicial and summary execution, sexual assault, slavery, torture, illegal detention, deportation, forced labour or any other inhumane act or omission that is committed against any civilian population or any identifiable group of persons, and that constitutes a contravention of customary international law or conventional international law; and

(c) Acts which violate the Convention on the Prevention and Punishment of the Crime of Genocide and the Convention against Torture and Other Cruel and Inhuman or Degrading Treatment or Punishment.

10. Canada suggests that no person should be tried for an offence in respect of a serious violation of international humanitarian law within the competence of the ad hoc tribunal if he or she was under the age of 12 years when the act or omission occurred. Any prosecution of young persons, over the age of 12 years when the act or omission occurred, should be conducted in accordance with the Convention on the Rights of the Child.

Law to be applied for purposes of interpretation

11. For the purposes of prosecution, offences within the subject-matter of the tribunal should be defined and interpreted in accordance with international conventions, international custom as evidence of a general practice accepted as law and the general principles of law recognized by civilized nations. Prosecutions should be conducted as violations of international law rather than national law. However, if necessary for interpretive purposes, reference may be made to appropriate national law.

Principles of liability

12. Principles of liability and forms of complicity, instigation and conspiracy to commit a crime within the jurisdiction of the tribunal must be specifically and clearly defined. Guilt by association, or the creation of offences based purely on membership in a de jure or de facto group whose primary or subordinate goal is to commit crimes coming within the jurisdiction of the tribunal is not acceptable. In the context of the jurisdiction of the ad hoc tribunal, Canada supports the position that the principles governing criminal liability which hold superiors accountable for the crimes of their subordinates and generally exclude the defence of acting pursuant to superior order should be applied.

Procedural guarantees

13. Canada places great importance upon safeguarding the defendant's procedural guarantees as provided for in article 14 of the International Covenant on Civil and Political Rights and similar provisions in other international conventions or national law. On this basis, we would oppose the possibility of taking proceedings against defendants in their absence, despite the practical difficulties that may exist with respect to transfer of the accused for trial. Canada is also against creating "rebuttable presumptions" or "reverse onus" crimes on the basis that this infringes on a defendant's right to be presumed innocent until proven guilty. Although Canada does not insist that the adversarial system of procedure be adopted, we do take the position that both the prosecution and the defence should have a residual right to call and cross-examine witnesses if the court controls this process.

14. Canada takes the position that adequate procedural guarantees must be in place to protect witnesses so as to avoid exacerbating harm already suffered by the victims.

Penalties

15. Canada strongly opposes the imposition of the death penalty, notwithstanding that the offence committed may be of a particularly heinous nature.

Appeals

16. Procedures for appeal, review and revision must be established for the ad hoc tribunal despite any practical difficulties that these proceedings may present.

N. LAWYERS COMMITTEE FOR HUMAN RIGHTS

19 April 1993.

H.E. Boutros Boutros-Ghali
Secretary-General
The United Nations
New York, New York 10017

Dear Mr. Secretary-General:

In United Nations Security Council Resolution 808, the Council expressed its desire to receive proposals for the establishment of an international tribunal to prosecute violations of international humanitarian law in the former Yugoslavia. The Lawyers Committee for Human Rights submits this letter, which outlines some of our broad concerns, and an appendix, which provides more detailed recommendations.

The Lawyers Committee is an independent, non-governmental organization. Its work is impartial, holding each government to the standards affirmed in the International Bill of Human Rights. This letter was prepared with assistance from the law firm of Cravath, Swaine & Moore. We submit our comments after having reviewed submissions that have already been made by the Organization of the Islamic Conference, the Commission on Security and Cooperation in Europe, and the governments of France, Italy and the United States.

We believe that the most important priority for the United Nations is to act expeditiously to establish an independent tribunal. The continuing violence against civilian non-combatants, including rape, torture and killing, constitutes grave breaches of international law, and the perpetrators of these crimes must be held accountable.

We view the establishment of an international tribunal, as proposed under Resolution 808, as an important undertaking which should begin as soon as possible. By establishing the Tribunal, the Security Council will send a clear signal to the combatants, and those who direct them, that persons who have committed rape, torture, killing or other acts in violation of international law will be tried and punished. The immediate establishment of the Tribunal may also deter future violations.

We recognize that the ongoing war in the former Yugoslavia imposes significant limitations. In the near term, these limitations will impair the Tribunal's ability to conduct meaningful trials of many potential defendants. We do not favor the trial of defendants *in absentia*.

At the same time, we strongly urge that the Tribunal be established now and immediately begin its work with the full support of the United Nations and with adequate resources and independence to carry out successfully its important mandate. In cases where prosecutors can quickly compile sufficient evidence to prosecute and where jurisdiction can be obtained over specific defendants, trials should go forward.

An Office of the Chief Prosecutor should be established immediately. The Chief Prosecutor's office should begin gathering, analyzing and preparing existing evidence for use in future trials. The Chief Prosecutor's office should prepare and publicly disseminate detailed indictments.

The United Nations should commit itself, as a matter of priority, to assist the Office of the Chief Prosecutor and the Tribunal in their efforts to arrest and extradite all persons indicted by the Chief Prosecutor. In addition, every Member State of the United Nations should be obliged to take all necessary steps to enforce the orders and decisions of the Tribunal and to arrest and transfer indicted persons in their countries to the jurisdiction of the Tribunal.

The Tribunal will be effective only if it is genuinely independent and fully funded -- insulated from outside political pressure or influence from the Security Council or any other entity. The Tribunal must also be viewed as independent by each of the parties to the conflict and by others in the international community. Both the Tribunal and the Office of the Chief Prosecutor must be structured, financed and administered to avoid the appearance of outside pressure or influence.

We have identified several principles that we believe should guide the establishment of the Tribunal and the Office of the Chief Prosecutor to help ensure their independence.

- There should be a full discussion of the process for the selection of trial court and appellate judges and the criteria for their selection. In the appendix to this letter, we set out one possible selection system. Several of the proposals you have already received describe other approaches. The particular approach the United Nations chooses to adopt is less important than achieving a broad consensus that the selection process is fair and reinforces the Tribunal's independence. A decision on the selection process should be made expeditiously.

- There should be a similar discussion of the process and criteria for the selection of the Chief Prosecutor. In the appendix to this letter, we propose one possible selection process; you have before you several other proposals. As with the selection of the judges, there should be an open discussion of the various proposals. It is more important that the selection process is widely viewed as fair, than that any one procedure or set of criteria be adopted.

- Once these selection procedures and criteria are in place, the judges and the Chief Prosecutor should be selected as expeditiously as possible. The United Nations, through your Office and the Security Council, should underscore the high priority for the immediate establishment of the Tribunal and Office of the Chief Prosecutor and the commitment of adequate funds and other necessary resources to help ensure the effective operation of these bodies.

- We favor allowing the Tribunal, once established, to carry out its own administrative functions, a measure which will reinforce its independence. Similarly, the Chief Prosecutor should have the authority to administer his or her office, including the recruitment and selection of staff.

- The funding of both the Tribunal and the Chief Prosecutor's office must be adequate to carry out this effort in a meaningful way. These funds should be allocated immediately from the United Nations' general operating budget. In the appendix, we propose that funds allocated to the Tribunal be held in an account established under the auspices of the International Court of Justice. Funds allocated at the outset to pay for the work of the Chief Prosecutor's office should be maintained in an account established under the auspices of the Security Council.

- We favor delegating substantial decision-making authority to the Tribunal to establish its own rules of procedure. The Tribunal's discretion should be limited only by a few broad requirements consistent with the right of fair trial as guaranteed by the International Bill of Human Rights.

The attached appendix provides a brief outline of several areas where the Lawyers Committee believes that the articulation of broad requirements may be necessary.

We hope these comments and suggestions are useful. We stand ready to assist the United Nations, the Tribunal or the Chief Prosecutor's office in whatever ways we can to help advance this important process.

Respectfully submitted,

Marvin E. Frankel
Chairman

Michael Posner
Executive Director

APPENDIX

Composition of the Trial Court

The Trial Court should have fifteen members, who should preside over trials in three-judge panels.

Composition of the Appeals Court

The Appeals Court should have nine judges, who should preside over appeals in three-judge panels. In cases of important or controlling questions of law, or where there are special circumstances, the Appeals Court may decide to sit *en banc*.

Criteria for Selection of Judges

Judges should be persons of high moral character, integrity and independence. They should have legal competence and qualifications in criminal law, as well as relevant international law. The selection criteria should be designed to ensure diversity in terms of geographic origin, gender and religion.

Appointment of Judges

The Secretary-General should select the judges, subject to approval by a two-thirds majority of the Security Council. The judges should be selected from a pool of candidates submitted by the Presidents or Chairs of the International Court of Justice, the European Court of Human Rights, the Inter-American Court of Human Rights, the African Commission on Human and Peoples' Rights and the Human Rights Committee (representing the various United Nations treaty bodies). There should be no more than one judge from any one country on the Trial Court and no more than one judge from any one country on the Appeals Court.

Term of Service

Members of the Tribunal should be appointed for a renewable term of three years. They should be removable only for cause, by a two-thirds vote of the Security Council.

Administration of the Tribunal

The Chief Judge of the Tribunal should be a member of the Appeals Court. He or she should be selected by a majority of the members of the Trial and Appeals Courts.

The Chief Judge should have administrative responsibility for the Tribunal. Funds for the Tribunal should be drawn from a special account established by the United Nations and administered through the International Court of Justice.

The Office of the Chief Prosecutor

The Office of the Chief Prosecutor should be responsible for the investigation and prosecution of defendants before the Tribunal. It will be expected to collect and develop evidence relating to the violations. When the evidence warrants, the Chief Prosecutor's office should issue public indictments and, for defendants who are before the Tribunal, conduct trials of indicted defendants.

The Chief Prosecutor should have administrative responsibility for the office. Funds for the Office of the Chief Prosecutor should be drawn from a special account established by the United Nations and administered through the Security Council.

Criteria for the Selection of the Chief Prosecutor

The Chief Prosecutor should be a person of high moral character, integrity and independence. He or she should have criminal law experience, including experience in the investigation and prosecution of criminal cases. He or she should also have a working knowledge of relevant international law.

Appointment of the Chief Prosecutor

The Chief Prosecutor should be appointed by a two-thirds vote of the Security Council. He or she should be selected from a pool of candidates submitted by the Presidents or Chairs of the International Court of Justice, the European Court of Human Rights, the Inter-American Court of Human Rights, the African Commission on Human and Peoples' Rights and the Human Rights Committee (representing the various United Nations treaty bodies).

Term of Service

The Chief Prosecutor should be appointed for a renewable term of three years. He or she should be removable with or without cause by a two-thirds vote of the Security Council.

Applicable Law

The Tribunal should have power to try and punish persons for violations of war crimes, crimes against humanity and any other violations of international law arising out of the conflict. The Tribunal's jurisdiction should include acts of torture, rape, killing, prolonged arbitrary detention or other violations of customary human rights law.

The Tribunal should not be precluded from trying those who were previously tried and acquitted by national courts or tribunals.

Provision of Legal Assistance

From the time of coming into the custody of the Tribunal, accused persons should have the right to legal assistance and to counsel of their choice. If they do not have sufficient means to pay for such assistance, it should be provided, without cost to the accused, by the Tribunal.

Rules of Evidence

The members of the Tribunal should determine the rules of evidence subject to the following principles:

A. The Tribunal should admit all probative evidence. It should endeavor to balance this broad rule of admissibility against the defendant's right to confront accusers. We recommend that a rule be adopted that would require convictions to be based on substantial testimony from percipient witnesses. This would forbid a conviction based solely on evidence that was not subject to cross-examination.

B. The rules of evidence should include measures for the protection of victims and witnesses from reprisal, particularly with respect to victims of torture and rape.

Extradition and Trials in Person

United Nations Member States should be obliged to take all necessary steps to enforce the orders and decisions of the Tribunal. Member States should establish extradition procedures which will enable them to arrest and transfer indicted persons to the jurisdiction of the Tribunal. The Tribunal should not initiate the trial of a person in his or her absence.

Principles of Criminal Liability

Individual defendants should be charged and tried for their own conduct and not solely for their membership in a group or association. Individuals should be held responsible for their acts and should not be permitted to assert a defense that their acts were those of a sovereign for which they individually are not responsible. The Tribunal should adhere to the requirements of *mens rea* and *actus reus*.

The defense of superior orders should not be available if the accused knew or should have known that the order he was given was unlawful. A superior officer should be held criminally responsible for crimes committed by a subordinate if the superior was in a command position, had the ability to prevent the crimes, and had actual knowledge, or intentionally avoided knowledge, of the commission of the crimes.

Judgment and Sentencing

The Trial Court should have the power to sentence convicted persons to imprisonment or other appropriate punishment. The death penalty should not be imposed.

Appeals

A convicted person should have the right to appeal his or her conviction to the Appeals Court. The Appeals Court should reverse a conviction if the Trial Court committed an error of law or fact that has caused a serious miscarriage of justice.

O. LETTER DATED 20 APRIL 1993 FROM THE PERMANENT REPRESENTATIVE OF SLOVENIA TO THE UNITED NATIONS ADDRESSED TO THE SECRETARY-GENERAL

S/25652, 22 April 1993.

Pursuant to paragraph 2 of the Security Council resolution 808 (1993), I would like to transmit, enclosed herewith, the letter from H.E. Mr. Lojze Peterle, Minister for Foreign Affairs of Slovenia, dated 16 April 1993, addressed to the Secretary-General, expressing the views of Slovenia with regard to the establishment of an ad hoc international tribunal for war crimes committed on the territory of some States in the region of the former Socialist Federal Republic of Yugoslavia.

I should be grateful if you would have this letter and its annex circulated as a document of the Security Council.

(Signed) Danilo TÜRK
Permanent Representative

Annex

Letter dated 16 April 1993 from the Minister for Foreign Affairs of Slovenia addressed to the Secretary-General

Pursuant to paragraph 2 of Security Council resolution 808 (1993), dated 22 February 1993, I should like to report on certain views that Slovenia holds with regard to the establishment of an ad hoc international tribunal for war crimes committed in the territory of some States created in the region of the former Socialist Federal Republic of Yugoslavia.

As I have already made clear in my letter of 26 February 1993, Slovenia supports the establishment of such a tribunal, which would prosecute those responsible for grave war crimes committed in the territories of Bosnia and Herzegovina and Croatia. My Government is convinced that the establishment of such a tribunal is a necessary and very important step, given the fact that those responsible for such crimes would be judged by an impartial judicial body as well as the fact that it could also contribute positively to the finding of solutions for the restoration of peace in the above-mentioned regions. In connection with the resolution and the material which has been prepared on the founding of the tribunal and which my Government has studied (proposals of France (S/25266), Italy (S/25300) and Sweden, on behalf of the Conference on Security and Cooperation in Europe (S/25307)), I should like to inform you of certain suggestions and comments of my Government.

The idea of the establishment of the tribunal has arisen because of the grave, systematic and mass violations of international humanitarian law, violations which have been committed and are still being committed in the territories of Bosnia and Herzegovina and Croatia. Slovenia is not involved in the present conflict in the territory of the aforementioned States. It is true that a few days of armed conflict occurred in Slovenia at the end of June 1991 as a result of the aggression of the Yugoslav People's Army, but the dimensions of this are not comparable with what is happening in the two above-mentioned States. In addition to Slovenia, the former Yugoslav Republic of Macedonia is not nor has been involved in these conflicts and has suffered no armed conflicts in its own territory. We are of the opinion that these facts are not sufficiently reflected in resolution 808 (1993), nor in the aforementioned documents.

These documents continuously speak of crimes committed in the territory of former Yugoslavia. Thus the territorial jurisdiction of the future international court is also determined as being for the entire territory of former Socialist Federal Republic of Yugoslavia.

We think that it would be more logical for the facts noted above to be reflected also in the territorial jurisdiction of the proposed tribunal, so that it would be limited to those regions where mass and grave breaches of humanitarian law and law of armed conflicts have actually taken place and are continuing, for which reason the court is being established, at which point it would also be worth adding that these crimes have been committed after the dissolution of the former Socialist Federal Republic of Yugoslavia. The purpose of these comments is not for Slovenia to avoid the jurisdiction of the tribunal but for us to express our desire that the tribunal's jurisdiction is balanced more with the actual state of affairs.

I should like to once again assure you that Slovenia will cooperate most surely and fully with the tribunal, even if the Security Council decides on some other territorial jurisdiction than the one here proposed. In such a case we would expect our suggestions to find an appropriate place in your report, which will be prepared in accordance with paragraph 2 of the resolution, as well as in the documents which will define the work of the future tribunal in greater detail.

In certain materials, 25 June 1991 is proposed as the starting date for the jurisdiction of the international tribunal. This is the day independence was declared in Slovenia as well as in Croatia. We would like to stress that this day was not associated with any kind of violence, that the declaration of independence was a peaceful act and that this was not an act aimed against anybody. Given this, we are of the opinion that this date is most unsuitable to be linked with the establishment of the tribunal for war crimes.

More suitable would be dates when conflicts arose which mark the beginning of war in the aforementioned States created on the territory of the former Socialist Federal Republic of Yugoslavia. A different approach could also be possible, that is, that the preparations for war are taken into consideration (the sabre-rattling of politicians in Serbia, violence in Kosovo) by way of analogy with the solutions at the trials in Nürnberg in respect of the responsibilities of the political leaders of the Third Reich for making war.

With regard to the jurisdiction of the tribunal _ratione materiae_, we are of the opinion that it should be limited only to those grave breaches committed _en masse_ and systematically. Other violations would fall under the competence of national legislation or courts.

In our opinion the principle of legality (_nullum crimen nulla poena sine lege_) would be most consistently served if the international court applied the provisions of chapter XVI of the Penal Code of the former Socialist Federal Republic of Yugoslavia in the text which was enacted in July 1990. These provisions are in total accordance both with the valid international law governing genocide as well as war crimes and crimes against humanity. Such a course of action is also envisaged in the Swedish proposal, but the authors themselves recognize that they have not been able to study carefully the provisions of the penal code and thus a few changes will have to be suggested. We propose that the international court applies the following articles: 141, genocide; 142, war crimes against the civilian population; 143, war crimes against the wounded and sick (which the Swedish proposal does not mention); 144, war crimes against prisoners-of-war; and 145, organizing groups for and inciting to genocide and war crimes, which includes the policy-makers, the designers of and implementers of plans for executing war crimes, conspiracy, etc.). Apart from this, the following criminal acts would fall within the jurisdiction of the international tribunal: article 148, use of prohibited means of war; article 152, destruction of cultural and historical monuments; and article 152, inciting to military aggression.

The provisions of chapter XVI also differentiate between grave breaches, which are included in the above-mentioned articles, and other criminal acts which are not committed en masse and systematically. The latter are incriminated in the following provisions of this law: article 146, illegal killing and causing of wounds to the enemy; article 147, illegal confiscation of possessions of those killed and wounded in the battlefield; article 148, use of prohibited means of war, if such acts are not committed en masse and systematically; article 149, violation of parliamentary rights; article 150, brutality towards the wounded, patients and prisoners-of-war, if such acts are not committed en masse and systematically.

The above-stated provisions of the Penal Code of the former Socialist Federal Republic of Yugoslavia are valid law in all the States that have been created in the territory of former Yugoslavia. All these States have in their Acts of Independence, in one way or another, and with certain restrictions and appropriate adaptations, accepted the previously valid penal code, but such restrictions do not refer to the above-mentioned acts. The only exception here is the death penalty, which in some States, including Slovenia, has been abolished, but not in Bosnia and Herzegovina. We are of the opinion that this should not be an obstacle to the application of the aforementioned valid legislation, while the international legal document on the establishment of the court could determine the highest and lowest sentence of imprisonment.

We trust that our suggestions and comments will contribute to the most appropriate mandate of the international tribunal and to its effectiveness.

(Signed) Lojze PETERLE
Minister for Foreign Affairs

P. NOTE VERBALE DATED 30 APRIL 1993 FROM THE PERMANENT REPRESENTATIVE OF THE NETHERLANDS TO THE UNITED NATIONS ADDRESSED TO THE SECRETARY-GENERAL

S/25716, 4 May 1993.

The Permanent Representative of the Kingdom of the Netherlands to the United Nations presents his compliments to the Secretary-General of the United Nations and has the honour to submit herewith the observations of the Government of the Kingdom of the Netherlands on the establishment of an international ad hoc tribunal for the prosecution and punishment of war crimes in the former Yugoslavia.

The Permanent Representative would appreciate it if the Secretary-General could have this letter and its annex circulated as a document of the Security Council.

Annex

Observations of the Government of the Kingdom of the Netherlands on the establishment of an international ad hoc tribunal for the prosecution and punishment of war crimes in the former Yugoslavia

1. Introduction

Security Council resolution 808 (1993) states "that an international tribunal shall be established for the prosecution of persons responsible for serious violations of international humanitarian law committed in the territory of the former Yugoslavia since 1991".

In order to contribute to the preparation of a report on the establishment of such a tribunal, as requested in paragraph 2 of the resolution, the Netherlands would put forward the following observations. Given the fact that the Secretary-General has already received several proposals containing draft charters for such a tribunal, the Netherlands will limit its observations to those issues which, in the opinion of the Netherlands, require further consideration. These observations relate to the following topics:

- The legal foundation for a charter;
- The law to be applied by and the competence of the ad hoc tribunal;
- The persons to be prosecuted;
- Trial in absentia;
- The sanctions to be applied;
- The investigation;
- The cooperation of States with the ad hoc tribunal;
- Institutional issues.

2. Legal basis for a charter

The Netherlands is of the opinion that in principle a treaty is the most solid legal basis for the establishment of a tribunal. This applies primarily to permanent tribunals, but would also be preferable in the case of an ad hoc tribunal. Since it is clear that the conclusion of a treaty would be complicated and time-consuming, and since the Security Council has already declared violations of international humanitarian law to be a threat to international peace and security, it seems appropriate under these circumstances for the Security Council to take the further necessary measures with regard to the establishment of an ad hoc tribunal for the former Yugoslavia. Establishment on this basis will also have clear consequences for the functioning and duration of the court.

3. Applicable law and competence of the ad hoc tribunal

As far as the law to be applied by the ad hoc tribunal is concerned, the following considerations should, in the opinion of the Netherlands Government, play an important role.

First, it must be observed that international law itself contains a series of substantive norms, that is to say: provisions explicitly prohibiting certain conduct and declaring this conduct a crime under international law. The application of these international norms by the ad hoc tribunal will not therefore constitute a violation of the principle of *nullum crimen sine lege*. However, these norms lack a specific sanction; they are not formulated in such a way as to allow for direct application by judicial bodies to specific situations and persons. Such specific sanction norms are normally contained in the national law of countries which are party to the relevant treaties. Such treaties limit themselves to imposing an obligation on the parties to "translate" the substantive norms of the treaty into sanction norms (criminal offences) under national law.

Second, it may be observed that the former Yugoslavia was party to a considerable number of universal conventions relating to human rights and humanitarian law. It was, for example, a party to the Convention on the Suppression and Punishment of the Crime of Genocide and to the four Geneva Conventions of 1949 and the 1977 Additional Protocols thereto. On the basis of the principles relating to the succession of States in respect of treaties, the republics which emerged from the former Yugoslavia may be considered to be equally bound by the above-mentioned conventions.

Third, it may be observed that the former Yugoslavia has given effect to the above-mentioned conventions by providing in its national criminal law for sanction norms relating, *inter alia*, to genocide and war crimes. However, it is at the moment unclear to what extent the criminal law which was applicable in the former Yugoslavia is still in force in the new republics.

On the basis of these considerations, the Netherlands favours a system whereby the ad hoc tribunal would prosecute suspects on the basis of violations of substantive norms under international law but would as far as the available sanctions are concerned refer to the national law of the former Yugoslavia, it being understood that in principle the court would not be allowed to impose sanctions of greater severity than those provided for under national law for similar offences. Only if this system is adopted will optimal effect be given to the principle of *nullum crimen, nulla poena sine lege*.

On the basis of the preceding considerations, the competence *ratione materiae* of the ad hoc tribunal would extend to the following:

- War crimes;

- Crimes against humanity.

As far as the definition of war crimes is concerned, reference may be made to the grave breaches enumerated in the Geneva Conventions of 1949 and the First Protocol of 1977. Crimes against humanity, on the other hand, are not explicitly elaborated in international law in substantive norms, with the exception of the crime of genocide. However, it is clear that the crimes which are considered to be crimes against humanity (such as murder, manslaughter, deprivation of liberty, rape and deportation) are prohibited and punishable under the national law of any self-respecting State. In the former Yugoslavia too, these crimes were offences under the criminal code. Although violations of national norms of criminal law will not in general amount to crimes against humanity, under exceptional circumstances they will. Such circumstances are present if the offences are committed as part of the deliberate, systematic persecution of a particular group of people and/or are designed systematically to deprive that group of people of their rights, and if the government, which under national law is bound to prevent and suppress such crimes, tolerates or even assists the commission of such crimes against that group of people. Acts of this kind undermine the norms and principles of the international community. In such cases, therefore, the international community has the right to deal with these offences and to undertake to prosecute and try those who commit them.

4. Persons to be prosecuted

In the French proposal for an ad hoc tribunal (report of the Committee of French Jurists set up to study the establishment of an international criminal tribunal to judge the crimes committed in the former Yugoslavia (see S/25266)) a distinction is made between three categories of perpetrators of the crimes to be prosecuted. The report observes that at both the Nuremberg and the Tokyo trials, the prosecution was limited to the "major war criminals", that is to say to the first of the three categories mentioned in section H of the report.

In the opinion of the Netherlands, a comparable approach might be taken by the ad hoc tribunal in the prosecution of war crimes committed in the former Yugoslavia. This would imply that the following offences in particular should be within the competence of the ad hoc tribunal:

- The fact of having ordered, authorized or permitted the commission of war crimes and/or crimes against humanity, and

- The fact of being in a position "to influence the general standard of behaviour" and having culpably neglected to take action against crimes of that kind. This is the case if the persons concerned should have known of the relevant acts, and could have prevented, terminated, or repressed the commission of those acts, and were duty-bound thereto, but failed to do so.

The fact that prosecution should, in the opinion of the Netherlands, focus on major war criminals does not mean that no action should be taken to investigate offences committed by subordinate personnel. On the contrary, such offences have to have been established, after all, before efforts can be made to determine where the responsibility for these crimes lay. It is advisable, however, to consider from the outset, while investigating individual crimes, whether and to what extent such crimes were committed within a systematic pattern of action or other context which could indicate that responsibility was shared by persons in senior positions. In short, it would be advisable to try to establish from the outset whether the offence was an initiative of the offender (and possibly a number of co-perpetrators) or whether his superiors (leaders) may be considered to have been guilty of complicity in or procuring the commission of the crime.

In the opinion of the Netherlands, such "minor" offenders should not of course remain unpunished. Their prosecution and punishment might, however, be left in principle to national judicial bodies, as soon as the circumstances allow for an impartial and fair trial.

As far as the jurisdiction of the tribunal in relation to the jurisdiction of national courts is concerned, the Netherlands therefore proposes that there should be concurrent jurisdiction, with a primary role for the international tribunal with respect to major war criminals.

5. Trial in absentia

A special problem relates to the question of whether the tribunal should also try suspects in absentia. On the one hand such a procedure may create a situation in which a person, convicted in absentia although not punished, will at least feel unsafe. On the other hand, it is to be expected that such a procedure will be perceived by the public as a sign of the tribunal's weakness. Furthermore, because during the trial in absentia the accused cannot defend himself and cannot contest the evidence, any conviction resulting from such a trial will also be questionable from a legal point of view. It also seems that the verdict will have to be served on the convicted person, in order for the period within which an appeal can be lodged to commence. This will lead to difficulties if that person cannot be found in good time, given that the ad hoc tribunal will only be in existence for a certain period. Given these considerations, the Netherlands prefers not to provide for trial in absentia. After all, the effects of a conviction in absentia on the person concerned can also be achieved in a less time-consuming way. In other words, it would suffice for the prosecuting office to prepare a file on the suspect and to conclude that on the basis of that file serious suspicions exist that the person concerned has committed war crimes or crimes against humanity. As a result of such suspicions, the tracing and prosecution of the suspect may be organized. If the suspect is subsequently arrested, trial can follow.

6. Sanctions to be applied

An appropriate sanction norm has to be created both for war crimes and for crimes against humanity to be applied by the ad hoc tribunal. In the opinion of the Netherlands this sanction norm should be derived from the norms which were applicable under former Yugoslav national law: the sanctions should not be more severe in principle than those imposed under national norms, in order to safeguard the nulla poena sine lege principle. As far as the death penalty is concerned, which was applicable in former Yugoslavia, the Netherlands agrees with the other proposals already submitted to the Secretary-General that this sanction should be ruled out.

A particular problem arises with respect to the prosecution of persons who have already been tried and sentenced by a national judicial body. Although the principle of non bis in idem is not applicable at international level, it would in the opinion of the Netherlands be highly unfair if these national sanctions were not taken into account. Given the primary responsibility of the ad hoc tribunal for the trial of major war criminals in particular, the Netherlands favours the proposals on this issue contained in the report of France (see S/25266) and the United States of America (see S/25575).

7. Investigation and prosecution

The success of the tribunal will largely depend on the question of whether investigation of the atrocities committed in the former Yugoslavia will provide sufficient evidence for the prosecution of the individuals considered responsible for those offences. In the opinion of the Netherlands, after the adoption by the Security Council of a charter for an ad hoc tribunal, priority should be given to the creation of an effective investigation and prosecution apparatus. The later investigations begin, the more difficult it will be to find the necessary evidence for the prosecution of suspects. It is therefore proposed that the investigation and prosecution of crimes committed in the former Yugoslavia should start immediately after the adoption of the charter. At the same time, however, the Netherlands observes that it will be impossible to start trials of suspects before the hostilities in former Yugoslavia have ended.

The investigation and prosecution apparatus should consist of at least several hundred investigators, comprising inter alia public prosecutors, policemen and medical specialists, all with considerable experience in the investigation of serious crimes. At least some of these investigators should have an active knowledge of the languages spoken in the former Yugoslavia in order to avoid problems relating to the translation of statements by witnesses and suspects.

In order to function effectively, the investigators should be invested with the powers of house-search, pre-trial detention, etc., laid down in the code of criminal procedure of the former Yugoslavia. The right to exercise these powers should be conferred by the Security Council resolution adopting the charter of the ad hoc tribunal. This resolution should furthermore provide for an obligation on local authorities to provide all assistance possible to the international investigators.

8. Cooperation of States with the ad hoc tribunal

Chapter VII of the Charter is needed as a legal basis to ensure that all States will cooperate in every possible way with the investigation and prosecution of war crimes in the former Yugoslavia. It is emphasized here that this obligation does not apply only to the former Yugoslav republics but to all United Nations Members. Although most of the evidence must be found in the former Yugoslavia, thousands of former Yugoslav nationals who have witnessed the commission of war crimes and crimes against humanity have fled the country. Furthermore, people suspected of offences may have fled or will flee or attempt to flee to other countries. It is of major importance that these witnesses too may be involved in the investigation and prosecution of the offences and it is of course also very important that persons against whom prima facie evidence is collected relating to the commission of serious offences will be brought before the tribunal either as witnesses or as suspects and will not escape simply by fleeing from former Yugoslav territory.

9. Institutional issues

Composition of the tribunal

The tribunal should be composed in such a way that it will fulfil the requirements which are laid down in several universal and regional human rights instruments. This means inter alia that at least three chambers must be established, dealing with several stages of the criminal proceedings. One chamber should deal with questions relating to pre-trial procedure, such as the need for pre-trial detention of suspects, etc. Another chamber should try the cases at first instance. This investigation must relate to both questions of fact and questions of law. The third chamber should act as a chamber of cassation and appeal. The Netherlands would prefer a procedure which would in principle be linked to questions of law. Only if the judgement of the "second" chamber were to be annulled on this basis, would the "third" chamber be required to issue a final decision on both questions of fact and questions of law.

Whatever system of appeal is chosen, it follows from the "equality of arms" principle that appeal must be equally accessible to the defendant and to the prosecuting office.

The first chamber may be composed of three to five judges, the other two chambers preferably of five judges. When composing these chambers it should be kept in mind that the major legal systems should be represented. Furthermore, it would be advisable to include judges from the former Yugoslavia in these chambers.

In addition, a review and/or a pardon procedure should be available at the request of the convicted person on the basis of new facts or circumstances.

Seat

In the opinion of the Netherlands it is important that the tribunal be a suborgan of the United Nations, entrusted with duties which have to be fulfilled independently. Furthermore, the composition of the tribunal should reflect its universal character. This character derives in the first place from the fact that the tribunal will be established on the basis of a Security Council resolution. Whatever location is chosen as the seat of the tribunal, the possibility should be left open of holding preliminary investigations and trials either in the former Yugoslavia or elsewhere, wherever it is most convenient and efficient.

Q. LETTER DATED 19 MAY 1993 FROM THE CHARGÉ D'AFFAIRES A. I. OF THE PERMANENT MISSION OF YUGOSLAVIA (SERBIA AND MONTENEGRO) TO THE UNITED NATIONS ADDRESSED TO THE SECRETARY-GENERAL

A/48/170,* S/25801,* 21 May 1993.

I have the honour to transmit herewith the letter from His Excellency Mr. Vladislav Jovanović, Deputy Prime Minister and Minister for Foreign Affairs of the Federal Republic of Yugoslavia, addressed to you (see annex).

I should be grateful if you would have the text of the present letter and its annex circulated as an official document of the General Assembly, under item 146 of the preliminary list, and of the Security Council.

(Signed) Dragomir DJOKIĆ
Ambassador
Chargé d'affaires a.i.

ANNEX

Letter dated 17 May 1993 from the Deputy Prime Minister and Minister for Foreign Affairs of the Federal Republic of Yugoslavia to the Secretary-General

Following your report of 3 May 1993 (S/25704) relating to paragraph 2 of Security Council resolution 808 (1993) of 22 February 1993, I am writing to apprise you of the position of the Yugoslav Government.

The establishment of an ad hoc international tribunal by the Security Council for the prosecution of persons responsible for grave breaches of international humanitarian law committed in the territory of the former Yugoslavia since 1991 is a precedent in international law and the work of the United Nations.

Yugoslavia considers that all perpetrators of war crimes committed in the territory of the former Yugoslavia should be prosecuted and punished under national laws, which are harmonized with international law and by competent judicial authorities, in accordance with the principle of territorial jurisdiction.

Since Yugoslavia has already accepted the jurisdiction of international commissions for the investigation of war crimes, which has not been the case with other States, this constitutes additional pressure by the international community on the work of its national judicial authorities engaged in the prosecution and punishment of perpetrators of war crimes.

Yugoslavia is one of the advocates of the idea concerning the establishment of a permanent international tribunal and respect for the principle of equality of States and universality and considers, therefore, the attempts to establish an ad hoc tribunal discriminatory, particularly in view of the fact that grave breaches of international law of war and humanitarian law have been committed and are still being committed in many armed conflicts in the world, whose perpetrators have not been prosecuted or punished by the international community

---

* Reissued for technical reasons.

(Korea, Viet Nam, Algeria, Cambodia, Lebanon, Afghanistan, the Belgian Congo, Iraq, Panama etc.). War crimes are not committed in the territory of one State alone and are not subject to the statute of limitations, so that the selective approach to the former Yugoslavia is all the more difficult to understand and is contrary to the principle of universality.

Yugoslavia has its doubts about the impartiality of the ad hoc tribunal, particularly because of the one-sided approach of the United Nations Security Council to the responsibility for armed conflicts in the territory of the former Yugoslavia and the fact that numerous initiators and advocates of the idea of its establishment have openly stated that this was going to be a tribunal for Serbs. Besides, reports of various international commissions investigating war crimes are biased and unsubstantiated.

In view of the fact that, under the Charter of the United Nations, the Security Council has no mandate to set up such a tribunal or to adopt its statute, it is quite legitimate to question the legal basis for the establishment of the ad hoc tribunal. This is borne out by the opinions of many States and a number of draft tribunal statutes, including the draft of the Conference on Security and Cooperation in Europe (CSCE), to the effect that such a tribunal could be established only by a convention or as a result of decisive influence of the United Nations General Assembly.

In the report by the Secretary-General of 3 May 1993, submitted under paragraph 2 of Security Council resolution 808 (1993), it is said that the international tribunal has been set up on the basis of Chapter VII and Article 29 of the United Nations Charter (S/25704, sect. I).

Yugoslavia wishes to reiterate that the Security Council has no mandate to establish an international tribunal, nor does Chapter VII of the United Nations Charter provide for the establishment of that tribunal. Invocation of Article 29 of the United Nations Charter is legally unfounded and arbitrary, since Article 29 only provides that the Security Council may establish subsidiary organs as it deems necessary for the performance of its functions. It is obvious that such a tribunal is not a subsidiary organ of the Security Council. No independent tribunal, particularly an international tribunal, can be a subsidiary organ of any body, including the Security Council.

The ongoing drive to establish an international tribunal is politically motivated and without precedent in international legal practice, so much so since members of the international community have not been able to agree on the establishment and statute of an international criminal court for decades. The proposed statute of the international tribunal is inconsistent and replete with legal lacunae to the extent that makes it unacceptable to any State cherishing its sovereignty and dignity.

I would like to recall that the international community has held Yugoslav criminal legislation and its judiciary in very high esteem, inter alia, because it has adopted all solutions and achievements of modern criminal law and all international conventions pertaining to international humanitarian law.

The establishment of an ad hoc tribunal is also contrary to the provisions of the Constitution of the Federal Republic of Yugoslavia, which prohibits extradition of Yugoslav nationals. Yugoslavia is not convinced of the need that it alone should amend its constitutional provisions pertaining to extradition, which are otherwise contained in appropriate legal documents of other States as well, even less so if the same obligation is not provided also for other members of the international community.

Yugoslavia is a signatory State of all international conventions in the field of international humanitarian law, its legislation is in full harmony with the provisions of those conventions and it is prepared to comply fully with its international commitments under these conventions.

In advising you of the remarks of the Federal Government on the proposals contained in your report, I wish to inform you that any decision of the Security Council on this issue related to Yugoslavia will have to be approved by the Parliament of the Federal Republic of Yugoslavia as the supreme authority under its Constitution.

PART VIII

PROPOSALS OF STATES AND ORGANIZATIONS FOR THE RULES OF PROCEDURE AND EVIDENCE OF THE INTERNATIONAL TRIBUNAL

A. PERMANENT MISSION OF THE ARGENTINE REPUBLIC TO THE UNITED NATIONS

27 July 1993.
IT/4, 16 November 1993.

The Government of the Argentine Republic wishes to express its satisfaction at the resolve shown by the Security Council in ensuring the establishment and rapid functioning of an international tribunal for the prosecution of those persons responsible for extremely serious violations of humanitarian law committed in the territory of the former Yugoslavia.

Argentina wishes to stress, first of all, its support for resolution 808 (1993) containing the decision to establish this tribunal, and for the effective work carried out by the Secretary-General in compliance with the mandate assigned to him under paragraph 2 of that resolution. It also wishes to express its support for resolution 827 (1993) establishing the International Tribunal and adopting its Statute.

The Argentine Government attaches the utmost importance to the proper functioning of the Tribunal, whose work will be crucial to the prosecution of those persons individually responsible for committing atrocious violations of the laws of war and humanitarian laws.

Argentina further stresses that this Tribunal will be the first such tribunal to function since those established immediately after the Second World War. Hence, it will necessarily serve as a very valuable precedent for other similar initiatives that might be taken in future in other parts of the world. Moreover, despite its character as an ad hoc Tribunal, the influence it would have on the proceedings of a permanent international criminal court, should such a Court be established, is not to be underestimated.

It is therefore of paramount importance that the International Tribunal conduct its proceedings so as to gain the utmost confidence and credibility of international public opinion.

The provisions of the Statute of the International Tribunal, adopted by the Security Council in resolution 827 (1993), are designed to ensure the due legitimacy and transparency of the Tribunal's decisions.

Another essential element in the pursuit of these objectives will be the rules of procedure and evidence applicable to all phases of the proceedings, which must be adopted by the judges of the Tribunal in accordance with the provisions of Article 15 of the Statute.

There is no comprehensive, internationally accepted body of law that can satisfy all these requirements. Therefore, taking into account the urgency with which the International Tribunal must begin to function and render judgements, there is probably no alternative but to rely - as regards certain aspects - on national law or the general practice of tribunals in the former Yugoslavia, with the exception of those proceedings incompatible with the general principles of law recognised by the international community.

In this regard, there is no doubt that, at all times, the work of the International Tribunal should be carried out in full respect for the human rights and fundamental freedoms of the accused.

Consequently, the Argentine Government notes with satisfaction that the Statute, in Article 10, embodies the fundamental principle of "non bis in idem". Furthermore, Article 21 of the Statute includes the minimum guarantees to which the accused is entitled, contained in article 14 of the International Covenant on Civil and Political Rights, which constitute the core of human rights guarantees in the context of criminal justice.

None the less, although such principles have been incorporated in the Statute and despite the international consensus that exists on the protection of the basic rights of the accused, there may be very different approaches to the technical aspects of criminal proceedings.

It is important to recall the at times opposing trends that characterize the Anglo-Saxon and continental legal systems on fundamental questions of procedure, such as those relating to the powers of the parties and of the Tribunal in the conduct of the proceedings, the consideration of pre-trial evidence during the trial, the admission of illegally obtained evidence, etc.

In seeking to provide solutions to these questions, consideration should be given to the need to conduct the proceedings so as to ensure, as already mentioned, the absolute transparency and legitimacy of each and every one of the Tribunal's actions. Nevertheless, the Tribunal should have sufficient flexibility under the rules of procedure established to be able to carry out its work with reasonable effectiveness in the light of the countless material problems that will be posed by the situation in the territory of the former Yugoslavia.

Concerning the distribution of powers between the parties and the Tribunal, the Argentine Government considers that, in order to take the most logical and appropriate approach to discovering the truth in each specific case, an intermediate system must be formulated - one that lies somewhere between the continental and common law systems - which would provide for shared responsibility between the parties and the Tribunal in determining the admissibility of evidence.

Rules should also be established to define the relationship that will exist between the pre-trial and the actual trial phases. In certain systems, all places of evidence that might help to determine the Tribunal's verdict must be adduced during the trial and evidence that is not available to the Tribunal may not be replaced by pre-trial evidence.

In this connection, the Argentine Government believes that the special circumstances in which the tribunal will have to function in the territory of the former Yugoslavia justify the selection of those systems that would allow for the consideration of pre-trial evidence, even if it is later introduced indirectly in the proceedings.

The Argentine Government wishes to stress the need to protect victims and witnesses. Written testimony and videotapes might be useful in preserving evidence and guaranteeing protection.

In some cases, the anonymity of witnesses might have to be preserved by restricting public access and banning the publication of the victims' identity or of any material from which their identity could be inferred.

Another question of great importance is related to the consideration of "illegally" obtained evidence. In this connection, the Argentine Government favours the avoidance of extreme measures that might pose merely formal obstacles to the work of the Tribunal. In this regard, at every phase of the proceedings, evidence should be rejected only if it has been gathered through serious violations of human rights, especially torture, and cruel or inhuman treatment or punishment.

Accept, Sir, the assurances of my highest consideration.

(*Signed*) EMILIO J. CARDENAS
Ambassador
Permanent Representative

B. PROCEDURAL AND EVIDENTIARY ISSUES FOR THE YUGOSLAV WAR CRIMES TRIBUNAL:

Resource Allocation, Evidentiary Questions and Protection of Witnesses

Helsinki Watch, August 1993.

INTRODUCTION

The United Nations has issued nearly thirty declarations on the former Yugoslavia; it has thus far failed to follow through with a single one of them.[1] From promises to create "safe havens" to threats of retaliation against continuing acts of aggression, the U.N. has, for the most part, been all talk. The Security Council's call for an international tribunal to investigate and try war criminals seems headed for the same dead end. Eight months have passed since the U.N. first called for the tribunal;[2] three months have passed since the U.N. gave a tribunal its final stamp of approval.[3] Still, as of this writing, the tribunal has yet to get off the ground.

On July 29, 1993, Helsinki Watch, a division of Human Rights Watch, released a report on eight cases ready for investigation by the tribunal, naming 29 individual defendants, linking each defendant to specific violations of the law governing the tribunal[4] and summarizing evidence collected by Helsinki Watch to date. That report demonstrates that a prosecutorial office could obtain sufficient evidence for a war crimes tribunal, if the U.N. allocates adequate resources for uncovering, preserving and preparing evidence before it disappears.

Integral to any investigatory effort is a parallel commitment to the safety and integrity of the witnesses who will testify, and to the development and implementation of fair procedural and evidentiary rules. The U.N. attempted to address these issues in the Statute of the International Tribunal

---

[1]See Human Rights Watch, *The Lost Agenda: Human Rights and U.N. Field Operations,* June 1993, pp. 85-103, detailing failure of U.N. actions in the former Yugoslavia.

[2]Security Council Resolution 808 of February 22, 1993.

[3] Security Council Resolution 827 of May 25, 1993.

[4] See *Prosecute Now!, Helsinki Watch Releases Eight Cases for War Crimes Tribunal on Former Yugoslavia,* News from Helsinki Watch, Vol. 5, no. 12, August 1, 1993.

("the Statute"),[5] the law governing the tribunal. However, many concerns remain, including several of particular interest to groups like Helsinki Watch that have been working closely with witnesses and survivors, and that understand the practical obstacles to mounting successful and fair investigations in the context of the Balkan conflict.[6]

In this document, Helsinki Watch discusses some of the major flaws in the Statute that stand in the way of fair and adequate preparation of evidence, particularly poor resource allocation, vague and inadequate procedural and evidentiary rules, and insufficient protection of witnesses. While the document does not attempt to address every possible area of concern,[7] it highlights those of most immediate and particular interest to Helsinki Watch and, in these areas, offers concrete suggestions for improvement.

Above all, the work of the war crimes tribunal must begin immediately, in order to individualize what too often is seen as collective guilt and, in this manner, to diffuse ethnic tensions.[8] And, at all times, the

---

[5] The Statute of The International Tribunal, in Security Council Resolution 827 of May 25, 1993 (incorporating The Report of the Secretary General pursuant to Security Council Resolution 808 of February 22, 1993). Among other substantive provisions, the statute incorporates a list of "grave breaches" of the 1949 Geneva Conventions and their 1977 First Additional Protocol (Article 2); enumerates specific violations of the laws of war (Article 3); specifies that the tribunal shall have the power to prosecute persons committing genocide (Article 4); lists nine crimes that will be considered "crimes against humanity" when committed in armed conflict against civilians (Article 5); and specifies when persons shall be liable for aiding and abetting "grave breaches" under Article 2 and "crimes against humanity" under Article 5 (Article 7).

[6] Helsinki Watch has released portions of the extensive testimony gathered by its field representatives in *War Crimes in Bosnia-Hercegovina, Volumes I and II* (released in August 1992 and April 1993, and available from Human Rights Watch, 485 Fifth Avenue, New York, New York 10017). On August 29, 1993, Helsinki Watch updated these volumes with a report entitled *Abuses Continue in the Former Yugoslavia* (detailing accounts of human rights abuses spreading into Serbian-controlled Yugoslavia and including previously unreleased testimony from Montenegro and Bosnia-Hercegovina).

[7] In particular, Helsinki Watch leaves to a later day commentary on elements of the crimes under the Statute, although this area is extremely important. The Statute leaves to the judges the responsibility of drafting the elements of crimes; once they do so, Helsinki Watch will offer its commentary if necessary.

[8] As Helsinki Watch has pointed out elsewhere, regardless of whether the accused can be forced to stand trial, investigations will serve a purpose in diffusing ethnic tensions. Indictments and arrest warrants -- which can be issued without the presence of the accused --

investigations should proceed in line with protections accorded the accused in international conventions and customary law. The tribunal's investigations will be largely exemplary: they can never hope to prosecute all offenders and, as such, must strive instead to reestablish the rule of law by prosecuting a select number of offenders with strictest regard to the due process rights of the accused.

Whether the public will perceive that the present war crimes investigations[9] and subsequent trials have been conducted fairly and appropriately will largely be determined by the rules of evidence that direct their course. Helsinki Watch offers the following suggestions guided by the understanding that to withstand the test of time, investigations and trials must be conducted fairly and without even the slightest appearance of impropriety. Yet, beyond this, Helsinki Watch recognizes that full due process is important in and of itself, as an essential component to reestablishing the rule of law.

RECOMMENDATIONS FOR THE WAR CRIMES TRIBUNAL

Resources for Effective Prosecution

Thus far international bodies have spent most of their time and resources establishing the mechanism of the tribunal -- giving it a statute, establishing its jurisdiction and the substantive law it is to apply, and discussing procedural matters. These are necessary tasks. Indeed, much of this memorandum is devoted to such issues. But the tribunal will have no work to do unless time, energy, and financial resources are devoted to investigating and developing cases that can be brought before the tribunal for prosecution. Courts can indict and try individuals only on the basis of evidence. Despite the efforts of the Commission of Experts convened by the Secretary-General, neither that body nor any other has had the necessary resources to develop the evidence needed to prosecute cases. Helsinki Watch therefore cannot emphasize strongly enough that the greatest single need in order to press forward the work of the tribunal is for the Security Council to

---

can be a successful deterrent in and of themselves. As long as amnesty for alleged war criminals is never put on the bargaining table, those indicted by the tribunal would be subject to arrest once they leave their country. See "Introduction," in *Prosecute Now!, Helsinki Watch Releases Eight Cases for War Crimes Tribunal on Former Yugoslavia,* News from Helsinki Watch, Vol. 5, no. 12, August 1, 1993.

[9] Since Helsinki Watch believes that investigations alone will serve a purpose, its commentary is not limited to the trials themselves, but instead also addresses protections needed during the investigatory stage.

make available the resources required for thorough and immediate investigations.

Nongovernmental organizations such as Helsinki Watch have been able to do a certain amount of investigatory work, identifying a number of cases where the evidence against particular individuals appears both clear cut and easily documented.[10] Still, the efforts of human rights groups cannot substitute for the work of an international investigatory team, which can focus on the type of information gathering necessary for proving criminal charges at trial. Such investigations include the collection and preservation of physical evidence, identification of witnesses, the collection of testimony that can be presented at trial and the identification of alleged perpetrators for indictment. While the work of nongovernmental human rights organizations such as Helsinki Watch may prompt investigations and provide collateral information and assistance, the work of collecting evidence for trial should be done by a well-financed prosecution team, with cooperation of many governments, including those with access to physical evidence and witnesses.

As time goes by, physical evidence becomes harder to collect; the sites of atrocities are altered, making forensic investigation more difficult and less conclusive; and contact may be lost with witnesses, especially refugees, who move from one place to another. Accordingly, efforts must be undertaken immediately to find witnesses and to ensure their safety so that they can provide preliminary information for the investigation, and also remain willing and available to testify when the time comes.

The commitment of the international community to holding a tribunal covering war crimes in the former Yugoslavia will be measured not by the amount of discussion and refinement of the legal machinery of the tribunal, necessary as that is, but rather by the political willingness to commit the resources required to investigate alleged crimes. Every word that follows in this memorandum thus is meaningless, unless the tribunal and its investigatory staff receive financial and technical support.

Rules of Procedure and Evidence

While resource allocation garners top priority at this point, the U.N. cannot afford to neglect thorny procedural and evidentiary questions that

---

[10] See *Prosecute Now!, Helsinki Watch Releases Eight Cases for War Crimes Tribunal on Former Yugoslavia,* News from Helsinki Watch, Vol. 5, no. 12, August 1, 1993.

remain unaddressed. In this section, Helsinki Watch highlights some of the major shortcomings of the Statute under widely accepted international law, and suggests that the Security Council amend its decision to address these issues.

The Statute

The judges of the international tribunal have the task of developing rules of evidence and procedure for every stage of the proceedings. Specifically, Article 15 of the Statute provides that the judges of the tribunal

> shall adopt rules of procedure and evidence for the conduct of the pre-trial phase of the proceedings, trials and appeals, the admission of evidence, the protection of victims and witnesses and other appropriate matters.

The Statute includes no provision for either the Security Council or any other international body to scrutinize and reject the rules adopted by the judges. Indeed, the Statute does not provide for public input and comment on the rules of evidence.

Nevertheless, other articles of the Statute circumscribe the power of the judges. In particular, the judges are bound to follow provisions which specify the rights of the accused (Article 21).[11] Under Article 21, the accused enjoys the following rights:

* "equal treatment" before the tribunal;
* a "fair and public hearing;"[12]
* the "presumption of innocence;"
* prompt information in detail and in an understandable language of the nature and cause of any charge against him;
* adequate time to prepare for trial;
* notification of the right to counsel;

---

[11] In addition, the power of the justices is circumscribed by the provisions pertaining to jurisdiction (Articles 6, 8, and 9); organization and composition of the tribunal (Articles 11, 12, 13 and 14); general pretrial requirements and investigation, preparation, and review of indictment (Articles 18 and 19); and conduct of trial proceedings (Article 20). In this document, Human Rights Watch concentrates on Article 21 and 22, touching only briefly on related sections.

[12] Article 21 specifically provides that the right to a public hearing is "subject to Article 22 of the statute." (Article 22 provides for the protection of witnesses.)

* counsel of his own choosing;
* appointed counsel "where the interests of justice so require," and without charge when the defendant is indigent;
* trial without "undue delay;"
* to be present at his own trial;
* "to examine or have examined the witnesses against him;"
* "to obtain the attendance and examination of witnesses on his behalf under the same conditions as witnesses against him;"
* free assistance of an interpreter; and
* the right not to be compelled to testify against himself.

This list, for the most part copied verbatim from Article 14 of the International Covenant on Civil and Political Rights ("the ICCPR"), appears exhaustive at first glance. Nevertheless, a direct comparison of the ICCPR and the Statute illustrates that a few major gaps remain unaddressed.

First, the Statute does not indicate when proceedings may be held *in camera*. In contrast, the ICCPR specifically restricts the use of such proceedings:

> The press and the public may be excluded from all or part of a trial for reasons of morals, public order *(ordre public)* or national security in a democratic society, or when the interest of the private lives of the Parties so requires, or to the extent strictly necessary in the opinion of the court in special circumstances where publicity would prejudice the interests of justice...,[13]

The Statute contains no such limitations; instead, it states only that trials need not be public when "the Trial Chamber decides to close the proceedings in accordance with its rules of procedure and evidence." The Statute itself, however, never offers exactly what those rules should be. At best, the Statute implies only that trials may be closed in order to protect the identity of victims and witnesses. (See Article 22.)

Second, in a related matter, the Statute fails to indicate when, if ever, *ex parte* affidavits may be used. The ICCPR does not directly address this issue, instead it simply reiterates the basic principle that in general trials

---

[13] This section further states that "any judgment rendered in a criminal case or in a suit at law shall be made public except where the interest of juvenile persons otherwise requires or the proceedings concern matrimonial disputes or the guardianship of children." ICCPR, Article 14(1). Thus, even cases that hold private hearings are usually required to make public *judgments*.

should be open and that the accused shall have the right to examine witnesses against him. (See ICCPR, Article 14(3)(e).[14]) This approach makes sense under the ICCPR, as it is a general statute, drafted to encompass all scenarios. The Statute, however, was created only to address a single and unique war crimes tribunal, a court burdened with the difficulty of investigating war crimes during an ongoing conflict and while the aggressors remain, at least in part, victorious.[15] Given that the issue of admissibility of *ex parte* affidavits is of paramount concern under such circumstances (and especially because some commentators have suggested that *ex parte* affidavits be used when witnesses are too afraid to testify), the Statute should provide more explicit instructions. Helsinki Watch suggests that, in order to comply with the highest international standards of due process, courts never admit *ex parte* affidavits as substitutes for live testimony, because the admission of *ex parte* affidavits violates the rights of the accused to confrontation and cross-examination.

Third, in contrast to the ICCPR, the Statute apparently does not contemplate compensation of a person whose conviction is overturned or who is pardoned "on the ground that a new or newly discovered fact shows conclusively that there has been a miscarriage of justice." (See ICCPR, Article 14(6).) The ICCPR has placed great priority in this safeguard; the Statute is wholly silent on the matter.

Commentary

Given the importance of the rules of evidence in guiding the war crimes tribunal on a fair and just course, Helsinki Watch cannot accept the Security Council's near-complete abdication of responsibility in drafting rules of evidence and procedure. Although Helsinki Watch is confident that an independent and fair judiciary can be chosen for the tribunal, it disagrees with the Security Council's decision to grant the judiciary plenary authority to draft rules of evidence and procedure.

Helsinki Watch thus urges the Security Council to amend the Statute to retain oversight authority over the judiciary's adoption of rules of evidence and procedure, or to issue a statement that makes clear that it intends to

---

[14] The European Convention for the Protection of Human Rights and Fundamental Freedoms includes the same provision, see Article 6(3)(d).

[15] No other international war crimes investigation and/or trial has ever taken place under these conditions.

exercise oversight responsibilities over rulemaking. Ideally, the Security Council would accept an active role in crafting the most important rules; but, at the very least, it should review the judiciary's rules. Grave concerns about fairness and legitimacy may arise if the judges' actions in this crucial area are not monitored.

Omissions in the Statute include the standard of proof to be used at trial and the standard of review to be used in appellate proceedings.[16] In addition, although the Statute indicates that judgments must be "rendered by a reasonable opinion in writing," no guidelines are provided as to what constitutes an adequate record of decision that will allow for meaningful review, such as a verbatim transcript, a full summary of evidence considered and a detailed account of the court's reasoning.

In addition, Helsinki Watch is concerned about the limited and vague nature of the few procedural safeguards specified in the Statute, and accordingly suggests that the Security Council issue supplementary decisions addressing these matters. As noted above, the Statute fails to provide at least the minimum protections recognized by the ICCPR. These shortfalls include, but are not limited to, the failure of the Statute to adopt:

* specifications as to when trial proceedings may be closed and as to what particular safeguards may be employed to protect witnesses;
* a direction that *ex parte* affidavits, offered as substitutes for live testimony that can be subject to cross-examination, are not admissible;
* a provision allowing for compensation of those unjustly accused, similar to that found in the ICCPR. (See ICCPR, Article 14(6).)

Protection of Witnesses and Related Procedural and Evidentiary Issues

No war crimes investigations can succeed unless witnesses receive adequate protection in exchange for their testimony. Based on its extensive field work in the former Yugoslavia, Helsinki Watch understands that the safety concerns of witnesses to war crimes committed in the Balkans are particularly acute.

---

[16] Since the trials are criminal proceedings, the standard of evidence should be the strictest possible, i.e. proof "beyond a reasonable doubt."

Helsinki Watch has released over 800 pages of testimony and analysis on war crimes in the former Yugoslavia.[17] Although the purpose of Helsinki Watch missions has been to document human rights abuses generally, not to amass evidence for a trial, many of the same witnesses and victims will be asked to testify about the same events at the tribunal. Helsinki Watch thus has intimate familiarity with many of the men, women, and children who ultimately will provide the tribunal with needed evidence. Through this close and ongoing contact, Helsinki Watch has come to an understanding of what types of protections will be needed for victims and witnesses in order to persuade them to testify, to guarantee their safety, and to provide for their return to society. Drawing form its field work, Helsinki Watch details a range of suggestions below.

The Need to Balance Competing Interests

The full text of the provision of the Statute providing for the protection of witnesses and victims (Article 22) reads as follows:

> The International Tribunal shall provide in its rules of procedure and evidence for the protection of victims and witnesses. Such protection measures shall include, but shall not be limited to, the conduct of *in camera* proceedings[18] and the protection of the victim's identity.

The only provisions of the Statute bearing further on what trial measures would be appropriate to protect witnesses seem contradictory on their face. Article 20, the main article establishing the appropriate conduct of the trial proceedings, anticipates closed trial proceedings by specifying that "[t]he hearings shall be public *unless the Trial Chamber decides to close the proceedings in accordance with its rules of procedure and evidence.*" (See Article 20(4)(emphasis added).) In contrast, Article 21(2) grants the accused the right to a "public hearing" and Article 21(4)(e) and allows the accused the

---

[17] See *War Crimes in Bosnia-Hercegovina, Volumes I and II* (released in August 1992 and April 1993, and available from Human Rights Watch, 485 Fifth Avenue, New York, New York 10017).

[18] Trial proceeding held in the judge's chambers or in some other area closed to the public.

right "to examine and have examined, the witnesses against him...."[19]

In crafting rules of evidence and procedure to fill in the gaps in the Statute, the tribunal must somehow appropriately balance the interests of the accused and those of the witnesses. The accused's interests, in addition to the right to cross-examination, include an interest in being able to confront the accuser (the "right to confrontation"), to prepare a defense (which may necessitate knowing the names of witnesses), to be present at trial (and at all of the stages in which facts are being weighed), and to have the trier of fact accord appropriate weight to the evidence.[20]

Witnesses' interests, commonly called "privacy" interests,[21] are three-fold. First, they include interests associated with personal safety. Many of the people of the former Yugoslavia who will be called on to testify at the tribunal fear reprisal against themselves and their families. This fear, which may arise at any trial, warrants particular attention here, where the accused may be closely acquainted with witnesses and thus knowledgeable about where they may be located; where members of government, military officers, and others with access to weapons and other means of punishment are among the

---

[19] The later provision, however, may also allow for restrictions on cross-examination which are intended to protect witnesses' safety. As one commentator has explained:

> ...this provision aims at ensuring for the defense, in this respect, complete equality of treatment with the prosecution.... On the other hand, it does not imply the right to have witnesses called without restriction. The provision does not therefore mean that municipal law cannot lay down conditions for admission and examination of witnesses, provided that such conditions are identical for witnesses on each side. (Paul Sieghart, *The International Law of Human Rights,* 1983.)

[20] One of the reasons courts exclude hearsay testimony in jury trials is that juries may be ill-equipped to weigh evidence differentially, granting first-hand testimony the highest weight and hearsay testimony less weight. Here, where the trier of fact is a panel of judges, this concern is not present; the judges could accept hearsay testimony and merely grant it little weight. However other concerns mitigate against this approach. Courts also exclude hearsay evidence in non-jury trials in order to protect the right of the accused to cross-examine witnesses against him or her, a right specifically provided for by the Statute, see Statute, Article 21(4)(a), as well as the right of the accused to confront the accusers.

[21] The word "privacy" is both too limited and too vague in this case. Witnesses do not need privacy in the sense that they need to be left alone. On the contrary, what they may desire most is government protection and assistance in order to preserve their security and dignity, and to help them reestablish their lives.

accused; and where some of the supporters of the accused have already taken revenge as a matter of course. The possibility of retaliation will only be magnified if the trial should take place before the war has ended. Under these circumstances, public testimony not only endangers the physical safety of witnesses and their family members, but also their job security, pension, housing, and ability to travel.

Second, witnesses and victims are entitled to what could be called "dignity" interests -- the interest in being treated with respect, with not being publicly humiliated. This need may be especially great for witnesses who are survivors of rape and other forms of sexual abuse. Before they can even talk about their abuse, such witnesses must come to terms with many layers of shame. Some fear that if they admit to having been raped or otherwise sexually abused, no one will marry them or their husbands will divorce them, their families will disown them, and their communities ostracize them. In addition, based on knowledge of the conduct of counsel in previous local trials, many women anticipate that they will be subject to probing and even brutal questioning about their own sexual conduct. Unlike other survivors who may not have been able to hide their suffering -- their bullet-ridden limbs, their bruises, their broken legs -- survivors of rape may have successfully concealed their trauma. To testify necessitates disclosure and possibly the end of a long process of self-denial.[22] Accordingly, for all of these reasons, rape survivors may be extremely reluctant to come forward for a war crimes trial unless the tribunal takes steps to safeguard them from public humiliation.

Third, along with the immediate "safety" and "dignity" interests, witnesses have an interest in life itself, which here means assistance in being able to start their lives anew. To do so, many witnesses need a full array of social services, especially trauma counseling and other health care. Some witnesses also need assistance with relocation, a grant of asylum, and even a new identity. Although such assistance serves safety and privacy interests, it also addresses witnesses' struggle to resume their lives, a struggle that could be seen as an important interest in and of itself.

---

[22] And potential witnesses may realize that after they testify, they are unlikely to receive the kind of counseling and other social services they need. See *Meeting the Health Care Needs of Women Survivors of the Balkan Conflict,* The Center for Reproductive Law & Policy, New York, April 1993.

Toward General Principles on Protection

Although the Statute permits the tribunal to fashion protections for witnesses, the Security Council does not *require* that witnesses who legitimately desire it be protected. For this reason, Helsinki Watch urges the Security Council to amend the Statute to provide a general mandate on protection.

Since cases before the tribunal will be exemplary cases, intended to reestablish the rule of law in what has been a lawless society, the strictest regard must be paid to the due process rights of defendants at all times. Thus, in weighing the rights of witnesses and accused, if due process compromises are needed to entice certain witnesses to testify, then it is better to let the case drop and to prosecute other defendants against whom witnesses are willing and able to testify. Accordingly, Helsinki Watch urges that the tribunal be *required* to provide protection for witnesses whenever needed, but *only* in line with the rights of the accused.

The standard should be that all witnesses shall be granted the degree of protection they need at all stages of the trial, including investigatory, indictment, and trail. Although some commentators have advocated "special" safeguards for rape victims, Helsinki Watch cautions against an approach that would treat all rape survivors alike and grant them seemingly "extra" protections. The general standard of protection for all witnesses can be applied to survivors of rape, with the recognition that the degree of protection needed by some rape survivors may be greater than other witnesses. At all times, the court should focus on the particular need of *all witnesses,* weighed against the rights of the accused.[23]

Concrete Suggestions for Applying Protection Rules

The main priority in any investigation and subsequent trial should be ensuring that the proceedings are fair and that the rights of the accused are adequately protected. In line with these goals, courts have designed several safeguards to protect witnesses, many of which may be applicable here. Juridical measures to protect witnesses include the power of the court to order persons under its jurisdiction to stay away from the witness, with an attendant power of contempt, fine and jail, and court orders or requests to governments

---

[23] This approach will be useful in those cases in which witnesses testify about several war crimes at once, and for those in which a woman in the investigatory stage may claim to be a witness to rapes, but later reveals that she was a victim. Such a witness is entitled to protection through every stage of the proceedings.

to protect witnesses or to arrest persons who harass witnesses. These tactics, however, may be inadequate for many witnesses who will be called to testify before the tribunal. To the extent that such standard provisions fail, the tribunal may draw from the following array of more novel protective measures.

In-Camera Proceedings

The expense of closed proceedings is the accused's right to an open trial; however, closed proceeding preserve the defendant's rights to cross-examination and confrontation. The testimony of a witness given outside the public view can in part guarantee his safety, but it can scarcely be considered an adequate protection in many cases, especially taken into account the fact that once the accused discovers the witness's identity, so will others who may wish him harm. Thus, *in-camera* proceedings, without more, will frequently be insufficient when a witness's safety is threatened.

Modified *In-Camera* Proceedings

In-Camera proceedings may be modified as necessary to address the particular needs of a witness. For example, in cases in which the witness's identity is not critical to the defendant's right to cross-examination, such as when there was no personal relationship between the accused and the witness prior to the alleged crime and there are not extraordinary issues about the witness's motive to testify truthfully, a witness may be introduced by a pseudonym during an *in-camera* proceedings.[24] While this method adds extra protection for the witness, the witness remains identifiable by sight. For witnesses needing even greater protection, the use of *in-camera* proceedings may be combined with other safeguards, such as the use of screens (see below),[25] when doing so is consistent with the defendant's due process rights. Also, when possible the use of *in-camera* proceedings may be modified to enhance the accused's right to a public trial. In particular, the testimony of an *in-camera* proceeding could be made public, possibly with the name and any other identifying characteristics of the witnesses omitted.

---

[24] Pseudonyms may be used in public proceedings as well.

[25] Screens also may be used outside in public proceedings.

Alteration of Image or Voice of Witness

Whenever a video or audio tape is used, either in the investigatory stage or at trial, the tribunal may alter the voice or image in order to further protect the witness. This will help conceal the witness's identity once the evidence is used at trial, but will not protect the witness from being identified by anyone present at the taping. Because both the accused and the accused's counsel should have the right to be present at videotaped depositions or videotaped trial testimony, they will be able to identify the witness regardless of whether the tape is eventually altered.

Use of Screens

To resolve some of the difficulties noted above, witnesses whose identity is not critical to a defendant's right of cross-examination may be permitted to give trail or deposition testimony, or other statements to investigators behind a screen which presents only their silhouettes[26] Their voices can also be altered and their identity further concealed through use of a mask, wig, and/or body padding. In this way, the general public and the press can hear the contents of the testimony while not discovering the witnesses' identities. In addition, the judges, by sitting parallel to the screen, can observe the demeanor of each witness.

Designation of an Alternative Site to Take Testimony

The tribunal may designate another site at which to take testimony from a witness, in an effort to minimize public attention. However, because the public's attention may still be drawn to the presence of the judge, counsel and the defendant in the place of questioning, this system is unlikely to provide much safety unless it is combined with other protective measures.

Designation of a Special Rapporteur

The Court may designate a special rapporteur to investigate general conditions and report to the court. Such a rapporteur would decrease the need

---

[26] Recently in the U.S., Judge Royce Lamberth, from the United States District Court for the District of Columbia, allowed testimony of witnesses in a criminal case involving an investigation nicknamed "Irangate" or "Contragate." It involved two agents of the Central Intelligence Agency (CIA), whose identity had to be protected for national security reasons. Both agents eventually testified behind a screen under assumed names.

to expose witnesses to the possibility of reprisal for testimony on peripheral matters. Witnesses thus would need to be called only to testify about the conduct of the defendant himself.

Sealing or Expunging Witnesses' Names from Public Records

In conjunction with the measures outlined above, the tribunal could seal or expunge witness's names from public records when necessary to ensure their safety. Any records identifying witnesses could be kept in a designated safe in a neutral country, to be opened only upon an emergency and after a decision by the Security Council, or after a set time period, such as 100 years.

Use of Pseudonyms

In so far as the identify of a witness is not critical to a defendant's right of cross-examination, pseudonyms for witnesses maybe used throughout the investigatory and trial stages, alone or along with any of the other protective devices detailed above.

Use of U.N. Guards

At every stage in which a witness is called upon to give testimony, his or her safety may be secured through use of U.N. guards.

In addition to the above measures, which concern the presentation of testimony, several other procedural and evidentiary issues bear upon preserving the interests of the witnesses and the rights of defendants. Five of those issues -- use of "rape shield laws," admission of expert testimony, use of other third party testimony, *ex-parte* affidavits, and relocation of witnesses -- are addressed below.

"Rape Shield" Laws

In order to protect rape victims from public humiliation, the tribunal may supplement its rule on relevance of evidence with a so-called "rape shield law." These laws, used in a number of U.S. states, generally prohibit defense counsel from presenting evidence on the past sexual history of the witness in order to prove consent or otherwise discredit the witness. Although in cases before the tribunal evidence of witnesses' past sexual conduct is likely to be excludable as irrelevant, the adoption of a general prohibition of such evidence would add a safeguard for witnesses.

Admission of Expert Testimony

The tribunal should admit expert testimony to explain the manner in which some trauma victims testify. For example, one effect of trauma is that victims may blank out a part of their testimony, temporarily or forever. Trauma experts could help the tribunal assess lapses in rape victims' and other trauma victims' testimony, and illuminate whether and how such lapses can be justified.[27]

Use of Third Party Testimony

The tribunal may accept testimony of human rights advocates, social service workers and other third parties for background and supplementary information about general conditions that are material to the case.

Ex-Parte Affidavits

Ex-parte affidavits, offered as substitutes for live witnesses, should never be permissible because they directly violate the rights of the accused.

Relocation of Witnesses

In general, secrecy may be enhanced if testimony is taken close to a witness's residence (so that he or she need not stay overnight to give the testimony) in a hospital, school, or other public building to which the witness is likely to travel. This procedure, however, will be inadequate in many cases. Witnesses with the greatest security needs should be removed from their country with their family members at the earliest stage of investigation. Family members should not be left behind as they may be identified and subject to harassment and abuse. The tribunal should bear full responsibility for housing, health care, and other social services for such witnesses and their families immediately upon their temporary relocation prior to trial and through their permanent relocation.

A Commitment to Witnesses Beyond Trial

The above safeguards, standing alone, are inadequate to preserve fully the rights of witnesses and victims. In addition to their interests in safety and dignity, witnesses and victims have an interest in being able to resume normal

---

[27] See Glen Randall and Ellen Lutz, *Serving Survivors of Torture,* 1991.

lives. In order to do so, many of them, and many of their family members, need social services, housing, legal assistance, long-term trauma counseling and other health care.

Given the heavy psychiatric burden of testifying about war time abuses, the tribunal should bear the responsibility of providing free psychiatric care. Trained trauma counselors can help prevent witnesses from being re-traumatized by their experience before the tribunal. Such counseling must be culturally and ethnically appropriate, gender-sensitive, and in an understandable language; witnesses and their family members should have a choice of counselors and should be able to switch counselors; and the counseling should begin as soon as witnesses are contacted in the investigatory stage and continue as long as necessary past the trial stage. The United Nations must commit the financial resources necessary to provide such needed care. The tribunal could also be given the power to order defendants convicted of crimes to reimburse the U.N. for the costs of such care.

In addition, witnesses and their families may need to be relocated after testifying. Of paramount concern is that there be a place for the witnesses to go. To this end, the Security Council should ensure that witnesses quietly be granted asylum in various pre-arranged countries. As part of a complete "witness protection program," the Security Council should also arrange for new identities for witnesses and their family members when necessary, and assist with their integration into a new society. In order to prevent the public from perceiving such arrangements as attempts to "buy witnesses," the tribunal should offer witnesses such protections as the need arises on an equal basis, no matter how they testify.

CONCLUSION

Helsinki Watch offers the above suggestions for the war crimes tribunal with the hope that the United Nations will make good on its promise to get the war crimes investigations off the ground. In order to do so, the U.N. must first commit the financial and technical resources necessary for thorough investigations. Then, in order to ensure that witnesses are adequately protected and that investigations and trials are fair to the accused, the U.N. should address the concerns enumerated above. Compared with other dilemmas that the U.N. has faced in the Balkans, the war crimes tribunal can easily become a reality. All that is needed is the political will.

* * *

This report was written by Julie Mertus, Counsel for Helsinki Watch.

Helsinki Watch was established in 1978 to monitor domestic and international compliance with the human rights provisions of the 1975 Helsinki Accords. The chair of Helsinki Watch is Jonathan Fanton and the vice chair is Alice Henkin. Jeri Laber is executive director; Lois Whitman is deputy director; Holly Cartner and Julie Mertus are counsel; Erika Dailey, Rachel Denber, Ivana Nizich and Christopher Panico are research associates; and Pamela Cox, Christina Derry, Ivan Lupis and Alexander Petrov are associates.

Helsinki Watch is a division of Human Rights Watch, which includes Africa Watch, Americas Watch, Asia Watch, and Middle East Watch. The chair of Human Rights Watch is Robert L. Bernstein and the vice chair is Adrian W. DeWind. Kenneth Roth is acting executive director; Holly J. Burkhalter is Washington director; Gara LaMarche is associate director; Ellen Lutz is California director; Susan Osnos is press director; Jemera Rone is counsel; Michal Longfelder is development director; Dorothy Q. Thomas is Women's Rights Project director; Joanna Weschler is Prison Project director; Kenneth Anderson is Arms Project director.

Helsinki Watch is affiliated with the International Helsinki Federation in Vienna, Austria.

C. PERMANENT MISSION OF FRANCE TO THE UNITED NATIONS

28 October 1993.

IT/4, 16 November 1993.

The Permanent Mission of France to the United Nations presents its compliments to the United Nations Secretariat and has the honour to refer to Security Council resolution 827 approving the Statute of the International Tribunal for the former Yugoslavia.

Under that resolution, the States Members of the Organization can address to the Secretariat, for transmission to the judges of the International Tribunal for the former Yugoslavia, their comments concerning the rules of procedure of the Tribunal.

Attached hereto, for transmission to the judges of the Tribunal, you will find the comments of the Government of France, which concern in particular the possibility of the Tribunal taking proceedings against certain defendants in their absence, in certain conditions.

The Permanent Mission of France to the United Nations takes this opportunity to convey to the United Nations Secretariat the renewed assurances of its highest consideration.

New York, 28 October 1993

Note of the Government of France concerning the rules of procedure of the International Tribunal established by Security Council resolutions 807 and 827 (1993)

1. In its resolution 827 (1993) of 25 May 1993, the Security Council requested "the Secretary-General to submit to the judges of the International Tribunal, upon their election, any suggestions received from States for the rules of procedure and evidence called for in Article 15 of the Statute of the International Tribunal" (para. 3).

According to that article:

> "The judges of the International Tribunal shall adopt rules of procedure and evidence for the conduct of the pre-trial phase of the proceedings, trials and appeals, the admission of evidence, the protection of victims and witnesses and other appropriate matters."

2. The Government of France considers the wording of these rules of procedure to be particularly important, for the Statute of the International Tribunal has left open questions of the greatest significance. The attainment of the objectives set by the Security Council, as defined in its resolutions 808 and 827 (1993), will depend largely on the answers to those questions.

The Government of France relies entirely on the judges of the Tribunal, in their wisdom, to devise appropriate rules of procedure which usefully expand and clarify the provisions of the Statute. Nevertheless, in accordance with the aforementioned paragraph 3 of resolution 827 (1993), it wishes to draw the attention of the Tribunal to a point of crucial importance.

3. In the report which it prepared at the request of the Minister of State and Minister for Foreign Affairs, the Committee of French Jurists set up to study

the establishment of an International Criminal Tribunal to judge the crimes committed in the former Yugoslavia 1/ did not exclude the possibility of judgement in the defendant's absence, although it described that possibility as a "last resort", since "every effort must be made to ensure that the defendant effectively appears, so that the judgement cannot be challenged and the trial is of an exemplary nature". 2/

4. The Statute of the Tribunal does not explicitly exclude the possibility of judgement in the defendant's absence, but does not actually provide for it. The report of the Secretary-General states:

> "A trial should not commence until the accused is physically present before the International Tribunal. There is a widespread perception that trials in absentia should not be provided for in the statute as this would not be consistent with article 14 of the International Covenant on Civil and Political Rights, which provides that the accused shall be entitled to be tried in his presence." 3/

5. The Government of France considers that this argument - which the Secretary-General does not endorse - is based on a misunderstanding: the right of the accused to be present at his trial - which is not called in question - should not make it possible for the accused (or the authorities to whom he is answerable) to prevent the trial from taking place by refusing to attend. This consideration is of particular importance in the context in which the Tribunal will be required to perform its functions: the arrest or transfer of the accused may be hypothetical and the lack of any in absentia procedure may paralyse the Tribunal.

6. It would therefore doubtless be appropriate for the rules of procedure of the Tribunal, which are designed to clarify the provisions of the Statute, to eliminate any possible ambiguities and to fill any gaps, should provide for the possibility of judgement in the absence of the accused in cases where the latter refuses to appear (and cannot be compelled to do so) or cannot be contacted after a certain period of time.

Such a procedure should, of course, be accompanied by all the desirable guarantees. In accordance with the general principles of criminal law, it should be stated that the sentence will be nullified or the trial resumed if the accused is arrested or appears spontaneously.

7. If the Tribunal were nevertheless to decide to exclude any possibility of judgement in the absence of the accused, it would probably seek means of remedying the resulting serious disadvantages, in so far as possible, in particular the risk that its action might be rendered ineffective, by seeking means of exerting pressure on the accused (or on the authorities to whom he is answerable) in order to ensure his effective appearance.

To that end, the Tribunal could provide that when the accused cannot be served with an order or warrant of arrest within a specified period of time, or does not comply with the order or warrant of arrest, the indictment will be read out (or may be read out, if the Tribunal so decides) in a public hearing of the Trial Chamber.

1/ The report of this Committee was circulated as Security Council document S/25266 of 10 February 1993.

2/ Para. 108 of the report; see article XV, para. 2, of the draft Statute.

3/ Document S/25704 of 3 May 1993, para. 101.

D. AUSTRALIAN COMMENT ON THE RULES OF EVIDENCE AND PROCEDURE FOR THE INTERNATIONAL TRIBUNAL

IT/5, 16 November 1993.

Operative paragraph 3 of Security Council resolution 827 requested the Secretary-General 'to submit to the judges of the International Tribunal, upon their election, any suggestions received from States for the rules of procedure and evidence called for in Article 15 of the Statute of International Tribunal'.

Pursuant to OP 3 of SCR 827, Australia submits the following comment concerning the rules of procedure and evidence for the International Tribunal.

Australia considers that the rules of procedure and evidence for the International Tribunal should draw on internationally recognised norms and standards. In its work on a draft statute for an international criminal tribunal, the International Law Commission has incorporated many of these norms and standards in the preliminary versions of the draft statute which will be considered by the Sixth Committee at UNGA 48. Australia suggests that the judges of the International Tribunal should take into account this work of the ILC when developing the rules of procedure and evidence for the International Tribunal.

E. SUGGESTIONS MADE BY THE GOVERNMENT OF THE UNITED STATES OF AMERICA RULES OF PROCEDURE AND EVIDENCE FOR THE INTERNATIONAL TRIBUNAL FOR THE PROSECUTION OF PERSONS RESPONSIBLE FOR SERIOUS VIOLATIONS OF INTERNATIONAL HUMANITARIAN LAW COMMITTED IN THE FORMER YUGOSLAVIA

IT/14, 17 November 1993.

PREFACE

The Statute of the International Tribunal establishes a modified adversarial system for prosecuting persons responsible for serious violations of international humanitarian law committed in the former Yugoslavia. Accordingly, this proposal represents a compromise between common law adversarial systems and civil law systems. This proposal takes into consideration the types of offenses to be tried before the International Tribunal, the form the evidence is most likely to take, and the difficulties of prosecuting cases in the less than perfect environment of on-going hostilities.

The goal is to provide, without being overly detailed and burdensome, a comprehensive body of rules governing the trial before the International Tribunal, as well as a guide for lawyers practicing in that forum.

A Commentary accompanies this proposal in an attempt to provide guidance to the International Tribunal regarding the interpretation of these Rules. Accordingly, the International Tribunal may wish to reproduce the Commentary along with the Rules in order to assist the judges and practitioners before the International Tribunal.

The Commentary also highlights particular issues which the judges of the International Tribunal may wish to consider during the approval process for these or any other rules. That portion of the Commentary which describes these issues is enclosed in brackets. Depending on how these issues are resolved, changes to the rules and Commentary may be needed.

We have also undertaken to define the elements of the various offenses over which the International Tribunal has jurisdiction and to recommend the maximum punishment which should be imposed for each offense. These definitions and maximum sentence recommendations will be submitted in a separate proposal.

TABLE OF CONTENTS

AUTHORITY OF THE TRIBUNAL

MISCELLANEOUS POWERS

INVESTIGATIONS AND SUSPECTS' RIGHTS

INDICTMENT AND PRETRIAL PROCEEDINGS

INDICTMENT AND PRETRIAL PROCEEDINGS (continued)

TRIAL PROCEDURES

TRIAL PROCEDURES (continued)

POST-TRIAL PROCEDURES

Rule 1: General Provisions

1.1 Authority. The present Rules of Procedure and Evidence for the International Tribunal for the Prosecution of Persons Responsible for Serious Violations of International Humanitarian Law Committed in the Former Yugoslavia, established by Resolution 827 of the Security Council acting under Chapter VII of the Charter of the United Nations, are hereby promulgated by the International Tribunal in accordance with the provisions of Article 15 of the Statute of the International Tribunal.

1.2 Entry into force. These Rules shall take effect upon their approval by a majority of the judges of the International Tribunal.

1.3 Amendment of rules. Where necessary in the interests of a fair and expeditious trial, a Trial Chamber may issue a written order amending a procedural provision of these Rules, in such form and upon such notice as it may determine. An amendment made pursuant to the provisions of this rule is applicable only to the proceeding for which it was formulated.

1.4 Effect of violation. A failure to comply with these Rules shall not require the dismissal of charges or the exclusion of evidence unless specifically provided for in these Rules, or unless the failure to comply is so inconsistent with fundamental principles of fairness and due process that dismissal or exclusion is required in order to prevent a miscarriage of justice or serious damage to the integrity of the proceedings.

1.5 Language. All proceedings before a judge or Chamber of the International Tribunal and all indictments, orders, warrants, motions, requests and judgments shall be in English and French, unless otherwise specified in these Rules or authorized by a Trial or Appeals Chamber.

1.6 Purpose and interpretation. These Rules are intended to provide for the just determination of cases before the International Tribunal. They shall be interpreted to ensure simplicity in procedure, fairness to the parties and the elimination of unjustified expense and delay.

1.7 Definitions. For purposes of these Rules:

(A) Accused. An "accused" is an individual indicted in accordance with Rules 12 and 13.

(B) Arrest. "Arrest" is defined as the physical seizure of the accused for the purpose of taking him or her into custody in order to be forthcoming to answer the indictment.

(C) Commutation. The term "commutation" shall mean an act of the International Tribunal mitigating its sentence from a certain term of imprisonment to a lesser term.

(D) International Tribunal. The term "International Tribunal" shall refer to the International Tribunal for the Prosecution of Persons Responsible for Serious Violations of International Humanitarian Law Committed in the Former Yugoslavia, established by United Nations Security Council Resolution 827 on May 25, 1993.

(E) Lesser Included Offense. A "lesser included offense" is an offense, each element of which must be proven in order to prove another offense.

(F) Pardon. The term "pardon" shall mean an act of the International Tribunal releasing a person it sentenced from the remaining term of imprisonment and from any disabilities consequent on his or her conviction.

(G) Party. A "party" is defined as the prosecutor, or the accused and his or her counsel.

(H) Prima Facie. "Prima facie" evidence is evidence which, if unexplained or uncontradicted, establishes each element of the offense with which an accused is charged.

(I) Prosecutor. The term "prosecutor" shall refer to the Prosecutor as set forth in Article 16 of the Statute, or an attorney on the staff of the Prosecutor.

(J) Statute. The term "Statute" shall refer to the Statute of the International Tribunal issued pursuant to United Nations Security Council Resolution 827 on May 25, 1993.

(K) Suspect. A "suspect" is an individual concerning whom the Prosecutor possesses information which would lead a reasonable person to believe that the individual committed an offense over which the International Tribunal has jurisdiction.

COMMENTARY

Rule 1.1 restates the authority under which these Rules are promulgated.

Rule 1.2 provides for the judges of the International Tribunal to approve Rules of Evidence and Procedure. The Rules will enter into force immediately upon formal approval.

Rule 1.3 provides the Trial Chambers with the necessary flexibility to conduct proceedings in the less than perfect setting of ongoing hostilities and their aftermath. To ensure that the necessary measures are available in a particular case, a Trial Chamber may amend procedural aspects of the Rules; however, a written order upon notice to the Parties is required in order to do so. An order issued by a Trial Chamber is subject to post-trial review by the Appeals Chamber.

In addition, the judges of the International Tribunal can make permanent amendments under the authority of Article 15 of the Statute. Such amendments should be enacted in accordance with the procedure set forth in Rule 1.2.

or exclusion of evidence. For example, a breach of the discovery provisions found in Rule 17 would not, unless exceptionally egregious, require such remedies. In general, then, a chamber should provide a remedy which is proportional to the detriment suffered as a result of the breach.

Rule 1.5 requires that proceedings be conducted in English and French. In addition all writings issued by the International Tribunal shall be made available in English and French. Other Rules may provide for particular proceedings or writings to be in a language other than these official languages (for example, Rule 15, Rule 23).

Rule 1.6 is intended to serve as a guide when a Chamber is called upon to interpret the Rules. If, for example, a party seeks to have the Rules interpreted in a excessively technical manner or in a manner which would result in great expense or waste of time, such an interpretation should be rejected in favor of a interpretation which is less elaborate, or more cost effective.

Rule 1.4 makes clear that a breach of the Rules does not automatically require the imposition of the drastic remedies of dismissal

Rule 1.7 defines certain terms used frequently in the Rules.

[We have suggested that approval be by majority vote of the judges. Of course, the International Tribunal may decide to require a two thirds majority, or some other standard of approval. Also, Security Council action may be desirable for entry into force.

The Appeals Chamber has not been given the power to amend the Rules in an individual case, since that decision is not subject to further review. In the event that a Chamber wishes to make a permanent amendment to these Rules, the eleven judges should convene as a body to consider and vote on the proposed amendment.]

Rule 2: Personal and Subject Matter Jurisdiction

2.1 Personal jurisdiction. The International Tribunal may try any natural person.

2.2 Subject matter jurisdiction. The International Tribunal shall have jurisdiction to try serious violations of international humanitarian law committed in the territory of the former Yugoslavia from January 1, 1991, including, but not limited to:

(A) all humanitarian law agreements in force in the territory of the former Yugoslavia at the time the acts were committed, including the 1907 Hague Convention (IV) Respecting the Laws and Customs of War on Land and the Regulations annexed thereto, the 1949 Geneva Conventions, and the 1977 Additional Protocols to those conventions;

(B) all customary international law of armed conflict, including the law interpreted and applied by the International Military Tribunals at Nuremberg and Tokyo;

(C) genocide, as defined in Article 4 of the Statute; and

(D) crimes against humanity as enumerated in Article 5 of the Statute when committed contrary to law as part of a widespread or systematic campaign against any civilian population on national, political, ethnic, racial, gender, or religious grounds, during a period of armed conflict, whether internal or international in character, including all acts committed in the territory of the former Yugoslavia during the time of armed conflict whether or not in execution of or in connection with that armed conflict, all acts committed in preparation of such armed conflict, and all acts committed not during such armed conflict but in execution of or in connection with (as interpreted by tribunals applying the Charter of the International Military Tribunal at Nuremberg or Control Council Law No. 10) that armed conflict.

2.3 Territorial and temporal jurisdiction. A crime is considered to have been committed in the territory of the former Yugoslavia if any part of the planning, instigation, ordering, execution, or completion of the crime took place within the territory of the former Socialist Federal Republic of Yugoslavia, including its land surface, airspace and territorial waters. The temporal jurisdiction of the International Tribunal shall extend from the period beginning January 1, 1991.

COMMENTARY

Rules 2.1, 2.2 and 2.3 are included in order to clarify the limitations set forth in the Statute upon the exercise of jurisdiction by the International Tribunal. Since substantive rather than procedural, Rule 2 is not subject to amendment pursuant to the provisions of Rule 1.3 ("Amendment of rules").

Rule 3: Limitations of Actions

There shall be no period of limitations within which a prosecution must be initiated or completed.

COMMENTARY

Rule 3 codifies customary international law. Moreover, the principle that war crimes are subject to no statute of limitations has been made the subject of the Convention on the Non-Applicability of Statutory Limitations to War Crimes and Crimes Against Humanity (entered into force November, 1970). Although often considered procedural, the limitations provision is of such significance in determining the scope of permissible action by the International Tribunal that it should not be subject to amendment pursuant to Rule 1.3 ("Amendment of rules").

[Statutes of limitations are treated as procedural by some legal systems, and substantive by others. We have included this provision since the Statute is silent on this issue and customary international law considers there to be no limitations period for this class of offenses.]

Rule 4: Primacy of the International Tribunal

4.1 Generally. The International Tribunal and national courts have concurrent jurisdiction over serious violations of international humanitarian law committed in the territory of the former Yugoslavia since 1 January 1991; however, the International Tribunal may, at any time, request the national court to defer to the primacy of the International Tribunal.

4.2 Procedures for requesting deferral

(A) The decision to request deferral of a national court proceeding is within the sole discretion of the International Tribunal.

(B) Requests for deferral shall be issued by the President of the International Tribunal in writing and filed with the Permanent Representative to the United Nations of the nation concerned or, if the State has filed a written request with the Registry and the President of the International Tribunal, with the central authority designated by that State. In the event that a State has no permanent representative to the United Nations, the President of the International Tribunal shall forward a request directly to the Minister of Foreign Affairs of the State.

(C) If, within 30 calendar days after the request for deferral has been filed as set forth in subsection (B), the State fails to file a written response which satisfies the International Tribunal that the State is taking adequate steps to comply with the request, the International Tribunal shall so inform the Secretary General, for transmission to the Security Council.

(D) The determination which court will exercise jurisdiction is a matter for resolution by the International Tribunal and the national courts, and is not a right of the accused.

(E) Requests for deferral may be accompanied by such orders, warrants, or requests as a Trial Chamber or the International Tribunal may deem appropriate.

4.3 Determinations in national courts. Neither factual nor legal determinations made in national courts shall be binding upon the International Tribunal or any Chamber thereof.

COMMENTARY

Rule 4.1 is derived from Article 9 of the Statute, which provides for the exercise of primacy by the International Tribunal over proceedings in national courts.

Rule 4.2, subsections (A), (B) and (C), set forth procedures for requesting deferral. Subsection (D) is designed to prevent an accused from attempting to obtain judicial relief from either the International Tribunal or from a national court by arguing that deferral should (or should not) have been requested in his case. Subsection (E) permits the International Tribunal to, if it wishes, submit other communications to a State at the same time as a request to defer.

Rule 4.3 is intended to prevent an accused from successfully arguing that the International Tribunal is bound by a factual or legal ruling made by a national court prior to deferral. This Rule does not apply to situations in which the International Tribunal is precluded from trying an accused by Article 10(2) of the Statute.

Rule 5: Non Bis In Idem

5.1 Prosecutions by the International Tribunal

(A) Impediments based upon prior proceedings in national courts

(1) In the event that the Chamber before which an indictment is pending determines that Article 10(2) of the Statute precludes further proceedings by the International Tribunal, it shall dismiss the indictment and provide such other relief as may be necessary.

(2) Following the dismissal of an indictment under this subsection, the Prosecutor is prohibited from bringing new charges based upon the acts underlying the dismissed indictment.

(3) A determination regarding this issue made by a national court is not binding upon the International Tribunal or any Chamber thereof.

(B) Impediments based upon prior proceedings before the International Tribunal. After the commencement of the presentation of evidence at trial by the Prosecutor on the general issue of guilt, an accused may not be retried for the same charge set forth in the indictment unless the new trial arises from an appeal or request for a new trial, or unless the first trial was terminated prior to judgment either at the request of the defense or, for extraordinary cause shown by the prosecutor, by the Trial Chamber.

5.2 **Prosecutions by national courts**. When the International Tribunal becomes aware that criminal proceedings are pending against an individual before a national court for the same crimes for which the individual has been tried by the International Tribunal, the International Tribunal shall, in accordance with the procedures for requesting deferral under Rule 4, request that the national court permanently discontinue its proceedings.

COMMENTARY

Rule 5.1(A) permits a Chamber of the International Tribunal to dismiss charges pending before it, if an accused has already been tried by a national court for a war crime in a proceeding which the International Tribunal views as being adequate. The provision clearly indicates that the determination that the appropriate circumstances exist is by the Trial Chamber and not the national court or some combination thereof. The decision by the Trial Chamber is subject to review by the Appeals Chamber.

Rule 5.1(B) is designed to preclude the Prosecutor from initiating a trial and then withdrawing the case if it appears during trial that conviction is unlikely. Retrial would be barred under these circumstances once the prosecution begins to present evidence (either documentary or testimonial) at trial on the issue of guilt. This protection does not preclude retrial when it results from a motion for a new trial or an appeal, since Articles 25 and 26 of the Statute explicitly permit it. Moreover, offenses not included in the indictment before the Trial Chamber, even though known at the time of trial, are not affected.

Rulings by the Trial Chamber on any motion to dismiss made after the commencement of the Prosecutor's presentation on the issue of guilt, should, if possible, be reserved until after judgment. This procedure saves judicial resources in the event that the granting of a motion to dismiss is later reversed by the Appeals Chamber. In that case, the Appeals Chamber can merely reinstate the judgment of the Trial Chamber.

Rule 5.2 recognizes the International Tribunal's obligation to request a national court to discontinue proceedings once an individual has already been tried by the International Tribunal.

Rule 6: Miscellaneous Provisions

6.1 Scheduling, appointment of officials. The President of the International Tribunal, in accordance with these Rules, shall determine the mode of and procedure for:

(A) the scheduling and assignment of matters to a judge or Chamber;

(B) the appointment of officials necessary for the functioning of proceedings; and,

(C) the disqualification, recusal, or reassignment of a judge.

6.2 Disqualification, recusal of judges

(A) Under extraordinary circumstances by which it appears that a judge may not be capable of impartially carrying out the duties of office, or mentally or physically carrying out the duties of office, a judge of the Trial Chamber may, on his or her own motion or on motion of a party, be disqualified from participating in proceedings related to the charges against an accused.

(B) The judge who reviews an indictment under Rule 13 may not sit as part of the Trial Chamber before whom the accused is later tried.

(C) In the event of disqualification or recusal, another judge of the International Tribunal may act in the matter in place of the disqualified or recused judge.

6.3 Compulsion of testimony. In the event that a witness in a proceeding before the International Tribunal refuses to give evidence requested of him on the grounds set forth in Rule 25.9(B), the witness may nonetheless be compelled to give evidence if immunity from the use of that testimony, direct or indirect, at a subsequent prosecution of the witness by the International Tribunal, is conferred by the Trial Chamber presiding over the proceeding after a determination that there is no substantial risk that the testimony will be used in a prosecution of the witness by a national authority.

6.4 Contempt. Contempt of court may be punished by any Chamber of the International Tribunal.

COMMENTARY

Rule 6.1 is intended to give to the President of the International Tribunal control over assignment of cases, scheduling of judges for the issuance of warrants, confirmation of indictments and the like. In addition, the President should devise procedures for maintaining staff such as officers to maintain the security and decorum of court proceedings, the services of doctors or other professionals in order to determine the competence of an accused to stand trial, translators, interpreters, court stenographers, clerks of court, photographers, etc.

Rule 6.2 sets forth the instances in which a judge may not take part in a case. The mere fact that a judge is of the same religion or ethnic group as that of an accused or victim should not in and of itself be a basis for disqualification.

Rule 6.3 permits a witness to be compelled to answer questions which may incriminate him or her once immunity is bestowed by the Chamber and the Chamber has determined that there is no founded risk of prosecution related to the testimony in a national court. If the witness nonetheless refuses to answer, this provision is made enforceable through the inherent power of a Chamber, recognized in Rule 6.4, to punish contempt.

Rule 6.4 recognizes the inherent power of the court to punish contempt. The need to maintain the authority and dignity of and respect for the Chambers of the International Tribunal and their decrees requires that Chambers have the authority to punish contempt. For example, a witness is granted immunity under Rule 6.3 yet continues in his or her refusal to testify, the witness could be held in contempt and jailed until he or she agrees to testify. In addition, any disregard for, or disobedience of, the orders or commands of a Chamber of the International Tribunal constitutes a contempt of court. Given the limited subject matter jurisdiction of the International Tribunal, the contempt power is the only mechanism available to insure the freedom of proceedings from perjury, witness tampering or intimidation and other offenses which affect the integrity of the proceedings.

Rule 7: Protection of Victims and Witnesses

The Trial Chamber shall employ reasonable measures necessary to ensure the protection of victims and witnesses.

(A) Protection of the identity and location of a victim or witness. The Trial Chamber may conceal the identity and location of an alleged victim or witness of an offense when necessary to ensure the safety, physical health, or mental health of the victim or witness. To that end, the Trial Chamber may issue protective orders under Rule 8 or employ alternatives to live testimony under subsection (B).

(B) Alternatives to live testimony. *In camera* proceedings, the use of one-way closed circuit television and other measures designed to protect victims and witnesses are permitted upon a showing of good cause.

COMMENTARY

Rule 7 provides for the protection of victims and witnesses, as mandated by Article 22 of the Statute. It recognizes the tension between the accused's right to cross-examine witnesses under Article 21(4)(e) of the Statute, and the use of alternatives to live testimony, *in camera* proceedings, or concealment of the identity of a victim or witness. Use of protective measures should be limited to situations where the measures are considered necessary and always be balanced against the accused's rights. There may be cases in which protection cannot be afforded consistent with the rights of the accused. In such an instance, the Prosecutor may have to consider using other evidence in place of the witness.

The need to employ protective measures will arise for a variety of reasons, such as threatened reprisal by the accused or others acting on behalf of the accused, or because testifying in the accused's presence may cause the victim or witness substantial emotional or psychological distress or will impair his or her ability to communicate.

Rule 7 should be read in conjunction with Rule 17, regarding discovery of the Prosecutor's witnesses, and Rule 25, regarding use of stipulations and the protection of witnesses from reprisals. The use of protective measures should be balanced against the accused's rights and permitted only when necessary to ensure the protection of a particular victim or witness.

This Rule contemplates a variety of measures. Therefore the following discussion of particular methods should not be considered an exclusive list or an endorsement of any particular method:

Alteration of Image or Voice of Witness. Whenever a video or audio tape is used, either in the investigatory stage or at trial, altering the voice or image of the witness should be considered. Identity may be further concealed through use of a mask, wig, and/or body padding.

Use of Screens. Witnesses whose identity is not critical to the defense may be permitted to give trial or deposition testimony behind a screen which presents only their silhouettes. In this way, the general public and the press could hear the contents of the testimony while not discovering the witness's identity. In addition, the judges, by sitting parallel to the screen, could still observe the demeanor of the witness.

Designation of an Alternative Site to Take Testimony. The Trial Chamber should consider designation of another site at which to take testimony from a witness in an effort to minimize pubic attention. However, because the public's attention may still be drawn to the presence of the judges, counsel and the accused in the place of questioning, this system would be unlikely to provide much safety unless combined with other protective measures.

Sealing or Expunging Witnesses' Names From Public Records. The Prosecutor should seek protective orders to seal or expunge a name from public records when necessary to ensure that person's safety. Any records identifying witnesses could be kept in a secure location for a lengthy period of years.

Use of Pseudonyms. Insofar as the identity of a witness is not critical to an accused's defense, pseudonyms for witnesses may be used throughout the investigatory and trial stages.

The Trial Chamber should consider the protection of victims and witnesses and the accused's right to represent himself or herself pursuant to Article 21(4)(d) prior to permitting an accused to proceed *pro se*. For example, the Trial Chamber should consider not permitting an accused to proceed *pro se*, or appointing defense counsel for the limited purpose of conducting cross examination of a victim or witness, when an alternative to live testimony of the victim or witness is used by the Prosecutor. Particular care should be given to ensure the accused does not abuse the right to proceed *pro se* to intimidate, harass, or embarrass the alleged victim or witness.

Rule 8: Protective Orders

8.1. Issuance. In order to ensure the safety and security of a particular victim or witness, protect the national security of a State, protect the confidentiality of investigations, or prevent the flight of suspects or accused, a Trial Chamber or, if prior to the initial appearance of the accused, the judge who confirmed the indictment may issue an order:

(A) preventing the disclosure of the identity or location of a particular victim or witness;

(B) preventing the disclosure of a State's national security information, provided to the International Tribunal by a State on condition of confidentiality;

(C) sealing an indictment against public disclosure; or,

(D) protecting from disclosure such other documents or information as may be necessary.

8.2. Disclosure

(A) State national security information. State national security information cannot be disclosed to the public without the prior approval and consent of that State.

(B) Indictments. Disclosure of sealed indictments is permitted:

(1) to the extent necessary for the issuance and execution of a warrant or order;

(2) when the accused has been brought into custody or has been released pending trial; or

(3) when the authority who originally sealed the indictment determines that sealing is no longer required.

(C) Other documents or information. Disclosure of other sealed documents or information is permitted only in accordance with the specific provisions of the protective order or when the authority which originally sealed the document or information determines that sealing is no longer required.

8.3 Duties of Registrar. The Registrar will retain material subject to a protective order and protect from disclosure its contents and, with respect to a sealed indictment, the fact that an indictment has been confirmed pursuant to Rule 13.

COMMENTARY

Rule 8 is based in part upon Article 22 of the Statute, governing protection of victims and witnesses, and in part upon Article 19 of the Statute, which provides that the Trial Chambers can issue any orders as may be required for the conduct of the trial.

Rule 8 contemplates that some matters which come before the court may require protection from disclosure, since, for example, the information (1) is protected by a State, or (2) if known to the suspect or accused, is capable of increasing the risk of flight.

Information provided to the International Tribunal by a State, which the State believes necessary to protect as a matter of national security, *ordre public*, or other essential interest, may initially be reviewed by the Trial Chamber in closed proceedings or *in camera*. If the Trial Chamber determines the information is relevant, it should notify the State of the action it intends to take which may result in disclosure of the information to the accused or to the public.

Rule 9: Investigations

9.1 Conduct of Investigations. In the conduct of any investigation, the Prosecutor may, without further order of the International Tribunal or Chamber thereof,

(A) question victims, witnesses, and, subject to Rule 10, suspects;

(B) collect, examine, and test evidence;

(C) conduct on-site investigations;

(D) seek assistance from authorities of a State;

(E) conduct any other investigatory activity not inconsistent with these Rules.

9.2 Retention of information. The Prosecutor shall make arrangements for the retention, storage, and security of information and physical evidence obtained in the course of investigations or proceedings. The arrangements shall be consistent with the Agreement between the United Nations and the Government of the Netherlands of [date] and, if information is provided by a State, with the request of that State.

COMMENTARY

Rule 9.1 set forth a non-exhaustive list of the powers of the Prosecutor (including investigators or other persons acting at the direction of the Prosecutor) in conducting an investigation pursuant to Articles 16 and 18 of the Statute.

In the event that the Prosecutor exceeds his or her authority or engages in misconduct, Article 19(2) of the Statute permits the Trial Chamber to enter any order required for the conduct of a fair trial or to protect the rights of the suspect or accused.

In addition, Rule 10.2 permits a Chamber to exclude evidence obtained in violation of a suspects rights during questioning, while Rule 25 permits a Chamber to exclude other evidence obtained during the course of an investigation.

This Rule, when viewed in conjunction with Articles 18, 29 and 30 of the Statute of the International Tribunal, should protect the Prosecutor from legal liability for actions carried out in the course of an investigation.

This Rule also emphasizes that the Prosecutor has the power to directly seek assistance from States without the approval or sanction of a Chamber of the International Tribunal. The Prosecutor may make requests for international legal assistance under the procedure specified in the domestic law of the State from which assistance is requested. In the event that a State's domestic law requires such a request to emanate from a judicial as opposed to prosecutorial authority, Article 19 of the Statute authorizes the Chambers to do so upon request of the prosecutor.

Rule 9.2 requires the Prosecutor to store information or evidence obtained in the course of investigation or judicial proceedings. Stored evidence or information may be used for future proceedings against any individual. Information may be used in future proceedings, regardless of whether the investigation or proceeding in which it was obtained resulted in conviction. The Prosecutor should make every effort to return physical evidence to its true owner when it is no longer needed for evidentiary purposes.

Rule 10: Suspect's Rights During Investigatory Questioning

10.1 Suspect's rights. Prior to a suspect being questioned by or on behalf of the Prosecutor, the suspect shall be informed of the following:

(A) the nature of the violations of the Statute as to which he or she may be considered a suspect;

(B) the right to remain silent;

(C) the right to assistance of legal counsel, including the right pursuant to Rule 11 to request assignment of counsel if indigent; and

(D) the right to translation in a language he or she speaks and understands.

10.2 Remedy for violation of suspect's rights. Statements of a suspect obtained in violation of Rule 10.1, or evidence derived therefrom, are not automatically inadmissible in subsequent proceedings against him or her. Admissibility of such evidence is governed by the provisions of Rule 25.

10.3 Undercover investigations. The provisions of Rule 10.1 shall not apply to any undercover investigatory action that may be carried out by the Prosecutor or by any agent or informant acting at the direction of the Prosecutor, provided that the action is not carried out for the purpose of circumventing Rule 10.1.

COMMENTARY

Rule 10.1 incorporates the safeguards set forth in Articles 18 and 21 of the Statute which protect a suspect from compelled self-incrimination and provide for the assistance of legal counsel. The suspect is also entitled to translation in a language which he or she understands. Translations should include consideration of physical handicaps which preclude the suspect from engaging in normal oral communication.

Rule 10.2 reaffirms the principle that a violation of a rule of procedure does not automatically require exclusion of the evidence obtained by the failure to comply with the rule.

Rule 10.3 makes clear that legitimate undercover investigations are not to be hampered by the requirements of this Rule. Thus, for example, the Rule does not require an investigator to break off the undercover operation designed to identify persons who were not previously suspects or to investigate continuing criminal activity if a known suspect appears and makes admissions. However, the undercover activity should not be a mere subterfuge to permit the Prosecutor to circumvent the suspect's exercise of his or her rights.

It should also be emphasized that this Rule does not prohibit a private person acting on his or her own initiative from obtaining statements from a suspect. Nor, barring reprehensible methods, does it prohibit national police acting in a domestic investigation from using methods to obtain statements which may not technically comply with this Rule.

Rule 11: Right to and Qualifications of Counsel

11.1 Right to counsel. Regarding a suspect's right to counsel during questioning and an accused's right to counsel during any post-indictment proceeding where the accused's presence is required or permitted, the suspect or accused shall have:

(A) the right, at no expense to the International Tribunal or other United Nations entity, to qualified, reasonably available counsel of his or her choosing, or

(B) the right, subject to Rule 11.3, to have counsel assigned to him or her free of charge.

11.2 Qualifications of counsel

(A) Subject to Registrar verification, an attorney is considered qualified to represent suspects and accused if he or she is a lawyer in good standing, admitted to the practice of law of a State.

(B) Counsel appointed by the International Tribunal pursuant to Rule 11.3 must further satisfy the Registrar that he or she possesses appropriate training and familiarity with the general principles of criminal law.

11.3 Determination of indigency and appointment of counsel. The Registrar shall formulate the criteria, subject to the approval of the International Tribunal, to be used in determining whether a suspect or accused has sufficient means to pay for counsel. In determining whether a suspect or an accused lacks sufficient means to pay for counsel, the following procedures shall be followed:

(A) a request for assignment of counsel shall be made to the Registrar;

(B) the Registrar shall make the determination, based on the approved criteria, whether a suspect or accused has sufficient means to pay for counsel;

(C) an adverse determination may be appealed by the suspect or accused to a judge of a Trial Chamber whose determination shall be binding and not subject to further appeal;

(D) a further request may be made and considered upon a showing of a change in circumstances from the earlier request;

(E) the Registrar shall maintain a list of attorneys meeting the criteria of Rule 11.2, who have indicated their willingness to be appointed, and, in consultation with the President of the International Tribunal, shall assign counsel from that list; and

(F) the assignment of particular counsel may be appealed to a judge of a Trial Chamber whose determination shall be binding and not subject to further appeal.

11.4 Power to disqualify and discipline counsel. Nothing in these Rules shall be construed to restrict the inherent power of a Trial Chamber or the Appeals Chamber to disqualify or discipline counsel when necessary to protect the integrity of the proceedings.

COMMENTARY

Rule 11.1 provides for the right to assistance of counsel, as guaranteed by Articles 18 and 21 the Statute. The right to appointment of counsel at no cost is limited by Articles 18 and 21 to circumstances in which the suspect or accused is without sufficient means to pay for it. The right to be represented by a particular counsel is not absolute. If the counsel hired by an accused is not available for trial within a reasonable time, the Trial Chamber may require the accused to obtain counsel that is available. In this way, the accused's right to counsel cannot be used to circumvent the ability of the Trial Chamber to execute its responsibilities.

Rule 11.2 sets forth very liberal criteria for determining whether an attorney retained by a suspect or accused is qualified to appear before the International Tribunal. In general, retained counsel should be permitted to appear before the International Tribunal if he or she is an attorney in good standing in the State in which he or she is admitted to practice.

Rule 11.3 sets forth the procedures by which counsel may be appointed to an indigent suspect or accused. The criteria to be used in determining whether an individual has sufficient means to pay for counsel is best delegated to the Registrar. Appointed counsel should be selected from a list of qualified practitioners. Many of these practitioners may, over time, become familiar with practice before the International Tribunal and be appropriate choices for appointment in particularly difficult cases.

Rule 11.4 recognizes the inherent authority of the International Tribunal to discipline or disqualify counsel if necessary.

Rule 12: Form and Contents of Indictments

12.1 *Prima facie* evidence required. Upon a determination that *prima facie* evidence exists for prosecution of a suspect, the Prosecutor may prepare an indictment.

12.2 Form of indictment. The indictment shall be in writing and shall consist of a separate count or statement for each of the crimes with which the accused is charged. Each count shall set forth:

(A) a plain, concise, and definite statement of the essential facts constituting the crime, and

(B) the specific provision of the Statute which the accused is alleged to have violated.

12.3 Minor changes to the indictment

(A) Minor changes to the indictment may be made by the Prosecutor without prior approval of the Trial Chamber at any time prior to arraignment. After arraignment, any minor change may be made only upon approval of the Trial Chamber. A "minor change" is any change which does not add a party, offense, or substantial matter not fairly included in the indictment and which is not likely to mislead the accused as to the offense or offenses charged.

(B) Upon permitting such change or changes, the Trial Chamber shall, upon motion of the defense, order any adjournment of the proceedings which may, by reason of such amendment, be necessary to accord the defense adequate opportunity to prepare for trial.

12.4 Additional charges against an accused

(A) Once an indictment has been confirmed, additional charges may be brought against the accused only upon a separate indictment issued and confirmed under these Rules.

(B) Charges brought under separate indictments may be joined for trial at any time prior to trial. After the commencement of trial but prior to final judgment, charges brought under a separate indictment may be joined to the existing indictment only if the new indictment alleges an additional legal theory of liability, as opposed to the commission of different acts.

(C) In the event that the Prosecutor joins separate indictments after the trial of an indictment has commenced, the Trial Chamber shall, upon motion of the defense, order any adjournment of the proceedings which may, by reason of such joinder, be necessary to accord the defense adequate opportunity to defend against the charges.

12.5 Joinder of accused, consolidation of indictments

(A) Two or more accused may be jointly charged in a single indictment and jointly tried if the crimes charged overlap sufficiently to justify a single indictment or trial.

(B) When two or more accused are charged in separate indictments who could have been charged in a single indictment, the Trial Chamber may, upon motion of the prosecutor, order that such indictments be consolidated for trial.

12.6 Severance. The Trial Chamber may, in the interest of justice, grant an accused's request for severance.

COMMENTARY

Rules 12.1 and 12.2 are derived from Article 18 (4) of the Statute. They standardize the form and content of the indictment in order to provide adequate notice to the accused of the offenses with which he or she is charged. Pursuant to Rule 13, the indictment must, at a minimum accompanied by a summary of the evidence which makes out a *prima facie* case.

It should be noted that the Prosecutor is an independent entity, who has sole discretion to determine whether or not to charge an individual.

The Prosecutor may charge in the alternative, meaning the Prosecutor may allege that the accused's acts constitute at least one of several charged offenses. For example, the Prosecutor may charge in separate counts of the indictment that a killing was either (1) part of a systematic effort of "ethnic cleansing" constituting a violation of the Genocide Convention or (2) wilful killing as a grave breach of the Geneva Conventions. Based upon such an indictment, the Trial Chamber could find the accused guilty of a grave breach even if, due to the inability to prove that the accused was motivated to exterminate an ethnic group, a genocide offense has not been proven.

Rule 12.3 sets forth the circumstances under which an indictment can be amended, as opposed to withdrawn and reissued under Rule 13.

Rule 12.4 permits a new indictment charging different acts or crimes to be joined with an existing indictment for trial.

Unrestricted joinder of indictments once the trial of an indictment has commenced is permitted in some legal systems (in the interest of judicial economy), while others permit no new charges to be brought. In yet other jurisdictions, adding of charges is permitted only if the new charge alleges an additional legal theory of liability, as opposed to the commission of different acts. In proposed Rule 12, we have opted for a variant on the last of these procedures: We have not permitted the amendment of an indictment after trial commences; instead, we permit the Prosecutor to issue a new indictment charging a different legal theory -- but no new acts -- which can thereafter be joined with the existing indictment. The reason why we have done so is that if the Prosecutor has charged the incorrect violation of law (which at the conclusion of the trial will result in acquittal on that charge), the operation of *non bis in idem* would preclude reprosecution even though the accused could have been convicted for the same acts if the Prosecutor had charged the correct violation of law. By permitting the Prosecutor, in essence, to amend the legal theory of the prosecution during trial, potential miscarriages of justice can be avoided. However, by prohibiting the Prosecutor from joining indictments based upon other acts, the proposed rule protects the accused from being surprised at a late stage of trial preparation.

This Rule should not be interpreted to restrict the right of an accused to consent to any change proposed by the Prosecutor.

Rule 12.5 creates criteria by which the composition of joint trials can be determined. In essence, accused can be joined in one indictment and thereafter tried together; alternatively, separate indictments can be consolidated for trial if the accused could have been charged in a single indictment. This Rule should not be interpreted to restrict the right of accused to consent to joinder or consolidation.

Rule 12.6 provides that in the event of multiple charges, joinder of indictments, joinder of accused, the Trial Chamber may grant a defense request for severance.

[The judges should consider whether the Rules should permit joinder of a new indictment with an indictment as to which trial has already commenced (1) under no circumstances; (2) only when the new indictment alleges an additional legal theory of liability; or (3) also when the new indictment alleges the commission of additional acts.]

[The judges may wish to define more precisely the circumstances under which different accused can be joined for trial.]

Rule 13: Confirmation, Dismissal and Withdrawal of Indictments

13.1 Transmittal. Upon completion of the indictment, the Prosecutor shall transmit the indictment and so much of the evidence he or she deems necessary to support the indictment to a judge of a Trial Chamber for review.

13.2 Confirmation or dismissal. On the basis of his or her review, the judge to whom the indictment has been transmitted shall either confirm or dismiss the indictment.

(A) The judge shall confirm only so much of the indictment for which he or she finds that a *prima facie* case exists and which alleges an offense over which the International Tribunal has jurisdiction.

(B) The accused may not challenge the validity of an indictment on the grounds that it was confirmed in whole or in part on the basis of evidence subsequently determined to be inadmissible at trial.

(C) The judge shall dismiss any allegation which does not meet the requirements of subsection (A). However, before dismissing any allegation, the judge shall allow the Prosecutor the opportunity to present additional evidence on the allegation, and to be heard.

(D) The dismissal of an indictment under subsection (C) shall not preclude the Prosecutor from subsequently bringing a new indictment based upon the acts underlying the dismissed indictment.

13.3 Withdrawal. An indictment or one or more counts thereof may only be withdrawn by the Prosecutor. Following the withdrawal of an indictment or one or more counts thereof, the Prosecutor is permitted to bring new charges based upon the acts underlying the withdrawn indictment or portions thereof, except as provided in Rule 5.

(A) Prior to an accused's initial appearance before the Trial Chamber, the decision to withdraw an indictment is within the sole discretion of the Prosecutor.

(B) Thereafter, an indictment may be withdrawn only with the approval of the Trial Chamber upon a showing of good cause by the Prosecutor.

COMMENTARY

Rules 13.1 and 13.2 are based upon Article 19 of the Statute.

Rule 13.3 permits the Prosecutor to withdraw an indictment. The offenses alleged in a withdrawn indictment may be the basis for a subsequent indictment against the accused. A subsequent indictment must be confirmed in accordance with this Rule. In cases in which major changes to an indictment are required prior to the commencement of trial, it is anticipated that the Prosecutor will withdraw the indictment and subsequently reindict. As a matter of practice, there should be no reason why the subsequent indictment cannot be prepared and confirmed prior to withdrawal of the existing indictment, in order to avoid having to release an accused who is in pretrial detention.

Withdrawal of an indictment once the presentation of evidence has been commenced at trial results in a prohibition against retrial of an accused on the same charges, except in limited circumstances. A more thorough discussion of this issue can be found in the commentary to Rule 12.4.

Rule 14: Procuring Presence of the Accused

14.1 General Procedure. Upon confirmation of an indictment and request of the Prosecutor, a judge of a Trial Chamber may issue any warrant or order required to procure the presence of the accused for trial. Any warrant or order shall be in writing, accompanied by a copy of the indictment.

14.2 Warrants for Arrest. A Warrant for Arrest shall be issued in all cases unless the judge is satisfied that the accused will appear voluntarily and will not pose a danger to a victim, witness or any other person, in which case an Order to Appear may be issued. Warrants for Arrest shall include an order for the confinement of the accused pending trial.

14.3 Orders to Appear. Orders to Appear shall provide the accused sufficient notice of the time, date, and place to appear for initial appearance before a Trial Chamber.

14.4 Other orders. The judge may issue such other orders, warrants, or requests required to secure the presence of the accused for trial.

14.5 Transmittal to States

(A) The Prosecutor shall promptly communicate with the State in whose territory the accused is believed to be located to arrange for compliance with the order or warrant.

(B) All requests for assistance in obtaining the presence of the accused shall be accompanied by a true copy of the indictment and arrest warrant, a statement of the evidence upon which the indictment is based, and information as to the identity and, to the extent available, the location of the accused. In addition, the request for assistance may contain a statement regarding the arrangements for the transfer of the accused.

(C) The Prosecutor may take such action as necessary to obtain permission from a State to transport through its territory an accused surrendered by another State to the International Tribunal.

14.6 Notification of the Secretary General. If the International Tribunal concludes that a State is not making substantial and good faith efforts to comply with a request or order, the International Tribunal may notify the Secretary General for transmission to the Security Council.

COMMENTARY

Rules 14.1, 14.2, 14.3 and 14.4 are based upon Article 19(2) of the Statute, which grants judges of the Trial Chambers the power to "issue such orders and warrants for the arrest, detention, surrender or transfer of persons, and any other orders as may be required for the conduct of the trial." Rule 14 treats only those orders, warrants and requests necessary to ensure the presence of the accused at trial.

Rules 14.5 and 14.6 set forth the procedure by which the International Tribunal requests the surrender of an accused who is believed to be located in the territory of a State. We recognize that surrender of an accused may not be automatic; a State whose assistance has been requested in obtaining the surrender of the accused may wish to conduct an extradition or other proceeding in conformity with its laws. However, in the event that the International Tribunal concludes that a State is not taking adequate steps to locate and surrender an accused, it may notify the Secretary General in order that the Security Council may take appropriate action.

[The judges may wish to clarify whether a communication to the Security Council under Rule 14.6 should be by the Trial Chamber responsible for the case, the President of the International Tribunal, or after a vote of the entire body of judges.]

Rule 15: Accused's Initial Appearance

Following the issuance of a Warrant for Arrest, an Order to Appear, or any order, warrant or request which restricts the liberty of the accused, the accused's initial appearance before a Trial Chamber shall take place without undue delay. During the accused's initial appearance the Trial Chamber shall:

(A) satisfy itself that the rights of the accused, particularly the right to counsel, are respected;

(B) provide the accused with a copy of the indictment in a language which the accused speaks and understands;

(C) unless waived, ensure that the indictment is read to the accused in a language the accused speaks and understands;

(D) satisfy itself that the accused understands the indictment;

(E) call upon the accused to enter a plea;

(F) should the accused fail to enter a plea or make an irregular plea, enter a plea of not guilty on behalf of the accused;

(G) satisfy itself that the accused understands that if he or she fails to appear for any post-indictment proceeding, the proceedings can continue in his or her absence; and

(H) set dates for completion of production of evidence, resolution of motions, and commencement of trial.

COMMENTARY

Rule 15 is based upon Article 20 of the Statute and sets forth the procedures to be followed during the initial appearance of the accused.

Under this Rule, an accused who, having initially appeared before a Trial Chamber and been given notice of the charges and the date of trial, voluntarily absents him or herself prior to or during trial, may nonetheless be tried. This is not trial *in absentia*, which is specifically prohibited by the Statute, since the accused has been brought before the International Tribunal and given the opportunity to defend against the charges.

The term "irregular plea" in subsection (F), refers to situations in which, rather than entering a plea of guilty or not guilty, an accused makes ambiguous or non-responsive remarks.

Rule 16: Confinement Prior to Judgment

16.1 Authority for confinement. Upon the execution of a Warrant for Arrest, the accused shall be confined.

16.2 Place of confinement. Confinement will be either in facilities provided pursuant to the Agreement between the United Nations and the Government of the Netherlands of [date] or in facilities of a State.

16.3 Conditions of confinement. Upon motion of either party, the Trial Chamber may modify the conditions of an accused's confinement.

16.4 Release. Once confined, an accused may not be released except upon order of the Trial Chamber before which the indictment will be tried. Release may be ordered by the Trial Chamber only in extraordinary circumstances, or if it is satisfied that the accused will appear for trial and, if released, will not pose a danger to a victim, witness or any other person. The Trial Chamber may impose such conditions upon the accused's release as it may determine. If necessary, the Trial Chamber may issue a Warrant for Arrest to secure the presence of the accused who was previously released or otherwise permitted to remain at liberty.

16.5 Credit against sentence. In the event that a sentence of confinement is imposed, the accused's sentence shall be reduced by the number of days previously spent in confinement under this Rule.

COMMENTARY

Rule 16.1 is based upon Articles 19 and 20 of the Statute. Confinement is mandatory in cases in which a Warrant for Arrest has been issued.

Rule 16.2 anticipates arrangements between the Prosecutor and States regarding the location and conditions of accused's confinement within in those States.

Rule 16.3 permits the Trial Chamber to respond to unforeseen events affecting the confinement of an accused.

Rule 16.4 establishes the criteria for releasing an accused from confinement. A State may at any time prior to or during the pretrial confinement of the accused, request that the accused be released from pretrial confinement. Such requests should only be honored upon a sufficient showing that the State can ensure that the accused will appear at trial. The Trial Chamber may impose conditions upon the release of an accused and may subsequently order confinement if required.

Rule 16.5 makes clear that the amount of time spent in confinement prior to trial, conviction or sentence shall be credited against the sentence ultimately imposed.

Rule 17: Production of Evidence

17.1 Disclosure by the Prosecutor. Except as otherwise provided in these Rules, the Prosecutor shall provide the following information or matters to the defense:

(A) Evidence which accompanied the indictment. As soon as practicable after the initial appearance of the accused, the Prosecutor shall provide the defense with copies of evidence which accompanied the indictment at the time confirmation was sought.

(B) Documents, tangible objects, and reports. Upon request of the defense, the Prosecutor shall, within a reasonable time thereafter, permit the defense to inspect any books, papers, documents, photographs, tangible objects, buildings or places, or copies or portions thereof, which are in the possession, custody or control of the Prosecutor, and which are either material to the preparation of the defense, are intended for use by the Prosecutor as evidence at trial on the issue of guilt, or were obtained from or belonged to the accused. For purposes of this subsection, matters filed with the Registry by the Prosecutor are considered in the control of the Prosecutor and subject to disclosure.

17.2 Exculpatory evidence. The Prosecutor shall, as soon as practicable, disclose to the defense the existence of evidence known to the Prosecutor which reasonably tends to:

(A) negate the guilt of the accused of an offense charged in the indictment; or

(B) mitigate the guilt of the accused regarding an offense charged in the indictment.

17.3 Witnesses

(A) Prior to the commencement of trial, the Prosecutor shall, subject to the protections accorded to a particular witness under Rules 7 and 8, notify the defense of the names of and means of contacting witnesses the Prosecutor intends to examine:

(1) in the Prosecutor's presentation of the evidence of guilt; and

(2) in order to rebut a defense of which the Prosecutor has received notice under Rule 17.4(A).

(B) The fact that an individual's name appears on a list of witnesses provided to the defense shall not be grounds for an adverse inference in the event that the individual does not testify at trial.

17.4 Disclosure by the defense. Except as otherwise provided in these Rules, the defense is required to provide disclosure only in the following situations:

(A) Notice of defenses. No later than the date set by the Trial Chamber for the completion of production of evidence, the defense shall notify the Prosecutor its intent to offer:

(1) the defense of alibi, including the specific place or places at which the accused claims to have been present at the time of the alleged offense and the names and addresses of witnesses upon which the defense intends to rely to establish the alibi;

(2) the defense of diminished or lack of mental responsibility, including the names and addresses of witnesses upon which the defense intends to rely to establish the diminished, or lack of, mental responsibility;

(3) a special defense, including the names and addresses of witnesses and documentary evidence upon which the defense intends to rely to establish the special defense; however, failure of the defense to provide notice under this Rule shall not limit the right of the accused to testify.

(B) Inadmissibility of withdrawn notice. Evidence of the fact that the defense previously provided and then withdrew notice of a defense is not admissible at trial.

(C) Reciprocal production of evidence. If the defense requests disclosure under Rule 17.1(B), the Prosecutor, upon compliance with the defense request, is entitled to inspect any books, papers, documents, photographs, tangible objects, or copies or portions thereof, which are within the possession, custody, or control of the accused and which the defense intends to introduce at trial on the issue of guilt.

17.5 Continuing duty to disclose. If a party discovers additional evidence or material previously requested or required to be produced pursuant to these Rules, that party shall promptly notify the other party and the Trial Chamber of the existence of the additional evidence or material.

17.6 Matters not subject to disclosure. Notwithstanding the provisions of Rules 17.1 through 17.5, the following matters are not subject to disclosure:

(B) reports (other than scientific or medical reports), memoranda, or other internal documents prepared by a party, its assistants or representatives in connection with the investigation or preparation of the case.

17.7 Production of evidence in the control of a State. Either party may move before the Trial Chamber to issue a request to a State for legal assistance for the purpose of obtaining evidence which is in the control of that State. The failure of a State to produce the evidence sought shall not require dismissal of charges or the postponement of proceedings except in extraordinary circumstances.

17.8 Regulation of the production of evidence. The Trial Chamber may prescribe such terms and conditions as are just and equitable to facilitate and control the production of evidence process.

COMMENTARY

Rules 17.1 through 17.7 provide for broad disclosure of information by both parties. Each party should have an adequate opportunity to prepare its case and equal opportunity to interview witnesses and inspect evidence. No party should be permitted to unreasonably impede the access of another party to a witness or evidence; however, access by the defense may be limited, under Rule 7, if required for the protection of a victim or witness.

Inspection under this rule contemplates allowing the parties to make copies and photographs of the adverse party's evidence, except for material subject to a protective order pursuant to Rule 8.

Rule 17.7 permits the defense, as well as the Prosecutor, to request the Trial Chamber to seek production of evidence from a State (of course under Rule 4 and Article 19 of the Statute, the Prosecutor may seek information or evidence from a State either with or without the assistance of Chambers). Before granting the defense motion, the Trial Chamber should be satisfied that the request is not speculative, *i.e.* that the evidence does in fact exist, is located within the State, and is critical to the defense. If a State determines that its domestic law or other essential interest prohibits production of the evidence sought, this should have no adverse impact on the Prosecutor's case. Dismissal would only be appropriate in the face of an intentional and wholly unjustified refusal to produce evidence so critical to the defense case that its absence cannot be compensated.

Rule 17.8 gives the Trial Chamber broad powers to control the process by which evidence is produced. It may issue orders to compel compliance with a production request, such as ordering production, granting a continuance, prohibiting the introduction of evidence, and other orders as are just under the circumstances. It may also order that the production be denied, restricted, or deferred, or make such other order as may be required by the interests of justice.

A party may request that the Trial Chamber inspect evidence *in camera* prior to its determination that a production request should be granted or denied. If the party's motion contains information which may not be subject to disclosure, the motion, or the pertinent portion thereof, may be sealed.

Rule 18: Motions Practice

18.1 Time for making motions

(A) Generally. After the accused's initial appearance, either party may move before the Trial Chamber for appropriate relief or ruling. Such motions may be written or oral at the discretion of the Trial Chamber.

(B) Prior to initial appearance. Notwithstanding the provisions of subsection (A), under extraordinary circumstances where the accused has made allegations which create a substantial likelihood that he or she will prevail, the Trial Chamber may, prior to the accused's initial appearance, entertain motions for dismissal or other relief based upon jurisdictional defects.

(C) Prior to trial on the issue of guilt. Failure by the defense to make the following motions within 30 days after the initial appearance of the accused or prior to the commencement of trial, whichever occurs first, shall constitute waiver, although the Trial Chamber for good cause shown may grant relief from the waiver:

(1) Defenses or objections based on defects in the indictment;

(2) Motions to suppress evidence obtained from or belonging to the accused;

(3) Motions for severance of charges or accused; and

(4) Objections based on the denial of request for appointment of counsel pursuant to Rule 11.

18.2 Opportunity to respond. Upon the submission of a motion, the other party shall be afforded a reasonable opportunity to respond to the motion.

18.3 Ruling on motions. Motions shall be decided as expeditiously as possible. A motion may be summarily denied on the grounds that insufficient allegations of fact or law have been set forth to justify further inquiry by the Trial Chamber. Otherwise, a motion may be granted or denied either on the basis of the representations made in the motion and response, or after such further proceedings as the Trial Chamber may specify, or both.

18.4. Prosecutor's appeal of adverse ruling. The prosecutor may immediately appeal from an order of the Trial Chamber which:

(A) dismisses all or part of an indictment and prohibits the prosecutor from bringing new charges based on the acts underlying the dismissed indictment, or portion thereof; or

(B) suppresses, excludes or precludes evidence, if the prosecutor represents to the Trial Chamber that the appeal is not taken for the purpose of delay and that the evidence is a substantial proof of a fact material in the proceeding.

18.5. Limitations

(A) With the exception of a motion for dismissal pursuant to Rule 18.1(B), an accused who has voluntarily failed to appear for proceedings before the International Tribunal is precluded from making any motions pursuant to these Rules.

(B) The provisions of Rule 18.1 through 18.4 do not apply to motions or requests by the prosecutor for the issuance of orders, warrants or requests by the International Tribunal which:

(1) are made prior to the accused's initial appearance; or

(2) justify consideration ex parte.

COMMENTARY

Rule 18 governs the conduct of motions practice, based upon the principles that follow. Generally, motions or requests by the prosecutor (1) made prior to the accused's initial appearance, (2) related to the issuance of orders to secure the attendance of the accused and for the protection of victims and witnesses, and (3) for the assistance of Chambers in obtaining international legal assistance, may be made *ex parte*. Other motions must be made after the accused's initial appearance, with the exception of claims that prosecution by the International Tribunal is barred under Rule 5.

With the exception of *ex parte* motions, each party must be given the opportunity to respond to motions. A motion may be denied out of hand by the Chamber if insufficient allegations of fact or law are made to justify further hearing. In accordance with the general rule that fugitives may not seek relief, fugitives may not file motions or objections while they refuse to submit themselves to the International Tribunal's authority.

Rule 18 also provides for the interlocutory appeal by the Prosecutor of the granting of motions to suppress, exclude or preclude, if this deprives the Prosecutor of an important item of proof. It also provides for interlocutory appeal of the granting of motions to dismiss indictments. The execution of the Trial Chamber's order can be stayed under the provisions of Rule 29.

Rule 19: Depositions

19.1 Authority. The Trial Chamber may order a deposition whenever, due to exceptional circumstances of the case, it is in the interests of justice that the testimony of a prospective witness be taken and preserved for use at trial.

19.2 Submission

(A) In writing. Either party may submit a written motion for the taking of a deposition.

(B) Content. The motion shall include the name and location of the person whose deposition is requested, the proposed date and place at which the deposition is to be taken, a statement of the matters on which the person is to be examined, and of the exceptional circumstances justifying the taking of the deposition.

(C) Notice. The party at whose request the deposition is being taken shall give reasonable notice to the other party and to the person who is to be examined.

(D) Ruling. The motion shall be decided pursuant to the criteria set forth in Rule 18.3.

19.3 Conduct. Subject to any conditions that the Trial Chamber may provide, a deposition shall be carried out under the same conditions as the examination of a witness at trial. Objections and the grounds for the objections shall be stated at the time of the deposition; rulings on objections, if any, shall be made at the time of trial.

19.4 Payment of expenses. Whenever a deposition is taken at the request of the Prosecutor or at the request of an accused determined to be indigent pursuant to the provisions of Rule 11, the Trial Chamber may direct that the International Tribunal bear the expense of the deposition.

COMMENTARY

Rule 19 permits measures to be taken to ensure that the testimony of victims or other witnesses is available for trial or sentence. Given the preference for "live" testimony as opposed to second-hand accounts, it may be important to the Prosecutor's case to memorialize a witness's testimony in this manner if there is reason to believe the witness will be unavailable for trial.

Depositions should be carried out under circumstances as close as possible to those at trial, including the right to cross-examination, and giving the accused the opportunity to be present, or if impracticable since in detention, giving the accused voice or other access to the proceedings and to consultation with counsel.

This provision permits filmed, taped or otherwise transcribed depositions to be taken in advance of trial if there is reason to believe that the victim or witness may not be available for trial by reason of absence, illness or other good cause.

Rule 20: Public Trial

20.1 Open sessions. All post-indictment proceedings before the International Tribunal, other than deliberations of a Chamber, shall be open to the public, except as otherwise provided in these Rules.

20.2 Closed sessions. The Trial Chamber may close a session of trial to protect the safety, security, or identity of particular victims or witnesses and for reasons relating to the national security of a State. The Trial Chamber may conduct *ex parte, in camera* hearings or consider *ex parte* briefs and affidavits on the issue of whether there is a need for protection of national security information or the identity of any particular witness or victim.

20.3 Control of spectators. In order to protect the accused's right to a fair trial or maintain the dignity and decorum of the proceedings, the Trial Chamber may limit the number of spectators in, exclude specific persons from, restrict access to, or, subject to Rule 20.2, close the courtroom.

20.4 Photography or other recordings. Photography, video recording or audio recording of the trial, other than by the Registry, is within the discretion of the Trial Chamber.

COMMENTARY

Rule 20 is derived from Articles 19(2) and 20 of the Statute. The Rule grants broad discretion to the Trial Chamber in determining whether to close proceedings when it finds that the potential harm to either a victim, witness, or the essential interests of a State, outweighs the public's interest in, and the accused's right to, a public trial.

Rule 21: Presence of the Accused

Except as otherwise provided in these Rules, the accused is entitled to be present at all post-indictment proceedings before a Chamber, other than deliberations. However, the accused shall be considered to have waived the right to be present whenever:

(A) the accused is voluntarily absent after his or her initial appearance; or

(B) having been warned by the Trial Chamber that disruptive conduct will cause the accused to be removed from the courtroom, persists in conduct which justifies exclusion from the courtroom.

COMMENTARY

Rule 21 is based upon Article 21 of the Statute's guarantee of the right of an accused to be tried in his or her presence. As recognized by numerous legal systems, this right is not absolute; therefore, Rule 21 specifies the circumstances under which a trial can continue without the presence of the accused.

Rule 22: Abbreviated Proceedings

[Under many common law systems, the prosecutor enjoys broad powers to offer immunity to, and enter into plea-bargain agreements with, accused who provide meaningful and substantial cooperation in the investigation or prosecution of other cases. Most civil law systems, however, do not permit such activities, although cooperation of lower and mid-ranking accused in exchange for significant mitigation of punishment is an important tool in building successful prosecutions against high-ranking suspects and accused.

Without such mechanisms, the International Tribunal may be unable to successfully prosecute a significant number of high-level figures. Accordingly, in Appendix I to these Rules, we have set forth two proposals for encouraging cooperation of accused in exchange for favorable treatment regarding their cases. Option One, containing provisions for the granting of immunity by the Prosecutor, the making of pretrial agreements between an accused and the Prosecutor, and the acceptance by the Trial Chamber of a plea of guilty, provides a common law approach. Option Two, permitting an abbreviated proceeding in which an accused may acknowledge guilt and provide cooperation in exchange for mitigation of punishment, but in which the prosecutor may not unilaterally grant immunity, may be more compatible with civil law systems. The judges may, of course, adopt aspects of both proposals if they desire.]

Rule 23: Case Presentation

23.1 In general. The Trial Chamber shall control the mode and order of the presentation of evidence as necessary to ascertain the truth, avoid needless consumption of time, and protect victims and witnesses from harassment or undue embarrassment.

23.2 Joint trials. In joint trials, each accused shall be accorded rights and privileges as if tried separately.

23.3 Opening statements. Before presentation of evidence by the Prosecutor has begun, each party may make an opening statement to the Trial Chamber. The defense may elect to make its statement after the prosecution has concluded its presentation and before the presentation of evidence for the defense.

23.4 Presentation of evidence. Each party is entitled to present evidence. Unless otherwise required by interests of justice, evidence on the issue of guilt shall be presented in the following sequence:

(A) Presentation of evidence for the prosecution;

(B) Presentation of evidence for the defense;

(C) Presentation of prosecution evidence in rebuttal;

(D) Presentation of defense evidence in surrebuttal;

(E) Additional rebuttal evidence in the discretion of the Trial Chamber; and

(F) Presentation of evidence requested by the Trial Chamber.

23.5 Argument by counsel on findings. After the closing of evidence, the Prosecutor shall be permitted to make an initial argument. The defense shall be permitted to reply. The Prosecutor shall then be permitted to make a rebuttal argument. Arguments may properly include any fair comment on the evidence in the case, including inferences to be drawn therefrom, in support of a party's theory of the case.

23.6 Deliberations, standard of proof

(A) Generally. After argument by both parties on findings, the Trial Chamber shall deliberate in closed session. A finding of guilty of any offense may be reached only when a majority of the Trial Chamber is satisfied that guilt has been proved beyond a reasonable doubt.

(B) Resolution of charges. The Trial Chamber shall vote separately on each charge contained in the indictment. If two or more accused are tried together, separate findings shall be made as to each.

(1) If the evidence presented at trial constitutes a minor variation from the allegations contained in the indictment, an accused may nonetheless be found guilty provided that the variation has not affected a substantial right of the accused. Upon such finding, the Trial Chamber shall modify the indictment accordingly.

(2) If the evidence fails to prove the accused's guilt of the offense charged, but proves the accused's guilt of a lesser included offense, the Trial Chamber may find the accused guilty of the lesser included offense. Upon such finding, the Trial Chamber shall modify the indictment accordingly.

23.7 Judgment and written opinion

(A) The judgment shall be delivered in public and in the accused's presence.

(B) Subject to the provisions of Rule 23.6, the judgment shall specify whether or not the accused is guilty of each offense contained within the indictment.

(C) The judgment shall be accompanied by a reasoned written opinion, to which separate or dissenting opinions may be appended. At a minimum, the opinion shall state whether the accused is guilty of each offense contained within the indictment, the evidence upon which this judgment is based, and the reasons for and the degree of weight given to the evidence upon which the judgment is based.

COMMENTARY

Rule 23.1 provides that the Trial Chamber controls the presentation of evidence. In an adversarial system, a Trial Chamber acts as a neutral referee between the parties: sustaining or overruling objections to the form of questions, the admissibility of testimonial and other evidence; determining the appropriateness of arguments and conduct of counsel; conduct of other persons in the courtroom; setting the order of proof; ruling on motions, etc.

Rule 23.2 restates the maxim that the proof introduced in a joint trial against one accused, but not the other, should be kept separate within the minds of the judges of the Trial Chamber.

Rules 23.3, 23.4, and 23.5 set the order of presentation of proof. Since, under Article 21.3 of the Statute, the accused is presumed innocent until proven guilty beyond a reasonable doubt, the accused need not present any evidence, let alone before the Prosecutor has completed his or her initial presentation.

The testimony of witnesses shall be taken orally in open session, unless otherwise provided in these Rules (a discussion of the alternatives to live testimony can be found in the commentary to Rule 7). Each witness must testify under oath or affirmation. The party calling the witness first conducts direct examination of the witness, followed by cross-examination of the witness by the opposing party. Redirect and recross-examination are within the discretion of the Trial Chamber. In addition to any examinations by the Prosecutor and defense counsel, the Trial Chamber may conduct any questioning it deems necessary.

Documentary and physical evidence, whenever practicable, should be marked for identification and included in the record of trial whether admitted in evidence or not. If it is impracticable to attach an item of documentary or real evidence to the record, the item should be clearly and accurately described by testimony, photographs, or other means so that it may be considered on appeal.

In compensation for the high burden of proof on the prosecution, Rule 23.5 grants to the Prosecutor a second "rebuttal" argument.

Rules 23.6 and 23.7 govern the conduct of the Trial Chamber's deliberations, voting, the announcement of the judgment and preparation of the written opinion.

Rule 24: Accused's Rights

The accused is entitled, subject to the limitations set forth elsewhere in these Rules, to the following minimum guarantees:

(A) the right to be treated equally with all other accused;

(B) the right to be presumed innocent throughout all portions of the trial until such time as a Trial Chamber finds him or her guilty beyond a reasonable doubt;

(C) the right to be tried without undue delay;

(D) the right, subject to Rule 20, to a public trial;

(E) the right to counsel throughout all portions of the trial, including counsel assigned by the Registrar upon a determination of indigency in accordance with Rule 11;

(F) the right to adequate time and facilities for the preparation of his or her defense and to communicate with counsel;

(G) the right, in accordance with Rule 17, to full and open production of evidence in a timely fashion to allow the defense to fully prepare for trial;

(H) the right to examine the evidence and cross-examine the witnesses against him or her, subject to the protections accorded victims and witnesses under Rules 7 and 8;

(I) the right to obtain attendance and examination of witnesses on his or her own behalf under the same conditions as witnesses against the accused and to have such witnesses made available, upon timely notice to the Prosecutor, at the expense of the International Tribunal;

(J) the right to free assistance of an interpreter if the accused cannot understand or speak the language of the International Tribunal;

(K) the right not to be compelled to testify against him or herself, not to confess guilt, and not to have his or her silence held against him or her in determining findings or sentence.

COMMENTARY

Rule 24 is based upon Article 27 of the Statute.

When determining whether the accused has been brought to trial without undue delay under subsection (C), the Trial Chamber shall consider all circumstances and exigencies, excluding time attributed to the defense and those delays outside the control of the Prosecution and the Tribunal. The Trial Chamber shall not dismiss any charges with prejudice because of undue delay except under exceptional circumstances.

An accused's right to counsel contained in subsection (E) is governed by Rule 11.

The right to examine the evidence under subsection (G) includes the right to inspect, copy, conduct scientific testing, etc.

Although the accused has a right, set forth in subsection (H), to cross-examine the witnesses against him, this is limited by Rules 7 and 8, which provides for the protection of victims and witnesses. The Trial Chamber should use a means for cross-examination which protects victims and witnesses, yet maximizes the accused's right of confrontation. A full discussion of protective measures is found in the commentary to Rule 7.

Before granting a request for the production of witnesses under subsection (I), the Trial Chamber should require the defense to establish that the witness's testimony is admissible under Rule 25. If the Trial Chamber determines that the witness is reasonably available, is material and relevant to the defense of the accused, and that the witness's testimony is the best means to introduce such evidence, the Trial Chamber should order the production of the requested witness.

In an effort to grant full meaning to the accused's right to remain silent under subsection (K), the Trial Chamber must not draw any adverse inference from the accused's election to remain silent. The burden of proving guilt always remains on the Prosecutor, and the burden to prove his innocence never shifts to the defense. Accordingly, the accused never assumes a duty to testify in his behalf.

Rule 25: Evidence

25.1 Purpose and interpretation. This Rule shall be interpreted to ensure fairness to the parties and to the end that the truth may be ascertained and cases justly decided.

25.2 Secondary sources. Insofar as not contrary to the Statute or these Rules, a Chamber shall have the power to rely on the following sources of international law in interpreting or supplementing Rule 25:

(A) international conventions, whether general or particular;

(B) international custom, as evidence of general practice accepted as law;

(C) general principles of the laws of nations; and

(D) judicial decisions and the teachings of other international tribunals and States.

25.3 Rulings on evidence

(A) The admissibility of evidence in accordance with these rules shall be determined by the presiding judge of the Trial Chamber. A majority of the judges sitting on the Trial Chamber may overrule a determination made by the presiding judge.

(B) The party seeking to introduce evidence shall have the burden of satisfying all requirements for its consideration by the Trial Chamber.

(C) The Trial Chamber shall set forth its reasons for rejecting evidence or admitting evidence over the objection of a party orally in the record or in a written opinion attached to the record.

25.4 Joint trials. In joint trials, evidence which is admissible against only one or some of the joint or several accused may be considered only against the accused concerned.

25.5 Acceptance of facts without introduction of evidence. The Trial Chamber may, without the production of evidence, recognize the existence in truth of certain facts having a bearing on the issue of guilt, which are not subject to reasonable dispute, and which are either:

(A) generally known universally, locally, or in the area pertinent to the event, or

(B) capable of accurate and ready determination by resort to sources whose accuracy cannot reasonably be questioned.

25.6 Agreements as to admissibility

(A) The defense and the prosecution may make oral or written agreements that a fact, the contents of a document, or the expected testimony of a witness should be considered as evidence by the Trial Chamber.

(B) The Trial Chamber may, in the interest of justice, decline to accept an agreement under subsection (A).

(C) Before accepting an agreement under subsection (A), the Trial Chamber must be satisfied that the accused understands the nature and effect of the agreement, and that both the accused and the Prosecutor consent to its consideration by the Trial Chamber.

(D) Either party may withdraw from an agreement offered under subsection (A) any time before it is accepted by the Trial Chamber. After it has been accepted, a party may withdraw from it only if permitted to do so by the Trial Chamber.

(E) Expected testimony or the content of a document presented to and accepted by the Trial Chamber under this Rule may be attacked, contradicted, or explained in the same way as if the witness had testified at trial or the document had been accepted as evidence and viewed by the Trial Chamber. The fact that the parties agreed that a witness would give certain testimony or that a document has certain contents does not constitute an admission of the truth of the testimony or document's contents.

(F) Except as provided by subsection (E), any fact presented to and accepted by the Trial Chamber under this Rule is binding on both parties and may not be contradicted.

25.7 Relevance

(A) The Trial Chamber shall in general admit any oral, written or physical evidence having a bearing on the issues before it. Irrelevant evidence shall not be admitted.

(B) Relevant evidence may nonetheless be excluded if required by any other provision of these Rules, or for other good cause, including that it would constitute a needless presentation of cumulative evidence, would result in undue delay, or would otherwise represent a waste of time.

25.8 Primary evidence

(A) The Trial Chamber shall prefer the presentation of primary evidence of a fact. "Primary evidence" means original or first hand evidence. A copy of a document certified as being a true and accurate reproduction of the original shall be considered to be original evidence.

(B) Testimony from a witness as to assertions made by another person, other than the accused, is admissible to prove the truth of the assertions only when the Trial Chamber is satisfied that, as to the assertions,

(1) circumstantial guarantees of their trustworthiness exist,

(2) their admission does not undermine the interests of justice and the accused's right to a fair trial, and

(3) they are more probative on the relevant fact for which they are offered than any other evidence which the proponent can procure through reasonable efforts or they are corroborative of other evidence already admitted.

(C) Written statements of an individual not testifying before the Trial Chamber are admissible only when the Trial Chamber is satisfied that the criteria in subsection (B), as applied to the statements, are met.

(D) When a writing or recorded statement or part thereof is introduced by a party, the Trial Chamber may require that party to introduce any other part or any other writing or recorded statement which ought in fairness to be considered contemporaneously with it.

25.9 Witnesses

(A) Every person is presumed competent to be a witness and shall present his or her testimony orally under oath or affirmation.

(B) Unless granted immunity under Rule 6.3, a witness has the right against self-incrimination and may decline to make any statement which might tend to incriminate him or her.

(C) If scientific, technical, or other specialized knowledge will assist the Trial Chamber to understand the evidence or to determine a fact in issue, a witness qualified as an expert by knowledge, skill, experience, training, or education, may testify thereto in the form of an opinion or otherwise.

(D) Witnesses shall be protected from reprisals, but measures taken to protect witnesses shall be balanced by the Trial Chamber with the accused's right to a fair trial, including, but not limited to, the accused's right to confront and cross-examine adverse witnesses.

25.10 Victim's past behavior in cases involving sexual assault

(A) In a case in which a person is accused of rape or sexual assault, evidence of the past sexual behavior of an alleged victim of such rape or assault is not admissible unless it is evidence of:

(1) past sexual behavior with persons other than the accused, offered by the accused upon the issue of whether the accused was or was not the source of semen or injury with respect to the alleged victim;

(2) past sexual behavior with the accused, offered by the accused upon the issue of whether the alleged victim consented to the sexual behavior with respect to which the rape or assault is alleged; or

(3) past sexual behavior, offered by the accused to rebut evidence by the Prosecutor that the alleged victim did not engage in sexual activity during a given period of time.

(B) Before admitting evidence of the victim's past sexual behavior, the Trial Chamber shall satisfy itself through an offer of proof made by the defense outside the presence of the public that the evidence meets the requirements of subsection (A).

25.11 Lawyer-client privilege

An individual has a privilege to refuse to disclose and to prevent any other person from disclosing confidential communications made for the purpose of facilitating the rendition of professional legal services to that individual.

25.12 Confessions and admissions. A confession is an out-of-court acknowledgement of guilt of any element of a criminal offense or any out-of-court self-incriminating statement made by an individual. An admission is any other statement made by an individual with respect to his or her participation or lack of participation in an offense charged.

(A) A confession or admission may be admitted as evidence only if voluntarily given.

(B) The Trial Chamber, in determining the issue of voluntariness, shall take into consideration all the circumstances surrounding the giving of the confession or, including, but not limited to: (1) the existence of any use or threatened use of physical force upon the individual or another person, or undue pressure which undermines the individual's ability to make a choice whether or not to make a statement, (2) the existence and circumstances of custody of the individual at time of the confession, (3) whether the individual knew the nature of the offense with which he or she was charged or of which he or she was suspected at the time of confession, (4) whether the individual was advised of his or her rights under Rule 10, and (5) whether the individual was without the assistance of counsel at the time of questioning. The presence or absence of any of the above factors need not be conclusive on the issue of voluntariness of the confession.

25.13 Evidence resulting from electronic surveillance, undercover investigations, informant information or search and seizure. Relevant evidence seized from the person or control of the accused or obtained as a result of the use of electronic surveillance, undercover investigators, informant information, or search and seizure is admissible unless obtained by methods so offensive to fundamental principles of fairness and due process that its admission is antithetical to, and would seriously damage, the integrity of the proceedings.

25.14 Special Defenses. If a special defense, such as those listed below, is placed in issue by credible evidence, the Prosecutor shall have the burden of proving beyond a reasonable doubt that the defense is not valid.

(A) Obedience to orders. It is a defense to any offense that the accused was acting pursuant to orders unless the accused knew the orders to be unlawful, or a person of ordinary sense and understanding would have known the orders to be unlawful.

(B) Duress or coercion. It is a defense to any offense, except any crime involving killing, that the accused's participation in the offense was caused by a reasonable apprehension that the accused or another innocent person would be immediately killed or would immediately suffer serious bodily injury as a result of the accused's refusal to commit the act. The Trial Chamber may consider as a matter of mitigation in offenses involving killing the extent to which the accused was compelled by duress to commit the crime.

(C) Mistake of fact. It is a defense that the accused held, as a result of ignorance or mistake, an incorrect belief regarding a fact such that, if the true facts were as the accused believed them, the accused would not be guilty of the offense. The ignorance or mistake must have been reasonable under all the circumstances. Ignorance of the requirements of international humanitarian law is not a defense.

COMMENTARY

Rule 25 is derived from Article 15 of the Statute, which provides that the judges of the Tribunal shall adopt rules of procedure and evidence.

Rule 25.1 is intended to provide a general guideline to be used in construing the rules of evidence for the International Tribunal. It is, however, only a rule of construction and not a license to disregard the Rules in order to reach a desired result.

Rule 25.2 gives a Chamber the power to use recognized sources of international law in order to interpret or supplement this Rule. We foresee that individual judges will resort to these sources to the extent necessary to interpret a provision of this Rule.

Rule 25.3, subsection (A) allows for the efficiency of proceedings by permitting the presiding judge to rule upon the admissibility of evidence. The second part of this Rule, however, permits the presiding judge to be overruled by a majority of the judges sitting on that Trial Chamber. This procedure will ensure that all rulings encompass the views of the majority of the judges, while eliminating the requirement that the judges of the Trial Chamber must discuss each objection or issue which arises concerning the admissibility of evidence.

Subsection (B) requires the party seeking to introduce evidence to establish a proper predicate. A "proper predicate" means preliminary questions to a witness which, for example, establish the admissibility of evidence and the qualifications of an expert witness. We have not attempted to provide guidance as to the prerequisites for all types of evidence. For example, we have not specified what types of documentary evidence may be accepted by the Trial Chamber without being accompanied by the testimony of a custodian or other person familiar with the document.

Subsection (C) requires the presiding judge to state for the record the reasons for denying the admission of evidence. This ensures a clear and concise record in case either party appeals an adverse ruling.

Rule 25.4 provides that evidence presented against only one accused in a joint trial is not to be considered against any others. When it is impossible to effectively delete all references to a co-accused, alternative steps must be taken to protect the co-accused. Alternative steps may include the granting of a severance and trial by a separate Trial Chamber.

Rule 25.5 discusses the circumstances under which a fact or testimony can be accepted for consideration by a Trial Chamber without proof presented by a party, a doctrine known in common law systems as "judicial notice." The following are examples of matters of which judicial notice may be taken: The ordinary division of time into years, months, weeks and other periods; general facts and laws of nature, including their ordinary operations and effect; general facts of history; generally known geographical facts; such specific facts and propositions of generalized knowledge as are so universally known that they cannot reasonably be the subject of dispute; such facts as are so generally known or are of such common notoriety in the area in which the trial is held that they cannot reasonably be the subject of dispute; and specific facts and propositions of generalized knowledge which are capable of immediate and accurate determination by resort to easily accessible sources or reasonable indisputable accuracy.

Rule 25.6 deals with the rule of judicial economy known in common law systems as "stipulations." This Rule permits the parties the flexibility to introduce evidence not in dispute in a manner which may save substantial time and money.

Rule 25.7 sets forth fundamental principles of relevancy which govern the admissibility of all evidence. The general standard is that relevant evidence is generally admissible. "Relevant evidence" is that evidence which has any tendency to make the existence of any fact that is of consequence to the determination of the action more probable or less probable than it would be without the evidence. This qualified admissibility of relevant evidence is intended to require a balancing between the degree of the probative value of the proffered evidence and the judicial efficiency of the Trial Chamber in determining whether relevant evidence should be admitted.

Rule 25.8 expresses a preference for "primary evidence." However, depending upon the circumstances, the only available evidence may be the testimony of a witness, an *ex parte* affidavit, a document certified by a State as an official document, or evidence of the kind described in subsection (B) known in common law systems as hearsay evidence.

It is critical that the principle that relevant evidence should be considered by a Chamber be balanced against the rights of the accused to have a fair trial. Specifically, the Trial Chamber should balance the accused's rights of confrontation and cross-examination against the type of evidence offered. The more the evidence in question bears on issues directly related to guilt, the higher the standard of admissibility that should be applied by the Trial Chamber.

For example, should an *ex parte* witness statement be offered to prove an essential element of the offense charged, then the Trial Chamber should consider refusing to consider it if the person who made the statement is available to give testimony. Even if admitted, the Chamber should give less weight to secondary evidence such as *ex parte* affidavits, since it has not had the opportunity to fully judge the reliability of the individual making the statement. In contrast, testimony by a witness in another judicial proceeding, whom the accused had the opportunity to cross-examine, should be admitted and given a greater degree of weight. With regard to documents, a duplicate of a document proven to be an accurate reproduction of the original should be admissible to the same extent as the original.

Rule 25.9 sets forth a general rule of competency of witnesses. The oath or affirmation requirement is to help the Trial Chamber ensure that the witness knows the difference between truth and falsehood, and understands the moral importance of telling the truth. The oath or affirmation shall be administered in a manner calculated to awaken the witness's conscience and impress the witness's mind with the duty to tell the truth.

Subsection (B) permits a witness to refuse to testify where the answer may tend to incriminate the witness. In such cases immunity may be an option to acquire the testimony of the witness.

Subsection (C) should not be read as requiring the admission of testimony merely because it comes from an individual who purports to be expert in a particular area. Expert testimony may be excluded for any ground under these Rule, including that the methods utilized by the expert are not reliable enough.

Subparagraph (D) should be read in conjunction with Rules 7 and 8 regarding protection of victims or witnesses.

Rule 25.10 is designed to protect a victim of a sexual assault or rape from undergoing needless suffering as a result of defense cross-examination regarding the victim's prior sexual history. Although originally designed for common law systems in which a jury could be unduly swayed by such examination, even in a non-jury system, the procedure operates to protect the victim from essentially irrelevant yet emotionally damaging questioning before a large audience. The defense must make an "offer of proof" before such evidence may be presented, meaning that the defense must either describe the evidence with sufficient particularity or produce the witness or other evidence for preliminary examination by the court so it can determine that the evidence may be heard in open court. The Trial Chamber may of course outline how the victim may be examined or cross-examined with respect to the evidence.

Rule 25.11 specifies that communications between a client and his or her lawyer are privileged, and may not be admitted in evidence unless the privilege is waived by the client. Other privileges recognized in various jurisdictions were considered and specifically rejected.

Rule 25.12 permits confessions to be accepted as evidence only if the confession is voluntary, thus ensuring that the accused's right to remain silent has been honored. It should be noted that statements in which a suspect or accused attempts to exculpate him or herself, but which, given other evidence, establish deception or some other damaging fact, should normally be considered to fall outside the scope of this Rule.

Rule 25.13 specifically provides that evidence resulting from electronic surveillance, undercover investigations and search and seizure shall be admissible unless obtained by extraordinarily offensive methods. The provision was necessary in order to make clear that these investigatory methods can be utilized, although the domestic law of some nations which acceded to the Statute would not necessarily permit the use of such evidence in their national courts.

Rule 25.14 treats the issue of the burden of proving special defenses. Any defense may be raised by credible evidence presented by the defense, the Prosecutor, or the Trial Chamber. Placing upon the Prosecutor the burden of proving the invalidity of a special defense is in keeping with the Prosecutor's burden of proving beyond a reasonable doubt that the accused committed the crime or crimes charged in an indictment.

Subsection (A): While Article 7 of the Statute states that "the fact that an accused person acted pursuant to an order of a government or of a superior shall not relieve him of criminal responsibility, but may be considered in mitigation of punishment," it is a recognized principle of international law, dating from the Nuremberg "subsequent proceedings," that under some circumstances the defense of obedience to superior orders is legitimate. In order to be a valid defense, however, the accused must have neither subjective or objective knowledge of the superior order's unlawfulness.

Subsection (B): It is a fundamental principle of many legal systems that commission of a crime while under duress is a factor that should also be considered in mitigation of punishment. This principle is applied, in one context, to narrow the effect of an imperfect obedience to superior orders defense. Thus, even if an accused knew, or should have known, that the orders he or she was given were unlawful, it remains a matter for the Trial Chamber to consider in mitigation that the accused committed offenses while under duress.

Subsection (C): The defense of ignorance or mistake of fact is particularly important in armed conflict where the "fog of war" sometimes clouds the true nature of a situation. For example, a reasonable mistake of fact that an object is a legitimate military target should not lead to prosecution, or, if it does, should allow a defense.

Rule 26: Sentencing

26.1 Production of evidence. Upon request of either party, the other party shall:

(A) permit the requesting party to inspect such matters as the other party will present to the Trial Chamber during the sentencing phase of the trial; and

(B) notify the requesting party, subject to the protections accorded to a particular witness under Rules 7 and 8, of the names of and means of contacting the witnesses the other party intends to call during the sentencing phase of the trial.

26.2 Presentencing procedure. If any findings of guilty have been announced, the prosecution and the defense may present or submit matter to aid the Trial Chamber in determining an appropriate sentence. Such matter may include aggravation, extenuation or mitigation evidence, or evidence concerning rehabilitative potential. The Trial Chamber may, upon request of the Prosecutor or the defense, permit a presentencing hearing. If such a hearing is permitted, the Prosecutor and the defense shall ordinarily present matter in the following order:

(A) Presentation by the Prosecutor;

(B) Presentation by the defense;

(C) Rebuttal/Surrebuttal;

(D) Argument by the Prosecutor on sentence; and

(E) Argument by the defense on sentence.

26.3 Adjudging sentence. The sentence imposed shall be determined by majority vote of the judges of the Trial Chamber. In reaching a sentence, the Trial Chamber shall take into account such factors as the gravity of the offense, the individual circumstances of the convicted person, and the evidence submitted during presentencing, such mitigating circumstances as meaningful and substantial cooperation provided to the Prosecutor by the accused, and the extent to which any penalty imposed by a national court on the same person for the same act has already been served. The sentence shall be announced in the presence of the accused, and subject to the protections accorded to a particular witness under Rules 7 and 8, in public.

26.4. Status of accused after conviction or sentence. Where the accused is at liberty during the pendency of proceedings, the Trial Chamber, upon conviction or sentence of the accused, may order that the accused be immediately taken into confinement, that the execution of the judgment be stayed pending appeal as set forth in Rule 29, or that the accused surrender pursuant to such terms as the Trial Chamber may impose. If necessary, the Trial Chamber may issue a Warrant for Arrest to secure the presence of the accused.

COMMENTARY

Rule 26 establishes a separate sentencing phase of trial, after a finding of guilty. This separate phase ensures that the parties have the opportunity to present evidence which, while not relevant to the issue of guilt, is pertinent to the determination of the appropriate penalty. It also offers the Trial Chamber the opportunity to take a fresh look at the evidence it considered during the trial.

Rule 26.1 provides for open discovery between the parties prior to the sentencing phase.

Rule 26.2 sets the order of presentation of evidence during the sentencing phase.

Rule 26.3 sets forth a non-exhaustive list of the factors which may be considered by a Chamber in imposing sentence. It is important to note that cooperation by the accused in the investigation and prosecution of other individuals is a significant mitigating factor. As noted in the commentary to Rule 22, cooperation of lower and mid-ranking accused in exchange for significant mitigation of punishment is an important tool in building successful prosecutions against high-ranking suspects and accused. Rule 27 provides the permissible range of penalties.

Rule 26.4 sets forth the procedure for taking an accused into custody who was previously at liberty upon conviction or sentence. Once an individual has been convicted, the risk of flight obviously becomes much higher. Accordingly, this provision permits liberty to be immediately revoked and the convicted person taken into custody. This provision also makes it clear that the Chamber may issue a Warrant for Arrest if the accused does not comply with conditions set for his or her surrender.

[The judges may determine that separate guilt adjudication and sentencing phases are not required.]

Rule 27: Penalties and Enforcement of Sentences

27.1 Scope of Imprisonment

(A) The Trial Chamber may adjudge a sentence or sentences of imprisonment for a term up to and including the remainder of the convicted person's natural life.

(B) In imposing sentence, the Trial Chamber shall have recourse to the general practice regarding prison sentences in the courts of the former Yugoslavia.

(C) The Trial Chamber shall indicate whether multiple sentences shall be served consecutively or concurrently.

(D) The Trial Chamber shall credit the convicted person with the period of detention pending trial solely attributable to the charges brought by the International Tribunal. The Trial Chamber shall also credit the convicted person with the period of detention pending surrender of that person from a State to the International Tribunal.

27.2 Place of imprisonment. Imprisonment shall be ordered to be served in and according to the laws of a State designated by the International Tribunal from a list of States which have indicated to the Security Council their willingness to accept convicted persons.

27.3 Supervision of imprisonment. All sentences of imprisonment shall be supervised by the International Tribunal or an entity designated by the Security Council.

27.4 Confiscation of property. In addition to or in place of a sentence of imprisonment the Trial Chamber may order the confiscation from the convicted person of any property, real or personal, acquired through criminal conduct, including duress. Such orders shall also direct the return of such property to its lawful owners or their successors in interest.

27.5 Restitution. Compensation to victims by a convicted person may be an appropriate part of decisions regarding sentencing, the reduction of a sentence, parole, or commutation. The Trial Chamber shall consider the offender's ability to pay and shall not make any other part of its adjudged sentence contingent upon successful payment. Nonetheless, successful payment or nonpayment may be considered at a later time in determining whether to grant clemency or parole.

COMMENTARY

Rules 27.1 and 27.2 are based on Articles 24 and 27 of the Statute.

The maximum penalty is life imprisonment and the Trial Chamber may consider the "general practice regarding prison sentences in the courts of the former Yugoslavia" in fixing general sentencing guidelines. The accused receives credit for the time spent in pretrial detention, as well as the time spent in detention pending extradition to the Tribunal.

Rule 27.3 recognizes that the International Tribunal retains jurisdiction over the accused, although imprisonment is served in and according to the laws of States agreeing to accept convicted persons.

Rule 27.4 is derived from paragraph 114 of the Secretary General's Report, which states that in addition to imprisonment, "property acquired by criminal conduct should be confiscated and returned to its rightful owners."

Rule 27.5 emphasizes that whether or not a convicted person make restitution is an appropriate factor to consider in determining future parole and clemency requests.

Rule 28: Record for Post-trial Proceedings

28.1 Generally. A record shall be prepared in every case prosecuted before the International Tribunal.

28.2 Contents

(A) The record shall consist of:

(1) a verbatim transcript of every in-court session of the Trial Chamber;

(2) a copy of the indictment and any other documents submitted in the proceedings;

(3) any exhibit offered or submitted to or used by the Trial Chamber, or a certified copy, photographic reproduction, or detailed description thereof;

(4) a copy of the judgment of the Trial Chamber; including separate and dissenting opinions.

(B) Videotape, audiotape or any other transcriptions of the proceedings not directed to be made by the Trial Chamber shall not be considered part of the record.

28.3 Authentication. The record shall be forwarded for review and authentication to the Trial Chamber which heard the matter. Prior to authentication, the Prosecutor, the defense and each judge of that Trial Chamber shall have the opportunity to review the record of proceedings and to propose any changes necessary to accurately reflect the course of the proceedings. A judge designated by the presiding judge of the Trial Chamber shall authenticate the record.

28.4 Release. A record shall not be released, in whole or part, to any person until it has been authenticated and, then, only with the approval of the International Tribunal. The accused, if indigent, shall, at no expense, be provided a copy of such portion of the record of proceedings as may be required for preparation for and to conduct an appeal pursuant to these Rules.

COMMENTARY

Rule 28 governs the preparation of the record which will be used to determine all post-trial matters. The record should include the actual exhibits used during trial; where this is not practicable, accurate photographs, copies and the like, can be substituted. It is not necessary that an exhibit have been introduced into evidence for it to be made part of the record. Any item which was marked by the clerk of court as a potential exhibit may be included.

Rule 29: Appeal

29.1 Basis for appeal. The Appeals Chamber shall hear appeals from the Prosecutor, or persons convicted by a Trial Chamber, brought on the following bases:

(A) an allegation of error on a question of law, the nature of which would invalidate the judgment or sentence of a Trial Chamber;

(B) an error of fact which has resulted in a miscarriage of justice; or

(C) an order of the Trial Chamber pursuant to Rule 18.4.

29.2 Notice of appeal

(A) A party seeking to appeal a judgment or sentence, must, within 30 days after the announcement of such judgment or sentence, file with the Appeals Chamber and serve upon other parties a written notice of appeal. The Appeals Chamber may extend the period up to an additional 30 days for good cause shown, or for a further period up to 120 days if the failure to comply with this provision resulted from improper conduct by an employee of the International Tribunal, the death or disability of the accused's counsel or the inability of the accused and his or her counsel to have communicated, in person or by mail, concerning whether an appeal should be taken.

(B) If a notice of appeal is not filed in a timely fashion, or if a properly filed appeal is withdrawn in all respects, the judgment and sentence shall be deemed to be final and not further appealable.

29.3 Record on appeal

(A) Where the appeal is based upon an allegation of an error of law, the Appeals Chamber shall make its determination after review of the record authenticated by the Trial Chamber.

(B) Where the appeal is based upon an allegation of an error of fact, the Appeals Chamber shall make its determination after review of the record authenticated by the Trial Chamber, and where appropriate, after review of additional evidence presented to it.

29.4 Permissible actions

(A) The Appeals Chamber may, with respect to each count of the indictment pending at the time of the Trial Chamber's judgment:

(1) affirm the decision of the Trial Chamber;

(2) reverse the decision of the Trial Chamber and enter a judgment and, if necessary, a sentence;

(3) modify a conviction or sentence imposed by the Trial Chamber;

(4) remit a case to the Trial Chamber to resolve controverted factual issues which cannot be resolved from the record, to permit the Trial Chamber to make other factual or legal determinations, or to take other action directed by the Appeals Chamber.

(B) The Appeals Chamber shall not reverse a judgment of conviction on the basis of an error of law unless it is satisfied that the error materially affected the substantial rights of the accused at trial. The Appeals Chamber shall not reverse a judgment of conviction on the basis of an error of fact unless it is satisfied that the error has resulted in a miscarriage of justice.

(C) The decision of the Appeals Chamber shall be accompanied by a reasoned written opinion to which separate or dissenting opinions shall be appended.

29.5 Finality of review. A decision by the Appeals Chamber issued under Rule 29.4(A)(1), (2), or (3) shall be deemed to be final and not further appealable.

29.6 Stay of judgment

(A) Upon motion of an accused who has taken an appeal to the Appeals Chamber, a majority of the members of the Trial Chamber, or a member of the Appeals Chamber, may issue an order both:

(1) staying or suspending the execution of the judgment pending the determination of the appeal, and

(2) fixing such conditions of confinement or release as provided for in Rule 16.

(B) A motion pursuant to subsection (A) shall be denied if the accused does not establish:

(1) a probability of success on appeal, and

(2) that the likelihood of irreparable injury if the stay is denied outweighs the public interest in prompt execution of the judgment.

(C) A motion under this Rule shall be made in accordance with the provisions of Rule 18.

29.7 Surrender following appeal. Where the accused is at liberty during the pendency of an appeal as a result of an order issued pursuant to this Rule, the Appeals Chamber, upon affirmance or revision of the judgment and sentence must promptly order that the accused surrender to the International Tribunal, or to an authority designated by it, in order that the execution of the judgment be commenced or resumed. If necessary, the Appeals Chamber may remit the case to the Trial Chamber in order to issue a Warrant for Arrest to secure the presence of the accused.

29.8 Appeal; mode of submission and argument. The mode of and procedure for submission of briefs, reconciliation of errors in the transcript of proceedings, circumstances in which oral argument is required, the effect of the failure to present oral argument, the amount of time for oral argument allowed to each party, the number of counsel entitled to be heard, and such other procedures as may be required for the orderly litigation of appeals, shall be determined by such regulations as drafted and adopted by the Appeals Chamber.

COMMENTARY

Rule 29 treats appellate procedure and is based on Article 28 of the Statute.

Rule 29.1 specifies the bases upon which an appeal may be made.

Rule 29.2 requires a party to make its appeal within a specified time frame, so that, in the event that no appeal is made within that time frame, decisions of the Trial Chamber become final.

Rule 29.3 discusses the evidence which the Appeals Chamber can consider during its determination of the appeal. In most cases where further fact findings need to be made, it will be appropriate to permit the Trial Chamber which originally considered the case (and which has seen the demeanor of the witnesses) to carry out the fact-finding process. However, the Appeals Chamber has been given the power to hear evidence itself for the rare cases in which this would be more efficient.

Rule 29.4 gives the Appeals Chamber a wide range of powers. It may affirm, reverse or modify the decision of a Trial Chamber, or remit the case to the Trial Chamber for a particular action. The reversal or revision of a Trial Chamber's decision, based on an assertion of a "miscarriage of justice", should only be granted when the Appeals Chamber determines that, but for the error, a result more favorable to the appellant would have been reached.

Rule 29.5 specifies that a judgment becomes "final," thus absolutely precluding a national court from further prosecution for the same acts, once the Appeals Chamber makes a dispositive ruling, which does not remit the case to the Trial Chamber for further proceedings.

Rules 29.6 and 29.7 govern the granting of stays pending appeal and of taking a convicted person into custody during or after appeal.

Rule 29.8 leaves to the Appeals Chamber itself the development of uniform rules for the orderly progression of the appellate process.

Rule 30: Review Proceedings

(A) Where evidence has come to light which was not known to the moving party at the time of the proceedings before a Trial Chamber and could not have been discovered through the exercise of due diligence, the defense, or, within one year after the entry of a final judgment, the Prosecutor may make a motion to the Trial Chamber for reconsideration of the judgment or sentence, or for a new trial.

(B) If two judges of the Trial Chamber that adjudicated the case agree that the new evidence is credible and would probably have caused a different result on some or all of the charges or in the imposition of a substantially different sentence, the Trial Chamber shall either reconsider the case in light of the new evidence or order a new trial.

(C) A motion under this Rule shall be made in accordance with the provisions of Rule 18.

(D) The judgment of the Trial Chamber upon reconsideration shall be accompanied by a reasoned written opinion to which separate or dissenting opinions shall be appended.

(E) The judgment and sentence of the Trial Chamber upon reconsideration may be appealed from in accordance with the provisions of Rule 29.

(F) In the event that the judgment is pending appeal at the time the motion is filed, the Appeals Chamber may return the case to the Trial Chamber for disposition of the motion.

COMMENTARY

Rule 30 is based upon Article 26 of the Statute and sets forth the criteria upon which review proceedings can be conducted. Rehearing shall be limited to a determination of the admissibility of the new fact or facts and the consideration of them in light of the Trial Chamber's original decision. The right of appeal from the Trial Chamber's determination shall be the same as in any case before the International Tribunal.

The Chamber reviewing the case should initially attempt to determine whether the claim can be resolved on the basis of the allegations made in the supporting motion, *i.e.* dismissal for failure to make sufficient factual or legal allegations to provide the relief requested or dismissal because the issue was already adjudicated in an appeal. If it cannot dismiss the motion on that basis, only then should further proceedings be held.

Rule 31: Pardon and Commutation of Sentences

31.1 Generally. Only the International Tribunal, or an entity designated by the Security Council, may, after consideration of the standards set forth in Rule 31.3, pardon or commute the sentence of any person convicted.

(A) Individual States in which convicted persons are imprisoned have no unilateral authority to pardon, commute the sentences of, or otherwise release such persons prior to the expiration of their sentences.

(B) If, according to the laws of the State in which the convicted person is imprisoned, he or she is eligible for pardon or commutation of sentence, the State shall notify the International Tribunal or the entity designated by the Security Council of such eligibility and state its views regarding the advisability of granting pardon or commutation. The International Tribunal or the entity designated by the Security Council shall, upon such notice, determine whether pardon or commutation is appropriate.

31.2 Periodic review. Notwithstanding a convicted person's eligibility under the laws of the State in which the convicted person is imprisoned, the International Tribunal, or the entity designated by the Security Council, shall periodically review all its sentences to determine whether it should grant pardon or commutation. The period after which sentences shall be reviewed is determined as follows:

(A) Sentences of less than one year: no review.

(B) Sentences of one year or more: review after a period of six months or the expiration of one-third of the term, whichever is greater. In no case shall the period be greater than ten years. After the initial review of a particular sentence, the International Tribunal or the entity designated by the Security Council shall continue to review it annually.

(C) Sentences of life imprisonment: review after a period of ten years.

31.3 Standard of review. The following standards are advisory only, and do not constitute an exhaustive list of the factors to be considered in granting pardon or commutation. This Rule should be interpreted to ensure that all convicted persons, regardless of where imprisoned, are treated fairly and equally.

(A) Gravamen of offense. The International Tribunal should consider whether pardon or commutation is consistent with the gravamen of the offense or offenses for which the prisoner was convicted.

(B) Treatment of similarly-situated prisoners. The International Tribunal should consider whether pardon or commutation would be inconsistent with the continuing imprisonment of persons it convicted of similar offenses. In particular, it should determine whether the prisoner has served a sufficient term of imprisonment as punishment for his or her crime. If the International Tribunal's review is conducted prior to the expiration of one-third of the sentence, release may be ordered only in exceptional circumstances.

(C) Demonstration of rehabilitation. The International Tribunal should consider whether the prisoner has demonstrated rehabilitation sufficient to warrant his or her release and reentry into international society. In this connection, it is not necessary that the prison in which the prisoner was incarcerated offer particular rehabilitation programs.

(D) Cooperation. The International Tribunal should consider whether the prisoner has provided meaningful and substantial cooperation to the Prosecutor in the investigation or prosecution of other cases before the International Tribunal. The International Tribunal may also consider such cooperation rendered to authorities of a State.

COMMENTARY

Rule 31 is based on Article 28 of the Statute, which states that if "pursuant to the applicable law of the State in which the convicted person is imprisoned, he or she is eligible for pardon or commutation of sentence, the State concerned shall notify the International Tribunal accordingly." Since Article 28 vests ultimate decision authority in the President of the International Tribunal in consultation with his judges, the notification is merely a recommendation.

This Article, standing alone, might result in the unequal treatment of prisoners incarcerated in different States. Unless a particular State recommends a prisoner for release under its laws, the matter might never be considered by the International Tribunal. To remedy this potential equal protection problem, Rule 31.2 establishes the requirement that the International Tribunal periodically review every imprisonment sentence.

The standards of review are offered as examples of factors that should be considered in the pardon and commutation decisions. In general, the International Tribunal should try to balance leniency against the need to continue imprisonment as a matter of equal treatment among similarly-situated prisoners, general deterrence (the need to prevent future war crimes), and specific deterrence (preventing the specific offender from committing more crimes).

In addition, given the administrative burdens acting as a "parole board" are likely to impose on the International Tribunal, it should be stated that this responsibility may be delegated to any subsidiary organ that may be created.

The use in this Rule of the term "the International Tribunal or the entity designated by the Security Council" is offered to call attention to the concern that the International Tribunal must not be dissolved until some body is established to continue its supervision of sentences. The form of a successor body is left to the Security Council.

APPENDIX I

OPTION ONE

22.1 Acceptance of a plea of guilty. An accused may be found guilty of an offense based on his or her entry of a plea of guilty. Before accepting a plea of guilty, the Trial Chamber shall:

(A) address the accused personally and inform the accused of the nature of the offense to which the accused is pleading guilty, that the accused has the right to plead not guilty, and that by pleading guilty the accused waives his or her rights to confront and cross-examine witnesses.

(B) address the accused personally and determine that the plea is voluntary and not the result of promises apart from a plea agreement under Rule 9, force, or threats.

(C) if a plea agreement exists,

(1) require disclosure of the entire agreement, except the appendix containing any sentence limitation, before the plea is accepted.

(2) address the accused personally and satisfy itself that the accused understands the agreement, that the accused entered into the agreement voluntarily, that the parties agree to the terms of the agreement, and that the written agreement (including the appendix containing any sentence limitation) contains all the terms and understandings of the parties.

(D) determine that there is a factual basis for the plea. The factual basis for a plea may be determined by questioning the accused, through the use of stipulations, through the use of any evidence that would be admissible on the merits, or through a combination thereof.

22.2 Judgment. Judgment based on a plea of guilty may be entered immediately upon acceptance of the plea by the Trial Chamber. If the Trial Chamber does not accept a plea of guilty, it shall not enter a judgment acquitting the accused. Instead, it shall restore the matter to its previous procedural status. An accused may not appeal the validity of a judgment of guilt entered pursuant to this Rule.

22.3 Sentencing. Sentencing shall be conducted in accordance with the provisions of Rule 26. In the event that a plea agreement exists, after sentence is announced the Trial Chamber shall inquire into the sentence limitations, if any, of any pretrial agreement, and shall, if the sentence adjudged by the Trial Chamber is greater that the sentence agreed upon by the parties, conform the sentence adjudged, to the limitations contained in the agreement.

> NOTE: In common law systems, an accused will often plead guilty to some but not all counts under an indictment, in exchange for a promise by the Prosecutor to provide such benefits as withdrawal of the remaining counts of the indictment, agreement

not to engage in further prosecutions (known as a "grant of immunity"), and agreement to an upper limit for the sentence which will be imposed. In the event that an accused pleads guilty to some but not all charges, the Trial Chamber should defer sentencing until the trial on the remaining counts is completed. In order to obtain the cooperation of an important witness in a prosecution before the International Tribunal, the Prosecutor may need the authority to make such agreements with a suspect or an accused. If Option One is adopted, the following provisions should be added to Rule 9.

Added to Rule 9.1:

(F) grant immunity in accordance with the provisions of Rule 9.3; and,

(G) enter into pretrial agreements in accordance with the provisions of Rule 9.4.

Added to Rule 9 following Rule 9.2:

9.3 Immunity. The Prosecutor may grant any person immunity; however, an immunity granted is binding only upon the International Tribunal and is not binding upon any State without the express agreement of that State.

(A) Full immunity. The Prosecutor may grant immunity from prosecution by the International Tribunal for any acts over which the International Tribunal has jurisdiction.

(B) Testimonial immunity. The Prosecutor may grant immunity from use in a prosecution of an individual of testimony, statements, and any information directly or indirectly derived from such testimony or statements by that individual.

(C) Procedure. A grant of immunity shall be in writing in the language of the International Tribunal and in a language the suspect or accused speaks and understands, signed by the Prosecutor, and shall identify the matters to which it extends. A grant of testimonial immunity may also contain an order of the International Tribunal that the Trial Chamber shall be closed during the testimony of the immunized witness and that the protected portions of an immunized witness's testimony shall be redacted from any transcriptions of the record of proceedings released to the public.

9.4 Pretrial agreements. The Prosecutor may enter into pretrial agreements with an accused; however, such agreements are binding only upon the International Tribunal and are not binding upon a State without the express agreement of that State.

(A) Nature of the agreement. A term or condition in a pretrial agreement shall not be enforced if the accused did not freely and voluntarily agree to it, or if it deprives the accused of the right to counsel, the right to due process, or the right to challenge the jurisdiction of the International Tribunal.

(B) Permissible terms. A pretrial agreement may include:

(1) a promise by the accused to plead guilty to one or more charges;

(2) a promise by the Prosecutor to grant immunity for one or more offenses, to limit the amount of confinement which may be imposed for particular offenses; and,

(3) such additional terms or conditions to which the parties may agree and which are not prohibited under subsection (A) above.

(C) Procedure. Either party may initiate negotiations concerning a pretrial agreement; however, all negotiations with the accused shall be in the presence of defense counsel unless the accused is not represented by counsel. The pretrial agreement shall:

(1) be in writing in the language of the International Tribunal and in a language the accused speaks and understands;

(2) be signed by the accused, defense counsel, and the Prosecutor; and

(3) contain all terms, conditions, and promises between the parties, except that any limitation as to the amount of confinement which may be imposed for a particular offense shall be written as an appendix to the agreement.

(D) Withdrawal

(1) The accused may withdraw from a pretrial agreement at any time, but may not withdraw from a plea of guilty entered pursuant to a pretrial agreement once the plea has been accepted by the Trial Chamber.

(2) The Prosecutor may withdraw from a pretrial agreement at any time before the accused begins performance of promises contained in the agreement, if the accused fails to fulfill any material promise or condition in the agreement, or if inquiry by the Trial Chamber under Rule 22 discloses a disagreement as to a material term in the agreement other than the sentence limitation.

(E) Further limitations. The fact that an accused offered to enter into a pretrial agreement or entered into a pretrial agreement and then withdrew from such agreement shall not be considered against the accused in determining findings or sentence. Neither shall the agreement itself be admissible into evidence against the accused.

(F) Inquiry by the Trial Chamber. A plea agreement may not be accepted by a Trial Chamber pursuant to Rule 22, unless the agreement conforms to the provisions of this Rule.

OPTION TWO

22.1 When permitted

(A) Upon motion of the Prosecutor, with the concurrence of the accused and his or her counsel, the Trial Chamber may, in an abbreviated proceeding, make a determination that the accused is guilty of an offense or offenses set forth in an indictment or indictments. The Trial Chamber may conduct this proceeding when (1) the accused wishes to acknowledge his or her guilt, and (2) the Trial Chamber determines that it is in the interests of justice to make an abbreviated determination of guilt. If the Trial Chamber determines that the criteria of this Rule have not been fulfilled, such determination shall have no legal effect other than to restore the matter to its previous procedural status.

(B) In determining whether the conducting of such an abbreviated proceeding is in the interests of justice, the Trial Chamber may consider any relevant factor including:

(1) the contrition of the accused;

(2) the extent of cooperation provided by the accused in the investigation and prosecution of other persons by the International Tribunal, or the ability and intention of the accused to provide such cooperation in the future;

(3) the gravity of the acts committed by the accused relative to those of other persons investigated or prosecuted with the cooperation of the accused;

(4) the gravity of the acts committed by the accused relative to those of other persons prosecuted by the International Tribunal;

(5) the nature of the proof of guilt.

22.2 Procedure

(A) If the Trial Chamber determines that it is appropriate to conduct an abbreviated proceeding under this Rule, it shall address the accused personally and satisfy itself that the accused wishes to acknowledge his or her guilt with full understanding:

(1) of the nature of the offenses charged,

(2) that the accused has the right to be proven guilty beyond a reasonable doubt after a full trial pursuant to these Rules, and

(3) that the accused enjoys other substantial rights including the right to remain silent and to confront the witnesses against him or her.

(B) The Trial Chamber shall also determine that, apart from any agreement with the Prosecutor regarding cooperation or regarding the Prosecutor's agreement to recommend a particular sentence, the accused's decision to acknowledge his or her guilt is not the result of promises, force, or threats. In this regard, the Trial Chamber may require the Prosecutor to disclose the substance of any agreement entered into with the accused.

(C) The Trial Chamber shall also determine that there is a factual basis for the finding the accused guilty. The factual basis for a plea may be determined by questioning the accused, through the use of stipulations, any evidence that would be admissible under Rule 25, or through a combination thereof.

(D) The Trial Chamber may advise the accused of the sentence it anticipates imposing pursuant to Rule 22.4. If the Trial Chamber subsequently determines that it must impose a greater sentence, it shall permit the accused, if he or she desires, to have the matter restored to its previous procedural status and proceed to a full trial. If, however, prior to the determination that a greater sentence is required, the accused has substantially performed an agreement with the Prosecutor under subsection (B) to provide cooperation in the investigation and prosecution of other persons by the International Tribunal, the Trial Chamber shall impose the sentence it had originally anticipated imposing.

(E) A judgment of guilty pursuant to this Rule may be entered immediately upon the Trial Chamber's determination of the accused's guilt in accordance with this Rule and need not be accompanied by a written opinion.

22.3 Closed proceedings. Upon motion of the defense, the Trial Chamber may, in order to safeguard an accused who may be endangered if the abbreviated proceeding were to be conducted in public, proceed *in camera*, notwithstanding any provision of these Rules to the contrary.

22.4 Sentence. If the Trial Chamber enters a finding of guilty pursuant to this Rule, it may conduct a sentencing proceeding pursuant to Rule 26. Upon motion of the Prosecutor, the imposition of sentence may be postponed pending the rendering of cooperation by the accused to the Prosecutor.

22.5 Non-appealability of judgment of guilt. An accused may not appeal the validity of a judgment of guilt entered pursuant to this Rule.

22.6 Review of sentence. The Prosecutor may make a motion pursuant to Rule 30 seeking the modification of the sentence of an accused who has been sentenced pursuant to a finding of guilt under this Rule, in order to reflect cooperation by the accused subsequent to sentence.

22.7 Effect of determination. For the purpose of the provisions of Article 10 of the Statute, the judgment and sentence resulting from a proceeding under this Rule shall have the same effect as a conviction after trial; however, in the event that the accused does not fully comply with his or her agreement to cooperate, the Trial Chamber, upon the motion of the Prosecutor, may, vacate the judgment and continue the prosecution of the accused in accordance with the applicable provisions of these Rules. Upon such further proceedings, the fact that an accused offered to enter into a pretrial agreement or entered into an agreement and then did not fulfill such agreement shall not be considered against the accused in determining findings or sentence. Neither shall the agreement itself or any admissions made by the accused pursuant to Rule 22.2(C) be admissible in evidence against the accused.

F. MEMORANDUM OF THE LAWYERS COMMITTEE FOR HUMAN RIGHTS TO THE INTERNATIONAL TRIBUNAL FOR THE PROSECUTION OF PERSONS RESPONSIBLE FOR SERIOUS VIOLATIONS OF INTERNATIONAL HUMANITARIAN LAW IN THE TERRITORY OF THE FORMER YUGOSLAVIA SINCE 1991

IT/INF 4, 19 November 1993

I. Introduction

Article 15 of the Statute of the International Tribunal provides that "[t]he judges of the International Tribunal shall adopt rules of procedure and evidence for the conduct of the pre-trial phase of the proceedings, trials, and appeals, the admission of evidence, the protection of victims and witnesses and other appropriate matters." This Memorandum is respectfully submitted by the Lawyers Committee for Human Rights to set forth recommendations for these rules.

The Lawyers Committee for Human Rights is an independent, non-governmental organization. Its work is impartial, holding each government to the standards affirmed in the International Bill of Human Rights.

The Lawyers Committee believes that the rules of procedure and evidence of the International Tribunal should reflect a fair balancing of the interests of the international community and individual victims in punishing and deterring war crimes against the interests of the accused in having a full and fair opportunity to defend against any accusation. The Committee believes that the following rules achieve that balance.

II. The Pre-Trial Phase

A. *Right to Counsel*: Article 18 of the Statute of the International Tribunal (the "Statute") authorizes the Prosecutor to "question suspects, victims and witnesses," and Article 18(3) provides that "if questioned, the suspect shall be entitled to be assisted by counsel of his own choice, including the right to have legal assistance assigned to him without payment by him in any such case if he does not have sufficient means to pay for it."

1. *Rights of Suspects*: The Lawyers Committee suggests that the Tribunal interpret this to mean that, as a matter of procedure, the Prosecutor should advise any person who appears before him for questioning whether that person is a "suspect" (*i.e.*, a person considered at the time to be a potential target for prosecution), and, if so, of that person's right to counsel before questioning begins. Questioning of such a person should not proceed unless the suspect either waives his right to counsel or fails to obtain counsel after having a reasonable opportunity to do so. Questioning of a suspect who has declined or failed to obtain counsel should cease if the suspect expresses the desire to consult counsel in the course of the questioning and should not resume unless the suspect either consents to the resumption or fails to obtain counsel after a reasonable time. Suspects should be given a reasonable opportunity to consult with their counsel. In the interests of justice the Tribunal might consider establishing an office of Defense Counsel which would, inter alia, have authority to determine when a suspect has insufficient means to pay for counsel, and to assign defense counsel in such cases. If the suspect does not have sufficient means to pay for counsel, the Prosecutor must arrange for counsel to be provided at the expense of the Tribunal.

2. *Rights of Witnesses*: Because the Prosecutor may not always be able to determine *ex ante* who will be the subject of an indictment, any person who is questioned by the Prosecutor should have a reasonable opportunity to consult with a lawyer, and a right to have a lawyer present at any interrogation.

3. *Privilege*: All communications between a suspect or witness and his lawyer in connection with obtaining legal advice should be regarded as privileged, and hence, not subject to discovery or admission at trial, unless (1) the suspect consents to such discovery or admission or (2) one or both parties to the communication has voluntarily disclosed the content of the communication to one or more third parties.

B. Right to Remain Silent: Immunity: The Lawyers Committee reads Article 21(4)(g) as recognizing a general right to silence for those accused of war crime offenses. The Prosecutor may request, and the Tribunal may require (by exercise of its contempt powers), a witness, suspect, or potential suspect to answer questions that might incriminate the person if the Prosecutor grants the answerer immunity from prosecution, which may, in the discretion of the Prosecutor, be limited to immunity from use of the statement in any prosecution of the answerer, or may extend to immunity from prosecution with respect to any matter in the jurisdiction of the Tribunal. The Trial Chamber should be required to respect such promises.

C. Pretrial Detention: Bail: Any person arrested in connection with an investigation should be detained under conditions that conform to the Standard Minimum Rules for the treatment of Prisoners and the body of Principles for the Protection of All Persons Under Any Form of Detention or Imprisonment. The Tribunal, or any Judge of the Tribunal, should have the power to permit release of any such person upon the posting of sufficient bail. No person arrested at the initiative of the Prosecutor prior to indictment should be detained for more than 72 hours except upon a finding by a Judge of the Tribunal of probable cause to believe that the named suspect has committed a triable offense. Where the suspect is detained under the jurisdiction of the Tribunal, judges of national courts should not have the ability to grant release upon bail without the authorization of the Tribunal in the particular case.

D. Preparation of an Indictment: Article 18(4) authorizes the Prosecutor to "prepare an indictment" upon "a determination that a prima facie case exists." The rules should provide that the Prosecutor should not state publicly that any person is suspected of a crime, except by indictment. An indictment should contain a plain, concise, and definite written statement of the essential facts constituting the offense charged. For each count, the indictment should also state the official citation of the statute or other provision of applicable law which the defendant is alleged to have violated.

E. *Retrial of Person Acquitted by National Tribunals*: Pursuant to Article 10 of the Statute the Lawyers Committee believes that the Prosecutor should be empowered to indict person who have already been acquitted by a national court. The Tribunal should then inquire into whether, in view of the prior acquittal, the interests of justice preclude the current indictment from proceeding. In addressing this issue, the Trial Chamber should consider, among other factors, the diligence with which the national case was prosecuted, the extent to which the national case involved war crimes or only ordinary crimes, and the history and practices of the specific national court with similarly-situated -- that is, similar in nationality, ethnicity, or race -- criminal defendants. The Trial Chamber should permit such an indictment to proceed only if it makes the determination that, in view of the above-described factors, the prior national proceeding fundamentally violated the norms of justice.

F. *Extradition:* Pursuant to Article 29 of the Statute, which provides that "States shall comply" with requests for assistance or an order of the Trial Chamber, including requests or orders for the transfer of the accused to the International Tribunal, the Trial Chamber may require any national government with appropriate jurisdiction to surrender or transfer any person who has been indicted. As the Tribunal is established on the basis of a decision made under Chapter VII of the Charter of the United Nations, this provision of the Statute prevails over national laws, extradition treaties, and other international covenants.

G. *Post Indictment Right to Counsel*: After indictment, an accused should have the assistance of counsel in connection with each phase of the proceedings, including the right to have counsel appointed if s/he lacks the means to pay for counsel, and the right to have counsel present at all stages of the proceeding in the Trial Chamber.

H. *Disclosure of Exculpatory Evidence:* The Rules should require that the Prosecutor disclose to the accused any exculpatory information known to the Prosecutor and that such disclosure should be made a reasonable time in advance of trial sufficient to permit review of the information.

III. Procedure at Trial

A. *Prohibition of Trials in absentia*: Article 21(4)(d) of the Statute provides that the accused is "entitled...to be tried in his presence." This provision should be read as a blanket prohibition on trials *in absentia*. That is, the trial cannot begin if the defendant, for whatever reason including the refusal by a nation to extradite him, is not in the courtroom. However, the further progress of the trial, including the return of the judgment, shall not be prevented and the defendant shall be considered to have waived the right to be present whenever a defendant, initially present, (1) is voluntarily absent after the trial has commended or (2) after being warned by the court that disruptive conduct will cause the exclusion of the defendant from the courtroom, persists in conduct which is sufficient to justify his exclusion. A defendant is not required to be present at a conference, argument upon a question of law, or at an appellate proceeding.

B. *Trial of Multiple Defendants*: The Prosecutor should be empowered to seek a single trial proceeding for multiple defendants accused of related crimes. In such a case, the Trial Chamber should be required to make separate findings as to the guilt or innocence of each individual defendant. In addition, the Trial Chamber should have the discretion to require separate trials if the interests of justice so require.

C. *Right to Cross-Examine Witnesses*: At trial, the accused or counsel for the accused should have the right to cross-examine witnesses called by the Prosecution. The Prosecution should provide to the accused any records of prior statements by those witnesses in the possession of the Prosecutor. Such disclosure should be made a reasonable time prior to the witness giving testimony. The accused should have the right to call, and the power to compel the appearance of, witnesses in his or her own behalf. The accused should be able to subpoena documents or other evidence held by third parties; the Tribunal should provide all necessary assistance in this respect.

D. *Witness Protection*: With due regard for the rights of cross-examination and confrontation, the Trial Chamber, pursuant to Article 22, should be empowered to protect the identity of witnesses and victims and the contents of sensitive documents. The Lawyers Committee recommends that, upon request of the Prosecutor, the Trial Chamber should hold a non-public adversarial hearing at which it determines whether a person or document warrants such treatment. The Trial Chamber should have wide discretion to take whatever precautions are necessary to ensure the confidentiality of such sensitive information.

E. *Adverse Inference from a Failure to Testify by Accused:* The Prosecutor may call the accused as a witness but may not compel the witness to testify against himself or to confess guilt. The Trial Chamber should not be precluded from drawing an adverse inference from a failure to testify, but should inform the accused that it may do so.

IV. Evidentiary Rules at Trial

A. *General Rules of Admissibility:* The Lawyers Committee recommends that the Tribunal not be bound by technical rules of evidence. It should admit any evidence which it deems to be relevant and reliable. It should exclude any evidence which is not relevant, or not reliable, or whose probative value is substantially outweighed presentation of cumulative evidence.

B. *Procedure for Evidentiary Objections:* The Tribunal may exclude evidence on the objection of the opposing party, or on its own initiative. A party that does not object to the admission of evidence tendered to the Tribunal by the other party should be deemed to have waived its objection unless the Trial Chamber or the Appeals Chamber determines that the interests of justice require otherwise.

V. Burdens and Penalties

A. *Presumption of Innocence:* Pursuant to Article 21(3), defendants shall be considered innocent until proven guilty. The Lawyers Committee believes that the Prosecutor should have the burden of establishing that the accused is guilty of the specific offenses for which s/he has been indicted.

B. *Procedural Errors*: The fact that a procedural or evidentiary error has occurred during the trial should not render the judgment invalid *per se*. Rather, if the defendant can demonstrate that discovery, misconduct or trial error was probably prejudicial to the defendant's right of fair trial, the International Tribunal should be empowered to order a new trial. There should be no exclusionary rule for violations of procedure and evidence. The Tribunal shall have exclusive power to discipline the Prosecutor and members of his staff for violations of procedural and evidentiary rules, and shall so discipline whenever appropriate to deter or punish such violations.

C. *Penalties: Imprisonment: Fines*: The Statute provides for incarceration as the only penalty for war crime offenses. The Lawyers Committee believes, however, that Article 24(3), which provides for the "return of any property and proceeds acquired by criminal conduct ...to their rightful owners" should be read broadly to require convicted defendants to disgorge all economic gains achieved as a result to the commission of war crimes and that the Tribunal should have the authority to assess and determine damages in such cases. Upon conviction of any defendant, the Trial Chamber should hold a special hearing to identify which of the defendant's assets are properly characterized as having been acquired due to his unlawful; conduct. At such a hearing the burden of proof should rest with the prosecutor, and disputes shall be resolved on the basis of a preponderance of the evidence. Once received by the Tribunal, such disgorged funds, if not identifiable as the property of one or more specific persons, should be placed in a trust fund for all victims to draw upon. A custodian should be appointed to disburse funds in an equitable manner upon proof of claim.

G. LETTER DATED 29 NOVEMBER 1993 FROM THE PERMANENT REPRESENTATIVE OF CANADA TO THE UNITED NATIONS ADDRESSED TO THE SECRETARY-GENERAL

IT/15, 29 November 1993.

Further to paragraph 3 of Security Council resolution 827 (1993) of 25 May 1993, I enclose recommendations of the Government of Canada on rules of procedure and evidence for the International Tribunal for the Prosecution of Persons Responsible for Serious Violations of International Humanitarian Law Committed in the Territory of the Former Yugoslavia since 1991.

I should be grateful if the recommendations were forwarded to the judges of the International Tribunal and circulated, with this letter, as a document of the Security Council.

(Signed) Louise FRECHETTE
Ambassador and
Permanent Representative

Annex

Recommendations of the Government of Canada on rules of procedure and evidence for the International Tribunal for the Prosecution of Persons Responsible for Serious Violations of International Humanitarian Law Committed in the Territory of the Former Yugoslavia since 1991

INTRODUCTION

1. In paragraph 3 of Security Council resolution 827 (1993) of 25 May 1993, the Security Council invited Member States to provide suggestions for the rules of procedure and evidence called for in article 15 of the Statute of the International Tribunal for the Prosecution of Persons Responsible for Serious Violations of International Humanitarian Law Committed in the Territory of the Former Yugoslavia since 1991.

2. In providing its specific response to the request in paragraph 3, Canada has focused in part I of its submission on issues arising out of gender-based crimes. Canada has, during the last decade, introduced fundamental substantive and procedural changes to its criminal justice system in the areas of sexual-assault crimes and witness testimony. Canada believes that its experience in this area and elements of these provisions could be of assistance to the Tribunal in its precedent-setting prosecution of gender-based crimes in the context of international humanitarian law.

3. Part I of Canada's recommendations to the Tribunal recognizes the fact that laws and societal perceptions of victims of rape and other gender-based crimes can affect both the behaviour of victims and of practitioners within the criminal justice system. Canada's recommendations, which encompass some matters of substance as well as issues of evidence and procedure, are designed to increase the reporting of such crimes and to provide for fairer and more effective prosecution of offences, having regard to the rights of both the victim and the accused.

4. Part II of Canada's submission is intended to address the admissibility of certain evidence, having regard to the limitations arising directly from the ongoing armed conflict in the former Yugoslavia and the necessity to balance the probative value of such evidence against the rights of the accused.

5. Parts III and IV of Canada's submission address the particular needs of victims. Having regard to the nature of the conflict in the former Yugoslavia; the fact that lawlessness and violations of humanitarian law continue there; the circumstances of ethnic conflict, which have frequently pitted neighbour against neighbour; and the psychological disadvantage suffered - particularly by women victims when faced with their abusers - Canada urged the Tribunal to exercise the utmost sensitivity to the trauma suffered by victims and witnesses in the past, their potential need for protection from retribution, and to the ordeal they will likely undergo when reliving their experience during the tribunal process.

PART I

SUBSTANTIVE DESCRIPTION AND EVIDENTIARY STANDARDS APPLICABLE TO CRIMES OF SEXUAL ASSAULT

6. Canada invites the Tribunal to address rape and other gender-related offences, such as forced pregnancy or forced prostitution, as distinct offences against international humanitarian law, whether or not they have the potential of also constituting an aspect of the crime of genocide.

7. Characterization of the offence. Canada urges the Tribunal to adopt and use a broad definition of the term "rape" in its proceedings. While recognizing that the Statute uses the term "rape", which in some legal systems refers to forced vaginal intercourse, this term should be interpreted broadly to encompass any non-consensual sexual activity, whether vaginal, anal or oral. The Tribunal may wish to employ the term "sexual assault" for such offences. This could increase reporting; lessen the impact on the victim, her family and her community; and lead to more successful prosecutions.

8. The defence of consent. Canada recommends that, in the event that the defence of consent is raised, the Tribunal regard the following factors as vitiating consent:

(1) The application of force to the complainant or to a person other than the complainant;

(2) Threats or fear of the application of force to the complainant or to a person other than the complainant;

(3) The exercise or abuse of a position of power or authority;

(4) The incapacity of the victim to consent;

(5) Expression by the victim, by words or conduct, of a lack of agreement to engage in sexual activity;

(6) Expression of "consent" by the words or conduct of a person other than the victim.

9. Addressing the issue of consent is particularly important if the victim submits to sexual activity on one or numerous occasions because of prior threats or violence, as in the case of forced prostitution. In determining whether or not a threat of force occurred or was feared by the victim, the Tribunal should thus have regard not solely to immediate events surrounding one specific instance, but also to the victim's state of mind in the light of all the surrounding circumstances.

10. Corroboration. Corroboration of the victim's testimony by "independent witnesses" should not be required. Requirements for corroboration in the prosecution of the crime of "rape" - compared to the lack of such requirements in instances of other assault offences - reflect an assumption that women are inherently untrustworthy when it comes to making complaints of sexual offences. A requirement for corroboration in sexual assault cases may violate established tenets of international human rights law that guarantee equality before the law regardless of gender. Any issue relating to corroboration should therefore go only to the weight of the evidence.

11. Previous sexual history. Canada urges the Tribunal to find evidence concerning a victim's previous sexual history to be irrelevant in challenging or supporting her credibility, assessing the gravity of the offence, determining the likelihood of consent, or as a consideration in sentencing. Such evidence should be prima facie inadmissible, unless the Tribunal has determined, at a closed hearing, that the evidence has significant probative value which is not substantially outweighed by the danger of prejudice to the proper administration of justice.

12. Sentencing. Canada requests that if the Tribunal convicts an accused or rape and the rape has resulted in a pregnancy which the victim may subsequently be forced to carry to term, the Tribunal consider the victim's pregnancy as a particularly aggravating circumstance for the purpose of sentencing the accused.

PART II

ADMISSIBILITY OF OUT-OF-COURT AND SIMILAR FACTUAL EVIDENCE

13. The recommendations in this section are intended to pertain to evidence in all cases tried before the Tribunal, and are not limited to cases involving sexual assault.

14. Canadian investigating teams have noted that, due to the ongoing communications and security problems in the former Yugoslavia, it is extremely difficult to contact or make arrangements to meet victims and witnesses. Such problems may be exacerbated when it becomes necessary to transport victims or witnesses in order to enable them to appear before the Tribunal. As a result, viva voce evidence may not always be available. Canada therefore recommends that evidence given out of court, via written statements, audio transcription or videotape should be admissible before the Tribunal, provided certain conditions are met in order to safeguard the rights of the accused.

15. The Tribunal should consider establishing criteria for the admission of out-of-court evidence, in cases where its probative value would be so high as to displace the prejudice that may result from its admission and it is required for the proper administration of justice. For this purpose, Canada suggests that a two-part text of "necessity" and "reliability" be adopted by the Tribunal:

(1) The "necessity" of accepting out-of-court evidence could be determined based on factors such as present unavailability of the witness due to death or medical reasons; inability to locate the witness due to displacement; inability to attend or be brought before the Tribunal because of security and logistical problems arising out of the armed conflict in the former Yugoslavia.

(2) The "reliability" of such evidence would be determined by factors such as the circumstances under which it was obtained; location; identity and/or independence of the questioner; the presence of other persons; and the apparent physical and mental condition of the witness.

16. Given that the crimes to be addressed by the Tribunal are likely to involve patterns of conduct, Canada recommends that the Tribunal permit the introduction of similar factual evidence in circumstances where its probative value would be so high as to displace the prejudice that may result from its admission and where it is necessary for the proper administration of justice.

PART III

PROCEDURES FOR ENSURING THE PROTECTION OF WITNESSES

17. Due to the nature and circumstances of the prosecutions in which the Tribunal will engage - whether in respect to prosecutions of sexual offences or other crimes - it is likely that situations will arise where victims or witnesses are unable, unwilling or afraid to testify before the Tribunal unless certain protective measures are taken. Canada therefore recommends that the Tribunal, in establishing its rules of procedure and evidence, include a number of protective measures.

18. The Tribunal should consider according special protection to victims or witnesses who would have a reasonable fear of retribution if their identity were published or, in certain circumstances, known to the accused. In such cases, the Tribunal should exercise its powers to exclude the public and the media from the courtroom, and/or to order a ban on the publication of any information that may lead to the witness' identity becoming known.

19. In cases where the Tribunal forms the opinion that the safety of the witness demands special protective measures, testimony from outside the courtroom, or from behind a screen in the courtroom, should be permitted. Pursuant to existing provisions in the Canadian Criminal Code, for example, such testimony is permissible only if the accused and the Court are able to watch the testimony, ordinarily by means of closed-circuit television, and the accused is able to communicate with counsel while watching. The addition of technical means of concealing the witness' facial features, in order to prevent identification by the accused, should be considered in special circumstances.

20. Canada recommends that the Tribunal also permit testimony to be given from outside the courtroom or from behind a screen in the courtroom - with the accused being able to watch the testimony by means of closed-circuit television and to communicate with counsel while watching - where the victim or witness is too distressed to face the accused, and the Tribunal forms the opinion that such protective measures are necessary to obtain a full and candid account of the events.

PART IV

VICTIMS' SUPPORT SERVICES

21. Canada recommends that prosecutorial and investigative staff tasked with prosecuting sexual-assault crimes be given special training to encourage sensitivity and receptiveness to the trauma experienced by victims and to their special needs and interests.

22. Canada further recommends that the Tribunal, through the Prosecutor's Office, encourage the establishment of and cooperation with out-of-court victim-witness support programmes, which may be staffed by local volunteers or non-governmental organizations. Such programmes have been found in Canada to assist witnesses in preparing for the ordeal of court testimony by familiarizing them with the legal process. In addition, they can provide psychological support during and after the victim's involvement in the criminal justice process.

H. PERMANENT MISSION OF SWEDEN TO THE UNITED NATIONS

9 December 1993.

The Permanent Representative of Sweden to the United Nations presents his compliments to the Secretary-General of the United Nations and has the honour to inform him of the following.

Pursuant to paragraph 3 of Security Council resolution 827 (1993), a translation of the Swedish Act concerning counsel for the injured party is hereby transmitted, which could be of assistance to the Tribunal when drafting its Rules of Procedure.

This Act, originally adopted by the Swedish Parliament in 1988, and amended thereafter, has shown to be of great help to victims, especially in cases concerning sexual abuse. It has also been of assistance to the courts, since the hearing of the injured party has been facilitated.

Please note under Section 1 that in cases concerning offences which fall under Chapter 6, (sexual crimes) of the Swedish Penal Code, when a preliminary investigation has been initiated, a special counsel shall be appointed for the injured party unless it is apparent that the injured party does not need such counsel. In crimes other than sexual crimes, a counsel for the injured party is most commonly appointed when the crime victim is a relative of the suspect (or, for other reasons, is in an inferior position to the suspect).

Please also read under Section 3 that the counsel for the injured party shall protect the interests of the injured party in the case and support and assist him/her.

The Permanent Representative wishes to underline the importance for the Tribunal to perform its functions independently without interference from any Government or any other source. The enclosed Act should therefore not be seen as any intention on the part of Sweden to direct the Tribunal's work, but as a possible guideline to protect and support witnesses and victims of rape and sexual assault in the former Yugoslavia.

The Permanent Representative of Sweden to the United Nations avails himself of this opportunity to renew to the Secretary-General of the United Nations the assurances of his highest consideration.

SWEDEN

Act concerning counsel for the injured party (No. 1988:609)

Section 1

In cases concerning offences which fall under Chapter 6 of the Penal Code, when a preliminary investigation has been initiated, a special counsel shall be appointed for the injured party (counsel for the injured party) unless it is apparent that the injured party does not need such counsel.

If, in view of the personal relationship of the injured party to the suspect or in view of other circumstances, it can be assumed that the injured party needs a counsel, after a preliminary investigation has been initiated, a counsel for the injured party shall also be appointed in cases concerning

1. crimes under Chapter 3 or 4 of the Penal Code, punishable by imprisonment,
2. crimes under Chapter 8 Sections 5 or 6 of the Penal Code, or attempt, preparation or conspiracy to commit such crimes.

Section 2

A counsel for the injured party may not be appointed after the prosecutor has decided that public prosecution will not be instituted or that such a prosecution shall be withdrawn or after the prosecutor has waived appeal against the sentence pronounced in the case.

Section 3

The counsel for the injured party shall protect the interests of the injured party in the case and support and assist him/her. The counsel's responsibilities do not include assisting the injured party to prosecute in a civil claim pertaining to the crime, if this action is conducted by the prosecutor.

Section 4

The counsel for the injured party shall be appointed at the request of the injured party or when there are other reasons for doing so. In connection with the appointment, Section 21, paragraph one, of the Legal Aid Act (1972:429) applies.

As regards change of counsel for the injured party and the right of such a counsel to put someone else in his stead, Section 21, paragraphs 2 and 3, of the Legal Aid Act apply.

The counsel for the injured party shall be dismissed if this is required in view of the circumstances of the case or if there are other reasons for doing so.

Otherwise, regarding the counsel for the injured party, the rules contained in the Code of Judicial Procedure concerning counsels apply.

Section 5

The counsel for the injured party is entitled to remuneration in accordance with the applicable provisions in Section 22 of the Legal Aid Act (1972:429) with reference to counsels in connection with general legal aid. Regarding remuneration, Sections 19, 23, 49, 49 a, and 49 c of the Legal Aid Act also apply.

Section 6

If a counsel for the injured party is appointed, the injured party's subsequent costs for evidence and investigation in connection with civil claims are compensated to the same extent as is the case when an injured party has been granted general legal aid in connection with such claims.

Section 7

Decisions on questions referred to in this Act are taken by the court. However, in the cases referred to in Section 6, the counsel for the injured party may decide on an investigation himself to the same extent as applies for a counsel engaged in general legal aid under Section 24 of the Legal Aid Act (1972:429).

Section 8

The provisions of Chapter 31 of the Code of Judicial Procedure concerning the defendant's or other persons' liability to repay the Treasury the sums paid out of public funds by order of the court also apply regarding costs under this Act.

Notes

- The reference in Section 1, paragraph one to Chapter 6 of the Penal Code concerns sexual crimes.

- The reference in Section 1, paragraph two, item 1 concerns crimes of violence; crimes against personal liberty and integrity.

- The reference in Section 1, paragraph two, item 2 concerns robbery.

I. PERMANENT MISSION OF NORWAY TO THE UNITED NATIONS

22 December 1993.

The Permanent Representative of Norway to the United Nations presents his compliments to the Secretary-General of the United Nations, and has the honour to submit the following observations regarding the elaboration of the rules of procedure for the International Tribunal for Crimes in the Former Yugoslavia, established pursuant to Security Council Resolution 827 (1993).

The Norwegian government trusts that basic principles concerning the rights of victims and witnesses will be taken into due account when drafting of the rules takes place as planned in the January/February 1994 session of the Tribunal. In maintaining and broadening certain significant principles set forth in the annex of the United Nations General Assembly Resolution 40/34 entitled Declaration of Basic Principles of Justice for the Victims of Crime and Abuse of Power, it is vital that both victims and witnesses be treated with dignity and compassion by the prosecutors handling the case and the Tribunal. Furthermore, proper assistance and support must be provided throughout the legal process.

It would be greatly appreciated if the Secretary-General would have the text of this note conveyed to the International Tribunal for Crimes in the Former Yugoslavia.

The Permanent Representative of Norway to the United Nations avails himself of this opportunity to renew to the Secretary-General of the United Nations the assurances of his highest consideration.

40/34. Declaration of Basic Principles of Justice for Victims of Crime and Abuse of Power

The General Assembly,

Recalling that the Sixth United Nations Congress on the Prevention of Crime and the Treatment of Offenders recommended that the United Nations should continue its present work on the development of guidelines and standards regarding abuse of economic and political power,

Cognizant that millions of people throughout the world suffer harm as a result of crime and the abuse of power and that the rights of these victims have not been adequately recognized,

Recognizing that the victims of crime and the victims of abuse of power, and also frequently their families, witnesses and others who aid them, are unjustly subjected to loss, damage or injury and that they may, in addition, suffer hardship when assisting in the prosecution of offenders,

1. *Affirms* the necessity of adopting national and international measures in order to secure the universal and effective recognition of, and respect for, the rights of victims of crime and of abuse of power;

2. *Stresses* the need to promote progress by all States in their efforts to that end, without prejudice to the rights of suspects or offenders;

3. *Adopts* the Declaration of Basic Principles of Justice for Victims of Crime and Abuse of Power, annexed to the present resolution, which is designed to assist Governments and the international community in their efforts to secure justice and assistance for victims of crime and victims of abuse of power;

4. *Calls upon* Member States to take the necessary steps to give effect to the provisions contained in the Declaration and, in order to curtail victimization as referred to hereinafter, endeavour;

(a) To implement social, health, including mental health, educational, economic and specific crime prevention policies to reduce victimization and encourage assistance to victims in distress;
(b) To promote community efforts and public participation in crime prevention;
(c) To review periodically their existing legislation and practices in order to ensure responsiveness to changing circumstances, and to enact and enforce legislation proscribing acts that violate internationally recognized norms relating to human rights, corporate conduct and other abuses of power;
(d) To establish and strengthen the means of detecting, prosecuting and sentencing those guilty of crimes;
(e) To promote disclosure of relevant information to expose official and corporate conduct to public scrutiny, and other ways of increasing responsiveness to public concerns;
(f) To promote the observance of codes of conduct and ethical norms, in particular international standards, by public servants, including law enforcement, correctional, medical, social service and military personnel, as well as the staff of economic enterprises;
(g) To prohibit practices and procedures conducive to abuse, such as secret places of detention and incommunicado detention;
(h) To co-operate with other States, through mutual judicial and administrative assistance, in such matters as the detection and pursuit of offenders, their extradition and the seizure of their assets, to be used for restitution to the victims;

5. *Recommends* that, at the international and regional levels, all appropriate measures should be taken:

(a) To promote training activities designed to foster adherence to United Nations standards and norms and to curtail possible abuses;

(b) To sponsor collaborative action-research on ways in which victimization can be reduced and victims aided, and to promote information exchanges on the most effective means of so doing;

(c) To render direct aid to requesting Governments designed to help them curtail victimization and alleviate the plight of victims;

(d) To develop ways and means of providing recourse for victims where national channels may be insufficient;

6. *Requests* the Secretary-General to invite Member States to report periodically to the General Assembly on the implementation of the Declaration, as well as on measures taken by them, to this effect;

7. *Also requests* the Secretary-General to make use of the opportunities, which all relevant bodies and organizations within the United Nations system offer, to assist Member States, whenever necessary, in improving ways and means of protecting victims both at the national level and through international co-operation;

8. *Further requests* the Secretary-General to promote the objectives of the Declaration, in particular by ensuring its widest possible dissemination;

9. *Urges* the specialized agencies and other entities and bodies of the United Nations system, other relevant inter-governmental and non-governmental organizations and the public to co-operate in the implementation of the provisions of the Declaration.

96th plenary meeting
29 November 1985

ANNEX

Declaration of Basic Principles of Justice for Victims of Crime and Abuse of Power

A. *Victims of crime*

1. "Victims" means persons who, individually or collectively, have suffered harm, including physical or mental injury, emotional suffering, economic loss or substantial impairment of their fundamental rights, through acts or omissions that are in violation of criminal laws operative within Member States, including those laws proscribing criminal abuse of power.

2. A person may be considered a victim, under this Declaration, regardless of whether the perpetrator is identified, apprehended, prosecuted or convicted and regardless of the familial relationship between the perpetrator and the victim. The term "victim" also includes, where appropriate, the immediate family or dependants of the direct victim and persons who have suffered harm in intervening to assist victims in distress or to prevent victimization.

3. The provisions contained herein shall be applicable to all, without distinction of any kind, such as race, colour, sex, age, language, religion, nationality, political or other opinion, cultural beliefs or practices, property, birth or family status, ethnic or social origin, and disability.

Access to justice and fair treatment

4. Victims should be treated with compassion and respect for their dignity. They are entitled to access to the mechanisms of justice and to prompt redress, as provided for by national legislation, for the harm that they have suffered.

5. Judicial and administrative mechanisms should be established and strengthened where necessary to enable victims to obtain redress through formal or informal procedures that are expeditious, fair, inexpensive and accessible. Victims should be informed of their rights in seeking redress through such mechanisms.

6. The responsiveness of judicial and administrative processes to the needs of victims should be facilitated by:

(a) Informing victims of their role and the scope, timing and progress of the proceedings and of the disposition of their cases, especially where serious crimes are involved and where they have requested such information;

(b) Allowing the views and concerns of victims to be presented and considered at appropriate stages of the proceedings where their personal interests are affected, without prejudice to the accused and consistent with the relevant national criminal justice system;

(c) Providing proper assistance to victims throughout the legal process;

(d) Taking measures to minimize inconvenience to victims, protect their privacy, when necessary, and ensure their safety, as well as that of their families and witnesses on their behalf, from intimidation and retaliation;

(e) Avoiding unnecessary delay in the disposition of cases and the execution of orders or decrees granting awards to victims.

7. Informal mechanisms for the resolution of disputes, including mediation, arbitration and customary justice or indigenous practices, should be utilized where appropriate to facilitate conciliation and redress for victims.

Restitution

8. Offenders or third parties responsible for their behaviour should, where appropriate, make fair restitution to victims, their families or dependants. Such restitution should include the return of property or payment for the harm or loss suffered, reimbursement of expenses incurred as a result of the victimization, the provision of services and the restoration of rights.

9. Governments should review their practices, regulations and laws to consider restitution as an available sentencing option in criminal cases, in addition to other criminal sanctions.

10. In cases of substantial harm to the environment, restitution, if ordered, should include, as far as possible, restoration of the environment, reconstruction of the infrastructure, replacement of community facilities and reimbursement of the expenses of relocation, whenever such harm results in the dislocation of a community.

11. Where public officials or other agents acting in an official or quasi-official capacity have violated national criminal laws, the victims should receive restitution from the State whose officials or agents were responsible for the harm inflicted. In cases where the Government under whose authority the victimizing act or omission occurred is no longer in existence, the State or Government successor in title should provide restitution to the victims.

Compensation

12. When compensation is not fully available from the offender or other sources, States should endeavour to provide financial compensation to:

(a) Victims who have sustained significant bodily injury or impairment or physical or mental health as a result of serious crimes;
(b) The family, in particular dependants of person who have died or become physically or mentally incapacitated as a result of such victimization.

13. The establishment, strengthening and expansion of national funds for compensation to victims should be encouraged. Where appropriate, other funds may also be established for this purpose, including in those cases where the State of which the victim is a national is not in a position to compensate the victim for the harm.

Assistance

14. Victims should receive the necessary material, medical, psychological and social assistance through governmental, voluntary, community-based and indigenous means.

15. Victims should be informed of the availability of health and social services and other relevant assistance and be readily afforded access to them.

16. Police, justice, health, social service and other personnel concerned should receive training to sensitize them to the needs of victims, and guidelines to ensure proper and prompt aid.

17. In providing services and assistance to victims, attention should be given to those who have special needs because of the nature of the harm inflicted or because of factors such as those mentioned in paragraph 3 above.

B. Victims of abuse of power

18. "Victims" means persons who, individually or collectively, have suffered harm, including physical or mental injury, emotional suffering economic loss or

substantial impairment of their fundamental rights, through acts or omissions that do not yet constitute violations of national criminal laws but of internationally recognized norms relating to human rights.

19. States should consider incorporating into the national law norms proscribing abuses of power and providing remedies to victims of such abuses. In particular, such remedies should include restitution and/or compensation, and necessary material, medical, psychological and social assistance and support.

20. States should consider negotiating multilateral international treaties relating to victims, as defined in paragraph 18.

21. States should periodically review existing legislation and practices to ensure their responsiveness to changing circumstances, should enact and enforce, if necessary, legislation proscribing acts that constitute serious abuses of political or economic power, as well as promoting policies and mechanisms for the prevention of such acts, and should develop and make readily available appropriate rights and remedies for victims of such acts.

J. REPORT OF THE AMERICAN BAR ASSOCIATION TASK FORCE ON WAR CRIMES IN THE FORMER YUGOSLAVIA, COMMENTING ON THE UNITED STATES' DRAFT RULES OF PROCEDURE AND EVIDENCE FOR THE INTERNATIONAL TRIBUNAL*

IT/INF.6/REV. 2, 18 January 1994.

Report on the Proposed Rules of Procedure and Evidence of the International Tribunal To Adjudicate War Crimes Committed in the Former Yugoslavia

The ABA Task Force on War Crimes in Former Yugoslavia ("ABA Task Force" or "Task Force")[1/] met on December 15, 1993 and December 20, 1993 to consider the draft Rules of Procedure and Evidence ("Rules") for the International Tribunal for the Prosecution of Persons Responsible for Serious Violations of International Humanitarian Law Committed in the Former Yugoslavia ("International Tribunal" or "Tribunal"), prepared by the United States Department of Defense, in consultation with the Department of Justice and the Department of State. The Task Force also considered amendments to the draft Rules suggested by Judge Gabrielle McDonald, the United States judge on the International Tribunal.

This report sets out the views of the ABA Task Force on the Rules. Many of the Rules specifically considered are those which the Task Force feels should be amended or redrafted by the International Tribunal. Where appropriate, alternative language is suggested. In general, the Task Force endorses the Rules proposed by the United States government. In particular, it is appropriate that the rules of procedure adopted by the International Tribunal be based largely on common law principles, because the Statute of the International Tribunal ("Statute") establishes a court which employs adversary procedures of the common law model.

The ABA Task Force is aware that other nations have offered suggestions to the International Tribunal regarding rules of procedure and evidence, and that additional suggestions are likely to be forthcoming in the future. This report considers such suggestions only to a limited extent and focuses primarily of the Rules proposed by the United States government. However, the Task Force urges the International Tribunal to give proper

* The membership of the ABA Task Force on War Crimes in the Former Yugoslavia, contained in an annex to this Document, is not reproduced.

1/ A list of the membership of and liaisons to the ABA Task Force on War Crimes in the Former Yugoslavia is attached hereto as Annex 1.

consideration to all proposals which it receives. In particular, the Rules discussed here are based largely upon the common law justice system of the United States. Those nations which have civil law justice systems will be better able to communicate the advantages of such systems to the International Tribunal.

1. **Rule 1.2 -- Approval of Rules**

Rule 1.2 states that the Rules "shall take effect upon their approval by a majority of the judges of the International Tribunal." Because of the centrality of the Rules to the functioning of the International Tribunal, the Task Force recommends that the Tribunal adopt the alternative suggestion of the drafters that two-thirds majority approval be required.

Furthermore, after approval by the International Tribunal, the Rules should be submitted to the Security Council for approval to ensure that the procedures of the Tribunal have the mandate of the Security Council -- since it is under the authority of the United Nations and the Security Council that the International Tribunal was established. Such a process would also give the Security Council the opportunity to address any potential conflicts between the Rules and the Statute.

2. **Rule 1.3 -- Amendments to Rules**

Rule 1.3 permits a Trial Chamber to "amend" the Rules for the purposes of an individual proceeding. However, the word "amend" suggests a change that is more permanent. The Task Force recommends that this verb be replaced with "adapt" or "adjust".

Because of the potentially significant impact which a rules change may have on a criminal proceeding, the International Tribunal may also wish to consider permitting interlocutory appeal in appropriate cases from a decision of a Trial Chamber pursuant to Rule 1.3.

3. **Rule 2.2(A) -- Enumeration of Crimes**

Rule 2 is a substantive, rather than procedural, provision which sets out the jurisdiction of the International Tribunal. The Task Force is concerned that Rule 2.2(A) refers to crimes which are not enumerated in the Statute. Specifically, Rule 2.2(A) refers to the Hague Regulations and the 1977 Additional Protocols to the Geneva Conventions.

In accordance with the principle of nullum crimen sine lege, it is important that the Rules not permit prosecution and punishment of crimes which are not clearly within the International Tribunal's jurisdiction under the Statute. It is also important that the Rules, which are procedural in nature, not contain a provision which conflicts with the Statute in the important substantive area of the Tribunal's subject matter jurisdiction. Therefore, the Task Force believes that it is important to ascertain that Rule 2.2(A) properly states the Tribunal's subject matter jurisdiction in accordance with the Security Council's understanding of the Statute. Thus, this concern provides an additional reason for submitting the Rules to the Security Council for approval.

In its July 1993 Report on the International Tribunal to Adjudicate War Crimes Committed in the Former Yugoslavia ("1993 Report"), the Task Force recommended that certain offenses specified in the Hague Regulations be included in the Statute.[2] The Task Force stands by this recommendation and further recommends that Rule 2.2(A) refer to the text of the Statute.

Furthermore, the ABA Task Force agrees with the view of the Secretary-General of the United Nations that the International Tribunal should have competence to punish only conduct which constitute crimes under established principles customary international law.[3] The Task Force believes that the Additional Protocols to the Geneva Conventions, which set out extensive obligations regarding treatment and protection of victims of armed conflict but which have not been ratified by the United States, have not attained this status. For this reason, and to achieve consistency with the Statute, the Task Force recommends that the reference to the Additional Protocols be deleted from Rule 2.2(A).

4. **Rule 2.4 (new) -- Amendment to Rule 2**

The commentary to Rule 2 indicates that the rule is not subject to amendment under Rule 1.3. The ABA Task Force recommends that this limitation be made explicit in the text of the rule:

> **2.4** Rule 2 is not subject to amendment pursuant to Rule 1.3.

5. **Rule 4.2**

See comments on Rule 14.6 below, regarding notification of the Security Council.

6. **Rule 6.1**

The phrase "in accordance with these Rules" gives the impression that the procedures which the President is empowered to establish are in some way defined by the other proposed Rules. The ABA Task Force recommends that the phrase be deleted.

7. **Rule 6.2(A) -- Recusal of Judges**

Rule 6.2(A) allows a motion for recusal of a judge by a party or by the judge himself or herself. It is also possible that a member of the International Tribunal may become aware of circumstances suggesting that the recusal of a colleague would be appropriate. The Task Force believes that the Rules should provide for such a possibility.

The Task Force recommends that the President of the International Tribunal be empowered to call for the recusal of other judges of Tribunal. Limitation of this power to the

---

[2] 1993 Report (bound version) at 13-14.

[3] Report of the Secretary General Pursuant to Paragraph 2 of Security Council Resolution 808 ("Secretary-General's Report"), U.N. Doc. S/25704, ¶ 34 (3 May 1993).

President would promote orderliness of the recusal procedures and would limit the possibility of intramural disputes between judges. A judge who believes that a colleague should be recused would be able to communicate the basis for his or her belief to the President.

The Tribunal may also wish to consider a mechanism to permit judges to move for recusal of the President. The ABA Task Force does not make a recommendation as to such a procedure.

8. **Rule 6.4 -- Contempt**

Under United States law, the exercise of a court's contempt powers may take the form of criminal or civil contempt proceedings. Criminal contempt is penal in nature and generally requires the imposition of a term of imprisonment or a fine, or both. Civil contempt sanctions are intended to compel compliance with a court's order and may include imprisonment, fines, or other remedial measures. Unlike criminal contempt penalties, civil contempt sanctions cease upon compliance with the court's order.

The general remedial jurisdiction of the International Tribunal is limited to imposition of imprisonment.[4] However, the Statute also implies equitable powers; for example, Article 24(3) permits the Tribunal to "order the return of any property and proceeds acquired by criminal conduct . . . to their rightful owners." The imposition and enforcement of civil fines, possibly through attachment of assets, would be an important tool for enforcement of the Tribunal's contempt power. Furthermore, the availability of civil fines could alleviate potential unwillingness of the Tribunal to punish contempt if the only available sanctions are criminal ones.

The ABA Task Force recommends that Rule 6.4 be revised to indicate that the International Tribunal possesses both criminal and civil contempt power:

> **6.4 Contempt.** Contempt of court may be punished by imposition of fines, imprisonment, or other measures by any chamber of the International Tribunal.

9. **Rule 7 -- Protection of Victims and Witnesses**

Rule 7 is the primary provision which presents an important tension in the Rules: between the right of victims and witnesses to protection and the right of the accused to effective cross-examination. The ABA Task Force calls attention to its detailed comments on this issue in its previous report.[5] The general principles set out in those comments should be borne in mind by the International Tribunal as it confronts the tension between witness protection and cross-examination on a case-by-case basis.

4/ Statute, art. 24(1).

5/ 1993 Report (bound version) at 29-36.

In addition, in order to note the importance of cross-examination within the text of Rule 7, the Task Force recommends that two additional sentences be added to the end of Rule 7(A):

> However, there may be cases in which protection cannot be afforded consistent with the rights of the accused. In such instances, the Prosecutor may have to consider using other evidence in place of the witness.

This language is drawn substantially from the Commentary to Rule 7.

10. **Rule 8 -- National Security**

The ABA Task Force recognizes that states may have legitimate reasons for seeking protection of confidential information which is provided to the International Tribunal. However, the Task Force believes that the provisions of proposed Rule 8 which relate to protection of "national security" information raise two areas of concern.

First, the Task Force believes that all evidence offered against an accused should be made available to him or her and, if used at trial, be presented in open court. Trials based on information which is not publicly disclosed could seriously impair the credibility and apparent integrity of the International Tribunal.

Second, a decision by a Trial Chamber to protect information based specifically upon "national security" should be avoided, because of the widely varying and often expansive interpretations of that term by various states. Information for which a national security privilege is asserted should be protected in the same manner as other confidential information which is provided by a state. It is not necessary to have a separate category of "national security" information. Indeed, the presence of such a provision in the Rules would impair the credibility of the International Tribunal because of the potential for abuse of the protection. In practice, it would be extremely difficult for the International Tribunal to second guess a state's claim of national security.

a. Proposal

In accordance with the above concerns, the Task Force proposes that Rule 8 be amended as follows:

> **8.1 Who may issue.** In order to ensure the safety and security of a particular victim or witness, protect the confidentiality of information supplied by a State, protect the confidentiality of investigations, or prevent the flight of suspects or accused, a Trial Chamber or, if prior to the initial appearance of the accused, the judge who confirmed the indictment may issue an order:
>
> . . .
>
> (B) preventing the disclosure of confidential information provided by a State;

8.2 Disclosure. . . .

(A) State confidential information. Confidential information provided by a State may not be disclosed to the public without the prior approval and consent of that State. Provided, that

(1) Any confidential information which is offered to the Tribunal to support the issuance of an indictment and any confidential information which the Prosecutor intends to use at trial must be provided to the accused in advance of trial, at such time as ordered by the Tribunal; and

(2) No confidential information shall be offered at trial in a closed proceeding under Article 20(4) of the Statute or Rule 20.

Confidential information may be disclosed to the accused or before the Trial Chamber in summarized or edited form if the Trial Chamber determines that the accused will not be prejudiced by summarization or editing of the evidence.

b. Rationale

i. Terminology

The proposed modification to Rule 8 uses the term "confidential information" in place of the term "national security information." This modification indicates that all information which a state may regard as confidential should be treated under the same procedural framework. Confidential information which does not involve national security may include, among other things, information relating to the identity of sources, proprietary information of a corporation or national of a state, information protected by a state evidentiary privilege (attorney-client, physician-patient, etc.), and other information that has been provided to a state on the condition that it be kept confidential.

ii. Disclosure Requirements

The proposed requirement of disclosure to the accused of information which supports issuance of an indictment or which is to be offered at trial ensures that the accused will be able to adequately answer the charges against him. United States law recognizes the right of an accused to obtain classified information that will be used against him. The Classified Information Procedures Act (CIPA) provides that a court may determine that disclosure of classified information to an accused is required.[6]

The proposed requirement of disclosure in a public session of confidential information offered against the accused ensures the integrity of proceedings involving confidential information. The Task Force recognizes that this requirement may limit the ability of the Prosecutor to proceed in cases where a state refuses to consent to disclosure of confidential

---

[6] 18 U.S.C. App. § 6. See also United States v. Poindexter, 727 F. Supp. 1470, 1476-81 (D.D.C. 1989) (requiring disclosure of certain classified documents to defendant); United States v. North, 698 F. Supp. 322, 325 (D.D.C. 1988) (same).

information which it has provided. However, United States law also contemplates such a possibility. CIPA provides for dismissal of an indictment (or other lesser sanctions) when the Attorney General refuses to permit disclosure of classified information.[7]

The requirement of public disclosure would also circumscribe the discretion that is available to the International Tribunal under Art. 20(4) of the Statute: "The hearings shall be public unless the Trial Chamber decides to close the proceedings in accordance with its rules of procedure and evidence." Although closed sessions are thus within the International Tribunal's power, the Task Force believes that the Rules should not allow closed sessions to protect confidential information of a state.

Closed sessions may be appropriate for certain purposes. For example, in camera proceedings to protect witnesses are specifically authorized by the Statute, see Art. 23. Furthermore, the substance of the witness' testimony at such a session could be disclosed to the public in some form. In contrast, closure of a session on the ground that evidence is too sensitive for public disclosure does not advance any important purpose of the Statute and could seriously impair the appearance of integrity of the International Tribunal.

iii. Limits on Disclosure of Confidential Information

The Task Force recognizes that states may have legitimate interests in restricting disclosure of confidential information which is provided to the International Tribunal. The proposed modification of Rule 8 accommodates these interests.

First, the revised rule would not require disclosure of information which is transmitted to the Prosecutor but which is not used against the accused. Although the Prosecutor has an independent obligation to provide exculpatory evidence to the accused, under Rule 17.2, the International Tribunal would be able to deny disclosure in cases where the evidence in question is not relevant to the accused's defense. United States courts frequently make such determinations.[8]

Second, revised Rule 8 would permit required disclosures of evidence to be "in summarized or edited form if the Trial Chamber determines that the accused will not be prejudiced by summarization or editing of the evidence." The Trial Chamber would have substantial discretion in determining the manner of disclosure. United States courts may handle this type of situation under CIPA by permitting summarization of classified evidence,[9] or by allowing admission of "a statement admitting relevant facts that the specific classified information

---

[7] 18 U.S.C. App. § 6(e)(2).

[8] See United States v. Fowler, 932 F.2d 306, 311-12 (4th Cir. 1991) (excluding documents in trial for unauthorized conveyance of classified documents); United States v. Yunis, 924 F.2d 1086, 1095 (D.C. Cir. 1991) (excluding classified tapes of conversations between control tower and hijackers of airplane).

[9] 18 U.S.C. App. § 6(c)(1)(B); see also Socialist Workers Party v. Attorney General of the United States, 642 F. Supp. 1357, 1377-79 (S.D.N.Y. 1986) (allowing summarization of information regarding FBI informants).

would tend to prove."[10] Special procedures might also be developed to facilitate disclosure under such circumstances. For example, in Socialist Workers Party, the court appointed a special master to consider and summarize the classified evidence at issue.[11]

11. Rule 8.2(B) -- Sealed Indictments

Rule 8.2(B)(2) permits the disclosure of a sealed indictment "when the accused has been brought into custody or has been released pending trial." The ABA Task Force believes that unsealing of sealed indictments should be required, rather than merely permitted, at the time an accused is brought into custody. It could substantially impair the credibility of the International Tribunal to give it the power to detain an accused on undisclosed charges.

12. Rule 9.4 (new) -- Confidentiality of Investigations

Rule 9 does not impose an obligation to maintain the confidentiality of information secured in the course of an investigation. In order to protect the rights of those not charged as well as the interests of victims, witnesses, and other sources, the ABA Task Force recommends that the International Tribunal devise measures to assure the confidentiality of the information provided. Possible language might be as follows:

> **9.4 Confidentiality of matters under investigation.** Matters under investigation or subject to trial shall not be disclosed by the Prosecutor, the Registry, and members of their staffs, except as otherwise provided for in these Rules:
>
> (A) Disclosure otherwise prohibited by this rule may be made to --
>
> (i) the Prosecutor and his staff for use in the performance of their duties;
>
> (ii) such government personnel of a state or subdivision of a state as are deemed necessary by the Prosecutor in the performance of his duties to carry out the mandate of the International Tribunal; or
>
> (iii) other persons authorized by the International Tribunal under such procedures as it may establish.
>
> (B) Any person to whom matters are disclosed under Rule 9.4(A) shall not disclose the matters to other persons except in accordance with this rule.

The ABA Task Force suggests that such a rule could be supplemented by commentary such as the following:

> Rule 9.4 authorizes the disclosure of confidential information obtained in an investigation only in order

---

[10] 18 U.S.C. App. § 6(c)(1)(A); see also United States v. North, 713 F. Supp. 1442, 1443-44 (D.D.C. 1989) (approving admissions of fact as substitution for classified material).

[11] 642 F. Supp. at 1377-79.

> to further the investigation itself or for other purposes which the International Tribunal deems proper. However, Rule 9.4 should not be construed to bar disclosures by any person to counsel by whom the person is represented. A knowing violation of Rule 9.4 may be punished as contempt under Rule 6.4.

13. **Rule 11.1 -- Right to Counsel**

The use of the conjunction "or" between Rule 11.1(A) and Rule 11.1(B) obscures the fact that an indigent accused has both the right to attempt to acquire counsel of choice at no expense to the International Tribunal <u>and</u> the right to have counsel assigned to him. Therefore, the ABA Task Force recommends that Rule 11.1 be redrafted to provide:

> . . . the suspect or accused shall have the right, at no expense to the International Tribunal or other United Nations entity, to qualified, reasonably available counsel of his or her choosing. An indigent suspect or accused who is unable or unwilling to obtain such counsel shall have the right, subject to Rule 11.3, to have counsel assigned to him or her free of charge.

14. **Rule 12.3 -- Changes to Indictments**

Rule 12.3 permits certain types of changes to an indictment without issuance and confirmation of a separate indictment. It is the view of the ABA Task Force that any subsequent changes to the indictment must be confirmed by the judge who confirmed the indictment pursuant to Article 19 of the Statute and Rule 13.2 (proposed by Judge McDonald). Furthermore, even to the extent changes are approved by a Trial Chamber rather than by the initial confirming judge, the Task Force does not agree that the Prosecutor should be permitted to make changes to an indictment prior to the accused's initial appearance "without prior approval of the Trial Chamber." An accused should be charged based only upon an indictment that has been confirmed in its entirety by the International Tribunal.

15. **Rule 12.4(C) -- Adjournment or Continuance Upon Joinder**

In order to avoid prejudice to the accused from joinder of an indictment, the accused should be permitted to move for adjournment or continuance regardless of the stage of the proceedings at the time of joinder -- that is, such a motion should be permitting before the commencement of trial. Accordingly, the ABA Task Force recommends that Rule 12.4(C) be modified as follows:

> In the event that separate indictments are joined in accordance with Rule 12.4(B), the Trial Chamber shall, upon motion of the accused, order any adjournment or continuance of the proceedings which may, by reason of such joinder, be necessary to accord the defense adequate opportunity to defend against the charge.

16. **Rule 14.6 -- Notification of Security Council**

Rule 14.6 provides that where a state does not provide adequate assistance in procuring the presence of an accused, "the International Tribunal may notify the Secretary General for transmission to the Security Council." However, as a subsidiary body of the Security Council, the Tribunal has the power to send communications directly to the Council. Furthermore, direct transmission would avoid any bureaucratic delay and avoid the possibility that the Secretary General would exercise discretion not to transmit the Tribunal's communication to the Council in a particular case. For these reasons, the ABA Task Force recommends that Rule 14.6 be amended as follows:

> **14.6 Notification of the Security Council.** If the International Tribunal concludes that a State is not making substantial and good faith efforts to comply with a request or order, the International Tribunal may notify the Security Council for appropriate action.

Furthermore, the Rules omit to provide the International Tribunal with similar powers of notification in other situations in which the failure of states to cooperate could be a problem. The primary relevant areas are deferral by states to International Tribunal proceedings (Rule 4.2) and production of evidence (Rule 17). The Task Force proposed two alternative approaches to this omission. First, Rules 4 and 17 could be amended to contain provisions similar to Rule 14.6. Second, a new rule of general applicability could be added, permitting the Tribunal to notify the Security Council upon failure of a state to cooperate.

17. **Rule 16.4 -- State Requests for Release from Confinement**

The Commentary to Rule 16.4 states that a State may request release of an accused from pretrial confinement. The ABA Task Force believes that the Commentary should make clear whether the standards for release upon request by a State are the same as the standards for other pretrial release determinations.

18. **Rule 17.2 -- Exculpatory Evidence**

Rule 17.2 provides that the Prosecutor must provide exculpatory evidence to the accused. The ABA Task Force recommends that International Tribunal draft Commentary specifying in more detail the types of evidence that must be produced by the Prosecutor.

Specifically, the Task Force calls attention to the treatment of two categories of such evidence under United States law. First, in United States v. Giglio,[12] the Supreme Court held that the requirement of production of exculpatory evidence extends generally to evidence which tends to impeach the testimony of a prosecution witness[13] and specifically to promises of immunity from prosecution.[14] Second, the Jencks Act[15] requires the prosecution to produce, after a government witness has testified, any prior statements of the witnesses. Such statements could assist cross-examination and permit impeachment on the basis of prior inconsistent statements.

---

[12] 405 U.S. 150 (1972).

[13] Id. at 154.

[14] Id. at 154-55.

[15] 18 U.S.C. § 3500.

19. **Rule 17.7**

See comments on Rule 14.6 above, regarding notification of the Security Council.

20. **Rule 18.4(B) -- Prosecutorial Appeals of Evidentiary Rulings**

To limit the circumstances in which the Prosecutor may appeal an evidentiary ruling, the ABA Task Force recommends that the Rules require an explicit Trial Chamber finding that excluded evidence is important to the prosecution, as a condition precedent of the Prosecutor's right to appeal. To this end, Rule 18.4(B) might be amended as follows:

> (B) suppresses, excludes or precludes evidence, if the Trial Chamber finds that the evidence is a substantial proof of a fact material in the proceeding and if the prosecutor represents to the Trial Chamber that the appeal is not taken for the purpose of delay.

21. **Rule 18.5(B) -- Motions**

Rule 18.5(B) makes the provisions of Rules 18.1 to 18.4 inapplicable to certain motions by the Prosecutor which are "made prior to the accused's initial appearance" or "justify consideration ex parte." Though far more limited, there are also likely to be situations in which the accused may be justified in making motions under these circumstances. To provide balance, the ABA Task Force recommends that the words "by the prosecutor" be deleted from Rule 18.5(B) and the second sentence of its Commentary.

22. **Rule 20.2 -- Closed Sessions**

The ABA Task Force believes that it is crucial to the credibility of the International Tribunal that a record be kept of any closed sessions of the Tribunal. Therefore, the Task Force recommends that an additional sentence be added to Rule 20.2:

> Except for deliberations, a record shall be kept of all closed sessions and shall be available for review on appeal by the Appellate Chamber.

Furthermore, in accordance with its comments on Rule 8 above, the ABA Task Force recommends that the words "the national security of a State" be replaced with "the confidentiality of information provided by a State."

23. **Rule 20.4 -- Conditions on Photography and Video Recording**

The ABA Task Force believes that the Rules should make clear that the International Tribunal has the power to impose appropriate conditions on photography and video recording which a Trial Chamber permits during trial or other proceedings. State courts in the United States have experimented with use of television cameras in courtrooms for more than ten years. Every state that permits televised trials imposes requirements related to the location, number, and size of the cameras, as well as the types of witnesses (e.g., rape victims and children) whose photography is prohibited.

The Task Force recommends that the phrase "and conditions imposed thereon," be inserted following the comma after "Registry." Furthermore, the International Tribunal may wish to consider drafting Commentary regarding the appropriate use of cameras, in order to establish guidelines in advance for dealing with what is certain to be a large number of requests for photography and broadcast of Tribunal proceedings.

24. Rule 22 -- Abbreviated Proceedings

a. Discussion

Prosecutions by the International Tribunal are likely to present serious problems of securing evidence against individuals at higher levels of command responsibility. These will often be the individuals that directed or, at the very least, gave impetus to the offenses committed by others. However, without the cooperation of the less culpable, such as those who received illegal orders, the successful prosecution of the more culpable may be very difficult. The cooperation of the former is essential to provide investigative leads and admissible evidence.

Regardless of the structure of a system of criminal justice, the process of securing such cooperation may be difficult where, quite appropriately, the right against self-incrimination exists. Generally, those with the most probative evidence against other individuals also bear responsibility for having engaged in criminal acts. Because of their exposure to possible criminal prosecution, they can effectively block the progress of an investigation by a proper exercise of their right against self-incrimination.

Even if not blocked, an investigation may be impeded by the exercise of the right against self-incrimination by less culpable individuals. This may require that alternative sources of evidence be secured in order for the investigation to proceed. It may also mean that substantial time will be lost and substantial resources diverted to full-scale prosecutions of those less culpable, because only after convictions are secured can cooperation be expected and, if necessary, legitimately induced. Such a diversion of resources would be significant in view of the breadth of the allegations and the scope of the crimes which the International Tribunal is mandated to consider. Moreover, the International Tribunal is not likely to remain in existence on an indefinite basis.

For these reasons, a mechanism for abbreviated proceedings is essential to permit the Prosecutor to carry out his responsibilities under the statute. In most respects, either of the two proposed options in the Rules is acceptable.

The advantage of Option Two is that it more closely approaches the practice in many civil law countries. Furthermore, a judgment of conviction under Option Two is more likely to be given deference under the principle of non bis in idem -- because the proceeding would be less summary in nature and would involve more substantial participation by the judges of a Trial Chamber -- and therefore provides the accused with greater certainty as to the treatment of the disposition by national courts. At the same time, for purposes of facilitating an investigation, Option Two provides a means for expediting the disposition of a case.

However, the ABA Task Force expresses a strong preference for availability of immunity provisions along the lines of those in Option One. The basis for the preference is the experience in the United States of conducting complex criminal prosecutions. Where a right against self-incrimination exists and due deference is given to the exercise of such a right, the investigation of higher level or more remote individuals is nearly impossible.

As a compromise between the public's interest in having all relevant evidence produced and the right against self-incrimination, a practice of providing immunity to witnesses at the investigatory stage has evolved.[16/] This practice has played a critical role in enabling prosecutions against large or complex organizations. Further, in countries of the civil law tradition, there has recently been increased adoption of aspects of common law systems of criminal procedure.[17/]

While there may be uses for what is known under U.S. law as "transactional" immunity -- full immunity from prosecution as to particular conduct -- reliance on "use" immunity will be sufficient in most situations. Use immunity, which is the type of immunity generally bestowed under U.S. law, is intended to be as broad as, but no broader than, the right against self-incrimination.[18/] Use immunity prevents the prosecution from using against a witness any evidence secured from him pursuant to the grant of immunity.[19/] The witness is also protected against the use of evidence derivatively obtained.[20/] A grant of use immunity does not free a witness from prosecution for crimes about which testimony is given. It only provides that in any future prosecution against the witness, the Prosecutor will have the burden of proving that evidence offered against an accused was not derived from the accused's immunized testimony.[21/]

[16/] See H.R. Rep. No. 91-1549, 91st Cong., 1st Sess., reprinted in 1970 U.S.C.C.A.N. 4007, 4017-18.

[17/] See Craig M. Bradley, The Emerging International Consensus as to Criminal Procedure Rules, 14 Mich. J. Int'l L. 171 (1993).

[18/] See Kastigar v. United States, 406 U.S. 441, 453-62 (1972) (statutory use immunity leaves witness and prosecutorial authorities in substantially the same position as if witness had claimed right against self incrimination); United States v. Underwood, 880 F.2d 612, 617 (1st Cir. 1989) (use immunity afforded witness same protection entitled to under right against self-incrimination); United States v. Papadakis, 802 F.2d 618, 621 (2d Cir. 1986) (defendant cannot be prosecuted for truthful statements protected by immunity because use immunity is coextensive with the right against self-incrimination).

[19/] See Murphy v. Waterfront Commission, 378 U.S. 52 (1964).

[20/] See note 17, supra; see also H.R. Rep. No. 91-1549, 1970 U.S.C.C.A.N. at 4018.

[21/] Kastigar v. United States, 406 U.S. 441, 461-462 (1972). Compare, e.g., United States v. Schwimmer, 882 F.2d 22, 25-26 (2d Cir. 1989) (dictum) (no violation of right against self-incrimination if government proves that evidence derived from sources independent of immunized testimony), cert. denied, 493 U.S. 1071 (1990); United States v. Brimberry, 803 F.2d 908, 916 (7th Cir. 1986) (no violation of right against self-incrimination when government had independent source established by building strong case against defendant that included witness testimony obtained independently of defendant's immunized cooperation), cert. denied, 484 U.S. 896 (1987).

The ability to resort to a grant of immunity has the added advantage of minimizing investigative abuses, which are more likely where there is no legal means of securing critical evidence. Improper inducement or coercion of evidence is likely both to infringe on the right against self-incrimination and to produce evidence of questionable reliability. Regardless of the reliability of the evidence produced, such practices would undermine the integrity of the International Tribunal and its processes.

b. Recommendation

For the above reasons, the ABA Task Force recommends that the International Tribunal adopt Option Two, supplemented with the immunity provisions of Option One. Thus, Rules 9.1(F) and 9.3 of Option One would be added to Option Two, with the modifications discussed below.

The modifications of the Rules proposed by Judge McDonald include the recommendation that Rules 9.1(G) and 9.4 of Option One, regarding pretrial agreements between the Prosecutor and the accused, be included regardless of which option is chosen. The ABA Task Force is not opposed to this proposal, in particular because Rules 22.4(B) and 22.7 of Option Two refer to such agreements.

i. Rule 9.3 -- Immunity

Care must be taken to assure that immunity is not improvidently granted. Therefore, the ABA Task Force recommends that the International Tribunal be required to approve grants of immunity. Furthermore, by limiting grants of immunity to use immunity, the right against self-incrimination and the need to gather evidence can be accommodated with the goal of prosecuting all culpable parties.

An additional consideration is that evidence provided pursuant to a grant of immunity could be used in a prosecution before a national court which is not bound by the grant of immunity. The International Tribunal should consider that such circumstances may require protection of the information pursuant to Rule 8 or proposed Rule 9.4 (see above), or requests for deference to the primacy of the Tribunal pursuant to Rule 4. However, unlike Rule 6.3, the grant of immunity is primarily for investigatory purposes. Orders may be tailored to meet the particular needs of the situation and to afford a witness sufficient protection.

Consistent with these concerns, language that might be considered for Rule 9.3 is as follows:

9.3 Immunity.

(A) Grant of Immunity. If any person refuses, on the basis of his privilege against self-incrimination, to provide evidence to the Prosecutor and the Prosecutor determines that such evidence is important to an investigation or prosecution before the International Tribunal, the Prosecutor may apply to the International Tribunal for a grant of immunity. An order granting immunity shall provide that no testimony or other evidence provided under the order (or any information directly or indirectly derived from such testimony or other evidence) may be used against the witness in any criminal case, except a prosecution for perjury, giving a false statement, or otherwise failing to comply with the order. The person to whom the order is directed may not refuse to comply with the order on the basis of his privilege against self-incrimination.

(B) Approval. A grant of immunity shall be subject to approval by the member or members of the International Tribunal who at the time are responsible for approving an indictment. A request of the Prosecutor for a grant of immunity shall specify the grounds for the request and shall be denied only when the interests of justice so require. The denial of a request for a grant of immunity shall not preclude the Prosecutor from subsequently seeking a grant of immunity based upon the acts underlying a prior request.

(C) Procedure.

(1) A grant of immunity shall be in writing in the language of the International Tribunal and in a language the suspect or accused speaks and understands, signed by a member of the International Tribunal, and shall identify the matters to which it extends.

(2) If the judge or judges issuing the grant of immunity determine that there is a substantial risk that evidence or testimony provided pursuant to the grant of immunity will be used in a prosecution by a national authority, or that there will be other substantial risk to the witness, the order granting immunity may also contain provisions protecting the testimony of the immunized witness in the manner authorized by Rules 7 and 8, or limiting the use of the evidence produced to investigatory purposes. Such protection shall cease when the reason for protecting the testimony no longer exists, or when otherwise ordered by the Trial Chamber.

(D) Failure to comply. The failure of a witness to comply with the terms of the grant of immunity shall be subject to the contempt provisions of Rule 6.4. Any sanctions thus imposed shall cease at such time as there is compliance with the grant of immunity.

ii. Rule 22.3 -- Closed Proceedings

It is important that a record be kept of closed proceedings. See comments on Rule 20.2 above. Furthermore, the fact that abbreviated proceedings represent a disposition of a prosecution against an accused suggests a need for public accountability. Therefore, where possible, the record of a closed proceeding should within a reasonable period of time be available to the public. The ABA Task Force recommends that consideration be given to adding the following language to Rule 22.3:

> A record shall be kept of the closed proceeding and shall be subject to appellate review. The record shall, where possible, be subject to public disclosure within a reasonable period. Public disclosure shall be required when the reason for protecting the testimony shall cease to exist or when the the accused testifies in an open proceeding of the International Tribunal as to the matters subject to protection.

iii. Rule 22.7

To encourage the veracity of statements made pursuant to a cooperation agreement, provision should be made to permit the use of such statements in a prosecution for perjury or giving a false statement. Accordingly, the ABA Task Force recommends that consideration be given to modifying the final sentence of Rule 22.7 as follows:

> Except for use in a prosecution for perjury or giving a false statement, neither shall the agreement itself or any admissions made by the accused pursuant to Rule 22.2(C) be admissible in evidence against the accused.

25. Rule 23.2 -- Confessions in Joint Trials

It is an important principle of United States law that introduction in a joint trial of a confession by one defendant which implicates another defendant is prohibited.[22] The concerns which animate this rule are substantially attenuated in a trial without a jury. Nevertheless, it remains true that in a joint trial before the International Tribunal, there may be no opportunity to cross-examine an accused as to the substance of a confession, in view of the right against self-incrimination.[23] Therefore, the ABA Task Force recommends that consistent with the Bruton principle, Rule 23.2 be amended, or that Commentary to Rule 23.2 be adopted, along the following lines:

> No conviction of an accused after a joint trial may be based in whole or in part on evidence contained in a confession or admission of a different accused who is tried in the same proceeding, if that different accused does not take the stand to testify in his defense. Howwever, this Rule shall not prohibit admission of such a confession or admission against the accused by whom it was made.

26. Rule 23.4 -- Order of Proof

The order of proof set out in Rule 23.4 does not permit the parties to offer evidence in rebuttal to evidence requested by the Trial Chamber. To allow such evidence, the ABA Task Force recommends that the order of proof be changed by moving Rule 23.4(F) to the current position of Rule 23.4(C) and renumbering the other provisions of Rule 23.4 accordingly.

27. Rule 23.6(A) -- Reasonable Doubt Standard

Rule 23.6(A) requires proof "beyond a reasonable doubt," but does not define that standard. The reasonable doubt standard is one with which the members of the Tribunal who are from civil law jurisdictions may be unfamiliar. Members of the ABA Task Force are of the view that many civil law jurists regard the reasonable doubt standard as being very stringent -- more so than it is in application. For these reasons and to promote

---

[22] See Bruton v. United States, 391 U.S. 123 (1968).

[23] Statute, art. 21(4)(g); Rule 24(K).

consistency in the weighing of evidence, the Task Force recommends that the International Tribunal adopt Commentary which defines the reasonable doubt standard. One possible formulation is:

> It is not required that the [Prosecutor] prove guilt beyond all possible doubt. The test is one of reasonable doubt. A reasonable doubt is a doubt based upon reason and common sense -- the kind of doubt that would make a reasonable person hesitate to act. Proof beyond a reasonable doubt must, therefore, be proof of such a convincing character that a reasonable person would not hesitate to rely and act upon it in the most important of his or her own affairs.[24]

28. **Rule 25.2 -- Sources of Law**

Rule 25.2 is based on Article 38 of the Statute of the International Court of Justice ("ICJ"). To bring Rule 25.2 more closely in line with the ICJ Statute, the ABA Task Force recommends two changes. First, the Task Force recommends that Rule 25.2(C) be modified to indicate that it refers to principles common to the domestic law of many nations. Second, the Task Force recommends that Rule 25.2(D) be modified to recognize the role of publicists in the development on international law. The revised provisions would read as follows:

> (C) general principles of law recognized by civilized nations; and
>
> (D) decisions of other international tribunals and of national courts, and the teachings of the most highly qualified publicists of the various nations.

29. **Rule 25.5 -- Acceptance of Facts Without Evidence**

Rule 25.5 permits what is known in United States law as judicial notice. The ABA Task Force agrees that the International Tribunal should have the power of judicial notice; however, in particular cases it is possible that there will be dispute as to whether a particular matter is properly subject to judicial notice. Therefore, the Task Force recommends that the Tribunal consider revising Rule 25.5 as follows:

> **25.5 Acceptance of facts without introduction of evidence.** The Trial Chamber may on its own motion or on the motion of a party, without the production of evidence, recognize the existence in truth of certain facts having bearing on the issue of guilt, which are not subject to reasonable dispute, and which are either:
>
> (A) generally known universally, locally, or in the area pertinent to the event, or
>
> (B) capable of accurate and ready determination by resort to sources whose accuracy cannot reasonably be questioned.

---

[24] Edward J. Devitt et al., <u>Federal Jury Practice and Instructions</u> § 12.10 (4th ed. 1992).

> When a Trial Chamber accepts facts in this manner on its own motion, it shall, where practicable, give the parties notice and an opportunity to respond as to the matter accepted.

30. **Rule 25.6 -- Agreements as to Admissibility or Facts**

Rule 25.6 combines and confuses stipulations to a fact and stipulations as to admissibility of evidence. Rule 25.6(E) relates to stipulations as to admissibility and allows the evidence at issue to be contradicted. Rule 25.6(F) relates to stipulations to facts themselves and states that facts accepted in this manner are generally binding. Because Rules 25.6(E) and 25.6(F) do not distinguish these differing situations, they are in conflict.

To resolve this conflict, the ABA Task Force suggests three changes to Rule 25.6. First, Rule 25.6(A) should indicate that two separate cases are addressed:

> (A) The defense and the prosecution may make oral or written agreement:
>
> (1) that the contents of a document, the expected testimony of a witness, or any other matter should be considered as evidence by the Trial Chamber, or
>
> (2) that a fact may be deemed conclusively proved by the Trial Chamber.

Second, "this Rule" in the first sentence of Rule 25.6(E) should be replaced by "Rule 25.6(A)(1)" -- to indicate that Rule 25.6(E) relates to stipulations as to admissibility. Third, "this Rule" in Rule 25.6(F) should be replaced by "Rule 25.6(A)(2)" -- to indicate that Rule 25.6(F) relates to stipulations to a fact.

31. **Rule 25.7(B) -- Evidence More Prejudicial Than Probative**

The ABA Task Force recommends that the types of relevant evidence which may be excluded under Rule 25.7(B) be expanded to include evidence which is more prejudicial than probative:

> (B) Relevant evidence may nonetheless be excluded if required by any other provision of these Rules, or for other good cause, including that it would constitute a needless presentation of cumulative evidence, would result in undue delay, or would otherwise represent a waste of time, or that its probative value is substantially outweighed by the danger of unfair prejudice.

32. **Rule 25.8(D) -- Complete Documents**

Admission of a complete document, as contemplated by Rule 25.8(D), is generally sought by the party not introducing the document. Rule 25.8(D) does not make it clear that such a party has a right to request a complete document. To clarify this rule, the ABA Task Force recommends that the International Tribunal replace "may require that party" with "on motion of an opposing party or on its own motion may require the party introducing the writing or statement . . . ."

33. **Rule 25.8(E) (new) -- Non-Primary Evidence**

Rule 25.8 implements a version of the hearsay rule that is far simpler than the rule as applied under United States law. This simplification is particularly appropriate in that many of the hearsay concerns which are raised by a jury trial will be absent in a proceeding before the International Tribunal. However, to clarify that the right of confrontation must be carefully balanced when admitting hearsay as evidence, the ABA Task Force recommends that the International Tribunal consider adding a new Rule 25.8(E):

> (E) The Trial Chamber should balance the accused's rights of confrontation against the type of evidence offered, and may assign appropriate weight to evidence that is of lesser probative value because it is non-primary evidence or, in the judgment of the Trial Chamber, is lacking in credibility for any reason. If the accused challenges the introduction of any non-primary evidence on the ground that its probative value is outweighed by the prejudice the accused will suffer if it is admitted, the Trial Chamber shall, upon notice and an opportunity to respond, make a determination of admissibility. If the Trial Chamber determines that the prejudice to the accused from the introduction of the evidence outweighs the probative value, the evidence shall be excluded.

34. **Rule 25.10 -- Rape Shield Rule**

a. Discussion

Rule 25.10 sets out what is known as a rape shield provision in United States courts. Because of the likelihood that numerous offenses of rape will be prosecuted by the International Tribunal, the ABA Task Force believes that this provision must be carefully considered to preserve the rights of both rape victims and of potential accuseds. Three primary areas are of concern.

First, although the Task Force assumes that it is evidence of prior consensual sexual behavior that is made inadmissible by this rule, this principle should be made explicit. The Prosecutor should be able to introduce evidence of non-consensual sexual behavior -- e.g., to show command responsibility for mass rape, or to show the requisite intent for genocide.

Second, the rule should take into account that "consent" to rape in proceedings before the International Tribunal may involve situations in which women are subject to extreme physical and psychological duress. For example, in the situation where a person is raped or sexually assaulted (by someone other than another prisoner) while detained in one of the "rape camps" that have reportedly been set up in the former Yugoslavia, "consent" to the sexual activity is subject to conditions of physical and psychological duress, and the accused should only be allowed to introduce evidence prior consent by the victim in extraordinary circumstances. An analogous case would be a claim that subjects of medical experimentation in a concentration camp consented to the experimentation.

Third, Rule 25.10(A)(3) would allow evidence of "past sexual behavior . . . to rebut evidence by the Prosecutor that the alleged victim did not engage in sexual activity during a given period of time." This provision would allow impeachment evidence of a type that would ordinarily be barred by Rule 25.10, on the basis that the Prosecutor has brought such evidence into issue. The ABA Task Force believes that the protections of Rule 25.10 should not be circumvented through the presentation of impeachment evidence. Federal Rule of Evidence 412, which has provisions similar to Rule 25.10(A)(1) and 25.10(A)(2),[25] has no provision analogous to 25.10(A)(3). Instead, the Task Force recommends that the International Tribunal adopt a fundamental fairness exception parallel to the constitutional exception of Federal Rule of Evidence 412(b)(1).

b. Recommendation

For the above reasons, the ABA Task Force recommends that Rule 25.10(A) be modified as follows:

> (A) In cases which a person is accused of rape or sexual assault, evidence of past consensual sexual behavior of the alleged victim of such rape or assault is not admissible unless it is evidence of:
>
> (1) past sexual behavior with persons other than the accused, offered by the accused upon the issue of whether the accused was or was not the source of semen or injury with respect to the alleged victim;
>
> (2) past sexual behavior with the accused, offered by the accused upon the issue of whether the alleged victim consented to the sexual behavior with respect to which the rape or assault is alleged; or
>
> (3) past sexual behavior which is otherwise so probative on the issue of guilt or innocence that failure to admit it would be fundamentally unfair.
>
> Provided, that in the case of an alleged rape or sexual assault of a person in detention by a person not in detention, the exception set out in Rule 25.10(A)(2) shall not apply unless the accused demonstrates to the Trial Chamber by clear and convincing evidence that consent to the prior sexual behavior was not affected by coercion.

In addition, the Task Force recommends that the Commentary to Rule 25.10 be amended by adding two new paragraphs after ". . . questioning before a large audience":

> The rule distinguishes the case in which an alleged victim who is in detention is raped or sexually assaulted by a person not in detention. In such a case, the accused is permitted to introduce evidence of the victim's prior consensual sexual behavior with the accused only in extraordinary circumstances. Such extraordinary circumstances might include the case of a consensual sexual relationship between the accused and

---

[25] Fed R. Evid. 412(b)(2)(A) & (B).

the victim at a time when the victim was not in detention. The rationale for this distinction is that in cases in which the alleged victim is in detention, "consent" to sexual activity is subject to conditions of physical and psychological duress. The situation is analogous to a claim that an inmate of a concentration camp consented to medical experimentation.

Rule 25.10(A)(3) is intended to permit admission of the prior sexual history of the victim only in extraordinary circumstances. Where admission is not authorized under subsection (1) or (2), but the evidence is so probative on the issue of guilt or innocence that failure to consider it would be manifestly unjust, subsection (3) would apply. Rule 25.10 recognizes in principle that a victim's past sexual behavior is typically of little or no relevance, and that its admission has historically been based on unjustified assumptions that the testimony of rape victims is unreliable. Thus, for such evidence to be admitted pursuant to subsection (3), the evidence sought to be introduced must be so compelling that its relevance cannot reasonably be questioned. Great care must be taken by the Tribunal to ensure that the general rule of inadmissibility of prior sexual conduct evidence not be eviscerated through overutilization of subsection (3).

Furthermore, the words "such evidence," now at the beginning of the third paragraph, would be replaced by "any evidence of a victim's prior consensual sexual activity."

35. **Rule 25.12(B)**

The words "or admission" should be added after each appearance of the word "confession." The omission of reference to admissions in Rule 25.12(B) appears to have been inadvertent.

36. **Rules 25.14(A) and (B) -- Obedience to Orders and Duress**

Rules 25.14(A) and (B) and their Commentary, relating to the special defenses of obedience to orders and duress or coercion, are consistent with United States military law, the U.S. position on the defense of superior orders under international law (as articulated by both U.S. Army Field Manual 27-10, The Law of Land Warfare, and the statement of Madeleine Albright, U.S. ambassador to the U.N., on Article 7(4) of the Statute[26/]), and the 1993 Report's treatment of these issues.[27/] Indeed, the text of Rule 25.14(A) is identical in substance to Rule for Courts-Martial 916(d), Manual for Courts-Martial, United States (1984).

26/ 1993 Report (bound version) at 39-40.

27/ Id. at 36-41.

However, as more fully explained in the 1993 Report, the recognition of a defense of superior orders and the treatment of the defense of duress in Rule 25.14 is not consistent with the literal terms of Article 7(4) of the Statute or the Secretary-General's Report.[28] The ABA Task Force endorses Rule 25.14 as drafted, but advises the International Tribunal to ensure that the rule is consistent with the Statute, if necessary by seeking an interpretation of the Statute by the Security Council.

37. **Rule 27.1(B) -- Prison Sentences in Former Yugoslavia**

Rule 27.1(B) provides that "the Trial Chamber shall consider the general practice regarding prison sentences in the courts of the former Yugoslavia." However, the maximum prison sentence in the former Yugoslavia was fifteen years, because more serious crimes were punishable by death. The International Tribunal, in contrast, may not impose a death sentence[29] but is specifically authorized in Rule 27.1(A) to impose sentences up to life imprisonment. The ABA Task Force recommends that the commentary to Rule 27.1 state that the maximum prison sentence of fifteen years in the former Yugoslavia does not bar the imposition of a longer sentence of imprisonment by the International Tribunal.

38. **Rule 28.2(A)(1)**

In accordance with the above comments on Rule 20.2, regarding the making of a record of closed sessions of the International Tribunal, the ABA Task Force recommends that "every in-court session" be replaced with "every session, whether in court or in camera (with the exception of deliberations), ..."

39. **Rule 28.2(A)(2) -- Interlocutory Orders**

Rule 28.2(A)(2) should unambiguously indicate that interlocutory orders of the Trial Chamber are part of the record on appeal. To this end, a comma and the words "any interlocutory orders," should be inserted after "indictment."

40. **Rule 28.3 -- Changes to Record**

The ABA Task Force believes that Rule 28.3 should be construed to permit only clerical and other non-substantive changes to the record on appeal. The integrity of the adjudicative process could be compromised if the judges of a Trial Chamber were permitted to make substantive changes to conform the record to their view of the proceedings. Therefore, the Task Force recommends that the word "non-substantive" be inserted before the word "changes" in the second sentence of Rule 28.3.

---

[28] Id.

[29] Statute, art. 24(1).

41. Rules 29 and 30 -- Appeals After Acquittal

The ABA Task Force's 1993 Report reviewed the historical basis and philosophical rationale underlying the double jeopardy protection afforded by the U.S. Constitution, and the related international law concept of non bis in idem.[30] The Report concluded that the sound principles underlying those protections conflict with provisions of the Statute which allow prosecutorial appeals from a judgment of acquittal and allow the Prosecutor to reopen a case after acquittal if new evidence is discovered. Rules 29 and 30 maintain the positions the ABA Report found objectionable. Because the principles on which the prohibition against double jeopardy are based apply with particular force to the prosecution of individuals before the International Tribunal, the ABA Task Force maintains its opposition to prosecutorial appeals from judgments of acquittal and to allowing the Prosecutor to reopen a case after acquittal on the basis of newly discovered evidence.

a. The Traditional Rationales for the Double Jeopardy Doctrine

The 1993 Report identified two primary purposes underlying the double jeopardy doctrine which are relevant here. First, respect for the accused's legitimate desire for finality:

> The underlying idea . . . is that the State with all its resources and power should not be allowed to make repeated attempts to convict an individual for an alleged offense, thereby subjecting him to embarrassment, expense and ordeal and compelling him to live in a continuing state of anxiety and insecurity. . . .[31]

Second, the 1993 Report recognized that the double jeopardy doctrine is designed to guard against the increased probability of an erroneous conviction that might arise if the state, with its superior resources, were allowed to subject an individual to retrials until it finally won a conviction.[32] These factors apply with particular force to persons accused before the International Tribunal.[33]

---

[30] 1993 Report (bound version) at 41-43.

[31] Green v. United States, 355 U.S. 184, 187-88 (1957).

[32] See United States v. DiFranesco, 449 U.S. 117, 130 (1980); Burks v. United States, 437 U.S. 1, 16 (1978).

[33] In certain cases, the U.S. Supreme Court has allowed prosecutorial appeals from rulings in favor of the accused other than an acquittal on the merits. See United States v. Scott, 437 U.S. 82 (1978) (government may appeal from dismissal of case for preindictment delay; motion could be made prior to trial and dismissal was not on ground related to guilt or innocence); United States v. Wilson, 420 U.S. 332 (1975) (government may appeal dismissal of indictment for preindictment delay, entered after jury verdict of guilty, because no new trial would be required if favorable appellate ruling obtained). In these cases, the Supreme Court evaluated the burdens on the accused and the risk of government oppression and concluded that government appeals in certain limited situations are permissible. These decisions underscore the central concern of our double jeopardy clause that persons once tried and acquitted not be subjected to further proceedings.

b. Application of the Traditional Principles to the International Tribunal

i. The Power of the Prosecutor

The power of the Prosecutor under the Rules will be significant, as it should be. The Prosecutor will have a full opportunity to develop the case. The Prosecutor can bring his or her case against an accused at any time. Under Rule 3, there is no statute of limitations. Thus the Prosecutor can make whatever investigations he or she believes appropriate before bringing a case. Rule 9 gives the Prosecutor extensive investigatory powers, and no approval for the exercise of these powers need be obtained from the Trial Chamber of the International Tribunal before any investigation is undertaken. In addition, the Prosecutor may be given the power to develop evidence through grants of immunity from prosecution.[34] The Prosecutor has at his or her disposal not just the resources of a nation-state but of the United Nations. Finally, Rule 12 allows the Prosecutor to add a new legal theory of liability even after the trial has commenced.

ii. The Role of the Prosecutor

The Statute clearly contemplates that the Prosecutor will have an independent adversarial role, typical of the role of a prosecutor in a common law system, as opposed to the less partial role of a civil law prosecutor (or standing judge).[35] In the adversarial system set up by the Statute, particularly in high visibility cases such as the ones that would be before the International Tribunal, the Prosecutor can fairly be expected to become deeply committed to obtaining a judgment of conviction. There is little evidence that the Prosecutor will be expected to prepare, try, and pursue a case on appeal with any less zeal than a prosecutor in a common law jurisdiction. Nor is there reason to think that the Prosecutor will decline available opportunities to attack acquittals on appeal or to seek to reopen cases once lost at the trial level. The double jeopardy doctrine blocks a prosecutor from giving reign to those understandable but potentially oppressive instincts.

iii. The Significant Burdens on a Defendant From a Retrial

Concerns about embarrassment, expense, ordeal, anxiety, and insecurity resulting from additional appellate proceedings or a second trial after a judgment of acquittal may prove even more burdensome in proceedings before the International Tribunal than in proceedings before a domestic court. An accused may be isolated geographically, culturally, and linguistically. The accused may well be imprisoned both prior to and during the trial, without a presumption in favor of release. Further, because of international attention to events occurring in the former Yugoslavia, the accused will likely by subject to extensive scrutiny.

---

[34] Draft Rules, Appendix I, Option 1.

[35] Statute, art. 16.

c. <u>The Moral Authority of the International Tribunal</u>

Considerations unique to the nature and purpose of the International Tribunal argue against retrial of an acquitted defendant. The Tribunal is composed of eleven judges from eleven different nations divided into two Trial Chambers and an Appeals Chamber.[36] These judges are charged with interpreting both the law and facts and deciding when, in the judgment of the civilized world, a person has beyond a reasonable doubt violated international humanitarian law.[37] The diverse backgrounds of these judges assure all concerned that a person convicted of violating international humanitarian law has truly violated such law, not just one locality's moral sensibilities.

An acquittal by a Trial Chamber is a clear finding of these respected jurists that reasonable doubt exists that a violation of international humanitarian law has occurred. A conviction after acquittal could undermine the moral force of the International Tribunal's decisions. A person would stand convicted of a violation of international humanitarian law, despite the fact that one of the chambers of the court appointed to render this judgment, representing a segment of that international community, had reasonable doubt that a violation of international humanitarian law had in fact occurred. A change in membership of the Trial Chamber, or a change in the panel from one trial to the next, may occasion a change in result. In contrast, reversal of a conviction does not undermine the moral force of the Tribunal's judgments. Rather it assures all that a violation of international humanitarian law will be found only when both the trial and appellate Chambers of the International Tribunal combine to find the conviction proper.

d. <u>Conclusions</u>

The principles which have led United States courts to prohibit prosecutorial appeals after a judgment of acquittal and to prohibit retrial of a once-acquitted defendant on the basis of newly-discovered evidence apply with even greater force to prohibit prosecutorial appeals and retrial of a defendant before the International Tribunal. For the reasons stated above, the ABA Task Force urges the International Tribunal to consider revisions to Rules 29 and 30. The Task Force believes that the respect given by the international community to the proceedings of this International Tribunal may be undermined if its deliberations are not seen as promoting the significant interest of finality. If a defendant, once acquitted, may be brought back for a second or subsequent trials -- possibly before a Trial Chamber having a different composition than the one that has already acquitted the accused -- critics will be able to state with apparent justification that this body values convictions more highly than it values justice and the appearance of even-handedness.

---

[36] Statute, arts. 11, 12.

[37] Rules 2, 23.6, 23.7.

K. PROPOSALS RELATING TO THE PROSECUTION OF RAPE AND OTHER GENDER-BASED VIOLENCE TO THE JUDGES OF THE INTERNATIONAL TRIBUNAL FOR THE PROSECUTION OF PERSONS RESPONSIBLE FOR SERIOUS VIOLATIONS OF INTERNATIONAL HUMANITARIAN LAW COMMITTED IN THE TERRITORY OF THE FORMER YUGOSLAVIA SINCE 1991.[1]

3 February 1994.

I. INTRODUCTION

This document is intended to identify a number of issues relating to prosecutions by this Tribunal[2] of rape and gender-based violence perpetrated in the former Yugoslavia. It suggests approaches to articulating and defining the subject-matter jurisdiction of the Tribunal as to gender-specific violations under international law; developing certain rules of procedure and evidence for the Tribunal; adopting mechanisms for protection of witnesses and victims who provide testimony to the Tribunal, while maintaining fair due process standards for the accused; and providing appropriate redress including compensation to victims of these crimes. These suggestions are presented to assist the Judges of the International Tribunal in developing rules and mechanisms which make explicit the application of established international law principles of violations of women's human rights; reflect the gender-specific nature of certain violations; and properly implement the imperatives of precluding gender bias, protecting both the dignity and security of witnesses, and guaranteeing the rights of the accused.

Specifically, in devising the substantive rules for the prosecution of these offenses, the Tribunal must guard against adopting standards which are the product of sex discrimination and sex-stereotyping. The international guarantees against sex discrimination contained in the Universal Charter, the International Covenant on Civil and Political Rights and, more pointedly,

---

[1] These proposals are submitted by a USA-based working group of legal scholars and attorneys associated with non-governmental human rights organizations including Professor Rhonda Copelon and law student members, Karen Lesley-Loyd and Leila Maldonado on behalf of the International Women's Human Rights Law Clinic (IWHR) of City University of New York Law School (CUNY), Queens, New York; Jennifer Green, Administrative Director of the Harvard Human Rights Program, Cambridge, MA; Kathleen Pratt, of Heller, Ehrman, White & McAuliffe and associated with the International Human Rights Law Group, Washington, D.C.; Patrick Cotter, former prosecutor and Visiting Assistant Professor, Chicago-Kent College of Law, Chicago, Ill.; Beth Stephens, Center for Constitutional Rights, New York City and Carin Kahgan. The authors wish to acknowledge as well the contributions of Christopher Blakesley, Rachel Pine of the Center for Reproductive Law and Policy, Jennifer Schirmer, Center for European Studies, Harvard University, and others including Harvard Law Students Inbar Schwartz, Deborah Solomon and David Weinstein, and Yale Students Bethany Berger, Natalie Coburn, Tim Holbrook, Wesley Hsu, Heidi Kitrosser, Steven Parker, Giovanni Seinelli, and Wendy Wesler.

[2] For all purposes herein, the authors refer to the Tribunal either by as the "International Tribunal" or simply as "Tribunal". See, "Report of the Secretary-General Pursuant to Paragraph 2 of Security Council Resolution 808," S/25704 (May 3, 1993) approved by the Security Council, May 25 1993. (Hereinafter "Report".)

in the Convention for the Elimination of All Forms of Discrimination Against Women and the UN Draft Declaration on the Elimination of Violence Against Women, scheduled to be adopted during this session of the General Assembly, preclude countries, and through them this International Tribunal, from employing sex-stereotyped or sex-discriminatory rules. Moreover, the recognition by the 1993 World Conference of Human Rights in Vienna of the pervasiveness and gravity of gender-based violence and the duty of all international and national institutions to eliminate it underscores the obligation of the Tribunal to carefully fashion the rules.

This document is intended to build on the substantive analyses and suggestions which have already been put forth by other non-governmental organizations and governmental entities.[3]

This memo can only identify the problems and suggest solutions; it does not purport to be a thorough analysis of the problem or a comprehensive survey of the newer approaches to the problem. We urge, therefore, that in drawing up the rules in the area of sex crimes, the Tribunal seek the advice of persons having expertise in the fair and effective prosecution of sex crimes. Sex-stereotyped misconceptions about crimes of sexual violence are common in the absence of particular experience and expertise in this area of criminal law. The rules established for the investigation, trial and the protection of witnesses, and the understanding by all the Judges of the need for those rules, will determine whether war crimes of sexual violence will be fairly redressed with due regard for both the rights of the accused and the protection of the victims. These rules will thus be a very significant factor in whether women come forward as complainants.

II. SCOPE OF JURISDICTION

Article 1 of the Statute of the International Tribunal (herein "Statute"),[4] "Competence of the International Tribunal," gives the Tribunal power "to prosecute persons responsible for serious violations of international humanitarian law committed in the territory of the former Yugoslavia since 1991 in accordance with the provisions of the present Statute." The Statute then delineates, in Articles 2-5, certain categories of violations over which the Tribunal has

---

[3] *See, e.g.*, Amnesty International, "Memorandum to the United Nations: The Question of Justice and Fairness in the International War Crimes Tribunal for the Former Yugoslavia," April 1993 (herein "AI Memorandum"); Amnesty International, "From Nuremberg to the Balkans: Seeking Justice and Fairness in the International War Crimes Tribunal for the Former Yugoslavia," April 1993 (herein "Seeking Justice"); International Human Rights Law Group, *No Justice, No Peace: Accountability for Rape and Gender-Based Violence in the Former Yugoslavia*, June 1993 (herein "*No Justice, No Peace*"); Christopher L. Blakesley, "The Ad Hoc Tribunal for Crimes Against Humanitarian Law in the Former Yugoslavia: Report Prepared for the American Section of the Association International de Droit Penal and for the International Criminal Law Interest Group of the American Society of International Law" 7 (1993) (herein "Blakesley Report"); Helsinki Watch, "Procedural and Evidentiary Issues for the Yugoslav War Crimes Tribunal," August 1993 (herein "Helsinki Watch Report"); ABA Section of International Law and Practice, "Report on the International Tribunal to Adjudicate War Crimes Committed in Former Yugoslavia," July 1993 (herein "ABA Report"); The International Women's Human Rights Clinic of the City University of New York, "Gender Justice and the Constitution of the War Crimes Tribunal Pursuant to Security Council Resolution 808 (April 1993)," herein "CUNY Report"); Canadian Submission; French Submission; US Submission. Wherever possible, the authors of this submission have endeavored not to repeat the substance of what has already been put forth.

[4] *Id.* at Para. 29.

jurisdiction.

Rape is explicitly identified as a crime only in the definition of Crimes Against Humanity (Article 5). However, as discussed below, Article 2 (Grave Breaches), Article 3 (Violations of the laws and customs of war), Article 4 (Genocide), and Article 5 (Crimes against humanity) all contain provisions which implicitly authorize prosecuting rape and other gender-specific violations as crimes under the Tribunal's jurisdiction. It is critical that this implicit authority be made explicit, through adoption of rules of procedure which incorporate and articulate customary and conventional international law principles recognizing that rape and other gender-based violence constitute international law violations.[5]

Proposal

1. Rape, force impregnation, and forced maternity should be explicitly recognized as "grave breaches" under Article 2.

2. Rape, forced impregnation, and forced maternity should be recognized as violations of the laws and customs of war under Article 3.

3. Rape, forced impregnation and forced maternity, when committed as part of a campaign of genocide, should be explicitly acknowledged as genocidal acts under Article 4.

4. As recommended by the American Bar Association, the crimes of forced prostitution and forced impregnation should be specifically enumerated as crimes against humanity covered by Article 5 of the Statute of the Tribunal.[6]

Commentary

1. Conventional and customary international law recognizes that rape and other gender-specific crimes, such as forced impregnation and forced maternity, are acts prohibited by international law.[7] Rape is explicitly prohibited in the Geneva Conventions of 1949 and the

---

[5] The Judges of the Tribunal have the authority to perform such interpretive functions. Article 15 of the Tribunal's Statute mandates that the Judges establish, *inter alia*, rules of procedure, rules of evidence, and mechanisms for witness protection:

> The judges of the International Tribunal shall adopt rules of procedure and evidence for the conduct of the pre-trial phase of the proceedings, trials and appeals, the admission of evidence, the protection of victims and witnesses and other appropriate matters.

[6] *See* ABA Report, supra, at 18. Article 5(h), which identifies the categories of persecution-based offenses, should also be expanded to include gender.

[7] This Section is a slightly-modified adaptation Section I.B of the International Human Rights Law Group Report, *No Justice, No Peace: Accountability for Rape and Gender-Based Violence in the Former Yugoslavia*, June 1993, pages 5-10.

two Protocols thereto.[8] Rape is also encompassed in language of the Geneva Conventions designating as a "grave breach" of the Conventions, *inter alia,* "torture or inhuman treatment"[9] and "willfully causing great suffering or serious injury to body or health"[10] when committed against "protected persons". Significantly, the Security Council has repeatedly referred to these provisions as applicable to the situation in Bosnia.[11] Forced pregnancy and forced maternity

---

[8] Article 27 of the Geneva Convention Relative to the Protection of Civilian Persons in Time of War, *adopted* Aug. 12, 1949, 6 U.S.T. 3516, T.I.A.S. No. 3365, 75 U.N.T.S. 287 [hereinafter Fourth Geneva Convention], which applies to international armed conflicts, provides: "Women shall be especially protected against any attack on their honor, in particular against rape, enforced prostitution, or any form of indecent assault." This provision applies to women who are "protected persons," which Article 4 of the Convention defines as "those who, at a given moment and in any manner whatsoever, find themselves, in case of a conflict or occupation, in the hands of a Party to the conflict or Occupying Power of which they are not nationals." Article 76(1) of Protocol I, which also applies to international armed conflicts, similarly provides: "Women shall be the object of special respect and shall be protected in particular against rape, forced prostitution and any other form of indecent assault." Protocol I Additional to the Geneva Conventions of Aug. 12, 1949, and Relating to the Protection of Victims of International Armed Conflicts, *opened for signature* Dec. 12, 1977, 1125 U.N.T.S. 3 (*entered into force* Dec. 7, 1978). Article 4(2)(e) of Protocol II, which applies in situations of non-international armed conflict, prohibits "outrages upon personal dignity, in particular humiliating and degrading treatment, rape, enforced prostitution and any form of indecent assault" when committed against persons who do not take a direct part or who have ceased to take part in hostilities. Protocol II Additional to the Geneva Conventions of Aug. 12, 1949, and Relating to the Protection of Victims of Non-International Armed Conflicts, *opened for signature* Dec. 12, 1977, 1125 U.N.T.S. 609 (*entered into force* Dec. 7, 1978).

[9] Statute, para. 48 includes rape and torture. *See* T. Meron, Rape As A Crime Under International Humanitarian Law, 87 A.J.I.L. 424, 425 n. 70; Deborah Blatt, Recognizing Rape As A Method of Torture, 19 N.Y.U. Rev. Law & Social Policy 821 (1992); Andrew Byrnes, "The Committee Against Torture, in P. Alston (ed.) *The United Nations and Human Rights, 509.519 & n. 38 (1992)*: "Question of Human Rights of all Persons Subjected to Any Form of Detention or Imprisonment, Torture and Other Cruel, Inhuman or Degrading Treatment or Punishment," "*Report by the Special Rapporteur, Hum. Rts. Comm.*, U.N. ESCOR, U.N. Doc. E/CN.4/1986, cited in Blatt, *supra.* at 847 n. 151. *See also European Commission of Human Rights, Cyprus v. Turkey. Applications Nos. 6780/74 and 6950/75* (1976); Amnesty International, *Women on the Frontline* (1991).

[10] *See* INTERNATIONAL COMMITTEE OF THE RED CROSS, AIDE MEMOIRE, Dec. 1992. As indicated in footnote 10, *supra*, the *Aide Memoire* recognized that the act of rape is an extremely serious violation of international humanitarian law, as it violates the mandate in Article 27 of the Fourth Geneva Convention providing special protection for women against "any attack on their honor, in particular against rape, enforced prostitution, or any form of indecent assault." In addition, the ICRC explicitly acknowledged that the "grave breaches" definition in Article 147 "obviously covers not only rape, but also *any other attack on a woman's dignity.*" *Aide Memoire*, at ¶ 2 (emphasis added). As acts which clearly attack a woman's dignity and "willfully caus[e] great suffering or serious injury to body or health," forced impregnation and forced maternity would qualify as "grave breaches" when committed against "protected persons."

[11] Fourth Geneva Convention, *supra*, Art. 147. These provisions apply only to situations of international armed conflict. Various resolutions of the United Nations Security Council and other U.N. documents relating to ongoing violations in Bosnia appear to assume that these violations are governed by provisions of the Geneva Conventions that are applicable in situations of international armed conflict. *See, e.g.*, U.N. Doc. S/RES/771 (1992); U.N. Doc. S/RES/780 (1992); U.N. Doc. S/RES/808 (1993); *Letter Dated 9 February 1993 from the Secretary-General Addressed to the President of the Security Council*, U.N. Doc. S/25274 (1992); *Interim Report of the Commission of Experts Established Pursuant to Security Council*

resulting form rape constitute additional violations of these grave breach provisions.[12]

2. The laws and customs of war make clear that, irrespective of the nature of the conflict (international, internal, or some hybrid thereof), certain acts -- such as torture and willfully causing great suffering or serious injury to body or health -- are strictly prohibited. Rape has also consistently been prohibited as a violation of these laws and customs of war.[13]

3. As defined under customary international law, "Crimes against humanity" include rape committed on a mass or systematic scale. [14] Where committed on a mass or systematic scale, forced impregnation and forced maternity should also be recognized as crimes against humanity, as they (like rape) are inhumane acts on the same level of severity as murder and torture. Standing alone, all these crimes should also be recognized as persecution based on gender.[15] Where, as in Bosnia, rape and other sex crimes are a tactic of genocide, it is also a persecution based on "racial or religions" grounds. Statute, Art. 5(h).

4. To the extent that rape, forced impregnation and/or forced maternity have been committed as part of a campaign "to destroy, in whole or in part," a national, religious or ethnic

---

Resolution 780 (1992), Annex I, at 14, para. 45, U.N. Doc. S/25274 (1993); INTERNATIONAL COMMITTEE OF THE RED CROSS, AIDE MEMOIRE, Dec. 1992; *see also* WATCH REPORT VOL. II, at 20; AMNESTY INTERNATIONAL, JUSTICE & FAIRNESS IN THE WAR CRIMES TRIBUNAL FOR THE FORMER YUGOSLAVIA, Apr. 1993, at 15; *see further* Letter from Robert A. Bradtke, Acting Assistant Secretary for Legislative Affairs, to Senator Arlen Specter (Jan. 27, 1993) (recognizing that all parties to the conflict in the former Yugoslavia are bound by the Geneva Conventions and customary international law principles applicable to an international conflict).

To dispel any remaining ambiguity over whether the provisions governing international or internal armed conflicts apply to specific violations, the authors of this document urge that the various parties to the conflict in the former Yugoslavia be affirmatively held to their earlier agreement to be governed by the provisions of the Geneva Conventions relating to international armed conflict, including the "grave breaches" provision.

[12] *See* Center for Reproductive Law & Policy, "Recognizing Forced Impregnation as a War Crime Under International Law" (prepared by Anne Tierney Goldstein) (New York City, 1993).

[13] *See* T. Meron, "Rape as a Crime under International Humanitarian Law," 87 A.J.I.L.424, 425 (1993) ("Rape by soldiers has of course been prohibited by the laws of war for centuries"); Y. Khusalani, *Dignity and Honour of Women As Basic and Fundamental Human Rights* (Boston, Martinus Nijhoff, 1982).

[14] Statute, Art 5 (g). As interpreted by the International Military Tribunal and U.S. Military Tribunals in Nuremberg, "Crimes Against Humanity" as defined in the Nuremberg Charter and Control Council Law No. 10, consisted of inhumane acts on the same level of severity as murder and torture, committed on a mass scale against civilians, particularly when carried out as part of a pattern of persecution or discrimination. *See Diane F. Orentlicher, Settling Accounts: The Duty to Prosecute Human Rights Violations of a Prior Regime,* 100 YALE L.J. 2537, 2587-2588 (1991).

[15] *See* R. Copelon, "Surfacing Gender: Reconceptualizing Crimes Against Women in Time of War," in A. Stiglmayer (ed.) (Lincoln, NB: University of Nebraska Press, 1994) (forthcoming).

group "as such," these acts also constitute genocide as defined under the Convention on the Prevention and Punishment of the Crime of Genocide and under customary international law.[16]

Finally, certain international human rights law principles that are widely recognized to be part of customary international law are applicable in characterizing the nature of rape and other gender-specific violations. Rape and other gender-specific crimes violate the prohibition against "torture and other cruel, inhuman or degrading treatment or punishment," which is set forth in both the International Covenant on Civil and Political Rights[17] and the Convention Against Torture and Other Cruel, Inhuman or Degrading Treatment or Punishment.[18] The former Yugoslavia was a party to both of these conventions, and the successor states have recognized that they are bound by these treaties' provisions.[19]

---

[16] *Adopted* Dec. 9, 1948, G.A. Res. 260 A (III), 78 U.N.T.S. 227 (*entered into force* Jan. 12, 1951). On April 8, 1993, the International Court of Justice issued a provisional ruling that implied, without actually finding, that Yugoslavian Serbs were committing acts in violation of the Genocide Convention by virtue of their involvement in "ethnic cleansing" in Bosnia. The Court indicated, by a vote of 13 to 1, that

> The Government of the Federal Republic of Yugoslavia (Serbia and Montenegro) should . . . ensure that any military, paramilitary or irregular armed units which may be directed or may be subject to its control, direction or influence, do not commit any acts of genocide, of conspiracy to commit genocide, of direct and public incitement to commit genocide, or of complicity in genocide, whether directed against the Muslim population of Bosnia and Herzegovina or against any other national, ethnical, racial or religious group....

Application of the Convention on the Prevention and Punishment of the Crime of Genocide (Bosnia-Herzegovina v. Yugo. (Serbia and Montenegro)), Provisional Measures, Order of 8 April 1993, I.C.J. Report 1993, at 3, para. 52.A.(2).

[17] *Adopted* Dec. 16, 1966, art. 7, G.A. Res. 2200, 21 U.N. GAOR Supp. (No. 16), at 52, 999 U.N.T.S. 171, *reprinted in* 6 I.L.M. 368 (1967) [hereinafter ICCPR].

[18] *Opened for signature* Feb. 4, 1985, *reprinted in* 23 I.L.M. 1027 (1984), *as modified,* 24 I.L.M. 535 (1984), 39 U.N. GAOR Supp. (No. 51), at 197, U.N. Doc. A/39/51 (1984) (*entered into force* June 26, 1987) [hereinafter, "Torture Convention"].

[19] *See* Statement on respect of humanitarian principles made by the Presidents of the six republics in the Hague on 5 November 1991; Memorandum of Understanding, dated 27 November 1991, signed in Geneva by representatives of the Republic of Croatia, Federal Republic of Yugoslavia and Republic of Serbia; Addendum to the Memorandum of Understanding of 27 November 1991, signed by representatives of the Federal Republic of Yugoslavia and the Republic of Croatia; Agreement reached under ICRC auspices on 28 & 29 July 1992, signed by Prime Minister of Federal Republic of Yugoslavia and Vice-Prime Minister of Republic of Croatia; Agreement signed on 22 May 1992 by representatives of the Presidency of the Republic of Bosnia-Herzegovina, the Serbian Democratic Party, the Party of Democratic Actions and the Croatian Democratic Community; U.N. Doc. A/Conf.157/PC/60/Add.4, para. 37 (1993).

III. SUGGESTED PROCEDURAL RULES

A. Substantive Definitions Of Gender-Specific Offenses

In the case of rape and other gender-specific crimes, the Tribunal faces a critical task of definition. Because rape and other gender-specific crimes have not been separately charged and tried before other International Tribunals, international law does not provide specific codification from which to draw. The Report of the Secretary-General provides that the Tribunal shall apply international law.[20] Thus, in developing the rules and procedures for adjudicating rape and other sex crimes, the Tribunal must interpret and develop international law consistent with the principle *nullem crimen sine lege.*

Guidance for this task can be found in the Revised Draft Statute for an International Criminal Court and the 1953 Report of the drafting committee. Article 2 of the Revised Draft provides: "The Court shall apply international law, including international criminal law, and, where appropriate, national law."[21] The Report of the Committee makes the exposition of international law the primary concern. Further, the debate among the drafters makes clear that national law was intended to apply in very limited circumstances, such as where the international instrument specifically requires it or where a state party specifically requests it.[22] Developing international law is important to providing stability, permanence, independence, effectiveness and universality.[23]

In applying international law the Tribunal follows Article 38(1) of the Statute of the International Court of Justice.[24] Moreover, in this case where criminal responsibility is at issue, the Tribunal must develop criteria consistent with the principle against retrospective responsibility. In this respect, both international law, as noted in the Secretary-General's Report

---

[20] *Report*, note 3, Para. 29.

[21] United Nations, "Report of the 1953 Committee on International Criminal Jurisdiction," General Assembly Official Records: Ninth Session Supplement No. 12, Annex (A/2645), 27 July-20 August, 1953, A/AC.65/1.13 (Aug. 24, 1953).

[22] *Id.* The Report refers to the provision of the Genocide Convention, which provides for the application of domestic penalties. The implication is that states bear the burden of requesting application of international law. *See* M. Cherif Bassiouni, (ed.) *International Criminal Law*, Vol. III, Dobbs Ferry, New York: Transnational Publishers, Inc., at 224 (1987).

[23] *Id.* at 214.

[24] It provides:

> "The Court, whose function is to decide in accordance with international law such disputes as are submitted to it, shall apply: (a) International conventions, whether general or particular, establishing rules expressly recognized by the contesting states; (b) International custom, as evidence of a general practice accepted as law; (c) the general principles of law recognized by civilized nations; (d) . . . judicial decisions and the teachings of the most highly qualified publicists."

Statute of the International Court of Justice, Article 38(1)(a)(b)(c)(d), 59 Sta. 1055, T.S.993, 2 Bevans 1179.

as well as Part I herein, and the laws of the former Yugoslavia provide clear notice of grave wrongdoing. Indeed, international law violations were explicitly encompassed in Yugoslavia's constitutional and criminal laws, and, in some cases, in more expansive terms.[25] The Yugoslav code not only punished the sex crimes at issue here as domestic crimes;[26] they also identified them separately and punished them more harshly as war crimes.[27] There is accordingly no issue of retrospective responsibility.

In discerning and applying international law standards for the prosecution of these recognized offenses, care must be taken not to perpetuate the traditional sex-stereotype and sex-discriminatory treatment of crimes of sexual violence. Attention should focus, therefore, on the newer developments in national laws relating to the prosecution of sexual violence as well as the writings of jurists over the past 25 years who have elucidated the problems and potential solutions. This approach is entirely consistent with the principle against retrospective liability. Our recommendations are limited to assuring fair prosecution of these atrocious and recognized crimes and guarding against the introduction of prejudicial, inflammatory and irrelevant evidence and to protecting the complainants and witnesses from harassment and humiliation, none of which serves a legitimate prosecutorial purpose or protects legitimate rights of the accused.

Proposals

The crimes which constitute or are constitutive of sexual torture[28] (and their

---

[25] With respect to genocide and persecution-based offenses, for example, the constitution prohibited public and private action which stirred up national, racial or religious hatred or intolerance. *See e.g.*, Arts. 154, 174, 198, and 203. The former Yugoslavia not only ratified the Genocide Convention, Convention on the Prevention and Punishment of the Crime of Genocide, 78 U.N.T.S. 277, New York, Dec. 9, 1948., Entered into force Jan 12, 1951; Ratified without qualification by Yugoslavia, 8/29/50. It also expanded the definition of genocide in the domestic law to include forcible displacement or deportation as genocidal acts. See, Yugoslavian Criminal Code, Chap. 11, Art. 124 [Original Title: *Krivicni zakonik*]. *Collection of Yugoslavian Laws,* vol. ii (Beograd: Institute of Comparative Law, 1964) (hereinafter "1962 Code"); and Criminal Law, Socialist Federative Republic of Yugoslavia, 16th Heading, Art. 141, *The People's Newspaper* (Zagreb, 1978) (hereinafter "1978 Code"). Moreover, the Constitution prohibited other violations of protected rights, as did the codes.

[26] *See 1962 Code,* Chapter 16 (Offenses Against the Dignity of the Person and Morality).

[27] *See 1962 Code,* Chapter 11 (Criminal Offenses Against Humanity and International Law); *1978 Code,* 16th Heading (Criminal Acts Against Humanity and International Law). *See* Penalties, Part VI, *infra.* Both explicitly include, among others, rape and forced prostitution, while forced impregnation and other sex crimes are encompassed within "tortures or inhuman treatment of the civilian population, causing great suffering or serious injury to body or health, use of measures of intimidation and terror, unlawful taking to concentration camps and other unlawful confinements, coercion to compulsive labor.

[28] Article 1 of the UN Convention Against Torture and Other Cruel, Inhuman or Degrading Treatment or Punishment defines torture as:

> any act by which severe pain or suffering, whether physical or mental, is intentionally inflicted on a person for such purposes as obtaining from him or a third person information or a confession, punishing him for an act he or a third person has committed or is suspected of having committed, or intimidating or coercing him or a third person, or for any reason based on discrimination of any kind, when such pain or suffering is inflicted by or at the instigation of or with the consent of acquiescence of a public official or other person acting in an official capacity...."

substantive definitions) include:

1. RAPE

a. Rape is any form of forced sexual intercourse. The requisite coercion can be shown through evidence of force, deceit, deprivation, or threats of any of the above, as well as promise of better treatment.[29]

b. Rape encompasses a range of non-consensual sexual acts or conduct including the introduction of the penis into the mouth, vagina or anus of the victim or the introduction of other parts of the body or of weapons or objects into the vagina or anus of the victim.[30]

c. Rape occurs when there is introduction (described above) to any extent. Proof of rape does not require penetration or the emission of semen.[31]

2. FORCED PROSTITUTION

Forced Prostitution may consist of the following:

a. Subjecting a person to repeated acts of rape.

b. Forcing a person to comport themselves in such a way as to invite or solicit and engage in sex in an apparently voluntary way.

c. Detaining a person for the purpose of or under threat of subjecting them to repeated acts of rape or to comporting themselves so as to invite, solicit or engage in sex in an apparently voluntary way.

G.A. Res. 46, U.N. GAOR, 30th Sess, Supp. No. 51 at 197, 23 U.N. Doc. A/39/51 I.L.M. 535 (1985).

Rape has been identified in international law as a form of torture. See n. 12, *supra*. Sexual torture can also involve a range of sexual abuse involving physical, psychological and verbal methods, against the person or against persons close to the person, including forced commission of sexual assaults on others close to the person, forced nudity and other forms of exposure designed to punish, humiliate, degrade, and intimidate the subject.

[29] The law of Bosnia-Herzegovina provides in Chapter XI, "(1) Whoever coerces a female person with whom he is not married to, into sexual intercourse by force or threat to endanger her life or body of that or someone close to her will be sentenced to between one to ten years in prison." Small Sokolovie, Krivicnizakon SRBIH Socialist Republic of Bosnia and Herzegovina, Sarajevo, 1988. For the evidentiary implications of this standard, *see* Part IV, B, *infra*.

[30] *See, e.g.*,Australia Crimes Act of 1958 (Vic) section 36.

[31] *Id.* section 37(2) and 36(3).

3. FORCED IMPREGNATION AND ATTEMPTED FORCED IMPREGNATION

Forced Impregnation may be shown by the following[32]:

a. An impregnation that results from an assault or series of assaults on a woman perpetrated with the intent that she become pregnant. The assault may take the form of rape, including forced insemination.[33]

b. As long as the intent to impregnate can be established, the crime of attempted forced impregnation may be shown even if pregnancy does not result.

4. ABDUCTION OR DETENTION FOR SEXUAL PURPOSES

Abduction or detention accompanied by sexual abuse or the threat thereof is an exacerbated form of unnecessary detention.[34]

5. GENOCIDE

As discussed previously, rape, forced prostitution and forced pregnancy are not only war crimes and crimes against humanity in themselves; in the context of the war in the former Yugoslavia, they are also one of the most potent means of accomplishing genocide.[35] These crimes "caus[e] serious bodily and mental harm to the members of the group" and "deliberately inflict...on the group conditions of life calculated to bring about its physical destruction in whole or in part. They do this to women and through women with the intent to destroy the group. Moreover, specific threats to impregnate women with children of another ethnicity and the use of rape to drive them from their families and community are measures "intended to prevent births within the group" and a form of "forcibly transferring children to another

---

[32] This definition is excerpted from Center for Reproductive Law & Policy, *Recognizing Forced Impregnation as a War Crime Under International Law* (1993) (prepared by Anne Tierney Goldstein).

[33] The requisite criminal intent can be established either directly, through admissions or statements of the perpetrators, or indirectly, through circumstantial evidence. Forcible removal of a woman's IUD or contraceptive implant, or destruction of other means of birth control or access to birth control, would constitute evidence of intent to impregnate. The intentional detention of a pregnant woman until she was beyond the time limit in which local law or practice permits abortion would also constitute evidence of violation. Mandatory pregnancy tests following a rape, or attempts to keep track of a detained woman's menstrual cycle (especially if she were assaulted more frequently around the time she ovulated) similarly would be evidence of the requisite intent.

[34] Detention of civilians beyond what is strictly necessary is a violation of the Geneva Conventions. *See* Statute, Art. 2(g), Article 42 of the Fourth Geneva Convention provides: "The internment or placing in assigned residence of protected persons may be ordered only if the security of the Detaining Power makes it absolutely necessary." Geneva Convention Relative to the Protection of Civilian Persons in Time of War, *adopted* by the Diplomatic Conference for the Establishment of International Conventions for the Protections of Victims of War, August 12, 1949, *entered into force,* October 21, 1950. Where the practice or threat of sexual abuse is involved, the crime is distinct and more severe.

[35] "Recognizing Forced Impregnation as a War Crime Under International Law," note 14, *supra.*

group."[36] For these reasons, it is important that sex crimes be recognized as acts of genocide.

B. Conspiracy, Incitement, Attempts and Complicity Should Be Charged As To Gender-Specific Crimes

Proposal

Prosecutions for Conspiracy, Incitement, Attempts, and Complicity in regard to rape, forced pregnancy, and forced prostitution are justified by the known evidence and consistent with the United Nations Resolution establishing this Tribunal, international law, and historic precedent. We, therefore, recommend adoption of a rule comparable to that embodied in the Tokyo Charter, which extended the jurisdiction of the Military Tribunal to:

> "Leaders, organizers, instigators and accomplices participating in the formulation or execution of a common plan or conspiracy to commit any of the foregoing crimes are responsible for all acts performed by any person in execution of such a plan."[37]

Commentary

The enormity and nature of the evidence of the use of mass or systematic rape, forced pregnancy, and forced prostitution by parties in the former Yugoslavia as a military and political tool demands that these crimes be prosecuted not only against the individual perpetrators of the attacks, but also against all persons who conspired to carry out such crimes, as well as all those who incited, attempted, demonstrated complicity or had command responsibility in those crimes. Failure to so charge would result in culpable parties evading justice and would fail to serve the legitimate goal of deterring future war crimes, as set forth in the Resolution establishing this Tribunal.

In establishing this Tribunal, the United Nations recognized the propriety of charges of conspiracy, incitement, attempts, and complicity with regard to the War Crimes. Article 4 of the Statute establishes that the Tribunal "shall have the power to prosecute persons committing genocide" including those committing, "conspiracy to commit genocide; direct and public incitement to commit genocide; attempt to commit genocide; complicity in genocide."[38] The Tribunal further has the power to punish persons responsible for Crimes Against Humanity, including "torture; rape," and "other inhuman acts."[39]

The Statute of the Tribunal also explicitly relies upon "international humanitarian law," and international "customary" and "conventional" law, both "customary" and

---

[36] Convention on the Prevention and Punishment of the Crime of Genocide, 78 U.N.T.S. 277, *adopted* by the U.N. General Assembly on Dec. 9, 1948, G.A. Res. 2670, 3GOAR, Part 1, U.N Doc. A/810, 174, *entered into force* on Jan. 12, 1951. Art. II(a)(b)(c)(d)(e).

[37] *See* Charter of the International Military Tribunal for the Far East, Article 5, (c); *see also, Indictment,* Count One, and *Indictment,* Count One, of the International Military Tribunal, Nuremberg.

[38] *See* Article 4.

[39] *See* Article 5.

"conventional," such charges are within the Tribunal's jurisdiction.[40]

C. Command Responsibility For Gender-Specific Violations

Article 7, section 3 of the Statute of the Tribunal states that a superior will be held responsible for the acts of his subordinate,

> if he knew *or had reason to know* that the subordinate was about to commit such acts or had done so and the superior *failed to take the necessary and reasonable measures to prevent such acts or to punish the perpetrators* thereof.

(Emphasis added). This standard is adapted from that applied in the Nuremberg and Tokyo proceedings, and incorporated into the Geneva Conventions and the Protocols thereto, as well as the military codes of many nations.

Proposals

1. Superior responsibility attaches to civilians as well as to military commanders. The Genocide Convention, for example, states in Article IV that those responsible shall be punished "whether they are constitutionally responsible rulers, public officials or private individuals."

2. Superior officials bear a high level of responsibility for the actions of their forces. One Canadian case concluded that the fact that a war crime had been committed by a subordinate established *prima facie* evidence of the commander's responsibility.[41]

3. The commander has a duty to obtain information about what is happening in the area under his or her command. He or she "will not ordinarily be permitted to deny knowledge of reports received at his headquarters... [or] happenings within the area of his command while he is present therein."[42] In sum, "He cannot ignore obvious facts and plead ignorance as a defense."[43]

4. Commanding officers are responsible for educating their forces about the laws of

---

[40] Conspiracies to commit various war crimes (including war crimes which encompass rape, forced pregnancy, and forced prostitution) were successfully prosecuted at Nuremberg and Tokyo. The Nuremberg Indictment charged the defendants with being:

> "[L]eaders, organizers, instigators or accomplices in the formulation or execution of a common plan or conspiracy to commit, or which involved the commission of, Crimes against Peace, War Crimes, and Crimes against Humanity."

See e.g., International Military Tribunal, Nuremberg: *Indictment*, Count One.

[41] *See Abbaye Ardenne Case, quoted in* Green, *War Crimes. Extradition and Command Responsibility,* 14 Is. Y.B. 17, 36 (1984).

[42] *Hostage Case (United States v. List)* (Case No. 7, 1948), *reprinted in* 11 *Trials of War Criminals Before the Nurenberg Military Tribunals* 1260 (1951).

[43] *Id.* As applied to the former Yugoslavia, from time that widespread rapes and other sexual abuse in Bosnia received international publicity, if not before, all superior officials should be presumed to have known of them. They thus should be held liable for their failure to punish those responsible and for their failure to take reasonable measures to prevent future rapes.

war.[44] Under the laws of the former Yugoslavia, as well as humanitarian law treaties and customary international law, a commanding officer was required to inform his or her subordinates that rape and other sexual abuse constitute war crimes, and about their liability to punishment should they commit these offenses.

5. Superior officials are criminally liable for the failure to punish war crimes, as well as the failure to prevent them.[45] At a minimum, superior officials under the laws of the former Yugoslavia have an obligation to investigate the reports of widespread rapes and punish those responsible. The failure to do so constitutes a war crime.

6. Command responsibility requires taking all necessary steps to prevent war crimes; empty gestures (such as issuing orders which the subordinates know are not serious) are not adequate. As stated in the judgment of the Tokyo tribunal, where a commander knows of the criminal action of his forces, his duty "is not discharged by the mere issue of routine orders."[46]

7. It is also not sufficient to report abuses and simply rely on assurances by others that the criminal activity has stopped, without taking effective action to stop the activity.[47]

8. Command responsibility covers all forces under the superiors' command and *"under their control"* (Protocol I, Art. 87(1)). Where a military unit occupies a territory, it is responsible for the actions of all forces within that area, even if they are not directly under the officer's command.[48] Further, control can be shown through evidence other than that for chain

---

[44] Protocol I, Art. 87(2). The United States Army, for example, requires commanding officers to provide instruction in the laws of war, to insure that your men are aware of the law of war, of their duty to disobey orders that would require them to commit acts in violation of that law, and of their obligation to report any such violator of which they become aware." Army Subject Schedule 27-1; *See also* The Geneva Conventions of 1949 and Hague Convention of 1907, at 10.

[45] Protocol I, Art. 87(3).

[46] II Judgment *of the IMT for the Far East* 1176 (1948). Similarly, convictions in *United States v. List* were based on the failure to investigate incidents, and the failure "to take *effective steps* to prevent their execution or recurrence." 11 T.W.C. 757, 1256 (1948) (emphasis added).

Similarly, General Matsui, Commander-in-Chief of the Central China Area Army which captured and occupied Nanking, was convicted of a failure to protect the civilian population even though he ordered his forces to conduct themselves in accordance with the law, since he knew or should have known that his orders were ineffective. *The Tokyo Judgment: The International Military Tribune for the Far East,* B.V.A. Roling & C.F. Ruter, eds., 447-48, 453 (1977).

[47] For example, immediately after Japanese forces entered Nanking in December 1937, Foreign Minister Hirota informed the War Ministry of widespread abuses and was assured that the misconduct would cease. He Was found guilty of criminal negligence for relying on this assurance and failing to take effective action to stop the criminal activity. *The Tokyo Judgment: The International Military Tribune for the Far East,* B.V.A. Roling & C.F. Ruter, eds., 447-48, 983 (1977).

[48] *See Hostage Case (United States v. List)* (Case No 7, 1948), *reprinted in 11 Trials of War Criminals Before the Nurenberg Military Tribunals* 759, 1256, 1260, 1271 (1951). In that case, the court found that

> The commanding general of occupied territory, having executive authority as well as military command, will not be heard to say that a unit taking unlawful orders from someone other than himself was responsible for the crime and that he is therefore absolved from responsibility. It is claimed, for example, that certain SS units under the direct command of Heinrich Himmler

of command.[49] Finally, as in the Shabra and Shatilla massacres,[50] if superior officials allowed paramilitary and civilian groups to commit rape and other sexual abuse, they may be held responsible for those crimes.

Commentary

Explicitly acknowledging that these principles of command responsibility are applicable to rape and other gender-specific crimes is critical. If the Tribunal fails to do so, it risks implicitly enforcing the dangerous misperception that rape and other sexual abuse of women is a normal and uncontrollable product of warfare. This erroneous perception flies in the face of both conventional and customary international law, which condemn such abuses and holds commanding officers responsible for preventing and punishing such behavior by their forces. For a discussion of some of the evidentiary implications of this standard, see IV, A & C.

IV. SUGGESTED EVIDENTIARY RULES

A. Admissibility of Evidence

Article 15 of the Statute of the International Tribunal grants the Judges of the Tribunal broad authority to determine the evidentiary standards that will govern the prosecutorial process.[51] Given the extraordinary circumstances that wartime imposes on the gathering of evidence, and the particular needs of victims and witnesses of sex crimes, it is necessary and appropriate that a flexible standard should be adopted.[52]

> committed certain of the atrocities herein charged without the knowledge, consent or approval or these defendants. But this cannot be a defense for the commanding general... [whose] responsibility is general and not limited to control of units directly under his command....

This same analysis can be instructive to this Tribunal.

[49] For example, the Israeli government investigation of the 1982 massacres committed by the Phalangist military forces in the Shabra and Shatilla refugee camps in Lebanon found Israeli military officials responsible for failing to stop the massacres -- even though the Phalangists were not a part of the Israeli military -- because the Israeli investigators found a "symbiotic relationship" between the two forces. *The Commission of Inquiry into the Events at the Refugee Camps in Beirut 1983; Final Report (Kahan Report)* (Authorized Translation), *reprinted in* The Jerusalem Post, Feb. 9, 1983 (Supplement) and in 22 Int'l Legal Materials 474 (1983).

Recently-published information details the link between supposedly independent paramilitary groups and the government of Serbia, including both the Serbian army and police. *See* "Rival Serbs Are Admitting Bosnia-Croatia Atrocities" *The New York Times,* Nov. 13, 1993, at 6. Further evidence of this link could be developed by examining who has profited from the commission of atrocities, as recent reports indicate that senior officials of the government of Yugoslavia have profited from the pillage of Bosnian and Croatian villages. *Id.*

[50] *See* footnote 52, *supra.*

[51] *See* Section I, *supra.*

[52] This conclusion is supported by the precedent set by the International Military Tribunal (IMT) of the Nuremberg trials. As the first modern international tribunal for the prosecution of war crimes, the IMT offers an appropriate starting point for analyzing admissibility of evidence for this Tribunal. The IMT operated under a very liberal standard. Article 18 of the Charter of the IMT allowed it to admit any evidence

We recommend that, consistent with the due process rights of the defendants, the judges exercise their discretion in favor of the protection of victims or other witnesses at all stages of the proceedings. All of the recommendations below pertain throughout the proceedings, from the pre-trial phase through trials, appeals, and sentencing.

Proposals

1. With exceptions and conditions specified hereinafter, the Tribunal should admit evidence that it considers relevant and then assess its weight. There is no need for the type of rigid evidentiary rules developed in systems which make use of lay juries.

2. Not withstanding the foregoing general principle, the Tribunal should refuse to admit that which threatens serious harm to a witness or victim, including both physical danger (e.g. a fear of retaliation for testifying) and psychological harm. The Tribunal should also exclude evidence which is so tainted by sexual stereotypes that it is of no evidentiary value, inflammatory, or threatens serious harm to the trial of the case or to the victim or witness.

3. To ensure the fairness of a flexible standard of admissibility, the Tribunal should, upon motion of counsel or upon its own motion, at any time, hold a separate hearing, *in camera* if appropriate, to consider the probative value of the evidence and whether the evidence should be excluded for any of the reasons set forth in point 2 or whether if received, protections may be necessary for the victims, other witnesses, and defendants.

4. Efforts should be made to prove cases against the defendant with evidence other than the direct testimony of survivors of the atrocities. Such evidence could include documentary evidence, eye witness testimony, medical records, and "spontaneous utterances." The adequacy of these alternative forms of proof should be considered before the Tribunal requires that the victim testify.

5. Evidence such as hearsay, unsworn statements, or in some case *ex parte* affidavits should be allowed wherever there are sufficient indicia of reliability such as other similar hearsay statements, lack of motive to lie or significant circumstantial evidence. Such a rule would fall within the Nuremberg "any probative value" standard while safeguarding the interests of the defendant.

---

which it deemed to have probative value. The article states:

> The Tribunal shall not be bound by technical rules of evidence. It shall adopt and apply to the greatest possible extent expeditious and nontechnical procedure, and shall admit any evidence which it deems to have probative value.

It should be noted that the need for a liberal standard is even greater here since the Nuremberg Tribunal had access to official documentary evidence because the accused had been defeated in war.

The authors recognize, however, that the standard is subject to certain limitations, such as other obligations in the Statute and by other agreements, such as the International Covenant on Civil and Political Rights. These limitations include ones that are intended to protect the rights of the defendant (*see* ABA Report, *supra*, at 30), as well as restrictions intended to protect the rape victim, such as limits on the admissibility of the victim's sexual history. Part V, *infra*.

6. The use of experts in international tribunals is acknowledged and well-accepted.[53] Expert testimony should be admitted to explain relevant aspects of the impact of coercive circumstances and the resulting atrocities on the victims and witnesses.

B. Specific Evidentiary Considerations For Sex Crimes

By contrast to other issues where liberal rules of admissibility are both fair and necessary, certain aspects of the trial of sexual violence require strict limits to protect against the introduction of traditionally inflammatory and irrelevant evidence.[54] Without such rules, women will be inevitably discouraged from bringing their cases to the Tribunal. Even if this evidence were insulated from prejudicial effect because the Tribunal is the trier of fact, its very solicitation and introduction inflicts trauma and harm. Beyond that, the rules are important because sexual biases about rape run very deep and are difficult to extirpate. Thus it is imperative that the Tribunal make clear -- through adoption of pertinent procedural and evidentiary rules -- its rejection of sex-stereotypes and discrimination as a basis for receiving evidence in the prosecution of war crimes. The Tribunal should consider consulting with experts who could provide training to ensure its own understanding of the fallacies, prejudice, and harm to traumatized witnesses that can result from the traditional approach.

Proposals

1. In determining whether sexual conduct charged is forced or coerced, it is sufficient if the woman says "no" or if the act(s) were committed under conditions where the victim reasonably believed that she was not free to leave or refuse without risk of harm to herself to another person. Coercion may be established by the fact of detention, the appearance of authority, or the conduct of the accused and others acting in concert with him. The victim need not resist to establish coercion.

2. When coercion is shown, the Tribunal shall not permit the defendant to cross-examine the victim to establish consent or otherwise present a consent defense, unless he submits *in camera* the evidence of consent apart from the victim's proposed testimony and the Tribunal determines that he has shown that consent was likely.

3. If the Tribunal permits the defense of consent, it shall exclude all evidence of prior sexual conduct of the victim with the accused or others, except evidence which tends to demonstrate voluntary sexual relations with the defendant within a reasonable period of time. The Tribunal shall not infer from such an act or acts of voluntary intercourse that subsequent sexual acts are voluntary, but rather must scrutinize the circumstances to assure that each occasion of sexual intercourse was consensual.

4. Mandatory corroboration of the elements of these offenses is unnecessary.

---

[53] *See generally* Gilliam M. White, *The Use of Experts by International Tribunals* (1965); Durward V. Sandifer, *Evidence before International Tribunals* (1975).

[54] Among the traditional beliefs are that women invite and fabricate rape and that the "good" woman is chaste and resists to the utmost. These prejudices have given rise to rules requiring corroboration of the woman's testimony and permitting introduction of evidence of prior sexual conduct to show consent as well as lack of credibility. They have also justified inflammatory, suggestive and humiliating cross-examination of the complainant, which has been increasingly recognized as transcending the defendant's legitimate rights. *See e.g.*, S. Estrich, *Real Rape* (1987).

5. Expert evidence relating to trauma should be admissible to inform the Tribunal concerning the particular impact of trauma.[55] Its absence should not be seen as establishing the defendant's innocence.

Commentary

i. Coercion, which includes force, threats of force, deceit, deprivation or promise of reward or better treatment, can be established based on evidence of the totality of the circumstances of war, detention, occupation and other acts of terror against the civilian population and through evidence of coercive conduct directed at the victim.

ii. Coercive circumstances properly give rise to rebuttable evidentiary presumptions against consent (i.e., it was more likely than not that there was no consent). Defendants can present evidence in an *in camera* proceeding (described above) to rebut the presumption. Such presumptions reflect the probability of intimidation of civilians by persons with official authority, as well as to the extremely small probability of consent under such coercive circumstances. Examples of presumptions of nonconsent include the provision in the Geneva Conventions which treats as a "grave breach" any form of medical experimentation on prisoners even where consent is given,[56] and proposed rules concerning the treatment of prisoners outside the context of war which preclude recognizing consent.[57]

iii. A strong presumption against consent is appropriate because, in the circumstances of sex crimes in the former Yugoslavia, the possibility of non-coercive or voluntary sexual intercourse is extremely remote. Beyond that, the possibility that false charges will be brought or that they will survive the investigative process is made more remote by the powerful obstacles faced by complainants.[58]

---

[55] For example, sexual violence can produce extreme shame, numbness and denial which may, alone or with fear of reprisal or the absence of an accountable or regularly functioning judicial system, preclude or be inconsistent with prompt reporting. In addition, experts on post traumatic stress syndrome and the testimony of trauma victims could explain the ability of a victim or witness to remember clearly the appearance of the perpetrator, but to blur surrounding facts, even though such facts could appear unforgettable to the outside observer; or the existence of discrepancies in differing accounts as a result of victims' memory of differing levels of detail at different stages of their healing processes; or the demeanor of traumatized witnesses.

[56] Art. 11(2) prohibits "medical or scientific experiments" on persons in the power of an adverse party who are deprived of liberty "even with their consent." This is subject to an exception where the procedure is necessitated by health and consistent with accepted medical standards that would apply to the party's nationals who are not deprived of their liberty. Protocol II, note 10, *supra*.

[57] The Working Group of the General Assembly's Sixth (Legal) Committee, which revised the Draft Body of Principles for the Protection of All Persons Under Any Form of Detention or Imprisonment proposed: "No detained or imprisoned person shall, *even with his consent*, be subjected to any medical or scientific experimentation which may be detrimental to his health." U.N. Doc. A/C.6/39/L/10, para. 20 (1984). *See* Nigel Rodley, *The Treatment of Prisoners Under International Law* 232-235 (Paris, UNESCO, 1987).

[58] Paramount among these are the emotional effect on survivors, often shared by direct witnesses. Human rights reports have emphasized the profound shame, denial and trauma, as well as the well-founded fear of publicity, exploitation and re-traumatization. To bring a claim before the International Tribunal carries an additional set of obstacles; for example, the alien nature and formality of the legal process; anticipation of repeated and hostile questioning; the trauma of confrontation with the perpetrator; the need to leave one's home or community; the possibility of not being believed; the lack of confidence in

iv. It is fair to the accused and essential to the dignity and participation of the survivors to limit strictly the circumstances under which the presumption of inherent coercion can be overcome and a defense of consent by entertained. Cross-examination of the complainant as to possible consent should be allowed only where the accused can show that it was more likely that not that the sexual activity was not coerced. Furthermore, the appearance of voluntary meetings or a personal "relationship" between the accused and the complainant must be strictly scrutinized before a consent defense is permitted, given the pervasiveness of fear and the unequal status of the parties: both as men and women and as conquerors and conquered.

v. Evidence of the prior sexual conduct with anyone other than the defendant should be excluded because it is irrelevant, inflammatory and based on sex-stereotypes which deprive a woman of her right of bodily integrity and because the impact of producing or eliciting this testimony from the complainants is a sever barrier to participation.[59]

C. Evidentiary Considerations For Proving Command Responsibility

Proposals and Commentary

1. *Evidence of a policy or pattern of ordering, authorizing, tolerating, encouraging or failing to punish rape and other sexual abuse may prove command responsibility for the crimes.* This evidence can be found in the testimony of witnesses stating that commanders knew of rapes and did little to stop them, that commanders ordered rapes, or that commanders participated in the rapes themselves. Much of this testimony may be in the form of hearsay and unsworn statements. The Tribunal should adopt the evidentiary standards discussed above, allowing this testimony when sufficient indicia of reliability are present.

2. *Relevance of evidence should also be construed broadly to allow for the wide range of evidence required to show a relationship between the rapes and military activity.* Evidence should be allowed to show the timing of the rapes in relation to troop movements and military takeovers of the relevant territory in order to establish patterns and evidence of coordinated activities. Similarly, evidence should also be admitted to show the contemporaneous existence of other violations of international humanitarian law in prison camps, battlefields and civilian regions of occupied areas where rapes have occurred.

3. *Expert testimony should be admitted on the psychological effects of rape.* This information is relevant to prove a policy of using or permitting rape as a weapon of war. The psychological effects are allegedly a significant reason why commanders have chosen to use or allow rape in their campaigns. Rape is an effective means of destroying and driving out communities, outcomes which are consistent with a campaign of ethnic cleansing.

4. *Media reports (newspapers, radio and video) should also be admitted to show that commanders had or should have had knowledge of the mass rapes.*

---

the possibility of redress; the fear of retaliation.

[59] *See e.g.* S. Estrich, *Real Rape* (1987); H. Field & L. Bienen, *Jurors and Rape: A Study In Psychology and Law* (1980). Strict controls in non-emergency contexts can be found, for example, in the Australian Evidence Act, See 37a No. 6248 (1958). LAN 107-458 (1980).

V. SUGGESTED MECHANISMS FOR PROTECTION OF VICTIMS AND WITNESSES

A. General Protections

The physical security and psychological well-being of victims and witnesses must be protected at all stages of the proceedings. While some victims and witnesses may regard public accusation of those who committed atrocities as an important part of their recovery, others may consider it to exacerbate the trauma they have suffered.[60] Those victims and witnesses who wish to come forward must be physically protected and provided the necessary support services to allow their testimony to expedite their recovery rather than to be a source of retraumatization. Those victims and witnesses who do not wish to come forward to testify or present evidence should not be pressured to do so. The decision of those who wish to give testimony but remain anonymous must also be respected to the extent consistent with the rights of the accused.

Proposals and Commentary

1. *A security system to be developed for those giving testimony and preparing documentation.*[61] This should include the use of U.N. guards, or the issuance and enforcement of restraining orders.[62] If necessary, victims, witnesses, and their families should be physically relocated.[63]

2. *Victims' right to representation.*[64] To fully protect the rights of victims and witnesses, they, like the defendants, should have the right to representation. This representation could help ensure that the procedures and evidentiary rules for victim and witness protection are implemented, protecting any rights and interests that may be distinct from that of the prosecution. Victim and witness advocates would also work to ensure that physical and psychological needs are met during the investigation and trial process.

3. *All participation by victims and witnesses must be voluntary and given with fully informed consent.*[65] For the Tribunal to consider consent genuine, victims and witnesses should receive careful counseling about the implications of participating in the Tribunal, or as relevant, relinquishing their anonymity. Such counseling could be done by victim and witness advocates, described above.

4. *The confidentiality of the victims and witnesses should be guarded.* Victims and witnesses should not be publicly identified without their consent -- to protect both their security and their privacy. They have a right to keep their identity from the public, and in extreme cases,

---

[60] CUNY Report, at 3-4; *No Justice, No Peace,* at 35.

[61] ABA Report at 37-44; AI Memorandum at 6, 27-28; *No Justice, No Peace,* at 45-46.

[62] Helsinki Watch Report, at 10.

[63] ABA Report, at 45; Helsinki Watch Report, at 13.

[64] CUNY Report, at 4.

[65] *No Justice, No Peace,* at 27-30; CUNY Report, at 4.

from the alleged perpetrator.[66]

5. *There must be a commitment to witnesses and victims throughout and after the investigation and trial process.*[67] The Tribunal should commit itself to minimizing the trauma of participating in all phases of the Tribunal's process. The Tribunal should assure that witnesses be accompanied by a family member or person of their choice and that separation from their communities be minimized (unless, of course, people are afraid to return to their communities). It should also provide services necessary to help them through the Tribunal processes and to rebuild their lives during and after trial, e.g., trauma counseling and other health care, assistance with relocation, and assistance with political asylum claims.[68] This could be accomplished in part through the appointment of counsel for victims, described above.

B. Pre-trial phase

Proposals and Commentary

1. *Interviews to collect evidence should be done in a manner sensitive to victim and witness needs.* Interviewers should have experience or be given training in working with victims of sex crimes. Interviewers must try to ascertain the treatment needs of the person being interviewed and not simply "extract" the information necessary to proceed with a prosecution. Interviewers should make clear that a rape survivor need not speak of her ordeal at all, and can end the interview at any time she chooses. Victims should be assured that they have complete control over the future use of their testimonies, including the terms of confidentiality.[69]

2. *Women interviewers.* Women victims should be interviewed by women who have been trained in how to work with women victims and survivors.[70]

3. *Videotaped depositions.*[71] Depositions may be videotaped if it would assist the victim or witness to avoid testifying in public and in the presence of her alleged attacker. This type of deposition has been allowed in U.S. and other courts. The general principle of allowing evidence other than the direct testimony of the victim or witness is discussed below.

C. Trials and appeals

It is important not to ignore or exaggerate the critical tension between the security and privacy rights of victims and witnesses on the one hand and the due process rights of the defendant on the other; one particular tension is that between the right of a defendant to

---

[66] *No Justice, No Peace,* at 31; CUNY Report, at 4.

[67] ABA Report, at 44; CUNY Report, at 5; Helsinki Watch Report, at 9; AI Memorandum, at 27-28.

[68] Helsinki Watch Report. at 9.

[69] *No Justice, No Peace,* at 16.

[70] *No Justice, No Peace,* at 30; AI Memorandum, at 7, 29.

[71] ABA Report at 40.

confront his or her accuser. We are committed to the protection of the rights of the defendant as well as to the rights of victims and witnesses. We believe, however, that once the likely probative value of the evidence is weighed against the potential harm to the victim or witness, there will be few instances of serious conflict between the due process rights of the accused and the security and privacy rights of victims and witnesses. Numerous criminal codes have established procedures which strike this balance, such as those of Australia, Canada and the United States, and human rights organizations have also addressed these issues. The following procedures supplement the protections discussed in the section on evidentiary standards.

Proposals and Commentary

1. *In-camera proceedings should be allowed to protect the privacy interests of victims and witnesses.*[72] Article 20 gives the Trial Chamber discretion to close hearings to the public: "the hearings shall be public *unless the Trial Chamber decides to close the proceeding in accordance with its rules of procedure and evidence;*" Article 22 explicitly provides for *in camera* proceedings. In its procedural rules, the Tribunal should make clear that the detrimental psychological impact of a public hearing on a victim or witness is a reason to close the proceedings to the press and/or general public.

2. *Other mechanisms to conceal the identity of victims and witnesses from the public and press should be allowed.* These include alteration of the image or voice of witness in a video or audio tape presented at trial[73] and sealing or expunging witnesses' names from public records.[74] Records identifying the victim should be secured and kept from the public.

3. *Concealing the identity of the victim or witness form the defendant.* As mentioned above, many victims and witnesses fear retribution from the defendants, or would find it extremely traumatic (endangering their psychological and/or physical survival) to confront their alleged attacker(s). For both their physical safety and psychological well-being, as well as that of their family and friends, in some of the most extreme cases it may be necessary for the Tribunal to conceal the identity from the defendant and his or her attorneys.

Possible procedures include testimony by one-way observation methods and closed circuit television,[75] use of screens so that the defendant and the public cannot see the victim or witness,[76] and the use of pseudonyms.[77] Because of the serious implications for the due process

---

[72] ABA Report, at 41-42 AI Memorandum, at 6, 27; CUNY Report, at 4; Helsinki Watch Report, at 10; *No Justice, No Peace,* at 19, 45, 47. *See* ABA Report for discussion of sexual assault cases as an exception of the U.S. constitutional right of access to criminal trials.

[73] Helsinki Watch Report, at 11.

[74] ABA Report, at 42; *No Justice, No Peace,* at 46.

[75] ABA Report, at 39; AI Memorandum, at 27; CUNY Report, at 4; *No Justice, No Peace,* at 45. The American Bar Association and the International Human Rights Law Group reports discuss these methods as protecting the privacy of the victims and witnesses; they do not advocate concealing identification from defendants. The ABA Report discusses use in U.S. courts.

[76] Helsinki Watch Report, at 11-12.

[77] ABA Report, at 42; Blakesley, at 7; Helsinki Watch Report, at 12.

rights of the defendants, these procedures should only be implemented after an *in camera* hearing in which the court assesses the compatibility of these procedures with the defendant's rights as well as the danger to the victim and/or witness.

4. *Reasonable Limitations on Examination of Victims and Witnesses.* The Tribunal should adopt procedures to protect witnesses and victims from the further brutalization of harassing and irrelevant questioning which can occur during rape trial proceedings. See Part IV, B.1 *supra*. Specifically, the Tribunal is urged to consider the following procedures:

a. *The Tribunal should adopt a format which vests in the Tribunal the sole, or at least primary, responsibility for questioning witnesses/victims/defendants.* Such a system is consistent with legal systems now in use around the world. Counsel for all parties should be allowed to submit proposed questions to the Tribunal, but the Tribunal must be granted authority to put only truly relevant questions to all persons testifying. Such a format and procedure would provide for a full and fair opportunity for parties to have all relevant questions put to witnesses/victims in as non-threatening a manner as possible.

b. *Tribunal judges should have, and exercise, wide discretion in limiting questioning of witnesses/victims to evidentiary matters directly related to the substantive charges against the defendants.* This standard should be adopted whether the Tribunal itself puts all questions to the witnesses/victims, as suggested above, or counsel for parties before the Tribunal are allowed to question. Questions related to the background, character, past sexual history, or other irrelevant considerations, should be ruled to be expressly prohibited.

c. *Repetitious questioning of witnesses/victims, which will exacerbate the trauma of recounting the atrocities committed against them, and discourage witnesses/victims from coming forward, should be prevented.* This will be particularly important in situations where witness/victims are testifying against numerous defendants in the same, or separate, proceedings. Such situations are inevitable given the many instances of mass or successive rapes currently alleged and likely to come before the Tribunal.

d. *Victim/witness testimony, both direct and cross-examination, should be held admissible against all similarly situated defendants.* Provisions should be made for additional and successive defendants to submit additional, non-repetitive, relevant questions to be put to the witness/victim. Such a procedure would insure fairness to defendants while limiting the further suffering of witnesses/victim. Such a procedure would insure fairness to defendants while limiting the further suffering of witnesses/victims, thus encouraging more witnesses/victims to come forward.

VI. PROPOSED PENALTIES

Article 24(1) of the Statute of the Tribunal provides that the Trial Chambers "shall have recourse to the general practice regarding prison sentences in the courts of the former Yugoslavia." While the Statue does not make Yugoslavian law the exclusive source of penalty, and the Tribunal should preserve the power to apply international law in case of discrepancy, Yugoslavian law appears to provide the court with a broad rage of discretion.

Most importantly, war crimes under Yugoslav law carry penalties from 5 years to the death penalty.[78] Rape and forced prostitution are explicitly listed as war crimes and are, therefore, subject to must greater penalty than the 10 year maximum applied to rape as a domestic crime.[79]

A. Aggravating Factors

The laws of the former Yugoslavia also recognize a broad range of aggravating factors. Where rape is committed together with lewd acts,[80] unnatural concupiscence of sodomy,[81] carnal knowledge or unnatural concupiscence with a minor under fourteen years of age,[82] or upon a helpless person who is in a state of being unable to offer resistance,[83] of if the rape occurred through the misuse of the perpetrator's position,[84] additional sentence(s) can be imposed[85] Intermediation, or the recruiting, inducing, inciting or luring of women for prostitution,[86] and the procuring and/or pandering of a female for illicit sex[87] are also offenses carrying penalties if the female was under fourteen years of age.[88] In addition, when crimes were "exceptionally dangerous" due to the perpetrator's particular determination, persistence or ruthlessness, or if particularly grave circumstances attached to the crime, heavier penalties are required.[89]

Extrapolating from the breadth of aggravating factors recognized under Yugoslavian law and applying them to the circumstances of the war in the former Yugoslavia, the following are among the factors that ought to be recognized under Article 24 (2) as aggravating factors which should increase the sentence.

1. The possession of arms, offensive weapons, explosives or imitations thereof.

---

[78] *1962 Code,* note 27, *supra.*, Chap. 11, Art. 123; *1978 Code.* 16th Heading, Art. 142. We agree with the Tribunal Statue that no matter how heinous the offense, the death penalty should not applied. Art. 241 (1).

[79] 1962 Code, Chap. 16 179(1)(2), note 27, supra. As a purely domestic crime, there is no minimum sentence for forcible rape; a minimum of three years is required where grievous bodily injury or death was inflicted upon the woman.

[80] *Id.* at Art. 183.

[81] *Id.* at Art. 186.

[82] *Id.* at Art. 181.

[83] *Id.* at Art. 180.

[84] *Id.* at Art. 182.

[85] *Id.* at Art. 46.

[86] *Id.* at Art. 188.

[87] *Id.* at Art. 187.

[88] *Id.* at Arts. 181-188.

[89] *Id.* at Art. 41.

2. Acts or threats to inflict additional violence to life or well-being of the victims or others.

3. Acts or threats accompanying the physical sexual attack which are intended or likely to inflict additional degradation or humiliation of the victim(s) or others.

4. A prior relationship between the victim and the defendant.[90]

5. The presence of other persons, including family members and intimates, bystanders, or aiders and abettors.

6. The communication of the fact of the rape to others under circumstances where the identity of the victim is revealed or could be surmised.

7. The consequence of forced pregnancy.

8. The fact of and conditions of detention.

9. The victim is a minor child under the age of fourteen years.

B. Mitigating Circumstances

With regard to factors which should mitigate the offense under Article 24(2) of the Statute of the Tribunal, it is significant that the Yugoslavian Criminal Code recognized a soldier's obligation to follow superior orders or face up to a year of imprisonment.[91] No punishment would be imposed if a criminal offense was committed under the orders of a superior officer *unless* that order was directed at committing a war crime or any other grave criminal offense.[92] In such an instance it would be the subordinate's responsibility to refuse to execute the order.

When, however, a soldier reasonably believed, based on the information available at the time, that he or she was facing imminent bodily harm or death if he or she were to refuse to carry out the orders of a superior officer, the totality of those circumstances should be taken into consideration as a mitigating circumstance related to the commission of a war crime. However, this defense should not be made available to individuals who merely faced humiliation or embarrassment in front of other military personnel or civilians.

Other mitigating circumstances should include:

1. Youth of the defendant

2. Coercion to enter the military

3. IQ (borderline incompetence)

4. Level of education of the defendant.

---

[90] The evidence is that trauma is enhanced by the breach of an earlier relationship that involved an element of trust. *See* R. Copelon, "Surfacing Gender: Reconceptualizing Crimes Against Women in Time of War," in A. Stiglmayer (ed.) (Lincoln, NB: University of Nebraska Press, Forthcoming, 1994).

[91] *Id.* at Art. 327.

[92] *Id.* at Art. 352.

VII. COMPENSATION FOR VICTIMS

It is also necessary to establish procedures for compensation to the victims of atrocities in the former Yugoslavia. Article 24(3) of the Tribunal's Statute provides:

In addition to imprisonment, the Trial Chambers may order the return of any property and proceeds acquired by criminal conduct, including by means of duress, to their rightful owners.

Proposals

1. The Tribunal should be empowered to order violators to pay compensation to victims.

2. The Tribunal should seek to have the United Nations create a fund or compensation commission through which to compensate the losses to victims.

Commentary

As a result of the gender-specific crimes perpetrated against them, women suffered both tangible and intangible losses. They have lost their bodily integrity; their physical and mental health; their self-esteem; their sexuality; their right of personal security; and their right of sexual, ethnic, and religious equality. They have lost or been forced to separate from family members; they have lost or fear the loss of their capacity to form families or bear children in the future; they have fled their homes and communities, lost their work, their livelihoods, their possessions, and the security of their identity in their communities.

These losses must be recognized in the interpretation of this provision of the Statute. In accordance with basic principles of humanitarian and human rights law, the concept of "property and proceeds" could be expanded by the Tribunal. This would entail interpreting the concept of property to encompass rights or entitlements. We acknowledge, however, a certain discomfort with categorizing rights as property. Alternatively, the Tribunal could request that the Security Council either expand its jurisdiction to grant compensation or establish a separate compensation mechanism to ensure that reparations are made for these types of injuries. Any other result privileges property over the deprivation of human rights, and ignores the principle of reparation embodied in Article 24(3) and in other international instruments.

The right to compensation is one which has been codified in numerous international human rights instruments[93] and supported by the decisions and commentary of various international human rights bodies.[94] Illustrative of the scope of damages previously granted are the German reparations to Holocaust victims and the Compensation Commission for Victims of the 1991 Gulf War.

Laws by the Federal Republic of Germany compensated for "loss of life, damage to limb or health, loss of liberty, property or possessions, or harm to professional or economic

[93] Article 8 of the Universal Declaration of Human Rights (1948); article 5, par. 5 of the European Convention for the Protection of Human Rights and Fundamental Freedoms (1950); article 6 of the International Convention on the Elimination of all Forms of Racial Discrimination (1965); article 2, par. 3(a) and article 9, par. 5 of the International Covenant on Civil and Political Rights (1966); articles 8, 10, 25, 63, 68 of the American Convention on Human Rights (1969); article 31, par. 2 of the African Charter on Human and Peoples' Rights (1981); article 14, par. 1 of the Convention against Torture and Other Cruel, Inhuman or Degrading Treatment or Punishment (1984); articles 15 and 16 of the ILO Convention 160; Indigenous and Tribal Peoples Convention (1989); article 39 of the Convention on the Rights of the Child (1989).

[94] Such human rights entities include the UN Human Rights Committee, the Committee on the Elimination of Racial Discrimination, the Committee against Torture, the Committee on the Elimination of Discrimination Against Women, the Commission of Inquiry established under the Constitution of the International Labour Organization, the European Court of Human Rights, the Inter-American Court of Human Rights. *See* Van Boven study, at 21-36.

prospects.[95] German reparations also included "death caused by a deterioration in health resulting from emigration or from living conditions detrimental to health...[and] suicide prompted by persecution, including suicide caused by economic difficulties which the victim could not overcome in the country to which he emigrated.[96]

The Compensation Commission established in the aftermath of the 1991 Gulf War can also be instructive. The UN included in their definition of damages "serious personal injury and mental pain and anguish." Serious personal injury included "Dismemberment; Permanent or temporary significant disfigurement, such as substantial change in one's outward appearance; Permanent or temporary significant loss of use or limitation of use of a body organ, member, function or system; and, Any injury which, if left untreated, is unlikely to result in the full recovery of the injured body area, or is likely to prolong such full recovery.[97] In addition, "... serious personal injury also includes instances of physical or mental injury arising from sexual assault, torture, aggravated physical assault, hostage-taking, or illegal detention ... or being forced to hide...."[98]

Compensation for mental pain and anguish was provided for both financial losses (such as loss of income and medical expenses) and non-financial losses (in cases where "(a) A spouse, child or parent of the individual suffered death; (b) The individual suffered serious personal injury involving dismemberment, permanent or temporary disfigurement, or permanent or temporary significant loss of use or limitation of use of a body organ, member, function or system; (c) *The individual suffered a sexual assault or aggravated assault or torture.)*[99]

Gender-based violence in the former Yugoslavia, both in itself and as part of a campaign of genocide, falls within these categories, including "sexual assault", "mental pain and anguish", "aggravated physical assault," "torture", "hostage-taking", and "illegal detention", and serious personal injury.

In order to effect the rights to reparation and compensation recognized in international law, it would be appropriate for the Tribunal to request that the United Nations Security Council establish a fund to be administered by the Tribunal itself or separately (perhaps through the Compensation Commission).

---

[95] Van Boven study at 107.

[96] *Id.* These categories encompass at least some of the victims of the atrocities in the former Yugoslavia. "Damage to limb or health" Includes "lasting impairment of the victim's mental or physical faculties" (i.e.: post-traumatic stress disorder). "Damage to liberty" includes detention in concentration camps, forced stay in ghettos, forced labor, and having to live "underground". This definition of damages can be applied to women who were deprived of their liberty by being detained in camps where they were repeatedly raped, as well as to those who were detained n their own homes or any other location and raped or otherwise subjected to sexual torture an cruel, inhuman or degrading treatment. It applies as well to the losses suffered as a result of flight and the need to reestablish their lives in new or foreign settings.

[97] *Id.* at ¶ 99.

[98] *Id.* at ¶ 100

[99] *Id.* at ¶ 101 (emphasis added).

PART IX

INTERNATIONAL TRIBUNAL DOCUMENTS

A. First Session, 17–30 November 1993

A.1. DECISIONS ADOPTED AT THE FIRST PLENARY SESSION OF THE INTERNATIONAL TRIBUNAL

IT/6/Rev. 2, 1 September 1994.

The following decisions were taken by the Members of the International Tribunal at its meetings:

1. Adoption of the provisional agenda contained in Document IT/1.

2. The term of the President of the International Tribunal would be two years, renewable only for a further period of two years. This decision was taken unanimously.

3. Judge Antonio Cassese was unanimously elected as President for a two year term. (Article 14, para. 1.)

4. The assignment of the Judges to each of the Chambers would be for a period of one year. This decision was also unanimous.

5. It was unanimously decided that the two Trial Chambers would be constituted as follows:

   One Chamber would comprise

   Judge Gabrielle McDonald,
   Judge Rustam Sidhwa
   Judge Lal Chand Vohrah

   and the other Chamber would comprise

   Judge Adolphus Karibi-Whyte
   Judge Germain le Foyer de Costil
   Judge Elizabeth Odio-Benito,

   with Judge Gabrielle McDonald being unanimously elected President of the former and Judge Adolphus Karibi-Whyte unanimously elected President of the latter.

* This document replaces documents IT/6/Rev.1, IT/6/Add.1/Rev.1, IT/6/Add.2.

6. It was also unanimously decided that the Appeals Chamber would be constituted as follows:

   Judge Antonio Cassese
   Judge Georges Abi-Saab
   Judge Jules Deschênes
   Judge Li Haopei
   Judge Sir Ninian Stephen

   As the President of the Tribunal Judge Cassese is *ex officio* President of the Appeals Chamber.

7. Judge Elizabeth Odio-Benito was unanimously elected as Vice President of the Tribunal.

8. In the light of the Report on the Practice of the International Court of Justice made by Dr. G.A. Fleischauer, and taking into account that

   (a) the Tribunal has been set up on an ad hoc basis, and

   (b) the term of office of the Judges is relatively short (4 years),

it was agreed that:

   1. Judges should not take up or continue permanent engagements incompatible with their duties as Judges.

   2. They may be allowed to engage in ancillary activities such as arbitrations on an ad hoc basis, scholarly writing, teaching on a part-time basis, speaking engagements etc.

   3. The activities referred to in (2) above should, however, in no way prevent Judges from fully participating in the Tribunal's activities.

   4. The undertaking of any of those activities should be reported to the President who, in case of doubt, may submit the matter to the Tribunal.

   5. Furthermore, it was decided that allowance should be made for an initial period of "phasing out". During this period, Judges may be authorized by the President to fulfil engagements taken prior to the election to the Tribunal, provided that this does not involve a protracted absence from the Tribunal's meetings.

9. It was agreed that each Judge should be assisted by a duly qualified professional legal assistant, at a level lower than P5. However, in view of the need to adopt an

"evolutionary approach", that is to proceed gradually in the recruitment of staff, it was decided that priority should be given to legal assistants for members of the Trial Chambers. It is, therefore, hoped that by March 1994 at least six can be hired.

Furthermore, it was agreed that Judges may also be helped by research assistants. They might be highly qualified final year law students or law graduates, who would work on a temporary basis and be paid by their own University or by a Foundation (such as the Ford Foundation) without any financial obligation on the Registry. They would be given such assignments as research, preparation of background material, bibliographical notes, etc.

As for the recruitment of legal assistants and research assistants, it was decided that all applications or curricula vitae should be transmitted to the Registrar. He will prepare a consolidated list, to be circulated to all Judges. The appointment of legal assistants will be made in accordance with normal United Nations practice, after due consultation of a Selection Committee consisting of the President, the Vice-President, the Presiding Judges of the Trial Chambers and the Registrar.

The appointment of the research assistants will be made after consulting the aforementioned Selection Committee.

Legal assistants and research assistants shall be duty bound to observe strict confidentiality about the functioning of the Tribunal.

10. The Tribunal adopted the schedule for its sessions in 1994 as follows:

    17 January through 11 February
    25 April through 24 July
    19 September through 4 November

11. The January - February session of the Tribunal will be a plenary session to resume with the drafting of the Rules of Procedure and Evidence.

12. The Tribunal adopted the provisional agenda of the January - February session contained in document IT/12.

13. The Tribunal adopted the draft press communiqué that would be issued at the end of the session (doc. IT/13).

14. The Tribunal decided to adopt a shorter name for the Tribunal for informal use. The name adopted in English is: International Tribunal for Crimes in former Yugoslavia" and in French "Tribunal International pour les crimes en ex-Yougoslavie".

A.2. NOTE FROM THE PRESIDENT
Statute's Provisions Requiring National Action
IT/11/Rev. 1, 29 November 1993.

	Action Required
- Art.9 para 2 (concurrent jurisdiction)	
Primacy of the IT.	National legislation
- Art.10 para 2 (non-bis in idem)	
Re-trial by the IT.	National legislation on extradition or surrender to IT of a convicted person.
- Articles 18 and 29 (right of the Prosecutor to conduct on-site investigations)	Legislative or administrative action.
- Art. 20 para. 2 (taking suspects into custody following an arrest warrant of the Tribunal)	Legislative (or administrative) action
- Art. 24 para. 3 (return of property acquired by criminal conduct and protection of the rights of third parties)	Legislative action
- Art. 27 (enforcement of sentences)	
States indicating to the SC their willingness to accept convicted persons.	Administrative (in some countries legislative) action.
- Art. 28 (pardon or commutation of sentences)	
Communication of national legislation on the matter.	Administrative action.
- Art. 29 (co-operation and judicial assistance.	National legislation and administrative action.

-	Art. 30 (extension to members of Tribunal and staff, of the privileges and immunities provided for in the 1946 UN Convention).	Legislative action.

A.3. PRESS COMMUNIQUE

IT/13, 30 November 1993.

The International Tribunal for Crimes in former Yugoslavia communicates the following for the information of the Press:

The Inaugural meeting of the Tribunal was held on 17 November 1993. The meeting opened with the presentation of the statement of the Secretary-General, by his representative, Mr. Carl-August Fleischhauer, Under Secretary-General, and Legal Counsel of the United Nations.

Thereafter each Judge took the oath of office. The elected Judges, who are Georges Michel Abi-Saab (Egypt), Antonio Cassese (Italy), Jules Deschenes (Canada), Adolphus Godwin Karibi-Whyte (Nigeria), Germain Le Foyer De Costil (France), Li Haopei (China), Gabrielle Kirk McDonald (United States), Elizabeth Odio Benito (Costa-Rica), Rustam S. Sidhwa (Pakistan), Ninian Stephen (Australia) and Lal Chand Vohrah (Malaysia) each read the solemn declaration and signed the document which was witnessed on behalf of the Secretary-General by Mr. Carl-August Fleischhauer.

The Prosecutor designate, Ramon Escovar-Salom (Venezuela) was present and so were a few dignitaries including the President of the International Court of Justice, Sir Robert Jennings, and the Dean of the Corps Diplomatique, Ambassador of the Republic of Yemen, H.E. Mr. M.A.R. Al-Robaes.

The Minister for Foreign Affairs of the Kingdom of the Netherlands, Dr. P.H. Kooijmans representing the Government of the Netherlands addressed the gathering.

The Minister of Justice, H.E. Mr. E.M.H. Hirsch Ballin, the Secretary-General of the Ministry of Foreign Affairs, Mr. D.J. van den Berg, the Secretary-General of the Ministry of Justice, Mr. G.J. van Dinter, the President of the High Court of Justice, Mr. S. Royer, the Attorney General of the High Court of Justice, Mr. T.B. ten Kate, and other senior officials of the Government of the Netherlands were also present. Officiating at the session as Secretary of the Tribunal was Mr. Gritakumar Chitty.

The inaugural meeting adjourned thereafter. The Tribunal continued its session in closed meetings. The representative of the Secretary-General, Mr. C-A Fleischhauer, chaired the meeting pending the election of the President. On 18 November 1993 the Tribunal elected Antonio Cassese as its President by acclamation. It had previously decided that the term of the presidency would be two-years renewable only for a further period of two-years.

The Tribunal has three Chambers which are, an Appeals Chamber consisting of five members and two Trial Chambers with three members each. The President of the Tribunal also presides over the Appeals Chamber. Under the Tribunal's Statute the President in consultation with the Members would determine who is assigned to each of the Chambers and each of the Trial Chambers elects its own President.

At its next meeting the Members decided that assignments to the Chambers would be for a period of one-year and thereafter there would be a rotation. Following this it was unanimously decided that the two Trial Chambers would be constituted as follows: One would comprise Judges Gabrielle McDonald, Rustam Sidhwa and Lal Chand Vohrah, with Judge Gabrielle McDonald elected Presiding Judge. The other Trial Chamber would comprise Judges Adolphus Karibi-Whyte, Germain Le Foyer de Costil and Elizabeth Odio Benito, with Judge Adolphus Karibi-Whyte as its Presiding Judge.

The Appeals Chamber, under the presidency of Judge Antonio Cassese has as its members Judges Georges Abi-Saab, Jules Deschenes, Li Haopei and Sir Ninian Stephen.

Judge Elizabeth Odio Benito was unanimously elected as Vice President of the Tribunal.

Having established its organizational structure and elected its officials, at its further meetings the Tribunal decided *inter alia* that its title should be abbreviated as "The International Tribunal for Crimes in former Yugoslavia".

Other matters under consideration of the Tribunal included *inter alia* the urgency for the early appointment of a Registrar and a Deputy Prosecutor. They also considered the appointment of legal assistants, researchers and support staff to serve their needs.

The members thereafter commenced an initial consideration of the rules of procedure and evidence. They had before them several informal proposals and suggestions from Member States, non-governmental organizations and others. Many major issues were discussed. The President and other judges have allocated among themselves the tasks of formulating various aspects of the rules which are to be carried out between the end of the first session and the commencement of the next session in January 1994.

The future sessions in 1994 are scheduled for:

17 January - 11 February
25 April - 29 July
19 September - 4 November

Consistent with its Provisional Agenda, the Tribunal expects to take up and conclude its consideration of the Rules of Procedure and Evidence at its January/February 1994 Session. Thereafter it will await the bringing of cases before it by the Prosecutor.

The Tribunal had before it several documents and background materials compiled by the Secretariat and several others distributed at the request of the President.

The Tribunal has addressed a letter to the Secretary-General and through him to the Security Council requesting that States be asked to urgently adopt enabling national legislation to give effect to the Statute of the Tribunal. States should also be called upon to appoint high level officials who would serve as liaison with the Tribunal in fulfilling its mandate. By this means it is intended to expedite communication and interaction in order to deal with matters which fall within the competence of the different governmental ministries or agencies responsible for foreign affairs, justice and national or internal affairs.

B. SECOND SESSION, 17 JANUARY–11 FEBRUARY 1994

B.1. STATEMENT BY THE PRESIDENT MADE AT A BRIEFING TO MEMBERS OF DIPLOMATIC MISSIONS

IT/29, 11 February 1994.

SUMMARY OF THE RULES OF PROCEDURE

OF THE INTERNATIONAL CRIMINAL TRIBUNAL

FOR THE FORMER YUGOSLAVIA

Introductory Remarks

On behalf of all of the Judges of the International Criminal Tribunal for the Former Yugoslavia, I welcome you to the close of our Second Session. The primary aim of this Session has been to prepare and approve the draft Rules of Procedure and Evidence of the Tribunal and I am delighted to be able to inform you that, after unstinting efforts from everyone involved, we have completed our task and the Rules were formally adopted by us today.

We have tried to capture the international character of the Tribunal by adopting only measures on which there is a broad consensus of agreement, thus, we hope, reflecting concepts which are truly recognised as being fair and just in the international arena. We have also attempted to strike a balance between the positivist and innovative approaches to the interpretation of our founding Statute and the customary international law it reflects.

Lastly, but most important of all, we have looked to the Rules to provide the necessary structure for our functions and to indicate both to the people of the former Yugoslavia and to the community of nations that we mean business!

As a body unique in international law, we have had little in the way of precedent to guide us. The two other international criminal tribunals that preceded us, at Nuremberg and Tokyo, both had very rudimentary rules of procedure: the rules of procedure of the Nuremberg Tribunal scarcely covered three and a half pages, and all procedural problems were resolved by individual decisions of the tribunal; in Tokyo, there were only nine rules of procedure, which formed part of the statute of the tribunal and, again, all other procedural matters were left to the case-by-case decision of the tribunal.

As far as our Tribunal is concerned, it is important, in the interests of the proper administration of justice, to adopt precise and detailed rules to govern the principal aspects of the proceedings and to provide a solid basis for the rights of the defence. Therefore, the Rules of Procedure have been arranged in a logical sequence to reflect the actual steps in the proceedings, so as to assist both the accused and counsel appearing before us, and we have made every attempt to draft them in plain, accessible language. Only time will tell how successful we have been.

Specific Issues

1. The adversarial system versus the inquisitorial system

Based on the limited precedent of the Nuremberg and Tokyo Trials, and in order for us, as judges, to remain as impartial as possible, we have adopted a largely adversarial approach to our procedures, rather than the inquisitorial approach found in continental Europe and elsewhere, The task of investigating allegations of offences and obtaining the necessary evidence will fall mostly on the Prosecutor. He is the one who will submit indictments to us for confirmation and he is the one who will argue the case before us. We have made considerable efforts to put both the prosecution and the defence on the same footing, with full disclosure of documents and witnesses by both sides, so as to safeguard the rights of the accused and ensure a fair trial. In this respect we have made a conscious effort to make good the flaws of Nuremberg and Tokyo.

However, there are two important adaptations to that general adversarial system. The first is that, as at Nuremberg and Tokyo, we have not laid down technical rules for the admissibility of evidence. I have been told that the common law rule of thumb is:"All relevant evidence is admissible unless it is inadmissible". When I remarked that that was somewhat unclear to me and not very helpful, I was told that was the point! Be that as it may, this Tribunal does not need to shackle itself to restrictive rules which have developed out of the ancient trial by jury system. There will be no jury sitting at the Tribunal, needing to be shielded from irrelevancies or given guidance as to the weight of the evidence they have heard. We, as judges, will be solely responsible for weighing the probative value of the evidence before us. <u>All</u> relevant evidence may be admitted to this Tribunal unless its probative value is substantially outweighed by the need to ensure a fair and expeditious trial. An example of this would be where the evidence was obtained by a serious violation of human rights.

Secondly, the Tribunal may order the production of additional or new evidence *proprio motu*. This will enable us to ensure that we are fully satisfied with the evidence on which we base our final decisions and to ensure that the charge has been proved beyond reasonable doubt. It will also minimise the possibility of a charge being dismissed on technical grounds for lack of evidence. We feel that, in the international sphere, the interests of justice are best served by such a provision and that the diminution, if any, of the accused's rights is minimal by comparison.

2. A "tailor-made" set of Rules

I have already mentioned that this Tribunal is a unique institution. As an ad hoc Tribunal we have been able to mould our Rules and procedures to fit the task in hand. That task is not, as at Nuremberg and Tokyo, to apply "victors' justice". This Tribunal is charged with sole responsibility for judging the perpetrators of some of the most heinous crimes known to man, committed not on some foreign battlefield but their own home ground, acts of terror and barbarism committed not against total strangers (which, of course, is still inexcusable) but against their own neighbours, in a civil, inter-state, war which is further complicated by ethnic and religious conflict.

(a) Patterns of conduct

An issue we were determined to address was that of crimes consisting of patterns of conduct. The Rules provide for the admission of evidence of a consistent pattern of criminal conduct if it is of high probative value and its admission is consistent with the interests of justice.

(b) Immunity

The question of the grant of immunity from prosecution to a potential witness has also generated considerable debate. Those in favour contend that it will be difficult enough for us to obtain evidence against a suspect and so we should do everything possible to encourage direct testimony. They argue that this is especially true if the testimony serves to establish criminal responsibility of those higher up the chain of command. Consequently, arrangements such as plea bargaining could also be considered in an attempt to secure other convictions.

However, we always have to keep in mind that this Tribunal is not a municipal criminal court but one that is charged with the task of trying persons accused of the gravest possible of all crimes. The persons appearing before us will be charged with genocide, torture, murder, sexual assault, wanton destruction, persecution and other inhumane acts. After due reflection, we have decided that <u>no one</u> should be immune from prosecution for crimes such as these, no matter how useful their testimony may otherwise be. This will apply to both testimonial and use immunity. The degree of cooperation received from an accused will, however, be taken into account as a mitigating factor in sentencing.

(c) Protection of witnesses

As I have just mentioned, we are very much aware that there may be considerable reluctance on the part of witnesses to come to the Tribunal to testify. One of our overriding concerns has been how to encourage witnesses to do this. Often the principal witness against the perpetrator of a crime will be the victim himself, who may feel threatened, either directly, or indirectly, for example, if the witness has family still within an area held by forces sympathetic to the accused. This will be especially important if we are successful, as I hope we are, in bringing to trial political and military leaders and those who are higher in the chain of command.

We have tried to deal with these problems in a number of ways.

(i) Depositions

One method is to permit the Prosecutor to submit evidence by way of deposition in exceptional circumstances. This has the added advantage that it may enable the Tribunal to proceed on the basis of such evidence in cases where the witness has subsequently disappeared or is reluctant or unable to testify in open court. Depositions may be made locally and may be taken by means of video-conference if appropriate. In order to protect the rights of the accused, the procedure for taking depositions allows for cross-examination.

Another protection is that arrangements may be made for the identity of a witness who may be at risk not to be disclosed to the accused until such time as the witness can be brought under the protection of the Tribunal. Witnesses may also be protected from public identification if appropriate.

(ii) The Victim Unit

However, the most important provision for the protection of witnesses in our Rules of Procedure, and the most innovative in international law, is the establishment of a Victims Unit within the Office of the Prosecutor. We have never allowed ourselves to lose sight of the fact that victims and witnesses also have rights, rights which, often, have been grossly violated by the accused. Therefore, we have created a special unit to provide counselling, not only on their legal rights but also psychological help and support, and to recommend protective measures where required. As it is intended that this Unit will deal mainly with female victims of rape and sexual assault, we are planning to hire qualified women for this Unit whenever possible.

(d) Sexual Assault

This leads me to my final point on this particular topic, crimes of sexual assault.

The Tribunal recognises that many of the victims of the conflict in the former Yugoslavia are women and we have placed special emphasis on crimes against women in our Rules of Procedure. We have chosen to talk of crimes of sexual assault, rather than rape, and have made special provision as to the standard of evidence and matters of credibility of the witness which may be raised by the defence.

In particular, no corroboration of the victim's testimony is required in matters of sexual assault and the victim's previous sexual conduct is irrelevant and inadmissible. If a defence of consent is raised, the Tribunal may take note of factors which vitiate consent, including physical violence and moral or psychological constraints. A victim or witness to a charge of sexual assault may not be questioned as to prior sexual conduct or reputation, or any failure to report the incident to authorities or to seek medical attention.

In view of the highly specialised nature of the legal issues to be determined by it, the Tribunal has also made provision in its Rules for the appearance before it of *amicus curiae* on request. Not only will this enable the Tribunal to have access to independent expert advice on any matter it may wish but will also permit other interested parties, such as States and Non-Governmental Organisations, to present their views.

3. Trial by default

One of the questions I am asked most frequently is: "What will the Tribunal do if an accused refuses to appear before it?" This is one of the most contentious issues we have had to address in our deliberations, whether to provide in our Rules for trial in absentia or, as I prefer to call it, trial by default.

No one is more aware than the judges of this Tribunal of the practical difficulties we may face if an accused absconds or, as is more likely, a State refuses to hand over a suspect, on the ground that it is contrary to its own national laws to do so. Consequently, a provision for trial by default, coupled always with the necessary protections as to due process and a right of review, has a certain attraction. However, the overriding need to ensure that justice is not only done but is seen to be done has led us, after considerable debate, I must say, to the conclusion that we should not include such a provision in our Rules.

This is not to say that transgressors may evade our jurisdiction with impunity. Our founding Statute imposes a specific obligation on each Member State of the United Nations to cooperate with the Tribunal and to comply with its orders, including those for the arrest or detention of suspects. These obligations prevail over any internal national law impediment to the surrender or transfer of the accused. The Rules of Procedure lay down detailed requirements for the issue and publication of the indictment. Details of each and every indictment will be made public upon confirmation unless, exceptionally, the confirming judge is satisfied that an order of non-disclosure is necessary in the interests of justice.

A warrant for the arrest of the accused will be sent to the State in which the accused lives or was last known to be present. That State is required to notify the Tribunal if it is unable to execute the warrant. Failure to report to the Tribunal within a reasonable time will be deemed failure to execute the warrant, in which case the Tribunal Prosecutor may take all reasonable steps to inform the accused of the indictment, including notification in appropriate newspapers.

The indictment may then be submitted to one of the three-man Trial Chambers of the Tribunal for reconfirmation. At that time the indictment and all supporting evidence will be submitted in open session. If the Trial Chamber is satisfied that a *prima facie* case has been established, it shall issue an international arrest warrant to be transmitted to all States. Furthermore, if the Trial Chamber is satisfied that the failure to execute the warrant was the result of failure by a State to cooperate with the Tribunal, the President shall notify the Security Council accordingly.

We are confident that these measures will establish the firm resolve of this Tribunal and full compliance with its orders and decisions. It may be that nothing can sway the hearts and minds of the hardened criminals who are responsible for the atrocities reported daily from the former Yugoslavia. However, we are optimistic that the steps we have included, and which we are fully prepared to implement, will go a long way towards bringing those persons to justice or effectively imprisoning them within the borders of a State which will be regarded as a pariah among nations.

4. The need for State cooperation

We have tried to take the special historical and practical circumstances of the situation into account when drafting our Rules of Procedure. The Rules place strong emphasis on the obligation of all States, under international law, to cooperate with the Tribunal and comply with its orders. For this reason, the Rules repeat the duty laid down in its founding Statute to act promptly in executing a warrant for arrest, or any other Order of the Tribunal, and restate the principle that the obligation of States to surrender the accused prevails over any legal impediment in its national legislation.

I have already mentioned the power to report to the Security Council cases of State inaction or refusal to cooperate. This applies as much to the six republics of the former Yugoslavia as to any other State. If such a step proves necessary, we will look to the members of the Security Council for support on an international scale.

The Tribunal may request a State to provide it with any information the State has acquired in the course of its own investigations or proceedings and the State is required, under the Statute, to transmit all information so requested.

The Tribunal has primacy over national court proceedings on the same subject matter and decisions of national courts are not binding on it. We may require a State to defer to the Tribunal's jurisdiction and request a stay or deferral of proceedings, particularly if it appears that the national court proceedings are not impartial or are designed to shield the accused from international criminal responsibility. Again, any failure on the part of a State to comply with such a request may be reported to the Security Council.

B.2. PRESS COMMUNIQUE

IT/30, 11 February 1994.

The International Criminal Tribunal for the Former Yugoslavia communicates the following for the information of the Press.

The second session of the Tribunal was held from 17 January to 11 February 1994, in The Hague, the Netherlands, in the Aegon Building.

1. Visit of United Nations Secretary-General

During the first week of the second session, the Secretary-General of the United Nations visited the Tribunal during an official three-day visit to the Netherlands. He expressed strong support for the Tribunal and placed considerable emphasis on its role in meeting the challenge of a new world order based on democracy and human rights.

2. Rules of Procedure and Evidence

The primary aim of this session has been to prepare and approve the draft Rules of Procedure and Evidence of the Tribunal. These Rules are based on both the Statute adopted by the Security Council in its resolution 827 (1993) of 25 May 1993, and customary international law. Not only do the Rules provide the necessary structure for the functioning and organisation of the Tribunal, but also for the conduct of the pre-trial phase of the proceedings, including investigation and indictment by the Prosecutor, trials and appeals, the admission of evidence, the protection of victims and witnesses, orders and warrants, and the appointment of counsel.

Given the limited precedent value of the Nuremberg and Tokyo trials, the Judges have taken into consideration the major legal systems of the world, and have adopted in the Rules a largely adversarial approach, rather than the inquisitorial approach.

The Rules place a strong emphasis on the obligation of nation States, pursuant to Article 29 of the Statute, to cooperate with the Tribunal and to take whatever steps may be necessary to comply with any of its orders. This includes the enactment of national legislation where necessary to remove any impediment which may exist to the surrender or extradition of suspects or accused. In cases of inaction or refusal to cooperate, the Tribunal will report the matter to the Security Council for such action as the Security Council may wish to take.

The Rules confirm, pursuant to the Statute, the primacy of the Tribunal over national court proceedings on the same subject matter. The Tribunal may require a State to defer to the Tribunal's jurisdiction and may request a stay or deferral of proceedings, particularly if it appears that the national court proceedings are not impartial or are designed to shield the accused from international criminal responsibility.

The Rules have been adopted by the Tribunal meeting in plenary, on Friday, 11 February 1994. After final editing, to be completed in the following weeks, the Rules will be published in English and in French, both texts being authentic.

3. Registrar

Professor Theo van Boven, of the University of Limburg in the Netherlands, has been appointed as Acting Registrar of the Tribunal. He will be responsible for the administration and servicing of the Tribunal, and will serve as its channel of communication.

4. Deputy Prosecutor

A Deputy Prosecutor, Mr. Graham Blewitt, former Director of the Australian War Crime Prosecution Unit, has been appointed. Mr. Blewitt has already commenced work and is expected to arrive in The Hague next week to set up the Office of the Prosecutor. In addition to an Investigation Unit and a Prosecution Unit, the Office of the Prosecutor will include a Victims and Witnesses Unit, which will recommend protective measures for victims and witnesses and provide counselling and support for them.

5. Tribunal's Budget

The question of the budget remains a matter of great importance and urgency. The Tribunal is currently working on the basis of its initial funding. The draft budget for 1994 - 1995 is now awaiting United Nations approval, expected in March. Until it is approved, the Tribunal cannot exercise its mandate fully. The budget includes provision for immediate recruitment of staff for Judges and for the Offices of the Registrar and the Prosecutor. Financial provision will also be made for the Tribunal premises and construction of a prison block for detainees. Construction of the prison block has now commenced. Completion is currently anticipated for the end of June 1994.

6. States' contributions to the Tribunal

A number of countries have now made contributions to the special United Nations fund from which the Tribunal is financed, in particular, the United States of America, Pakistan and Italy. Others have confirmed their commitment to such funding.

7. Adoption of national legislation for the implementation of the Statute

While Italy has already passed a law in this respect, a number of other countries (including the Netherlands, Spain, France, Great Britain) are in the process of doing so.

8. Future plenary meetings of the Tribunal

Subject to the scheduling of sessions of the Trial Chambers for cases to be brought before them by the Prosecutor, the future plenary meetings of the Tribunal in 1994 have been rescheduled for:

25 April - 13 May
18 July - 28 July

Hearings will commence as soon as the Prosecutor has completed pre-trial investigations pursuant to the Rules of Procedure and Evidence, hopefully in mid-1994.

C. Third Session, 25 April–5 May 1994

C.1. LIST OF DECISIONS ADOPTED DURING THE THIRD PLENARY SESSION OF THE INTERNATIONAL CRIMINAL TRIBUNAL FOR THE FORMER YUGOSLAVIA (Item 19 of the agenda) (Document IT/33/REV. 1) (The Hague, 25 April–5 May 1994)

IT/54, 5 May 1994.

1. The Tribunal adopted the Rules Governing the Detention of Persons Awaiting Trial or Appeal Before the Tribunal or Otherwise Detained on the Authority of the Tribunal (IT/38/Rev. 3)* pursuant to Item 7 of the Agenda.

2. The Tribunal adopted the Report relating to Item 10 of the Agenda (Questions relating to the Assignment of Counsel) (IT/59)*.

3. The Tribunal adopted the Report relating to Item 6 (Questions relating to the Building of the Courtroom and Accessory Facilities), Item 13 (Seal of the Tribunal), Item 14 (Robes of the Judges) and Item 15 (Conduct of Proceedings) of the Agenda (IT/60)*.

4. The Tribunal adopted a provisional schedule for its future activities and has set the dates of the Fourth plenary session for 18 - 28 July 1994.

5. The Tribunal adopted the provisional agenda for the Fourth plenary session (Item 17 of the Agenda) (IT/58/Rev.1)*.

6. The Tribunal decided to amend Rule 96 of the Rules of Procedure and Evidence and adopted the amended text of this Rule (IT/53/Rev.1)*.

7. The Tribunal adopted, as amended, the resolution concerning the difficulties encountered by the Tribunal and requested the President to send a copy of the resolution to the Secretary-General of the United Nations, the President of the Security Council and the President of the General Assembly (IT/57/Rev.1).

8. The Tribunal adopted the List for Assignment of Trial Chambers' Judges for the Review of Indictments (Rule 28 of the Rules of Procedure and Evidence) (IT/48)*.

9. The Tribunal adopted the minutes of the First session and the verbatim records of the Second session.

10. The Tribunal adopted a final Press Communique (IT/61)* to be issued at the end of its session.

* These documents, which were annexed to the List of Decisions, are not included here.

C.2. PRESS COMMUNIQUE

IT/61/Rev. 1, 5 May 1994.

The International Criminal Tribunal for the Former Yugoslavia communicates the following for the information of the Press.

1. General

The Third session of the Tribunal was held from 25 April to 5 May 1994, in The Hague, the Netherlands, the seat of the Tribunal. At this session the Tribunal continued to make the necessary preparations for its future operational tasks.

Following the adoption of its Rules of Procedure and Evidence at its Second session, the Tribunal has now discussed and adopted Rules Governing the Detention of Persons Awaiting Trial or Appeal Before the Tribunal or Otherwise Detained on the Authority of the Tribunal ("Rules of Detention"). The Tribunal also discussed and adopted Guidelines for the Assignment of Counsel pursuant to Rule 45 of its Rules of Procedure and Evidence.

In addition, the Tribunal met with the recently appointed Under-Secretary-General for Legal Affairs and Legal Counsel of the United Nations, Mr. Hans A.V. Corell and had an exchange of views with Mr. Graham T. Blewitt, the Deputy Prosecutor.

Furthermore, the Tribunal reviewed with representatives of the Netherlands authorities issues of common interest and, in particular, progress made with regard to such infra-structural matters as the construction of a courtroom and the building of detention facilities.

In addition, the Tribunal adopted a list of the Trial Chambers' Judges who, as from 1 July 1994, are assigned, on a monthly basis, the task of reviewing any indictment that might be issued by the Office of the Prosecutor.

The Tribunal also discussed various aspects of the organisation and functioning of the Registry.

By adopting these measures, the Tribunal has taken all the steps within its powers necessary to make it possible for trials to start as soon as feasible.

2. Rules of Detention

The Tribunal adopted a detailed set of 91 rules which will govern the administration of the detention unit for detainees awaiting trial or appeal and which will also ensure the protection of their individual rights while in detention. In general terms, the rules are intended to regulate the conditions of detention of inmates, including their rights and obligations, at all stages from reception to release, and to provide the basic criteria for management of the detention unit.

The Rules of Detention contain a series of basic principles, a section on the management of the detention unit, a section on the rights of detainees and a section on removal and transportation of detainees.

In drawing up the Rules of Detention, the Tribunal paid particular attention to existing relevant international standards, such as the United Nations Standard Minimum Rules for the Treatment of Prisoners, the Body of Principles for the Protection of All Persons under Any Form of Detention or Imprisonment and the Basic Principles for the Treatment of Prisoners. The Tribunal also took into account the European Prison Rules of the Council of Europe and rules and regulations which form part of the Dutch prison system. Furthermore it should be noted that a number of recommendations made by the European Committee for the Prevention of Torture and Inhuman or Degrading Treatment or Punishment (CPT) have been included in the detention regime.

It should be emphasized that this is the first time that such a detailed set of binding Rules has been adopted by an international body to regulate the day-to-day operation of an international detention institution.

The text of the Rules of Detention will become available within the next few days.

3. <u>Guidelines for the Assignment of Counsel</u>

Rule 45 of the Rules of Procedure and Evidence contains a number of provisions relating to the assignment of counsel to indigent suspects or accused. The Tribunal has now adopted guidelines relating to such issues as:

- criteria of indigency;
- procedure for granting legal assistance;
- criteria for fees and expenses to be paid to assigned counsel;
- disciplinary measures applicable to assigned counsel;
- facilities to be provided to assigned counsel;
- assignment of counsel to a suspect (as distinct from assignment of counsel to an accused).

The text of the guidelines will become available within the next few days.

4. <u>Amendment of the Rules of Procedure and Evidence</u>

Since the publication of its Rules of Procedure and Evidence, the Tribunal has received a number of comments and suggestions from Governments and NGOs for possible improvement. They will be duly taken into account, also in the light of the Tribunal's practice which will develop over a period of time. At the present session the Tribunal unanimously adopted an amendment to Rule 96(ii) of its Rules of Procedure and Evidence. As a consequence, this Rule now reads as follows:

Rule 96

Evidence in Cases of Sexual Assault

In cases of sexual assault:

(i) no corroboration of the victim's testimony shall be required;

(ii) consent shall not be allowed as a defence if the victim

a) has been subjected to or threatened with or has had reason to fear violence, duress, detention or psychological oppression, or

b) reasonably believed that if she did not submit, another might be so subjected, threatened or put in fear;

(iii) prior sexual conduct of the victim shall not be admitted in evidence.

5. **Fourth plenary session of the Tribunal**

The Fourth session of the Tribunal is scheduled to start on 18 July 1994. Among the items to be discussed is the First Annual Report of the Tribunal.

C.3. RESOLUTION ADDRESSED TO THE GENERAL ASSEMBLY AND SECURITY COUNCIL OF THE UNITED NATIONS

IT/57/Rev. 2, 5 May 1994.

THE INTERNATIONAL CRIMINAL TRIBUNAL FOR THE FORMER YUGOSLAVIA, at the end of its third session (25 April - 5 May 1994)

RECALLING

- its creation by Security Council resolution 827 of 25 May 1993 and its inauguration on 17 November 1993,

- the adoption of its Rules of Procedure and Evidence at its second session on 11 February 1994;

- the adoption, at the present session on 5 May 1994, of its Rules Governing the Detention of Persons Awaiting Trial or Appeal Before the Tribunal or Otherwise Detained on the Authority of the Tribunal and its Guidelines on Assignment of Counsel;

- the completion of all those other steps that are within its powers in preparation for the effective operation of the Tribunal and the fulfilment of the mission entrusted to it by the Security Council;

- the full cooperation of the Government of the Kingdom of the Netherlands in all respects, including the imminent conclusion of the Headquarters Agreement;

NOTES nevertheless the following difficulties which, despite the efforts to date of all parties, prevent the Tribunal from embarking on its mission:

first, two matters which it is now too late to remedy, namely:

- that despite the full cooperation of the Dutch authorities, the detention facilities for accused awaiting trial will not be ready until August at the earliest;

- that the Courtroom, the only one at present proposed for use by all three Chambers of the Tribunal and the layout of which has been approved by the Tribunal, will not be ready before mid-October at the earliest;

secondly, three matters requiring urgent attention:

- the Tribunal still awaits the appointment of the Prosecutor, who is an essential organ of the Tribunal;

- the Deputy Prosecutor, despite his best efforts, does not yet have at his disposal any staff of investigators and assistant prosecutors;

- the budgetary situation of the Tribunal has been left shrouded in regrettable uncertainty;

EMPHASIZES that the whole process of investigation, indictment and, ultimately, trial cannot begin until these three matters have been attended to.

CONSIDERS that the population suffering from the continuing armed conflict in the Former Yugoslavia would not understand that the Tribunal, which gave rise to such high expectations, is thus being delayed in fulfilling its mission.

IN CONSEQUENCE, THE TRIBUNAL FERVENTLY HOPES that the competent United Nations authorities, once apprised of the aforementioned situation, will undertake determined action in order urgently to solve those problems and to enable the Tribunal to fulfil the important mission entrusted to it.

D. Fourth Session, 18–29 July 1994

D.1 LIST OF DECISIONS ADOPTED DURING THE FOURTH PLENARY SESSION OF THE INTERNATIONAL CRIMINAL TRIBUNAL FOR THE FORMER YUGOSLAVIA (Item 16 of the Agenda) (Document IT/69) (The Hague, 18–29 July 1994)

IT/80, 28 July 1994.

1. The Tribunal adopted its First Annual Report (IT/68)* pursuant to Item 6 of the Agenda.

2. The Tribunal adopted the report relating to Item 11 of the Agenda (Instructions on the Assignment of Counsel) (IT/77)*, together with the Directive on Assignment of Counsel (IT/73)*.

3. The Tribunal authorized the President to proceed with the Appointment of an Inspecting Authority for the Detention Unit (Item 12 of the Agenda).

4. The Tribunal authorized the President to send a letter to the United Nations Office of Legal Affairs concerning the terms and conditions of employment of Judges (Item 18 of the Agenda).

5. The Tribunal considered a report from the Chairman of the Working Group relating to Practical Matters of Concern to Judges (Item 18 of the Agenda) and adopted its recommendations as to pensions, death-in-services benefits, travel benefits and use of official cars.

6. The Tribunal decided to establish an Inter-sessional Working Group to review requests for amendment of the Rules of Procedure and Evidence (Item 7 of the Agenda).

7. The Tribunal decided to establish an Inter-sessional Working Group on the preparation of Judicial Forms (Item 20 of the Agenda).

8. The Tribunal adopted the revised List for Assignment of Trial Chambers' Judges for the Review of Indictments (Rule 28 of the Rules of Procedure and Evidence) (IT/48/Rev.2)*.

9. The Tribunal adopted the summary minutes of the Third session (Item 5 of the Agenda).

10. The Tribunal has set provisional dates for three judicial sessions in 1995, being from mid-January - mid-April, mid-May - mid-July and mid-September - mid-December. Within those judicial sessions, the Tribunal has set the dates of the Fifth plenary session for 16 January - 3 February 1995 and the Sixth plenary session for 3-14 July 1995.

11. The Tribunal adopted the provisional agenda for the Fifth plenary session (Item 15 of the Agenda) (IT/81)*.

12. The Tribunal adopted a final Press Communique (IT/790)* to be issued at the end of its session.

* These documents, which were annexed to the List of Decisions, are not included here.

D.2. PRESS COMMUNIQUE
International Tribunal for the Former Yugoslavia Operational as a Criminal Court as of this Autumn

IT/82, 28 July 1994.

The Fourth Plenary Session of the International Criminal Tribunal for Yugoslavia, which commenced on Monday 18 July, closed on Friday 29 July, at the Tribunal's Seat.

This Session was the last scheduled prior to the commencement of proceedings, and to this end the Judges have completed the necessary legal and the operational framework of the Tribunal.

Basic law texts completed

The Judges have approved the Directive on the Assignment of Defense Counsel, which will be published by the Registry to enter in force by 1 August 1994.

This text sets out the content of the right to legal assistance granted to suspects or accused recognized indigent, and governs its practical application.

The Directive is additional to the Rules of Procedure and Evidence (adopted during the Second Plenary Session) and to the Rules of Detention (adopted at the end of the Third Plenary Session): they establish the legal basis which is essential for the effective functioning of the Tribunal.

Courtroom and Detention Unit ready by October

From an operational point of view, the Judges have agreed on the installation and the equipment of the courtroom; the building works are engaged. They have also monitored the progress made in the construction of the Detention Unit.

The Tribunal expects that the Detention Unit will be ready by 1 October 1994, and the Courtroom 21 October 1994. The functioning of the Tribunal as a criminal court will thus be possible in the coming weeks.

"Decisive step towards the first proceedings"

The Judges officially welcomed the Honourable Mr. Justice Richard J. Goldstone, who was appointed as the Prosecutor of the Tribunal on Friday 8 July by the Resolution 936 of the Security Council. It was a major highlight of the Meeting.

The Judges took note with deep satisfaction of this appointment, and held with the Prosecutor an intense working session. They welcomed warmly his decision to start working as of 15 August 1994.

The fact that Mr. Goldstone is going to take up his duties very soon means, as he put it himself, "decisive step towards the first proceedings".

Adoption of the first Annual Report

The Judges have adopted the first Annual Report of the Tribunal. This document takes stock of the installation phase of the Court, and mentions both the difficulties encountered and the prospect of being operational.

It will be submitted to the Security Council and the General Assembly prior to be made public.

Indictments possible by this autumn

As of 1 September 1994, the presence of the Judges in The Hague will be organized to proceed with the indictments required by the Prosecutor.

PART X

THE NUREMBERG PRECEDENT

A. LONDON AGREEMENT OF 8 AUGUST 1945

Agreement by the Government of the United States of America, the Provisional Government of the French Republic, the Government of the United Kingdom of Great Britain and Northern Ireland, and the Government of the Union of Soviet Socialist Republics for the Prosecution and Punishment of the Major War Criminals of the European Axis.

WHEREAS the United Nations have from time to time made declarations of their intention that war criminals shall be brought to justice;

AND WHEREAS the Moscow Declaration of 30 October 1943 on German atrocities in Occupied Europe stated that those German officers and men and members of the Nazi Party who have been responsible for or have taken a consenting part in atrocities and crimes will be sent back to the countries in which their abominable deeds were done in order that they may be judged and punished according to the laws of these liberated countries and of the free Governments that will be created therein;

AND WHEREAS this Declaration was stated to be without prejudice to the case of major criminals whose offenses have no particular geographic location and who will be punished by the joint decision of the Governments of the Allies;

NOW THEREFORE the Government of the United States of America, the Provisional Government of the French Republic, the Government of the United Kingdom of Great Britain and Northern Ireland, and the Government of the Union of Soviet Socialist Republics (hereinafter called "the Signatories") acting in the interests of all the United Nations and by their representatives duly authorized thereto have concluded this Agreement.

Article 1. There shall be established after consultation with the Control Council for Germany an International Military Tribunal for the trial of war criminals whose offenses have no particular geographical location whether they be accused individually or in their capacity as members of organizations or groups or in both capacities.

Article 2. The constitution, jurisdiction, and functions of the International Military Tribunal shall be those set out in the Charter annexed to this Agreement, which Charter shall form an integral part of this Agreement.

Article 3. Each of the Signatories shall take the necessary steps to make available for the investigation of the charges and trial the major war criminals detained by them who are to be tried by the

International Military Tribunal. The Signatories shall also use their best endeavors to make available for investigation of the charges against and the trial before the International Military Tribunal such of the major war criminals as are not in the territories of any of the Signatories.

Article 4. Nothing in this Agreement shall prejudice the provisions established by the Moscow Declaration concerning the return of war criminals to the countries where they committed their crimes.

Article 5. Any Government of the United Nations may adhere to this Agreement by notice given through the diplomatic channel to the Government of the United Kingdom, who shall inform the other signatory and adhering Governments of each such adherence.*

Article 6. Nothing in this Agreement shall prejudice the jurisdiction or the powers of any national or occupation court established or to be established in any Allied territory or in Germany for the trial of war criminals.

Article 7. This Agreement shall come into force on the day of signature and shall remain in force for the period of one year and shall continue thereafter, subject to the right of any Signatory to give, through the diplomatic channel, one month's notice of intention to terminate it. Such termination shall not prejudice any proceedings already taken or any findings already made in pursuance of this Agreement.

IN WITNESS WHEREOF the Undersigned have signed the present Agreement.

DONE in quadruplicate in London this 8th day of August 1945 each in English, French, and Russian, and each text to have equal authenticity.

For the Government of the United States of America
/s/ ROBERT H. JACKSON

For the Provisional Government of the French Republic
/s/ ROBERT FALCO

For the Government of the United Kingdom of Great Britain and Northern Ireland
/s/ JOWITT

For the Government of the Union of Soviet Socialist Republics
/s/ I. NIKITCHENKO
/s/ A. TRAININ

* In accordance with Article 5, the following Governments of the United Nations have expressed their adherence to the Agreement: Greece, Denmark, Yugoslavia, the Netherlands, Czechoslovakia, Poland, Belgium, Ethiopia, Australia, Honduras, Norway, Panama, Luxembourg, Haiti, New Zealand, India, Venezuela, Uruguay, and Paraguay.

CHARTER OF THE INTERNATIONAL MILITARY TRIBUNAL

I. CONSTITUTION OF THE INTERNATIONAL MILITARY TRIBUNAL

Article 1. In pursuance of the Agreement signed on the 8th day of August 1945 by the Government of the United States of America, the Provisional Government of the French Republic, the Government of the United Kingdom of Great Britain and Northern Ireland, and the Government of the Union of Soviet Socialist Republics, there shall be established an International Military Tribunal (hereinafter called "the Tribunal") for the just and prompt trial and punishment of the major war criminals of the European Axis.

Article 2. The Tribunal shall consist of four members, each with an alternate. One member and one alternate shall be appointed by each of the Signatories. The alternates shall, so far as they are able, be present at all sessions of the Tribunal. In case of illness of any member of the Tribunal or his incapacity for some other reason to fulfill his functions, his alternate shall take his place.

Article 3. Neither the Tribunal, its members nor their alternates can be challenged by the Prosecution, or by the defendants or their counsel. Each Signatory may replace its member of the Tribunal or his alternate for reasons of health or for other good reasons, except that no replacement may take place during a Trial, other than by an alternate.

Article 4.

(a) The presence of all four members of the Tribunal or the alternate for any absent member shall be necessary to constitute the quorum.

(b) The members of the Tribunal shall, before any trial begins, agree among themselves upon the selection from their number of a President, and the President shall hold office during that trial, or as may otherwise be agreed by a vote of not less than three members. The principle of rotation of presidency for successive trials is agreed. If, however, a session of the Tribunal takes place on the territory of one of the four Signatories, the representative of that Signatory on the Tribunal shall preside.

(c) Save as aforesaid the Tribunal shall take decisions by a majority vote and in case the votes are evenly divided, the vote of the President shall be decisive: provided always that convictions and sentences shall only be imposed by affirmative votes of at least three members of the Tribunal.

Article 5. In case of need and depending on the number of the matters to be tried, other Tribunals may be set up; and the establishment, functions, and procedure of each Tribunal shall be identical, and shall be governed by this Charter.

II. JURISDICTION AND GENERAL PRINCIPLES

Article 6. The Tribunal established by the Agreement referred to in Article 1 hereof for the trial and punishment of the major war criminals of the European Axis countries shall have the power to try and punish persons who, acting in the interests of the European Axis countries, whether as individuals or as members of organizations, committed any of the following crimes.

The following acts, or any of them, are crimes coming within the jurisdiction of the Tribunal for which there shall be individual responsibility:

(a) *CRIMES AGAINST PEACE:* namely, planning, preparation, initiation or waging of a war of aggression, or a war in violation of international treaties, agreements or assurances, or participation in a Common Plan or Conspiracy for the accomplishment of any of the foregoing;

(b) *WAR CRIMES:* namely, violations of the laws or customs of war. Such violations shall include, but not be limited to, murder, ill-treatment or deportation to slave labor or for any other purpose of civilian population of or in occupied territory, murder or ill-treatment of prisoners of war or persons on the seas, killing of hostages, plunder of public or private property, wanton destruction of cities, towns, or villages, or devastation not justified by military necessity;

(c) *CRIMES AGAINST HUMANITY:* namely, murder, extermination, enslavement, deportation, and other inhumane acts committed against any civilian population, before or during the war,* or persecutions on political, racial, or religious grounds in execution of or in connection with any crime within the jurisdiction of the Tribunal, whether or not in violation of domestic law of the country where perpetrated.

Leaders, organizers, instigators, and accomplices participating in the formulation or execution of a Common Plan or Conspiracy to commit any of the foregoing crimes are responsible for all acts performed by any persons in execution of such plan.

* Comma substituted in place of semicolon by Protocol of 6 October 1945.

Article 7. The official position of defendants, whether as Heads of State or responsible officials in Government departments, shall not be considered as freeing them from responsibility or mitigating punishment.

Article 8. The fact that the defendant acted pursuant to order of his Government or of a superior shall not free him from responsibility, but may be considered in mitigation of punishment if the Tribunal determine that justice so requires.

Article 9. At the trial of any individual member of any group or organization the Tribunal may declare (in connection with any act of which the individual may be convicted) that the group or organization of which the individual was a member was a criminal organization.

After receipt of the Indictment the Tribunal shall give such notice as it thinks fit that the Prosecution intends to ask the Tribunal to make such declaration and any member of the organization will be entitled to apply to the Tribunal for leave to be heard by the Tribunal upon the question of the criminal character of the organization. The Tribunal shall have power to allow or reject the application. If the application is allowed, the Tribunal may direct in what manner the applicants shall be represented and heard.

Article 10. In cases where a group or organization is declared criminal by the Tribunal, the competent national authority of any Signatory shall have the right to bring individuals to trial for membership therein before national, military, or occupation courts. In any such case the criminal nature of the group or organization is considered proved and shall not be questioned.

Article 11. Any person convicted by the Tribunal may be charged before a national, military, or occupation court, referred to in Article 10 of this Charter, with a crime other than of membership in a criminal group or organization and such court may, after convicting him, impose upon him punishment independent of and additional to the punishment imposed by the Tribunal for participation in the criminal activities of such group or organization.

Article 12. The Tribunal shall have the right to take proceedings against a person charged with crimes set out in Article 6 of this Charter in his absence, if he has not been found or if the Tribunal, for any reason, finds it necessary, in the interests of justice, to conduct the hearing in his absence.

Article 13. The Tribunal shall draw up rules for its procedure. These rules shall not be inconsistent with the provisions of this Charter.

III. COMMITTEE FOR THE INVESTIGATION AND PROSECUTION OF MAJOR WAR CRIMINALS

Article 14. Each Signatory shall appoint a Chief Prosecutor for the investigation of the charges against and the prosecution of major war criminals.

The Chief Prosecutors shall act as a committee for the following purposes:

(a) to agree upon a plan of the individual work of each of the Chief Prosecutors and his staff,

(b) to settle the final designation of major war criminals to be tried by the Tribunal,

(c) to approve the Indictment and the documents to be submitted therewith,

(d) to lodge the Indictment and the accompanying documents with the Tribunal,

(e) to draw up and recommend to the Tribunal for its approval draft rules of procedure, contemplated by Article 13 of this Charter. The Tribunal shall have power to accept, with or without amendments, or to reject, the rules so recommended.

The Committee shall act in all the above matters by a majority vote and shall appoint a Chairman as may be convenient and in accordance with the principle of rotation: provided that if there is an equal division of vote concerning the designation of a defendant to be tried by the Tribunal, or the crimes with which he shall be charged, that proposal will be adopted which was made by the party which proposed that the particular defendant be tried, or the particular charges be preferred against him.

Article 15. The Chief Prosecutors shall individually, and acting in collaboration with one another, also undertake the following duties:

(a) investigation, collection, and production before or at the Trial of all necessary evidence,

(b) the preparation of the Indictment for approval by the Committee in accordance with paragraph (c) of Article 14 hereof,

(c) the preliminary examination of all necessary witnesses and of the defendants,

(d) to act as prosecutor at the Trial,

(e) to appoint representatives to carry out such duties as may be assigned to them,

(f) to undertake such other matters as may appear necessary to them for the purposes of the preparation for and conduct of the Trial.

It is understood that no witness or defendant detained by any Signatory shall be taken out of the possession of that Signatory without its assent.

IV. FAIR TRIAL FOR DEFENDANTS

Article 16. In order to ensure fair trial for the defendants, the following procedure shall be followed:

(a) The Indictment shall include full particulars specifying in detail the charges against the defendants. A copy of the Indictment and of all the documents lodged with the Indictment, translated into a language which he understands, shall be furnished to the defendant at a reasonable time before the Trial.

(b) During any preliminary examination or trial of a defendant he shall have the right to give any explanation relevant to the charges made against him.

(c) A preliminary examination of a defendant and his trial shall be conducted in, or translated into, a language which the defendant understands.

(d) A defendant shall have the right to conduct his own defense before the Tribunal or to have the assistance of counsel.

(e) A defendant shall have the right through himself or through his counsel to present evidence at the Trial in support of his defense, and to cross-examine any witness called by the Prosecution.

V. POWERS OF THE TRIBUNAL AND CONDUCT OF THE TRIAL

Article 17. The Tribunal shall have the power:

(a) to summon witnesses to the Trial and to require their attendance and testimony and to put questions to them,

(b) to interrogate any defendant,

(c) to require the production of documents and other evidentiary material,

(d) to administer oaths to witnesses,

(e) to appoint officers for the carrying out of any task designated by the Tribunal including the power to have evidence taken on commission.

Article 18. The Tribunal shall:

(a) confine the Trial strictly to an expeditious hearing of the issues raised by the charges,

(b) take strict measures to prevent any action which will cause unreasonable delay, and rule out irrelevant issues and statements of any kind whatsoever,

(c) deal summarily with any contumacy, imposing appropriate punishment, including exclusion of any defendant or his counsel from some or all further proceedings, but without prejudice to the determination of the charges.

Article 19. The Tribunal shall not be bound by technical rules of evidence. It shall adopt and apply to the greatest possible extent expeditious and non-technical procedure, and shall admit any evidence which it deems to have probative value.

Article 20. The Tribunal may require to be informed of the nature of any evidence before it is offered so that it may rule upon the relevance thereof.

Article 21. The Tribunal shall not require proof of facts of common knowledge but shall take judicial notice thereof. It shall also take judicial notice of official governmental documents and reports of the United Nations, including the acts and documents of the committees set up in the various Allied countries for the investigation of war crimes, and the records and findings of military or other Tribunals of any of the United Nations.

Article 22. The permanent seat of the Tribunal shall be in Berlin. The first meetings of the members of the Tribunal and of the Chief Prosecutors shall be held at Berlin in a place to be designated by the Control Council for Germany. The first trial shall be held at Nuremberg, and any subsequent trials shall be held at such places as the Tribunal may decide.

Article 23. One or more of the Chief Prosecutors may take part in the prosecution at each trial. The function of any Chief Prosecutor may be discharged by him personally, or by any person or persons authorized by him.

The function of counsel for a defendant may be discharged at the defendant's request by any counsel professionally qualified to conduct cases before the Courts of his own country, or by any other person who may be specially authorized thereto by the Tribunal.

Article 24. The proceedings at the Trial shall take the following course:

(a) The Indictment shall be read in court.

(b) The Tribunal shall ask each defendant whether he pleads "guilty" or "not guilty".

(c) The Prosecution shall make an opening statement.

(d) The Tribunal shall ask the Prosecution and the Defense what evidence (if any) they wish to submit to the Tribunal, and the Tribunal shall rule upon the admissibility of any such evidence.

(e) The witnesses for the Prosecution shall be examined and after that the witnesses for the Defense. Thereafter such rebutting evidence as may be held by the Tribunal to be admissible shall be called by either the Prosecution or the Defense.

(f) The Tribunal may put any question to any witness and to any defendant, at any time.

(g) The Prosecution and the Defense shall interrogate and may cross-examine any witnesses and any defendant who gives testimony.

(h) The Defense shall address the Court.

(i) The Prosecution shall address the Court.

(j) Each Defendant may make a statement to the Tribunal.

(k) The Tribunal shall deliver judgment and pronounce sentence.

Article 25. All official documents shall be produced, and all court proceedings conducted, in English, French, and Russian, and in the language of the defendant. So much of the record and of the proceedings may also be translated into the language of any country in which the Tribunal is sitting, as the Tribunal considers desirable in the interests of justice and public opinion.

VI. JUDGMENT AND SENTENCE

Article 26. The judgment of the Tribunal as to the guilt or the innocence of any defendant shall give the reasons on which it is based, and shall be final and not subject to review.

Article 27. The Tribunal shall have the right to impose upon a defendant on conviction, death or such other punishment as shall be determined by it to be just.

Article 28. In addition to any punishment imposed by it, the Tribunal shall have the right to deprive the convicted person of any stolen property and order its delivery to the Control Council for Germany.

Article 29. In case of guilt, sentences shall be carried out in accordance with the orders of the Control Council for Germany, which may at any time reduce or otherwise alter the sentences, but may not increase the severity thereof. If the Control Council for Germany, after any defendant has been convicted and sentenced, discovers fresh evidence which, in its opinion, would found a fresh charge against him, the Council shall report accordingly to the Committee established under Article 14 hereof, for such action as they may consider proper, having regard to the interests of justice.

VII. EXPENSES

Article 30. The expenses of the Tribunal and of the trials, shall be charged by the Signatories against the funds allotted for maintenance of the Control Council for Germany.

PROTOCOL RECTIFYING DISCREPANCY IN TEXT OF CHARTER

Whereas an Agreement and Charter regarding the Prosecution of War Criminals was signed in London on the 8th August 1945, in the English, French, and Russian languages;

And whereas a discrepancy has been found to exist between the originals of Article 6, paragraph (c), of the Charter in the Russian language, on the one hand, and the originals in the English and French languages, on the other, to wit, the semicolon in Article 6, paragraph (c), of the Charter between the words "war" and "or", as carried in the English and French texts, is a comma in the Russian text;

And whereas it is desired to rectify this discrepancy:

NOW, THEREFORE, the undersigned, signatories of the said Agreement on behalf of their respective Governments, duly authorized thereto, have agreed that Article 6, paragraph (c), of the Charter in the Russian text is correct, and that the meaning and intention of the Agreement and Charter require that the said semicolon in the English text should be changed to a comma, and that the French text should be amended to read as follows:

c) *LES CRIMES CONTRE L'HUMANITE:* c'est à dire l'assassinat, l'extermination, la réduction en esclavage, la déportation, et tout autre acte inhumain commis contre toutes populations civiles, avant ou pendant la guerre, ou bien les persécutions pour des motifs politiques, raciaux, ou réligieux, lorsque ces actes ou persécutions, qu'ils aient constitué ou non une violation du droit interne du pays ou ils ont été perpetrés, ont été commis à la suite de tout crime rentrant dans la competence du Tribunal, ou en liaison avec ce crime.

IN WITNESS WHEREOF the Undersigned have signed the present Protocol.

DONE in quadruplicate in Berlin this 6th day of October, 1945, each in English, French, and Russian, and each text to have equal authenticity.

For the Government of the United States of America

/s/ ROBERT H. JACKSON

For the Provisional Government of the French Republic

/s/ FRANÇOIS de MENTHON

For the Government of the United Kingdom of Great Britain and Northern Ireland

/s/ HARTLEY SHAWCROSS

For the Government of the Union of Soviet Socialist Republics

/s/ R. RUDENKO

B. RULES OF PROCEDURE
(Adopted 29 October 1945)

Rule 1. *Authority to Promulgate Rules.*

The present Rules of Procedure of the International Military Tribunal for the trial of the major war criminals (hereinafter called "the Tribunal") as established by the Charter of the Tribunal dated 8 August 1945 (hereinafter called "the Charter") are hereby promulgated by the Tribunal in accordance with the provisions of Article 13 of the Charter.

Rule 2. *Notice to Defendants and Right to Assistance of Counsel.*

(a) Each individual defendant in custody shall receive not less than 30 days before trial a copy, translated into a language which he understands, (1) of the Indictment, (2) of the Charter, (3) of any other documents lodged with the Indictment, and (4) of a statement of his right to the assistance of counsel as set forth in sub-paragraph (d) of this Rule, together with a list of counsel. He shall also receive copies of such rules of procedure as may be adopted by the Tribunal from time to time.

(b) Any individual defendant not in custody shall be informed of the indictment against him and of his right to receive the documents specified in sub-paragraph (a) above, by notice in such form and manner as the Tribunal may prescribe.

(c) With respect to any group or organization as to which the Prosecution indicates its intention to request a finding of criminality by the Tribunal, notice shall be given by publication in such form and manner as the Tribunal may prescribe and such publication shall include a declaration by the Tribunal that all members of the named groups or organizations are entitled to apply to the Tribunal for leave to be heard in accordance with the provisions of Article 9 of the Charter. Nothing herein contained shall be construed to confer immunity of any kind upon such members of said groups or organizations as may appear in answer to the said declaration.

(d) Each defendant has the right to conduct his own defense or to have the assistance of counsel. Application for particular counsel shall be filed at once with the General Secretary of the Tribunal at the Palace of Justice, Nuremberg, Germany. The Tribunal will designate counsel for any defendant who fails to apply for particular counsel or, where particular counsel requested is not within ten (10) days to be found or available, unless the defendant elects in writing to conduct his own defense. If a defendant has requested particular counsel who is not immediately to be found or available, such counsel or a counsel of substitute choice may, if found and available before trial, be associated with or substituted for counsel designated by the Tribunal, provided that (1) only one counsel shall be permitted to appear at the trial for any defendant, unless by special permission of the Tribunal, and (2) no delay of trial will be allowed for making such substitution or association.

Rule 3. *Service of Additional Documents.*

If, before the trial, the Chief Prosecutors offer amendments or additions to the Indictment, such amendments or additions, including any accompanying documents shall be lodged with the Tribunal and copies of the same, translated into a language which they each understand, shall be furnished to the defendants in custody as soon as practicable and notice given in accordance with Rule 2 (b) to those not in custody.

Rule 4. *Production of Evidence for the Defense.*

(a) The Defense may apply to the Tribunal for the production of witnesses or of documents by written application to the General Secretary of the Tribunal. The application shall state where the witness or document is thought to be located, together with a statement of their last known location. It shall also state the facts proposed to be proved by the witness or the document and the reasons why such facts are relevant to the Defense.

(b) If the witness or the document is not within the area controlled by the occupation authorities, the Tribunal may request the Signatory and adhering Governments to arrange for the production, if possible, of any such witnesses and any such documents as the Tribunal may deem necessary to proper presentation of the Defense.

(c) If the witness or the document is within the area controlled by the occupation authorities, the General Secretary shall, if the Tribunal is not in session, communicate the application to the Chief Prosecutors and, if they make no objection, the General Secretary shall issue a summons for the attendance of such witness or the production of such documents, informing the Tribunal of the action taken. If any Chief Prosecutor objects to the issuance of a summons, or if the Tribunal is in session, the General Secretary shall submit the application to the Tribunal, which shall decide whether or not the summons shall issue.

(d) A summons shall be served in such manner as may be provided by the appropriate occupation authority to ensure its enforcement and the General Secretary shall inform the Tribunal of the steps taken.

(e) Upon application to the General Secretary of the Tribunal, a defendant shall be furnished with a copy, translated into a language which he understands, of all documents referred to in the Indictment so far as they may be made available by the Chief

Prosecutors and shall be allowed to inspect copies of any such documents as are not so available.

Rule 5. *Order at the Trial.*

In conformity with the provisions of Article 18 of the Charter, and the disciplinary powers therein set out, the Tribunal, acting through its President, shall provide for the maintenance of order at the Trial. Any defendant or any other person may be excluded from open sessions of the Tribunal for failure to observe and respect the directives and dignity of the Tribunal.

Rule 6. *Oaths; Witnesses.*

(a) Before testifying before the Tribunal, each witness shall make such oath or declaration as is customary in his own country.

(b) Witnesses while not giving evidence shall not be present in court. The President of the Tribunal shall direct, as circumstances demand, that witnesses shall not confer among themselves before giving evidence.

Rule 7. *Applications and Motions before Trial and Rulings during the Trial.*

(a) All motions, applications or other requests addressed to the Tribunal prior to the commencement of trial shall be made in writing and filed with the General Secretary of the Tribunal at the Palace of Justice, Nuremberg, Germany.

(b) Any such motion, application or other request shall be communicated by the General Secretary of the Tribunal to the Chief Prosecutors and, if they make no objection, the President of the Tribunal may make the appropriate order on behalf of the Tribunal. If any Chief Prosecutor objects, the President may call a special session of the Tribunal for the determination of the question raised.

(c) The Tribunal, acting through its President, will rule in court upon all questions arising during the trial, such as questions as to admissibility of evidence offered during the trial, recesses, and motions; and before so ruling the Tribunal may, when necessary, order the closing or clearing of the Tribunal or take any other steps which to the Tribunal seem just.

Rule 8. *Secretariat of the Tribunal.*

(a) The Secretariat of the Tribunal shall be composed of a General Secretary, four Secretaries and their Assistants. The Tribunal shall appoint the General Secretary and each Member shall appoint one Secretary. The General Secretary shall appoint such clerks, interpreters, stenographers, ushers, and all such other persons as may be authorized by the Tribunal and each Secretary may appoint such assistants as may be authorized by the Member of the Tribunal by whom he was appointed.

(b) The General Secretary, in consultation with the Secretaries, shall organize and direct the work of the Secretariat, subject to the approval of the Tribunal in the event of a disagreement by any Secretary.

(c) The Secretariat shall receive all documents addressed to the Tribunal, maintain the records of the Tribunal, provide necessary clerical services to the Tribunal and its Members, and perform such other duties as may be designated by the Tribunal.

(d) Communications addressed to the Tribunal shall be delivered to the General Secretary.

Rule 9. *Record, Exhibits, and Documents.*

(a) A stenographic record shall be maintained of all oral proceedings. Exhibits will be suitably identified and marked with consecutive numbers. All exhibits and transcripts of the proceedings and all documents lodged with and produced to the Tribunal will be filed with the General Secretary of the Tribunal and will constitute part of the Record.

(b) The term "official documents" as used in Article 25 of the Charter includes the Indictment, rules, written motions, orders that are reduced to writing, findings, and judgments of the Tribunal. These shall be in the English, French, Russian, and German languages. Documentary evidence or exhibits may be received in the language of the document, but a translation thereof into German shall be made available to the defendants.

(c) All exhibits and transcripts of proceedings, all documents lodged with and produced to the Tribunal and all official acts and documents of the Tribunal may be certified by the General Secretary of the Tribunal to any Government or to any other tribunal or wherever it is appropriate that copies of such documents or representations as to such acts should be supplied upon a proper request.

Rule 10. *Withdrawal of Exhibits and Documents.*

In cases where original documents are submitted by the Prosecution or the Defense as evidence, and upon a showing (a) that because of historical interest or for any other reason one of the Governments signatory to the Four Power Agreement of 8 August 1945, or any other Government having received the consent of said four signatory Powers, desires to withdraw from the records of the Tribunal and preserve any particular original documents and (b) that no substantial injustice will result, the Tribunal shall permit photostatic copies of said original documents, certified by the General Secretary of the Tribunal, to be substituted for the originals in the records of the Court and shall deliver said original documents to the applicants.

Rule 11. *Effective Date and Powers of Amendment and Addition.*

These Rules shall take effect upon their approval by the Tribunal. Nothing herein contained shall be construed to prevent the Tribunal from, at any time, in the interest of fair and expeditious trials, departing from, amending, or adding to these Rules, either by general rules or special orders for particular cases, in such form and upon such notice as may appear just to the Tribunal.